A HISTORY OF THE PRESIDENCY FROM 1788 TO 1897

BY

EDWARD STANWOOD, Litt. D. (Bowdoin)

The Riverside Press

BOSTON AND NEW YORK
HOUGHTON MIFFLIN COMPANY
The Riverside Press Cambridge

PREFACE

THE basis of this book is the "History of Presidential Elections," originally published in 1884. In the preparation of that work the meagreness and comparative inaccessibility of material concerning the early elections made the chapters that deal with that period somewhat barren. Increasing abundance of material and greater familiarity with the political history of more recent times caused a broadening of the plan, and led to the result that the later chapters of the original work, and still more the chapters added in subsequent editions, in 1888, 1892, and 1896, were much more than a history of the elections.

I have thought that the usefulness of the book might be greatly enhanced by rewriting a large part of it, supplying deficiencies by a more diligent search for and study of the facts relating to the presidency in the early days of the government, and enriching it throughout with new personal, explanatory, and other enlightening matter, thus making the whole work uniform in method. This has enabled me to introduce a fuller discussion of some of the political problems to which the constitutional provisions regarding the presidential office have given rise. More important still, the revision and expansion of the work have given me a much-desired opportunity to modify some opinions expressed in the original book which a more careful and thorough examination of original sources of information has led me to regard as not well founded. The last consideration has the more weight in view of the use that has been made of the book in the history departments of our colleges.

The changes and additions here noted have given the book

so much greater scope than it had in its first form, that a broader title seems necessary. If it be urged that a history of the presidency should include an account of the development of the presidential office, and of the successive expansions or limitations of the President's powers and duties, the reply may be made that there has been no such development to record, since the office is now what it was in the time of Washington, — neither of greater nor of less weight in the government than it was then.

I have endeavored to collect and present all important matters relating to the presidency, beginning with the constitutional history of the office, covering every public event and discussion which had a perceptible influence in determining who should hold the office, and in connection therewith to note the origin and sketch the history of all political parties, however ephemeral, that rose above the rank of a local faction. And, since one President is different from another, I have tried to show wherein and in what manner the personal qualities of the Presidents have affected the course of public events and of the national history.

E. S.

BROOKLINE, MASSACHUSETTS, July, 1898.

CONTENTS

A HISTORY OF THE PRESIDENCY

I

THE ELECTORAL SYSTEM

THE evolution of the Constitution of 1787 forms one of the most interesting chapters in the history of human government. For the first time, the representatives of an inchoate nation, meeting to ordain and establish a fundamental law for themselves and their posterity, could write that law upon *tabula rasa*. They had to expunge nothing, — to abolish no old institutions, to violate no traditions, to reform no long-standing abuses. Their task was not made easier by their unexampled freedom from the trammels of an established order; on the contrary, it was thereby rendered more difficult. To know what is not liked goes far toward teaching one what will be liked. The members of the Philadelphia Convention had no indication of what would be agreeable to those for whom they acted. Yet they proceeded, first to draw in the rough, and afterward to fill in and refine the detail, of a constitution that has converted the unorganized communities of a congeries of mutually repellant States into a united nation, under a government more conservative and less subject to change than that of any other self-governing people in the world.

Particularly worthy of study is the process by which the executive department of the government to be created was moulded, as the perfect statue is developed from the rough block of marble. By successive resolutions the convention determined that there should be an executive; consisting of one person; holding office for a limited period; reëligible; elected; endowed with certain powers. The Convention hesitated upon many points; the decisions first reached were not always, not even usually, final. Indeed, almost every feature of the plan

ultimately adopted was at least once rejected, after full debate.
Yet it cannot be said, after a full study of the debates, that
the Convention was unduly vacillating. The truth is that it
was a series of independent propositions which was rejected in
all these çases, but that when they were combined in a whole,
the scheme became that toward which the Convention was all
the time working. This will explain why Hamilton, whose
plan of a government was widely different from that which
formed the basis of the Convention's deliberations, who, indeed, had but little part in the formation of the Constitution,
could without great inconsistency become a defender of the
instrument as a whole, and could write : [1] " The mode of the
appointment of the Chief Magistrate of the United States is
almost the only part of the system of any consequence which
has escaped without some censure, or which has received the
slightest mark of approbation from its opponents." Notwithstanding this statement, which was strictly true, it is now to
be said that the only part of the machinery of government,
ordained by the people when they adopted the Constitution,
that has suffered the least change since the government came
into being, is the article which then gave universal satisfaction ;
and that no part of the Constitution has been so earnestly and
so continuously criticised as this same article, already once
amended to remove a supposed defect.

The plan of a national government submitted to the Convention on the 29th of May, 1787, by Mr. Edmund Randolph,
provided for " a national executive to be chosen by the national
legislature for the term of —— years," " and to be ineligible
the second time."   Charles Pinckney proposed, at the same
time, " that the executive power be vested in a ' President of
the United States of America,' which shall be his style ; and
his title shall be ' His Excellency.'   He shall be elected for
——years, and shall be reëligible." In some of the propositions
made during the early days of the Convention the proposed
executive was styled the " governor ; " but it was a mere suggestion, resulting from the fact that as there was not, and
never had been, a model from which to copy the executive
which the Convention intended to create, no precedent existed
to guide them in giving him a title.   The first question was,
In how many persons should the executive power be vested ?
One voice was raised in favor of three, — one to be chosen

[1] *Federalist*, No. 67.

from the North, one from the Middle States, and one from the South. It was speedily determined that there should be a single chief magistrate, and the decision was not reopened or criticised afterward.

The questions concerning the executive department of the government divided themselves into two classes : What should be the powers and duties of the President ? and, How and by whom should he be chosen ? With the first class we have nothing to do, save incidentally. To understand why the Convention was puzzled, and why it changed its mind, apparently, so often, it is necessary to inquire briefly what it was the purpose of the Convention to accomplish, and against what apprehended evils it endeavored to guard. It was one of the guiding principles, early adopted and rigidly adhered to, that the legislative, executive, and judicial departments of the government should be separate and mutually independent. There were two, and only two, natural ways of selecting the President : by popular vote, and by the national legislature. At no time was the proposition of a popular election received with favor, although it had the support of powerful advocates, particularly of Mr. Gouverneur Morris. The chief objections urged against it were three : the great advantage this method would give to the large States ; the probable ignorance of the people at large as to the comparative merits of candidates, and the consequent likelihood that they would in all cases give a preference to a candidate each from his own State ; and the general incompetence of the populace to decide a question of such moment. Superficial writers are responsible for a popular impression that the third of these reasons was the controlling one, — that the Convention by its action registered its distrust of the people, that if the members had felt a greater confidence in the people, the decision would have been different. From this it is plausible to draw an argument that the present generation, which knows that the people may be trusted, should introduce the popular election. In truth, a distrust of the good judgment of the people was expressed by one member only, Colonel Mason, of Virginia, who happens to have been one of the three members of the Convention who did not sign the Constitution,[1] in the often quoted remark that it would be " as unnatural to refer the proper character for chief magistrate to the people as it would be to refer a trial

[1] The others were Randolph and Gerry.

of colors to a blind man." On the other hand, the fear of aggrandizement by the large States was ever present as a controlling principle; for unless the frame of government were such as the smaller States would adopt, the Convention must be a failure. The consideration that the public characters of the country were not generally known, save in the neighborhood of their homes, was also potent, and was founded upon a real condition.

Yet the alternative, an election by the legislature, was equally objectionable on other grounds. To require that the Executive should be independent of the law-making power, and at the same time to give the election to the legislature, was an inconsistency so glaring as to shock the Convention whenever the clause relating to the choice of a President came under consideration. The only escape from it, and that but a partial one, was to forbid the reëlection of a chief magistrate, — a provision which, as was pointed out, might and would sometimes exclude from the office the person best fitted to exercise it. The proposition to avoid these difficulties by creating a body of electors for the sole purpose of choosing a President was made early in the session. On the 2d of June, James Wilson proposed that there should be "certain districts in each State which should appoint electors to elect outside of their own body." The objection was made that, inasmuch as the most eminent citizens would be already serving as senators, representatives, and State governors, the choice of a President would, by this plan, be committed to a body of inferior men, ignorant of the merits of citizens in all parts of the country, and therefore apt to vote for candidates living in their own State. Dealing with the conditions that prevailed in their time, — a dearth of men capable of filling so many new positions as it was necessary to create, and an absence of the means by which information regarding public men and public affairs is now disseminated, — they were right.

The statement of the perplexities by which the Convention was confronted prepares us to understand the frequent reversal of its decisions. The first resolution, adopted before the objections to it had occurred to the members, was that the Executive should be chosen by the legislature. Then Elbridge Gerry brought forward a suggestion that the President should be elected by the governors of the States; this was negatived. Hamilton's plan of a government, offered on the 18th of June, which was never considered by the Convention, committed the election to a body of electors to be chosen by the people, by districts. These electors were to meet, those for each State within that State, and vote not only for a President of the United States, but also for two " second electors." A majority of all the " first electors" was to be necessary to make choice of a President. Should such a majority not be obtained, the "second electors " were to meet in one place, be presided over by the Chief Justice, and effect a choice.

The convention returned to the subject of the Executive on the 17th of July, and after a debate rejected a motion that he should be chosen " by electors appointed by the legislatures of the several States." On the 19th it adopted a motion in almost the identical words of the rejected proposition : " to be chosen by electors appointed for that purpose by the legislatures of the States." The question as to the length of the President's term, as well as that of his reëligibility, was closely involved with the consideration of the body to which he was to owe his election. A long term and ineligibility for a second term were both measures to insure the President's independence of the legislature. The bugbear of legislative tyranny was held up before the Convention almost as frequently as was that of a control of the government by the larger States. Seven years, therefore, was the term first agreed upon ; and the question of reëligibility was left open. After the second vote, above noted, committing the choice to independent electors, the term was reduced to six years ; and an amendment that a President should not hold office more than six years of any twelve years was rejected. This was on the 19th of July. The next day the Convention adopted Mr. Gerry's proposition regarding the number of electors : Massachusetts, Pennsylvania, and Virginia were to have three each ; Connecticut, New York, New Jersey, Maryland, North Carolina, and South Carolina, two each ; Rhode Island, Delaware, and Georgia, one each. On the 26th the Convention reverted to the seven years' term, with the provision of ineligibility for reëlection. Then, on the same day, the whole subject was referred to a committee of five. The committee reported a draft of a Constitution on the 6th of August. The article relating to the election of President was in these words : —

ART. X., SECT. 1. The executive power of the United States shall be vested in a single person. His style shall be " The President of the United States of America;" and his title shall be "His Excellency." He shall be elected by ballot by the legislature. He shall hold his office during seven years, but shall not be elected a second time.

This section, which combined Mr. Randolph's and Mr. Pinckney's plans, but which contained no trace of the electoral plan adopted by the Convention, was the basis of future discussions. But the scheme of a choice by the legislature was still as objectionable as ever. It was at this point that Mr. Hugh Williamson of North Carolina made a suggestion in which was the germ of the plan ultimately adopted. He proposed to refer the election to popular vote, each elector to vote for three persons, and the choice to fall on him who obtained a majority of all the persons voting. He thought this would be a cure for the evil that the large States would govern. Gouverneur Morris at once caught up the idea, but suggested that two votes only be allowed to electors, and that it be provided that one at least of the two should not be given to a citizen of the voter's own State. Mr. Madison also thought that something valuable might be made of Mr. Williamson's suggestion, with Mr. Morris's amendment. He advanced the idea that the second best man would probably be the first, that is, a voter would place a citizen of his own State first, but would give his second vote to a man selected on account of his fitness for the place, and not on account of his residence. The voter might give the preference to a local candidate in the hope that he would get a majority; but he would not throw away his second vote also. The first judgment of the Convention was against the proposition, yet it was defeated by one majority only, — five States supporting and six opposing it.

On the 24th of August the question of the Executive was again considered. The Convention rejected a proposition by Mr. Morris to refer the election to electors chosen by the people of the several States, and also a motion that the President be chosen "by electors." It rejected moreover a plain election by the people, a motion to give to each State one vote for President (in the election by "the legislature," which in all this discussion meant the House of Representatives and not both branches of Congress), and another motion that when the legislature should be equally divided the President of the Senate should have the casting vote. It adopted two amendments to the section quoted above, which made the third sentence read as follows: "He shall be elected by joint ballot by the legislature, to which election a majority of the votes of the members present shall be required." In the clause as amended, it will be seen, the phrase "the legislature" signifies both branches.

Up to this point no proposition had been made to appoint a Vice-President. On August 31 "the questions not yet settled" were referred to a committee of eleven, which reported, on the 4th of September, a scheme for the election of the Executive radically different from anything that had been sanctioned by the Convention, — as different as the report of a Congressional committee of conference, in our day, sometimes is from any version of a bill passed in non-concurrence submitted to it. The committee proposed to strike all out of the section printed above after the word "Excellency," and to insert the following provisions: —

Each State shall appoint, in such manner as its legislature may direct, a number of electors equal to the whole number of senators and members of the House of Representatives to which the State may be entitled in the legislature. (A)

The electors shall meet in their respective States, and vote by ballot for two persons, of whom one at least shall not be an inhabitant of the same State with themselves; and they shall make a list of all the persons voted for, and of the number of votes for each, which list they shall sign and certify, and transmit, sealed, to the seat of general government, directed to the President of the Senate. The President of the Senate shall, in that house, open all the certificates: and the votes shall then and there be counted. (B) The person having the greatest number of votes shall be President, if such number be a majority of the whole number of electors; and if there be more than one who have such majority, and have an equal number of votes, then the Senate shall choose by ballot one of them for President; but if no such person have such majority, then, from the five highest on the list, the Senate shall choose by ballot the President. And in every case, after the choice of a President, the person having the greatest number of votes shall be the Vice-President; but if there should remain two or more who have equal votes, the Senate shall choose from them the Vice-President.

The legislature may determine the time of choosing and assembling the electors, and the manner of certifying and transmitting their votes.

When the article was taken up for consideration on the

following day, September 5, many amendments were offered. Those which were adopted show again most clearly that the Convention now discerned definitely what it desired to accomplish, and that it could move directly to that end. At the place marked (A) a provision was inserted that " no person shall be appointed an elector who is a member of the legislature of the United States, or who holds any office of profit or trust under the United States." At the place marked (B) was added the phrase, " in the presence of the Senate and House of Representatives," — an important clause, in that it implies that the President of the Senate was to count the electoral vote, and that the members of the two houses were to be present as witnesses only. The word " immediately " was inserted in the direction to the Senate to choose the President in case of a failure of the electors to give a majority to one person. A motion to commit the election to the " legislature " instead of to the Senate was rejected by seven States against three. The reason for this vote was evidently a determination that when the electors did not effect a choice, the result should be determined by a poll of States, each having an equal voice ; for when Roger Sherman moved that the election be made by the House of Representatives, each State to have one vote, the motion was carried by ten States to one. Then it was suggested that inasmuch as a majority of the House of Representatives constituted a quorum, the election might be carried, when the members of three large States only were present, by a vote of two States to one. Madison met this by offering an amendment, which was accepted, providing that when the House was assembled for the purpose of electing a President, a quorum should consist of a member or members from two thirds of the States, and that a majority of all the States should be necessary to effect a choice.

Thus all the points of objection were met, and the scheme as a whole was regarded with almost universal satisfaction. The whole Constitution was referred to a committee " to revise the style and arrange the articles agreed to by the House." The committee, appointed on the 8th of September, reported on the 12th. The articles were " read, debated by paragraphs, amended, and agreed to," and the Convention adjourned on the 17th of September. The article, as finally adopted and ratified, under which the first four elections were held, is, in full, as follows : —

Art. II., Sect. 1. The executive power shall be vested in a President of the United States of America. He shall hold his office during the term of four years, and, together with the Vice-President, chosen for the same term, be elected as follows: —

Each State shall appoint, in such manner as the legislature thereof may direct, a number of electors, equal to the whole number of senators and representatives to which the State may be entitled in the Congress; but no senator or representative, or person holding an office of trust or profit under the United States, shall be appointed an elector.

The electors shall meet in their respective States, and vote by ballot for two persons, of whom one at least shall not be an inhabitant of the same State with themselves. And they shall make a list of all the persons voted for, and of the number of votes for each; which list they shall sign and certify, and transmit, sealed, to the seat of the government of the United States, directed to the President of the Senate. The President of the Senate shall, in the presence of the Senate and House of Representatives, open all the certificates, and the votes shall then be counted. The person having the greatest number of votes shall be the President, if such number be a majority of the whole number of electors appointed; and if there be more than one who have such majority, and have an equal number of votes, then the House of Representatives shall immediately choose by ballot one of them for President; and if no person have a majority, then from the five highest on the list the said House shall in like manner choose the President. But in choosing the President, the votes shall be taken by States, the representation from each State having one vote; a quorum for this purpose shall consist of a member or members from two thirds of the States, and a majority of all the States shall be necessary to a choice. In every case, after the choice of the President, the person having the greatest number of votes of the electors shall be the Vice-President. But if there should remain two or more who have equal votes, the Senate shall choose from them by ballot the Vice-President.

The Congress may determine the time of choosing the electors and the day on which they shall give their votes; which day shall be the same throughout the United States.

What the electoral system has accomplished, and wherein it has proved more or less defective, may be learned in detail from the historical events narrated in subsequent chapters. It is desirable, nevertheless, to consider in this place the general working of the system, and its development in practice. In the first place, let us see how far it has fulfilled the purposes and expectations of the framers of the Constitution. No doubt it is unsafe to declare in precise terms what they intended to accomplish by every clause and word of the remarkable instrument they left for the use of their country-men: nor is it just or expedient to regard their work as imperfect in those parts of the Constitution wherein later generations have departed from what seems to have been their original intention, provided the modification, not in-consistent with the letter of the Constitution, result in a workable and equitable system. Bearing in mind these pre-liminary cautions, we may say that the Convention sought to accomplish, (1) the independence of the Executive; (2) the choice of the President by an electorate which (*a*) should be intelligent, and free to choose the best, and (*b*) should not be controlled by the large States; (3) that in the event of a failure of the electors to make a choice, each State should have an equal voice.

The first of the above-enumerated objects has been realized, although at one time it seemed to be defeated. In the Chap-ter on the Convention System (XIV) it will be seen how the Congressional Caucus became so obvious a necessity that it would have been contrary to the plainest dictate of political wisdom not to make use of it; and yet it was directly in vio-lation of the principle that the President must not owe his election to the legislative department of the government. The national convention has restored to the President as large a measure of independence of Congress as is possible under any system. So long as the strongest, wisest, and best-informed public men have the greatest influence upon the choice, as they ought to have, and so long as the people send such men to Congress, as they ought to do, so long will the absolute independence of the President be impossible; but not his in-dependence of Congress as a whole, or of his own party mem-bers in Congress.

The most difficult requirement was that the electors should be free agents, and qualified to make a wise choice by acquaint-ance with the public men of the country. In the strictest sense, the first part of this condition was not realized even at the earliest elections. There was no second where Washington was first; but when he retired, the intelligence of the electors needed to be instructed. It was many years before acquaint-ance with public men was sufficiently general to enable all the

States to appoint electors who were competent to judge for themselves. It is notorious that almost from the beginning, the electors have been subject, in giving their votes, to a moral stress so powerful that not one of them could separate himself from his fellows and vote for any other than the candidate of his party, without being held guilty of unpardonable political treachery. The intrigues to detach Federal electors from Adams, eight years only after the Constitution went into effect, and the absolute unanimity of the anti-Federal electors in support of both Jefferson and Burr, in 1800, show how quickly the scheme of independent, free-acting electors came to naught. Shall we say that it is surprising that the sagacious statesmen of the Convention did not foresee that the government they were instituting would be a government by party, and that the success of parties would depend as much on their discipline as on their principles ? They did foresee it. Or rather, they feared, as some of them expressed it in debate, that the electors would be influenced and controlled in their action by designing men ; and they hoped only that the votes would be free.

No argument is needed to prove that the scheme of the fathers is not only impracticable, but that in its operation it would now be intolerable. Were electors to be chosen merely as party men, uncommitted to any candidates, one of two things must happen. Either the choice of these candidates, after the appointment of electors, would be made in the utmost confusion, and would be attended with scandalous intrigues, perhaps with corruption ; or, the election of a President would be thrown into the House of Representatives, not occasionally, but always. The most casual consideration of the subject will convince every thinking man that the system we have is far better than that which the fathers planned. We have, in the convention system, a device which substitutes the judgment of a whole party for that of the individual elector, and which enables the wishes of the largest party to be carried into effect, instead of being scattered and wasted. The new system may not, does not, carry out the exact intention of the Fathers, but it conforms to the letter of the Constitution.

Four elections only were held under the provisions of the Constitution as ratified by the States. Then a change was made, in order to meet in a different way a state of affairs which the Convention had foreseen. The circumstances in which the will of the victorious party was nearly frustrated at the election of 1800–1801 are fully narrated in a subsequent chapter. It was to prevent a recurrence of the scandal, for it was a scandal, in spite of the fact that it was constitutional, that the change was made. Nevertheless the amendment cast away the very feature which induced the Convention to entrust the choice of President to a created body of electors, and which was to make it certain that the large States should not control. Consequently, it seems at first sight illogical to amend the Constitution by ordaining a different course of procedure, for the sole reason that something had happened which was distinctly foreseen and provided for.

It seemed both illogical and unwise to Gouverneur Morris, who was at that time a member of the United States Senate from New York.[1] The twelfth amendment was proposed by New York. Mr. Morris voted against it, and the resolution of the House of Representatives was first defeated by his vote. In a letter to the President of the Senate and Speaker of the Assembly of New York, dated December 25, 1802,[2] he gives his reasons for his vote, three in number, of which one only is pertinent. The evils complained of were foreseen in the Convention. " The Convention not only foresaw that a scene might take place similar to that of the last presidential election, but even supposed it not impossible that at some time or other, a person admirably fitted for the office of President might have an equal vote with one totally unqualified, and that, by the predominance of faction in the House of Representatives, the latter might be preferred. This, which is the greatest supposable evil of the present mode, was calmly examined, and it appeared that however prejudicial it might be at the present moment, a useful lesson would result from it for the future, to teach contending parties the importance of giving both votes to men fit for the first office." Mr. Morris was a Federalist, but his judgment in the crisis of 1801 had been decidedly against the course pursued by the members of his party in the House of Representatives. Thus he had seen an example of that which he characterizes as " the greatest supposable evil of the present mode." He must also have been aware of the strenuous efforts put forth by men of his own party to secure for Mr. Pinckney a larger electoral vote than

[1] He represented Pennsylvania in the Convention of 1787.
[2] Sparks's Life of Gouverneur Morris, vol. iii., p. 174.

that for Mr. Adams, in the year preceding that crisis. That which he calls a " useful lesson " was then, and has at almost every subsequent election been greatly needed, and usually unheeded. No doubt, if a party victorious in the choice of electors were always liable to the accident of having to submit to an assembly politically hostile the choice between its two candidates for the presidency, the nominations would be more carefully made. But it is clearly evident that, with the abandonment of the theory of independent voting by electors, and the consequent certainty that there would always be a tie between two candidates, and an election ultimately by the House of Representatives, the change made after the Jefferson-Burr contest was a wise one.

It has been said that to this change is to be attributed the semi-degradation of the office of Vice-President. In support of the assertion it may be stated with truth that not more than two or three candidates for Vice-President of all parties, during the last three quarters of a century, have been men who, at the time of their nomination, had even been suggested as candidates for President. Mr. Tyler, Mr. Wheeler, and Mr. Hendricks may be named ; is there a fourth ? It may nevertheless be urged that under the original system there surely would have been an evil greater than the choice of second-rate men for the vice-presidency. Consider what would have happened had two such men as Clay and Webster been the candidates, and the successful candidates, of the Whig party, in 1840. Receiving an equal vote from the electors, the House of Representatives must have made choice between them. One of the two would have gone to the White House ; the other would have been condemned to the obscurity of the vice-presidency. One can hardly conceive of a situation more conducive to intrigue on the part of both, — to an effort of the successful man to retain power by putting down his rival, of the unsuccessful to supplant him. This consideration alone, — and others might be mentioned, — should be sufficient to reconcile the country to the change that resulted from the tie vote between Jefferson and Burr.

No strong movement has ever been made to substitute a direct popular vote for the existing system. The suggestion is so clearly impracticable that a discussion of its merits is useless. A three fourths vote of the States is needed for an amendment of the Constitution. Under the present apportionment there are fifteen States which have no more than two members each in the House of Representatives. One third of the States, then, have a vastly greater power in determining who shall be President than they would exercise under the system of popular election. Not one of them would give its consent to the change. Nor has there ever been a time in our history when the number of small States which would lose political power by the adoption of a system of popular election was not large enough to foredoom the proposition.

Numerous have been the suggestions of amendment of the Constitution with a view to dispensing with the machinery of electors, at the same time preserving to the States their relative weight in the election. The leading idea in the most of them is: a direct vote by the people for President and Vice-President; the result in each State to be determined by a plurality; the candidates who receive such plurality to be credited with as many votes from that State as the electoral votes they would have under the present system. The sole practical advantage to be anticipated from any of these propositions is relief from the possibility of treachery on the part of men designated as electors. Never but once has this danger threatened. A complete remedy, much more easily applied than an amendment of the Constitution, is the election of men of high character as electors.

The language of the Constitution relative to the counting of the votes is extremely precise up to the point of designating by whom they shall be counted. It does not seem to have suggested itself to any member of the Convention that there might be a controverted election in any State, and consequently that authority to make a decision should be lodged somewhere. The vagueness of the direction led to a variation in practice at the early elections, as will be observed in the account of each election. Gradually Congress asserted its right to make the count and to determine all questions arising. If this is not clearly the intention of the framers of the Constitution — who provided merely that the certificates of votes should be opened in the presence of Congress — it is certainly safer to entrust the decision to the two Houses than to the discretion of one man. The process by which Congress assumed the power will be most conveniently set forth in the history of the successive elections.

The theory of the Constitution undoubtedly is that the electors are officers of their respective States. As such the method of their appointment is left entirely to the legislatures. From the beginning there was a marked difference in the States in this regard, for while in most of them the legislature itself made the choice, some entrusted the election to the people. It will be seen from what follows that the tendency to the system of popular election was not strong at first; but in Monroe's time it became general. When the election of 1824 took place three fourths of the State legislatures had renounced the privilege of appointment. During the whole period prior to 1824 there were numerous cases of the resumption of the right of choice directly, by the legislatures of States in which a political advantage was to be gained by so doing. At the election of 1828, in Delaware and South Carolina alone were the electors chosen by legislature. South Carolina clung to that method of appointment until the civil war. Another change in the mode of appointment accompanied or followed that just mentioned. Originally, in most of the States where the popular system prevailed, each voter cast his ballot for three electors — two for the State at large, and one for the congressional district in which he resided. But politicians soon discovered that the weight of the State's influence was increased by a general election of the whole number, by the plan known in France as the *scrutin de liste*. As soon as a few of the States had adopted this method it was necessary for the rest to do the same, for self-protection. Maryland was the last State to give up the district system, which she did after the election of 1832. Since then no State has reverted to it, with one exception, namely, Michigan in 1892. The party accidentally in power adopted this device with the express purpose of dividing the electoral vote of the State, which it had no hope of obtaining upon a general popular vote. It is in this feature that the electoral plan of 1787 fails most conspicuously. The general ticket greatly increases the power of the large States. Since the first election of Jackson, when it became the usual rule of election, no President has been chosen in opposition to the vote of both New York and Pennsylvania, and but four in opposition to the vote of either of them. Nevertheless, it cannot be asserted that the general result would have been different in many cases, if the district method of election had prevailed universally. Gerrymandering might effect almost as much as the general ticket. Inasmuch as the power to choose between the district and the general ticket system rests exclusively with the legislatures, and since the evil — whatever it may be — can be reached by amendment of the Constitution only, the plan adopted will undoubtedly continue in use.

Since the electors of President and Vice-President are state officers, whose appointment is certified by the governor; who meet, discharge their one duty, and adjourn, within the State and under state authority, it follows that a fraud perpetrated with the connivance of the chief officers of a State is subject to no effective revision. Unfortunately there have been too many instances of subversion of the will of the people by fraudulent elections, falsified returns, and disfranchisement of citizens by rejection of their legal votes, to admit of this being regarded as a fanciful danger. Indeed, it may be asserted that from the time of the Plaquemines affair in 1844 to the present time there have been few presidential elections which are not believed by members of one party or another to be tainted with electoral frauds. So long as the elections are under state control this evil is beyond remedy. To introduce the system of popular election of the President would not be a cure, even in appearance. Moreover, the jealousy and alarm that are always excited by every proposition to put elections under national supervision, render the only possible remedy wholly impracticable. Yet it needs no argument to prove that fraud which gives the electoral vote of New York or Nevada, the largest or the smallest State, to electors who have not a plurality of votes, and by so doing changes the result of the presidential election, entails a political injury not merely upon the people of the State whose will has been nullified, but upon the whole country. The wrong must go unpunished and unredressed, because there is no appeal from the acts of state authority. There was no apprehension of such wrong when the Constitution was framed; but it has been suffered, repeatedly, if not frequently. In 1876 a complication of electoral disorders and controversies, in which neither party was innocent, brought the country to the verge of a terrible crisis. It would be sheer optimism to believe that evils equally perilous to peace will not occur hereafter.

In the early days of the Republic most of the States required election to all offices by a majority of votes; and when no candidate had more than a plurality, a fresh election was held, and repeated until a majority appeared. At that time it would have been thought a peril to the Republic, had any candidate for President, elected under a popular system, obtained the office supported by less than a majority of the people. It is needless to repeat that the framers of the Constitution required a majority of electoral votes, representing the States as units in the Federal Union; or failing that, a majority of States represented in the lower House of Congress. In practice almost every President since Polk — the first on the list — has had less than a majority of all the votes. The exceptions are Pierce, Lincoln (in 1864), Grant at both his elections, and McKinley. Two Presidents entered office backed by less than a plurality of popular votes : Hayes, and Benjamin Harrison. Even this cannot be deemed an argument for a change from the present electoral system, unless we are to abandon altogether the principle of election by States and adopt that of election by a plurality of individuals.

One phase of the practical working of the electoral system should, in conclusion, be mentioned and examined. It is customary for the newspapers, after each election, to draw attention, in the tone of an alarmist, to the fact that the change of a certain small number of votes from one candidate to another in a few States, would have given the election to that second candidate. The successful party in the contest of 1896 affected, to an unusual degree, to regard the result as a narrow escape, and the defeated party mourned that it missed a victory by so small a margin. Yet, as a matter of fact, Mr. McKinley was the first President since 1872 to receive a clear majority of votes ; and he also had a larger electoral majority than any President during the same period, except Mr. Cleveland at his second election. The answer to the ever-repeated arithmetical speculation is that the votes never do have a tendency to redistribute themselves in the way suggested. One election does not resemble another ; but the tendency in one State at any given election is substantially the same as in other States. It increases the majority of the winning party in its own States ; it carries some States over to the opposition ; it reduces majorities in the States held by the losing party, — these changes all being, at any election, in the same direction. It appears that something less than nineteen thousand votes transferred from McKinley to Bryan in the States of California, Delaware, Indiana, Kentucky, Oregon, and West Virginia, would have given Bryan the election. It is overlooked that five of the six States named were gained by the Republicans from the Democrats, since they were carried by Mr. Cleveland in 1892; and that the change was a part of the movement which gave McKinley his election. It would have required a change of 8772 votes in Indiana to transfer that State from the Republican to the Democratic column. Since similar causes produce similar effects, we must suppose that in other States as well as in Indiana, the Republicans would have lost 2.7 per cent. of their vote, and the Democrats gained 2.9 per cent. That change throughout the country would have reduced McKinley's plurality by about 360,000 votes. Applying to the whole country the proportional change needed to give the vote of Delaware to Bryan, the position of the two candidates would be almost exactly reversed; Bryan would have a plurality of more than 600,000. This statement suggests strongly that the result in a single State cannot be dissociated from the result in other States. It is interesting as an arithmetical fact that twenty thousand voters, carefully located, might have reversed the verdict of 1896; but as a political fact it is valueless, and has no bearing upon the question of the practical working of the electoral system.

Almost identical conditions, it may also be observed, are found to exist at every election. In 1892, Mr. Cleveland had 277 electoral votes to 145 for Mr. Harrison — a larger excess than that of McKinley over Bryan in 1896. A change of 26,000 votes in California, Delaware, Illinois, Indiana, Kansas, North Dakota, and Wisconsin, would have given Harrison 226 votes, and an election. In 1888 a change of 7200 votes in New York alone would have elected Cleveland over Harrison. A change of 600 votes in New York, in 1884, would have elected Blaine over Cleveland. Garfield might have been defeated in 1880 by the loss to Hancock of 10,517 votes in New York, or by the loss of 11,452 votes in Maine, New Hampshire, Connecticut, Indiana, and Oregon. Hayes, but for circumstances favoring him, might have been replaced by Tilden without the loss of one popular vote. A study of the tables of popular votes in the following pages will reveal many similar facts, even back to 1836, when a slight change in

Pennsylvania would have compelled Van Buren to seek his election from the House of Representatives. It appears, then, that the situation in 1896 was nothing unusual, nor one to give the victors a lugubrious thrill, and the defeated a regretful sigh for what might have been. It is ordinarily the case at every election that some precincts, districts, counties, or States are carried by the victorious party by narrow margins ; and it is those which make the difference between victory and defeat. That the same thing is true of our Presidential elections is not a good ground for criticism of the electoral system.

Summing up the merits and faults of the system as modified by experience, we may at least say this : that it has almost always resulted in giving effect to the popular will, as well as to the will of the States — which was what it was designed to do. The restlessness which advocates radical change in any institution that has turned out not to be perfect, without due consideration of fresh evils that may be introduced by the reform, has devised many substitutes for the system which exists. Yet every substantial evil that has been experienced under the electoral clauses of the Constitution was introduced by politicians for party purposes, and might be cured — granting the desire to cure it — without altering these clauses. If any scheme can be presented which politicians might not pervert, it may be well to consider it.

II

THE FIRST ELECTION

It was provided by the Constitution of the United States that " the ratification of the conventions of nine States shall be sufficient for the establishment of this Constitution between the States so ratifying the same." The Constitution was adopted September 17, 1787. Before the close of the year it had been ratified by the conventions of three States. Two other States came to its support in January, 1788, one in February, one in April, and one in May, bringing the number up to eight. New Hampshire had the honor of giving the ninth vote, which made the Constitution effective, on June 21 ; Virginia followed closely on the 26th of the same month ; and New York yielded, after a memorable and bitter struggle, on July 26. The States of North Carolina and Rhode Island refused their assent to the Constitution, and adhered to the refusal until Congress had proposed a series of twelve amendments, ten of which were adopted. Neither of the two States participated in the first election.

The Constitution having become operative, it was the duty of the Congress of the Confederation, in obedience both to the advice of the Convention of 1787 and to its own resolution, to fix the time when the new government should come into being. A long and dreary discussion as to the place where the seat of government should be, caused a needless delay in starting the machinery, and, as will be seen presently, has resulted in a sudden stoppage of the legislative department on a fixed day, every alternate year, for more than a century. It was not until September 13, 1788, — New York City having at last been chosen as the temporary seat of government, — that a resolution was passed, reciting in a preamble that a sufficient number of States had ratified the Constitution, and directing that electors of President and Vice-President should be appointed on the first Wednesday in January, 1789, that they should meet in their respective States and give in their

votes on the first Wednesday in February, and that the new
Congress should meet in New York on the first Wednesday in
March.   The people everywhere had become impatient at the
tardy action of Congress, and hailed this resolution with great
satisfaction.

Nevertheless, the time allowed them was exceedingly short.
During the year that elapsed between the promulgation of the
Constitution by the Convention, and the summons to the first
political action under it, no preparations whatever had been
made for an election.   If it cannot be asserted positively that
no state legislature had passed a law providing for the election
of Representatives and the appointment of electors, prior to
the adoption of the resolution of Congress just referred to, it
is nevertheless believed that this is the fact.   Indeed, it must
have seemed to most people futile to pass laws providing for
elections under a Constitution that was bitterly opposed, and
that might never go into effect.   It may well be doubted if
Congress would have directed the establishment of a government in the nine States which first ratified the Constitution, if
Virginia and New York had not been included in the number.

Even in these days of railroads and telegraphs a period of
four months would be a short time in which to do all that was
to be done between September 13 and January 7.   The legislatures were to be summoned, laws were to be passed to
provide for elections, and candidates for the new positions
were to be canvassed and chosen.   At that time communication was slow.   Intelligence of the resolution of Congress
would hardly reach some of the distant state capitals in two
weeks.   The governor must then issue his proclamation sum-
moning the legislature, and here again allowance had to be
made both for the slowness of mails in notifying members in
the remote regions of the State, and for the time they must
necessarily consume in travelling to the capital.   All this before a discussion, perhaps prolonged, as to the manner in which
electors should be appointed ; and, if it should be determined
to give the people the privilege of choosing them, all the preparations for a popular election.   It seems to have been generally inferred from the shortness of the time allowed, that
Congress intended that the legislatures themselves should
make the choice.   " It is evident," wrote a newspaper correspondent at Philadelphia, on October 1, 1788, " that Congress
construe the Constitution that the legislatures of the several

States, not the people, are to choose the electors, as that body has ordered the choice of said electors to be on the first Wednesday of January, and their meeting for the choice of President four weeks later. For if the people, as hath been asserted, are to choose the electors, is it possible that in the large States of Massachusetts, Virginia, etc., the returns can be made for the choice, notice given to the persons chosen, and the persons thus chosen have time to meet together in the short space of one month? No, it is impossible, and can only be remedied by the legislature, who, in fact, are ' the States ' making the choice."

In five of the eleven States entitled to participate in the election the governors did not summon the legislature in time to provide for an election by the people, and thus they virtually required the legislature to make the appointment. These States were Connecticut, New Jersey, Delaware, South Carolina, and Georgia. The proceedings in some of the other States were interesting. The legislature of New Hampshire assembled on the 5th of November and passed an act for the election of representatives and electors on the third Monday in December (the 15th). The people were to bring in their votes for five electors, the full number to which the State was entitled. The votes were to be returned to the legislature, which was to be in session at the beginning of January; "and the persons having a majority of votes shall, on the first Wednesday of January next, be duly appointed and declared elected." In case the whole or any of the electors should not be chosen by a majority, then the General Court was to choose as many as might be wanting, from double that number of the candidates, having the highest number of votes. No elector received a majority, and it became the duty of the General Court to appoint a full list. The law had not prescribed the method of choice, and the two branches had great difficulty in coming to terms. The Senate claimed equal power with the House of Representatives in the appointment; the House insisted upon a joint ballot. The contest was prolonged far into the night, the House stubbornly refusing to admit the pretension of the Senate to a full negative upon its action. "The observations made by the members of the Senate, relative to their prerogative," writes one reporter, quoted by the Hartford "Courant," "were pertinent, manly, and firm — those of the House, ingenious, deep, and well-digested." It is not easy to decide between two sets of adjectives so well balanced, which branch of the General Court had the better of the argument Shortly before midnight, in order that the vote of the State might not be lost to Washington, "the Great American Fabius," the House yielded, with a protest against its action being regarded as a precedent, and concurred in the list of electors chosen by the Senate. They were all Federalists.

The plan adopted by the Massachusetts General Court was not unlike that of New Hampshire. The people in each representative district were to vote for two persons, inhabitants of the district. From the two persons in each district having the highest number of votes the General Court chose one; and it also chose, independently, two electors at large. The law prescribed that the choice should be by joint ballot.

The vote of New York was lost. The two branches of the legislature fell into a contest almost precisely like that in New Hampshire. The Assembly was willing to divide the electors with the Senate, when objection was made to its original proposition of a joint ballot. The Senate refused to agree to any plan which did not give it a full negative upon the action of the Assembly. The time for action was wasted in bitter contention. New York was not enthusiastic over the new Constitution, and many members of the legislature were rather glad than sorry that the deadlock was not broken until the time for an election had passed.

Pennsylvania, Maryland, and Virginia passed laws providing for popular elections, which took place without great excitement. Not only in these States, but in Massachusetts and New Hampshire, the vote was light. The two parties were made up of those who favored the Constitution on the one hand, and those who opposed it on the other. Political sentiment seems to have been largely one way or the other in each community. Here, the Federalists comprised nearly the whole population; there, scarcely a Federalist was to be found. There were thus present none of the elements necessary for a great political contest. The majority cast perhaps a half of their possible vote, the minority hardly appeared at the polls; in fact, they often had no candidates in the field.

The electors were, as the Constitution contemplated that they should be, free agents in the choice of President and Vice-President. Yet public opinion governed their action to a far greater degree than might have been anticipated in the

4783

discharge of a perfectly new function. One name, indeed, came spontaneously to the thoughts of all. The newspapers of the time and the private letters of statesmen show that it was universally regarded as fitting that George Washington should be President. As will be seen presently a suggestion of another result was made, but it came not from those who desired the defeat of General Washington, but from those who had or affected a fear that others might desire it. So far as can be ascertained, neither any elector nor any considerable number of the people countenanced opposition to Washington. It was from the first accepted as the obvious and proper course to give him a unanimous vote. But the electors were to vote for two persons, — he who received the highest number, being a majority, to be President; the candidate who received the next highest number, whether a majority or not, to be Vice-President. Public opinion gradually concentrated upon John Adams.

Most of the electors were, to use one of the phrases current at the time, men of "strong federal opinions," and it was but natural that they should desire to support a candidate who, like themselves, favored the new Constitution. Since the President was a citizen of a Southern State, it was deemed just to take the Vice-President from the North. These considerations, restricting the choice, were recognized early in the discussion. Hamilton was a most conspicuous leader of Federalist opinion; but he had not attained the age of thirty-five years, and therefore was not eligible to the office. A candidate from New England was indicated as desirable. The names of Governor Hancock, Samuel Adams, John Adams, and General Henry Knox, were canvassed. Knox was a soldier, like Washington, and was speedily rejected as a candidate. It was deemed necessary that Hancock should remain in the position of Governor of Massachusetts. Samuel Adams had been an opponent of the Constitution at the outset, and although he had subsequently advocated it, his early attitude on the question rendered him an unsuitable candidate. John Adams remained, — at least as conspicuous a figure in public life as any man in New England, qualified both by his talents and by his experience for the highest place, and open to none of the objections cited against the other Massachusetts candidates. He was a civilian; he would vacate no office where his services were needed, by becoming Vice-President; and he had written a book in defence of the Constitution. Moreover, his public services for many years, not the least of which had just been rendered as minister to England, and had ended not many months before in a dignified retirement, made him seem to most Federalists a peculiarly acceptable candidate. The sentiments of the friends of the Constitution are well set forth in an article in a Philadelphia paper under date of October 8, 1788, three months prior to the choice of electors : —

The electors of President of the United States on the part of the Commonwealth of Pennsylvania are to meet in the borough of Reading, where it is universally hoped and expected that one more tribute of merited approbation will be given to George Washington, Esq., by their unanimous suffrages. Of the several respected candidates in nomination for Vice-President, circumstances seem most in favor of John Adams, Esq. While the conciliating talents of Governor Hancock, and the attachment to him that prevails in Massachusetts, render him necessary to the peace of New England, Mr. Adams is perfectly at leisure to fill a seat for which nature, education, and the experience of several years and various courts in Europe have eminently and peculiarly qualified him.

Nevertheless there was another side of the question. Adams's relations to Washington during the Revolutionary war had been such that doubt was entertained if he would be acceptable to Washington. To an inquiry on this point there had come from Mount Vernon a cautious reply that —

Having taken it for granted that the person elected for that important place would be a true Federalist, in that case he was altogether disposed to acquiesce in the prevailing sentiments of the electors, without giving any unbecoming preference, or incurring any unnecessary ill-will.

Hamilton was consulted. He had generalized upon what he had seen of Mr. Adams ; and while admitting the merits of that gentleman, had an almost prophetic foresight of the political woes that would be caused by the infirmities of his temper. " On the whole," he wrote, " I have concluded to support him." It is impossible to say how much of American history would have been changed had Hamilton followed this resolution without modification. His distrust and misgivings led him to take a step which aroused the resentment of Adams and wounded his vanity. When we reflect how many of the acts of Adams which led to his defeat and the rout of the

Federalist party are to be ascribed directly to his rancor toward Hamilton, we seem almost to make the political history of the country for more than a generation turn on a trivial circumstance.

Although in all the newspaper references to the coming election, — one of which is quoted above, — Mr. Adams was spoken of as a candidate for Vice-President, that gentleman did not so regard himself, but rather as a candidate for the presidency. If he received more votes than Washington, he would be President ; if the votes were equal, the House of Representatives would choose one of the two. He showed plainly that he regarded his own merits as equal to those of Washington. Hamilton's offence was that he also foresaw the possibility that Adams's vote would be equal to Washington's, and took measures to prevent it. After the event it was clear that there had never been any danger ; but it does not, by any means, follow that Hamilton was over-anxious and officious. There was an understanding that the New York opponents of the Constitution would vote for George Clinton, and for Adams, or some other than Washington. Ultimately, as we have seen, New York chose no electors. It is said in the Life of Hamilton, by his son, that " for a time the pretensions of Franklin " to the presidency " were discussed in private circles. But the incomparably superior claims of Washington silenced this purpose, which there is no evidence was encouraged by Franklin, whose extreme age would alone have presented an insuperable objection." There is no evidence that Franklin was aware of the suggestion. Yet when such rumors were in the air, it was no more than common prudence on the part of Hamilton to do what he could to make Washington's election sure by cutting down the vote for Adams. This, moreover, was not only his right, but what almost every man in the country except Adams would thank him for accomplishing.

What Hamilton did was to send word into several States, advising that a unanimous vote be given to Washington, and that some of the votes which would naturally go to Adams be scattered. No doubt his advice was followed more extensively than was needful, and more than Hamilton himself intended. If we may take his own word for it, he did not at the time suppose that Mr. Adams would resent his action. In his famous letter on the character of John Adams, writter in 1800, with reference to the election of 1796 and the then pending election which resulted in the overthrow of Adams, he said, alluding to his interference in the first contest : —

Great was my astonishment and equally great my regret, when, afterwards, I learned from persons of unquestionable veracity that Mr. Adams had complained of unfair treatment in not having been permitted to take an equal chance with General Washington, by leaving the votes to an uninfluenced current.

No statement was ever made, so far as is known, how much of the scattering vote was due to Hamilton's advice. It is not difficult to attribute the seven votes given to other candidates by Connecticut and New Jersey electors to his influence. Those of Virginia seem rather anti-Federal than Hamiltonian vagaries. At all events, the long list of scattering votes shows how little reason there was for Hamilton's fears.

Under the Constitution the thirteen States were entitled to sixty-five representatives and twenty-six senators; and consequently to ninety-one electoral votes. Rhode Island and North Carolina, with three and seven votes, respectively, had not adopted the Constitution; the eight votes of New York were lost; and two electors of Maryland and two of Virginia failed to appear on the day of voting — the 4th of February. It was explained that the ice in the rivers and bay prevented one of the absent Maryland electors from attending, and gout held the other at home. The electoral votes were sixty-nine in number, and were cast as follows : —

STATES.	George Washington.	John Adams.	Samuel Huntington.	John Jay.	John Hancock.	Robert H. Harrison.	George Clinton.	John Rutledge.	John Milton.	James Armstrong.	Edward Telfair.	Benjamin Lincoln.
New Hampshire . . .	5	5	–	–	–	–	–	–	–	–	–	–
Massachusetts . . .	10	10	–	–	–	–	–	–	–	–	–	–
Connecticut	7	5	2	–	–	–	–	–	–	–	–	–
New Jersey	6	1	–	5	–	–	–	–	–	–	–	–
Pennsylvania	10	8	–	–	2	–	–	–	–	–	–	–
Delaware	3	–	–	3	–	–	–	–	–	–	–	–
Maryland	6	–	–	–	–	6	–	–	–	–	–	–
Virginia	10	5	–	1	1	–	3	–	–	–	–	–
South Carolina . . .	7	–	–	–	1	–	–	6	–	–	–	–
Georgia	5	–	–	–	–	–	–	–	2	1	1	1
Total	69	34	2	9	4	6	3	6	2	1	1	1

It may be well to note that, excepting John Jay and George Clinton, of New York, and John Hancock of Massachusetts, all the "scattering" candidates for Vice-President were "favorite sons" of the States which gave them votes. Georgia, in particular, distinguished itself by discovering four of its own citizens worthy to be placed second to Washington.

The consummation of the election of General Washington was an occasion of solemn joy throughout the country. The accounts of the voting are meagre. One description only of the scene has been found. In Massachusetts the electors had their ballots, for Washington and Adams, prepared before they came together. Having organized, they voted quickly and adjourned. "There was not a word spoken," reports the Worcester "Spy," "except in the choice of a chairman." Many of the newspapers expressed their feelings in the exuberant rhetoric of the day, when the election had taken place. Here is one example from Baltimore : —

The important day in the annals of America is past, which conferred on a single citizen those sovereign powers that require to be placed in one person, in order to render a nation happy in peace, and prosperous in war. Perhaps that day has exhibited what has never happened before in any part of the globe; above three millions of people, scattered over a country of vast extent, of opposite habits and different manners, all fixing their hopes on the same man, and unanimously voting for him only, without the intervention of force, artifice, plan, or concert. With what delight will the lover of mankind dwell on this period of history and cherish the memory of a people, who could thus feel and thus reward a life of great and virtuous actions?

The first Wednesday in March was the day fixed by the Congress of the Confederation for the meeting of the new Congress of the United States. It was more than a month after that date, on the 6th of April, 1789, that a quorum of senators appeared in their seats. It was nearly as difficult to secure the acceptance of the senatorial position by suitable persons, as it had been to persuade them to discharge the far less important duties devolved on members of the Continental Congress ; and the old vices of non-attendance and tardy attendance were still persistent. Nevertheless, since the fourth of March was the day appointed for the meeting, and since some of the senators appeared in their seats on that day, it was assumed that the whole government then came into being. Although Washington was not inaugurated until the 30th day of April, his first term was held to have ended on the 3d of March, 1793. The first Congress came to an end on the 3d of March, 1791; and every Congress since then has come to its constitutional term on the same day of that month. A more unfortunate period could not have been chosen, for the result has been that every alternate session is virtually limited to three months' duration. An earlier ratification of the Constitution by New Hampshire, Virginia, and New York, and greater promptness on the part of Congress, might have carried the day of the birth of the government back to December; and there might have been two sessions of full length. Or if the first Congress had taken the view that its term began when it completed its organization, that would have given a month more of time for the short session. Some half-hearted attempts have been made during the century to change the system which so greatly hampers and hurries Congress; but no action in that direction has ever been taken.

As soon as a quorum of senators was in attendance, immediate steps were taken for inducting the President and Vice-President into office. John Langdon, a senator from New Hampshire, was elected "president for the sole purpose of opening and counting the votes for President of the United States." A message was sent to the House of Representatives apprising that body of the presence of a quorum and of the temporary organization, "and that the Senate is now ready in the Senate Chamber to proceed, in the presence of the House, to discharge that duty; and that the Senate have appointed one of their members to sit at the clerk's table to make a list of the votes as they shall be declared, submitting it to the wisdom of the House to appoint one or more of their members for the like purpose."

The House appointed two tellers, and, having given notice to the Senate of its readiness to join that body, proceeded to the Senate Chamber. The President of the Senate opened and counted the vote. The Journal of the Senate reads that —

The Speaker and the House of Representatives attended in the Senate Chamber, and the president elected for the purpose of counting the votes declared the Senate and House of Representatives had met, and that he, in their presence, had opened and counted the votes of the electors for President and Vice-President of the United States, which were as follows : [The table given above is here inserted.]

Whereby it appeared that

George Washington, Esq., was elected President, and

John Adams, Esq., Vice-President, of the United States of America.

Notification to the President and Vice-President of their election was sent by the Senate by special messengers, and great preparations were made for the first inauguration. The journeys of Mr. Adams and General Washington — for Adams's was first in point of time — were like a triumphal progress. The Vice-President elect " sat out from Braintree," his home, escorted by the Roxbury troop of horse to Boston, where the cavalcade was received by a throng of applauding citizens, amid the ringing of the bells of the town. After a collation in his honor given by Governor John Hancock, another military company became his escort to Charlestown, and through Cambridge to Marlborough, where still another troop was waiting to receive him and accompany him on his way. The details of his journey through Connecticut are not preserved ; but he was met at the New York State line by the Light Horse of Westchester County, and escorted to the city. On April 21 he was introduced to the Senate. President Langdon left the chair and addressed Mr. Adams in a speech of congratulation ; and then the Vice-President took the chair and made a speech in reply. It is interesting to note that although he presided over the Senate thereafter, he did not take the oath of office until June 3. The Constitution prescribes a form of oath for the President, but not for other officers of the government. The act prescribing an oath of office was passed by Congress, and signed by the President on the first of June.

The journey of General Washington was much longer than Mr. Adams's, and was far more noteworthy for the popular demonstrations of love and devotion. Along the whole route he was greeted as only the sovereign of the people's hearts could be greeted. His progress from the New Jersey shore and his arrival in New York formed a fitting culmination of a journey, the like of which has never been seen on this continent. The ceremonies of inauguration soon followed, on the

30th of April. In the morning at nine o'clock, the people assembled in their respective churches for services of prayer for the success of the new government and the prosperity of the President. At noon, Washington was escorted from his house to the federal statehouse in Broad Street, where, upon a balcony and in the presence of a vast throng, the oath of office was administered by Chancellor Livingston. "I swear it. So help me, God!" ejaculated the first President. Then while the people shouted "Long live George Washington, President of the United States," he retired within the building to the Senate Chamber, where he delivered his inaugural address.

III

WASHINGTON RE-ELECTED UNANIMOUSLY

THE first administration was occupied chiefly in the organization of the new government, with the creation of departments, the formation of a revenue system, an adjustment of the public debt, and similar matters. Jefferson, at the head of the State Department, and Hamilton, at the Treasury, were the President's chief advisers. Circumstances gave to the younger man much greater prominence as the constructive statesman, at this momentous period, than to the author of the Declaration of Independence. The fact that to his department belonged naturally the duty of devising the financial measures which were of first importance ; the personal intimacy between the President and Hamilton ; and Washington's strong leaning to the Federalist view of public questions ; these all combined to render the Secretary of the Treasury conspicuous and successful, and to leave the Secretary of State in comparative obscurity. The line between parties was more clearly defined than one would have expected it to be in a country which had just been consolidated into a nation, and which had previously known no political divisions save those indicated by the terms " large States," " small States," " North," and " South." Not a few anti-Federalists were elected to Congress, and formed the nucleus of an active opposition. There is no doubt that Jefferson did what he could to thwart Hamilton and to defeat or modify the measures he devised, although those measures had the support of the President, the chief of both Secretaries. As governments are now organized, such a course of action would be regarded as base political treachery. It was not so at the time. The Secretaries did not form a cabinet, in the modern sense of the word ; Washington was not chosen President as the candidate of a party ; and being fully aware of Jefferson's dissent from the measures which he himself wished to be passed, he did not intimate a desire for the resignation of the Secretary of State.

Jefferson therefore felt free to organize and direct the party in opposition. It happened, unfortunately for Mr. Adams, that the Senate was closely divided, and that he was required, as Vice-President, to give the casting vote in favor of many of the most important measures of legislation devised by Hamilton. To no Vice-President since his time, it is believed, has fallen so large a share in active legislation. Mr. Adams was by nature and conviction a Federalist. He approved the measures brought forward, and, in spite of the grievance he had against Hamilton, loyally supported them. Hamilton himself, writing in the year 1800, expressed his entire satisfaction with Mr. Adams's course, and declared that it had the effect of modifying the unfavorable opinion of that gentleman which he had previously entertained. Indeed, while the canvass of 1796 was in progress he wrote to Mr. Adams, expressing a strong interest in his election; he referred to the Vice-President at this time as "a firm, honest, and independent politician;" and used all his influence to promote his success. But Adams's course had the opposite effect with the anti-Federalists. They could not or would not attack Washington; they trained all their guns on Adams.

The French Revolution was approaching one of its acute crises when the presidential canvass took place, for the king had already been deposed when the election took place, and was guillotined before the second inauguration. The great events in France were to have an important influence upon American politics. Mr. Adams was the first to suffer. His political enemies alighted upon some phrases in the published writings of the Vice-President which, they declared, proved him to be in favor of a monarchy, to have a liking for aristocracy, and to regard the Constitution as but a makeshift soon to be discarded for the system which they believed, or affected to believe, he preferred. They rang the changes on a passage in which he had extolled the working of government by "king, lords, and commons;" they jeered at his reference to the "well born;" and professed alarm lest he should be found conspiring against the Constitution which he had characterized as a "promising essay." Had such attacks been made before the outbreak of the French Revolution, it is doubtful if they would have caused anything but amusement. But now the warm approval of the uprising carried with it sympathy with the sentimental republicanism of the French people. The formality of the republican court at Philadelphia, the relations between the President and Congress which were a distinct imitation of those between king and parliament, — none of these things had offended the popular taste until sans-culottism began to triumph at Paris. Now the Republicans — the new name adopted by the anti-Federalist party — set up the spectre of monarchy for the express purpose of terrifying themselves into the eternal vigilance which is the price of liberty.

The opposition selected George Clinton of New York as their candidate in opposition to Mr. Adams. The preliminary electioneering was carried on in private letters between public men, and in communications in the newspapers. Rufus King wrote to Gouverneur Morris: "The opposition that now exists arises from other principles than those which produced an opposition to the Constitution, and proceeds from that rivalry which always has and will prevail in a free country. Washington and Adams will be re-chosen this winter : the first without opposition. Whether the opponents of Mr. Adams will combine their opposition I consider as uncertain. Should this be the case, Clinton will be their man." "A Citizen" wrote to the "Baltimore Advertiser" that all were in favor of Washington, but that "men who have a sense of equality and a disgust of supercilious superiority are, I am in hopes, linked as a strong chain against the Vice-President."

The leader among the newspapers opposing Adams was the "National Gazette," of Philadelphia, conducted by Philip Freneau. Freneau had gone to Philadelphia from New York, on an appointment by Jefferson as translator to the State Department, and had established his newspaper, which became the organ and mouthpiece of those who abused and vilified the Federalists and their measures, and particularly of those who hated Mr. Adams. Although the salary drawn by Freneau from the Government was a pitiful sum, his course as a protégé of the Secretary of State and as the editor of the most violent political newspaper in opposition to the administration was a public scandal. Both Freneau and Jefferson refused to see it in that light. The editor protested that his political course was uninfluenced by the secretary, and that his receipt of a salary from the government should not hamper him or deter him from expressing his opinions. Jefferson said nothing, and left Freneau's defence to stand for his own. It is not necessary to know whether Freneau's sworn denial that Jefferson had directly or indirectly dictated his course, was absolutely true or a disingenuous but skillfully worded evasion. Surely the situation, which either of the persons might have brought to a termination in a day, was not defensible. It is equally certain that Freneau was all the time faithfully serving Jefferson's purposes.

The other newspapers of the time had strong political leanings one way or the other, which can be detected by the prevailing tone of the communications printed by them. Yet they admitted to their columns letters on both sides of the question at issue. Classical signatures were much in vogue. A long series of articles signed "Catullus" was widely copied. That Hamilton was the author was suspected at the time. The letters are included in Hamilton's "Works." The discussion was carried on by "Lucius," "Marcus," "Mutius," "Antonius," "Philanthropos," and other Greeks and Romans. As the close of the canvass drew near, the virulence of party hatred became more intense, The enemies of Mr. Adams brought out one "local issue" to draw away a few votes. Congress had passed a bill apportioning members of the House of Representatives after the ascertainment of population at the first census. There was much bad feeling on this question. The bill passed by Congress encountered the first executive veto in the history of the government. Mr. Adams had, in the progress of the measure through the Senate, given a casting vote against a ratio of one representative to thirty thousand inhabitants. The defeat of that ratio reduced the representation of Virginia, and enraged the people of the State against Adams. Every electoral vote of Virginia was given to Clinton.

In most of the other States it was a strictly party contest. New England was solid for Federalism. New York had been carried, as before, by the Republicans. That is to say, it was counted for that party. At the spring election of 1792, the opposing candidates for governor were Clinton and Jay. There was a plurality of votes for Jay, but the canvassers threw out the returns from three counties and declared Clinton elected. Hamilton, writing to assure Adams of a wish for his success, intimated that the method of Clinton's election would not help his canvass for the vice-presidency. There is no evidence that it hurt his chances. The Middle States went for Washington and Adams. North Carolina and Georgia were carried for Clinton. This result was to have been anticipated in North Carolina, which had come into the Federal Union after the Constitution went into effect, and with unfeigned reluctance.

It was not until the last session of Congress before the election, that the following act regulating the election of President was passed. This law, modified and amended from time to time, as will be noted hereafter, remained in force until it was superseded by the act of 1887 : —

AN ACT *Relative to the Election of a President and Vice-President of the United States, and declaring the Officer who shall be President in case of Vacancies in the Offices both of President and Vice-President.*

SECTION 1. *Be it enacted*, etc., that, except in cases of the election of a President and Vice-President of the United States prior to the ordinary period, as hereinafter specified, electors shall be appointed in each State for the election of a President and Vice-President of the United States, within thirty-four days preceding the first Wednesday in December, 1792, and within thirty-four days preceding the first Wednesday in December in every fourth year succeeding the last election, which electors shall be equal to the number of senators and representatives to which the several States may by law be entitled at the time when the President and Vice-President thus to be chosen should come into office : *Provided always*, that when no apportionment of representatives shall have been made, after any enumeration, at the time of choosing electors, then the number of electors shall be according to the existing apportionment of senators and representatives.

SEC. 2. That the electors shall meet and give their votes on the said first Wednesday in December, at such place in each State as shall be directed by the legislature thereof ; and the electors in each State shall make and sign three certificates of all the votes by them given, and shall seal up the same, certifying on each that a list of the votes of such State for President and Vice-President is contained therein, and shall, by writing under their hands, or under the hands of a majority of them, appoint a person to take charge of and deliver to the President of the Senate, at the seat of government, before the first Wednesday in January then next ensuing, one of the said certificates ; and the said electors shall forthwith forward, by the post office, to the President of the Senate at the seat of government, one other of the said certificates ; and shall forthwith cause the other of the said certificates to be delivered to the judge of that district in which the said electors shall assemble.

SEC. 3. That the executive authority of each State shall cause three lists of the names of the electors of such State to be made and certified, and to be delivered to the electors on or before the said first Wednesday in December; and the said electors shall annex one of the said lists to each of the lists of their votes.

SEC. 4.   That if a list of votes from any State shall not have been received at the seat of government on the said first Wednesday in January, then the Secretary of State shall send a special messenger to the district judge in whose charge such list shall have been lodged, who shall forthwith transmit the same to the seat of government.

SEC. 5.   That Congress shall be in session on the second Wednesday in February, 1793, and on the second Wednesday in February succeeding every meeting of the electors, and the said certificates, or so many of them as shall have been received, shall then be opened, the votes counted, and the persons who shall fill the offices of President and Vice-President ascertained and declared agreeably to the Constitution.

SEC. 6.   That in case there shall be no President of the Senate at the seat of government on the arrival of the persons entrusted with the lists of the votes of the electors, then such persons shall deliver the lists of the votes in their custody into the office of the Secretary of State, to be safely kept and delivered over as soon as may be to the President of the Senate.

SEC. 7.   That the persons appointed by the electors to deliver the lists of votes to the President of the Senate shall be allowed, on the delivery of the said lists, twenty-five cents for every mile of estimated distance by the most usual road from the place of meeting of the electors to the seat of government of the United States.

SEC. 8.   That if any person appointed to deliver the votes of electors to the President of the Senate shall, after accepting his appointment, neglect to perform the services required of him by this Act, he shall forfeit the sum of one thousand dollars.

SEC. 9.   That in case of the removal, death, resignation, or disability both of the President and Vice-President of the United States, the President of the Senate, *pro tempore*, and, in case there shall be no President of the Senate, then the Speaker of the House of Representatives, for the time being, shall act as President of the United States until such disability be removed, or until a President be elected.

SEC. 10.   That whenever the office of President and Vice-President shall both become vacant, the Secretary of State shall forthwith cause a notification thereof to be made to the Executive of every State, and shall also cause the same to be published in at least one of the newspapers printed in each State, specifying that electors of the President of the United States shall be appointed or chosen in the several States within thirty-four days preceding the first Wednesday in December then next ensuing; *provided*, that there shall be a space of two months between the date of such notification and the said first Wednesday in December; but if there shall not be the space of two months between the date of such notification and the first Wednesday in December, and if the term for which the President and Vice-President last in office were elected shall not expire on the third day of March next ensuing, then the Secretary of State shall specify in the notification that the electors shall be appointed or chosen within thirty-four days preceding the first Wednesday in December in the year next ensuing, within which time the said electors shall accordingly be appointed or chosen; and the electors shall meet and give their votes on the said first Wednesday in December, and the proceedings and duties of the said electors and others shall be pursuant to the directions prescribed in this act.

SEC. 11. That the only evidence of a refusal to accept, or of a resignation of, the offices of President and Vice-President, shall be an instrument in writing declaring the same, and subscribed by the person refusing to accept or resigning, as the case may be, and delivered into the office of the Secretary of State.

SEC. 12. That the term of four years, for which the President and Vice-President shall be elected, shall in all cases commence on the fourth day of March next succeeding the day on which the votes of the electors shall have been given.

Fifteen States took part in the election of 1792. Rhode Island and North Carolina had ratified the Constitution; and Vermont had been admitted to the Union March 4, 1791, and Kentucky, June 1, 1792. Electors were appointed by the legislatures in Vermont, Rhode Island, Connecticut, New York, New Jersey, Delaware, South Carolina, Georgia, and Kentucky; by the people and the legislature in New Hampshire and Massachusetts; by the people alone in Pennsylvania, Maryland, Virginia, and North Carolina. In Massachusetts the people chose electors in five districts; in the other nine districts no one had a majority, and the General Court appointed electors for these districts and also two at large. In North Carolina a peculiar system was adopted which was never practiced anywhere else, nor at any other time. The apportionment, in accordance with the census of 1790, under which North Carolina was entitled to ten members of the House of Representatives, did not become law until April 13, 1792. The legislature was not then in session, nor did it meet again until the 15th of November. The electors were to meet, under the law of 1792, on the 5th of December. There was not time in the interval to provide for a popular election. Accordingly the legislature passed a law dividing the State into four districts, and directing the members of the legislature residing in each district to meet on the 25th of November and choose three electors.   This was a mere hasty makeshift, and the legislature made permanent provision at the same session for the choice of electors by the people by districts.

In the States where there was a popular election the vote seems to have been very light.   The largest number of votes given for any person as elector in Massachusetts was cast for Azor Orne, 693.   In Pennsylvania, where, two or three months before, forty thousand votes were cast for members of Congress, less than four thousand voted for electors.

It may be mentioned, as illustrating the extreme jealousy of state rights that prevailed at this time, that Governor Hancock sent a special message to the Massachusetts legislature, in the nature of a protest against the right of Congress to require the Executives of the several States to certify the lists required by section 3 of the act of 1792.   He was willing to perform the duty, but he would not concede the right of Congress to direct him to do it.

The election passed off without excitement or serious contest anywhere.   The result, by States, is indicated by the following table : —

STATES.	Washington.	Adams.	Clinton.	Jefferson.	Burr.
New Hampshire	6	6	–	–	–
Vermont	3	3	–	–	–
Massachusetts	16	16	–	–	–
Rhode Island	4	4	–	–	–
Connecticut	9	9	–	–	–
New York	12	–	12	–	–
New Jersey	7	7	–	–	–
Pennsylvania	15	14	1	–	–
Delaware	3	3	–	–	–
Maryland	8	8	–	–	–
Virginia	21	–	21	–	–
North Carolina	12	–	12	–	–
South Carolina	8	7	–	–	1
Georgia	4	–	4	–	–
Kentucky	4	–	–	4	–
Total	132	77	50	4	1

The counting of the electoral vote was for the first time a matter of previous agreement between the two Houses of Congress, and the system pursued in 1793 was, with occasional slight but sometimes significant modifications, that which was followed for a great many years. The House of Representatives proposed, February 5, 1793, the appointment of a joint committee " to ascertain and report the mode of examining the votes for President and Vice-President, and of notifying the persons who shall be elected of their election, and to regulate the time, place, and manner of administering the oath of office to the President." The Senate agreed, and the committee reported to the two Houses, February 11 : —

That the two Houses shall assemble in the Senate Chamber on Wednesday next at twelve o'clock; that one person shall be appointed a teller on the part of the Senate (two on the part of the House), to make a list of the votes as they shall be declared ; that the result shall be delivered to the President of the Senate, who shall announce the state of the vote, and the persons elected, to both Houses, assembled as aforesaid, which shall be deemed a declaration of the persons elected President and Vice-President, and, together with a list of the votes, be entered on the Journals of the two Houses.

This mode was observed.

The two Houses having accordingly assembled, the certificates of the electors of the fifteen States of the Union, which came by express, were, by the Vice-President, opened, read, and delivered to the tellers appointed for the purpose, who, having examined and ascertained the votes, presented a list of them to the Vice-President, which list was read to the two Houses, and is as follows : [Here follows the above table.]

Whereupon

The Vice-President declared George Washington unanimously elected President of the United States for the period of four years to commence with the 4th of March next; and

John Adams elected, by a plurality of votes, Vice-President of the United States for the same period, to commence with the 4th of March next.

It will be observed that in this case the Vice-President both opened *and read* the certificates, and that the tellers did no more than verify and tabulate the returns. The exclusive power of the Vice-President to count the votes was thus asserted and exercised in a marked manner. On the next occasion, as we shall see, the use of this power might have been a matter of some importance.

The inauguration of Washington at the beginning of his second term was almost scandálously unceremonious, yet not so informal as it came near to being.   The mad passion against outward show, an importation from France, led to frequent criticisms in the Republican newspapers of the semi-regal state in which the President was supposed to live.   Adams, of course, was not spared.   He too was denounced for the luxury of his mode of life, and the shafts aimed at him took effect.   He gave up his house in Philadelphia, sent his wife home to Massachusetts to manage the farm, and himself went to reside in lodgings.   When the day upon which the oath of office was to be taken a second time by the President elect drew near, the time and place of the ceremony became the subject of discussion in the cabinet.   Jefferson proposed that General Washington take the oath privately in his own house and send a certificate thereof to Congress. Hamilton fell in with this proposition; but the other members of the cabinet objected, and the plan was not adopted. At noon, precisely, on the 4th of March, Washington unattended entered the Senate Chamber, where were gathered many of the senators, some of the representatives who lingered after the adjournment of Congress, certain public officers, and " a number of private citizens."   He took the oath of office, delivered his inaugural address, and then retired as quietly as he had come.

IV

JOHN ADAMS

DURING Washington's first administration, domestic questions occupied the government chiefly and gave rise to party conflicts: the funding system and the excise law before all others. The first, which reduced the chaos of national finance to order, and restored the credit of the United States, nevertheless had necessarily some features which seemed a justification of the accusation that it was devised for the relief of the well-to-do. Accordingly it aroused the antagonism of the same class which, in modern times, denounces measures for the payment of national obligations in good faith, in order to maintain the credit of the country, as designed for the sole benefit of the bondholders. The excise law was passed in 1791, after violent opposition in Congress. Its execution was resisted more or less from the beginning; but it was not until 1794 that the situation became so acute that a large armed force became necessary to quell what has passed into history as the " Whiskey Insurrection." At that time occurred the first serious collision between federal and state authority. Governor Mifflin, of Pennsylvania, a Republican partisan, refused to take the initiative, and Washington called out the militia on the certificate of a federal judge that an insurrection existed. Little more than a display of force was required to put down the insurrection. The whole affair resulted, not a little to the surprise of both parties, in strengthening the government and making it popular. The people realized for the first time that they had created a power which was capable of making itself respected at home.

Meantime two most serious questions of foreign policy had been raised, and both of them had an important influence upon the elections which determined who should be the second President. The arrival, reception, and conduct of " Citizen " Genet, the French minister sent over by the Girondist government, excited the most bitter party controversy

the country had known. Although Jefferson himself, as
Secretary of State, wrote and signed the account of Genet's
diplomatic impertinences, and demanded his recall, yet his
political attitude toward the agitation and his strong sympathy for the French rendered it impossible that he should
remain in the cabinet as a loyal supporter of the administration. The appointment of Jay, the Chief Justice, to negotiate
a treaty with England, aroused but little public feeling. The
treaty which he negotiated was ratified by the Senate, by exactly the constitutional two-thirds majority, before its terms
were made public. But when it was published there arose
such a storm of opposition to its promulgation by the President as no Executive since Washington has had to encounter.
Public meetings at which the most violent language was used,
riots, burning the treaty and the effigy of Jay, — these were
every-day incidents in all parts of the country. This is not
the place to do more than refer to the events of the time and
indicate their bearing upon the ensuing election. The details
must be left to the general historian. It is sufficient to say
that the firmness of Washington was proof against the popular
clamor, against the personal abuse to which he was subjected,
even against the determination of a great majority of the
House of Representatives, as expressed in a resolution calling upon him for a copy of the instructions to Jay, with a
view to the impeachment of the ambassador. He promulgated the treaty, he remained calm and silent under vituperation, he returned a respectful but unflinching refusal to the
demand for Jay's instructions. In the end, too, the House
itself, by the narrowest of majorities, agreed to pass the measures necessary for carrying the treaty into effect. It is not
to be supposed that the sentiments of the American people
were expressed in the noisy outcries of the opposition. Events
proved that it was a minority only that displayed such violence of hostility toward measures which were greatly to the
benefit of the United States during the next ten years. But
the apparent strength of the democratic societies not only inspired the opposition party with a hope of capturing the government, but caused apprehension and anxiety throughout the
ranks of the Federalists.

It was made known by Washington to his closest intimates,
early in the year 1796, that he intended to decline a reëlection.
His purpose was rumored, but not definitely made public, early

in September. Those who had been aware of his intention had already canvassed the subject and were agreed upon their candidates. Several names were considered for the presidency. Hamilton was eligible, and he was the undoubted leader of his party. But he had made many enemies, and his candidacy would surely have aroused intense antagonism. There was a stain upon his private character; and a threat had been made that should he come forward as a candidate, certain papers alleged to be damaging to his integrity would be published. There is no evidence worthy to be regarded either that a truthful accusation against his financial honor could have been brought, or that a fear of exposure deterred him from becoming a candidate. He was rather a king-maker than a candidate for the throne.

If Hamilton were not to seek the office, the two most prominent candidates were Adams and Jay. It seems to have been universally felt that although Jay's talents fitted him for the office, his negotiation of the treaty with England would cost him enough votes to endanger his election. Adams was directly in the line of promotion; his services to the country during a long public life had given him as good title as any statesman had to the gratitude of his country; and his conduct in the Vice-President's chair had been fully acceptable to the Federal party. Accordingly it was agreed at a conference of Federalist members of Congress that Mr. Adams should be the candidate for President; and Thomas Pinckney of South Carolina was chosen as the candidate for Vice-President. The date of the nominations is not known. The time is fixed vaguely in a letter from Oliver Wolcott to Henry W. Edwards, quoted by Gibbs (vol. ii. p. 488), as the summer of 1796.

At about the same time, as we learn from the same authority, Jefferson and Burr were agreed upon by a conference of Republican members of Congress, as the candidates of their party. The Republicans seem to have arrived at a tacit understanding that Mr. Jefferson was to be their candidate, before the conference was held. Jefferson had been the leader and organizer of the party while still in Washington's cabinet. From his retirement at Monticello he had conducted a copious correspondence with the chief men of the party, full of comment on passing events and of advice as to their course of action. He was now the natural, and, indeed, the inevitable candidate. Republican opinion, in the North at all events, accepted Aaron Burr as the candidate for Vice-President. Burr had, by his political adroitness and activity, displaced George Clinton as the leader in New York of the Republican party. The second position was already regarded as one of importance vastly inferior to that of the first. Neither Mr. Pinckney nor Mr. Burr would have been generally regarded as possessing strong claims to the presidency. The names of the candidates for the vice-presidency were not usually coupled with those of the leaders. "It requires no talent at divination," said a writer in the "Boston Gazette," a Republican paper, in September, 1796, "to decide who will be candidates for the chair. Thomas Jefferson and John Adams will be the men, and whether we shall have at the head of our executive a steadfast friend to the rights of the people, or an advocate for hereditary power and distinction, the people of the United States are soon to decide." An unsigned letter from Virginia, dated September 24, published in all the papers, stated: "I have been informed that Mr. Edmund Randolph, who has lately visited Mr. Jefferson, says that Mr. Jefferson will serve in the office of President of the United States, if elected."

The canvass began tamely enough. For two or three weeks after the appearance of Washington's Farewell Address, which was dated September 17, 1796, the subject of the coming election was rarely even mentioned in the newspapers. But the contest soon became earnest and bitter. For the most part it took the form of an intensely partisan comparison of the records and views of the two candidates. The leading disputant on the Federal side wrote, over the signature "Phocion," a series of nearly thirty articles.[1] Although the papers consisted largely of attacks upon Jefferson, two or three of them were devoted to a strong defence of Adams. The stoutest opponent of the Vice-President adopted the signature "A Federalist." His position and arguments were anything but Federalist. Adams's record was assailed most virulently, and Jefferson was warmly praised. It must be said that the debate on both sides was disingenuous. Jefferson was not only berated for acts which in the minds of his opponents constituted real offences, but was accused of many things which it was easy to

---

[1] The authorship of the letters is not known. They are attributed by some historians to Hamilton; but they are not included by J. C. Hamilton in a list of his father's works, and Lodge, when preparing the memoir of Hamilton, could find no evidence that they were written by him.

show he had not done. But if he had reason to complain of a certain degree of unfairness on the part of his enemies, the misrepresentation of Adams's political opinions and public writings was shameful and scandalous. His expressions were garbled and deliberately misquoted. Perhaps no American public man has ever been treated more foully in this respect than was he. Bache's "Aurora" was a prototype of many a party newspaper edited with a conscienceless purpose to win political battles at any expense to the truth; but none of its successors have gone beyond it in malignity and unveracity.

There were some unconscious humors of the canvass, — among which may be classed the appeal to the voters of the country to support a " *Christian* President," — an attempt to rally the religious sentiment of the country against Jefferson. On the other hand nothing could have been more audacious, and nothing less convincing to men who knew anything of politics, than this warning, published in the Philadelphia papers shortly before the election : —

Freemen of Pennsylvania! Take caution! The aristocrats of our country are endeavoring to deceive you with the name of Washington. They presume to call theirs [the] " Washington ticket." Beware, fellow citizens, of the Washington ticket. It is intended to support the electors of the monarchist Adams, and begins with the name of Israel Whelen.

Our Republican ticket begins with the name of Thomas McKean, and is intended to support the election of the Republican Jefferson. Believe us, fellow citizens, that your President Washington loves a Republican and hates a monarchist. He therefore wishes that the Republican Jefferson may be his successor.

Shortly before the election a " bombshell " was thrown by the minister of France, " Citizen " Adet. He addressed a note to the Secretary of State, and also caused it to be published in all the newspapers which would print it, reproaching the administration with having violated its treaties with France, and with conducting itself in a most ungrateful manner toward a country which had rendered important assistance in the Revolutionary struggle. He also announced that he was directed by his government to suspend his diplomatic duties. The interruption of relations was, however, not to be interpreted " as a rupture between France and the United States, but as a mark of just discontent, which was to last until the government of the United States returned to sentiments and to measures more conformable to the interests of the alliance, and to the sworn friendship between the two nations."

What effect this manifesto had upon voters cannot be stated. Certainly it did not change the result, so far as Mr. Adams was concerned; but, considering the closeness of the vote in Pennsylvania, it is more than possible, indeed it is quite probable, that it contributed the electoral votes which made Jefferson Vice-President.

Some light is thrown upon the political machinery of the time by certain notices which appear in the newspapers. In Pennsylvania, on the day before the adjournment of the legislature, a conference of Republican members, together with citizens from different counties of the State, met and agreed upon a list of electors. This is the "ticket" just mentioned "which begins with the name of Thomas McKean." On the following day a similar meeting of Federalists made up a list of electors supposed to be favorable to Adams. Meetings of members of the two parties were afterward held at the county seats, and the tickets were ratified. In Virginia the practice of self-nomination, then and for a long time afterward followed with respect to seats in Congress, was in operation. Charles Sims offered himself as a candidate for elector in the Alexandria district, and announced that, if chosen, he should vote for Patrick Henry and John Adams. Ralph Wormeley, in another district, offered himself; and said that he preferred Washington for President, but that if he refused to stand, "it would be my part most diligently to search out for his successor a character the most resembling his in political principles, in sound judgment, in unexampled prudence, and in unshaken firmness." As this statement of his purpose seemed to be too vague, and he was asked for whom he would vote, he sent another communication to a Richmond newspaper, in which he discussed, and answered in the negative, the question whether an elector should disclose his intention. It did not become necessary for him to disclose it. He was not elected.

The appointment of electors was made, on various days, during the month of November, 1796. Sixteen States took part in the election, Tennessee having been admitted to the Union on June 1, 1796. The electors for that State were chosen by the legislature. Those for North Carolina were elected by the people. No other State changed its system, and there were, therefore, six States where there was a popular election, while in the other ten the choice was made by the legislature. The Federalists carried all the States north of Pennsylvania ; the Republicans all the States from Virginia southward. Pennsylvania was unexpectedly lost by the Federalists, who were nevertheless successful in Delaware, and in six of the ten districts of Maryland — one of which they carried by a majority of only four votes.

It is impossible to make a reasonably complete statement of the popular vote, even in the States where the people made the choice. But it is interesting to note how easily the result might have been different from what it was. In Pennsylvania the vote was extremely close. There were, as we have seen, two tickets, each bearing fifteen names. The highest number polled by any candidate for elector was 12,306; the lowest of the thirty had 12,071. Thus 235 votes only represented the greatest difference ; and two of the Federalist electors were chosen. The fact that, nevertheless, Adams received but one electoral vote in the State will be explained presently. It is necessary now merely to observe that a change of less than a hundred votes in Pennsylvania would have resulted in the election of Thomas Pinckney, instead of Thomas Jefferson, as Vice-President. It is even open to the student of history to maintain, basing an argument upon the events which intervened between the appointment of electors and the discharge of their duty, that the change might possibly have made Pinckney President and Adams Vice-President. Had Governor Mifflin complied strictly with the law requiring returns of the election to be made within fourteen days, when the governor was to proclaim the result, Jefferson would certainly have been defeated.

The contest in Massachusetts was fierce, and the Republicans showed unexpected strength. Governor Samuel Adams was a candidate for elector in the Boston district, but was defeated. The legislature chose electors for the districts in which no choice had been made by the people, in accordance with the system that had been in operation at the two previous elections. Among those thus appointed was Elbridge Gerry, who was inclined to support the Republicans. He voted, nevertheless, for Adams and Pinckney. The General Court passed a resolution authorizing the electoral college to fill any vacancies that might occur. Governor Adams signed the resolution ; but the next day, having, no doubt, perceived that every vacancy would subtract a vote from John Adams, he went to the office of the Secretary of State, erased his name from the resolution, and sent a message to the General Court communicating his reasons for so doing. Second thoughts are best, no doubt ; but the right of the governor to act upon them was not, in this case, admitted.

The canvass did not end with the appointment of the electors. "Phocion" still continued to give reasons why Jefferson should not be chosen ; but the articles made no impression upon the electors. The Republican candidate was sure of every opposition vote. The situation was far from clear on the Federalist side. Hamilton had, from the beginning, urged an equal support by the electors of Adams and Pinckney. He gave frankly his reason for the advice, "All personal and partial considerations must be discarded, and everything must give way to the great object of excluding Jefferson." New York would be unanimous for both the Federal candidates. "I hope New England will be so too. Yet I have some apprehensions on this point, lest the fear that he may outrun Mr. Adams should withhold votes from Pinckney. Should this happen, it will be in my opinion a most unfortunate policy. It will be to take *one* only instead of *two* chances against Mr. Jefferson ; and well weighed, there can be no doubt that the exclusion of Mr. Jefferson is far more important than any difference between Mr. Adams and Mr. Pinckney."

This is not the place to review in detail the points raised by the grandson of Mr. Adams and the son of Mr. Hamilton in the endeavor of each to cast upon the ancestor of the other the blame of a controversy which was fraught with disaster to the Federalist party. Mr. Adams himself did not think, after the election was over, that Hamilton had plotted his overthrow. In February, 1797, he wrote, "I believe they," including Hamilton, "honestly meant to bring in me, but they were frightened with a belief that I should fail, and they in their agony thought it better to bring in Pinckney than Jefferson." Mr. Adams changed his opinion on this point afterward ; and it should be remembered, lest the change should be counted against him, that when he wrote what has just been quoted he had no evidence on either side of the question. Hamilton himself supplied that evidence when his famous letter on John Adams was published four years later. "It is true," he wrote, "that a faithful execution of this plan " — an equal vote for the two candidates in the Northern States — " wouid have given Mr. Pinckney a somewhat better chance than Mr. Adams; nor shall it be concealed that an issue favorable to the former would not have been disagreeable to me; as indeed I declared at the time in the circle of my confidential friends. My position was that if chance should decide in favor of Mr. Pinckney, it probably would not be a misfortune; since he to every essential qualification for the office added a temper far more discreet and conciliatory than that of Mr. Adams."

It is only natural that Hamilton's cool disregard of Adams's sensibilities; his studied though veiled denial of Adams's superior merits; and his evident attempt to use Adams's own friends to carry out a policy which would have humiliated the Vice-President; — that all these things were resented at the time, and that they have been made the basis of serious accusations against Hamilton's good faith. But while, on the one hand, he cannot be exonerated from the charge that he was not straightforward and that he concealed one of the chief reasons of his action, on the other hand, it is not just to suppose that his motives were unworthy. They were not selfish. He sought no preferment for himself. In the circumstances of the selection of the two candidates his motives were not disloyal to the party. Moreover there is no reason to suppose that he had recurred, at this time, to his former unfavorable opinion of Adams, toward whom he cherished no personal animosity. Nevertheless, his course brought present disaster to the party; and it laid the foundation of the estrangement, the mutual distrust, and the bitter hatred between two men capable of large and long continued service to the country, which led to the ultimate ruin of the party.

Hamilton's plan failed. No less than eighteen electors in New England resolved that Pinckney's vote should not exceed Adams's, withheld their votes from the candidate for Vice-President, and scattered them upon others. Three Maryland electors did the same thing. Pinckney received, with Jefferson, the eight votes of South Carolina, and one vote more than Adams in Pennsylvania. He had therefore twelve votes less than Adams. Having also nine votes less than Jefferson, he failed of an election. One vote for Jefferson in Pennsylvania deserves notice, since it is believed to have been given by the only elector in the history of the country who has ever betrayed the trust reposed in him by those who supported him.

The closeness of the vote in Pennsylvania already has been recorded, and the fact that two Federalist electors slipped in. One of the two voted for Jefferson and Pinckney. The treachery of this elector was the subject of an exceedingly plain-spoken communication in the " United States Gazette " from an exasperated Federalist. " What ! " he exclaimed. " Do I chuse Samuel Miles to determine for me whether John Adams or Thomas Jefferson shall be President? No! I chuse him to *act*, not to *think*."

Not until a week or two after the electors had voted was the result definitely known, namely, that John Adams had one vote more than the number necessary to elect him; and that Jefferson, having the next highest number, only two less than a majority, was chosen Vice-President. The electoral votes were, by States, as follows: —

STATES.	John Adams, Mass.	Thomas Jefferson, Va.	Thomas Pinckney, S. C.	Aaron Burr, N. Y.	Samuel Adams, Mass.	Oliver Ellsworth, Conn.	George Clinton.	John Jay, N. Y.	James Iredell, N. C.	George Washington, Va.	Samuel Johnson, N. C.	John Henry, Md.	Charles C. Pinckney, S. C.
New Hampshire	6	–	–	–	–	6	–	–	–	–	–	–	–
Vermont	4	–	4	–	–	–	–	–	–	–	–	–	–
Massachusetts	16	–	13	–	–	1	–	–	–	–	2	–	–
Rhode Island	4	–	–	–	–	4	–	–	–	–	–	–	–
Connecticut	9	–	4	–	–	–	–	5	–	–	–	–	–
New York	12	–	12	–	–	–	–	–	–	–	–	–	–
New Jersey	7	–	7	–	–	–	–	–	–	–	–	–	–
Pennsylvania	1	14	2	13	–	–	–	–	–	–	–	–	–
Delaware	3	–	3	–	–	–	–	–	–	–	–	–	–
Maryland	7	4	4	3	–	–	–	–	–	–	–	2	–
Virginia	1	20	1	1	15	–	3	–	–	1	–	–	–
North Carolina	1	11	1	6	–	–	–	–	3	1	–	–	1
South Carolina	–	8	8	–	–	–	–	–	–	–	–	–	–
Georgia	–	4	–	–	–	–	4	–	–	–	–	–	–
Kentucky	–	4	–	4	–	–	–	–	–	–	–	–	–
Tennessee	–	3	–	3	–	–	–	–	–	–	–	–	–
Total	71	68	59	30	15	11	7	5	3	2	2	2	1

The proceedings in preparation for the count of the electoral votes were in all respects similar to those of four years previous, except that the proposition for a joint committee originated this time in the Senate. The count itself is interesting on account of the fact that Mr. Adams himself presided, opened, and read the certificates, and declared himself elected, when the rejection of four votes which had been called in question would have defeated him and elected his opponent. The legislature of Vermont had appointed electors, but had not previously passed a law directing how they should be appointed. It was contended privately, by some persons, that the appointment was invalid. But the question was not raised in Congress, or at the joint meeting for the count of the votes. Mr. Adams's opponents did not feel sure of their ground, and probably did not know how to proceed to make their objections effective. Mr. Madison wrote to Jefferson, January 8, 1797, " If the Vermont votes be valid, as is now generally supposed, Mr. Adams will have seventy-one and you sixty-eight, Pinckney being in the rear of both."

Mr. Adams himself could certainly not raise the question of the validity of the Vermont votes; but he seems to have given an opportunity for objections if anyone should see fit to raise them. The record shows this. When the tellers had reported the result, Mr. Adams thus addressed the assembled senators and representatives : —

Gentlemen of the Senate and House of Representatives, — By the report which has been made to me by the tellers appointed by the two Houses to examine the votes, there are 71 votes for John Adams, 68 for Thomas Jefferson [and so on to the end of the list]. The whole number of votes are 138; 70 therefore make a majority; so that the person who has 71 votes, which is the highest number, is elected President, and the person who has 68 votes, which is the next highest number, is elected Vice-President.

At this point Mr. Adams sat down for a moment. After an interval of silence, he arose again and said : —

In obedience to the Constitution and laws of the United States, and to the commands of both Houses of Congress, expressed in their resolution passed in the present session, I declare that John Adams is elected President of the United States for four years, to commence with the fourth day of March next; and that Thomas Jefferson is elected Vice-President of the United States for four years, to commence on the fourth day of March next.

And may the Sovereign of the Universe, the Ordainer of civil government on earth, for the preservation of liberty, justice and peace among men, enable both to discharge the duties of these offices conformably to the Constitution of the United States, with conscientious diligence, punctuality, and perseverance.

The inauguration took place in the chamber of the House of Representatives, which was crowded to its utmost capacity. The oath was administered by Chief Justice Ellsworth. General Washington was present, with a "countenance as serene and unclouded as the day," so Adams reports in a letter to his wife, descriptive of the ceremony, which he closes by saying, "All agree that, taken altogether, it was the sublimest thing ever exhibited in America."

THE JEFFERSON-BURR CONTEST

THE administration of John Adams witnessed the total wreck of the Federalist party, a result of divided leadership. Although Mr. Adams had become President by an extremely narrow majority of votes, yet his party was stronger in both branches of Congress than it had been during Washington's second administration. Of the sixth Congress, during the latter half of Adams's term, the Republicans formed but a small minority. The strength which the dominant party might wisely have used in consolidating its own power, through the adoption of a policy in harmony with its principles, was wasted in internal conflict. The blame, in a political sense, rested upon both the Federalist factions. Hamilton had become accustomed to exert a great, almost a controlling influence over Washington. He was consulted by the general quite as freely after his retirement from the cabinet as before. He was the leader of his own party in the same sense that Jefferson was the leader of the Republicans. That is to say, the chief men of the party sought his advice; he frequently volunteered counsel to them, upon the public questions that arose; and his opinion was usually followed. Mr. Adams was not one of Hamilton's coterie, nor was he a man either to seek advice as to his course of action, or to accept it with equanimity. From this situation arose all the bad feeling and secret intrigue that make this administration a period of political scandal.

Adams continued in office all the members of Washington's cabinet; Pickering, Secretary of State; Wolcott, Secretary of the Treasury; McHenry, Secretary of War; and Lee, Attorney-General. These men were in frequent correspondence with Hamilton. Before the first month of Adams's administration had closed, Hamilton wrote to Wolcott advocating strongly the sending of three ministers to France. Wolcott replied the next day; and in his letter revealed to Hamilton, "in the most perfect confidence," the fact that the President had already proposed to him the formation of such a commission to negotiate with France. In this incident is to be found the key of the whole situation within the administration during the ensuing four years. Hamilton could not, or would not, — at any rate, did not, — throw off the habit of advising the government and endeavoring to control its action. Since he had not the same influence over Adams as he had exercised over Washington, he operated through the secretaries who were already accustomed to receive and act upon his counsel. The secretaries, habituated to this influence, which had been so potent over the first President, whom they revered more than they did the second, dropped insensibly into the way of listening to Hamilton rather than to their chief, and — what wrought all the mischief — of measuring the intelligence and political sagacity of the President by the degree of deference he paid to Hamilton's judgment. It is not necessary to hold them base or even treacherous on this account, as does John Adams's grandson and biographer, and as all the anti-Federalist historians do. But the situation created was intolerable; and a much more even-tempered man than Mr. Adams might well be excused for losing control over himself when he discovered that his own subordinates were executing not his will, but that of another. In the very case under consideration, Mr. Wolcott had been approached by the President on the subject of a mission to France, and had shown a decided opposition to the measure. But in replying to Hamilton he wrote: "You know that I am accustomed to respect your opinions; and at any rate I am not so ignorant of the extent of your influence with the friends of government as not to be sensible that if you are known to favor the sending a commission, either nothing will be done or your opinion will prevail." Mr. Wolcott did not quite give up his opposition to the mission, but he was less strenuous after learning what Hamilton thought.

As time went on, the secretaries, particularly Pickering and Wolcott, besprinkled their correspondence with phrases indicating their contempt for their chief. That he was vain, indiscreet, opinionated, jealous, distrustful of many prominent men in his own party, yet guilelessly trustful toward some of the most artful of his political opponents, — all this must be admitted. Yet it might have been prevented from causing the confusion and disaster that followed, had the members of the cabinet themselves been discreet and wise politicians. When they found that they were unable to bend the President to Hamilton's will, because he was headstrong and they were his intellectual inferiors, they should have become the agents of the President's will, or retired from office.

The foregoing review of the situation is necessary, because in the relations between the President and the prominent men of the Federalist party is to be found the sole immediate cause of the political overturn in the year 1800. Adams's inaugural address was well received, even by those who had opposed his election. The popularity which he thus achieved increased and continued during the greater part of his term; although the dissatisfaction of the politicians of his own party grew more intense as the prejudice against him on the part of the people at large vanished. There was, all the time, an alert opposition, presided over by its ablest leader, whom circumstances had placed in the most favorable position for observation and for taking advantage of every mistake of the administration, and yet relieved of all responsibility for the course of public affairs.

The question which overshadowed all others during the administration was the relations with France. The insulting rejection of Gen. C. C. Pinckney as minister, and his expulsion from French territory, became known officially to the government on the 21st of March, 1797, before the administration had been three weeks in office. The appointment of Elbridge Gerry, John Marshall, and General Pinckney as a special embassy; the contemptuous treatment they received from the French directory; the corrupt proposals made to them by Talleyrand, acting through an agent; the X. Y. Z. letters; Adams's manly refusal to send another minister until assurance should be given that he would be received; his nomination of Murray as minister on the receipt of a vague intimation indirectly conveyed, that a minister would be received, without consultation with any member of the cabinet; the substitution of a commission for a single minister; the opposition of the secretaries to the step, and Pickering's studied delay in making ready for the departure of the envoys; and Adams's petulant order that they should sail before a specified day; this is a mere catalogue of the chief events in the history of the French negotiation. There were many echoes of the

affair in home politics : the resolution to organize an army, and
the ensuing difficulty relating to Hamilton's rank as a general
officer, ending with a victory for Hamilton, through the help
of Washington ; the establishment of a navy, a measure most
strenuously opposed by the whole Republican party, but heartily supported by Federalists of both factions; the Alien laws
and the Sedition act; and the Virginia and Kentucky resolutions of 1798 and 1799.

Of all these matters, as political issues between parties, the
last mentioned only survived the administration.   An examination of other pages in this book will show that the Democratic national platforms of 1848, 1852, and 1856 declared that
"every attempt . . . ought to be resisted with the same spirit
which swept the Alien and Sedition laws from our statute-
book."   The resolutions of 1798 and 1799 also appear in the
Democratic platforms of 1848 and 1852 as embodying principles to which the party still adhered.   There were two "Alien"
laws.   One of them authorized the President to "order such
aliens as he should judge dangerous to the peace and safety of
the United States, or should have reasonable grounds to suspect were concerned in any treasonable or secret machinations
against the government thereof, to depart out of the territory
of the United States."   The other act empowered the President, upon a declaration of war, to cause the subjects of the
hostile government " to be apprehended, restrained, secured,
and removed, as alien enemies."   The Sedition act declared it
an offence, and prescribed the punishment and its mode, to
combine or conspire, with intent to oppose the government,
when directed by the proper authority, to intimidate an officer
from the performance of his duty, to incite riots or insurrec-
tions against the laws of Congress, or to publish false, scandalous, and malicious writings against the government, either
House of Congress, or the President, with intent to bring them
into contempt, to stir up sedition, or to aid or abet a foreign
nation in hostile designs against the United States.   Inasmuch
as the Sedition act and the first of the Alien laws expired by
self-limitation before Jefferson took the oath of office, and since
the second Alien law was never repealed, but stands to-day
substantially unchanged, a commendation of the "spirit which
swept" them from the statute-book involves a historical blunder.   The resolutions of 1798 and 1799 were the first expressions of the doctrine which subsequently became known as
nullification.

The canvass of 1800 opened early. The first step, perhaps, was an attempt to draw General Washington from his retirement and induce him to stand again for the presidency. A suggestion to that effect was made, probably after a consultation among the Hamiltonians; but Washington refused to comply. Later, Gouverneur Morris wrote to him, December 9, 1799: "During a late visit to New York I learnt that the leading characters, even in Massachusetts, consider Mr. Adams as unfit for the office he now holds;" and he proceeded to urge him to become a candidate. It is probable that Washington never read the letter. He was taken ill on the 13th of December and died on the 14th. The scheme failed, and the leaders, seeing that it would be impossible to supplant Mr. Adams with any candidate of less authority than Washington, resigned themselves to the inevitable.

Early in March articles began to appear in the Republican papers, giving "dispassionate" reasons why Mr. Adams should not be elected. The articles were answered at length by correspondents of the Federalist newspapers. The discussion was extremely bitter, and unfounded charges were made on both sides. Probably the Federal ticket had been agreed upon at that time, although it was not authoritatively announced until June. General Charles Cotesworth Pinckney, a brother of Thomas Pinckney, who had been the candidate most voted for with Mr. Adams in 1796, was associated with Adams on the Federal ticket. The manner in which the ticket was formed is involved in much obscurity. Mr. Hezekiah Niles, whose "Weekly Register" is a treasury of facts for students of our early political history, tried to clear it up, but acknowledged his failure. Early in the year 1800 a meeting of a few Federalist members of Congress, for the purpose, as was said at the time, of influencing the Presidential election, was held in the Senate Chamber. So far as is known, no account of its proceedings was ever printed, but it was probably called for the purpose of strengthening Mr. Adams's cause; for Mr. Niles says in another place ("Register," Vol. 24, p. 277) that "it was well understood that many of the Federalists were opposed to the taking up of Mr. Adams for the presidency, — that they had nearly fixed on another person." Perhaps the naming a candidate for Vice-President may also have been one of the objects of the meeting. But it is all a matter of conjecture and uncertainty. Whatever may have been the purposes in view, the meeting excited the wrath of the Republicans, and was denounced in the Philadelphia " Aurora " as a "Jacobinical conclave," — for which and other insulting remarks the editor of the paper was arraigned at the bar of the Senate.

The Republican members themselves held a caucus somewhat later, — probably in February or March, 1800. It also was a secret meeting. It was attended by a small number of members only. It was called not so much for the purpose of nominating Mr. Jefferson, who was designated by the unanimous voice of his party as the natural candidate, as with the idea of causing a union upon Burr, as well as upon Jefferson. The situation and the course of events are explained in a letter, already cited in the preceding chapter, from Oliver Wolcott to Henry W. Edwards, printed in Gibbs's History, based on Wolcott's correspondence (Vol. ii., p. 488). Wolcott wrote that the division of the votes of Virginia in 1796 "gave great offence to Mr. Burr, who complained of bad faith. At the next conference, or caucus, of the Republican members of Congress, Mr. Burr required as a condition of his consent to be their candidate, that highly respectable members of the Republican party should write letters, stating that their honor was pledged to endeavor to procure for him an equal vote with Mr. Jefferson. I have no doubt, from information which I received (though I have never seen a letter to that effect), that this condition was complied with ; at any rate, an equal vote for Mr. Jefferson and Colonel Burr was in fact obtained."

Both parties entered upon the canvass with full confidence ; but the Federalists soon suffered a severe rebuff, when the New York election took place in May. Later their hopes revived and the Republicans became anxious. So well assured were the Federalists of success that the " Columbian Centinel," of Boston, on December 13, after the electors had actually voted, asserted that " there cannot be a doubt " of the election of Adams and Pinckney. One week later the "Centinel " was forced to " concede " the " bad news " that Jefferson and Burr were chosen. The result had finally been determined by the vote of South Carolina, on which the Federalists had counted as safe for their candidates.

In New York, the Republican assemblymen were successful in New York city. In a fit of faintheartedness the Philadelphia " Gazette " declared that the result " ascertains the election of Mr. Jefferson to the presidency," using the verb in a sense now obsolete. The suggestion filled other Federalists with indignant horror. " I trust," wrote one of them, " this country is not yet so abandoned of God." The disaster led Hamilton to write to Governor Jay, requesting him to call together the old legislature, which was Federalist, to pass a law giving the choice of electors to the people, by districts. Another letter, evidently inspired by Hamilton, was also sent to Jay urging the same step. The Governor replied to neither letter. He endorsed one of them, " proposing a measure for party purposes which I think it would not become me to adopt."

The politicians in other States were not so rigid in their morality as he. Virginia, where the district system of popular election had previously prevailed, and where the Federalists had made some inroads since 1796, amended its law and instituted the practice of election on a general ticket, thus ensuring its twenty-one votes for Jefferson. In Massachusetts a situation the reverse of that in Virginia existed. Several of its members of Congress were Republicans; a bye-election of a congressman in the spring of 1800 resulted in a Jeffersonian success; and when the State election took place, two or three weeks afterward, Governor Strong had a clear majority of only two hundred, and a plurality over Gerry of but 2611. In order to save the whole vote of the Commonwealth for Adams and Pinckney, it was necessary for the General Court to assume to itself the appointment of the electors. A special session was summoned, and a resolution changing the system was passed.

The situation in Pennsylvania was peculiar. It had been the practice in that State to pass a law regulating the mode of appointing electors just before each election, to be operative for that election only. At each prior election the people had enjoyed the privilege of choosing the electors by popular vote. In the year 1796, fourteen Jefferson electors had been chosen, and one Adams man. But in the time of Mr. Adams's popularity the Federalists had carried the State once or twice ; and, as the senators were elected by classes, for four years, it happened that, in the year 1800, although the Governor and the House of Representatives were strongly Republican, the Senate was still Federalist by 13 to 11. As no law had been passed providing for a popular election in time to enable the people to make a choice, it became the duty of the legislature itself to choose the electors. The House passed a law providing for an election by joint ballot, the only way in which the legislature of that State ever elected officers. The Senate rejected the bill and proposed, instead, an election by concurrent vote. The House refused to adopt that method. At last the Senate proposed that each House should name eight electors, and that the two Houses should vote together for the combined list, or for fifteen of the sixteen. The House was forced to yield, and the result was that eight Jefferson and seven Adams electors were chosen. The Federal senators — "the Federal thirteen," as they were proudly termed by their admirers — were loudly praised for this act by the party organs. The editor of the "United States Gazette," of Philadelphia, wrote on December 3, 1800, to his paper : —

The Federal thirteen deserve the praises and the blessings of all America. They have checked the mad enthusiasm of a deluded populace and the wicked speculation of designing demagogues. On reviewing the recent aspect of our political affairs, it may be figuratively said, *They have saved a falling world!*

It will be seen, from a consideration of what has been presented, that the Federalists had good reason to anticipate success. There were to be 139 electoral votes, of which 70 were necessary for a choice. The solid vote of New England, together with that of New Jersey and Delaware, gave them 49 votes ; Maryland, Pennsylvania, and North Carolina contributed 16 more ; and the eight votes of South Carolina, which the people of that State promised to them, again and again, would make up the majority. Reserving until a little later the story of the loss of those votes, let us say that it was only political chicanery, — or if that is too strong a word, exceedingly good play of the game of politics, that brought them so near to victory. New York told the story of the popular sentiment. Votes were saved to Adams in Pennsylvania and Massachusetts by taking advantage of earlier elections. On the other hand, not more than two or three votes were gained by the Republicans in Virginia by the adoption of the district system. On the surface it appears as if the Federalists were almost as strong as ever. In reality they were saved from a much more crushing defeat than they experienced by measures which the political morality of our time would condemn.

The progress of the canvass developed the usual number of

"campaign lies" and misrepresentations. When the overturn in Adams's cabinet occurred, the Trenton "Federalist" asserted its knowledge that the step was the outcome of an agreement between Adams and Jefferson. Adams was to be re-elected, and so was Jefferson; the President was to arrange the offices to the satisfaction of the Vice-President, who was to give his firm support to the measures of the administration. The statement was absurd, and might have been taken as a joke, had not the New Jersey paper been a serious organ of the party. Of the same category was the report circulated by the Federalist papers that Jefferson had discarded the Sabbath, together with the Christian division of time into weeks, and adopted in his household the French *decade*.

In May the Federalists expected to win by seventy-two votes against sixty-six. They counted on five votes in North Carolina, six in Pennsylvania, and four in Maryland, beside the eight of South Carolina. In June they claimed seventy-nine to fifty-nine. At about this time began to appear arguments to show that it was most necessary for all Federalist electors to give an equal vote to both candidates. For the most part the internal discussions of the Federalists were kept out of the newspapers. But occasionally something of the distrust between Adams's friends and the adherents of Hamilton appeared on the surface. It was not denied, because it was evident to the dullest apprehension that only by the most loyal adherence to the party programme could Jefferson be defeated. Yet when Hamilton made a tour of New England, extended as far as Maine, urging the equal support of both candidates, there was some criticism of his action in the Boston newspaper most devoted to Adams's fortunes. The Federalists of South Carolina, the State which had given its votes for Jefferson and Thomas Pinckney in 1796, now promised loyal support of Adams and C. C. Pinckney. Toward the close of the canvass a distinct offer was made to them to repeat the division of votes they had made at the former election, that is, to give an equal vote to Pinckney and Jefferson. General Pinckney refused to sanction the coalition, and gave it to be understood that he wished for no votes that were not given also to Adams. The expectation was that Adams and Pinckney, under the bonds of the agreement, would receive the same number of votes; whereupon the House of Representatives would elect Adams. It was in the warmest period of the canvass that Aaron Burr, in some way unknown, obtained possession of a part of Hamilton's letter on the character of John Adams, and gave it to the press. Hamilton then published the letter in full. An extract from it has been given already, in the account of the election of 1796. Two sentences only will be quoted here. They follow Hamilton's severe arraignment of the President : " Yet, with this opinion of Mr. Adams, I have finally resolved not to advise the withholding from him a single vote. The body of Federalists, for want of a sufficient knowledge of facts, are not convinced of the expediency of relinquishing him."

As had been the case in 1796, sixteen States took part in the election. New Hampshire, Massachusetts, and Pennsylvania took away from the people the appointment of electors. Rhode Island conferred the right upon them. There were, therefore, four States only in which electors were chosen by popular vote : Rhode Island, Maryland, Virginia, and North Carolina. The electors of both parties, with a single exception, voted equally for both candidates. One Rhode Island elector withheld his vote from Pinckney, and gave it to Jay. The result, by States, was as follows : —

STATES.	Thomas Jefferson, Va.	Aaron Burr, N. Y.	John Adams, Mass.	C. C. Pinckney, S. C.	John Jay, N. Y.
New Hampshire	–	–	6	6	–
Vermont	–	–	4	4	–
Massachusetts	–	–	16	16	–
Rhode Island	–	–	4	3	1
Connecticut	–	–	9	9	–
New York	12	12	–	–	–
New Jersey	–	–	7	7	–
Pennsylvania	8	8	7	7	–
Delaware	–	–	3	3	–
Maryland *	5	5	5	5	–
Virginia	21	21	–	–	–
North Carolina	8	8	4	4	–
South Carolina	8	8	–	–	–
Georgia	4	4	–	–	–
Kentucky	4	4	–	–	–
Tennessee	3	3	–	–	–
Total	73	73	65	64	1

* One Maryland elector did not attend.

Before entering upon a narrative of the exciting events that arose out of the equal vote for Jefferson and Burr, we must record a most promising attempt to remedy by law the deficiencies of the Constitution in the matter of the electoral count. Inasmuch as the legislation then proposed subsequently formed the basis of the "twenty-second joint rule," so famous in the counts of 1869 and 1873, and of the electoral commission law of 1877, it will be well to notice the proceedings at some length. A resolution introduced in the Senate January 23, 1800, by Mr. Ross of Pennsylvania, directed the appointment of a committee "to consider whether any, and what, provisions ought to be made by law for deciding disputed elections of President and Vice-President of the United States, and for determining the legality or the illegality of the votes given for those officers in the different States." The committee reported a bill, February 14, of which the provisions were, in brief, as follows : —

On the day before the second Wednesday in February of any year when there was to be a count of electoral votes, each House of Congress was to choose by ballot six of its own members, who, with the Chief Justice of the United States, or, in case of his disability from any cause, the next senior justice, would form a "grand committee," with "power to examine, and finally to decide, all disputes relating to the election."

Each House was next to elect two tellers, to whom the certificates of the electors, after they had been opened and read, were to be delivered ; and the tellers were to note the dates of the certificates, the names of the electors, the time and place of their meeting, and the governors' certificates accompanying, — these minutes to be read to the two Houses and entered on the two Journals.

After the certificates had been opened, read, and minuted, the President of the Senate was to administer to the members of the grand committee an oath to examine the certificates impartially, "together with the exceptions and petitions against them, and a true judgment give thereon, according to the evidence." All the certificates, papers, petitions, and testimony were then to be delivered to the chairman of the grand committee, which was to meet every day, sit with closed doors, have ample power to send for persons and papers, compel attendance of witnesses, and punish contempts. The powers of the grand committee were stated in the following section : —

SEC. 8. That the grand committee shall have power to inquire, examine, decide, and report upon the constitutional qualifications of the persons voted for as President and Vice-President of the United States ; upon the constitutional qualifications of the electors appointed by the different States, and whether their appointment was authorized by the state legislature or not ; upon all petitions and exceptions against corrupt, illegal conduct of the electors, or force, menaces, or improper means used to influence their votes ; or against the truth of their returns, or the time, place, or manner of giving their votes : *Provided always,* that no petition or exception shall be granted, allowed, or considered by the sitting grand committee, which has for its object to dispute, draw into question the number of votes given for an elector, or the fact whether an elector was chosen by a majority of the votes in his State or district.

The committee was to make a final report on the 1st of March, stating the number of legal votes for each person, the number rejected, and the reason for rejection ; such reasons to be signed by those who agreed to them. A majority of the committee was to decide finally all questions submitted, and on the day after the report was made the two Houses were to meet again in joint convention, when the result was to be declared, and, if no person had been chosen President, the House was to proceed immediately to make a choice according to the Constitution.

When the bill came under discussion, a motion was made to strike from it the first ten sections, — being all which contained any reference to a grand committee, — and to insert instead of them a single section, providing that when the two Houses should be assembled for the purpose of having the certificates of electors opened and counted, the names of the States should be drawn in order by lot ; that all petitions and exceptions should be read as well as the certificates themselves ; that, if no objection should be made, the votes should be counted ; but that " if the votes, or any of them, shall be objected to, the members present shall on the question propounded by the President of the Senate decide, without debate, by yea or nay, whether such votes are constitutional or not ; " and so on, each question being decided before the name of another State was drawn. This proposition was rejected. Various other amendments were offered, some of which were adopted, and the bill was passed substantially as it was reported, except that the constitution of the grand committee was changed so as to relieve the Supreme Court from duty in connection with the electoral count. Each House of Congress was to choose six of its members for this service, and the Senate was also to select three others of its members, of whom the House was to choose one by ballot as the thirteenth member of the grand committee.

The whole subject was considered with extreme care by the House of Representatives. After much debate upon it in Committee of the Whole, the bill was referred to a select committee, of which John Marshall, afterwards Chief Justice, was chairman. The committee reported back the bill, in a wholly new draft, on the 25th of April. It provided for a joint committee of four members from each House, with " power to examine into all disputes relative to the election of President and Vice-President of the United States, other than such as might relate to the number of votes by which the electors may have been appointed." To this committee all petitions, exceptions, and memorials against either the electors or the persons for whom they had voted, were to be delivered. The committee was to meet daily from the time of its appointment until it should make its report ; it was to have the powers for reaching witnesses and compelling the production of papers which the Senate had given to the grand committee. The report of the committee was to contain all the facts ascertained in the investigation, but no opinion. The count was to be made in presence of the two Houses immediately after this report was made — tellers having been previously appointed in the manner already established by precedent — in the following method : —

The names of the several States shall then be written under the inspection of the Speaker of the House of Representatives, on separate and similar pieces of paper, and folded up as nearly alike as may be, and put into a ballot-box, and taken by a member of the House of Representatives, to be named by the Speaker thereof ; out of which box shall be drawn the paper on which the names of the States are written, one at a time, by a member of the Senate, to be named by the President thereof, and so soon as one is drawn the packet containing the certificates from the electors of that State shall be opened by the President of the Senate, and then shall be read also the petitions, depositions, and other papers concerning the same, and if no exceptions are taken thereto, all the votes contained in such certificates shall be counted ; but if any exception be taken, the person taking the same shall state it directly and not argumentatively, and sign his name thereto ; and, if it be founded on any circumstance appearing in the report of the joint committee, and the exception be seconded by one member from the Senate and one from the House of Representatives, each of whom shall sign the said exception as having seconded the same, then each House shall immediately retire, without question or debate, to its own apartment, and shall take the question of the exception, without debate, by ayes and noes. So soon as the question shall be taken in either House, a message shall be sent to the other, informing them that the House sending the message is prepared to resume the count, and when such message shall have been received by both Houses, they shall again assemble in the same apartment as before, and the count shall be resumed. And if the two Houses have concurred in rejecting the vote or votes objected to, such vote or votes shall not be counted; but, unless both Houses concur, such vote or votes shall be counted. If the objection taken as aforementioned shall arise on the face of the papers opened by the President of the Senate in presence of both Houses, and shall not have been noticed in the report of the joint committee, such objections may be referred to the joint committee to be examined and reported on by them in the same manner and on the same principles as their first report was made; but if both Houses do not concur in referring the same to the committee, then such objections shall be decided on in like manner as if it had been founded on any circumstance appearing in the report of the committee. The vote of one State being thus counted, another ticket shall be drawn from the ballot-box, and the certificate and the votes of the State thus drawn shall be proceeded on as is hereinbefore directed, and so on, one after another, until the whole of the votes shall be counted.

The bill was carefully considered, and various amendments were proposed and negatived. It was passed on the 2d of May by a vote of 52 to 37. On being returned to the Senate, the bill was referred to a committee which reported several amendments, of which only one was adopted, but that was one of the greatest importance. The word " admitting" was substituted for " rejecting," in the passage quoted above, and the phraseology of the rest of the clause was changed to conform to the amendment; thus providing that, unless the two Houses concurred in *admitting* any disputed vote, it should not be counted. This was precisely the principle of the twenty-second joint rule of 1865, and the Senate adopted it in 1800 by a vote of 16 to 11. The House non-concurred, and a vote in each branch to adhere to the disagreement defeated the bill.

The proceedings preliminary to the count, and the count itself, were in all respects similar to those in former years up to the declaration of the result, which was in these words : —

· That the whole number of electors who had voted was one hundred and thirty-eight, of which number Thomas Jefferson and Aaron Burr had a majority; but, the number of those voting for them being equal, no choice was made by the people; and that, consequently, the remaining duties devolve upon the House of Representatives.

Already a committee had been appointed to prepare a set of rules for the House, in case the count should show that it was the duty of the House to elect a President ; and the rules, having been discussed in committee of the whole, were adopted as follows : —

First. In the event of its appearing, upon the counting and ascertaining of the votes given for President and Vice-President, according to the mode prescribed by the Constitution, that no person has a constitutional majority, and the same shall have been duly declared and entered on the Journals of this House, the Speaker, accompanied by the members of the House, shall return to their Chamber.

Second. Seats shall be provided in this House for the President and members of the Senate, and notification of the same shall be made to the Senate.

Third. The House, on their return from the Senate Chamber, it being ascertained that the constitutional number of States are present, shall immediately proceed to choose one of the persons from whom the choice is to be made for President; and in case upon the first ballot there shall not appear to be a majority of the States in favor of one of them, in such case the House shall continue to ballot for a President, without interruption by other business, until it shall appear that a President is duly chosen.

Fourth. After commencing the balloting for President, the House shall not adjourn until a choice is made.

Fifth. The doors of the House shall be closed during the balloting, except against the officers of the House.

Sixth. In balloting the following mode shall be observed, to wit : The representatives of the respective States shall be so seated that the delegation of each State shall be together. The representatives of each State shall, in the first instance, ballot among themselves, in order to ascertain the vote of that State; and it shall be allowed, where deemed necessary by the delegation, to name one or more persons of the representation to be tellers of the ballots. After the vote of each State is ascertained, duplicates thereof shall be made; and in case the vote of the State be for one person, then the name of that person shall be written on each of the duplicates; and in case the ballots of the State be equally divided, then the word " divided " shall be written on each duplicate, and the said duplicates shall be deposited, in manner hereafter prescribed, in boxes to be provided. That for the conveniently taking the ballots of the several representatives of the respective States, there be sixteen ballot-boxes provided; and that there be, additionally, two boxes provided for receiving the votes of the States; that after the delegation of each State shall have ascertained the vote of the State, the Sergeant-at-Arms shall carry to the respective delegations the two ballot-boxes, and the delegation of each State, in the presence and subject to the examination of all the members of the delegation, shall deposit a duplicate of the vote of the State in each ballot-box; and where there is more than one representative of a State, the duplicates shall not both be deposited by the same person. When the votes of the States are all thus taken in, the Sergeant-at-Arms shall carry one of the general ballot-boxes to one table, and the other to a second and separate table. Sixteen members shall then be appointed as tellers of the ballots, one of whom shall be taken from each State, and be nominated by the delegation of the State from which he was taken. The said tellers shall be divided into two equal sets according to such agreements as shall be made among themselves, and one of the said sets of tellers shall proceed to count the votes in one of the said boxes, and the other set the votes in the other box; and in the event of no appointment of teller by any delegation, the Speaker shall in such case appoint. When the votes of the States are counted by the respective sets of tellers, the result shall be reported to the House; and if the reports agree, the same shall be accepted as the true votes of the States; but if the reports disagree, the States shall immediately proceed to a new ballot, in manner aforesaid.

Seventh. If either of the persons voted for shall have a majority of the votes of all the States, the Speaker shall declare the same; and official notice thereof shall be immediately given to the President of the United States, and to the Senate.

Eighth. All questions which shall arise after the balloting commences, and which shall be decided by the House voting *per capita* to be incidental to the power of choosing the President, and which shall require the decision of the House, shall be decided by States, and without debate; and in case of an equal division of the votes of States, the question shall be lost.

An active intrigue had been in progress among the Federalists, dating back almost to the day when they learned of their defeat, which had for its purpose the prevention of the election of Mr. Jefferson. The first plan which occurred to them was that the House of Representatives should ballot fruitlessly for a President until the fourth of March had passed, when both the offices of President and Vice-President would become vacant. Then the law already passed by Congress in pursuance of the provisions of the Constitution [1] would become operative, and a new election would be held. This scheme was outlined in the "Columbian Centinel" in December, 1800. Some of the Federalist writers have denied that such a purpose as this was ever entertained; but the proof is too strong for denial that it was the first move made in the most indefensible and scandalous act in the history of the Federalist party. It was, nevertheless, soon abandoned; and another plan was adopted by preference. The plan was the support of Burr, and his election over Jefferson. The Federalists seem to have come slowly and reluctantly to the resolution to give Burr their votes. They did so in opposition to the most earnest remonstrances of Hamilton, who carried on an active correspondence with many public men. He argued directly with influential members of Congress, and endeavored to enlist the help of other prominent Federalists in dissuading the party from disgracing itself. No act of Hamilton's public life shows more conspicuously his high-mindedness and his political sagacity. His position is epitomized in a brief passage from a letter to Gouverneur Morris: "I trust the Federalists will not finally be so mad as to vote for Burr. I speak with an intimate and accurate knowledge of character. His elevation can only promote the purposes of the desperate and profligate. If there be a man in the world I ought to hate, it is Jefferson. With Burr I have always been personally well. But the public good must be paramount to every private consideration." The repugnance of the Federalists who persuaded themselves to support Burr is well expressed in a letter from Theodore Sedgwick, of Massachusetts, the Speaker of the House: "By a mode of election which was intended to secure to preëminent talent and virtues the first honors of our country, and forever to disgrace the barbarous institutions by which executive power is to be transmitted through the organs of generation, we have, at one election, placed at the head of our government a semi-maniac, and who in his soberest senses is the greatest marplot in nature; and

[1] Sec. 10. See p. 37.

at the next a feeble and false, enthusiastic theorist, and a
profligate without character and without property, bankrupt
in both."

Hamilton's most powerful efforts to detach the Federalists
from Burr were exerted upon the one member of the House of
Representatives from Delaware, Mr. James A. Bayard. Mr.
Bayard agreed with Hamilton in opinion; but as he wrote to
that gentleman, two or three weeks after the election: "I was
obliged to yield to a torrent which I perceived might be
diverted, but could not be opposed." He "contrived to lay
hold of all the doubtful votes in the House, which enabled
me, according to views which presented themselves, to protract
or terminate the controversy." The fact was that the Federalists made strenuous efforts to obtain assurances from Burr that
he would, if elected, administer the government as a Federalist. Burr could have been elected if he had committed himself to them. His character was such that his unwillingness
to do so must be attributed to doubts of success rather than to
principle. Letters written by him after his equality with
Jefferson in the race was ascertained, showed that he understood and acquiesced in the agreement that Jefferson was to be
President. Yet he carried on an intrigue with the Federalists,
without ever going so far as to leave open no way back into
the confidence of the Republican party. His adroitness over-
reached itself. When Mr. Bayard had satisfied himself that
Burr would not commit himself, he took a decided step which
resulted in the election of Jefferson.

When the House of Representatives retired to its own hall,
balloting for a President began immediately. Every member,
with two exceptions, was present, and one of the two, too ill to
attend, was in a committee-room adjoining the hall, where a
bed had been prepared for him. From the first several Federalists voted for Jefferson, but the most of them supported
Burr. A New Jersey member, whose defection Jefferson had
predicted two months before, gave the vote of the State to
Jefferson. Georgia was entitled to two representatives. One
of its members, a Republican, had died not long before. The
other, a Federalist, voted for Jefferson, and thus gave him the
vote of the State. Jefferson had, in all, the votes of eight
States. Burr had the votes of six States. Maryland and
Vermont were divided, — Maryland because of the defection
of another Federalist; the party division of the delegation was

three Federalists and three Republicans. As the Constitution required a majority of all the States to elect, the vote was not effective. The House balloted nineteen times on the 11th of February, nine times on the 12th, and once each on the 13th, 14th, 16th, and 17th, — thirty-five times in all. At every trial the result was the same. It is exhibited in the following table : —

STATES.	Jefferson.	Burr.	State voted for —
New Hampshire . . .	–	4	Burr.
Vermont	1	1	Divided –· Blank.
Massachusetts . . .	3	11	Burr.
Rhode Island	–	2	Burr.
Connecticut	–	7	Burr.
New York	6	4	Jefferson.
New Jersey	3	2	Jefferson.
Pennsylvania	9	4	Jefferson.
Delaware	–	1	Burr.
Maryland	4	4	Divided — Blank.
Virginia	16	3	Jefferson.
North Carolina . . .	9	1	Jefferson.
South Carolina . . .	–	5	Burr.
Georgia	1	–	Jefferson.
Kentucky	2	–	Jefferson.
Tennessee	1	–	Jefferson.
Total	55	49	

The thirty-sixth ballot, taken on the 17th of February, resulted in the choice of Mr. Jefferson. The Federalists, excepting those from New Hampshire, Massachusetts, Rhode Island, and Connecticut, declined to vote. This action gave the votes of Vermont and Maryland to Jefferson, raising his number to ten; it rendered blank the votes of Delaware and South Carolina; and left to Burr the four New England States above named. Mr. Bayard, in the account of the election which he gave to Hamilton, already quoted, says that when he became satisfied that Burr would not commit himself, he " came out with the most explicit and determined declaration of voting for Jefferson. You cannot well imagine," he continues, " the clamor and vehement invective to which I was subjected for some days. We had several caucuses. All acknowledged that nothing but desperate measures remained.

which several were disposed to adopt, and but few were willing openly to disapprove. We broke up each time in confusion and discord, and the manner of the last ballot was arranged but a few minutes before the vote was given." He reports that but for one Connecticut member, all the Federalists would have voted blank. When that member refused, the rest of his delegation refused also, and thereupon the other New England members, except the one from Vermont, joined them in their action, and voted for Burr to the last. "The means existed," he further declared, "of electing Burr, but this required his coöperation. By deceiving one man (a great blockhead) and tempting two (not incorruptible) he might have secured a majority of the States."

The inauguration was even more informal than that which took place in 1793, when Washington took the oath the second time. There is no evidence that either Washington on that occasion, or Mr. Adams in 1797, made use of a carriage to reach the Capitol. Nevertheless, an untrue story that Jefferson rode on horseback, unattended, to the building where Congress met, and that he hitched his horse to a fence post, has been the basis of an idea that the new President brought the style of government back to republican simplicity. The truth is, that at ten o'clock on the morning of the 4th of March, Burr appeared in the Senate Chamber, took the oath of office, and began to preside over the Senate. At noon Jefferson, clad in his usual dress, walked from the boarding-house, where, as Vice-President, he resided, accompanied by a company of artillery from Virginia. He went to the north wing of the Capitol where the House was in session, and was received by Vice-President Burr. Having taken a seat between Burr and Chief Justice Marshall, he soon rose and delivered his inaugural address. The oath was then administered by the Chief Justice. President Adams was not present to witness the ceremony. Early on the morning of the inauguration he left Washington on his journey to his home in Massachusetts.

VI

THE DEMOCRATIC REGIME

A POLITICAL era began with the inauguration of Jefferson. Forty years of uninterrupted ascendency of his party were followed by twenty years more, during which, although it was twice defeated in the electoral colleges, its adversaries enjoyed the sweets of power for four years only — one presidential term. The Republican party was in its origin merely a party of opposition. Its chosen designation had but a negative signification, for it was adopted rather to bring an accusation of monarchical tendencies against the party in power, than to embody a political programme of its own. It came into the possession of the government without a plan or a promise. Its adversaries applied to the members of the party the terms "Jacobins" and "Democrats;" perhaps not inappropriately, since much of their early political activity had been exerted through the medium of democratic societies formed on the model of the Jacobin clubs of Paris. Jefferson himself never adopted the democratic name; but gradually that which had been used as a term of reproach became the ordinary designation of the party, and ultimately a name proudly held. The Democratic party survived two great rivals, the Federalist and the Whig parties; and has come down to our own time in unbroken succession, although not without more than one radical change in its principles. For no one to-day holds the Jeffersonian creed. No one believes in strict construction of the Constitution, as he understood it; no one places the State above the nation, or accepts the doctrine of nullification, or denies the right of the Supreme Court to act as an arbiter and interpreter of the Constitution, or, in short, takes the view of Federalist legislation which Jefferson took. The strictest construction of our time concedes greater authority to the national government than Hamilton ever claimed for it.

One must carefully avoid judging the statesmen and politicians of the first quarter century under the Constitution by the standards which later generations have set up. If Jefferson and those who acted with him deemed the States safer repositories of ultimate authority than the general government, we must remember that the "more perfect union" was still an experiment. If the Virginia and Kentucky resolutions asserted a doctrine which was to imperil the existence of the government; and if some Federalists of the highest authority considered most seriously, although most secretly, a project having for its purpose the dissolution of the Union, and the establishment of a Northern confederacy; it must be borne in mind that the people had not had time to accustom themselves to an authority paramount to that set up in their state capitals, nor had the Union itself become an object of national love and devotion. Descending to the less important matter, what was the true interpretation of the Constitution, as it concerned the respective functions and jurisdiction of State and nation, it is not to be wondered at either that a most conservative view was taken at first; or that, as experience demonstrated both the safety of intrusting larger powers to the general government, and the necessity of conceding such powers to it, if the United States were to make itself respected at home and abroad, the more liberal construction prevailed.

Jefferson's inaugural address had in it a note of conciliation. "We have called by different names brothers of the same principle. We are all Republicans; we are all Federalists." But there was no conciliation in his administration. Congress proceeded, under his leadership, to undo all it could of the work of the Federalists. The judiciary system, established at the close of the last session of Congress, was an object of special detestation. The act was repealed and the judges deprived of their offices; and the attack upon the judiciary was followed up by impeaching judges obnoxious to the Republicans who could not be disposed of by the repeal. The taxing system was changed so as to get rid of a corps of Federal officeholders. Jefferson exercised the power of removal and appointment in order to reward party friends. The navy was treated with neglect. The President was always ostentatious in his efforts to restrain within most narrow bounds the authority of the general government, and to expand the function of the individual States; yet the most conspicuous act of his first administration, indeed, of his whole term, was the acquisition of Louisiana — a measure involving a construction of the Constitution far more latitudinarian than that which Hamilton put upon it. Many prominent Northern Federalists, in their anger, their helplessness, their apprehension that the rule of the Southern States was to be fastened upon the country permanently, entertained the idea of a separation from the rest of the Union, and the establishment of a new confederacy, to consist of New England and New York.

The course of the Federalists at this juncture was such as amply to justify the people in excluding them from the government. Their excesses in opposition were not the same as those' which had been a reproach to the Republicans during the administration of Washington and Adams. They did not fill the public journals with false charges against the national officers; nor garble and misrepresent their words, their acts, and their motives; nor did they load their political enemies with vituperative epithets. But they were childishly petulant in defeat; they tried to regain power by detestable intrigues and unnatural coalitions; and, as has just been said, some of them consulted together as to a separation from those whom they could not control, by breaking up the Union. Most of this was carried on in secret at the time; much of it has since been brought to light. Hamilton was aware of it. Not improbably it was his opposition to the scheme, in which Burr and leading Federalists were engaged, that prompted the Vice-President to challenge him to the fatal duel. Less than a week before his death he said to Colonel Trumbull, " You are going to Boston. You will see the principal men there. Tell them from me, as my request, for God's sake, to cease these conversations and threatenings about a separation of the Union."

With whatever bias or impartiality one may look upon the contentions and the actors of that era, one thing is evident. The people were with the President, and the administration grew stronger as time passed. This is shown abundantly by the progress which the Republican party made in the States where previously it had been weak. It is not to be supposed that the Federalist party was dead in Pennsylvania and the South; but the hopelessness of a struggle against the party in power was so fully recognized as to deter the opposition from nomi-. nating candidates, in many cases. In New England one Federalist stronghold after another was stormed ; some of them were captured ; from more than one other the enemy was repulsed with such effort as to exhaust the holders and encourage the assailants to hope that it would surrender at the next attack.

Jefferson's bearing in the presidential office pleased the people. He was informal and approachable. He discontinued the levees which had been a social feature of the preceding administrations — which, indeed, was a rather obvious thing to do, now that the seat of government had been removed to a small, ill-built little village in a vast swamp, which had no society worthy of the name. He also abolished the custom of a speech to Congress, to which each House was expected to reply, and substituted a written message. This change seemed, to the popular mind, a departure from a system borrowed from the English government, and the adoption of a more purely republican form. Jefferson learned a lesson from the failure of his predecessor, to which the attitude toward him of his cabinet ministers contributed. The Republican President sought from his secretaries advice, not their consent to his measures. He realized that he alone was responsible for results, and let it be known that the final decision rested with him. The Federalists had supposed him a shifty time-server. They found him a master in his own administration. They fancied that he was of a nature to shrink from responsibility. They saw him take boldly the great risk of purchasing Louisiana, which they, — and even he, at a period not many months earlier, — deemed a great violation of the Constitution. This measure, extremely popular in the South, and hardly less so in the North, beyond the somewhat narrow circle of Federalist leaders, determined the result of the election of 1804 beyond all doubt. Jefferson would probably have been elected easily ; the acquisition of Louisiana reduced the opposition to him almost to nothing.

The danger that the will of the people might be frustrated by the selection of an inferior man as President, was fully revealed by the election in 1800. It will be remembered that it was to prevent this very occurrence that the Convention of 1787 had adopted the device of a vote for two persons without designating who was to be President. The device had failed signally. It is an interesting fact that the first formal proposition of a change of system was made prior to that election, and proceeded from Vermont. The legislature of that State, in November, 1799, adopted a resolution urging an amendment of the Constitution to provide that the electors should designate for whom they voted as President, and for whom as Vice-President. On February 28 of the following year, 1800, the Massachusetts General Court passed a resolution approving the amendment. Nothing came of the movement at that time.

In 1801 Hamilton drafted two amendments, one of which closely resembled the Vermont resolution ; the other was intended to prohibit the choice of electors by legislatures or by general ticket. It provided that Congress — not the State legislatures — should divide each State into as many districts as the number of electors to which it should be entitled, and that one elector should be chosen by those qualified to vote for the more numerous branch of the state legislature. These two amendments were introduced in the New York legislature by De Witt Clinton, a Republican, and were adopted January 30, 1802. A resolution similar to the first was adopted December 15, 1801. Both sets of resolutions were presented in Congress in February, 1802, but the matter was not brought forward for consideration until just before the close of the session. On May 1, with little debate, the Committee of the Whole, in the House of Representatives, rejected a resolution of amendment briefly providing that in all future elections the votes given should designate for which person the elector voted as President and for which as Vice-President. The vote was : ayes 42, noes 22. It was held by the speaker — it is not now so held — that two thirds were necessary even on preliminary motions. Reported adversely to the House by the Committee of the Whole, the amendment was nevertheless passed the same day by 47 to 14. The resolution reached the Senate the next day, and was taken up and acted upon on the 3d, the last day of the session. It was rejected by 15 votes to 8, not two thirds. Gouverneur Morris, one of the New York senators, voted against the amendment; and felt bound, since the measure had come to Congress as a proposition of the New York legislature, to explain an act which defeated it. His letter to the Governor of the State has been quoted already (p. 12).

At the first session of the eighth Congress, which met in October, 1803, the question was considered at great length in both branches of Congress. An amendment of the Constitution, in substantially the form in which it was ultimately adopted, was introduced early in the session by DeWitt Clinton, who was now a senator from New York. Senator Pierce Butler, of South Carolina, a Federalist, proposed an amendment to the resolution, forbidding the election of any person as President who had held the office eight years, until a full term of four years had intervened ; and allowing him thereafter to be elected for only four years in eight. Senator Dayton of New Jersey moved to strike out of the amendment all that referred to a Vice-President, his object being to abolish the office. Neither of these propositions found favor, and the resolution, after slight verbal amendment, was passed by the Senate on December 2, by a vote of 22 to 10, — nearly a party division. The House of Representatives meanwhile had passed and sent to the Senate an amendment having the same purpose, but in a form much shorter, and more nearly resembling Hamilton's draft. Complaint was made in the House that the Senate had not acted upon this other resolution ; but the Senate version was taken up and was made the subject of a prolonged and acrimonious debate. It met with substantially unanimous opposition from the Federalist side of the House. The chief objection urged against it was based upon the clause providing that when, the choice of President devolving upon the House of Representatives, that body does not effect an election before the 4th of March, the Vice-President shall act as President. It was held that the proposed amendment would degrade the vice-presidency by inviting the nomination to the office of men who would never be thought of for President ; and the obnoxious clause would result in putting a second-rate man into the first office whenever the House failed to elect. Roger Griswold, of Connecticut, opposing the defeated amendment of 1802, had uttered prophetic words regarding the proposed change. " What," he exclaimed, " will be the effect of this principle ? The office of Vice-President will be carried to market to purchase the votes of particular States." It would be invidious to specify the numerous cases in which this prophecy has been verified ; but we need not go back many elections to find modern instances. Nevertheless, it was open to the advocates of the change, if it would have been in good taste to refer to the matter in Mr. Burr's presence, to say that the system under which they were then living had nearly brought to the presidential chair one whom no party would have selected deliberately for that position. Hamilton's comment on Morris's excuse for voting against the amendment in 1802 is to the point: "One such fact as the late election is worth a thousand beautiful theories."

In the course of the debate great stress was laid by Federalist speakers on the supposed tendency of the impending change to diminish the influence of the small States — an apprehension which was ever before them, since they were ever reminded of the dominance which Virginia, the greatest of the States, had already assumed. So far as the selection of presidential candidates is concerned, their expectation has been realized. Since the system of nominating conventions was introduced, three candidates only who were residents of small States have been made the " standard bearers " of either of the leading parties, — Pierce, of New Hampshire; Fremont, nominally of California, which was a small State in 1856; and Blaine, of Maine. But the constitutional system, in giving equal representation to the States in the Senate, has more than compensated the small States for any loss they may have suffered in other directions.

The amendment came to a vote in the House at last, and was carried by the exact constitutional majority — 84 to 42; but the vote of Mr. Speaker Macon was required to make up the number in the affirmative. As had been the case in the Senate, it was in general, a party division. Twenty-four of the negative votes were given by New England members, and only three members from that section supported the measure. Yet it will be observed that the noes exceeded the whole number of Federalist members in the House. Even among the Republicans of the North there was a fear of Southern rule, Virginia domination, and the control of the government by the large States. The amendment, as adopted, was in these words : —

The electors shall meet in their respective States and vote by ballot for President and Vice-President, one of whom, at least, shall not be an inhabitant of the same State with themselves; they shall name in their ballots the persons voted for as President, and, in distinct ballots, the persons voted for as Vice-President, and they shall make distinct lists of all persons voted for as President, and of all persons voted for as Vice-President, and of the number of votes for each; which lists they shall sign and certify, and transmit sealed to the seat of government of the United States, directed to the President of the Senate. The

President of the Senate shall, in the presence of the Senate and House of Representatives, open all the certificates, and the votes shall then be counted; the person having the greatest number of votes for President shall be the President, if such number be a majority of the whole number of electors appointed; and if no person have such majority, then from the persons having the highest numbers, not exceeding three on the list of those voted for as President, the House of Representatives shall choose immediately, by ballot, the President. But in choosing the President the vote shall be taken by States, the representation from each State having one vote. A quorum for this purpose shall consist of a member or members from two thirds of the States, and a majority of all the States shall be necessary to a choice. And if the House of Representatives shall not choose a President, whenever the right of choice shall devolve upon them, before the fourth day of March next following, then the Vice-President shall act as President, as in the case of the death or other constitutional disability of the President.

The person having the greatest number of votes as Vice-President shall be Vice-President, if such number be a majority of the whole number of electors appointed; and if no person have a majority, then from the two highest numbers on the list the Senate shall choose the Vice-President; a quorum for the purpose shall consist of two thirds of the whole number of Senators, and a majority of the whole number shall be necessary to a choice. But no person constitutionally ineligible to the office of President shall be eligible to that of Vice-President of the United States.

The resolution was not passed until December 8, 1803. It was extremely doubtful if the ratification of "three fourths of the legislatures of the several States" could be obtained so as to make the amendment operative at the next election. An effort was made, it may be remarked, in explanation of the quotation marks, to amend the resolution submitting the amendment, so as to read "the legislatures of three fourths of the several States." To correct the ambiguity and dispel the idea that a three-fourths vote was required of a State legislature, would have sent the resolution back to the Senate, and the objectionable phrase was allowed to stand. In order to provide for any contingency a law was passed, the following provisions of which remained in force until the passage of the act of 1887. It was enacted that the electors —

shall vote for President and Vice-President of the United States, respectively, in the manner directed by the above-mentioned amendment; and having made and signed three certificates of all the votes given by them, each of which certificates shall contain two distinct lists, one of the votes given for President and the other for Vice-President, they shall seal up the said certificates, certifying on each that lists of all the votes of such State given for President and of all votes given for Vice-President are contained therein, and shall cause the said certificates to be transmitted and disposed of, and in every other respect act in conformity with the provisions of the act to which this is a supplement. And every other provision of the act to which this is a supplement, and which is not virtually repealed by this act, shall extend and apply to every election of a President and Vice-President of the United States made in conformity to the above-mentioned amendment to the Constitution of the United States.

It was further provided by the same act that until electors should receive a notice that the amendment had been duly ratified by a sufficient number of States, they should vote in both ways, the old and the new, make out six certificates, and send two sets of each kind to the President of the Senate; but only those which should be in conformity to the Constitution at the time of the election were to be opened. This provision became inoperative by reason of the promptness of the States in ratifying the amendment, — which was declared adopted by the Secretary of State in a notification addressed to the several governors on the 25th of September, 1804. Thirteen of the sixteen States ratified the amendment. The dissenting States were Massachusetts, Connecticut, and Delaware.

The custom of selecting candidates for President and Vice-President by a caucus of congressmen was now well established. That which had previously been done secretly and informally was by the Republicans done openly for the first time. There was no need of a caucus for the choice of a candidate for President. All were in favor of Mr. Jefferson. But no one was in favor of Burr. The chief offences for the commission of which his memory is execrated, had not yet been committed; but he had, long before, lost the confidence of his early party friends. One hundred and eight members of the two Houses of Congress attended the caucus on the 25th of February, 1804. Mr. Jefferson was nominated unanimously. George Clinton of New York was nominated for Vice-President. The vote stood: —

For George Clinton, of New York 67
" John Breckenridge, of Kentucky 20
" Levi Lincoln, of Massachusetts 9
" John Langdon, of New Hampshire 7
" Giedon Granger, of Connecticut 4
" Samuel Maclay, of Pennsylvania 1

The Federalists agreed to support Charles Cotesworth Pinckney, of South Carolina, for President, and Rufus King, of
New York, for Vice-President. Where and by whom these
nominations were made is not known. The information is
not given in the newspapers of the time, nor is any meeting
for the purpose of nominating candidates referred to in the
published correspondence of public men.

There was no canvass. The Federalists deliberately withdrew from serious opposition to the election of Jefferson, save
that in the States where they were still strong they fought
desperately to retain their ascendency. The purpose not to
make a general canvass was foreshadowed a year earlier by
Gouverneur Morris, who wrote to Roger Griswold in November, 1803, that it was the wise course "to leave the arena free
for the Democrats to squabble in, at the next election," pre-
dicting that they either would " divide with mortal hatred "
and honest men would come by their own, or would " unite
in their present chief." He added that " the confidence in
spired by such appearance of universal approbation might take
from his vanity the snaffle which it now prances under, and
give you more mammoth expectations," — an excellent example of the rhetoric of the time, but, still better, an illustration of the delusion as to the sentiment of the people
under which most of the Federalists labored.

Seventeen States took part in the election, Ohio having
been admitted to the Union on November 29, 1802. A new
apportionment had been made, based upon the census of 1800,
increasing the number of Representatives from 106 to 142,
and the number of electors from 138 to 176. In seven of the
States electors were appointed by the legislature, — Vermont,
Connecticut, New York, Delaware, South Carolina, Georgia,
and Tennessee. They were chosen by the people on general
ticket in the other States, except in Maryland, North Carolina
and Kentucky, where they were chosen by districts. Kentucky was divided into two districts, eastern and western, and
four electors were chosen on general ticket in each. The

number of candidates was very large; but there was not a
Federalist among them. Disaster overtook the Federalists of
New Hampshire and Massachusetts. It was proposed to return to the system of popular election, abandoned in 1800 for
the purpose of making Adams's election sure. The Republicans urged that the electors be chosen by districts, but this
was refused. The Federalists had the mortification of seeing
both States carried by the Jeffersonians. A few election returns have been culled from the newspapers. They illustrate the onesidedness of the contest outside of New England.
Massachusetts gave 29,254 to Jefferson; 25,139 to Pinckney.
Pennsylvania, 22,081 to Jefferson; 1,239 to Pinckney. New
Jersey, 13,119 to Jefferson; 19 to Pinckney. Ohio, 2,093 to
Jefferson; 360 to Pinckney.

The electoral votes are shown in the following table: —

STATES.	PRESIDENT.		VICE-PRESIDENT.	
	Thomas Jefferson.	Charles C. Pinckney.	George Clinton.	Rufus King.
New Hampshire	7	–	7	–
Vermont	6	–	6	–
Massachusetts	19	–	19	–
Rhode Island	4	–	4	–
Connecticut	–	9	–	9
New York	19	–	19	–
New Jersey	8	–	8	–
Pennsylvania	20	–	20	–
Delaware	–	3	–	3
Maryland	9	2	9	2
Virginia	24	–	24	–
North Carolina	14	–	14	–
South Carolina	10	–	10	–
Georgia	6	–	6	–
Kentucky	8	–	8	–
Tennessee	5	–	5	–
Ohio	3	–	3	–
Total	162	14	162	14

The proceedings in connection with the electoral count were

noticeable for one incident only. The Vice-President said, addressing the two Houses assembled in joint meeting: "You will now proceed, gentlemen, to count the votes, as the Constitution and laws direct." This was different from the pracce of Mr. Adams, who himself counted the votes.

There were some irregularities in the certificates of the electors, and attention was called to them; but no objection was made to any votes, and the result was declared in accordance with the above list.

VII

JAMES MADISON

THE years of Jefferson's second administration were years of increasing trouble. At the end of it the Republican party escaped as by a miracle the fate which had overtaken the Federalists eight years before. During the whole term the President was nominally supported by an immense majority in Congress. The Senate in the ninth Congress numbered twenty-seven Republicans and seven Federalists; the House of Representatives, one hundred and nineteen Republicans and twenty-five Federalists. The division was nearly the same in the tenth Congress. Nevertheless, both in Congress and in the community at large the opposition to administration measures was large and powerful. In each of the three largest States of the Union the Republican party was rent by feuds. In New York, the Livingstons and Clintons having unitedly put down the Burr faction fell into a quarrel that lasted many years, and affected profoundly the politics of that State. In Pennsylvania the followers of Governor McKean, assisted by the Federalists, defeated the " regular " nomination of Snyder, who represented the more radical element, that styled itself " Friends of the People." This dissension was brought to an end by a shrewd piece of politics just in time to save the State to the party in 1808. Virginia, under the lead of John Randolph, was for a short time an opponent of the administration, and to the end of the canvass was divided between Madison and Monroe. It is not untrue to say that the impossibility of uniting the opposition rather than the strength of Mr. Madison saved that gentleman from defeat.

The chief events of the administration were occurrences in our foreign relations. Even before Mr. Jefferson had taken the oath of office a second time Mr. Monroe, with Mr. Charles Pinckney, began the negotiation with Spain for a recognition of American claims for spoliation and for a cession of Florida. Monroe was thwarted in his mission by France, and retired from Madrid in humiliation. At Paris he had no better fortune, and when he returned to his post at London he was confronted with judicial decisions, confirming the seizure of American vessels, which almost destroyed the rights of trade enjoyed by the shipping of neutral nations. Our ministers in France and Spain received hints which were duly transmitted to the President, that although both governments denied that West Florida was properly included in the Louisiana purchase, a few million dollars paid to Spain would effectuate a cession of the territory to the United States. Jefferson sent to Congress in December, 1805, a message which breathed a spirit of defiance toward Spain; but in a private conference with Randolph, the chairman of the Ways and Means Committee, he suggested that Congress offer to put two million dollars at his disposal for the purposes of the negotiation. Randolph from that moment turned against the administration. He saw in the President's two attitudes — one public and the other private — a purpose to gain credit with the people by a show of firmness and national self-assertion, meanwhile shifting upon Congress the responsibility of what popularly might be deemed a more craven policy, which he really desired to see adopted. Randolph also recognized in Mr. Jefferson's course a movement in behalf of Mr. Madison as the presidential candidate at the ensuing election. In spite of Randolph's vehement opposition the " two million act " — an appropriation of that sum for the foreign relations — was carried through both branches of Congress, sitting with closed doors. But although the nominal strength of the Republican party was nearly five to one in the House and nearly four to one in the Senate, the bill received a majority of fourteen only in the lower, and of six in the upper House.

The relations with England grew steadily worse. The doctrine that a neutral flag should protect the goods and the crew sailing under it, strenuously argued by American diplomatists, was contemptuously rejected and constantly disregarded by Great Britain. Vessels and their cargoes were seized and condemned; the crews of American ships were mustered on their decks by British naval officers, and all men who seemed worth taking were impressed into the service of the king and carried away. Congress thereupon passed a joint resolution forbidding the importation into the country, from Great Britain or elsewhere, of any of an enumerated list of articles of British manufacture. Shortly afterward Mr. Jefferson, hoping to come to terms with England, appointed William Pinkney, of Maryland, a joint commissioner with Mr. Monroe, to make a treaty with Great Britain. A stipulation that the visitation of American vessels by " press gangs " and the impressment of American sailors should cease was a *sine qua non* insisted upon in the instructions of the commissioners. This condition was rejected without qualification by Lords Auckland and Howick, the British commissioners, who nevertheless undertook that special instructions should be given and enforced, enjoining great caution in the exercise of the right of visitation ; and promised prompt redress in case the rights of native-born Americans should be violated.[1] The case before the American commissioners was similar to that which had confronted Jay when he was deputed by Washington to negotiate a treaty. If the instructions were strictly complied with, no treaty could be made. Monroe and Pinkney determined to accept what was offered, and conclude the treaty. The situation of American vessels at sea was steadily growing worse. Already a British Order in Council had been issued, blockading the coast from Brest to the Elbe, and prohibiting trade by neutrals from port to port along that coast. While the Monroe and Pinkney negotiation was in progress Bonaparte issued his Berlin decree, declaring the British islands in a state of blockade. Under this decree Americans, and all other neutrals, were forbidden to trade with the British islands ; and all vessels having British merchandise on board were liable to seizure. Other orders and other decrees followed, under which every American vessel found at sea became the lawful prize of any English or French naval vessel.

When the treaty negotiated by Monroe and Pinkney reached Jefferson, he refused to submit it to the Senate. He had decided to withhold it as soon as he learned from the letters of the envoys what its purport was to be. This action of the President greatly embittered the friends of Mr. Monroe, and left a rankling wound in the breast of the envoy himself.

Next came the outrage upon the Chesapeake by the British war vessel Leopard, an act of insolence almost unsurpassed in the relations of two nations nominally at peace with each other;

1 Great Britain never admitted, until many years after the War of 1812, that a native-born Briton could divest himself of his obligation to his sovereign. The right of expatriation and of naturalization in a foreign country was denied.

some weak and niggardly attempts at measures of defence ; and the Embargo. This last act, which was in its earliest form limited in its operation, though not by its terms limited in duration, was at first popular. As it was evaded, more stringent provisions were added ; and an act to enforce it was passed. It caused widespread distress and ruinous loss in all the commercial States. The first embargo act was passed in December, 1807 ; two supplementary acts were passed, one in January, and one in March, 1808. The evils caused by it began to be felt just as the presidential canvass was opening ; they were intolerable before the election took place.

Jefferson announced, after his second inauguration, that he should not again be a candidate. At no time thereafter did he make a secret of his wish that Madison should be his successor. There can be no doubt that many of his official acts were influenced by his desire to accomplish this object ; as little can it be questioned that a part of the opposition which he encountered in his own party was dictated by a wish of many Republicans to thwart this purpose. A large number of the Northern Democrats were becoming exceedingly weary of the Virginia dynasty. In the ninth Congress they broke away from Southern control and nearly defeated Macon for Speaker. He was elected on the third trial only, and then by a bare majority. In the tenth Congress they succeeded in defeating him and electing Varnum, of Massachusetts. George Clinton, who had been voted for at every election, and was now Vice-President, was evidently not averse to profiting by the growing dislike of Southern dictation. Moreover, by all the precedents he was the natural successor, as Adams had been to Washington, and Jefferson to Adams. Yet he could not count even on the support of New York, in pressing his claims, so fierce was the contention with the Livingstons.

There was still another candidate, Monroe, who, as has been already stated, had a grievance against the administration, and who was warmly supported by John Randolph and all other Southern Democrats who would not follow Jefferson and Madison implicitly. The situation did not promise harmony in the canvass of the ruling party. The Federalists adopted a waiting attitude. They had, until the Embargo began to be severely felt, no hope whatever of carrying through a candidate of their own ; but they did all that lay in their power to foster Democratic division, and evinced a purpose to use their force in defeating Jefferson's candidate, if the dissentient Republicans should organize an opposition. Later in the canvass, not only did they have hope for themselves, but they alarmed the supporters of the administration. At the end of June, 1808, Albert Gallatin, the Secretary of the Treasury, thought that " the Federalists will turn us out by 4th of March next," and in August he reckoned no States safe for Madison, save " the Western States, Virginia, South Carolina, and perhaps Georgia."

The canvass opened in January. On the 21st of that month the members of the Virginia legislature took the lead in nominating candidates for President. Two caucuses were held on that day. The first, attended by 119 members, unanimously recommended Mr. Madison ; the other, attended by 60, gave all but ten votes to Monroe. Two days before these caucuses were held, Senator Bradley of Vermont issued a notice to the Republican members of both Houses of Congress, requesting them to meet in the Senate Chamber on the 23d of the month at six o'clock. This call was issued " in pursuance of the powers vested in me." The purpose of the caucus, the anticipated result, and the assumption of " powers " by the Vermont senator, aroused instant opposition ; and then were heard the first vehement protests against the nomination of Presidents by congressional caucus, which were destined to grow in vigor and in the number of their supporters until the system was overthrown. Mr. Gray, a member from Virginia, published an answer to Mr. Bradley's summons, couched in the blustering style of the political literature of that day : " I take the earliest moment to declare my abhorrence of the usurpation of power declared to be vested in you — of your mandatory style, and the object contemplated. . . . I cannot consent, either in an individual or representative capacity, to countenance, by my presence, the midnight intrigues of any set of men who may arrogate to themselves the right, which belongs only to the people, of selecting proper persons to fill the important offices of President and Vice-President. Nor do I suppose that the honest people of the United States can much longer suffer, in silence, so direct and palpable an invasion upon the most important and sacred right belonging exclusively to them."

A member from New York published a burlesque upon Mr. Bradley's notification, in which, " in pursuance of a similar power vested in me," he deemed it expedient for the purpose of not nominating a President, not to call a Convention at the same time and place, and requested members not to attend it, "to aid and sanction an infringement of one of the most important features and principles of the Constitution of the United States." Nevertheless the caucus was held. It is said to have been attended by 94 senators and representatives, although only 89 votes were cast. Yet the attendance comprised not only a large majority of the Republican strength in both Houses of Congress, but more than one half of the whole membership of both bodies. On a ballot Mr. Madison had 83 votes, Mr. George Clinton 3, and Mr. Monroe 3. The first ballot for a candidate for Vice-President resulted in 79 votes for Mr. Clinton, 5 for John Langdon of New Hampshire, 3 for Henry Dearborn of Massachusetts, the Secretary of War, and 1 for John Quincy Adams. Messrs. Madison and Clinton were then formally declared nominated. An announcement of the action of the caucus was made in a resolution; and a statement was appended, which, in substantially the same form, was employed by every subsequent caucus of the kind as long as the system was in vogue. It declared "that, in making the foregoing recommendation, the members of this meeting have acted only in their individual characters as citizens; that they have been induced to adopt this measure from the necessity of the case; from a deep conviction of the importance of union to the Republicans throughout all parts of the United States in the present crisis of both our external and internal affairs; and as being the most practicable mode of consulting and respecting the interests and wishes of all upon a subject so truly interesting to the whole people of the United States."

Harmony was not restored by the nomination. Seventeen Republican members of Congress published a protest against the selection of Mr. Madison. They denied both the regularity and the expediency of the caucus. They asserted that the times demanded a man able "to conduct the nation with firmness and wisdom through the perils which surround it. . . . Is James Madison such a man? We ask for energy, and we are told of his moderation; we ask for talent, and the reply is, his unassuming merit; we ask what were his services in the cause of public liberty, and we are directed to the pages of the 'Federalist,' written in conjunction with Alexander Hamilton and John Jay, and in which the most extravagant of their doctrines are maintained and propagated!" The extent to which the revolt extended at this time is indicated by the fact that Clinton himself came out in a letter in which he disavowed consent to the proceedings of the congressional caucus. The candidate for the second place repudiated the proceedings by which he had been put in nomination.

Of calm consideration of the merits of the candidates, and of argument why one party rather than the other should be intrusted with power, there was none. The canvass was a game of politics from beginning to end. In Pennsylvania, for example, the " Constitutionalists," — that wing of the Democratic party which, allied with the Federalists, had put and kept Governor McKean in office, when they found that there was no other member of their faction who could command Federalist votes for governor, — suddenly changed their attitude and anticipated the other faction by coming out zealously for Madison. The "Conventionalists," as the anti-McKean faction was called, followed their example, but nominated a different set of electors. Then a harmonizing committee made up a list which favored McKean, while the McKean men gave their votes for Governor to Snyder, whom they had been fighting for years. In our day this would be called a " deal." It ensured to Madison the vote of Pennsylvania.

The friends of Mr. Monroe, in Virginia, were for a time encouraged by the refusal of their candidate to withdraw. When the nomination of Mr. Madison had been effected, Jefferson maintained at least the outward appearance of neutrality as between him and Monroe. Later in the canvass he exerted his influence to persuade Mr. Monroe to withdraw ; and when the election took place, Madison had an overwhelming majority in Virginia. So far as the candidacy of Mr. Clinton was concerned, the only hope was in securing Federalist support. The Livingstons were ardent Madisonians. Mr. Clinton's political fortunes at this time were in the keeping of his nephew, DeWitt Clinton, who did not — perhaps he would not, perhaps he could not — come to terms with the Federalists. It is to be hoped that it was the political virtue of the Federalists that prevented the arrangement. Yet a party that had espoused the cause of Aaron Burr could have had few qualms of conscience in promoting the candidacy of the man with whom their political opponents had once threatened to defeat George Washington.

The ultimate course of the Federalists was not decided until

October. It seems first to have been announced at the beginning of that month, less than five weeks before the appointment of electors, in the columns of the Charleston, South Carolina, "Courier": "We are authorized to say that certain accounts have been received in this city stating that Gen. Charles Cotesworth Pinckney of this State will be supported by the Federal Republicans throughout the several States at the ensuing election, as President of the United States."

Even while the efforts to patch up a peace in the Democratic party were proceeding with a fair degree of success there was much nervousness and anxiety among the leaders as to the result. State elections in New Hampshire and Rhode Island disappointed them greatly and caused them to fear the loss of all New England with forty-five electoral votes. Delaware was surely Federalist. It was feared that Maryland and North Carolina might give a majority of their votes against the administration. Then the loss of Pennsylvania and the giving of a few New York votes to Clinton would defeat Madison. But the Pennsylvania state election in October relieved them of their fears; and Vermont, although it chose a Federalist governor, had a Democratic legislature, owing to the system then prevalent of an equal representation of towns, large and small.

The number of States in 1808 was the same, seventeen, as in 1804. Electors were chosen by the legislature in Vermont, Massachusetts, Connecticut, New York, Delaware, South Carolina, and Georgia; by the people on general ticket in New Hampshire, Rhode Island, Pennsylvania, Virginia, and Ohio; by popular vote by districts in Maryland, North Carolina, Kentucky, and Tennessee. Kentucky, as before, was divided into two districts. In Massachusetts, as has been stated, there was no permanent law for the appointment of electors. Governor Sullivan was a Republican: the General Court, strongly Federalist. At its first session, in June, 1808, long before the usual time, it elected Mr. James Lloyd as senator to succeed John Quincy Adams. Mr. Adams had gone publicly over to the Republicans, and had even attended the congressional caucus, and voted for Madison. The legislature ignored the governor altogether in making arrangements itself to appoint the electors; and adjourned to meet in November for that purpose. When it re-assembled, Governor Sullivan sent in a message, advising that the appointment of electors be submitted to the people. The General Court not only disregarded the advice, but framed its order for the choice of the electors so as to dispense with the certification of the Governor. Nineteen Federalist electors were duly appointed. Governor Sullivan did not certify the appointment, but he sent to Congress a statement as to the method of appointment which was designed to serve as the basis of an objection to the votes in case of necessity. The alleged informality, which was no informality at all, as a reading of the Constitution will show, was brought to the attention of Congress by memorial, in December. A resolution was introduced for raising a joint committee "to examine the matter of said memorials and report their opinion thereon to both Houses," but it was not acted on. A few days later another resolution was introduced, directing the memorials to be sent to the Senate. After some debate, in which only one member expressed the opinion that Congress could take action in the premises, the resolution was passed and sent to the Senate with the memorials, where it was ordered that all the papers be laid on the table; and no action whatever was taken upon them.

In New York the Democrats had a majority of the legislature; but in the divided state of the party a compromise between the two factions was needful to save the vote of the State. There is no evidence that the Clintonians demanded a part of the electors as the price of abstaining from an alliance with the Federalists. The fact that a division was made indicates, nevertheless, that it was extorted. The "mixture list," to use the phrase employed by the Federalists, received sixty-five votes, the Pinckney ticket forty-six. There was a smaller admixture of Clinton men in the list of electors chosen than the Federalists supposed.

The case of New Jersey was peculiar. The law required electors to be appointed within thirty-four days before the first Monday in December. The legislature passed a law inadvertently fixing the election — by the people — thirty-six and thirty-five days [1] before the time for the electors to meet — on the 1st and 2d of November. Attention was called to the illegality of such action in ample season to remedy the oversight; but the legislature, — this was a year when political manœuvring was almost universal, — chose to leave things

---

[1] All elections in New Jersey, and in some other States, at that time, lasted two days.

as they were. If the Federalists were successful, the election would be null, and the vote of the State would be lost. If the Democrats should carry the State, the legislature could meet and appoint the same persons. The Democrats did have a majority; but the electoral vote depended for its validity on the choice of the electors by the legislature.

The count of electoral votes took place in the Hall of the Representatives, but by some oversight there was no provision in the joint resolution directing how the count should proceed, that the President of the Senate should take the chair. John Randolph, who could always be depended upon to create difficulties when there was opportunity, called attention to the fact, and objected to the chair being vacated by the Speaker without a vote of the House. "He did not wish the privileges of this House any way diminished." The case was provided for

	PRESIDENT.			VICE-PRESIDENT.				
STATES.	James Madison, Va.	George Clinton, N. Y.	C. C. Pinckney, S. C.	George Clinton, N. Y.	James Madison, Va.	John Langdon, N. H.	James Monroe, Va.	Rufus King, N. Y.
New Hampshire	–	–	7	–	–	–	–	7
Vermont	6	–	–	–	–	6	–	–
Massachusetts	–	–	19	–	–	–	–	19
Rhode Island	–	–	4	–	–	–	–	4
Connecticut	–	–	9	–	–	–	–	9
New York	13	6	–	13	3	–	3	–
New Jersey	8	–	–	8	–	–	–	–
Pennsylvania	20	–	–	20	–	–	–	–
Delaware	–	–	3	–	–	–	–	3
Maryland	9	–	2	9	–	–	–	2
Virginia	24	–	–	24	–	–	–	–
North Carolina	11	–	3	11	–	–	–	3
South Carolina	10	–	–	10	–	–	–	–
Georgia	6	–	–	6	–	–	–	–
Kentucky*	7	–	–	7	–	–	–	–
Tennessee	5	–	–	5	–	–	–	–
Ohio	3	–	–	–	–	3	–	–
Total	122	6	47	113	3	9	3	47

* One Kentucky elector did not attend. The State was entitled to eight votes.

by a formal vote, and the Senate was admitted. When the votes had all been opened and the returns tabulated, the President of the Senate was about to read the result, when one of the tellers remarked that one return was defective, not having a governor's certificate attached, referring, of course, to Massachusetts. Nothing further was said, and the President of the Senate, Mr. Milledge, senator from Georgia, proceeded to declare the result, as shown by the table on page 95.

Mr. Madison's inauguration was almost as informal as Mr. Jefferson's had been eight years before. He was conveyed in a carriage to the Capitol, escorted by two companies of militia, and went to the Representatives' Hall attended by two or three members of the cabinet. It is probable that Governor Clinton had already taken the oath of office as Vice-President, but no record of the ceremony is known to be in existence. At all events, Mr. Milledge still presided over the Senate. Mr. Madison delivered his inaugural address in the presence of a distinguished company, having Mr. Jefferson as his chief auditor; and the oath was then administered by Chief Justice Marshall.

VIII

AN ELECTION IN TIME OF WAR

It has been remarked by more than one historian that the government of the United States was never weaker in all its departments than during the first part of Madison's administration. The times required that it should be strong. The policy in the closing months of Jefferson's term had been feeble and vacillating. The embargo not only had failed to accomplish the object for which it was laid, but it had made a large contingent of the Democratic party semi-allies of the Federalists in opposing the administration measures. The last session of the tenth Congress — December, 1808, to March 4, 1809 — witnessed the passage of an act to enforce the embargo, and, just before the Congress expired, a complete change of policy in the substitution of non-intercourse for the embargo. A few only of the members knew the secret reason of this *volte-face*. It was designed to facilitate the negotiations about to begin with Mr. Erskine, the newly appointed British envoy. Mr. Madison made Robert Smith, of Maryland, his Secretary of State, — the weakest incumbent of that office in the history of the country. The agreement made with Mr. Erskine was one which the instructions the envoy had received did not authorize him to make ; and it was impatiently thrown out by Mr. Canning. From that time on, until war was declared in 1812, there was a diplomatic wrangle between the two governments. The relations of the United States with both England and France were hopelessly and equally bad. It would have puzzled much abler men than those who had the fortunes of America in charge to decide what was the wisest course, — to declare war against both the powers, to continue negotiations with a purpose to accept the best that could be obtained, or to submit to conditions against which we were too weak to struggle.

Madison chose none of these courses. He was sincerely desirous of peace, but he would not be satisfied to take what England would offer. Demanding more, he got nothing. Congress contained few strong men, almost none who supported the administration. Yet the party majority was large enough to give a subservient acquiescence in the measures proposed to Congress, even though it lacked leaders. The interminable controversy went on. Mr. Madison became weary of the war in his cabinet between Mr. Smith and Mr. Gallatin, and required the resignation of the Secretary of State. He had previously become reconciled with Mr. Monroe, and now appointed that gentleman to the State Department. Monroe entered office with the laudable purpose of bringing the long quarrel with England to a close, and with great confidence in his own power to hold the administration back from the war into which it was drifting. But a force greater than his own entered into public affairs just three weeks before his return to office, and soon swept him away. He entered the cabinet on November 25, 1811. On the 4th of the same month the twelfth Congress met. It contained in the House of Representatives a group of young Republicans, or Democrats, who assumed control of affairs in a masterful fashion : John C. Calhoun, William Lowndes, and Langdon Cheves, of South Carolina, and Henry Clay, of Kentucky. Cheves, the oldest of the four, was but thirty-five. Clay, who was thirty-four, was elected Speaker by a great majority. Felix Grundy, of Tennessee, a new member and also a young man, acted with this quartet of young men. William H. Crawford, a Senator from Georgia, — afterward the victim of "King Caucus," — who had been acting on somewhat independent lines, now became a stanch party man. All the efforts of this coterie of youthful leaders, of whom those just named were the most conspicuous, tended directly to war with England. They overbore the opposition of Mr. Madison, and carried Monroe along with the current. It was reported at the time on the authority of Mr. James Fisk, then a Republican member of the House from Vermont, that a committee waited upon Mr. Madison, and informed him that war was resolved upon ; that, unless such a step was taken, the Federalists might possibly carry the presidential election ; and that if he was not ready to adopt that policy he would be abandoned, and another candidate chosen for the pending election. It is not possible either to verify or to disprove this assertion. Mr. Quincy, of Massachusetts,

repeated the statement, in a form as distinct as the rules of the
House would allow, during the following year; and its truth
was not questioned. On the other hand, Mr. Clay is reported
to have denied the story; but the form of his denial is not
given. Carl Schurz, in his Life of Clay, says that there is " no
evidence " that coercion was applied to Madison; which is
true, but not conclusive. It is certain that the President
abandoned his settled policy at a time when nothing had been
changed except the attitude of the Democratic leaders in Congress; that he recommended an embargo, which was voted;
and that he followed the recommendation with a war message,
to which Congress responded promptly, though not by so large
a majority as he could have wished, with a declaration of war,
in June, 1812.

The Republican caucus for the nomination of candidates for
President and Vice-President was held on the 18th of May.
No opposition to the caucus manifested itself. The members
who did not intend to be bound by the action which they could
foresee, absented themselves. There were at least one hundred and thirty-three Republican senators and members, only
eighty-three of whom attended the caucus. New York was
represented by a single member, for New York had a plan of
its own. New England and New York combined did not
furnish as many members of the caucus as did Virginia alone.
Thus composed, the caucus was harmonious and unanimous.
Mr. Madison received eighty-two votes for President. Vice-
President George Clinton had died in office less than a month
before. In any event he would not have been nominated
again. On a ballot for Vice President the venerable John
Langdon, of New Hampshire, the first President *pro tempore*
of the Senate, received 64 votes; Elbridge Gerry, of Massachusetts, 16 votes; and two were scattering. The caucus
adopted a resolution recommending its candidates, and repeated
the declaration made four years before that the members acted
as private citizens. Mr. Langdon declined the nomination on
the ground of his age. A second caucus was held on the 8th
of June, when Mr. Gerry was nominated by 74 votes to 3
scattering. After the nomination was made, those who were
present who had not attended the first caucus were allowed an
opportunity to vote for a candidate for President. Ten members voted for Mr. Madison. He thus had the support of
ninety-two members, at least, out of one hundred and thirty-

three. It is an interesting fact, showing the ascendency of the Southern States in the Democratic party, that the original nomination of Mr. Langdon was attributed, by the "New Hampshire Patriot," which may have derived the information from Mr. Langdon himself, to the wish and influence of the Southern members. The Northern men preferred Mr. Gerry from the first ; but the South, helped by subservient Pennsylvania, not only dictated the nomination for the first place, but overruled the New England Democrats in their choice of a candidate for the second place.

The history of the canvass in opposition to Mr. Madison forms one of the most unpleasant chapters in American political history. The Democratic party in New York, for purely personal and local reasons, resolved not to train with the rest of the party. There was no question of principle involved. DeWitt Clinton had become, in the strictly modern sense, the " boss " of his party in New York ; and he willed to become its candidate for President. He was avowedly in favor of war when Madison was still for peace, and was quite willing to be nominated by the congressional caucus on a war platform. When Madison joined the war party Clinton shifted his ground, and based his candidacy on the impropriety of congressional caucuses and of Southern dictation. A caucus of Democratic members of the New York legislature was held at Albany on the 29th of May. Of ninety-five members of the party eighty-seven were present, and the absence of four others was accounted for satisfactorily. Mr. Clinton was nominated unanimously. A committee waited upon him after the caucus and informed him of the action taken. His reply was diplomatic in the extreme. He " sensibly felt and duly appreciated so distinguished a proof of their confidence." The canvass in behalf of Clinton was taken in charge by Martin Van Buren, then a young man of thirty, who thus made his entrance into national politics as the manager of a conspiracy to defeat the candidate of the party which afterward elevated him to the highest place in the nation.

It is not easy to reconcile Clinton's action with the most ordinary political prudence. His public life, even his course during that canvass, forbids us to attribute his conduct to any higher motive than personal ambition. Yet he refused overtures which were undoubtedly made to him to withdraw, with a promise of the succession on the retirement of Madison.

From being an advocate of war before war was declared, he proceeded to the point of becoming a critic of the administration because it did not prosecute the war with sufficient vigor, and sought the votes of dissatisfied Democrats on that ground. Then, since he would be in a hopeless minority without Federalist support, he stood willingly as the candidate of all who were in favor of peace. Gouverneur Morris records in his diary a conversation with De Witt Clinton just after the death of his uncle, the Vice-President, in the spring of 1812, in which an alliance between the Clintonians and the Federalists was discussed vaguely. It seems not improbable that Morris — who had come very near to the point of hating the Union and of desiring a separation from the South — had much to do in smoothing the way for a disgraceful coalition. The echo of Clinton's words denouncing the whole Federalist party as "fiends" had hardly died away when he was courting their support. On their part they made up their minds to give their votes to one who had no principles, — or, if that be too harsh a judgment, no principles not opposed to their own.

The coalition was brought about by a convention held at New York city in September, — a highly interesting meeting, as being the first convention of the same sort as those which now present presidential candidates. The meeting was strictly private, and no report of its proceedings was published in any newspaper. The fullest account of it is given in William Sullivan's "Public Men of the Revolution." In the summer of 1812 Mr. Sullivan and Jonathan Knight, both of Massachusetts, and Governor Roger Griswold and another gentleman of Connecticut, being at Saratoga Springs, talked over the state of the nation, and a convention of Federalists was proposed. The result was the assembling at New York in September of seventy persons representing eleven States of the Union, as follows: from New Hampshire, 2; from Massachusetts, 8; Rhode Island, 3; Connecticut, 6; New York, 18; New Jersey, 12; Pennsylvania, 12; Delaware, 2; Maryland, 3; South Carolina, 4. The convention held a session of three days. There was evidently great hesitation and opposition to the plan which was in the minds of the projectors of the meeting, since nothing whatever was done during the first two days. Rufus King, who had twice been the party candidate for Vice-President, denounced Clinton with such vehemence and passion that — so Mr. Sullivan reports — his knees trembled under him. King was supported by other members of the convention. As the meeting was on the point of breaking up, having come to no decision, Harrison Gray Otis arose, with his hat in his hand, as if about to depart, and began speaking in favor of Clinton. As he proceeded he became more earnest, and soon had the convention enchained by his eloquence. When he finished, the members decided by an almost unanimous vote to support Clinton. A Pennsylvania Federalist of somewhat mild type, Jared Ingersoll, was named as the candidate for Vice-President. The administration organ, the "National Intelligencer," got an inkling of what had been done, and published in connection with the affair a statement that Mr. Clinton had declared to a committee of the convention that "all political connection between him and the Democratic party in the United States had ceased and would not be renewed." Mr. Otis denied this statement as wholly false, and asserted that no communication had been had with Mr. Clinton, and that no statement had been made by him. We have had, in the most recent times, another example of the withholding from candidates of a notice of their nomination, expressly to relieve those candidates from the necessity of accepting the nominations in terms which might throw the party into confusion. All the facts that can be gathered from contemporaneous writers concerning the Federalist convention of 1812 are contained in an article by J. S. Murdock in the "American Historical Review" for 1896.

The opposition within the Federalist party to the candidacy of Clinton was not quenched by Otis's eloquence. Rufus King, in his correspondence, showed that his opinion was unchanged. When the electors were chosen by the New York legislature, forty-five votes were given for a "straight" Federalist ticket. Twenty-three blank votes were cast, most or all of them by Madisonians. The Clinton electoral ticket had seventy-four votes. A convention was held at Staunton, Virginia, on September 26, in which eighteen counties were represented. A Federalist electoral ticket was nominated; no formal nomination of presidential candidates was made, but the names of Rufus King, of New York, and General William R. Davie, of North Carolina, were "commended to the electors when appointed." Nevertheless, substantially the whole Federalist strength was bestowed upon Clinton. It may be remarked here that the coalition put an end forever to Clinton's prospects in national politics.   The canvass was a mere incident of the war, and of the efforts of its opponents to bring about peace.   No doubt men were then too strongly committed on one side or the other to be converted or perverted by argument or persuasion of any sort.   Nevertheless it is singular that the editors of political journals issued their papers week after week, in the autumn of 1812, devoid of all reference to the pendency of an important election.

Eighteen States took part in the election, Louisiana having been admitted to the Union on the 8th of April, 1812.   The mode of appointment of the electors was in general the same as in 1808, but there were some interesting exceptions.   In New Jersey the law of 1807 giving the election to the people, but fixing the date more than the designated thirty-four days before the meeting of the electors, (see p. 94) remained in force. At the State election in 1812 the Democrats had a popular majority, but the peculiarities of the apportionment gave the Federalists control of both branches of the legislature.   The annual meeting of the legislature was held in October; and on the 29th of that month, less than a week before the people were expecting to choose the electors, the legislature repealed the law of 1807, passed an act providing that electors should thereafter be chosen by the Council and General Assembly, and a few days afterward appointed eight federal electors.

North Carolina had always adhered to the system of a popular vote by districts.   But it was anticipated in 1811 that there would be an increase of electoral votes in consequence of a new apportionment, which would be made so late that the State could not be districted.   Accordingly it was then enacted that the electors in 1812 should be chosen by the legislature.   Such was the excuse given for the act, but it caused great excitement at the time; and when the legislature met in 1812 to appoint the electors there was much fear of a popular outbreak.

Massachusetts offered by far the most interesting case. Elbridge Gerry, the candidate for Vice-President with Madison, had been Governor of the State two years, and had been defeated for reëlection the month before the congressional caucus was held.   His administration had been made noteworthy, and his name historical, by the division of the Commonwealth into Senate districts, one of which was of so peculiar a construction that a certain member of the legislature likened its shape to that of a salamander. Another member exclaimed that it was a "gerrymander," and thus a new word was added to the language. The apportionment gave the Senate to the Democrats, although the House of Representatives was strongly Federal. Accordingly, when the question of establishing a method of appointing electors came up, the two Houses were unable to agree. The House made several propositions, all of which were rejected by the Senate, and the General Court adjourned to meet in October to settle the question. At the adjourned meeting the Senate was still in opposition. It was willing to let the vote of the State be lost by making no provision for an election, or to adopt any plan that promised to neutralize the vote by setting one part off against another. At last a proposition was made and accepted to make use of the districts into which the State was divided

STATES.	PRESIDENT.		VICE-PRESIDENT.	
	James Madison, Va.	De Witt Clinton, N. Y.	Elbridge Gerry, Mass.	Jared Ingersoll, Penn.
New Hampshire	–	8	1	7
Vermont	8	–	8	–
Massachusetts	–	22	2	20
Rhode Island	–	4	–	4
Connecticut	–	9	–	9
New York	–	29	–	29
New Jersey	–	8	–	8
Pennsylvania	25	–	25	–
Delaware	–	4	–	4
Maryland	6	5	6	5
Virginia	25	–	25	–
North Carolina	15	–	15	–
South Carolina	11	–	11	–
Georgia	8	–	8	–
Kentucky	12	–	12	–
Tennessee	8	–	8	–
Louisiana	3	–	3	–
Ohio	7	–	7	–
Total	128	89	131	86

for the purposes of the Courts of Common Pleas. Massachusetts proper was divided into three districts, — the western,
middle, and southern, which chose six, five, and four electors
respectively. The District of Maine had also three districts,
which chose three, three, and one, respectively. The Democrats hoped to get half the electors under this system, but
they were grievously disappointed. Every district chose Federal electors. The total popular vote was 50,333 for Clinton
electors, and 26,110 for Madison.

The electoral vote throughout the Union was much closer
than was anticipated. The "solid South" was arrayed in
favor of Madison; most of the North voted for Clinton. Vermont and Pennsylvania alone separated from their neighbors,
and the vote of Pennsylvania decided the election. The electoral votes were as shown in the table on the opposite page.

The count of electoral votes, which took place on the 10th
of February, 1813, in the Representatives' Hall, was marked
by no incident worthy of notice. It was a proceeding in all
respects similar to previous counts.

IX

THE LAST OF THE VIRGINIA "DYNASTY"

THE fate of the Federalist party is one of the most singular casualties in the history of politics. The party was destroyed by the success of its own principles in the hands of its opponents. The anti-Federalists began their existence by opposing the Constitution as destructive of the rights of the individual, and particularly of the smaller States ; when in power, they drove the Federalists near to the point of advocating a dissolution of the Union by perpetuating the domination of Virginia over the "confederacy." During the administrations of Washington and Adams the Federalists were champions of national supremacy, as opposed to the "State Rights" doctrines expressed in the resolutions of 1798 and 1799; Jefferson's policy in acquiring Louisiana, and the attitude of the Democrats toward New England particularism during the war of 1812, went far beyond the Federalism of Hamilton. Finally, the demand for peace on any terms, and a cessation of the war, denounced by the Democrats as "moral treason," and held up for the execration of all patriots, was precisely the policy which Mr. Madison finally adopted ; and the Treaty of Ghent did not even mention either of the objects for which war had been declared. Yet the party that had, as it were, led the way, was trampled in the dust by those who followed after. No doubt the gradual and unconscious adoption by the Democrats of the national principle which had been the original bond of union of the Federal party made it easy for Federalists to go over to the other side. But the disintegration of the organization did not take place until the conclusion of peace brought to an end the only issue that divided parties by a broad line.

The Hartford convention was, beyond a doubt, the event of Madison's second administration which had the most important influence upon the ensuing presidential election. Whether it should have been a death-blow to the Federal party is a question that requires a much fuller and more dispassionate discussion than it has ever had at the hands of a historian of high standing. Writers have been prone to take the superficial view that, since there were New England Federalists of the greatest prominence in the party who expected and desired a dissolution of the Union, — which is undoubtedly true, — and since those men were among the projectors and promoters of the Hartford convention; and since certain phrases in the report of the convention refer to a dissolution as among.the possibilities of the future, — therefore the convention was a treasonable assembly, whose members favored the formation of a confederation of Northern States. The other view deserves careful consideration, namely, that conservatives obtained control of a movement which radicals designed to be directed to the destruction of the Union. George Cabot, the head of the Massachusetts delegation and the president of the convention, expressed his own opinion of the duty set before him when he replied to a young friend who asked him what was to be done at Hartford, " We are going to keep you young hotheads from getting into mischief." Pickering, who was a disunionist, was displeased with the choice of delegates; and John Lowell, who shared Pickering's dislike of the turn the movement took, opposed the convention because he did not believe it would recommend the " effectual measures " which he desired. A study of the proceedings and of the report of the convention, with a prejudice born of these facts, leads one to quite a different conclusion from that of the historians who express themselves on the subject in terms of unqualified abhorrence of the convention and of all who took part in it.

Whatever be the view one holds of this unique assemblage, one thing is certain. It was the most unpopular convention ever held in the country, both during its session and ever since. The commissioners of Massachusetts and Connecticut, appointed to urge at the national capital the measures it recommended, arrived at Washington just as intelligence was received of the battle of New Orleans. Less than a fortnight afterward came the joyful news that a peace treaty had been signed. Nothing remained for Mr. Otis and his associates to do; and they returned home quietly, but pursued by shouts of derision from the Democratic press. The possibility of a return of the Federalists to power ceased from that moment.

The new questions which arose, as soon as Congress was able

to turn from the perilous and perplexing foreign problems
which had engaged its attention for many years, led ultimately
to a new party division. At the outset they merely broke
down the old lines. The incorporation of the second Bank of
the United States was carried by a great majority in a Congress nearly two to one Democratic, and the act was approved
by Madison. The position taken by the anti-Federalists in
Washington's time, that such an act was unconstitutional, was
completely abandoned. The war, with its necessary accompa-
niment of non-intercourse, cutting off the supply of foreign
manufactured goods, had greatly stimulated domestic manufactures. The resumption of commerce after the Treaty of Ghent
left the new industries exposed to violent foreign competition.
The urgent calls for protection by means of higher tariff duties
were responded to by the party in power, which thus adopted
another of Hamilton's principles. The protection sentiment
of that day had no more ardent supporter than John C. Calhoun. The question of internal improvements also began, at
this time, to acquire prominence ; but it was not until long
afterward that it became a party issue, and ranged the Democratic party, following its original doctrine of " strict construction," in opposition to the policy.

The only extensive stronghold of the Federal party, New
England, was endangered from within. A revolt against the
ecclesiastical supremacy of the Congregational Church gave
New Hampshire to the Democratic party ; it left the Federal-
ists but a meagre majority in Massachusetts ; even in ever-
faithful Connecticut it unsettled the hold of the Federalists.
Oliver Wolcott, Secretary of the Treasury in the cabinets of
Washington and Adams, became the candidate of the " tole-
ration " party for Governor, nominated by the influence of the
Episcopalians against his old Federal associates.

The presidential election drew near amid the general break-
ing-up of the Federal party. It had been understood between
Mr. Madison and Mr. Monroe that the Secretary of State was
to be brought forward for the succession with all the power of
the administration. Yet it was not so easy as it might seem
from a consideration merely of Mr. Monroe's apparent strength
in the electoral colleges, second only to that of Washington,
to bring about his nomination. He had two dangerous competitors. The Northern wing of the party, particularly the
New York contingent, was earnestly in favor of Governor

Tompkins, of New York. Mr. Monroe was not a favorite even with the Southern members ; and there was a great intrigue to bring forward William H. Crawford, of Georgia. The first step toward a nomination was the posting of an anonymous notice, dated March 10, 1816, inviting Republican senators and members of Congress to meet in the Representatives' Hall, on the 12th, " to take into consideration the propriety of nominating persons as candidates for President and Vice-President of the United States." Fifty-eight members attended this meeting, at which it was resolved to call a caucus for the 16th of the month, in the hope of a larger attendance. Of 141 Republican members, 119 attended the second caucus. The number was doubtless increased by the anxiety felt by the friends of the several candidates lest one or another should be nominated by a chance minority. The supporters of Mr. Monroe were out in force. The " National Intelligencer " manifested some trepidation lest the administration candidate should be defeated. " If ever doubted," it remarked, "the public opinion has been recently so decidedly expressed as to leave little doubt that the prominent candidate will, in the end, unite the suffrage of the whole Republican party." The " public opinion " in favor of the existing régime was as easily manufactured then as it is now, through the agency of the office-holders. The candidacy of Governor Tompkins was seen, even before the caucus was held, to be hopeless. He was known by but few of the persons who were to make the nomination. It is asserted in Hammond's " New York " that four fifths of the New York members preferred Crawford to Monroe. One of these members said that Martin Van Buren and Peter B. Porter, for reasons of their own, — but what their motives were is not known, — prevented the delegation from going to Crawford ; and thus they secured the nomination of Monroe.

Notwithstanding the inducements to attend the caucus, twenty-two Republicans were absent, of whom fifteen were known to be opposed to the caucus system of nomination. Immediately after an organization of the meeting was effected, Mr. Clay, and also Mr. John W. Taylor, of New York, moved resolutions that it is inexpedient to present candidates. The motions were rejected, — it is not recorded by what majority. The vote for a candidate for President was then taken. It resulted in the nomination of Mr. Monroe by the narrow majority of eleven votes. Monroe had sixty-five votes, Crawford fifty-four. Mr. Crawford's support came chiefly from five States, which gave him forty of his votes : New York, New Jersey, North Carolina, Kentucky, and his own State of Georgia. Had all the New York members voted freely, the nomination might have gone to him. Crawford himself professed afterward to have withdrawn from the contest before the caucus; but his friends seem not to have been aware of the fact when they voted. No intimation is given in any of the political literature of the day that it was proposed to him to keep out of the way of Monroe on a promise of future support. In view of the attempted employment of similar tactics on former occasions, in order to dispose of the pretensions of Monroe himself and of De Witt Clinton, and in view also of the events of 1824, it does not seem altogether improbable that his hesitation at the last moment was due to suggestions of this sort. Governor Daniel D. Tompkins, of New York, received eighty-five votes as candidate for Vice-President and was nominated. Governor Simon Snyder, of Pennsylvania, had thirty votes.

These proceedings startled the country, not so much because of what had been done, for that the people were ready to approve, but because the members who had assumed the right to make nominations had come near making recommendations which would not have been accepted. Numerous meetings were held in various parts of the country to protest against the caucus system, the most noteworthy of which, perhaps, was held in Baltimore, in which meeting Roger B. Taney, afterward Chief Justice, took a most prominent part. That, precisely, was happening, against which the Convention of 1787 had endeavored most scrupulously to guard, — the dependence of presidential candidates, and of Presidents desiring reëlection, upon the favor of Congress. Moreover, the latest nominations signified the perpetuation of a dynasty ; the rule of a single State of the Union ; the exclusion of every State except Virginia — which had now ceased being the State most numerously represented in Congress, although three fifths of her slaves were counted — from the privilege of furnishing a chief magistrate.

The nomination having been made, the election was decided. The elements of an effective opposition did not exist. Monroe would doubtless have won a victory had all who preferred another candidate formed a complete coalition. There was not a symptom of a wish to bring about such a union. The position

of the "old guard" of Federalists was indicated in a letter
from Gouverneur Morris to Rufus King, March 15, 1816.
This was Morris's latest utterance upon public affairs. His
death in November of the same year, just as the election was
to take place, closed a career which had begun at the Provin-
cial Congress in 1775. Mr. Morris wrote : —

That Mr. Madison's influence should decline is to be expected :
who is to be the successor? It seems to be acknowledged that no
Federal character can run with success. Nevertheless I believe
that if Howard of Maryland were started against Monroe he would
stand a tolerable chance. The Democrats can, I believe, be heartily united by nothing but the fear that a Federalist of superior
talents should be chosen. I have, at the same time, doubts
whether our friends in the Southern States would warmly support
a candidate from the North.

Nothing whatever was done to nominate candidates in opposition to Monroe and Tompkins. On December 3, the day
before the electors were to vote, the " Boston Daily Advertiser," published in one of the three States which had chosen
Federal electors, remarked : " We do not know, nor is it very
material, for whom the Federal electors will vote." They all
did vote for Rufus King, who had twice been their candidate
for Vice-President. For the second place the Massachusetts
electors supported Mr. Howard, of Maryland, suggested as a
candidate for President by Morris. Five Connecticut electors
voted for James Ross, of Pennsylvania, whom Morris mentioned in the letter above quoted as an available candidate for
the place.

In no State was there a real contest. The election of Monroe was entirely unopposed in the States from Virginia southward, and in Ohio. The legislatures of Massachusetts, Connecticut, and Delaware chose Federal electors ; those of Vermont
and New York, Democratic electors. In Rhode Island, which
the Federalists had just carried after a contest, no electors
were nominated in opposition to the Monroe ticket, which was
consequently chosen unanimously, not because the Federalists
doubted their ability to win, but because it was not worth
while, since the election of Monroe was assured. There was
an opposition ticket in Pennsylvania. The adage that politics
makes strange bedfellows was never more remarkably illustrated than by the fact that the ticket — which the Federalists
supported — was " under the patronage of Duane," as the

"Boston Advertiser" put it. Who was Duane? The famous editor of the "Philadelphia Aurora," the thick-and-thin advocate of Jefferson, the persistent slanderer of Adams and of all men and things "Federal," the Democrat to whose thinking Madison and Monroe were too mild and timid! The last appearance of the Federalist party in national politics was in alliance with its most virulent foe.

The number of States whose votes were counted at this election was nineteen. Indiana, which had adopted a constitution in June, 1816, was admitted to the Union December 11 of that year. The question whether or not its electoral votes should be counted gave interest to the joint meeting of the two Houses of Congress in February, 1817. The table of electoral votes was as follows: —

STATES.	PRESIDENT.		VICE-PRESIDENT.				
	James Monroe, Va.	Rufus King, N. Y.	Daniel D. Tompkins, N. Y.	John E. Howard, Md.	James Ross, Penn.	John Marshall, Va.	Robert G. Harper, Md.
New Hampshire	8	–	8	–	–	–	–
Vermont	8	–	8	–	–	–	–
Massachusetts	–	22	–	22	–	–	–
Rhode Island	4	–	4	–	–	–	–
Connecticut	–	9	–	–	5	4	–
New York	29	–	29	–	–	–	–
New Jersey	8	–	8	–	–	–	–
Pennsylvania	25	–	25	–	–	–	–
Delaware	–	3	–	–	–	–	3
Maryland	8	–	8	–	–	–	–
Virginia	25	–	25	–	–	–	–
North Carolina	15	–	15	–	–	–	–
South Carolina	11	–	11	–	–	–	–
Georgia	8	–	8	–	–	–	–
Kentucky	12	–	12	–	–	–	–
Tennessee	8	–	8	–	–	–	–
Louisiana	3	–	3	–	–	–	–
Ohio	8	–	8	–	–	–	–
Indiana	3	–	3	–	–	–	–
Total	183	34	183	22	5	4	3

The total number of electoral votes, it will be seen, was 217. A full vote would have been 221 ; but the three Federalist electors chosen in Maryland, and one of the Delaware electors, did not see fit to attend.

The preliminary arrangements in regard to the electoral count were made according to precedent. The two Houses met in the Representatives' Hall, and the certificates were duly opened. When all the returns except those from Indiana had been opened, Mr. Taylor, of New York, — a member of the House of Representatives, and afterward Speaker, — arose, and, addressing the Speaker, expressed his regret at being compelled to interrupt the proceedings, and to object to the vote from Indiana. He was proceeding to state his objections, when the Speaker (Mr. Clay) stopped him, and said that the two Houses had met for the single specified purpose of performing the constitutional duty which they were then discharging ; and that, while so acting in joint meeting, they could consider no proposition nor perform any business not prescribed by the Constitution.

At this point Mr. Varnum, of Massachusetts, concurring in what the Speaker had said, suggested the propriety of the Senate retiring, in order that the House of Representatives might deliberate upon the question raised by one of its members. The President of the Senate put the question to the senators, and in accordance with their vote the Senate withdrew. When the House was by itself, Mr. Taylor immediately took the floor, and urged that, since Indiana was not a State in the Union at the time the election took place, its votes were no more entitled to be counted than if they had come from Missouri or any other Territory. He maintained that the question should be considered and decided now, when the result would not be affected by it, and suggested that a joint resolution be passed declaring that the votes were illegal and ought not to be counted. A resolution was moved declaring the votes legal. On this a long debate took place. The suggestion was made that the resolution should not be a joint one, inasmuch as, by establishing a precedent, it might, at some time thereafter, when the House and Senate should be opposed to each other, " deprive this House of one of its powers by permitting the Senate to participate in this question." The discussion turned wholly upon the point whether or not Indiana was a State in the Union after it adopted its Constitution, and before it was admitted by a formal act of Congress. The power of Congress to reject the votes, if Indiana were not a State for purposes of the election, was questioned by no one. Finally, by an almost unanimous vote, the whole matter was indefinitely postponed, and the House sent a message to the Senate that it was prepared to resume the count.

Meanwhile a somewhat similar debate was taking place in the Senate; but, before a decision was reached, the message of the House was received. Thereupon the resolution which had been under discussion, declaring the votes of Indiana legal, was withdrawn by its mover, Mr. Barbour, of Virginia, and the Senate returned to the Representatives' Hall. After the two Houses had assembled, the Speaker informed them that the House of Representatives "had not seen it necessary to come to any resolution or to take any order on the subject which had produced the separation of the two Houses." Thereupon the count was completed, the result declared, and the proceedings were terminated.

The first full account of the inauguration of any President after Washington, to be found in the newspapers of the time, describes the ceremonial observed when Mr. Monroe took office. The order of proceedings on March 4, 1817, was almost exactly that which has now become the usual order. At half past eleven o'clock in the forenoon the President-elect left his residence and proceeded to the Capitol, escorted by "a large cavalcade of citizens on horseback," according to the tautological reporter for the "National Intelligencer." When Mr. Monroe arrived in the Senate Chamber the oath of office was first administered to the Vice-President, who delivered a short address on taking the chair. Then the Senate adjourned, and the whole assembled party proceeded without the building "to an elevated portico temporarily erected for the occasion, where in the presence of an immense concourse of officers of the government, foreign officers, strangers (ladies as well as gentlemen), and citizens, the President rose and delivered his address." After he had finished reading it, the oath was administered to him by the Chief Justice. "Such a concourse," declares the "National Intelligencer," "was never before seen in Washington, the number of persons present being estimated at from five to eight thousand." In the evening a great ball was given, and thus ended the events of the day.

X

THE "ERA OF GOOD FEELINGS"

DURING the last year of Mr. Madison's administration Congress passed an act changing the method of paying the members, and, as is usual in such cases, increasing the amount of their compensation. The change was from six dollars *per diem* to fifteen hundred dollars a year. The "compensation act" was exceedingly unpopular, and was repealed at the next session. Many members who voted for it were defeated. There was a large number of new members in the fifteenth Congress, but the balance of parties was nominally little changed. The new questions began to obliterate all party lines. The tariff united most of the Southern Democrats, the representatives of Pennsylvania and of the manufacturing districts, in favor of the protective policy. Commercial Massachusetts opposed it. The right to make "internal improvements" was rising into importance as a political issue; and here, too, the divisions cut across the old party lines. Many Federalists took an attitude of opposition, although logically, as broad constructionists, they should have been the supporters, and the Democrats should have been the opposers, of the policy. It is to be feared that the views of these Federalists were too greatly influenced by the prospect that the Middle and Southern States would profit most, and their own States least, by any appropriation Congress might make for the purpose. Congress declared itself in favor of internal improvements by a resolution that money constitutionally might be appropriated "for the construction" of post and military roads and of canals. But it rejected resolutions that the government constitutionally might "construct" these specified works. The distinction, rather fine-drawn and long ago abandoned by all parties, was that, while Congress might aid in such works, it could not undertake them.

Slavery loomed up for the first time, during Monroe's first term, as a great political issue. The clause of the Constitution which made the basis of representation in Congress the whole number of free persons, and three fifths of " all other persons," had been a constant source of complaint on the part of the Northern Federalists and those who chafed under the Virginia rule. Up to this time, nearly all the Southern ex-members, whenever they had had occasion to speak of the institution of slavery, had spoken of it as an evil, but one which could not be abolished without causing still greater evils than itself. Now the question of the admission of Missouri to the Union thrust itself upon Congress. Most of the representatives from the North, including those of both of the old parties, united to deny admission to Missouri except as a free State : the South was still more united in demanding that Missouri be admitted without restrictions. No previous debate upon a purely domestic question had been so exciting and passionate as that which took place on the Missouri bill. The whole country was aroused. Meetings were held and resolutions were adopted in cities and country towns ; state legislatures expressed their opinions in strong language. In Congress the contest was waged now with violence, now with strategy. The Southern members with their Northern allies, to whom John Randolph applied the term " doughfaces," — an appellation which stuck, — succeeded in linking together the bill for the admission of Maine as a separate State, to which there was no opposition, and that for the admission of Missouri. The outcome of the struggle was a compromise. An amendment was adopted which virtually permitted the existence of slavery in the proposed new State, but prohibited it forever in any of the remaining territory, ceded by France under the name of Louisiana, north of the line thirty-six degrees thirty minutes north latitude, — the northern line of Arkansas Territory. The amendment was carried against the opposition of the Southern extremists ; and the bill was then passed by the votes of all the Southern and a few Northern members. This was the famous Missouri Compromise, which became the line of defence of the anti-slavery sentiment of the country thirty years later, but which the South then stormed and captured. It was not the end of the contest over Missouri, for a clause in the Constitution framed for the State contained a provision forbidding admission into the State of free persons of color. The opposition aroused by this clause, which was held by the anti-slavery people to be inconsistent with the Constitution of the United States, was far more bitter than that manifested against the toleration of slavery in the new State. The legislature of Missouri was required to make a solemn pledge that no act should be passed that would exclude the citizens of any State from the privileges and immunities to which they were entitled under the Constitution. When this pledge had been given, and announced by a proclamation by the President, Missouri was to become a member of the Union.

All these exciting events took place in the year preceding the presidential election. It is not likely that, if Mr. Monroe had taken an active part in the great controversy on either side, he could have been defeated. The time was too short to organize a party of opposition with a prospect of success at the polls. As a matter of fact, the President held aloof altogether. When the "Enabling Act" for Missouri was laid before him he submitted two questions to his cabinet, — first, as to the constitutionality of an act to prohibit slavery in a Territory, which all the members, Calhoun as well as John Quincy Adams, answered in the affirmative; and, secondly, did the word "forever" in the compromising amendment extend to the time when the Territory should be erected into a State? Upon the second question there was a division, but the form of it was changed, at Calhoun's suggestion, to an inquiry if the proviso was constitutional. To this, again, all the cabinet agreed; and on March 2, 1820, Mr. Monroe signed the act. The popular excitement died out quickly, when it was supposed that the incident was closed. Had the subsequent action of the Missouri convention been foreseen, the public feeling might have found expression in the ensuing election. As it was, in one State only, Pennsylvania, was an electoral ticket nominated in opposition to Mr. Monroe; but there the ground of opposition was, expressly, that the President was the candidate of the slavery party.

The administration of Mr. Monroe was called at the time, and has since been known, as "the era of good feelings." The Federalists of New England were satisfied with his principles and with his conduct; and as the time drew near for an election they made no movement in opposition to him. In the spring of 1820 a caucus was called, to which were invited not only the Democrats, but such other members of Congress as might see fit to attend. Less than fifty members assembled. They adopted a resolution that it was not expedient to make any nomination, and adjourned.

It has been said already that there was an opposition ticket in Pennsylvania only. Where the electors were chosen by popular vote, the number of votes was exceedingly small. The largest number received by any elector in Connecticut was 3870, — about one vote to every seventy persons of the population. Only seventeen persons went to the polls in Richmond, Virginia. The fusion of parties was nowhere more pleasantly illustrated than in Massachusetts. A change was made once more in the method of appointment. Electors were chosen, one by each congressional district and two at large. The venerable President John Adams was elected unanimously as one of the two electors at large. Daniel Webster was one of the district electors. The college consisted, after vacancies had been filled, of eight Federalists and seven Democrats. They all voted for Mr. Monroe, but divided on the vice-presidency, the Federalists casting their votes for Richard Stockton, of New Jersey. One elector of New Hampshire gave his vote for John Quincy Adams for President, and thus deprived Monroe of the honor of a unanimous election. It has been reported — and the statement was repeated in the early editions of this history — that the dissenting elector withheld his vote from Mr. Monroe expressly to prevent that statesman from sharing an honor previously accorded to Washington alone. The statement is not correct. The "scattering" vote was given by William Plumer, formerly a senator in Congress and governor of the State, not because of his jealousy of Washington's record of unanimous election, but on account of his positive distrust of Monroe.

Five new States participated in this election, namely, Mississippi, admitted December 10, 1817; Illinois, admitted December 3, 1818; Alabama, admitted December 14, 1819; Maine, separated from Massachusetts and admitted as a State March 15, 1820; and Missouri, which adopted a Constitution in July, 1820, but was not proclaimed a State until August 10, 1821, when it had fulfilled the condition exacted of it by Congress as a prerequisite to admission. The situation in which Missouri stood at the time of the presidential election raised again, and in an exceedingly perplexing form, the question which had arisen in 1817 as to the right of Indiana to participate in the election. For whereas Indiana, although not fully admitted to the Union at the time the electors of 1816 voted, was a State in full standing when the votes were counted, Missouri had not performed the duty imposed as a condition of admission, and it was not certain that its legislature would ever give the pledge required. The inconvenience of a discussion of this question in the joint convention, and the doubts of members as to the result of an attempt to decide it either in joint meeting or by the two Houses separately, led to the invention of a method of avoiding the point altogether. The joint committee of Congress which was, in accordance with custom, appointed to ascertain and report a mode of examining the votes, reported, in addition to the usual resolution, the following : —

Resolved, That if any objection be made to the votes of Missouri, and the counting, or omitting to count, which shall not essentially change the result of the election, in that case they shall be reported by the President of the Senate in the following manner : Were the votes of Missouri to be counted, the result would be, for A. B. for President of the United States, —— votes ; if not counted, for A. B. for President of the United States, —— votes. But in either event A. B. is elected President of the United States. And in the same manner for Vice-President.

A long debate took place on this proposition in the Senate. The views advanced were various. But the Senate was persuaded to adopt the resolution upon the assurance of Mr. Barbour, who reported it, that it was his intention thereafter to bring up the matter of electoral votes objected to, to repair what he considered as a *casus omissus* in the Constitution, either by an act of Congress, if that should appear sufficient, or by an amendment to the Constitution.

The discussion in the House was of a different character. Mr. John Randolph attacked the resolution, providing for an alternative statement of the vote of Missouri, on constitutional grounds. He could not recognize in either House, or in both conjoined, the power to decide on the votes of any State. The electoral colleges were as independent of Congress as Congress was of them ; and he would rather see an interregnum, or that no votes should be counted, than that a principle should be adopted which went to the very foundation on which the presidential office rested. Several other gentlemen took similar views. The opposing argument was presented by Mr. Clay, then a private member, who said that Congress had been intrusted with the duty of enumerating the votes for President, and it was necessary for the two Houses to determine what were votes.

The resolution was adopted by a vote of 90 to 67, but the concurrence of the two Houses did not end the matter. When the votes of Missouri were announced by the President of the Senate and handed to the tellers, Mr. Livermore, of New Hampshire, a member of the House, addressing the President and the Speaker, objected to them on the ground that Missouri was not a State in the Union. The Senate thereupon retired, a motion to that effect having been put by the President. The Senate does not appear to have taken any action upon the objection, but in the House a long debate took place on a resolution that the votes ought to be counted. Mr. Randolph made himself the most conspicuous person in this discussion, and spoke upon the question with characteristic violence of language. Mr. Clay came to the rescue with an argument intended to show that the President of the Senate had acted erroneously in putting the question on the retirement of the Senate, the objection having been already provided for by the joint resolution. On his motion the subject was laid on the table, and the Senate was invited to return. The count then proceeded, and the result was declared in accordance with the prescribed form. The votes given are shown in the table on the opposite page.

As soon as the announcement had been made, Mr. Floyd, of Virginia, and after him Mr. Randolph, demanded to know what had become of the votes of Missouri. Their voices were drowned by cries of "Order!" and they were required to resume their seats. The Senate then retired, and Mr. Randolph made another violent speech, which he closed by proposing a series of resolutions reciting that the votes of Missouri have been counted, but that the announcement of the whole number of electors appointed, and of the votes given by them, has not been declared "agreeably to the provisions of the Constitution of the United States, and that therefore the proceeding has been irregular and illegal." While Mr. Randolph was reducing these resolutions to writing, a motion was made and carried to adjourn, and nothing more was heard of them.

The second inauguration of Mr. Monroe took place on the 5th of March, 1821, — the 4th was Sunday, — in the hall of the House of Representatives. The ceremony was a simple one, but the company was as large as could be crowded into a room which was by no means spacious. The President occupied a platform in front of the Speaker's chair, and the Chief Justice

STATES.	PRESIDENT.		VICE-PRESIDENT.				
	James Monroe, Va.	John Quincy Adams, Mass.	Daniel D. Tompkins, N. Y.	Richard Stockton, N. J.	Robert G. Harper, Md.	Richard Rush, Penn.	Daniel Rodney, Del.
Maine	9	–	9	–	–	–	–
New Hampshire	7	1	7	–	–	1	–
Vermont	8	–	8	–	–	–	–
Massachusetts	15	–	7	8	–	–	–
Rhode Island	4	–	4	–	–	–	–
Connecticut	9	–	9	–	–	–	–
New York	29	–	29	–	–	–	–
New Jersey	8	–	8	–	–	–	–
Pennsylvania *	24	–	24	–	–	–	–
Delaware	4	–	–	–	–	–	4
Maryland	11	–	10	–	1	–	–
Virginia	25	–	25	–	–	–	–
North Carolina	15	–	15	–	–	–	–
South Carolina	11	–	11	–	–	–	–
Georgia	8	–	8	–	–	–	–
Alabama	3	–	3	–	–	–	–
Mississippi *	2	–	2	–	–	–	–
Louisiana	3	–	3	–	–	–	–
Kentucky	12	–	12	–	–	–	–
Tennessee *	7	–	7	–	–	–	–
Ohio	8	–	8	–	–	–	–
Indiana	3	–	3	–	–	–	–
Illinois	3	–	3	–	–	–	–
Missouri	3	–	3	–	–	–	–
Total	231	1	218	8	1	1	4

* One elector in each of the States of Pennsylvania, Mississippi, and Tennessee died after appointment, and before the meetings of the electors.

stood by his side while he delivered his inaugural address. So dense was the throng that fears were entertained as to the safety of the crowd.

Questions concerning the presidential electoral system and the electoral count were much discussed during Mr. Monroe's administration, and at one time the prospect of submitting to the States for ratification an amendment of the Constitution, so that all elections might be uniform, seemed to be extremely good. The proposition had originated when the mishap at the election of 1800–01 was fresh in the minds of our public men, and when the necessity of guarding against a recurrence of it seemed imperative. It was then urged, as a part of the new system of choosing one person as President and another as Vice-President, that all the electors should be chosen by popular vote, the States to be divided for that purpose into districts. Although the matter was somewhat discussed in the newspapers from time to time, it does not appear to have been heard of again in Congress until the close of 1813. On December 20 of that year, Mr. Pickens, of North Carolina, introduced in the House a proposition to amend the Constitution in this respect, and made a long speech in support of the measure. He referred to the popular excitement which had prevailed in his State in consequence of the act of the legislature of North Carolina depriving the people of the right to choose electors, in 1812, as the reason for bringing the matter to the attention of Congress. The resolution for submitting the amendment to the States was negatived after some debate, 57 voting in favor of, and 70 against it.

Mr. Pickens introduced the subject again on one or two occasions after this defeat, but he did not press the amendment further until 1816. In December of that year he once more presented his resolution, in a new form, embracing two propositions. It provided that the States should be divided into districts for the choice of representatives in Congress, and also into single districts for the choice of electors. After some debate in Committee of the Whole, the House adopted the principle of the district system for representatives by a vote of 86 to 38. That part of the system which related to electors was approved by 87 votes against 51; but, as this was not a two-thirds majority, the House never took the subject up.

At the next session two amendments, in almost identical words, were introduced in the Senate by Mr. Dickerson, of New Jersey, and by Mr. Macon, of North Carolina. Subsequently the proposition relating to electors was changed so that one elector should be chosen from each representative district, and that the two additional electors for each State should be appointed " in such manner as the legislature thereof may direct," following the words of the Constitution. This amendment was negatived by 20 in favor to 13 opposed, — not two thirds. Again in 1818 Mr. Sanford, of New York, introduced the amendment in the Senate, by instruction of the New York legislature, as on previous occasions it had been introduced by others according to instructions from the legislatures of New Jersey and North Carolina.   This time a great deal of attention was paid to the matter.   It was debated at much length, three times referred to committees, and at last passed by a vote of 28 to 10.   In the House it was laid on the table by 79 to 73.   Introduced in the Senate again in 1819 by Mr. Dickerson, it was again passed, this time without debate, by 29 to 13.   Having been debated in the House, it was agreed to by the Committee of the Whole; but when it was reported to the House it was laid on the table, and never taken up.   Yet at the same session Mr. Smith, of North Carolina, introduced this identical amendment, and, after debate, it was passed to a third reading by a vote of 103 to 59; but on the question of its passage it was lost, 92 voting in favor of and 54 against it, — not two thirds.   The proposition never again came so near to success; but it was not abandoned, and as late as March, 1822, the Senate again passed the amendment by 29 to 11.   The House did not take the matter up for consideration.

Another effort was made during Mr. Monroe's administration to deal with the matter of the electoral count.   The Committee on the Judiciary, of the Senate, was instructed to consider the subject, and Mr. Van Buren reported a bill which, after amendment, was passed on April 19, 1824.   It covered the whole ground of the election and the count.   The electors were to make five lists of their votes instead of three.   One of these was to be sent to the seat of government by a messenger, two were to be deposited in the post office and forwarded by two successive mails to the President of the Senate, and the other two were to be delivered to the judge of the district in which the electoral meeting was held.   This was the only change proposed in the method of electing the President.   The important section was the fifth, as follows: —

SECTION 5. That at twelve o'clock of the day appointed for counting the votes that may be given at the next election for President and Vice-President, the Senate and House of Representatives shall meet in the hall of the House of Representatives, and on all future occasions in the centre room of the Capitol, at which meeting the President of the Senate shall be the presiding officer, but no debate shall be had nor question taken.   The packet containing the certificates from the electors of each State shall then be opened by the President of the Senate, beginning with the State of New Hampshire and going through to Georgia, in the order in which the thirteen original States are enumerated in the Constitution, and afterwards through the other States in the order in which they were respectively admitted into the Union; and, if no exceptions are taken thereto, all the votes contained in such certificates shall be counted; but if any exceptions be taken, the person taking the same shall state it in writing directly, and not argumentatively, and sign his name thereto; and if the exception be seconded by one member from the Senate and one member from the House of Representatives, and each of whom shall sign the said exception as having seconded the same, the exception shall be read by the President of the Senate, and then each House shall immediately retire, without question or debate, to its own apartment, and shall take the question on the exception, without debate, by ayes and noes. So soon as the question shall be taken in either House, a message shall be sent to the other informing them of the decision of the question, and that the House sending the message is prepared to resume the count; and when such message shall have been received by both Houses, they shall meet again in the same room as before, and the count shall be resumed. And if the two Houses have concurred in rejecting the vote or votes objected to, such vote or votes shall not be counted. The vote of one State being thus counted, another shall, in like manner, be called, and the certificate of the votes of the State thus called shall be proceeded on as is hereinbefore directed; and so on, one after another, in the order above mentioned, until the count shall be completed.

The bill was sent to the House for concurrence, where it was referred to the Committee on the Judiciary, and was reported back by Mr. Webster on the 10th of May without amendment. It was then referred to the Committee of the Whole, and was never taken up for consideration.

XI

THE DEFEAT OF "KING CAUCUS"

THE existence of a free government without a division into parties is an impossibility. The "era of good feelings" was a result, not of a radical change in human nature which permitted all Americans to think alike upon questions of national politics, but of a complete settlement of all the matters which had been the basis of party division. We have already seen that new issues began to loom into prominence even before Mr. Monroe's second election. In the latter part of his term they were causing differences, discussions, and divisions which were destined to become more definite and habitual, and eventually to range men on either side of a new party line. All these new issues — internal improvements, the tariff, slavery, and the rest — were to be decided one way or the other, according to the view one took of the scope and power of the Constitution. The two views were "strict construction" and "loose construction." Thus, when the Democratic party had substantially adopted the Federalist position in all the matters which pertained to the war of 1812, and the Federalists had crossed over to the position formerly occupied by their political opponents, the old question of interpretation arose in a new form, and ultimately reëstablished parties, greatly changed in personnel, in methods, in motives, and in aims. It will be seen, too, that issues not developed until years afterward were equally to be decided by an application of one or the other principle of interpreting the Constitution, — the Bank, nullification, the surplus revenue, the disposition of the public lands, in short, all the questions on which parties differed between 1830 and 1860.

No development of parties took place during Mr. Monroe's administration. In a few States the Federalist organization was maintained; but in no State was it in control of the government, nor did it ever regain control anywhere. It might and did exercise a certain influence by favoring one of two or more candidates, where the Democrats were divided. Except locally, it had no candidates of its own.

The election of 1824 was pending nearly three years. As early as April, 1822, Niles's Register remarked that there were already sixteen or seventeen candidates for the succession to Mr. Monroe. Soon after that the question how the candidates were to be nominated began to be discussed earnestly. The growth of an opposition to the system of nomination by congressional caucus has already been noted. The opposition was strong in 1816; but, inasmuch as the caucus had a result which a large majority of the people approved, little objection was heard after the nominations were made. No caucus was necessary in 1820. Now a determined resistance to the system was the only possible policy for the friends of all the candidates save one. It was understood universally that Mr. William H. Crawford, the Secretary of the Treasury, was the candidate preferred by the President; and, although Mr. Monroe did not obtrude his wishes upon the public in an unseemly manner, the very fact that his official support gave Crawford a larger body of partisans than any one of his rivals had, emphasized the objection to this mode of making nominations. It was foreseen that a caucus, should one be held, would be in Mr. Crawford's interest. Consequently the adherents of all the other candidates were opposed to the caucus.

Before the close of the year 1822, the minor candidates for the presidency had dropped out of the contest, and six only were left, for four of whom electoral votes were cast two years later. They were, in alphabetical order, John Quincy Adams, Secretary of State; John C. Calhoun, Secretary of War; Henry Clay, who had been Speaker of the House of Representatives most of the time during the previous ten years, but was just then in private life; De Witt Clinton, also in private life at that time; William H. Crawford, Secretary of the Treasury; and Andrew Jackson, who had been a representative and senator during Adams's administration, but who derived his fame and his prominence from his military achievements.

The first candidate who was put in formal nomination was Mr. Clay. The members of the Kentucky legislature, on the 18th of November, 1822, recommended him as "a suitable person to succeed James Monroe as President." In support of their resolution they issued an address to the people of the country in which they placed their preference upon "a warm affection for and a strong confidence in their distinguished fellow-citizen;" and their feeling that the time had come "when the people of the West may, with some confidence, appeal to the magnanimity of the whole Union for a favorable consideration of their equal and just claim to a fair participation in the executive government of these States." They nevertheless made the first consideration much the more prominent and important. The members of the Missouri legislature held a meeting about the same time, and adopted a resolution recommending Mr. Clay. Similar action was taken in Illinois and Ohio in January, 1823, and in Louisiana in March of the same year.

General Jackson seems first to have been nominated formally by the lower House of the Tennessee Legislature, on July 20, 1822, next by a mass convention of the people of Blount County, Tennessee, in May or June, 1823, and afterward by numerous conventions in all parts of the country. Mr. Adams was nominated by the legislatures of most of the New England States early in 1824; Mr. Clinton, by several counties in Ohio; Mr. Calhoun, by the legislature of South Carolina; Mr. Crawford, by the legislature of Virginia.

It will be seen that the situation closely resembled that, within each party, with which we of the present time are familiar at the beginning of every recurring presidential canvass. All the candidates professed the same political principles, at least to such an extent that any one of them might be heartily supported by the whole party, the only party in the country which had more than a local existence. A preference of one before the others might rest upon a conviction that he possessed superior qualifications; upon a personal liking for him; upon local pride; upon a disposition to be on good terms with the administration, — a consideration which helped Crawford only. Similar differences within a party are met nowadays, and they do not prevent a full and enthusiastic union of the whole organization in support of him whom the general voice of the party designates as the candidate. There then existed no body of men, and there was no way of forming a body of men, who could take the case in hand and determine which of the six candidates should be the candidate of all. The advocates of Mr. Crawford urged that the congressional caucus was the tried and approved mode, — not a perfect mode, but one which had previously harmonized differences and united the party. The adherents of all the others knew that a caucus would inevitably result in the choice of Crawford, and they were too wary to be drawn into that trap.

It thus became evident, a long while before the canvass should properly have begun, that the great question to be settled was whether or not a caucus should be held. It was discussed in every newspaper and in every political gathering. The state legislatures were a common means of expressing local sentiment. The first declaration in favor of a caucus was, it is believed, made by the legislature of New York, on May 23, 1823, when the following resolutions were unanimously adopted : —

That although a nomination by the Republican members of Congress is not entirely free from objections, yet that, assembled as they are from the different quarters of the Union, — coming from the various classes of community, — elected during the pendency and discussion of the question and in a great degree with reference to it, they bring into one body as perfect a representation as can be expected of the interests and wishes of all and of each ; and that a nomination made by them in a manner which has heretofore been usual is the best attainable method of effecting the object in view which has yet been suggested.

That we fully believe that a convention thus constituted will be less liable to be influenced by those sectional jealousies against which the Father of his Country has so solemnly and justly cautioned us ; more likely to cherish those purely national feelings which it is the interest and should be the pride of every State to protect ; and better calculated to preserve unbroken those political ties which bind together the Republicans of the North and the South, the East and the West, and are consecrated by the recollection of times and events dear to the Democracy of the nation which triumphed in the election and prospered under the administration of the illustrious Jefferson.

A few months later the legislature of Tennessee adopted a set of resolutions against the caucus, and instructing its members in Congress to use their influence to prevent the holding of such a meeting. The resolutions were sent to all the States for their approval. They were considered at the sessions of many legislatures in the earliest months of 1824. Maryland alone gave a cordial assent to them. Mr. Tyler, afterward President, offered resolutions in the Virginia House of

Delegates approving the caucus. Although the resolutions were not adopted, — owing to a delicate sense. of propriety which told the members that they ought not to take such action in their legislative capacity, — a meeting was held — perhaps it might be called a caucus — attended by three fourths of the members, who resolved almost unanimously in favor of the congressional caucus. Governor Troup, of Georgia, may be pardoned for manifesting some annoyance at being called upon to send to the legislature resolutions the sole purpose of which was to prevent the elevation of Georgia's favorite son to the presidency ; but the terms in which he communicated the resolutions were childishly petulant. He remarked in the course of this unique message that the word " caucus " was not in the dictionary, was not an English word, and he hoped would never be one. One branch of the South Carolina legislature approved the Tennessee resolutions ; the other threw them out with scorn. There was a like difference of opinion in the North. The Ohio and Indiana legislatures postponed the resolutions indefinitely. In Pennsylvania a report by a committee was rejected, by a vote of more than two to one, because it contained a clause which by implication sanctioned a caucus. The New York legislature expressed its dissent from the Tennessee resolutions and its approval of a caucus. In Massachusetts, and also in Maine, caucuses were held and John Quincy Adams was nominated ; subsequently in each State the Democratic members met again, and, while repeating their nomination of Mr. Adams, declared their wish that a congressional caucus should be held, and agreed to abide by the result.

Deep political excitement accompanied all these proceedings. The intensity of feeling is seen in the arguments on one side and the other with which for many months the newspapers were filled. There was no point in favor of the caucus or against it that was overlooked, and all of them were discussed and worked over until they were threadbare. The advocates of the caucus were entirely right when they said that the old method of nomination " tends to produce union, which the other mode has a tendency to destroy ; " and doubtless, if the Democratic party had been facing a strong and resolute enemy, the refusal to submit the claims of all the candidates to the arbitrament of the caucus would have been " bad politics." Since it was free from that danger, the violent struggle within the party was harmless, and it was useful in bringing to an end a dynasty which was making the government stale. The difficulty in the way of a better system of nomination, together with a hint as to the better way which was afterward adopted, is set forth in resolutions adopted by the Democrats of Lancaster County, Pennsylvania, in the winter of 1824 : " We believe the best and most unexceptionable method " to be " a convention of delegates from all the States of the Union ; " but as it would be " entirely impracticable, from the immense extent of our country, and from the great expense necessarily incident to an attendance from the extreme parts of the United States," they deemed " the old and tried mode," the caucus, the best that was attainable. When we reflect that at this time there was not a mile of railway in the country, and that weeks of travel were necessary to compass the distance from Louisiana and Missouri to the seat of government, the objection to a national convention does not seem overdrawn.

The call for a caucus, dated February 6, 1824, appeared in the " National Intelligencer " on the following morning. It was signed by six senators and five representatives, members from eleven States. It was addressed to the Democratic members of Congress, and invited them to meet in the Representatives' chamber on the evening of the 14th, " to recommend candidates to the people of the United States for the offices of President and Vice-President of the United States." Side by side with this notice appeared another, to which were appended the signatures of twenty-four senators and members, representing fifteen States, who asserted that they had satisfactory information that, of the two hundred and sixty-one senators and representatives, there were a hundred and eighty-one " who deem it inexpedient, under existing circumstances, to meet in a caucus " for the purpose named.

Although the accuracy of this canvass was impugned, the event showed that it was nearly correct. Sixty-six members only assembled in caucus. They represented sixteen States of the Union, but a large majority of them were from four States. New York supplied sixteen, from its delegation numbering thirty-six; Virginia, fourteen out of a possible twenty-four; North Carolina, ten of a delegation of fifteen ; eight of the nine Georgia members were present. These four States supplied forty-eight members, and the other twenty States only eighteen members of the caucus. Eight States were not represented at all; five States furnished one member each. A

motion was made to adjourn for six weeks, nominally in order
to wait for the action of the Pennsylvania State Convention,
really in order to drum up more members. Mr. Van Buren
spoke against the motion, and it was defeated. The caucus
then proceeded to ballot for a candidate for President. The
result was as follows: William H. Crawford had 64; John
Quincy Adams, 2; Andrew Jackson, 1; Nathaniel Macon, 1.
Two absent members, one each from Virginia and Georgia,
voted by proxy.

A ballot was next taken for a candidate for Vice-President.
Albert Gallatin of Pennsylvania had 57 votes; Erastus Root
of New York, 2; and the following named, one each: John
Q. Adams, William Eustis of Massachusetts, Samuel Smith of
Maryland, William King of Maine, Richard Rush of Pennsylvania, John Tod of Pennsylvania, and Walter Lowrie of
Pennsylvania. The caucus then adopted a resolution formally
recommending Messrs. Crawford and Gallatin, and declaring
that : —

In making the foregoing recommendation, the members of this
meeting have acted in their individual characters as citizens ; that
they have been induced to this measure from a deep and settled
conviction of the importance of union among Republicans throughout the United States, and as the best means of collecting and
concentrating the feelings and wishes of the people of the Union
upon this important subject.

A committee was appointed to prepare an address to the
people of the United States. The tone of the address was far
from reassuring. " We will not conceal our anxiety," the
committee declared. " To our minds, the course of recent
events points to the entire dismemberment of the party to
which it is our pride to be attached." They were right. The
caucus seems not to have added a vote anywhere to Mr. Crawford's strength. It seemed, indeed, to reveal his weakness,
even in Congress. The " National Intelligencer," the steadfast
advocate of Crawford, published a statement of the preferences
of the members of both Houses. It set down 40 of the 260
members — there was one vacancy — as Federalists, and divided the other 220 as follows : Crawford, 93 ; Adams, 38 ;
Clay, 32 ; Calhoun, 25 ; Jackson, 23. The canvass was
warmly disputed by the friends of the other candidates, one of
whom drew attention to the fact that the " Intelligencer " had
" lost " nine Democrats in its count, since the total number
accounted for was but 211.

Local and personal considerations predominated in the canvass that ensued. The caucus issue had served its purpose and was not made prominent. The "regularity" of the nomination was urged by Crawford's friends, but other men cared little about it. The "Boston Daily Advertiser" doubtless expressed the feelings of many of Mr. Adams's supporters in New England when it said they were going to vote for him "because he is a citizen of this Commonwealth," and "not so much because it is supposed that a majority of the electors have felt any strong attachment for him." It is fair to say that the "Advertiser" was a Federalist paper still, and spoke for its party friends, who still, perhaps, might have defeated the Adams electoral ticket in Massachusetts if they had been so disposed, and if it had been worth the effort.

The caucus ticket had been framed, in the selection of Mr. Gallatin for Vice-President, to capture the vote of Pennsylvania. But it did not strengthen the cause. Mr. Gallatin's eligibility was assailed, and he was forced to defend himself against the charge of being a "foreigner." Although he had been a resident of the United States since 1780, there was certainly a cloud upon his title as "a citizen of the United States at the time of the adoption of this Constitution." Nevertheless, he persisted in his candidacy until October, when he retired from the canvass, "understanding that the withdrawal of my name may have a favorable effect on the result" of the approaching election. Mr. Calhoun had withdrawn as a candidate for the presidency, and there was a general concentration upon him as the candidate for the second place on the part of all the anti-caucus forces, who had omitted, in their nominations, to name a Vice-President. It seems to have been in the minds of the Crawford party that they might effect a coalition with the supporters of Clay by giving the vice-presidency to the Kentucky statesman. A suggestion of such a union was rejected with scorn by the Clay men, and Mr. Gallatin's retirement had no perceptible effect on the canvass.

Long before the voting began, it was evident to all that there was to be no choice of President by the electors, and that the election would go, for the second time, to the House of Representatives; furthermore, that each of the four candidates — for Clinton had developed no strength in the canvass — would receive many electoral votes. Three only could go before the House. It therefore was the aim of every group to secure enough votes for its candidate to make him one of the three.

As in 1820, twenty-four States took part in the election. Electors were appointed by the legislatures in Vermont, New York, Delaware, South Carolina, Georgia, and Louisiana. In the other eighteen States they were chosen by the people ; by districts in Maine, Maryland, Illinois, Kentucky, and Missouri ; elsewhere, by general ticket.

The legislature of New York (entitled to 36 electors) contained supporters of three of the candidates. The law governing elections by the legislature required that each house should ballot separately until it made a choice by a majority of votes. If the two branches agreed in the election, they met in joint convention and declared the result. If different persons had been elected, the election was made by ballot in joint convention ; and here also a majority was required. The election began on the 10th of November. On that day the Senate made choice of the Crawford electors. The senators were divided in their preferences thus : for Crawford, 17 ; for Adams, 7 ; for Clay, 7. In the Assembly there was no choice : the Crawford ticket had 43 votes, the Adams 50, the Clay 32. Combined, therefore, the strength of the three candidates was : Crawford, 60 ; Adams, 57 ; Clay, 39. The balloting in the Assembly continued on the 10th, 11th, and 12th of November with the change of only a single vote. On the 12th, some of the Crawford men announced their purpose of voting for the Adams ticket in order to transfer the contest to a joint convention and to defeat Mr. Clay. This threat produced an effect upon the Clay men, who, on the following day, themselves supported the Adams ticket and gave it the required majority. The fact that an election had been effected by the Assembly was hurriedly communicated to some of the Crawford senators before the official notice could be sent, and the Senate hastily adjourned. On Monday, the 15th, the joint convention was held, and a ballot was taken. The whole number of ballots was 157, but three of them were blank votes. Seven friends of Mr. Clay, who had been placed upon the Crawford ticket in hope of inducing the Clay men to support the whole ticket, had 95 votes. The rest of the Crawford ticket had 76 votes. Twenty-five of the names on the Adams ticket had 78 votes each, which was exactly a majority of 154, the number of effective ballots, but one less than a majority of the whole number, including the blanks. A resolution was offered declaring the thirty-two electors who had 78 or more votes to be chosen. The Speaker of the Senate refused to put the question. A long debate and a scene of tumult and confusion such as has rarely taken place in a legislative body ensued ; and in the end the presiding officer, followed by the sixteen Crawford senators, left the Assembly Chamber. But at last the resolution was separately adopted by each House. The two branches met again, and completed the election by the choice of four Crawford men by a bare majority.

At the meeting of the electors, three of those who had been expected to vote for Clay deserted him and went, one each, to Adams, Crawford, and Jackson. It will be seen by reference to the table of electoral votes (page 140) that, if they had all voted for Mr. Clay, his vote and Crawford's would have been equal, and the names of Adams and Jackson only would have gone before the House of Representatives.

In Delaware there was a parliamentary problem of a character somewhat similar to that in New York. The number of members present at the joint meeting of the two houses of the legislature was 30. One elector (for Adams) received 21 votes, and was no doubt elected. Two Crawford men had 15 votes each, and seven other candidates had from 1 to 10 each. The law of Delaware provided that, "if an equal division of ballots shall appear for two or more persons, not being elected by a majority of the votes, the Speaker of the Senate shall have an additional casting vote." This was clearly not a case of the kind contemplated by the statute, which intended that the Speaker should decide between two or more equal and opposing candidates. If only one of the two Crawford men had received 15 votes, he could not have given a casting vote. As there were two equal candidates he gave an additional vote for each, and declared them elected. He followed the letter of the statute beyond a doubt.

The election of 1824 is the first with reference to which an attempt has been made to test the result by a comparison of the popular vote for the several candidates. The statement which is to be found in most of the political almanacs and compendiums of political information, even to the present day, is one which, it is believed, originated in an early number of Mr. Greeley's Whig Almanac, as follows : —

For Jackson 152,899
Adams 105,321
Crawford 47,265
Clay 47,087

The statement is inaccurate; and, when it has been corrected, it is misleading. No exact table of popular votes can be presented. In five States only were all four candidates represented at the polls. In six others there were three tickets; in seven there were but two tickets; in six States the electors were chosen by the legislature. Throughout New England the ticket in opposition to Adams was that supported by the caucus committee, and the votes should doubtless all be given to Crawford. In North Carolina there was a fusion of the friends of Jackson and Adams. The "old North State" had contained from the earliest times a strong body of Federalists, who were all opposed to Crawford, and were disposed to support Mr. Adams. It was estimated that at least five thousand of them voted for the fusion electoral ticket; but, inasmuch as the electors voted for Jackson, all their votes are credited to him. A careful study of the returns from all the States, in most cases official, and in every case a full return, results in the table given on page 136.

The difference in the totals of the two statements is not important. But neither statement is valuable as indicating the will of the people on the question of the presidency. Virginia, with a white population of 625,000, cast an aggregate of less than 15,000 votes; Pennsylvania, with a population of something more than a million, cast a few more than 47,000 votes, which was but a little larger number than that of Massachusetts, 37,000, with a population of less than 600,000; and Massachusetts, at the election of the previous year, had given more than 66,000 votes for governor. If to such inequalities as these we add those produced by the total omission from the list of all votes from six States which contained more than one fourth of the whole population of the country, the lack of significance of the statement of popular votes may be understood.

Mr. Calhoun was elected Vice-President by more than two thirds of the electoral votes. There was no choice of a President. Mr. Crawford, the caucus candidate, barely succeeded in securing a place among the first three candidates. Congress assembled on the 6th of December, five days after the

States.	Jackson.	Adams.	Crawford.	Clay.
Maine	—	10,289	2,336*	—
New Hampshire	—	9,389	643†	—
Vermont ‡	—	—	—	—
Massachusetts	—	30,687	6,616*	—
Rhode Island	—	2,145	200*	—
Connecticut	—	7,587	1,978*	—
New York ‡	—	—	—	—
New Jersey	10,985	9,110	1,196§	—
Pennsylvania	36,100	5,441	4,206	1,690
Delaware ‡	—	—	—	—
Maryland	14,523	14,632	3,364	695
Virginia	2,861	3,189	8,489	416
North Carolina	20,415‖	—	15,621	—
South Carolina ‡	—	—	—	—
Georgia ‡	—	—	—	—
Alabama	9,443	2,416	1,680	67
Mississippi	3,234	1,694	119	—
Louisiana ‡	—	—	—	—
Kentucky	6,455	—	—	17,331
Tennessee	20,197	216	312	—
Missouri	987	311	—	1,401
Ohio	18,457	12,280	—	19,255
Indiana	7,343	3,095	—	5,315
Illinois	1,901	1,542	219	1,047
Total	152,901	114,023	46,979	47,217

* Opposition ticket. † Opposition ticket, wrongly credited in former editions to Jackson. ‡ Electors appointed by legislature. § "Convention" ticket. ‖ "People's" ticket.

meeting of the electors. Although it was known that there had been no choice of a President, no notice was taken of the fact until the 13th of January, 1825, when Mr. Wright, of Ohio, offered a resolution for the appointment of a committee —

To prepare and report such rules as, in their opinion, may be proper to be observed by this House in the choice of a President of the United States, for the period of four years from the 4th day of March next, if, on counting the votes given in the several States in the manner prescribed in the Constitution of the United States, it shall appear that no person has received a majority of all the electors of President and Vice-President appointed in the several States.

This resolution was adopted on the 18th of January, and the committee was appointed, which reported, on the 26th, a plan that was in some respects different from that adopted in 1801, but the changes were not important.

The Senate proposed, on the 1st of February, to raise a joint committee " to ascertain and report a mode of examining the votes " in the usual form.   The committee was appointed, and reported a resolution similar to those adopted in former years, but containing a clause made necessary by the fact that there was no choice of a President.   When this resolution came up in the Senate, Mr. Eaton, of Tennessee, moved to add a new paragraph to the effect that, if objection should be made to any vote, it should be filed in writing and entered on the journals of the two Houses; that the two Houses should not separate until all the votes had been counted and reported; but that the report of the result should be " liable to be controlled and altered by the decision to be made by the two Houses, after their separation, relative to any objections that may be made," provided that no objection should be considered valid unless so voted by both Houses.

Mr. Van Buren opposed this clause, and after debate it was rejected.   No objections were made, it may be said here, to any votes at the time of the count; but in May, after the election, Mr. Wilde, of Georgia, introduced in the House of Representatives a resolution that a message be sent to the Senate requesting copies of all the certificates of electoral votes.   In a long speech he gave his reason for making this motion, which was that few of the certificates were strictly correct and in due form.   They either did not assert that the electors voted in distinct ballots for President and Vice-President, or they did not report a vote by ballot, — distinct ballots being required by the Constitution.   The resolution was opposed on the ground that it was too late, and that " the elections in the States were not subject to revision by Congress," and, on motion, was laid on the table.

Before the day for counting the votes, February 9, there was a great scandal in the House of Representatives.   The situation was one which invited intrigue, and no doubt there was much bargaining and attempted trading of votes.   The excitement ran high.   The votes of thirteen States were necessary for a choice.   Mr. Adams was sure of the unanimous votes of the six New England States, and of a majority in New York, Maryland, and Ohio.   Mr. Crawford would have Delaware, Virginia, North Carolina, and Georgia.   The universal expectation was that Mr. Adams would be chosen; and a desire to avoid such a long and perilous contest as had taken place in 1801, as well as a desire to be on the winning side, helped his cause. In the midst of the excitement a letter was published in the " Columbian Observer " of Philadelphia, on January 28, dated at Washington, from which the following is extracted : —

For some time past, the friends of Clay have hinted that they, like the Swiss, would fight for those who would pay best. Overtures were said to have been made by the friends of Adams to the friends of Clay, offering him the appointment of Secretary of State for his aid to elect Adams. And the friends of Clay gave this information to the friends of Jackson, and hinted that, if the friends of Jackson would offer the same price, they would close with them.

There was much more of the same sort, but this contains the substance of the charge. Mr. Clay at once published a card in which he asserted that he believed the letter was a forgery, " but, if it be genuine, I pronounce the member, whoever he may be, a base and infamous calumniator, a dastard, and a liar." Mr. George Kremer, of Pennsylvania, avowed himself the author of the letter, and asserted his ability to prove his assertions. The matter was brought to the attention of the House by Mr. Clay, who was Speaker of the House at the time, and a committee was raised to inquire into the matter. Mr. Kremer, in a long and labored but weak letter, declined to appear before the committee. In spite of the most positive denials of the truth of the story, and of an absolute lack of any evidence to support the accusation, the charge was persisted in and believed by all who had an interest in believing it. Three years afterward, in the midst of the ensuing canvass, General Jackson himself wrote a letter, which was made public, in which he gave an account of an interview in January, 1825, with a member of Congress whom he understood to intimate that Mr. Clay's influence might be detached from Mr. Adams and given to him on certain terms. Jackson thus not only revived the old scandal, but virtually affirmed his belief in the truth of the charge. He afterward asserted that the member of Congress was James Buchanan. Mr. Clay thereupon published a most emphatic and sweeping denial, one sentence of which will suffice to show its character: " I neither made, nor authorized, nor knew of any proposition whatever to either of the three candidates who were returned to the House of Representatives, at the last presidential election, or to the friends of either of them, for the purpose of influencing the result of the election, or for any other purpose." Mr. Buchanan himself then made a statement that it had "never once entered my head that he _General Jackson] believed me to be the agent of Mr. Clay or of his friends, or that I had intended to propose to him terms of any kind from them." One might suppose that this should have been conclusive. Even so thorough-going an admirer of Jackson as James Parton admits that "no charge was ever more plausible or more groundless . . . none was ever more completely refuted." Yet Jackson persisted in it to the end, and took pains, in 1844, only a year before his death, to deny that he had "recanted" it, and to affirm that his opinion "had undergone no change."

There is no need to rely on negative testimony to prove Mr. Clay's innocence; for almost immediately after the meetings of the electors he had announced to Senator Thomas H. Benton his intention to support Mr. Adams. Mr. Benton records, in his "Thirty Years' View," the fact that Mr. Clay made to him a communication of this intention before the 15th of December, 1824, which, Mr. Benton believes, was "probably before Mr. Adams knew it himself." It is a pity that Mr. Benton did not make public the evidence in his possession until November, 1827, when all possible harm to Mr. Clay's reputation which the false accusation could do had long been done. Of course the purpose of keeping the scandal alive was the defeat of Mr. Adams, who could not be innocent if Mr. Clay had been guilty of the corrupt bargain. It is only because of its bearing on the ensuing election, and because the accusation, if true, would have been an indelible stain upon the character of one of our Presidents, that so much attention has been given to it in these pages.

The electoral votes were counted on the 9th of February, 1825. The result as announced is given on page 140.

The President of the Senate, Mr. Gaillard, then declared that no person had received a majority of the votes given for President of the United States; that Andrew Jackson, John Quincy Adams, and William H. Crawford were the three persons who had received the highest number of votes, and that the remaining duties in the choice of a President now devolved upon the House of Representatives; and that John C. Calhoun was duly elected Vice-President.

STATES.	PRESIDENT.				VICE-PRESIDENT.					
	Andrew Jackson, Tenn.	J. Q. Adams, Mass.	W. H. Crawford, Ga.	H. Clay, Ky.	John C. Calhoun, S. C.	Nathan Sanford, N. Y.	Nathaniel Macon, N. C.	Andrew Jackson, Tenn.	M. Van Buren, N. Y.	H. Clay, Ky.
Maine	–	9	–	–	9	–	–	–	–	–
New Hampshire .	–	8	–	–	7	–	–	1	–	–
Vermont	–	7	–	–	7	–	–	–	–	–
Massachusetts . .	–	15	–	–	15	–	–	–	–	–
Rhode Island . .	–	4	–	–	3	–	–	–	–	–
Connecticut . . .	–	8	–	–	–	–	–	8	–	–
New York . . .	1	26	5	4	29	7	–	–	–	–
New Jersey . . .	8	–	–	–	8	–	–	–	–	–
Pennsylvania . .	28	–	–	–	28	–	–	–	–	–
Delaware	–	1	2	–	1	–	–	–	–	2
Maryland. . . .	7	3	1	–	10	–	–	1	–	–
Virginia	–	–	24	–	–	–	24	–	–	–
North Carolina. .	15	–	–	–	15	–	–	–	–	–
South Carolina . .	11	–	–	–	11	–	–	–	–	–
Georgia	–	–	9	–	–	–	–	–	9	–
Alabama	5	–	–	–	5	–	–	–	–	–
Mississippi . . .	3	–	–	–	3	–	–	–	–	–
Louisiana. . . .	3	2	–	–	5	–	–	–	–	–
Kentucky . . .	–	–	–	14	7	7	–	–	–	–
Tennessee . . .	11	–	–	–	11	–	–	–	–	–
Missouri	–	–	–	3	–	–	–	3	–	–
Ohio	–	–	–	16	–	16	–	–	–	–
Indiana	5	–	–	–	5	–	–	–	–	–
Illinois	2	1	–	–	3	–	–	–	–	–
Total	99	84	41	37	182	30	24	13	9	2

The Senate having retired, the House immediately proceeded to elect a President. A roll-call showed that every member of the House except Mr. Garnett, of Virginia, who was sick at his lodgings in Washington, was present. Mr. Webster, of Massachusetts, and Mr. Randolph, of Virginia, were appointed tellers. The House conducted the election according to the rules already adopted, and on the first ballot John Quincy Adams was chosen. The votes of thirteen States were given to him, those of seven to Jackson, and of four to Crawford. The Speaker declared Mr. Adams elected, and notice of the result was sent to the Senate. The votes of the States are shown by the following table, which indicates both the divisions within the delegations and the person for whom the vote of each State was given.

STATES.	Adams.	Jackson.	Crawford.	Vote for —
Maine	7	–	–	Adams.
New Hampshire	6	–	–	Adams.
Vermont	5	–	–	Adams.
Massachusetts	12	1	–	Adams.
Rhode Island	2	–	–	Adams.
Connecticut	6	–	–	Adams.
New York	18	2	14	Adams.
New Jersey	1	5	–	Jackson.
Pennsylvania	1	25	–	Jackson.
Delaware	–	–	1	Crawford.
Maryland	5	3	1	Adams.
Virginia	1	1	19	Crawford.
North Carolina	1	2	10	Crawford.
South Carolina	–	9	–	Jackson.
Georgia	–	–	7	Crawford.
Alabama	–	3	–	Jackson.
Mississippi	–	1	–	Jackson.
Louisiana	2	1	–	Adams.
Kentucky	8	4	–	Adams.
Tennessee	–	9	–	Jackson.
Missouri	1	–	–	Adams.
Ohio	10	2	2	Adams.
Indiana	–	3	–	Jackson.
Illinois	1	–	–	Adams.
Total	87	71	54	

The inauguration of Mr. Adams took place in the Representatives' Hall. A military escort accompanied the retiring President and the President-elect to the Capitol, where all the departments of the government and representatives of foreign powers had assembled. Mr. Adams, as all of his predecessors had been on a similar occasion, was arrayed in a full suit of plain cloth of American manufacture. Mr. Adams rose and read his inaugural address in a firm voice, after which the oath was administered to him by the venerable Chief Justice Marshall. Among the first to take the hand of Mr. Adams, after the ceremony, was Senator Andrew Jackson.

XII

JACKSON'S TRIUMPH

MR. ADAMS was foredoomed to defeat in 1828, — from the day of his inauguration. His political enemies were the most astute managers the country had produced. They had the chagrin of a failure to wipe out and avenge. They had a candidate ready for the canvass for whom it was easy to arouse popular enthusiasm. On the other hand, Mr. Adams, while supported by faithful and trusty statesmen, was surrounded also by officers whom he retained in the places to which they had been appointed by his predecessor, although he was fully aware of their treachery toward himself. Senators came to him to assure him that they were friendly to his administration, and then went to the Capitol and voted with the opposition, and assisted in passing some of the most malignantly insulting resolutions ever spread upon the records of the Senate. One member of the President's official family, the Postmaster-General, not then admitted to the cabinet, used the patronage of his office, during the whole of the four years' term, to the injury of the administration. More than once the members of the cabinet united in an earnest request to Mr. Adams to remove him; but he refused. The President would not, even when another man would have been goaded by desperation to turn upon his perfidious office-holders, remove any man because that man was not his personal supporter. There are numerous entries in his diary showing his steady adherence to a policy which is most completely set forth in this passage: "I see yet no reason sufficient to justify a departure from the principle with which I entered upon the administration, of removing no public officer for merely preferring another candidate for the presidency."

Another fact which would alone have been fatal to Mr. Adams's hopes of reëlection, if he had entertained such hopes, was his lack of the personal qualities that attract popular support. At best he had been, in 1824, but the candidate of a

minority. To ensure success at the next election it would
have been necessary to find new friends among those who had
been rather the adherents of other candidates than direct opponents of himself. He was not the man to conciliate. He was
made of too stern and uncompromising stuff. He would stoop
to none of the arts of the politician, not even to measures
which in these days of undoubtedly greater political virtue are
deemed innocent and harmless. He was too good for this
wicked world, — not too wise, not too tactful, not too tolerant.
He was nevertheless wise enough to be aware that he had little
or no chance of reëlection. His diary during 1828 abounds
in comments upon the hopeful assurances of his visitors, stating in plain language that he was not deceived by them. He
remarks upon Mr. Rush's preference for the mission to England to the chance of being elected Vice-President on the ticket
with himself: " I can easily conjecture what it is — the preference of the harbor to the tempest." Again, when he is
communing with himself upon the appointment of Governor
Barbour to the same place he says, May 1, 1828, " In my own
political downfall I am bound to involve unnecessarily none of
my friends." He thinks the effect of the appointment upon
the administration will be bad, — " violent, and probably decisive. But why should I require men to sacrifice themselves for
me ? "

The political questions that arose during Mr. Adams's administration were by no means of such importance as to justify
the formation of parties where none existed before. It is
impossible to comprehend how men who, at the outset, had no
complaint against Mr. Adams save that he had been successful
over their own candidate, could have worked themselves into
opposition so rancorous as they manifested to the proposition of the Panama mission, — a conference of American republics. It was a harmless scheme that promised good results ;
but these men jumped upon it and trampled it under their
feet with fury, for no better reason than that it was a project
which the President and Mr. Clay desired most earnestly to
see carried through. It was upon this measure that, as Mr.
Adams himself records, in January, 1826, the first attempt was
made " to unite the Jackson, Crawford, and Calhoun forces."
The tariff became an issue in politics in 1828 ; but that was
long after the opposition was fully organized and felt itself on
the eve of victory. Mr. Adams's position on the question of

internal improvements was not that of a majority of those who had supported other candidates; but the question was not one of sufficient importance to alienate any of them. It was an excuse rather than a reason for opposition. Moreover, General Jackson, as a senator, had voted for internal improvements, and had acted throughout with the protectionists in passing the tariff act of 1824. The opposition press teemed with falsehoods, absurd on their face or easily disproved, yet repeated in spite of ample proof of their untruth. The popular outcry against Freemasonry that arose after the affair of Morgan is a good example of the misrepresentation to which the President was subjected. He was not a Freemason; indeed he was actively opposed to the order. Yet in regions where the anti-masonic feeling was strong, he was published as being a member of the order, and a pretended transcript from the records of a lodge was issued, in which his admission was recorded. The old and oft disproved story of a "corrupt bargain" between himself and Clay was revived. No tale was too preposterous to be invented if it would make votes against this honorable, high-minded man, whose intentions were as good and whose patriotism was as pure as that of any man who ever sat in the President's chair.

The canvass of 1828 opened in October, 1825, before Mr. Adams had met Congress at all, and before he had indicated, except in his inaugural address, what was to be his policy. The Tennessee legislature nominated General Jackson for the succession. He accepted the nomination in an address which he delivered before the two Houses of the legislature, and resigned his seat in the Senate. Other legislatures, conventions, caucuses, and public meetings in all parts of the country also nominated the general. But in order to make his election certain it was deemed necessary to bring to his support the friends of Crawford. This is supposed to have been effected by a mission through the South undertaken after the close of the session of Congress in March, 1827, by Martin Van Buren and Churchill C. Cambreling, — the two most prominent New York politicians of the time. Mr. Van Buren, on his way through Washington in May, called on the President. Mr. Adams was not ignorant of the object of the tour. "They are generally understood to have been electioneering, and Van Buren is now the great electioneering manager for General Jackson, as he was before the last election for Mr. Crawford."

The basis of the campaign was the alleged "wrong" done to General Jackson in 1825 when, having the largest number of electoral votes and of popular votes, he was set aside in favor of Mr. Adams. Those who made this complaint paid but a poor compliment to the intelligence of those to whom it was addressed. If the framers of the Constitution had intended that a plurality of popular or of electoral votes should decide the election of President they would not have devised the elaborate system of election by the House of Representatives. Those who desire to see worked out the flimsy argument that the people were defrauded in 1825 by the defeat of a candidate who had but a plurality of votes, given under a system that did not contemplate popular elections, will find it in Benton's "Thirty Years' View." His exposition of what he calls "the *Demos Krateo* principle" is a brilliant specimen of reasoning from false premises.

The candidacy of Mr. Adams for reëlection was taken for granted. If there were any meetings, legislative or other, at which his name was formally presented, the nomination was of no value in the canvass. The question of the vice-presidency was much discussed. Calhoun, of course, was out of the question. From the beginning he had been an enemy of the administration; and it was plain to see that he was to be the candidate of the Jacksonians for reëlection. As early as February, 1826, Mr. Clay mentioned to Mr. Adams that he had been approached by many persons on the subject of the vice-presidency, and inquired what were the President's wishes. For his own part he preferred to retain his office of Secretary of State, but he was willing to do whatever would be best for the administration. Mr. Adams, without making a final decision, was inclined to think Mr. Clay more useful in the State Department. Mr. Clay reported also that Governor Barbour, the Secretary of War, was much considered for the vice-presidency. Two months later another caller upon the President referred to the question of who should have the second place on the ticket, "which, he says, W. H. Harrison looks to very earnestly." Still later the strange suggestion was made that Mr. W. H. Crawford should be nominated, and, more remarkable still, it was pressed rather urgently. Mr. Adams gave no countenance to this proposition, which he felt sure would result in nothing but treachery.[1] The matter was finally settled

[1] Mr. Adams, at the beginning of the administration, asked Mr. Crawford

by the nomination of Mr. Richard Rush, the Secretary of the Treasury, by the "administration" convention of Pennsylvania, which met at Harrisburg, January 4, 1828.

The friends of the administration believed, or professed to believe, to the last moment, that Mr. Adams would be re-elected. They classed Pennsylvania among the doubtful States, counted confidently upon the new States of the northwest, — Ohio, Indiana, Illinois, — and were encouraged, by the success of the administration party at the state election in Kentucky, as late as August, 1828, to believe that Mr. Clay's State would support them. The administration party was grossly deceived. Mr. Adams received fewer electoral votes than he had in 1824; and not one of the votes given for Clay four years before was transferred to him.

The last days of the canvass were made noteworthy by a political incident highly characteristic of Mr. Adams, — an incident which, in these times of rapid dissemination of intelligence, would have destroyed instantly any chances which a candidate in Mr. Adams's situation might have had. Probably it actually had but the slightest effect on the vote, and of course none whatever upon the result. In October, 1828, the month preceding the election, Mr. William B. Giles, of Virginia, a man intensely hostile to Mr. Adams, caused to be published a statement regarding the circumstances of that gentleman's secession from the Federalist party in 1808, and a part of certain correspondence between Mr. Jefferson and himself (Giles) in 1825. A lack of candor on Mr. Giles's part and a failure of memory on Mr. Jefferson's placed the conduct of Mr. Adams in a highly unfavorable light. The President authorized a reply which was printed in the "National Intelligencer," in the course of which he made against certain leaders of the Federal party in Massachusetts the grave charge of a purpose to dissolve the Union. Thirteen gentlemen, eleven of whom were certainly entitled to represent themselves as

---

to remain as Secretary of the Treasury. Some time afterward he learned, greatly to his surprise, that just before the close of Mr. Monroe's term Crawford had had a wordy altercation with the President, and had applied to him a term which one gentleman never addresses to another. After that affair the President and his Secretary of the Treasury were not on speaking terms, and transacted the public business through an intermediary. Mr. Adams, recording these facts in his diary, expresses regret that he had proposed to take Mr. Crawford into the cabinet. His knowledge of the affair explains his objection to the idea of the candidacy of Mr. Crawford for the vice-presidency.

among the chief Federalists of the State in 1808, while the others were sons of two such leaders, demanded that he should substantiate his charge, or retract it. An acrimonious correspondence ensued. Mr. Adams never gave to the world his final word on the subject, which he wrote at enormous length just at the close of his administration. It was first published in his grandson's "New England Federalism." A candid view of the case seems to be that disunion was discussed by some of the members of what was long known as the "Essex Junto;" but that the discussion was in an extremely narrow circle, and that even among them the idea found but the most limited acceptance. At all events Mr. Adams named but two or three men who had ever heard of the scheme, although he hinted at a larger number. Of course the assault by Mr. Adams upon the Federalists generally, when those who had been members of that party had but lately and reluctantly come to his support, was calculated to make them anything but zealous in his cause. Nevertheless it could operate upon the minds of voters in that community only where the name of Jackson symbolized all that was evil in politics; and for that reason it cost Adams few popular votes, and no electoral votes.

The number of States that participated in the election of 1828 was unchanged, — twenty-four. Since the preceding election, however, there had been a general change on the part of those States which had previously chosen electors through the medium of the legislature, to the popular system. Of the six States wherein the legislature had exercised this privilege in 1824, four changed to a popular election before 1828, — Vermont, New York, Georgia, and Louisiana. The change in New York was not effected without a great agitation of the people. The legislature held to the powers it exercised as long as it dared. Governor De Witt Clinton recommended the change to the legislature at a special session called in 1820, on which occasion the Senate of New York refused to perform any legislative duty whatever, and treated the Governor with such open disrespect as has hardly ever been shown toward a state executive by any department of government. A bill was passed once, perhaps twice, by one branch of the legislature, some years later, to confer the right on the people, but the other branch rejected it. At last, the legislature, affecting a doubt whether the people really cared for the privilege, passed an act formally submitting the question to them. If there had been any real doubt the result of the popular vote speedily dispelled it, and the legislature reluctantly yielded to the urgent demand.

But there still existed differences in the systems of election, even among those where there was an appointment of electors by popular vote. In the following States the election of 1828 was by general ticket, — the system which is now universal : New Hampshire, Vermont, Massachusetts, Rhode Island, Connecticut, New Jersey, Pennsylvania, Virginia, North Carolina, Georgia, Alabama, Mississippi, Louisiana, Kentucky, Ohio, Indiana, Illinois, and Missouri, — eighteen. Some of these, like Massachusetts, New Jersey, and North Carolina, having tried for many years to secure the district system by amendment of the Constitution, had despaired of success, and adopted the general ticket. Of the six States not named above, two, Delaware and South Carolina, clung to the old method of legislative appointment. In Maine and New York, an elector

STATES.	Jackson.	Adams.	Mode of Election.
Maine	13,927	20,733	Districts.
New Hampshire. . . .	20,922	24,134	General ticket.
Vermont	8,350	25,363	General ticket.
Massachusetts	6,016	29,876	General ticket.
Rhode Island	821	2,754	General ticket.
Connecticut	4,448	13,838	General ticket.
New York	140,763	135,413	Districts.
New Jersey	21,951	23,764	General ticket.
Pennsylvania	101,652	50,848	General ticket.
Delaware	—	—	Legislature.
Maryland	24,565	25,527	Districts.
Virginia	26,752	12,101	General ticket.
North Carolina	37,857	13,918	General ticket.
South Carolina	—	—	Legislature.
Georgia	19,363	No opposition.	General ticket.
Alabama	17,138	1,938	General ticket.
Mississippi	6,772	1,581	General ticket.
Louisiana	4,603	4,076	General ticket.
Kentucky	39,397	31,460	General ticket.
Tennessee	44,293	2,240	Districts.
Missouri	8,272	3,400	General ticket.
Ohio	67,597	63,396	General ticket.
Indiana	22,257	17,052	General ticket.
Illinois	9,560	4,662	General ticket.
Total	647,276	508,064	

was chosen for each representative district, and the members so appointed chose the two additional electors. In Maryland and Tennessee, the States were specially divided into districts for the choice of all their electors. There was, however, a divided vote of the electors in three only of the States.

The table on page 148 shows the popular vote of the States, and the manner of choosing electors in each State.

The electoral count was quite devoid of incident. The result, which was ascertained and declared in the usual manner, was as follows : —

	PRESIDENT.		VICE-PRESIDENT.		
STATES.	Andrew Jackson, Tenn.	John Quincy Adams, Mass.	John C. Calhoun, S. C.	Richard Rush, Penn.	William Smith, S. C.
Maine	1	8	1	8	–
New Hampshire	–	8	–	8	–
Vermont	–	7	–	7	–
Massachusetts	–	15	–	15	–
Rhode Island	–	4	–	4	–
Connecticut	–	8	–	8	–
New York	20	16	20	16	–
New Jersey	–	8	–	8	–
Pennsylvania	28	–	28	–	–
Delaware	–	3	–	3	–
Maryland	5	6	5	6	–
Virginia	24	–	24	–	–
North Carolina	15	–	15	–	–
South Carolina	11	–	11	–	–
Georgia	9	–	2	–	7
Alabama	5	–	5	–	–
Mississippi	3	–	3	–	–
Louisiana	5	–	5	–	–
Kentucky	14	–	14	–	–
Tennessee	11	–	11	–	–
Ohio	16	–	16	–	–
Indiana	5	–	5	–	–
Illinois	3	–	3	–	–
Missouri	3	–	3	–	–
Total	178	83	171	83	7

"Hurrah for Jackson!" had been the rallying cry of the campaign, and the answer to every campaign argument against him,— some of them true, many of them false.   Those who had worked to bring him in felt sure that they were to be rewarded, and they flocked to Washington for the inauguration in such throngs as the capital had never before seen.   General Jackson's own progress from Tennessee to the seat of government was one prolonged triumph.   Shouting crowds of delighted partisans were at every steamboat landing.   On the day of the inauguration the streets were so blocked that the procession which accompanied the President-elect could hardly make its way to the Capitol.   The ceremonies took place on the eastern portico of the building, in the presence of a vast multitude of men from every part of the country, who could not repress their joy at the prospect that "the rights of the people" were at last restored to them.

XIII

THE "OLD HERO" RE-ELECTED

THERE will always be two opinions concerning the character of Andrew Jackson and of his administration, — as to the fitness of the man for the position of President, as to the worthiness of the motives which actuated his official conduct, as to his influence upon the political morals of his country. His administration was a period of turmoil, and, whether he was right or wrong, he caused it. Another man than he would have taken the view that the good name of the government was of greater concern to him as its chief than that of any man — or woman ; and would not have deemed it in accordance with a dignified and high-minded conduct of public affairs that the smallest — to say nothing of the greatest — governmental questions should be involved with the question whether or not a certain woman, however unjustly accused, should be received in the society of the capital. Another man than he would not have sought a quarrel with the officer with whom he had been associated on the national ticket, on account of an opinion by that officer ten years before, in the privacy of a cabinet council, upon one of his — Jackson's — acts. These two incidents, the attempt to force the unwilling wives of his cabinet officers to associate with Mrs. Eaton, and the breach with Mr. Calhoun which was apparently planned deliberately by the President and Mr. Van Buren, are striking examples of the change that came over the government when Mr. Adams went out and General Jackson came in. They were both characteristic of the new régime ; neither would have been possible under the old.

The change was broad as well as deep. It began with the reign of terror among the office-holders. Yet the upheaval of the civil service effected by Jackson was the most logical and consistent change that was introduced at this time. There had been no reason for the rejection of Mr. Adams and the election of General Jackson, save a personal preference for

Jackson. If that was a good reason for substituting one President for another, it was surely sufficient to justify " rotation " in the minor offices, rotating out those who did not, and rotating in those who did, approve and assist in making the greater substitution. No President before Jackson had so good reason as he to regard his elevation as a personal triumph, or to assume that the whole responsibility of government was intrusted to him. That fact may explain why he felt justified in displaying anger when the Senate exercised its constitutional right to reject his nominations; why he adopted a dictatorial tone toward Congress; why he discarded the old custom of consulting the members of his cabinet on momentous public questions, and sought the advice of a coterie of politicians, his devoted slaves, who were derisively styled the " kitchen cabinet."

He was conscious of no scruples in violating rules which he himself had laid down for the conduct of others. In the letter in which he resigned his seat in the Senate, in 1825, he put more stress upon the importance of rendering the executive independent of Congress than upon anything else. This lesson came to him from the appointment of Mr. Clay, a member of the House of Representatives, to a cabinet office, by Mr. Adams. He urged, and argued at length in favor of, an amendment to the Constitution, " rendering any member of Congress ineligible to office under the general government during the term for which he was elected, and for two years thereafter." Yet when he made up his own cabinet he took four of its six members from Congress. A morbid suspicion of others; a combativeness of disposition that led him to see causes of quarrel where none existed, and to take up the quarrels of others in the intervals of his own; and a total lack of that sense of proportion which might have informed him what was and what was not worth fighting about; — this combination of personal qualities in the President had the effect of making his administration as turbulent a period as has been known in our history, and one on which those who enjoy a quiet life can never dwell with pleasure.

It would be uncandid not to add that most of those who have not studied the history of the time, and many of those who have studied it, take a radically different view of the matter from that which is here presented. To them Jackson is a man who rescued the country from great constitutional errors — the doctrines of his immediate predecessor ; who attacked and destroyed the " Monster," — the Bank of the United States ; who instituted a great reform when he made a clean sweep of the office-holders, and filled their places with " true Republicans ; " whose policy was, to use the words of one of his stanchest admirers, Mr. Benton, " to simplify and purify the workings of the government, and to carry it back to the times of Mr. Jefferson — to promote its economy and efficiency, and to maintain the rights of the people and of the States in its administration." That he was the sturdiest and most faithful of friends to those whom he liked and who were true to him, is attested by his zeal in doing favors for them at the sacrifice of his own dignity. Moreover, his masterful, overbearing character did not prevent — it might perhaps have been the cause of — a personal popularity that outlasted his administration and his life, and is perpetuated in a Jackson cult to this day. To his conduct in one emergency, nullification in South Carolina, none will give more unqualified and unstinted praise than those who regard the period of his administration as one of national demoralization.

Undoubtedly he was the man for his time. He had not the support of those who regarded government as a serious business, to be conducted from high motives and with calmness and decorum. But those people were a minority. His adoption of the principle first formulated by Marcy, that " to the victors belong the spoils of the enemy," was applauded and approved. He degraded national politics to the level of a game wherein the shrewdest and the strongest, rather than the best and the wisest, were to come off the victors ; yet he merely extended the operation of a principle that had long been dominant in the affairs of the great States of New York and Pennsylvania, and gave to a great majority of the people of the country a government of a sort which they preferred to that which had preceded it. Thus he attracted more than he repelled ; he pleased more of the men of his generation than he offended ; and when the appeal was made to the voters of the country to pass judgment upon his doings, a compact, enthusiastic body of his supporters confronted a disorganized and discordant opposition.

General Jackson, in his first message to Congress, December 8, 1829, expressed the opinion that " it would seem advisable to limit the service of the chief magistrate to a single term of either four or six years." [1]   Three months afterward, in March, 1830, Major W. B. Lewis, one of the "kitchen cabinet," wrote to a member of the Pennsylvania legislature, urging the importance of the reëlection of General Jackson in 1832. He enclosed a draft of a letter, addressed to the President, begging him to stand for reëlection, to be signed by the members of the legislature. It was signed by sixty-eight members, and sent to the general. Although he thought the liberties of the people would be safer if a President did not seek reëlection, he evidently did not fear that those liberties would be endangered by his own reëlection; for he acceded tacitly to the above-mentioned spontaneous demand.

Few of the measures of the period between 1829 and 1832 had a direct bearing upon the question of the presidential succession; for that was already settled. But they did have a great part in bringing about a division of the people into parties, and in determining which of these parties should be successful. General Jackson made the question of internal improvements one of leading importance by his veto of the Maysville-road bill, in May, 1830. He thus attached to the party of which he was the chief, all those who, in this particular, favored a "strict construction" of the Constitution. He took the part of Georgia and Alabama in their effort to possess themselves of the lands owned by the Creek and Cherokee Indians, and thereby gave encouragement to the Georgia nullifiers, which he afterward more than neutralized by his courageous and patriotic action against South Carolina nullification. Jackson's attitude on the question of the disposition of the public lands made him popular in the western States; although a disagreement between the two Houses of Congress prevented definite action.

The tariff of 1828, styled by its opponents a "tariff of abominations," had been passed amid great excitement during the last year of Adams's administration, but was by no means an administration measure. It was most bitterly denounced at the South, and caused the first steps toward nullification in South Carolina. The defiance of the national authority by that State became most serious when the tariff act of 1832 was

---

[1] He repeated this recommendation, in conjunction with one for an amendment of the Constitution providing for an election of President by the people, in the five succeeding annual messages.

passed, leaving untouched the protective duties that had caused
the greatest offence.

Jackson's most popular act was his assault upon the Bank
of the United States. It is not to the purpose to urge either
that he was right or that he was wrong ; that he undertook
the "war" because he thought Mr. Biddle, the president,
wished to thwart him, or because he believed the Bank endangered the liberties of the people.   The act was popular,
as assaults upon capitalists, "bloated bondholders," "trusts,"
and "the money power" have always been, in this country.

The candidacy of General Jackson for reëlection being
predetermined, the only matter which remained for the
Democrats to consider was the choice of a candidate for Vice-
President.   The President was in favor of Martin Van Buren,
the Secretary of State. It is clear that he allowed Mr. Van
Buren to have a free hand, and to make all his arrangements
with a view to the succession.   His letter resigning his seat
in the cabinet, April, 1831, was a skilfully worded announcement that he was a candidate for the place when General
Jackson should retire.   The President nominated him as
minister to England, and he departed for his post during the
recess of the Senate ; the Senate rejected the nomination, and
Jackson was more than ever determined that he should be
"Vice-President now, and President afterward."   Parton says
that there was a "programme" laid down before Jackson had
been a year in office, — "a programme of succession so long
that it would have required twenty-four years to play it out.
It was divided into three parts of eight years each : Andrew
Jackson, eight years ; Martin Van Buren, eight years ; Thomas
H. Benton, eight years."   He does not give his authority for
this statement, which can be neither proved nor disproved.

The chronological order of events requires that we should
mention first the formal nomination of opposition candidates.
The alleged abduction, in 1826, of William Morgan, who was
supposed to have revealed the secrets of Freemasonry, caused
the origin of an Anti-Masonic party.   From western New
York, the place of its birth, it spread over a large part of the
North and played an important part in some state elections.
In September, 1830, a national convention of Anti-Masons
was held in Philadelphia.   Four New England States, New
York, Ohio, New Jersey, Pennsylvania, Delaware, and Mary-
land, — ten States in all, — together with the Territory of

Michigan, were represented by 96 delegates. It was voted to hold a second national convention in Baltimore on the 26th of September, 1831, to be composed of delegates equal in number to the representatives in both Houses of Congress from each State, and to be chosen by the people opposed to secret societies, for the purpose of making nominations for the offices of President and Vice-President.

The convention was held at the time and place designated. Delegates to the number of 113 were present, representing all the New England and Middle States, Ohio and Indiana. It had been intended to nominate Judge McLean, of Ohio. McLean was Postmaster-General under Mr. Adams, but had nevertheless been a supporter of Jackson all through the administration. When he displayed an unwillingness to administer the Post-office Department as a part of the "spoils" with which the Democratic workers were to be rewarded, the President appointed him a justice of the Supreme Court. He seems to have passed at once to the opposition. At all events, after the convention of Anti-Masons in 1830, he had consented provisionally to become the candidate of the party, if nominated. It appears that certain influential "National Republicans," as the opposition now termed itself, gave notice that they could not support Judge McLean, and he accordingly wrote a letter to the Baltimore convention withdrawing his name. It was the avowed purpose of the Anti-Masons to present the name of one upon whom all the opponents of Jackson could unite. Their course was somewhat disingenuous, since by far the largest section of the opposition desired to vote for Mr. Clay.

The convention invited Chief Justice Marshall, who was in the city, to sit with the convention, and he accepted the invitation. A ballot was taken for a candidate for President. William Wirt, of Maryland, received 108 of 111 votes cast. Having more than the three fourths which it had been previously voted should be necessary for a choice, he was declared nominated. A committee was sent to inform him of his nomination, for he was in Baltimore. His answer was a very long and most remarkable letter, that must have been prepared in advance. He admitted that he had been made a Mason; confessed that he never saw any harm in the order until this political party was founded on the principle of opposition to secret societies; declared that Masonry as they conceived it "was not and could not be Masonry as understood by Washington;" and concluded by telling the delegates that if they had nominated him under a misapprehension he would permit them to substitute another name for his own. After his address the delegates unanimously voted to stand by the nomination. They completed the ticket by nominating Amos Ellmaker, of Pennsylvania, for Vice-President. The convention adopted no platform, but issued a long and verbose address to the American people.

The next convention, that of the National Republicans, was held at Baltimore on December 12, 1831. Seventeen States were represented by 167 delegates. South Carolina, Georgia, Alabama, Mississippi, Missouri, and Illinois were unrepresented. How many delegates attended from each State, and how they were chosen, cannot be ascertained. That it was not a gathering of volunteers is evident from the facts that a committee on credentials was appointed and that the convention adjourned to give the committee time to do its work. General Abner Lacock, of Pennsylvania, was the temporary chairman of the convention, and Governor James Barbour, of Virginia, the permanent president. The members voted for a candidate for President by rising in their seats as their names were called and announcing their vote. The nomination of Henry Clay was unanimous. In the same manner John Sergeant, of Pennsylvania, was unanimously nominated for Vice-President. A committee was raised, consisting of one member from each State, to inform Mr. Clay of the nomination ; and the committee was constituted by the delegation from each State naming its own member. Thus, in the earliest days of the convention system, one of the most striking features of the nomination was introduced in precisely the present form. In 1831, however, the notification was by mail instead of by a pilgrimage to the residence of the candidate. The convention adopted no resolutions, but it issued an address severely criticising the administration for its corruption, partisanship, and abuse of power ; for the hostility it had manifested to internal improvement, for treachery on the tariff question, for the war on the Bank, and for the humiliating surrender to Georgia in the matter of the Cherokee Indians.

By recommendation of this convention a national assembly of young men met in Washington in May, 1832, which accepted the nominations made by the National Republicans and adopted the following series of resolutions, — the first platform ever adopted by a national convention : —

1. *Resolved*, That, in the opinion of this convention, although the fundamental principles adopted by our fathers, as a basis upon which to raise a superstructure of American independence, can never be annihilated, yet the time has come when nothing short of the united energies of all the friends of the American republic can be relied on to sustain and perpetuate that hallowed work.

2. *Resolved*, That an adequate protection to American industry is indispensable to the prosperity of the country ; and that an abandonment of the policy at this period would be attended with consequences ruinous to the best interests of the nation.

3. *Resolved*, That a uniform system of internal improvements, sustained and supported by the general government, is calculated to secure, in the highest degree, harmony, the strength, and the permanency of the republic.

4. *Resolved*, That the Supreme Court of the United States is the only tribunal recognized by the Constitution for deciding in the last resort all questions arising under the Constitution and laws of the United States, and that upon the preservation of the authority and jurisdiction of that court inviolate depends the existence of the nation.

5. *Resolved*, That the Senate of the United States is preëminently a conservative branch of the federal government ; that upon a fearless and independent exercise of its constitutional functions depends the existence of the nicely balanced powers of that government ; and that all attempts to overawe its deliberations by the public press or by the national executive deserve the indignant reprobation of every American citizen.

6. *Resolved*, That the political course of the present Executive has given us no pledge that he will defend and support these great principles of American policy and the Constitution ; but, on the contrary, has convinced us that he will abandon them whenever the purposes of party require it.

7. *Resolved*, That the indiscriminate removal of public officers, for the mere difference of political opinion, is a gross abuse of power ; and that the doctrine lately " boldly preached " in the Senate of the United States, that " to the victor belong the spoils of the enemy," is detrimental to the interests, corrupting to the morals, and dangerous to the liberties of this country.

8. *Resolved*, That we hold the disposition shown by the present national administration to accept the advice of the King of Holland, touching the northeastern boundary of the United States, and thus to transfer a portion of the territory and citizens of a State of this Union to a foreign power, to manifest a total destitu

tion of patriotic American feeling, inasmuch as we consider the life, liberty, property, and citizenship of every inhabitant of every State as entitled to the national protection.

9. *Resolved*, That the arrangement between the United States and Great Britain relative to the colonial trade, made in pursuance of the instructions of the late Secretary of State, was procured in a manner derogatory to the national character, and is injurious to this country in its practical results.

10. *Resolved*, That it is the duty of every citizen of this republic, who regards the honor, the prosperity, and the preservation of our Union, to oppose by every honorable measure the reëlection of Andrew Jackson, and to promote the election of Henry Clay, of Kentucky, and John Sergeant of Pennsylvania, as President and Vice-President of the United States.

The Democratic convention, which was held at Baltimore on May 21, 1832, was a striking example of the hold which Jackson had on his party, perhaps still more of the authority which the general's agents were allowed to exercise in his name. Mr. Van Buren was not the free choice of the Democrats for the office of Vice-President. Every contemporary authority, except Benton, assures us of that fact. Yet Jackson desired his nomination, and the machinery was set in motion to effect it. In May, 1831, Major Lewis, second auditor of the Treasury, wrote from Washington to Amos Kendall, fourth auditor of the Treasury, who was then in New Hampshire, urging the propriety of having a convention to nominate a candidate for Vice-President, in May of the following year ; hinting that it would be well if the New Hampshire legislature were to propose such a convention, and advising him to " make the suggestion to our friend [Isaac] Hill." This scheme of the " kitchen cabinet " — for it was at this time composed of the three men named in the last sentence — was carried out. The result was communicated to the public in " a letter of a gentleman " in New Hampshire, printed in the " Globe," the President's organ, in June, 1831. The " gentleman " was Mr. Kendall, and the extract printed was as follows : —

The Republican members of the New Hampshire Legislature, to the number of about 169, met last evening. An address and resolutions approving of the principles and measures of the present administration, the veto of the President on the Maysville Road bill, disavowing the doctrine of nullification, disapproving Clay's American system, but recommending a judicious reduction of the duties, disapproving of the United States Bank, passed the convention unanimously. The convention also recommended a general convention of Republicans friendly to the election of General Jackson, to consist of delegates equal to the number of electors of President in each State, to be holden at Baltimore on the third Monday of May, 1832, to nominate a candidate for Vice-President, and take such other measures in support of the reëlection of Andrew Jackson as may be deemed expedient.

The suggestion of a convention, thus put forth with approval in the newspaper which had been established for the express purpose of being the mouthpiece of the administration, was seconded by all the party organs; and the delegates were chosen. Most of them were ready to register the will of the President, and measures were taken to secure the acquiescence of such as were inclined to oppose it. Major Eaton, lately the Secretary of War, and the husband of the famous Mrs. Eaton, already referred to, was a delegate from Tennessee. He went to Baltimore determined to oppose Van Buren; but he found there a letter from Major Lewis, advising him to support that gentleman "unless he wished to quarrel with the general." He yielded, and voted for Van Buren. At the "Jackson state convention" of Pennsylvania, held in March, 1832, Mr. Van Buren had no supporters. The Democrats of the State were in favor of the Bank, and were angry at Van Buren because the New York legislature had adopted resolutions against the institution. There was a long contest in the convention between the friends of Mr. Dallas, Mr. Buchanan, and Mr. Wilkins, which resulted in favor of Mr. Wilkins. So strong was the determination not to accept Mr. Van Buren that the electors nominated were pledged to vote for Mr. Wilkins, and, if he should be induced to withdraw, or if, for any other reason he should not be a candidate, to vote for Mr. Dallas. Yet when the convention was held, every vote of Pennsylvania was in favor of Van Buren. The electors nevertheless obeyed their instructions and gave Mr. Wilkins their votes.

The convention met on the day named in the saloon of the Athenæum. Every State except Missouri was represented; and the number of delegates is reported to have been 326. But according to the rules the States represented were entitled to but 282 delegates. The number of votes cast for a candidate for Vice-President exceeded this number by one. General Robert Lucas, of Ohio, was the temporary and also the

permanent president.   On the second day of the convention
the Committee on Rules reported the following : —

Resolved, That each State be entitled, in the nomination to be
made of a candidate for the vice-presidency, to a number of votes
equal to the number to which they will be entitled in the electoral
colleges, under the new apportionment, in voting for President and
Vice-President ; and that two thirds of the whole number of the
votes in the convention shall be necessary to constitute a choice.

This was the origin of the famous two-thirds rule, by which
all subsequent Democratic conventions have governed themselves in making nominations. On the first ballot for a candidate for Vice-President, Martin Van Buren had 208 votes,
Philip P. Barbour, of Virginia, 49, and Richard M. Johnson,
of Kentucky, 26 votes. Virginia and South Carolina voted
solidly for Mr. Barbour, who had also fifteen votes of delegates from Maryland, North Carolina, and Alabama. Colonel
Johnson had the full vote of Kentucky and Indiana, and two
votes from Illinois. Mr. Van Buren, having received more
than two thirds of all the votes, was declared the nominee.
General Jackson was recommended in the following resolution : —

Resolved, That the convention repose the highest confidence in
the purity, patriotism, and talents of Andrew Jackson, and that we
most cordially concur in the repeated nominations which he has
received in various parts of the Union as a candidate for reëlection
to the office which he now fills with so much honor to himself and
usefulness to his country.

No other resolution was adopted. A committee was appointed to prepare an address to the people in support of the
action of the convention ; but on the last day of the session
a report was made that the time had been too short to fulfil
that duty ; and this was accepted as satisfactory. Possibly the
difficulty of saying anything upon the Bank question without
sacrificing the electoral vote of Pennsylvania, and the absurdity
of issuing an address in which no mention should be made of
the Bank, had more to do than had the lack of time with the
failure of the committee to put the principles of the party in a
fitting form of words.

The convention accomplished the object for which it was
held, although it did not wholly overcome the repugnance of
Democrats in all the States to Mr. Van Buren, or suppress the
movement in favor of rival candidates. A Jackson-Barbour

convention was held in Charlottesville, Virginia, in June, by which Mr. P. P. Barbour was formally nominated as the candidate for the vice-presidency in conjunction with General Jackson for President. Later in the same month a similar convention was held in North Carolina, in which delegates from eighteen counties participated. The candidacy of Mr. Wilkins was purely local in Pennsylvania, and that of Mr. Barbour came to nothing.

The tone of political discussion during the canvass which preceded and followed these nominations was unexampled for its violence and rancor. The veto by the President of the bill rechartering the Bank of the United States, which had been passed by both Houses of Congress in spite of executive opposition, although there was a Democratic majority in each House, intensified the bitterness of the conflict. It also showed the strength of General Jackson's hold upon the people, that he could still retain, not only the support of the people, who were probably with him in his war on the Bank, but that of the politicians as well, — including that of men who had even voted to pass the Bank bill over the veto. Mr. Dallas was one of this class. He had introduced the bill for a new charter in the Senate, had supported it at every stage, and voted for it after the veto; and yet, within a month after the failure of the bill, he was found addressing a meeting in Philadelphia which adopted a series of resolutions referring to the Bank veto and expressing thanks to the President for his fearless discharge of duty. Nothing was too severe for the opponents of Jackson to say of him; and the violence of their denunciations was equalled by the angry vituperation which the Democrats poured out upon the National Republicans and all other advocates of the Bank.

The early elections were not clearly indicative of the result in November. In the Kentucky election, which took place in August, a "Jackson" governor and a "Clay" lieutenant-governor were chosen, each by a small majority. Maine was carried for the Jackson ticket in September, but by a greatly reduced majority. The October elections also gave the opposition hope, which the result in the ensuing month was not to justify; for Ohio, though giving a plurality to the Jackson ticket, seemed capable of being captured by the opposition if it could be united; and Pennsylvania gave to Governor Wolf, the Democratic candidate, but a few thousand majority, — less, in fact, than a third of that two years before. New Jersey and Maryland gave anti-Jackson majorities. The chance of success in defeating the President led to fresh combinations and coalitions where there was not already union among the several elements of the opposition. The National Republicans adopted the Anti-Masonic electoral ticket in New York, and there was a combination of the same kind in Ohio and elsewhere. But the Democrats professed a serene confidence in the result, and they were not mistaken. The doubtful States, with the exception of Kentucky, gave majorities, — some of them small but all-sufficient, — to the Jackson and Van Buren ticket. The Jackson party had, however, wisely determined not to put up a ticket in opposition to the Wilkins electors in Pennsylvania, and in South Carolina the contest for the legislature had been wholly between the Union men and the Nullifiers; the Nullifiers carried the legislature which

STATES.	Jackson.	Clay.*
Maine	33,291	27,204
New Hampshire	25,486	19,010
Vermont	7,870	11,152
Massachusetts.	14,545	33,003
Rhode Island	2,126	2,810
Connecticut	11,269	17,755
New York	168,497	154,896
New Jersey	23,856	23,393
Pennsylvania	90,983	56,716
Delaware	4,110	4,276
Maryland	19,156	19,160
Virginia.	33,609	11,451
North Carolina	24,862	4,563
South Carolina †	—	—
Georgia	20,750	—
Alabama ‡	—	—
Mississippi	5,919	No opposition.
Louisiana	4,049	2,528
Kentucky	36,247	43,396
Tennessee	28,740	1,436
Missouri	5,192	—
Ohio	81,246	76,539
Indiana	31,552	15,472
Illinois	14,147	5,429
Total	687,502	530,189

* The vote for Wirt is included in Clay's vote.   † By legislature.
‡ No opposition to Jackson.

was to appoint the electors. On the whole it was a great victory for the Democrats.

As before, twenty-four States took part in this election, but
the number of electors was enlarged by the new apportionment which had been made after the result of the census of
1830 was ascertained. Delaware joined the States which
permitted the people to choose the electors. South Carolina
alone followed the old system of appointment by the legislature; and she retained it until and including the election
of 1860. Maine, New York, and Tennessee also abandoned
at this time the district system of election. Maryland only

STATES.	PRESIDENT.				VICE-PRESIDENT.				
	Andrew Jackson, Tenn.	Henry Clay, Ky.	John Floyd, Va.	William Wirt, Md.	Martin Van Buren, N. Y.	John Sergeant, Penn.	William Wilkins, Penn.	Henry Lee, Mass.	Amos Ellmaker, Penn.
Maine	10	–	–	–	10	–	–	–	–
New Hampshire . . .	7	–	–	–	7	–	–	–	–
Vermont	–	–	–	7	–	–	–	–	7
Massachusetts	–	14	–	–	–	14	–	–	–
Rhode Island	–	4	–	–	–	4	–	–	–
Connecticut	–	8	–	–	–	8	–	–	–
New York	42	–	–	–	42	–	–	–	–
New Jersey	8	–	–	–	8	–	–	–	–
Pennsylvania	30	–	–	–	–	–	30	–	–
Delaware.	–	3	–	–	–	3	–	–	–
Maryland.	3	5	–	–	3	5	–	–	–
Virginia	23	–	–	–	23	–	–	–	–
North Carolina. . . .	15	–	–	–	15	–	–	–	–
South Carolina	–	–	11	–	–	–	–	11	–
Georgia	11	–	–	–	11	–	–	–	–
Alabama.	7	–	–	–	7	–	–	–	–
Mississippi	4	–	–	–	4	–	–	–	–
Louisiana.	5	–	–	–	5	–	–	–	–
Kentucky	–	15	–	–	–	15	–	–	–
Tennessee	15	–	–	–	15	–	–	–	–
Ohio	21	–	–	–	21	–	–	–	–
Indiana	9	–	–	–	9	–	–	–	–
Illinois	5	–	–	–	5	–	–	–	–
Missouri	4	–	–	–	4	–	–	–	–
Total	219	49	11	7	189	49	30	11	7

adhered to it. With the exception of South Carolina and Maryland, therefore, the method of choosing electors had now become uniform throughout the country, without the interposition of an amendment to the Constitution.

The count of electoral votes was conducted in strict accordance with precedent, without dispute or incident. The result of the popular and the electoral votes is exhibited on preceding pages.

XIV

THE CONVENTION SYSTEM

SINCE 1836 the system of nominating candidates for President and Vice-President by general party conventions has been universal. During the intervening sixty years no candidate, in whose favor an electoral ticket has been presented to the voters of any State, has been otherwise placed in nomination. It therefore becomes timely, at this point, to consider how the national convention came to supersede the earlier modes of nomination, and how it developed into the important adjunct of the government which it has become. Even so late as the time when the revolt against the congressional caucus began, a national convention, supposing it to have been possible to constitute such a body for such a purpose, would have been quite unsuitable. But just as the growth of our modern civilization has rendered necessary the invention and the immediate utilization of the improved instruments of rapid transportation, and of instantaneous communication between people at a distance from each other, so the evolution of political parties as compact and disciplined organizations enforced the adoption of the convention system. Neither could those parties exist in their present efficiency without a central authority; nor can we conceive of a body better adapted to the purpose than is the national convention. It is capable of improvement in details, but the general structure is a case of perfect adaptation to the end sought. Moreover, the proposition may be maintained that this extra-constitutional and extra-legal institution supplements the electoral system in such a way as to realize and make effectual the plans and purposes of the framers of the Constitution.

Let us note anew the successive steps in the process by which the necessity for this system arose. When the Constitution was adopted, the divergent interests of the people of the thirteen States were almost as many and as important as their common interests. The first division into parties was really upon the question whether the common welfare or the individual welfare of the States should be deemed paramount, — that is, whether the Constitution, establishing a more perfect Union, should be adopted. When that had been decided, the public men of the country fell apart over the discussion whether the Constitution should bind the States together closely or loosely. The conditions under which parties existed were widely different from those which prevail now; and these conditions affected every election in which national issues were involved. Party lines did not cut across families and neighborhoods to such an extent as they do now. Nor would it be true to say that they followed state lines. Yet party association was to a degree a matter more of state or of community public opinion than of individual opinion. A few leaders determined the political course to be pursued, the ground to be taken on public questions, and the candidates for office to be supported. The majority accepted the programme set forth by the leaders; and since the minority, recognizing the fact that it was outnumbered, rarely made a stubborn contest, and consequently did not force the dominant party to exhibit its full strength, the number of votes polled was usually small. One example will suffice to illustrate this fact. So late as 1824, when the most fiercely contested election of President known up to that time took place, eighteen States appointed electors by popular vote. In eight of those States the candidate locally successful had more than three times as many votes as the other three candidates combined. The population of the eighteen States was about 7,800,000, and their total vote was in round numbers 355,000, — less than one twentieth of the population. New York and New Jersey, having in 1896 about as many inhabitants as the eighteen States in 1824, gave a total of 1,783,000 votes. New Jersey alone, in 1896, cast more votes than were polled in the whole country in the great contest of 1824.

The framers of the Constitution expected that the electors of President and Vice-President would exercise an individual judgment in making a choice. But when the government was first formed, the only people who possessed a sufficient acquaintance with the public men of the land, save those of their own State or part of the country, were the officers at the seat of government and the members of Congress. Both of these classes were excluded from service as electors. Consequently, if the electors were left to themselves, it was inevitable that they would, in their lack of acquaintance with others, vote for candidates from their own or near-by States, and so fail to make a choice ; and the election would always be thrown into the House of Representatives. The selection of Washington was obvious and easy. When he retired it seemed so natural that the electors should choose Mr. Adams for the succession that members of his own party, exerting themselves against him, failed to effect his defeat. Thus the administration party was united in spite of itself. The opposition took the course of a nomination by caucus of its party members in both Houses of Congress, who were not merely the best but the only competent directors of the policy to be pursued, the only force that could prevent the strength of the party from being scattered and wasted, and the only means of enlightening the provincialism of the electors. Consequently the congressional caucus was in these times something more than a pardonable device for concentrating public opinion ; it was an instrument without which the party success of a great majority of the people would have been impossible.

Nevertheless the congressional caucus outlived its usefulness. It ceased to be a necessity when national concerns at last outweighed local interests, and when the people became acquainted with the character and ability of public men in all parts of the country. Always — in spite of its usefulness — contrary to the spirit of the Constitution, which enjoined a strict separation and the full independence of the three departments of government, it became a menace to popular liberty when it was used as a means of muffling the people, — depriving them of a voice in the selection of those who should fill the first places in the state, and usurping that power in behalf of men chosen for a different purpose altogether, and wholly irresponsible with reference to the choice of a President. The revolt came immediately upon a disregard of the will of the people, and upon the selection of second-rate men as candidates, to be accepted at the peril of a party defeat.

Nomination by state legislatures was the temporary makeshift of those who rebelled against the caucus. Save that it was not obnoxious to the spirit of the Constitution, it was inferior to the caucus in every respect. Those who made the nominations had, like the members of Congress, no commission to undertake the duty ; and they had not the qualification for the duty conferred upon congressmen by their opportunity to take a general survey of the field, and to compare the merits of candidates. Nomination by state legislature was either a movement to bring forward a conspicuous citizen of the State presenting his name, or, originating in that State, was a cunningly devised scheme to create an appearance of the candidate's popularity and importance by procuring his nomination by the legislature of another State.

John Quincy Adams and Jackson were the only Presidents whose nomination came exclusively from state legislatures. Adams was one of four candidates, three of whom were named for the office by the legislatures of their respective States; and he owed his election to the House of Representatives. Jackson's nomination in 1825 by the legislature of Tennessee merely gave his canvass an early start. He would have been elected in any event. Of the Vice-Presidents chosen at the same time as these two Presidents, Calhoun, having been nominated for the first place by the South Carolina legislature, was indebted for his first election to a concentration upon him, arranged by correspondence between the political leaders of the anti-caucus forces, after he had withdrawn as a candidate for the presidency. His second election came from an alliance with Jackson, without any nomination. Van Buren came in under the convention system. By no other means could he have been made the candidate of his party. The caucus was discredited and extinct. Nominations by friendly legislatures could be had easily; but there were unfriendly legislatures to be encountered, including that of the President's own State of Tennessee, which, despite Jackson's great political influence and strong preference for Van Buren, was never favorable to him. The first Democratic national convention was called to impose the President's will upon the whole party. From that time until, but not including, the year 1896, every national convention of the party in power for the time being has been more or less under the influence, in some cases under the control, of the administration; but the tendency has been and is toward freedom from dictation by President or Congress.

The idea of the nominating convention, commonplace as it is to us, was neither a part of our political inheritance from England, nor yet an early fruit of the new institutions that came with the Constitution. In Great Britain, until within a few years, candidates for Parliament offered themselves for election, or were presented to the constituency by the owner of the " pocket borough " or by the general leader of his party. The system of self-nomination, borrowed from Great Britain, was the usual mode of making candidates in many of the Southern States down to the time of the Civil War, and is even yet not altogether extinct. In the North a caucus presented candidates, but it was quite a different thing from the caucus as we understand the term. The principle was not recognized that all voters should be permitted to participate in the selection of candidates as well as in a choice between the candidates offered for their suffrages. The caucus was therefore a select gathering, to which those only were admitted who were invited. Its chief function was the selection of candidates for the legislature. In many of the States the governor and all other state officers were chosen by the legislature. Where they were elected by popular vote, the nominations were made either by a legislative caucus or — rarely — by a convention, which was not composed of elected delegates, but was virtually an enlarged and general state caucus, consisting, like the small local caucus, of persons bidden by the leaders and managers.

It is not easy, from the meagre materials at hand, to reconstruct the political machinery in use during the first thirty years under the Constitution. Nor must it be supposed that, where many communities were developing political institutions without much help from one another, because not in close intercourse, any general statement regarding their practice is true of all. We may trace back nearly to their origin institutions that have since been universally adopted. It may be stated — with some caution — that the earliest prototype of the delegate state convention, from which no doubt the national convention was derived, forms a part of the political history of Pennsylvania. Like many inventions in the arts, it was originally the result of accidental necessity and crude in form, but was afterward developed into a useful and efficient instrument. The Republican party of Pennsylvania was divided into two factions, one of which, by the help of the Federalists, who were few in numbers, kept Governor McKean in office from 1799 until 1808. His term was about to expire, and the war between the two factions was to be renewed. The partisans of Governor McKean determined to resort to the usual device of a caucus of members of the legislature, where they were strong, both in actual numbers and in the fact that most of the counties of the State were represented by one or more members of their faction. Their opponents also called a caucus; and, in order to make up the deficiency in their representation, invited their supporters in every county which would not be represented by a member of the legislature, to send delegates to the "convention." Although it is not essentially a part of the history of the development of the convention, it may be mentioned as an interesting series of facts that, in that year, 1808, the "constitutionalists" and "conventionalists" had a lively scramble for priority in adopting Mr. Madison as a candidate; that they composed their differences, put up a joint electoral ticket, united on Simon Snyder, the convention's candidate for governor, left the Federalists out of the government altogether, and ruled the State for more than thirty years thereafter.

The idea of the state convention was adopted, extended, and improved in New York and other States, and had already become an ordinary means of concentrating and organizing party action, when the necessity of adapting it to national politics arose, to be soon followed by the opportunity to introduce it. So far as can be ascertained, the first suggestion to this effect came also from Pennsylvania, in a resolution, already cited (p. 130), adopted by the Democrats of Lancaster County in 1824. The difficulties therein mentioned were already disappearing in 1832 with the construction of railway lines, and, before 1840, were unworthy a moment's consideration in comparison with the great advantages of the new system.

The national convention of to-day is in its essentials what it was at the beginning, seventy years ago; but it has been modified and reformed as the increasing refinement of party machinery rendered changes necessary. This remark is more accurate as applied to conventions of the older parties than to those of the newer. The aim is always to constitute conventions consisting wholly of duly elected delegates from every State in the Union, and in numbers proportioned to the representation of the States in Congress. The national and universal character of the assembly has from the first been the prime requisite; and, in order to render it national, it has been the custom of parties in the process of formation to relax the rigor of rules which would exclude delegates irregularly chosen, and volunteer members, from States that would otherwise be unrepresented. Indeed, most of the parties which have been formed during the last half-century — most of them to continue in existence but a few years — have been forced at first to resort to many devices to create an impression that they were national in character. In the extreme youth of more than one party, the national convention has consisted mostly or wholly of volunteers, who came together rather as representatives of their own opinions than as regularly chosen delegates. In such cases it has been usual to allow all the persons from any State, few or many, to cast a number of votes proportioned to the electoral vote of the State. The first Democratic convention, that of 1832, consisted of one delegate for each electoral vote. But the practice came gradually into vogue of enlarging the number of actual delegates, although their voting power could not so be increased. It was a device for exerting "pressure" upon a convention in favor of a particular candidate or a "plank" for the platform. In 1848, Virginia sent seventy delegates to the Democratic convention, to cast seventeen votes. Inasmuch as the system resulted in giving undue influence to the States which thus enlarged their delegations, since it made conventions unwieldy, and led to competition between the States by this means to increase their power, a reform was introduced. The present practice of all the national parties except the Populists is to constitute conventions of double the number of electors, and not to allow a larger membership than the number of votes to be cast.[1]

It is not easy, perhaps it is not possible, to ascertain how the delegates to early conventions were chosen. There was no uniform practice, and conventions were not over-particular in scrutinizing credentials. If there was a case of contesting delegations, which occasionally happened, the decision was not made according to an established rule, — for in the variety of methods of choice no rule could have been made, — but in favor of that faction whose votes were most needed by the majority of the convention. Or, if it were desirable to placate both factions, the two delegations were admitted to the convention, each member to have half a vote. In the early days, delegates were frequently chosen by the party members of the state legislatures. So late as 1864, some of the delegates to the Republican national convention were thus appointed. Delegate state conventions were called, from the beginning, in

[1] Save in cases where both rival delegations are admitted, with the privilege to each member of giving a fraction of a vote.

some parts of the country, to select delegates to national conventions.   In such cases the whole delegation for the State would be chosen by the state convention, either acting as a whole, or dividing itself into groups representing the several congressional districts.

These and other irregularities, which it is needless to specify, have disappeared.   Delegates are now almost universally chosen by conventions consisting of members elected in primary meetings to which the whole body of the party is admitted. Four delegates at large are appointed by a state convention, and two by a convention within each congressional district.   The Republican party not only prescribes this system, but requires that the conventions shall be held between two specified dates. The Democratic party has not adopted all these rules formally. Yet public opinion within the organization requires a general conformity to them.   In one noteworthy recent case, the Democratic convention for New York, prior to the national convention of 1892, was held long before the natural and usual time, in order to exercise a powerful influence upon the result.   It caused great indignation, and failed of its purpose after all.

In another important respect the practice of the two parties is different.   The principle of the "general ticket" in choosing electors was long ago introduced into national conventions, where it is known as the "unit rule."   The state convention instructs all the delegates for the State to vote "as a unit" on all questions that may arise.   Such an instruction was necessary to prevent confusion and collision when large delegations, which might not be numerically a multiple of the votes allowed to the State, were sent to national conventions. It may be suggested, although it is not asserted, that this was the origin of the rule.   Be that as it may, the unit rule is held to bind the district electors as well as those who represent the State "at large."   Its effect is, obviously, not only to nullify the will of any district which dissents from the general policy of the party in the State, but to employ its votes in carrying measures which it wishes to oppose.   The unit rule is still recognized in Democratic conventions as of binding force; and the presiding officers decline to permit the instructions of state conventions to be disregarded.   By no means all the States bind their delegates by an injunction to cast all their votes as a majority may decide; but more than once in the history of the party important results have been achieved or prevented in national conventions by the enforcement of this rule. The Republican party, which had already, on more than one occasion, permitted individual delegates to cast their votes in disregard of " unit " instructions, at last, in 1880, repudiated the rule altogether.

In the order of procedure all conventions are nearly alike. There is a temporary organization, under which committees are appointed — all committees consist of one member from each State, named by the delegation thereof — (a) to examine and report upon the credentials of members; (b) to nominate permanent officers; and (c) to prepare and present the platform. The business is transacted in the above order: first, contested elections are decided; next the permanent president of the convention is presented and installed; and then the platform of principles is reported, discussed, and adopted. Afterward the nomination of candidates is in order. The congressional caucus and the earliest conventions announced their principles in an address to the people of the country, which was not reported until after the nominations had been made. In modern times the issues of the pending campaign invariably are set forth before the candidates are named. It has become a custom to present the several candidates to the convention in nominating speeches, which are studiously contrived to have a dramatic effect upon the audience, and to evoke enthusiasm. In cases where there is a contest for the nomination, the partisans of each candidate endeavor to outdo their rivals in the loudness, the fervor, and the duration of their applause. When the time comes to vote, the roll of the States is called in alphabetical order, and the vote of each state delegation is announced by one of its members. The Republican party alone forbids the changing of votes once given. The prohibition is designed to allow some time for reflection when a sudden impulse seizes the members to " stampede " in favor of a certain candidate. It has always been believed that the nomination of Mr. Polk, in 1844, was carefully planned before the Democratic convention met. Few persons were in the secret, if the common belief as to the origin of the movement is to be accepted. The defeat of Van Buren was the one thing to be accomplished; how it was effected is told in the history of the election of 1844. There was a similar occurrence in 1852; and Seymour was nominated in

1868 by a stampede which was probably not planned long before it was set in motion. The purpose of bringing Pierce forward in 1852 was formed before the delegates came together, but he was held in reserve, and his name was not presented until the thirty-fifth vote. On the vote preceding that which gave him the nomination, he had the support of less than one fifth of the convention.

It will be observed, from the summary just made, that the Republican party has adopted several reforms in the constitution, the election, and the proceedings of national conventions, which have not commended themselves to the Democrats. Moreover, the Democrats cling still to one rule which has never been a part of the code of any other party ; that, namely, which requires that a nomination shall be made by two thirds of the convention. The origin and the history of this rule may be found in the proper places in this book. It is appropriate to say here, that it is a singular inconsistency, in a party which permits the majority of a state delegation to take full possession of all the votes allotted to that State, to refuse to a majority of the whole convention the right to name a candidate, and thus to enable a determined minority to enforce its own will or — as happened in 1860 — break up the convention.

It is easy to see in what features there is still room for useful reform in the convention system. The time favorable for making the necessary changes is not when a nomination is pending ; for then there will assuredly be a faction that stands to gain and another that stands to lose by the reform. It would be well for a carefully prepared scheme to be presented to a national convention, to be submitted to the conventions of the several States for adoption or rejection, somewhat as amendments to the Constitution are submitted. For example, the Democratic convention of the year 1900 might ask the state conventions of its party next to be held to vote whether the two-thirds rule should be retained or dropped, and direct that in case a majority, three fifths, two thirds, or any other specified fraction of the state conventions adopted the change, it should go into effect in the convention of 1904.

As for general reforms, it is clear that the undue influence of the local opinion of the city and State in which the convention is held should be neutralized ; that the "pressure" exerted by the too numerous outsiders, who constitute sometimes a body of participators in the proceedings, rather than an between self-constituted leaders who were not electors; next between the representatives of parties in Congress; after that, until the convention was devised, there was no agreement, and the electoral system bade fair to go to wreck. But the convention, taking its commission directly from the people, and giving an expression through one party or another to the will of all the people, furnishes a guide to the judgment of the electors which they do not and should not disregard. It is based really although unintentionally upon the theory of an indirect choice of the President by electors free to choose, which was the theory of the fathers of the Constitution. So long as the preliminary electors perform their duty well, it is not to be deplored that the official and final electors have merely the duty of giving formal effect to a choice already made for them. "The King reigns but does not govern" in a constitutional monarchy. It is not to be regretted that a committee of the two Houses of the British Parliament carry on the government subject to the will of the people, and that the nominal sovereign is merely an agent who gives formal assent to their plans, and may not overrule them. As in that case of the British government, so in this of our electoral system, safety lies in purifying and keeping pure the source of actual power, — not in overturning the electoral system because the intentions of the Fathers are not carried out in all their exactness. Parties have acquired great power in our government. That power would not be diminished by an abolition of the indirect election. And yet the goodness or badness of the choice of a President, and of the government as a whole, is to depend upon the question whether parties are honorable or corrupt. They are self-governing fractions of the State. They make the President, and will continue to make him under any system. Consequently it should be the concern of all good citizens to make the national convention, through which parties act directly upon the government, a free and independent body, expressive of the best thought, the highest motives, and the truest patriotism of the party.

XV

VAN BUREN

GENERAL JACKSON'S first term ended in the midst of a brief period during which he enjoyed almost universal popularity. His vigorous, patriotic, and effective proclamation against South Carolina nullification won for him unstinted praise from men who were wont to find in his acts nothing but evil. Parton quotes William Wirt (see p. 156) as saying at this time : " My opinion is, he may be President for life if he chooses." Yet in a few months he took another step which caused a recurrence of the opposition in more than its former violence. In a paper read to the cabinet in September, 1833, he said : " Whatever may be the opinions of others, the President considers his reëlection as a decision of the people against the Bank." No doubt he had a right so to consider it. But he had no right to fight ever the " monster," which the people had condemned, with the unfair and illegal weapons which he employed. He had resolved to remove the deposits of the United States from the Bank, in the face of the law which made the Bank the custodian of the public funds, and of a resolution of Congress, passed after an investigation, that the Bank was solvent and the funds safe. He was forced to remove Mr. McLane, the Secretary of the Treasury, to the State Department, because he was opposed to the removal of the deposits. Mr. Duane, whom he chose for the Treasury Department with the express purpose of ordering the removal, flatly refused to be the President's agent in the transaction, and was curtly dismissed from office. Roger B. Taney, afterward Chief Justice, was transferred from the Attorney-General's office to the Treasury, and gave the order. This step caused the greatest excitement, and stirred the opponents of the President to a pitch of anger almost unexampled in our history. The Senate refused to confirm Mr. Taney as Secretary of the Treasury, and it passed a resolution that the President, by his removal of the deposits, " has assumed upon himself authority and power not conferred by the Constitution and laws, but in derogation of both." This was the resolution which Thomas H. Benton soon afterward moved to "expunge" from the journal of the Senate, and which, three years later, was publicly expunged.

Another act, which marked the close of Jackson's first administration, should be mentioned here. Congress passed an act directing the distribution of the revenue derived from the sale of public lands among the several States. The policy of this act had been discussed long and earnestly. The opposition of the President was well known; yet the House of Representatives passed the bill by a vote of 96 to 40; and the vote of the Senate in its favor was 23 to 5. The bill was laid before the President so near the expiration of the twenty-second Congress that less time remained than the ten days which the Constitution allows the President to retain a bill. General Jackson neither signed nor returned the bill, and thus thwarted the will of more than two thirds of both Houses of Congress. This was the first case of a "pocket veto."

Almost all the measures adopted or even discussed during Jackson's second term arose directly or indirectly from the war on the Bank. The state bank question; the "Specie Circular," or order requiring all the land offices to receive gold and silver only in payment for public land; the widespread commercial distress following an era of wild speculation; the distribution of the surplus revenue, — these were the subjects that engaged the attention of Congress. The personal influence of the President was constantly felt in Congress, where he was supported by a strong and trustworthy body of adherents composing a majority of the House of Representatives, but, owing to the hostility of State-Rights senators, constituting a minority only of the upper branch. Among the people, too, he was regarded as a demigod. Not only were his acts approved, but his sturdy obstinacy and fearless pugnacity gave him favor with the masses of the people such as no other President before him or since his time has enjoyed.

But the opposition was earnest and active. The largest section of it was organized in 1834 as the Whig party. The name is not found in the public prints of the time before April of that year, when it is mentioned in Niles's Register, with a remark to the effect that the opposition party was so styled in Connecticut and New York. Horace Greeley's Whig Almanac

for 1838 describes the party as then constituted, consisting of
" (1) Most of those who, under the name of National Republicans, had previously been known as supporters of Adams and
Clay, and advocates of the American system ; (2) Most of
those who, acting in defence of what they deemed the assailed
or threatened rights of the States, had been stigmatized as
Nullifiers, or the less virulent State-Rights men, who were
thrown into a position of armed neutrality towards the administration by the doctrines of the proclamation of 1832 against
South Carolina ; (3) A majority of those before known as
Anti-Masons ; (4) Many who had up to that time been known
as Jackson men, but who united in condemning the high-
handed conduct of the Executive, the immolation of Duane,
and the subserviency of Taney ; (5) Numbers who had not
before taken any part in politics, but who were now awakened
from their apathy by the palpable usurpations of the Executive,
and the imminent peril of our whole fabric of constitutional
liberty and national prosperity."

The party, at the beginning of the presidential canvass,
was purely and simply an opposition party. Some of the
elements of its composition, enumerated above, were never
fully fused with the rest, and, under the stress of Tyler's administration, drifted back into the Democratic party. It was
not to be expected that the agreement of all the factions, in
hearty disapproval of General Jackson's policy, would hold
them together sufficiently to enable them to support one candidate heartily. Indeed, the sole motive to opposition, so far
as a large body of the so-called party was concerned, was an
objection to the President's quite unconcealed manœuvring to
designate his own successor. Leaving the plans of the opposition for a time, let us observe the course of events in the
Democratic party.

It was no secret that the President desired that Mr. Van
Buren should be his successor. It was rumored at one time,
and quite generally believed, that he contemplated resigning
and leaving the presidential office to the Vice-President, but
that he abandoned this project in order the better to secure
the succession to Van Buren. However this may have been,
it is certain that an opposition to Van Buren, not unlike that
which had existed in 1831 and 1832, threatened to make itself
felt and to thwart the President's plans. It manifested itself
in the President's own State of Tennessee, where, in October,

1835, the legislature formally presented Judge Hugh L. White, then a senator from Tennessee, as a candidate to succeed Jackson. On the day when this action was expected to be taken, there was placed on the desk of every member of the Tennessee legislature a package containing three copies of the Washington " Globe," in which was a series of gross attacks upon Judge White. The peculiarity of this circumstance lay in the fact that these precious documents bore the frank of the President, and some of them were addressed in his own hand. The supporters of Judge White maintained with much plausibility that he had stood by the administration, that he was as good a Democrat as the President himself ; that there was no established mode of nominating candidates ; and that General Jackson himself owed his nomination to the Tennessee legislature. Eight years had wrought a vast change in the general's attitude as to the respective rights of President and people ; and he could see in his old colleague and supporter only a " traitor." With characteristic determination he set about carrying into execution his purpose to seat Mr. Van Buren in the presidential chair. Prompt action was necessary. All but two of the Tennessee delegation favored Judge White, and the legislature of Alabama had followed Tennessee in giving him a nomination.

In February, 1835, the President wrote to a friend suggesting the holding of a national convention, to be composed of delegates "fresh from the people," — a phrase upon which the opposition played much during the ensuing canvass, — for the purpose of nominating candidates for President and Vice-President. The convention was called, and met in Baltimore on the 20th of May, 1835. Mr. Andrew Stevenson, of Virginia, late the Speaker of the House of Representatives, was called to the chair, and presided throughout all the sessions of the convention. Twenty-two States and two Territories — Michigan and Arkansas — were represented. No delegates were present from Illinois, South Carolina, or Alabama. The representation of the States would amuse those who are accustomed to the exact methods of the present day. A list of those who took part contains 626 names. Of these, 422 came from the States of Maryland, Virginia, New Jersey, and Pennsylvania. Maryland is mentioned first because it contributed 181 members. The state convention, called to select delegates, was apparently unwilling to deny any of its own members an opportunity to take part, and accordingly resolved that all of them should be delegates. Virginia sent 108, New Jersey 73, and Pennsylvania 60, being two contesting delegations of 30 each. On the other hand, Tennessee sent no delegates; but a citizen of the State who would vote for Van Buren, chancing to be in Baltimore, presented himself, was admitted, and cast the fifteen votes allotted to Tennessee. His name was Rucker; and he achieved fame through the verb "to ruckerize," which was coined at the time, a piece of political slang long since forgotten. Both sets of delegations from Pennsylvania were admitted. The vote of the State was allowed when they were on the same side, as in the choice of candidates, and excluded when they were on opposite sides.

The rules reported by the committee appointed for that purpose included one that each State should be allowed to cast as many votes as its number of electors; and "that a majority of two thirds shall be required to elect the candidates for President and Vice-President." The two-thirds rule was vigorously attacked as unrepublican. Mr. Saunders, of North Carolina, who reported it, defended it. He explained that it was designed to create "a more imposing effect." Continuing, he said that "it was to be presumed that no one had the most remote desire to frustrate the proceedings of the convention; and provided a majority should, on the first or second ballot, fix upon an individual, it was reasonably to be expected that the minority would be disposed to yield and unite with the majority, so as to produce the effect contemplated." In this view it seemed harmless; but Mr. Saunders did not foresee that nine years later he would himself employ the device, contrived to increase the "effect" of the nomination of Mr. Van Buren, to defeat that same gentleman. After debate, the two-thirds rule was rejected by a vote of 231 to 210; but the next morning the vote was reconsidered, and the rule reported by the committee was adopted. Nominations were then in order. Martin Van Buren received a unanimous vote as a candidate for President. Colonel Richard M. Johnson, of Kentucky, had 178 votes for Vice-President, and William C. Rives, of Virginia, 87. Before the voting began, Virginia gave notice that she would support no candidate who did not uphold the principles of the party; and after Colonel Johnson had received the necessary two thirds and been declared the nominee, her delegates further announced that she would not accept him as a candidate.

The opposition derided and denounced " the Van Buren convention." The office-holders who took part in it were counted and their names were published. The convention was declared to be a revival of the caucus in an equally objectionable form. The truth was that no convention could have brought the opposing factions into even a semblance of union, and that they did not wish to unite. Their idea was to take advantage of all the local elements of hostility to the reigning dynasty, to throw the election into the House of Representatives, and — to trust to luck for the rest. A Pennsylvania state convention of Anti-Masons held at Harrisburg, December 16, 1835, nominated General William Henry Harrison, of Ohio, for President, and Francis Granger, of New York, for Vice-President. The legislature of Ohio nominated, for President, Judge John McLean, of that State, who was " mentioned " for the presidency, off and on, from 1832 until 1860. The Whigs of Massachusetts nominated Daniel Webster. It was a cunning scheme. Tennessee, and perhaps one or two other Southern States, would vote for White. South Carolina was against Jackson, and was expected to throw its vote away on some one who had no other supporters.[1] Harrison or McLean would carry several States in the West, and perhaps Pennsylvania. Webster would hold New England. For Vice-President, Granger was accepted as the candidate in all the States where Harrison was supported, and in Massachusetts; while John Tyler, of Virginia, went on the ticket with Judge White. Although the scheme was a promising one and came near success, the margin of safety was on the side of the Democratic party once more, largely owing to the strictness of party discipline, and the determined use of the national patronage to perpetuate the Jackson dynasty under a new head. The battle between the contesting forces was a bitter one. Mr. Van Buren was the embodiment of all that was objected to on the part of the Whigs against General Jackson; and, on the other hand, the Democrats, honestly believing that the

[1] The expectation was realized, for on December 7, 1836, the South Carolina House of Representatives instructed the electors of the State not to vote for Van Buren, White, or Harrison ; and then both branches instructed them to vote for Willie P. Mangum, of North Carolina, for President, and for John Tyler, of Virginia, for Vice-President.

administration in power had acted for the best interests of the country, could find no words too severe to denounce those who would undo its work.   They made it a special accusation against the Whigs that they were for the Bank.   While it was true of the most of them, — and, considering what the Bank had done for the currency, and the great disasters which followed its overthrow, it was greatly to their credit that it was true, — they had not quite enough courage to avow their principles in the face of the manifest but strange hostility of the people to " Biddle's Bank."

As had happened in 1832, the early autumn elections did not promise a sweeping victory for the Democrats ; they even gave hope to the opposition that the election would be thrown into the House of Representatives.   Ohio and New Jersey, which had given their votes to Jackson four years before, were carried by the Whigs.   The Democratic majority in Pennsylvania was uncomfortably small, and in Maine there was no choice of a congressman at the September election in any one of the eight districts.   But the Democrats worked with extraordinary energy after these preliminary reverses and saved the day, although they came out of the contest with a largely reduced majority.

Twenty-six States took part in the election.   Arkansas had been admitted on the 15th of June, 1836.   Michigan, which had applied for admission as early as 1833, chose electors, and their votes were counted, as we shall see, in the same manner as were those of Missouri in 1821.   The State was formally admitted on the 26th of January, 1837, so that she was a State at the time the electoral count took place.   All the States except South Carolina, whose electors were appointed by the legislature, chose them by a popular vote and by general ticket.   The popular vote is given on page 185.

The usual resolution for the appointment of a committee to report upon the manner of conducting the count of votes was introduced in the Senate on the 26th of January, 1837.   An amendment offered by Mr. Clay, and adopted by the Senate, directed the committee also " to inquire into the expediency of ascertaining whether any votes were given at the recent election contrary to the prohibition contained in the second section of the second article of the Constitution ; and, if such votes were given, what ought to be done with them ; and whether any, and what, provision ought to be made for securing the

terms of the Constitution. In recent years parties have been careful not to place upon their electoral tickets any one who was even constructively " holding an office of trust or profit under the United States," — as, for example, a director in a national bank, or other corporation chartered by Congress. In the case before us the committee reported no bill or resolution on the subject. It merely reported the usual resolution for counting the vote, together with a second resolution, exactly like that which had been adopted in 1821 in regard to the votes of Missouri, to cover the case of Michigan. In the Senate this resolution provoked some discussion. Senators were divided over the question whether Michigan was or was not a State of the Union for the purposes of the election. The resolution was finally adopted by a vote of 34 to 9. In the course of the debate a senator asked Mr. Grundy, of Tennessee, who reported the resolutions, what course would have been pursued if the vote of Michigan would have varied the result ? Mr. Grundy replied that the gentleman could not expect him " to answer a question which the wisest of their predecessors had purposely left undetermined. What might be done under the circumstances adverted to, should they ever occur, the wisdom of the day must decide."

The official count of the electoral vote may be found on page 188.

The result was announced in the alternative form prescribed by the joint resolution, concluding with the declaration that, whether the votes of Michigan were counted or not counted, Martin Van Buren was elected President, and that no person had a majority of votes for Vice-President ; that an election to that office had not been effected ; that Richard M. Johnson, of Kentucky, and Francis Granger, of New York, were the two highest on the lists of electoral votes, and that it devolved on the Senate to choose a Vice-President from these persons.

On returning to its own chamber, the Senate adopted a resolution prescribing the manner in which an election should be made. The names of the senators were called in alphabetical order, and they voted *viva voce*. On the first trial, Richard M. Johnson, of Kentucky, was chosen by a vote of 33 to 16 for Francis Granger. This is the only occasion in our political history that the choice of the Vice-President has devolved upon the Senate.

STATES.	PRESIDENT.					VICE-PRESIDENT.			
	Martin Van Buren, N. Y.	William H. Harrison, O.	Hugh L. White, Tenn.	Daniel Webster, Mass.	Willie P. Mangum, N. C.	Richard M. Johnson, Ky.	Francis Granger, N. Y.	John Tyler, Va.	William Smith, Ala.
Maine	10	–	–	–	–	10	–	–	–
New Hampshire . . .	7	–	–	–	–	7	–	–	–
Vermont	–	7	–	–	–	–	7	–	–
Massachusetts	–	–	–	14	–	–	14	–	–
Rhode Island	4	–	–	–	–	4	–	–	–
Connecticut	8	–	–	–	–	8	–	–	–
New York	42	–	–	–	–	42	–	–	–
New Jersey	–	8	–	–	–	–	8	–	–
Pennsylvania	30	–	–	–	–	30	–	–	–
Delaware	–	3	–	–	–	–	3	–	–
Maryland	–	10	–	–	–	–	–	10	–
Virginia	23	–	–	–	–	–	–	–	23
North Carolina	15	–	–	–	–	15	–	–	–
South Carolina	–	–	–	–	11	–	–	11	–
Georgia	–	–	11	–	–	–	–	11	–
Alabama	7	–	–	–	–	7	–	–	–
Mississippi	4	–	–	–	–	4	–	–	–
Louisiana	5	–	–	–	–	5	–	–	–
Arkansas	3	–	–	–	–	3	–	–	–
Kentucky	–	15	–	–	–	–	15	–	–
Tennessee	–	–	15	–	–	–	–	15	–
Missouri	4	–	–	–	–	4	–	–	–
Ohio	–	21	–	–	–	–	21	–	–
Indiana	–	9	–	–	–	–	9	–	–
Illinois	5	–	–	–	–	5	–	–	–
Michigan	3	–	–	–	–	3	–	–	–
Total	170	73	26	14	11	147	77	47	23

The occasion of the inauguration of Mr. Van Buren was a great triumph for the " old hero." It was what Jackson's not too impartial and judicial biographer, James Parton, terms the election of Van Buren, — " the consummation of his most cherished hopes." There was no Jeffersonian simplicity in the ceremony. The general and the President-elect rode together, with a military escort, in the " Constitution phaeton," drawn by four grays. There was a great throng to witness the taking of the oath and to listen to the inaugural address.

General Jackson, infirm and ill and racked with pain, but still indomitable, sat uncovered during the delivery of the address. He had had the satisfaction to witness, what he had anticipated in a letter written to a friend two days before, "the glorious scene of Mr. Van Buren, once rejected by the Senate, sworn into office by Chief Justice Taney, also being rejected by the factious Senate."

XVI

TIPPECANOE AND TYLER TOO

THE canvass of 1840, the "log cabin" and "hard cider" campaign, stands unique in the political history of the country. It was marked by intense and extraordinary enthusiasm on the part of young men for a candidate who was close upon seventy years of age. The party which won the victory was a party in name only, for it had no other bond of union than opposition to the administration of the day. It announced no positive principles, it had no definite policy. Yet it triumphed over the closely organized party which had governed the country since the beginning of the century, — unless the four years' term of the second Adams is to be excepted, — which was strongly intrenched in the offices, and was using the public patronage without scruple to perpetuate its own power.

Many writers have put on record their estimate of Mr. Van Buren's character, and of his rank in the list of those who have occupied the presidential chair ; but neither his warm partisans nor those who have placed the lowest estimate upon him as a statesman attribute the disastrous defeat of the Democracy in 1840 to causes personal to him. That he drew the first breath of his public life in the atmosphere of political intrigue, bargain, treachery, and confusion, which has hung over the State of New York from the days of Washington to the days of McKinley, explains much in the story of his career. In his young manhood he was a distinguished party manager, and owed his advancement to the arts which he then cultivated. His adroitness in maintaining a non-committal attitude until it was practically certain which side was to win, and then coming out strongly on that side, was proverbial. Age, responsibility, and experience made him almost a statesman. He intended to make his administration a continuation of Jackson's.[1] In

[1] William Allen Butler, in his brief but beautiful tribute to his lifelong friend, remarks: " Mr. Van Buren 'followed in the footsteps of his illustrious predecessor.' The predecessor had been too illustrious, and his footsteps had so shaken the whole social system that a great shock was inevitable."

adherence to the political principles of his predecessor, the purpose was carried out. But Van Buren was a gentleman, in the sense of possessing culture and polished manners, and in preferring peace and order to quarrel and turmoil; and in this he differed so greatly from General Jackson that his administration could not be the same. He surrounded himself with gentlemen, bore himself with dignity, and evinced a most laudable desire to efface the memory of his achievements in the political field as " the Little Magician," and the subserviency to Jackson which insured him the succession. It was not unlikeness to his predecessor that caused his defeat. It had required all of Jackson's authority to carry him through in 1836, and his margin was small. To make use of an arithmetical calculation much in vogue at the present day, which is of little significance (see p. 17), a change of 2183 votes in Pennsylvania would have lost him the electors of that State and thrown the election into the House of Representatives. More than the small change necessary to defeat him was forthcoming in 1840, and the opposition had learned to unite for that one purpose. It was Van Buren's misfortune that the storm which Jackson had called from the sky, by his reckless use of high explosives, burst just as Jackson reached shelter and as the " Magician " stepped forth to take the great rainmaker's place. The terrible panic of 1837 began when the administration was but two months old, — a direct consequence of the financial disorder produced by Jackson's war on the Bank. The enforced liquidation of the greatest monetary institution in the country ; the transfer of the public funds to banks much weaker and far more loosely managed than the Bank of the United States; a wild speculation induced by the excessive note-issues of state banks which had a fictitious capital only ; and the inability of the banks to respond when called upon to refund the sums intrusted to them, under the law for " depositing " the surplus revenue with the States, — such were the events which brought about the suspension of specie payments on the 10th of May, 1837.

It is true, as the defenders of Mr. Van Buren say, that he met the crisis with courage. No man in his position was ever known to admit that the catastrophe which he had to face — and which in this case dealt his administration a deadly blow — was caused by the measures which he had supported. Rather, it confirmed him in his former opinions, and led him to recommend more radical steps in the direction of his previous policy. That the members of his party did not all agree with him is shown by the political history of his administration. Although, during his whole term, there was a Democratic majority in both Houses of Congress, he suffered repeated defeats in carrying through his one favorite scheme and great measure, the establishment of the Independent Treasury, — a device contrary then and ever since to all sound views of public and private finance. Nevertheless, it would be a mistake to represent either that Mr. Van Buren was abandoned by his party, or that his administration was an unpopular one among Democrats. On the contrary, a large majority of them believed in him, approved his measures, and desired his reelection. They were in favor of completing the work which Jackson had begun, by divorcing the state altogether from private banking corporations. Mr. Van Buren was then, and to the end of his life, as his "Political History" shows, an enemy of *banks* as well as of *The Bank*. It is probable that if the issue in the canvass of 1840 had been made wholly upon the bank question, the result would have shown that the people were with Van Buren. The Whigs were too shrewd to avow friendliness to *the* Bank, or to any bank. They took advantage of the opposition to, and the bad results of, the Jackson-Van Buren fiscal plans, without declaring themselves in favor of restoring what had been destroyed; and they also profited by the Southern hostility to the administration, without promising to reverse or even to modify the policy of the general government on the subject of State Rights. In short, the Democrats had principles and a policy, right or wrong, as people may think; the Whigs were united only in condemning, and, whatever they may have intended, whatever they may have done or attempted to do when they were in power, did not venture to declare principles or policy beforehand.

The state elections in 1837 and 1838 resulted unfavorably to the Democrats. The most of the elections of members of the twenty-sixth Congress took place in 1838; and they were so decidedly adverse to the Democrats that extraordinary exertions were required in the spring elections of 1839 to rescue their majority from extinction. So close was the contest that, when the House assembled in December, 1839, there were 119 Democrats, 118 opposition, and 5 members from New Jersey

whose seats were contested.   The certificates were held by
Whigs, who were not allowed to participate in the organization.
On that occasion Mr. Adams, the ex-President, who had returned to the House of Representatives, prevented anarchy
by calling the members to order and persuading them to choose
a temporary chairman, — a position which was assigned to Mr.
Adams himself.

Long before this time, the plans of the Whigs had been
forming; and, two days after the assembling of Congress, the
National Whig Convention met at Harrisburg, — on December 4, 1839.   The leaders were resolved on union, and the
only question was as to the candidate who would command
the largest support.   Mr. Clay had the advantage of a long
public service, and of having been a leader in national affairs
for almost thirty years; but he also labored under the double
disadvantage of being a Freemason, and as such not acceptable
to the faction which still mustered many followers in the
Eastern States, and of having been a conspicuous advocate
of the "American system," or protective tariff, which was
highly unpopular in the South Atlantic States.   General
William Henry Harrison was not a great leader; but he had
been more or less in the public service, military and civil, for
nearly half a century, and was well known throughout the
country.   Moreover, he had made a gallant run for the presidency in the Northern States in 1836, and was open to neither
of the objections urged against Mr. Clay.   It was evident that
one of these two would be selected to lead the Whig opposition.   Each had his strong partisans.   Not only they, but
the candidates as well, were anxious chiefly that the Whig
party should carry the election.   Mr. Clay's earnest and
laudable ambition to be President was not so great that he
would put it before the cause.   Moreover, he was aware of
the objections to his candidacy which some Whigs entertained.
When the autumn elections of 1839 indicated a reaction in
favor of the Democrats, and the necessity of a complete union
of the opposition, he wrote, in a letter which was read at the
Harrisburg Convention, that, "if the deliberations of the Convention shall lead them to the choice of another as the candidate of the opposition, far from feeling any discontent, the
nomination will have my best wishes and receive my cordial
support."   He further begged his friends to "discard all
attachment or partiality to me, and be guided solely by the

motive of rescuing our country from the dangers which now encompass it." Already, during the preceding summer, he had said in an address at Buffalo : " If my name creates any obstacle to union and harmony, away with it, and concentrate upon some individual more acceptable to all branches of the opposition." The action of the great " union and harmony " convention of Pennsylvania, held at Harrisburg on the 4th of September, probably did much to concentrate the Whig forces on Harrison ; for, while that convention extolled Clay in extravagant phrases, it expressed the opinion that General Harrison was the only man who could unite the anti-Van Buren party.

Two hundred and fifty-four delegates attended the Whig convention, from twenty-two States. South Carolina, Georgia, Tennessee, and Arkansas were not represented. The Whig committee of Arkansas sent a letter authorizing Judge Porter, of Louisiana, to cast the vote of Arkansas ; but the remembrance of the Whig derision of " ruckerizing," at the Democratic convention of 1835, forbade that the credentials should be accepted. Isaac C. Bates, of Massachusetts, was the temporary chairman, and Governor James Barbour, of Virginia, the permanent president, of the convention. After a long debate, a plan of nomination was agreed upon. As this scheme was peculiar, and is now quite obsolete, the order of the convention is given entire : —

That the delegates from each State be requested to assemble as a delegation, and appoint a committee, not exceeding three in number, to receive the views and opinions of such delegation, and communicate the same to the assembled committees of all the delegations, to be by them respectively reported to their principals. And that thereupon the delegates from each State be requested to assemble as a delegation, and ballot for candidates for the offices of President and Vice-President, and, having done so, to commit the ballot designating the votes of each candidate, and by whom given, to its committee. And thereupon all the committees shall assemble and compare the several ballots, and report the result of the same to their several delegations, together with such facts as may bear upon the nomination. And said delegations shall forthwith reassemble and ballot again for candidates for the above offices, and again commit the result to the above committees ; and if it shall appear that a majority of the ballots are for any one man for candidate for President, said committee shall report the result to the convention for its consideration. If there shall be no such majority, then the delegations shall repeat the balloting until such a majority shall be obtained, and then report the same to the convention for its consideration. That the vote of a majority of each delegation shall be reported as the vote of that State. And each State represented here shall vote its full electoral vote by such delegation in the committee.

It will be observed that this rule bears a resemblance to, although it is not precisely like, the " unit rule," which has caused so much trouble in Republican and Democratic conventions since that time. The action of the committees and of the delegations was not to be binding upon the convention until accepted by it. The scheme was adopted as a method of learning what candidate would be most acceptable to the States. An effort was made the next day, by Mr. Cassius M. Clay of Kentucky, to secure a reversal of the decision; but the convention by a strong vote adhered to its former resolution. The action of the committees and delegations is not a part of the official record; but it is known that on the first informal ballot, in which the wish of each delegate was expressed, without unifying the votes of the States, Mr. Clay had a small plurality. On the first ballot by States, Mr. Clay had 103, General Harrison 94, and General Winfield Scott 57. After repeated ballotings, late on Friday evening, the third day of the convention, a report was made by the committees that they had agreed upon a candidate. General Harrison had 148, Mr. Clay 90, and General Scott 16. On the next day a resolution was introduced declaring General Harrison the nominee of the convention, and it was supported in enthusiastic speeches by many of the friends of Clay. While the jubilee was still going on, the committees, which had been considering the question of Vice-President, made a report that John Tyler had received the unanimous vote of the convention.[1] His name was thereupon joined to that

[1] Henry A. Wise, in his " Seven Decades of the Union," asserts that the nomination of Mr. Tyler was prearranged, — that it had been agreed upon a year before. Mr. Tyler had resigned as senator from Virginia rather than obey the instructions of the legislature, and William C. Rives was elected to succeed him. The senatorial term was to end in 1839, and Mr. Rives and Mr. Tyler were candidates. Mr. Tyler discovered that the Whigs in Congress were favoring the election of Mr. Rives, in the hope that in consideration of their support he would act with them. According to Governor Wise a conference took place ; and Mr. Tyler withdrew from the contest and allowed Mr. Rives to be chosen, under an agreement — Mr. Clay is named as the other contracting party — that Mr. Tyler should be the candidate for Vice-President in 1840. Mr. Rives was elected, and acted with the Whigs.

of General Harrison in the pending resolution, and the vote was carried in a whirlwind of enthusiasm. The convention then adjourned, without having given expression in any form to the principles of the party which it represented. Even in the many speeches made during the four days' session, there was hardly a positive assertion of a principle made by any delegate. It was all hatred and opposition to Van Buren and the "Loco-Focos."

The nomination was received with great enthusiasm by the opposition. Meeting after meeting was held in many States, and the candidacy of the "Old Hero of Tippecanoe" was noisily ratified. The Whigs prepared to shout and sing their candidate into office. In February, 1840, the Whig Convention of Ohio, at Columbus, was made the occasion of a great "demonstration," a procession with banners, representations of log-cabins, coon-skins, pictures of the "old hero" drinking a mug of hard cider, and other equally logical appeals to the political sound sense of the voters of Ohio. A still more imposing affair was the great procession in Baltimore, on the 4th of May, in connection with the national convention of young men, which was nicely timed to occur simultaneously with the Democratic Convention in the same city. An excellent illustration of the political eloquence of the time is afforded by the ostentatious failure of the "Baltimore Patriot" to express the emotions which this great procession excited; but the editor certainly tried to do his subject justice : —

Monday was a proud day for Baltimore, for Maryland, for the Union. It was a day on which the Young Whigs of all the States were to meet in grand convention. Never before was seen such an assemblage of the people, in whose persons are concentrated the sovereignty of the government. In the language of the president of the day, "*Every mountain sent its rill*, — EVERY VALLEY ITS STREAM, and, lo! THE AVALANCHE OF THE PEOPLE IS HERE!"

It is impossible to convey the slightest idea of the sublime spectacle presented by the procession as it moved through the city. All that pen could write, all that the mouth of man could speak, all that the imagination can conceive of beauty, grandeur, and sublimity, would fall short, far short, of the reality. The excitement, the joy, the enthusiasm which everywhere prevailed, lighting up the countenance of every man in the procession; the shouts, the applause, the cheers, of those who filled the sidewalks and crowded the windows; the waving of handkerchiefs by the ladies; the responsive cries of the people; the flaunting banners; the martial music; the loud roar, at intervals, of the deep-mouthed cannon, — all these and more, much more, must be described, seen in the mind's eye, vibrate through the frame, fill the heart, before the reader can approach to any conception of the reality; and when all these are done, if they were possible, he has still but a faint and meagre impression of the scene that was presented. In no country, in no time, never before in the history of man, was there a spectacle so full of "natural glory." The aged veteran, whose declining years forbade his joining the procession, looked on; his feeble voice went to swell the general shout that penetrated even to the blue vault of heaven; his hand waved above his head, whilst down his furrowed cheek ran tears, the overflowing of a heart full even to bursting with joy and happiness and gladness, of all that goes to make up life's best pleasures, and these crowded, as it were, into one moment. The father who brought his children to see the patriots of the land; the mother to look upon her son, one of the patriot crew; the sister to behold the brother give vent to his youthful and extravagant joy,— were all there, and all went to make up the spectacle. Standing on an eminence commanding a view of the line of the procession in the whole extent of Baltimore Street, you beheld a moving mass of human beings. A thousand banners burnished by the sun, floating in the breeze, ten thousand handkerchiefs waved by the fair daughters of the city, gave seeming life and motion to the very air. A hundred thousand faces were before you, — age, manhood, youth, and beauty filled every place where a foothold could be got, or any portion of the procession be seen; and you gazed on the pageant with renewed and increasing delight, and words failed to express what your heart felt or your eyes beheld. Nothing was wanting, nothing left to be desired, — the cup of human joy was full. The free men of the land were there, — the fiery son of the South, the substantial citizen of the East, the hardy pioneer of the West, were all there. It was the epitome of a great nation, in itself realizing, filling up the imaginings, and may have been the very picture which the poet drew when he described our country, our institutions, and our people as a "land beyond the oceans of the West," where "freedom and truth are worshipped" by a "people mighty in their youth."

> That land is like an eagle, whose young gaze
>   Feeds on the noontide beam; whose golden plume
> Floats moveless on the storm, and in the blaze
>   Of sunshine gleams when earth is wrapped in gloom.
>   An epitaph of glory for the tomb
> Of murdered Europe, may thy fame be made,
>   Great people! as the sand shalt thou become!
> Thy growth is swift as morn, when night must fade;
> The multitudinous earth shall sleep beneath thy shade.

Thus much we may say in reference to what words can describe the procession to be, not what it was; for the reality we must give the dry details of the programme by which it was arranged. We can give nothing of the living spectacle, we can give nothing of the joy and gladness which —

> Spread through the multitudinous streets fast flying
> Upon the wings of hope —
>   from house to house replying
> With loud acclaim; the living shook heaven's cope,
> And filled the earth with echoes!

We can give nothing of these, and here all fail; but we must essay to present the scene, as far as feeble words can do it.

The procession does really seem to have been a grand affair, and there were numerous emblems of the Whigs, — log-cabins, barrels of hard cider, brooms to sweep the Augean stables, and others which it would be tedious to enumerate. The poet was with the Whigs that year. Among the mottoes on the banners was this : —

> Farewell, dear Van,
> You 're not our man;
> To guide the ship,
> We 'll try old Tip.

The Democrats, meanwhile, were in a situation which embarrassed them, but gave them no fear that they were about to suffer defeat. They had had the people with them at every election in forty years, excepting only in 1824; and they maintained that even then the popular judgment was for Jackson. They despised the opposition, and regarded the method of the canvass the Harrison party was carrying on as almost unworthy of the notice of serious-minded men. They had troubles of their own ; but Providence had always come to their aid at the critical moment, and it would do so again. So far as Van Buren was concerned, there was this time absolutely no opposition to him within the party. Tennessee, before unfriendly, would now give him its support ; and even South Carolina, which had sulked for eight years, was ready to vote for him. But there was a bitter opposition to the Vice-President, Colonel Johnson. Party discipline was not then what it is now. So hostile were many of the party to Johnson that it was certain that he, at least, would fail to be chosen by a majority of electors, whatever might be Van Buren's fate. The situation was such that it seemed wise to many of the leaders not to hold a convention at all, since to do so would merely advertise the party division. The Democrats were all in favor of Van Buren; the people had nominated him spontaneously. The Senate, which had once elected Colonel Johnson, could be trusted to choose that Democratic candidate who received the most electoral votes. It was asserted that there were ten States which had declined or would decline to send delegates to a convention. By some of them Mr. Van Buren had been named for reëlection in conjunction with William R. King, of Alabama, or James K. Polk, of Tennessee, or Littleton W. Tazewell, of Virginia, or Colonel Johnson himself.

There was then no such body as a national committee of the party, and in fact no constituted authority to decide whether a convention should be held or not. The conventions of 1831 and 1835 had both been called by the Democratic members of the New Hampshire legislature; and once again they issued a call for a convention to meet at Baltimore on the 4th of May, 1840. Delegates were present from twenty-one States. Connecticut, Delaware, Virginia, South Carolina, and Illinois were unrepresented. The membership corresponded to the number of votes allowed more closely than had ever before been the case. New Jersey alone was over-represented by fifty-nine delegates. There was but one member to cast the vote of Massachusetts, and several of the Western States were thinly represented. Governor Isaac Hill, of New Hampshire, was the temporary chairman, and Governor William Carroll, of Tennessee, the permanent president. Pending the preparation of business, there was an abundance of speech-making. All who addressed the convention were sure that a great victory for the Democratic party was impending, and each tried to outdo the rest in jeering at the Whigs. The great procession of the day before was referred to as an "animal show;" the Whigs were laughed at for shutting up their candidate and not allowing him the use of pen and ink; and one speaker said that he had tried to get an introduction to some of the log-cabin men in the procession "for the purpose of feeling their soft, delicate hands," but "as soon as he had done so he was pretty careful to put his hand on his purse."

On the second day of the convention the committee on resolutions reported the following platform of principles: —

1. *Resolved*, That the federal government is one of limited powers derived solely from the Constitution, and the grants of

power shown therein ought to be strictly construed by all the departments and agents of the government, and that it is inexpedient and dangerous to exercise doubtful constitutional powers.

2. *Resolved*, That the Constitution does not confer upon the general government the power to commence and carry on a general system of internal improvement.

3. *Resolved*, That the Constitution does not confer authority upon the federal government, directly or indirectly, to assume the debts of the several States, contracted for local internal improvements, or other State purposes; nor would such assumption be just or expedient.

4. *Resolved*, That justice and sound policy forbid the federal government to foster one branch of industry to the detriment of another, or to cherish the interest of one portion to the injury of another portion of our common country; that every citizen and every section of the country has a right to demand and insist upon an equality of rights and privileges, and to complete and ample protection of person and property from domestic violence or foreign aggression.

5. *Resolved*, That it is the duty of every branch of the government to enforce and practise the most rigid economy in conducting our public affairs, and that no more revenue ought to be raised than is required to defray the necessary expenses of the government.

6. *Resolved*, That Congress has no power to charter a United States Bank; that we believe such an institution one of deadly hostility to the best interests of the country, dangerous to our republican institutions and the liberties of the people, and calculated to place the business of the country within the control of a concentrated money power, and above the laws and the will of the people.

7. *Resolved*, That Congress has no power, under the Constitution, to interfere with or control the domestic institutions of the several States, and that such States are the sole and proper judges of everything appertaining to their own affairs not prohibited by the Constitution; that all efforts of the Abolitionists or others, made to induce Congress to interfere with questions of slavery, or to take incipient steps in relation thereto, are calculated to lead to the most alarming and dangerous consequences, and that all such efforts have an inevitable tendency to diminish the happiness of the people, and endanger the stability and permanency of the Union, and ought not to be countenanced by any friend to our political institutions.

8. *Resolved*, That the separation of the moneys of the government from banking institutions is indispensable for the safety of the funds of the government and the rights of the people.

9. *Resolved*, That the liberal principles embodied by Jefferson in the Declaration of Independence, and sanctioned in the Constitution, which make ours the land of liberty and the asylum of the oppressed of every nation, have ever been cardinal principles in the Democratic faith; and every attempt to abridge the present privilege of becoming citizens and the owners of soil among us ought to be resisted with the same spirit which swept the Alien and Sedition laws from our statute-book.

The vote was put on each of these resolutions separately, and every one of them was adopted by a unanimous vote. Another committee appointed to prepare an address to the people next presented its report, — an address which nearly fills a page of the Washington " Globe," in fine type, — and the pages of the newspapers of that day were of generous size. The address was listened to impatiently, for the convention was anxious to get at the question of nominations. Senator Clement C. Clay, of Alabama, chairman of a committee to which this subject had been referred on the previous day, reported two resolutions, to each of which a preamble was affixed. The first, having set forth that Mr. Van Buren had received many nominations for the position which he already filled to the satisfaction of the party and the country, and that he was the unanimous choice of the Democrats, formally presented him for reëlection. The preamble of the second resolution recited that several gentlemen had been put in nomination for the vice-presidency; that the States presenting some of these gentlemen had no representatives in the convention; and that all the candidates, by their discharge of public trusts, had shown themselves worthy to be elected to the office. The resolution itself was as follows: —

Resolved, That the convention deem it expedient at the present time not to choose between the individuals in nomination, but to leave the decision to their Republican fellow-citizens in the several States, trusting that, before the election shall take place, their opinions shall become so concentrated as to secure the choice of a Vice-President by the electoral colleges.

The first resolution was adopted unanimously without debate. The second was opposed and was warmly discussed. The friends of Colonel Johnson were not satisfied that he should not be commended to the electors, if a two-thirds vote in his favor could be had. But it presently appeared that the opposition to him was so determined that it would not be yielded even after such a nomination; whereupon opposition ceased and the resolution was unanimously adopted. The Whigs jeered at the Democrats as not being sufficiently united to name a candidate for Vice-President. They hurled back the rather neat reply that if they were not agreed upon men, they were united upon principles. That was more than the Whigs could say for themselves.

There was another convention, small in numbers and local in character, which made a third nomination for the office of President. Weak in numbers, the Abolitionists were bold and aggressive. As "Liberty men," in November, 1839, they met in Warsaw, New York, and nominated James G. Birney of New York for President, and Francis J. Lemoyne of Pennsylvania for Vice-President. For the second place Thomas Earle was afterward substituted. The question of slavery had been much discussed in Congress and by the press for many years, but the issue was not yet a really important one in presidential elections. As will be seen from the platform of the Democrats, that party was ready to take its stand against any federal interference with slavery; but the Whigs were not, so long as they constituted a party, willing to make an issue with the Democrats on that subject.

What the canvass had been from the beginning it continued to be to the end. On the part of the Whigs it was a season of great and enthusiastic meetings and stump-speeches. General Harrison himself appeared on the stump, and spoke at length in September and October, 1840, at Urbana, Dayton, Chillicothe, Columbus, and other places. In an address at Carthage, on August 20, he explicitly asserted the right of the people to discuss any subject, and to petition Congress for the redress of any grievance, including that of slavery; and for this he was roundly denounced as an Abolitionist. The Democrats were unable to understand, and still more unable to look with patience upon, the shouting campaign of the Harrison men. They affected to treat the party and its candidate with contempt, but they were really angry and alarmed. As State after State upon whose electoral vote they had counted gave the Whigs a majority, they became more desperate. They could not and would not believe that they were to be beaten, and predicted that "the bubble would burst" before November. That was a time when political slang was more current than it was ever before or has been since. The phrases, "Crow,

Chapman, crow," "The ball is rolling on," "Clear the kitchen," with numerous variations, and similar expressions, are still remembered by the men, now old, who took part in that famous canvass. The Whig song to the tune of "The Little Pig's Tail" has become historical, with its chorus: —

"For Tippecanoe and Tyler too — Tippecanoe and Tyler too;
And with them we 'll beat little Van, Van,
Van is a used up man;
And with them we 'll beat little Van."

The shouts of the Whigs over their success in Vermont, Kentucky, Maine, Ohio, and other States had hardly ceased ringing when the presidential election began. The choice of all the electors was still made on any day within thirty-four days preceding the meeting of the electors that might be fixed upon by the state legislature. The election began in Penn-

STATES.	Harrison.	Van Buren.	Birney.
Maine	46,612	46,201	194
New Hampshire	26,163	32,761	126
Vermont	32,440	18,018	319
Massachusetts	72,874	51,944	1,621
Rhode Island	5,278	3,301	42
Connecticut	31,601	25,296	174
New York	225,817	212,527	2,808
New Jersey	33,351	31,034	69
Pennsylvania	144,021	143,672	343
Delaware	5,967	4,874	–
Maryland	33,528	28,752	–
Virginia	42,501	43,893	–
North Carolina	46,376	33,782	–
South Carolina *	–	–	–
Georgia	40,261	31,021	–
Alabama	28,471	33,991	–
Mississippi	19,518	16,995	–
Louisiana	11,296	7,616	–
Kentucky	58,489	32,616	–
Tennessee	60,391	48,289	–
Missouri	22,972	29,760	–
Arkansas	5,160	6,766	–
Ohio	148,157	124,782	903
Indiana	65,302	51,604	–
Illinois	45,537	47,476	149
Michigan	22,933	21,131	321
Total	1,275,016	1,129,102	7,069

* Electors appointed by the legislature.

sylvania and Ohio on the 30th of October, and ended in North Carolina on the 12th of November, so far as popular elections were concerned. South Carolina, whose legislature made the choice of the electors for that State, appointed them a fort-night later. But it was evident as soon as the returns of Pennsylvania were in, showing a large gain for the Whigs, even since the state election, four weeks before, that Harrison was to be President. The popular vote is given on page 203.

The electoral count was conducted in the usual manner, and there was no incident to mark the proceedings. The result was declared as follows: —

STATES.	PRESIDENT.		VICE-PRESIDENT.			
	W. H. Harrison, Ohio.	Martin Van Buren, N.Y.	John Tyler, Va.	R. M. Johnson, Ky.	L. W. Tazewell, Va.	James K. Polk, Tenn.
Maine	10	–	10	–	–	–
New Hampshire	–	7	–	7	–	–
Vermont	7	–	7	–	–	–
Massachusetts	14	–	14	–	–	–
Rhode Island	4	–	4	–	–	–
Connecticut	8	–	8	–	–	–
New York	42	–	42	–	–	–
New Jersey	8	–	8	–	–	–
Pennsylvania	30	–	30	–	–	–
Delaware	3	–	3	–	–	–
Maryland	10	–	10	–	–	–
Virginia	–	23	–	22	–	1
North Carolina	15	–	15	–	–	–
South Carolina	–	11	–	–	11	–
Georgia	11	–	11	–	–	–
Alabama	–	7	–	7	–	–
Mississippi	4	–	4	–	–	–
Louisiana	5	–	5	–	–	–
Kentucky	15	–	15	–	–	–
Tennessee	15	–	15	–	–	–
Missouri	–	4	–	4	–	–
Arkansas	–	3	–	3	–	–
Ohio	21	–	21	–	–	–
Indiana	9	–	9	–	–	–
Illinois	–	5	–	5	–	–
Michigan	3	–	3	–	–	–
Total	234	60	234	48	11	1

The inauguration on the Fourth of March, 1841, was a great occasion for the Whigs.   They flocked to Washington in large numbers, many of them, alas! attracted thither by the hope of offices to be distributed by the new President to his party friends.   There was an imposing procession of volunteer militia to escort General Harrison to the Capitol.   The President-elect had himself arrived at the seat of government on the last day of February, apparently in the enjoyment of perfect health. He rode upon a white charger, flanked on either side by a body-guard of personal friends.   The ceremony, which was witnessed by a vast concourse of people, was preceded by the inauguration of Mr. Tyler as Vice-President, in the Senate Chamber.   After the long line of official and non-official witnesses had come from the building to the eastern portico, General Harrison rose and delivered his inaugural address, save the last paragraph.   Then the oath of office was administered by Chief Justice Taney, and the President pronounced the closing sentences of his address.   While the cheers of the victorious Whigs were still rising, he retired, entered his private carriage, and drove to the White House.

XVII

THE FIRST "DARK HORSE"

No election ever caused more disappointment, both to victors and to vanquished, than that of 1840. It would be difficult to describe the feelings of the Democrats. They were puzzled, they were grieved, they were angry. They honestly did not believe the Whigs capable of governing the country. It was almost too great a strain upon their trust in the fitness of the people for self-government that confidence had been withdrawn from them. As for the conduct of the campaign in which they were defeated, with its claptrap of processions, songs, emblems, and slang, words failed to express their disgust. They declared that the victory had been won by fraud, by the momentary madness of the people, by the power of money, — the first but not the last complaint of the sort, — by anything and everything except the excellent influences that had always carried elections for the Democrats. However much they might differ among themselves, and even with themselves, as to the cause of the defeat, upon one thing they were resolved, — that they would bring Van Buren forward again and elect him. The canvass of 1844 began, therefore, before Harrison was inaugurated. A St. Louis paper, almost as soon as the result of the election was known, placed Van Buren's name at the head of its columns as candidate for 1844, and "nailed its colors to the mast." Senator Benton thereupon wrote a letter to the editor commending his course, saying that twice before the Democratic party had won a victory, after its only two national defeats, by adopting at once the candidate in whose person it had suffered a reverse. This was the general sentiment of the party. In the three years ensuing, as the Washington "Globe" asserted just before the convention of 1844, twenty-four of the twenty-six States, in their state Democratic conventions, pronounced in favor of Van Buren, and more than three fourths of the conventions instructed their delegates to Baltimore to support him.

The disappointment of the Whigs was of a different character. It lay in the "Tyler too" part of their election programme. One month after General Harrison took the oath of
office he died, and John Tyler became President. Congress
was summoned in extraordinary session on the 31st of May,
1841. Among the first subjects to which the attention of
Congress was called by the President was the question what
should be substituted for the sub-treasury system, — a financial device which had certainly been condemned by the popular
voice in the recent elections. The Whigs took this to mean
also the creation of a bank. Mr. Tyler held a different view.
His course in Congress had never been favorable to the Bank
of the United States. The Whig leaders supposed that Mr.
Tyler had given them an assurance that he was in favor of a
bank erected on a proper basis. Mr. Tyler did not admit that
he had done so. The truth of the matter will never be known.
When a bill creating a bank, which the Whigs supposed to
have been drawn in accordance with his views, was presented
to him for approval he vetoed it, and the Whig majority was
not strong enough to pass it over the veto. A second bill was
prepared, after a conference with the President, submitted to
him after it was drafted and approved, and then passed without the alteration of a word. The President vetoed that bill
also, possibly in a fit of natural anger at a letter written by
John M. Botts, a leading Whig member from Virginia, — its
publication was a breach of confidence, — in which Mr. Botts
spoke with contempt of Mr. Tyler's "turns and twists."

It is needless to say that this act was received with uncon-
trollable indignation by the Whigs throughout the country.
All the members of the cabinet resigned, except Mr. Webster,
the Secretary of State, who retained office for reasons which
were approved by many of the Whigs. A caucus of members of the Senate and House of Representatives adopted an
address in which they announced that all political alliance between them and John Tyler was at an end, and that henceforth "those who brought the President into power can no
longer, in any manner or degree, be justly held responsible or
blamed for the administration of the executive branch of the
government." It is matter of history that Mr. Tyler continued to the end of his term to be what his early acts as
President had indicated that he would be. In fact his course
was what his whole political life had indicated that it would

be. He relied throughout upon those who had opposed him, and thwarted the measures of those who had elected him. The only inconsistency of which he was guilty was in supposing, honestly no doubt, that he was "a firm and decided Whig," when he was opposed to a bank, opposed to a protective tariff, opposed to the distribution of the proceeds of the public lands, opposed to internal improvements, and devoted to the principle of "strict construction" of the Constitution. The Whigs had not, to be sure, formally professed different principles from his in resolutions adopted by a national convention; but they were really unanimous, or substantially so, in holding all the views from which he dissented.

Whatever part an ambition to be reëlected, not by the Whigs, but by the Democrats, had in determining Mr. Tyler's course, he did not gain new political friends when he lost old ones. The Democrats were glad enough that the fruits of victory were snatched away from the Whigs; but, though they took advantage of the opportunity which chance threw in their way, they made no pretence of taking the President up as their own man. They loved the sin, but hated the sinner. There were some Democrats and Democratic papers slightly tinctured with "Tylerism," but they were few and uninfluential. By far the largest number of the Democrats were zealous and unwavering in their adherence to the fortunes of Mr. Van Buren. Yet it was not their unanimous sentiment. South Carolina was in favor of Mr. Calhoun, and so was Georgia; and that gentleman carried his sense of propriety so far that, in the autumn of 1843, he declined an invitation to visit Ohio in a semi-public way, on the ground that he ought not to do so while his name was before the country as a candidate for its highest office. Colonel R. M. Johnson, then lately Vice-President, was also advocated by the anti-Benton men of Missouri, as well as by partisans in his own State of Kentucky. He had no such scruples as those which restrained Mr. Calhoun, for he made a tour through the North, as far as Boston, in the course of which, if he was not belied, he assured the people that nothing could prevent the election of Mr. Clay in 1844 but his own candidacy. His belief in himself is shown by a letter written early in January, 1844, wherein he said that he had worn a certain "red vest" "when called upon to respond to my third unanimous nomination for the presidency by the annual convention of my native State." His friends always spoke of him as "the old hero" and "old Tecumseh." His willingness to be before the people was further exemplified in a letter, written in answer to an inquiry, in which he said plainly that he would accept the second place on the ticket if he did not get the first. The claims of General Lewis Cass were urged by some of those who did not think the nomination of Mr. Van Buren advisable. Finally, in Pennsylvania, Mr. James Buchanan was brought forward as a "favorite son."

In point of fact, while a most decided preference was shown for Mr. Van Buren before any and all others, those who opposed him were bitter and determined. They declared that he could not be elected, and that it would be suicide for the party to nominate him. When the question of a convention was under discussion, South Carolina refused to send delegates; and hot discussions arose in the Democratic newspapers whether delegates should be chosen by districts or by general ticket, and whether Virginia, which was for Van Buren, should be allowed to enter the convention with her delegation numbering five times the votes she would be allowed to cast.

Such was the situation late in 1843. The Democrats seemed to be, and were, in hopeless discord. The Whigs counted upon an easy victory, for they were absolutely united in supporting Mr. Clay, while the alleged treachery of Mr. Tyler had given them what was better than unanimity in respect of a candidate, — political union. The next succeeding events seemed to work in their favor, for they were as confident of their ability to defeat Mr. Van Buren as were that gentleman's enemies in his own party that he could not be elected. Mr. Buchanan formally withdrew his name in December, 1843; and in the following month Mr. Calhoun published a letter which was at first taken as a withdrawal, but was afterwards seen to be only a refusal to allow his name to go before the convention. His friends were thus left free to give him their independent support if they would. Meanwhile many state conventions were instructing their delegates to vote for Mr. Van Buren, and his nomination seemed to be inevitable. A clear majority of all the delegates could be counted for him beyond a question, and it was not doubted that he would receive the necessary two thirds.

But the situation was changed as if by magic. The question of the annexation of Texas loomed up suddenly. An overture by Texas for absorption had been once rejected, years before; a suggestion from the government of the United States that annexation might be acceptable, some time later, had come to nothing; and now Mr. Tyler thrust the matter again before the people by submitting to the Senate a treaty with Texas providing for its annexation to the United States. "*Re*-annexation" was the cry. Texas had been exchanged for Florida in a negotiation with Spain; it had in common with Mexico, of which it formed a part, been separated from Spain; it had been colonized by filibusters from the United States, had declared and achieved its independence in a war with Mexico, and was now a republic by itself. But Mexico had only suspended, not ceased, its efforts to reconquer Texas, and had not acknowledged the independence of the republic. To annex it, therefore, was to assume the obligation of a war with Mexico, or to overawe her weakness by our own strength.

The sentiment of the South was very strong in favor of "immediate re-annexation," for obvious reasons, chief among them being the additional strength which would thereby be acquired for the slavery interest. The question suddenly became a political issue of the first magnitude. Mr. Tyler sent the treaty to the Senate on the 22d of April, 1844, but the fact that such a treaty was under consideration was made public some weeks earlier. On the same day, April 27, letters were published from Henry Clay and Martin Van Buren, in which these two gentlemen, almost universally regarded as the two prospective rivals for the presidency, answered inquiries as to their views on the Texas question at length. Singularly enough, their views were similar in this, — that they both foresaw that annexation meant war with Mexico; that they regarded annexation without the consent of Mexico as dishonorable; and that, consequently, both were opposed to the pending measure. Mr. Clay went further, and expressed grave doubts as to the wisdom of annexation at all, for reasons partly financial (Texas having a debt which must be assumed) and partly political (the strong opposition that existed throughout New England, and the North generally). Mr. Van Buren's letter, perhaps the most courageous act of a public life which was not characterized by great courage, and therefore one of the most creditable, cost him the nomination. It was dated April 20, 1844, and made public a week later; and the convention met at Baltimore on May 27. The time was short, but it was long

enough to defeat him. The editor of the Richmond "En-
quirer," who had been as firm and steadfast a Van Buren man
as Senator Benton himself, presided at a meeting intended to
bring about a change in the instructions to the Virginia delegates, who had been directed to support Van Buren, and to
instruct them to vote for a candidate in favor of immediate
annexation. Some delegates from Southern States resigned
rather than obey the instructions already given them to vote
for Van Buren. Others declared that, although so instructed,
they knew that the wishes of their constituents would be modified by the disclosure of Mr. Van Buren's opinions, and that
they should support another candidate.

The convention was one of the most interesting ever held in
the country. The excitement among the arriving delegates
was intense. A great majority of them came with instructions
to support Van Buren; but it was known that many of them
would disobey, and how far the treachery — for so the real
advocates of Mr. Van Buren regarded it — extended made men
suspicious and anxious. Mr. Clay had already been nominated,
and the Whigs were earnest, enthusiastic, and confident. The
party organ of the Democrats at the capital, the Washington
"Globe," said truly, just before the convention met, that the
assertion that Mr. Van Buren had lost his standing with the
people by reason of his Texas letter was not supported by
evidence. Many politicians had turned against him, but the
rank and file of the party would be for him still, unless their
leaders advised them to desert him. The "Globe" attributed
the whole anti-Van Buren movement to Calhoun. "It is the
last card of his desperate competitor, who has been playing for
twenty-five years for the presidency with the frenzy of a game-
ster. It cannot win."

Three hundred and twenty-five delegates appeared at the
convention at Baltimore on May 27, 1844. Virginia and Kentucky only were greatly over-represented. For the most part,
the States sent exactly as many delegates as the electoral votes
to which they were entitled. South Carolina being unrepresented, there were 266 votes in the convention. Hendrick
B. Wright, of Pennsylvania, was the temporary chairman, and
was also appointed as the permanent president. As soon as
the temporary organization had been effected, General Saunders, of North Carolina, who had championed the two-thirds
rule in Van Buren's interest in the convention of 1835, moved

that the rules of the convention of 1832 be adopted for the government of this convention. The significance of the motion was recognized at once. It was a motion for the two-thirds rule. If it were not adopted, Van Buren was sure to be nominated; if it were adopted, he might be defeated. Consideration of the motion was postponed as premature; but General Saunders persisted in bringing it forward, and at last it was taken up. A warm debate ensued. The vote was taken at about noon of the second day of the convention. The rule was adopted by 148 votes against 118. Nearly two thirds of the Northern votes were in the negative; six sevenths of the Southern votes were in favor of the rule. The Northern delegates had it in their power to defeat the rule, and yet, being perfectly well aware that the adoption of the two-thirds requirement handicapped the candidate they professed to support, they lent themselves to the scheme of his opponents. The conclusion is inevitable that they were willing that he should be sacrificed, but that they did not quite venture to appear with daggers in their own hands.

"Balloting" for a candidate, as it was called, — although the voting was *viva voce*, — began in the afternoon. It will be seen from the table below that Mr. Van Buren received a majority of 26 on the first trial. He would have lacked but ten votes of a nomination had all those who came to the convention, instructed for him, given him their votes. He received but 12 votes of the 105 from Southern States; from the North, 134 votes out of 151. Seven trials took place before adjournment for the day, resulting as follows: —

	1st.	2d.	3d.	4th.	5th.	6th.	7th.
Whole number of votes	266	266	266	265	265	265	265
Necessary for a choice	178	178	178	177	177	177	177
Martin Van Buren, New York . .	146	127	121	111	103	101	99
Lewis Cass, Michigan	83	94	92	105	107	116	123
Richard M. Johnson, Kentucky . .	24	33	38	32	29	23	21
James Buchanan, Pennsylvania . .	4	9	11	17	26	25	22
Levi Woodbury, New Hampshire .	2	1	2	–	–	–	–
Commodore Stewart, Pennsylvania .	1	1	–	–	–	–	–
John C. Calhoun, South Carolina .	6	1	2	–	–	–	–

Early in the session on the following day an Ohio delegate moved a resolution that Martin Van Buren, having received a majority of votes on the first ballot, be declared the candidate.

It was ruled that this would require a two-thirds vote, as rescinding an order of the convention. An angry and confused debate took place over the point of parliamentary law, but an appeal from the decision of the chair was withdrawn, and the convention began once more to vote for a candidate.

The time had come to spring the sensation carefully prepared in advance of the convention. The States were called in geographical order, beginning with Maine. When New Hampshire was called, the delegates from that State gave all their votes to James K. Polk, of Tennessee. A member of the Maine delegation had remarked, just before the voting began, that " it was time to draw the fire of Tennessee." Seven Massachusetts delegates, all those of Alabama and Tennessee, and a few others, followed the lead of New Hampshire. The result was announced: Van Buren, 104; Cass, 114; Polk, 44. The ninth trial began without great evidence of excitement, until, upon the call of New York, the chairman of that delegation asked permission to retire for consultation. Meanwhile the roll-call proceeded. When the New York delegation returned, Mr. B. F. Butler made a speech, in the course of which he produced a letter from Mr. Van Buren which he had received before the convention met, authorizing the withdrawal of his name, if it would conduce to harmony. Accordingly Mr. Butler withdrew Mr. Van Buren, and cast the entire vote of New York for Mr. Polk. Then ensued a " stampede," — a scene repeated many times since that day in national conventions. Delegation after delegation changed its vote, and when the result was announced James K. Polk, of Tennessee, had every vote, and was nominated. A scene of wild confusion ensued. A despatch was sent by telegraph to Washington, — the first line built in the country had not long before been opened between the two cities, — and a congratulatory reply was received from the Democratic members of Congress twenty minutes after the nomination.

In the afternoon the convention voted for a candidate for Vice-President, and nominated Silas Wright, then a Senator from New York, almost unanimously, by 256 votes. Nine members of the Georgia delegation refused to vote for him, and supported Levi Woodbury, of New Hampshire. Mr. Wright was notified by telegraph, and declined the nomination peremptorily. Although he was requested to reconsider, and was waited upon that night by a committee of the convention, he persisted in his refusal to be a candidate. This is the only case in our history where a nomination for either the first or the second place on a presidential ticket, by a delegate convention of either of the great parties has been declined. Mr. Wright felt that he could not, in honor, accept the candidacy. He had been a sincere advocate of Mr. Van Buren's nomination. Moreover, a few days before the convention, he had been approached by some of his own personal friends, who suggested that the two-thirds rule might be adopted, that it might result in the defeat of Van Buren, and that it might be possible to turn the convention in his own favor. He rejected the overture, and wrote a letter to be used in case the contingency suggested were to arise. It did arise when New York was about to withdraw Van Buren, and the letter was read at the private meeting of the delegation. His determination was conveyed explicitly in these words: "I am not and cannot under any circumstances be a candidate before your convention for that office." The whole letter is published in Hammond's "Life of Silas Wright," which forms a part of the third volume of his "Political History of New York," and is highly creditable to Mr. Wright's sense of honor. He explained afterward that he felt that he could not accept the second place and so gain a profit from the defeat of his friend, Mr. Van Buren.

On the third day of the convention the members proceeded to vote again for a candidate for Vice-President. On the first trial, Governor John Fairfield, of Maine, had 107 votes; Levi Woodbury, of New Hampshire, 44; Lewis Cass, of Michigan, 39; R. M. Johnson, of Kentucky, 26; Commodore Stewart, of Pennsylvania, 23; George M. Dallas, of Pennsylvania, 13; William L. Marcy, of New York, 5. An inquiry was made whether Governor Fairfield was in favor of annexation, but the question could not be answered authoritatively, and he was dropped. The convention was evidently in a less conciliatory frame of mind than when it nominated Mr. Wright, who shared the views of Mr. Van Buren. On the second vote George M. Dallas had 220 votes; Governor Fairfield, 30; Mr. Woodbury, 6; and Mr. Dallas was nominated.

At the beginning of the morning session, before the nomination of Mr. Dallas, the following platform was reported and adopted. In most of our political text-books the platform appears in a mutilated form, and does not contain the first resolution, with its sarcastic allusion to the canvass of 1840 : —

Resolved, That the American Democracy place their trust, not in factitious symbols, not in displays and appeals insulting to the judgment and subversive of the intellect of the people, but in a clear reliance upon the intelligence, patriotism, and the discriminating justice of the American people.

Resolved, That we regard this as a distinctive feature of our political creed, which we are proud to maintain before the world, as the great moral element in a form of government springing from and upheld by the popular will; and we contrast it with the creed and practice of Federalism, under whatever name or form, which seeks to palsy the will of the constituent, and which conceives no imposture too monstrous for the popular credulity.

Resolved, therefore, That, entertaining these views, the Democratic party of this Union, through the delegates assembled in general convention of the States, coming together in a spirit of concord, of devotion to the doctrines and faith of a free representative government, and appealing to their fellow-citizens for the rectitude of their intentions, renew and reassert before the American people the declaration of principles avowed by them on a former occasion, when, in general convention, they presented their candidates for the popular suffrage.

[Here follow all the resolutions adopted by the convention of 1840; see p. 199.]

Resolved, That the proceeds of the public lands ought to be sacredly applied to the national objects specified in the Constitution; and that we are opposed to the laws lately adopted, and to any law, for the distribution of such proceeds among the States, as alike inexpedient in policy and repugnant to the Constitution.

Resolved, That we are decidedly opposed to taking from the President the qualified veto power by which he is enabled, under restrictions and responsibilities amply sufficient to guard the public interest, to suspend the passage of a bill, whose merits cannot secure the approval of two thirds of the Senate and House of Representatives, until the judgment of the people can be obtained thereon, and which has thrice saved the American people from the corrupt and tyrannical domination of the Bank of the United States.

Resolved, That our title to the whole of the territory of Oregon is clear and unquestionable; that no portion of the same ought to be ceded to England or any other power; and that the re-occupation of Oregon and the re-annexation of Texas at the earliest practicable period are great American measures, which this convention recommends to the cordial support of the Democracy of the Union.

After a formal resolution naming Polk and Dallas as the party candidates, the platform concludes with the following resolution : —

Resolved, That this convention hold in the highest estimation and regard their illustrious fellow-citizen, Martin Van Buren, of New York; that we cherish the most grateful and abiding sense of the ability, integrity, and firmness with which he discharged the duties of the high office of President of the United States, and especially of the inflexible fidelity with which he maintained the true doctrines of the Constitution and the measures of the Democratic party during his trying and nobly arduous administration ; that in the memorable struggle of 1840 he fell a martyr to the great principles of which he was the worthy representative, and we revere him as such; and that we hereby tender to him, in honorable retirement, the assurance of the deeply seated confidence, affection, and respect of the American Democracy.

In order to present the events of the opening of the Democratic canvass without a break, chronological order has been somewhat disregarded. Two conventions had already been held when that of the Democrats met. The Abolitionists had assembled at Buffalo at the end of August, 1843, and had nominated James G. Birney, of New York, for President, and Thomas Morris, of Ohio, for Vice-President. This action was to have a most important effect upon the ensuing canvass, unworthy of notice as the convention seemed. Only one hundred and forty-eight delegates were present, from twelve States. It adopted the following platform : —

Resolved, That human brotherhood is a cardinal principle of true democracy, as well as of pure Christianity, which spurns all inconsistent limitations; and neither the political party which repudiates it, nor the political system which is not based upon it, can be truly democratic or permanent.

Resolved, That the Liberty Party, placing itself upon this broad principle, will demand the absolute and unqualified divorce of the general government from slavery, and also the restoration of equality of rights among men, in every State where the party exists or may exist.

Resolved, That the Liberty Party has not been organized for any temporary purpose by interested politicians, but has arisen from among the people in consequence of a conviction, hourly gaining ground, that no other party in the country represents the true principles of American liberty, or the true spirit of the Constitution of the United States.

Resolved, That the Liberty Party has not been organized merely for the overthrow of slavery. Its first decided effort must indeed be directed against slaveholding as the grossest and most revolting manifestation of despotism, but it will also carry out the principle of equal rights into all its practical consequences and applications, and support every just measure conducive to individual and social freedom.

Resolved, That the Liberty Party is not a sectional party, but a national party; was not originated in a desire to accomplish a single object, but in a comprehensive regard to the great interest of the whole country; is not a new party nor a third party, but is the party of 1776, reviving the principles of that memorable era, and striving to carry them into practical application.

Resolved, That it was understood in the times of the Declaration and the Constitution that the existence of slavery in some of the States was in derogation of the principles of American liberty, and a deep stain upon the character of the country and the implied faith of the States; and the nation was pledged that slavery should never be extended beyond its then existing limits, but should be gradually, and yet at no distant day wholly, abolished by state authority.

Resolved, That the faith of the States and the nation thus pledged was most nobly redeemed by the voluntary abolition of slavery in several of the States, and by the adoption of the Ordinance of 1787 for the government of the territory northwest of the River Ohio, then the only territory in the United States, and consequently the only territory subject in this respect to the control of Congress, by which ordinance slavery was forever excluded from the vast regions which now compose the States of Ohio, Indiana, Illinois, Michigan, and the Territory of Wisconsin, and an incapacity to bear up any other than free men was impressed on the soil itself.

Resolved, That the faith of the States and nation thus pledged has been shamefully violated by the omission on the part of many of the States to take any measures whatever for the abolition of slavery within their respective limits; by the continuance of slavery in the District of Columbia, and in the Territories of Louisiana and Florida; by the legislation of Congress; by the protection afforded by national legislation and negotiation to slaveholding in American vessels, on the high seas, employed in the coastwise slave traffic; and by the extension of slavery far beyond its original limits by acts of Congress admitting new slave States into the Union.

Resolved, That the fundamental truth of the Declaration of Independence, that all men are endowed by their Creator with certain unalienable rights, among which are life, liberty, and the pursuit of happiness, was made the fundamental law of our national government by that amendment of the Constitution which declares that no person shall be deprived of life, liberty, or property without due process of law.

Resolved, That we recognize as sound the doctrine maintained by slaveholding jurists, that slavery is against natural rights and strictly local, and that its existence and continuance rest on no other support than state legislation, and not on any authority of Congress.

Resolved, That the general government has, under the Constitution, no power to establish or continue slavery anywhere, and therefore that all treaties and acts of Congress establishing, continuing, or favoring slavery in the District of Columbia, in the Territory of Florida, or on the high seas, are unconstitutional, and all attempts to hold men as property within the limits of exclusive national jurisdiction ought to be prohibited by law.

Resolved, That the provision of the Constitution of the United States, which confers extraordinary political powers on the owners of slaves, and thereby constituting the two hundred and fifty thousand slaveholders in the slave States a privileged aristocracy; and the provision for the reclamation of fugitive slaves from service, are anti-republican in their character, dangerous to the liberties of the people, and ought to be abrogated.

Resolved, That the practical operation of the second of these provisions is seen in the enactment of the act of Congress respecting persons escaping from their masters, which act, if the construction given to it by the Supreme Court of the United States in the case of Prigg *v.* Pennsylvania be correct, nullifies the *habeas corpus* acts of all the States, takes away the whole legal security of personal freedom, and ought therefore to be immediately repealed.

Resolved, That the peculiar patronage and support hitherto extended to slavery and slaveholding by the general government ought to be immediately withdrawn, and the example and influence of national authority ought to be arrayed on the side of liberty and free labor.

Resolved, That the practice of the general government, which prevails in the slave States, of employing slaves upon the public works, instead of free laborers, and paying aristocratic masters, with a view to secure or reward political services, is utterly indefensible and ought to be abandoned.

Resolved, That the freedom of speech and of the press, and the right of petition and the right of trial by jury, are sacred and inviolable; and that all rules, regulations, and laws in derogation of either are oppressive, unconstitutional, and not to be endured by free people.

Resolved, That we regard voting, in an eminent degree, as a moral and religious duty, which, when exercised, should be by voting for those who will do all in their power for immediate emancipation.

Resolved, That this convention recommend to the friends of liberty in all those free States where any inequality of rights and privileges exists on account of color, to employ their utmost energies to remove all such remnants and effects of the slave system.

Whereas, The Constitution of these United States is a series of agreements, convenants, or contracts between the people of the United States, each with all and all with each; and

Whereas, It is a principle of universal morality that the moral laws of the Creator are paramount to all human laws; or, in the language of an Apostle, that "we ought to obey God rather than men;" and

Whereas, The principle of common law, that any contract, covenant, or agreement to do an act derogatory to natural rights is vitiated and annulled by its inherent immorality, has been recognized by one of the justices of the Supreme Court of the United States, who in a recent case expressly holds that any "contract that rests upon such a basis is void;" and

Whereas, The third clause of the second section of the fourth article of the Constitution of the United States, when construed as providing for the surrender of a fugitive slave, does "rest upon such a basis" in that it is a contract to rob a man of a natural right, namely, his natural right to his own liberty, and is, therefore, absolutely void; therefore

Resolved, That we hereby give it to be distinctly understood by this nation and the world that, as Abolitionists, considering that the strength of our cause lies in its righteousness, and our hope for it in our conformity to the laws of God and our respect for the rights of man, we owe it to the Sovereign Ruler of the universe, as a proof of our allegiance to him in all our civil relations and offices, whether as private citizens or as public functionaries sworn to support the Constitution of the United States, to regard and to treat the third clause of the fourth article of that instrument, whenever applied to the case of a fugitive slave, as utterly null and void, and consequently as forming no part of the Constitution of the United States, whenever we are called upon or sworn to support it.

Resolved, That the power given to Congress by the Constitution, to provide for calling out the militia to suppress insurrection, does not make it the duty of the government to maintain slavery by military force, much less does it make it the duty of the citizens to form a part of such military force. When freemen unsheathe the sword it should be to strike for liberty, not for despotism.

Resolved, That, to preserve the peace of the citizens and secure the blessings of freedom, the legislature of each of the free States ought to keep in force suitable statutes rendering it penal for any of its inhabitants to transport, or aid in transporting, from such State, any person sought to be thus transported merely because subject to the slave laws of any other State; this remnant of independence being accorded to the free States by the decision of the Supreme Court in the case of Prigg *v.* The State of Pennsylvania.

The Whigs, as has been said already, were enthusiastic and completely united in the support of Mr. Clay. No other candidate was mentioned or thought of in connection with the nomination. The convention was held in Baltimore on the 1st of May, 1844. Every State in the Union was represented by a full delegation. The whole business of the convention was completed in a single sitting. Andrew F. Hopkins, of Alabama, was the temporary chairman, and Ambrose Spencer, of New York, the permanent president. Henry Clay was nominated unanimously by resolution, with the utmost enthusiasm. Four ballots were taken for a candidate for Vice-President. On the first, Theodore Frelinghuysen of New Jersey had 101; John Davis of Massachusetts, 83; Millard Fillmore of New York, 53; and John Sergeant of Pennsylvania, 38. Mr. Frelinghuysen gained on every ballot, and on the fourth received 155, against 116 for Fillmore and Davis combined. After numerous speeches had been made, in which the candidates were most highly commended and the triumph of the party was confidently predicted, Mr. Reverdy Johnson of Maryland moved the following series of resolutions, which were adopted : —

Resolved, That, in presenting to the country the names of Henry Clay for President, and of Theodore Frelinghuysen for Vice-President of the United States, this convention is actuated by the conviction that all the great principles of the Whig party — principles inseparable from the public honor and prosperity — will be maintained and advanced by these candidates.

Resolved, That these principles may be summed as comprising : A well-regulated currency; a tariff for revenue to defray the necessary expenses of the government, and discriminating with special reference to the protection of the domestic labor of the country; the distribution of the proceeds from the sales of the public lands; a single term for the presidency; a reform of executive usurpations; and generally such an administration of the affairs of the country as shall impart to every branch of the public service the greatest practical efficiency, controlled by a well-regulated and wise economy.

Resolved, That the name of Henry Clay needs no eulogy. The history of the country since his first appearance in public life is his history. Its brightest pages of prosperity and success are identified with the principles which he has upheld, as its darkest and more disastrous pages are with every material departure in our public policy from those principles.

Resolved, That in Theodore Frelinghuysen we present a man pledged alike by his Revolutionary ancestry and his own public course to every measure calculated to sustain the honor and interest of the country. Inheriting the principles as well as the name of a father who, with Washington on the fields of Trenton and of Monmouth, perilled life in the contest for liberty, and afterwards, as a senator of the United States, acted with Washington in establishing and perpetuating that liberty, Theodore Frelinghuysen, by his course as attorney-general of the State of New Jersey for twelve years, and subsequently as a senator of the United States for several years, was always strenuous on the side of law, order, and the Constitution; while, as a private man, his head, his hand, and his heart have been given without stint to the cause of morals, education, philanthropy, and religion.

The second only of these resolutions is printed in the political text-books, and always with a faulty punctuation, — the omission of a colon after the first phrase, — which makes nonsense of the whole resolution. The first resolution of the series is essential even to an understanding of the second, which stated the principles of the Whig party.

Although Mr. Tyler had not been mentioned as a candidate in the Democratic Convention, he had friends, — chiefly officeholders, it was said, by both Whigs and Democrats, — who held a convention, also in Baltimore, on the same day that the Democrats met there. It was a mass convention, rather than one of elected delegates. Mr. Tyler was unanimously nominated for the presidency, and accepted the nomination; but the movement fell dead, and Mr. Tyler withdrew his candidacy in a long, argumentative, and somewhat bitter letter, dated on the 20th of August.

The Democrats recovered themselves quickly from the surprise to which their convention had treated them. Van Buren's wrongs were soon forgotten. Immediately after his overthrow, Horace Greeley wrote in the New York "Tribune:" " We can with difficulty realize that this active, skilful, indomitable man, accustomed to organize victories out of the ruins of defeats which to another would seem annihilating, is to be henceforth a reminiscence. Verily, what shadows we are, what shadows we pursue!" The Democrats wasted no time even in reminiscence. The canvass began immediately, and it was to some extent a repetition of the campaign of 1840, with the difference that this time there were shouting and enthusiasm on both sides. Mr. Clay was undoubtedly the most popular man in the United States; but personal popularity did not decide the issue. The Democrats were much in earnest, both about the election and about Texas. Mr. Polk was a comparatively unknown man, although he had served as Speaker of the House of Representatives. He therefore excited no antagonisms. He was particularly acceptable to the South; and the Northern Democrats had nothing against him. It was believed and asserted that the movement in his favor in the convention had not been so spontaneous as its managers wished people to suppose, but that the matter had been carefully canvassed beforehand, and that the plan, as carried out, was laid some time before at Nashville. While, therefore, the Whigs made an enthusiastic canvass, there were not wanting signs that a majority of the people were still Democratic, and that the reverse of 1840 was merely a brief and half-thoughtless revulsion against certain abuses which had crept in, which the people did not like at the time, but to which they have since reconciled themselves most bravely. The early elections gave indications here and there of a slight Whig gain from the result in 1842, when the Democrats had been again successful in carrying a majority of Congress; but these gains were partially offset by Democratic successes, and were nowhere great enough to give the Whigs good ground for hope of a victory in November. Yet they continued to hope and to fight to the last.

The number of States voting was twenty-six, as before; but owing to the new apportionment, by which the number of representatives was cut down from 242 to 223, the number of electors was reduced to 275. The popular and the electoral votes are included in the same table, inasmuch as all the electors voted for both candidates of their respective parties: —

STATES.	POPULAR VOTE.			ELECTORS.	
	James K. Polk, Tenn.	Henry Clay, Ky.	James G. Birney, N. Y.	Polk and Dallas.	Clay and Frelinghuysen.
Maine	45,719	34,378	4,836	9	–
New Hampshire . .	27,160	17,866	4,161	6	–
Vermont	18,041	26,770	3,954	–	6
Massachusetts . . .	52,846	67,418	10,860	–	12
Rhode Island . . .	4,867	7,322	107	–	4
Connecticut	29,841	32,832	1,943	–	6
New York	237,588	232,482	15,812	36	–
New Jersey	37,495	38,318	131	–	7
Pennsylvania	167,535	161,203	3,138	26	–
Delaware	5,996	6,278	–	–	3
Maryland	32,676	35,984	–	–	8
Virginia	49,570	43,677	–	17	–
North Carolina . . .	39,287	43,232	–	–	11
South Carolina * . .	–	–	–	9	–
Georgia	44,177	42,100	–	10	–
Alabama	37,740	26,084	–	9	–
Mississippi	25,126	19,206	–	6	–
Louisiana	13,782	13,083	–	6	–
Kentucky	51,988	61,255	–	–	12
Tennessee	59,917	60,030	–	–	13
Missouri	41,369	31,251	–	7	–
Arkansas	9,546	5,504	–	3	–
Ohio	149,117	155,057	8,050	–	23
Michigan	27,759	24,337	3,632	5	–
Indiana	70,181	67,867	2,106	12	–
Illinois	57,920	45,528	3,570	9	–
Totals	1,337,243	1,299,062	62,300	170	105

* Electors appointed by the legislature.

It was not the closest election ever known in the country, but it was extremely close. There were but four States in which the plurality of Polk reached ten thousand; one State only gave Clay so large a plurality as that. Three States gave less than a thousand plurality each. Although Mr. Polk had 65 majority of the electoral votes, a change of 7918 votes, carefully distributed in the States of New York, Pennsylvania,

Georgia, and Indiana, would have given Clay a majority of 103 electoral votes. These were not the only peculiar features of the election. The Abolitionists defeated Clay. The Whigs were wroth against the new political faction before the election. The New York "Tribune" brought forward evidence satisfactory to itself that Birney sought a Democratic nomination in New York, and tried to catch Democratic votes. In all probability there was no truth in the charge, but it was believed at the time. Had the Abolitionists voted for Clay he would have had a popular majority of 24,119; he would have received the electoral votes of New York, 36, and Michigan, 5; and he would have been elected by 146 electoral votes against 129 for Mr. Polk. No doubt the Abolitionists acted with entire consistency in refusing to vote for Henry Clay, and no doubt it is as impossible to tell what might have happened if Clay had been elected as it would be to guess what would have been the course of history if Van Buren had not written his Texas letter; but at all events the election of Clay would have postponed the annexation of Texas, and possibly it would have averted the Mexican war.

Another noteworthy incident of the election was what was known as the Plaquemines fraud. It will be noticed in the above table that the Polk majority in Louisiana is 699. The parish of Plaquemines, below New Orleans on the Mississippi, had voted in previous years, and was returned as voting in 1844, as follows: —

	Democrat.	Whig.
Election of 1840	250	40
Election of 1842	179	93
Election of 1843	310	36
Election of 1844	1,007	37

The Democratic vote was larger by 697 than ever before, — almost exactly the whole Democratic majority in the State. The vote was also suspicious in this, that the Democratic vote returned was greater in number than the entire white male population, of all ages, in the parish in 1840. The explanation that was given by the Whigs was that the steamboat Agnes went down from New Orleans with a load of passengers under the charge of a political magnate of Plaquemines, and that these passengers stopped at three different places and cast each time a unanimous vote for Polk and Dallas. The steamboat Planter took down one hundred and forty others, who also voted early and often for the same ticket. These assertions were not only made, but sworn to, by many witnesses, including some persons, one of them a minor, who voted several times each, under the direction of the learned judge who managed the affair. The story bears all the marks of truth. If it is not true, it is at least singular that it was ten years after 1844 before Plaquemines parish could muster half as many Democratic votes as it gave that year to Polk.

Though the Whig newspapers rang with the charges of fraud, and though the accusation was supported by strong testimony, nothing was done about it. The election was lost, and a rectification of the fraud would not have changed the result. The Whigs submitted quietly; and when the electoral count took place in 1845, in the usual manner, no objection whatever was made, and Polk and Dallas were in due form declared elected.

The inauguration took place in the form which had now become usual. The President and the President-elect rode together, this time, in an open carriage; and a feature of the procession was a small band of Revolutionary veterans on foot. Inasmuch as this ceremony took place sixty-two years after the treaty of peace, the political enthusiasm of these aged men was as remarkable as was the inhumanity of the managers who suffered them to take such a part in the display of the day.

XVIII

THE "FREE SOIL" CAMPAIGN OF 1848

THE slavery question, which had been growing in importance fitfully, as a political issue, since the contest and compromise on the admission of Missouri in 1820, dominated the politics of the country in the election of 1844, and thereafter until it was decided by secession, war, and emancipation. Not that parties, statesmen, and politicians ranged themselves as advocates or opponents either of slavery as an existing institution or of the extension of slavery, until the critical moment of the struggle was near at hand. But every great measure, beginning with the annexation of Texas, was considered and decided with chief reference to the extension, the maintenance, the restriction, or the overthrow of the "peculiar institution" of the South. The opponents of slavery became bolder and more aggressive; its defenders more vigilant, more resentful of attacks upon it, more rigid in their ostracism of public men at the North who did not accept their principles, more resolute, in the event of a denial of their "rights," in their purpose to seek those rights by a separation from the Union. As the feeling grew more intense, and the language of extreme partisans increased in violence, well-meaning men tried to prolong the peace by compromises and by endeavors to turn the current of political thought to other subjects. How vain it was to attempt to reconcile irreconcilable things, to repress the "irrepressible conflict," the history of the next few years shows most plainly.

The South was better prepared for the conflict when it became acute than was the North. It was more united. It had control of one of the parties; it terrorized the other. It knew what it desired, and was ready to make demands and to insist upon them, no matter what might be the consequences. Thus it won the first victory of the great campaign, in the annexation of Texas, and followed it up during the next administration by the war with Mexico and the acquisition of more territory available, as was supposed, for the spread of the slavery system. Soon after the shocking accident on the "Princeton," on February 28, 1844, in which the Secretary of State, Mr. Upshur, and the Secretary of the Navy, Mr. Gilmer, lost their lives, Mr. Calhoun was made Secretary of State. Henry A. Wise asserts, in his "Seven Decades of the Union," that he offered the position to Mr. Calhoun without authority from the President, who nevertheless acquiesced in the selection so irregularly made of the most important member of his cabinet. Mr. Calhoun negotiated a treaty for the annexation of Texas, and was believed to be the active agent in defeating the nomination of Van Buren, who opposed the measure. The Senate rejected the treaty, 16 senators only favoring and 35 opposing it. Subsequently joint resolutions were offered, and passed by the House of Representatives, providing for the annexation. The resolutions would surely have failed in the Senate but for the addition of an amendment giving the President discretionary power to bring in Texas under a new treaty to be submitted to the Senate. Even this could not secure the bare majority required until Mr. Polk, the President-elect, was known to have pledged himself to act, not under the House resolutions, but under the Senate amendment. Mr. Tyler affixed his signature to the resolutions on March 1, 1845. The same night he dispatched a special messenger to Texas to consummate the annexation. Mr. Polk, inaugurated three days afterward, refused to recall the messenger. The opponents of annexation regarded the proceeding as a case of remarkably sharp practice.

Mr. Polk was not a great man. His Democratic supporters, and particularly the Southern men who controlled the party, had no cause of complaint either of unwillingness on his part to take the radical views they entertained on questions between the South and the North, or of lack of courage in acting upon those views. The Mexican war, which every one knew to be an inevitable consequence of the intrigue to annex Texas, was entered upon without hesitation. The Independent Treasury, — Van Buren's pet measure, — which had been overthrown by the Whigs, was reëstablished. The Secretary of the Treasury, Mr. Robert J. Walker, was given a free hand in drafting a tariff bill, and Congress passed it, — the famous tariff of 1846, framed in the most strict conformity to the wishes of the Southern Democrats. In the platform of the party the title of the United States to "the whole of the territory of Oregon" was asserted to be "clear and unquestionable;" and the "reoccupation" of Oregon was linked with the "reannexation" of Texas, as "great American measures." The whole of Oregon, as spoken of in those times, meant the territory lying north of Dakota, Montana, Idaho, and Washington, to the line of 54° 40' north latitude. "Fifty-four forty, or fight," was a Democratic rallying cry in the North, as the acquisition of Texas was in the South. After the election there was no enthusiasm on the Oregon question; an agreement was made, without a murmur of Democratic dissatisfaction, upon the line of 49°.

On every one of the three questions the Whigs were decidedly against the administration. They deprecated the Mexican war; they opposed the sub-treasury and the *ad valorem* low tariff of 1846; they jeered at the government for the meekness shown in accepting the northern boundary line offered by Great Britain. Yet slavery was to decide the canvass of 1848, not as a direct issue between the two great parties, but by dividing one of them and so giving the victory to the other. The opportunity of the anti-slavery men came to them from a peculiar situation developed in the politics of the State of New York. It would be almost true to say that there has never been a time when the Democrats of New York have not been divided into at least two factions. They have exhibited a remarkable power of getting together on election day, but at all other times they have been at war with each other. Some of their dissensions have already been mentioned. In the early days of the republic the contests were largely personal struggles between rival leaders, — Burr, the Clintons, and the Livingstons. During the second administration of Jackson a large faction was formed, professing extremely radical views, which called itself the Equal Rights party, but was termed by its adversaries the Loco-foco party. The name originated in an incident that occurred in New York city just before the election in 1835.[1] It was the custom to submit nominations to a general meeting of Democratic citizens. The Equal Rights men, determined to oppose the Tammany nominations, appeared in large numbers at the meeting called in Tammany Hall. A scene of great confusion

[1] Some authorities give the date erroneously as 1834. See *History of the Loco-foco Party*, by F. Byrdsall, chap. i.

between the two factions ensued.   At last the Tammany men withdrew, and as they left the hall extinguished the gaslights. The radicals, anticipating this, had provided themselves with candles and the then new "loco-foco" matches, by means of which the hall was relighted and the meeting proceeded.   Some years later the Whigs called all Democrats "Loco-focos."

The division of the party continued, with some changes in the causes of dissension, as well as changes in their designations.   During Polk's administration they were known as "Hunkers" and "Barnburners," — Hunkers, because they "hunkered" for office; Barnburners, because they were so much in earnest for the reforms they advocated that, as one of their orators put it, they were willing to imitate the Dutchman who burned his barn in order to destroy the rats which infested it.

It was narrated in the last chapter that Silas Wright refused to profit by the intrigue that defeated his friend Van Buren's nomination for the presidency.   Nevertheless, as a good party man, he did all in his power to help the Polk and Dallas ticket, and at the solicitation of the Democrats accepted reluctantly a nomination as governor of New York. He was elected by about twice the majority given to Mr. Polk. Whether intentionally or not, every step of the administration was hostile to the faction represented by Governor Wright and Mr. Van Buren, and in favor of the Hunkers.   Governor Marcy, a leader of the Hunkers, was Secretary of War; all the federal office-holders appointed were of the same faction. Silas Wright was regarded as one of the most promising candidates for the nomination in 1848; and if it had been the intention of the administration to prevent his success, it could not have employed more effectual measures than it did.   When he was again a candidate for governor in 1846, he was defeated.   His friends all believed that his defeat was the act of the President and his friends, although at the last moment a great show was made of anxiety for his election.   Indeed, a circular was sent to all office-holders in New York forbidding them, under penalty of dismissal, to vote against Governor Wright.

This long explanation of the situation in New York has been necessary because the Democratic division in that State lost the election of 1848.   It not only deprived the Democrats of electoral votes which would have changed the result, but it gave to the anti-slavery wing of the party in other States an opportunity to rally for their cause. Mr. Wright died suddenly in August, 1847; but his death, instead of bringing the serious party dissension to a close, aggravated it. As the war with Mexico drew to a close, the contest, minus its personal elements, extended into other States. David Wilmot, a Democratic member of the House of Representatives from Pennsylvania, proposed, as an amendment to a bill placing three million dollars at the disposal of the President for the negotiation of a treaty extending the territory of the United States, a proviso that slavery should not exist in any territory so acquired. The "Wilmot Proviso" played a great part in the debates of Congress, in the general struggle over the slavery question, and especially in the ensuing election of 1848.

Meanwhile all was not union and harmony in the Whig ranks. Henry Clay was still the most popular man in the party; but there was gradually springing up a feeling that, after his repeated defeats, and in the face of the uncompromising objections to him in anti-slavery quarters in the North, he could not be elected. Moreover there were those who thought that he should not have a permanent mortgage on the Whig party. Mr. Webster had strong friends and supporters to urge his pretensions. Judge McLean, General Scott, Mr. Clayton, of Delaware, and Thomas Corwin, of Ohio, were also put forward. But the movement in favor of General Taylor was of a character to disarrange all the calculations of the politicians. The campaign in his favor opened on February 22, 1848, when a state convention of Louisiana, consisting of delegates from thirty-six parishes (counties), elected in primary meetings "without regard to party distinction," brought forward General Taylor, and "decreed" in the name of their constituents that they nominated him as a candidate for President. Shortly afterward a mass meeting in Alabama, and the Whig members of the legislature of that State, nominated General Taylor, and recommended that the Whigs of Alabama should not send delegates to the national convention. A non-partisan mass meeting in Taylor's interest was also held in Baltimore. These movements created a serious situation. Apparently the nomination was to be taken out of the hands of the party. Taylor's supporters threatened to run him as a candidate whatever the Whig convention might do. It became important to know how far General Taylor lent himself to this feature of the canvass in his favor.   Letters were addressed to him to ascertain his purpose.   Two of his replies were made public.   In the first (April 20) he said that if nominated by the Whigs he "should not refuse acceptance," provided he were left free of all pledges, and permitted to maintain his independence of parties; that he did not design to withdraw his name if Mr. Clay should be nominated, nor in fact, "whoever may be the Whig or the Democratic candidate;" and — denying certain charges made against him — that he never said he was in favor of the tariff of 1846, or of the sub-treasury; nor had he asserted that he originated the war with Mexico, or that, if elected, he should select his cabinet from both parties.   In the second letter (April 22) he said that he was "a Whig, but not an ultra Whig;" and "on the subjects of the tariff, the currency, and the improvement of our great highways, the will of the people as expressed by their representatives in Congress ought to be respected and carried out by the executive."

All this was highly unsatisfactory to many of the Whigs. They had principles, — they had not all the same principles, to be sure, — and General Taylor apparently had none.   His election would mean nothing.   They could not be sure that their President would favor one of their measures.   But, on the other hand, the election of Mr. Clay would not mean much.   He was identified with contests over questions that had been decided.   Where would he stand when the new questions came to the front?   Texas had been annexed; the sub-treasury was reëstablished; the tariff of 1846, though soon to develop defects, was working well; the Oregon question was settled; and on the new issue then becoming prominent, Mr. Clay could not be acceptable to the "conscience Whigs."   All these considerations, and others which have not been mentioned, each in its own way, worked in favor of the Taylor movement; and his nomination was assured, although not conceded, before the Whig convention met.

The first convention preliminary to the canvass of 1848 was that of the Native Americans, — a party which had some strength in the Middle States, and which for some years past had even elected a few representatives in Congress from New York and Pennsylvania.   The convention met in Philadelphia in September, 1847, and nominated General Henry A. S. Dearborn, of Massachusetts, for Vice-President.

It recommended, but did not formally nominate, General Zachary Taylor for President.

In November of the same year the Liberty, or Abolition, party met at New York, and nominated for President John P. Hale, of New Hampshire, and for Vice-President Leicester King, of Ohio. After the Barnburners' convention, hereafter to be noticed, Mr. Hale withdrew from the canvass. It was given out at the time that Mr. Van Buren was a good enough Abolitionist for this party, though he " could not be regarded as a perfect embodiment of their principles." The " Liberty League," another Abolition body, held a convention at Rochester, N. Y., on the 2d of June, 1848, and nominated Gerritt Smith, of New York, for President, and the Rev. Charles E. Foote, of Michigan, for Vice-President. An " Industrial Congress " met at Philadelphia, June 13, 1848, and nominated Gerritt Smith for the first place, and William S. Waitt, of Illinois, for the second place on the ticket. So far as is known, no votes were cast for any of these minor candidates in any State.

The Democratic convention met at Baltimore on May 22, 1848. Judge J. S. Bryce, of Louisiana, was the temporary chairman, and Andrew Stevenson, of Virginia, the permanent president. All the States were represented, most of them fully, some by double or triple delegations. South Carolina had but one delegate, who was chosen at a little local gathering, numbering only eight or ten persons. There was not a little discussion whether or not he should be permitted to cast the nine votes of South Carolina ; he was finally allowed to do so, by a formal vote of the convention. Before the session closed, a resolution was adopted, 208 to 41, that in future conventions each State should be entitled to as many delegates only as the number of its electoral votes. This convention also directed the appointment of a central committee of one member from each State to take general charge of the canvass and of the party's interests. This was the first national committee ever organized.

The great question, which dominated all others, which raised before the convention the spectre of defeat, was that of the New York delegation. There had been two state conventions, and two full sets of delegates; thirty-six " Hunkers " and thirty-six " Barnburners " presented themselves, and each delegation demanded not only recognition as representing the

New York Democrats, but the absolute exclusion of the other faction.

The wrangling began as soon as the opening prayer had been offered, — over the constitution of the committee on credentials. Nothing was done on the first day beyond settling the membership of the convention, save as to the New York delegations and effecting a permanent organization. On the morning of the second day the two-thirds rule was adopted, after long debate, by 175 votes against 78. From that time until the evening of the 24th of May the convention devoted itself wholly to New York. On a resolution to admit the " Hunker " delegation, an amendment was offered to admit both delegations, the two combined to have only the vote to which New York was entitled. This was carried by two majority, — 126 to 124. Of the affirmative votes, 99 came from Northern States, and the other 27 from Maryland, Delaware, Kentucky, Tennessee, Missouri, and Texas. The North gave only 33 negative votes. Although this was, so far as it was a victory for either side, a triumph for the " Barnburners," they refused to take part in the proceedings, as did also the " Hunkers." The " Barnburners " openly withdrew from the convention.

As soon as the New York question was decided, balloting for a candidate for President began. Four trials were necessary, the result of which was as follows : —

	1st.	2d.	3d.	4th.
Whole number of votes . .	251	252	254	253
Necessary for a choice . . .	168	168	160	160
Lewis Cass, Mich.	125	133	156	179
James Buchanan, Penn. . .	55	54	40	33
Levi Woodbury, N. H. . . .	53	56	53	38
George M. Dallas, Penn. . .	3	3	–	–
W. J. Worth, Tenn.	6	6	5	1
John C. Calhoun, S. C. . . .	9	–	–	–
W. O. Butler, Ky.	–	–	–	3

It will be noticed that Mr. Polk received no votes. Like other Presidents, he had declared before his election his purpose not to be a candidate for a second term ; but, unlike some others, he had found, after a little manœuvring for a nomination, that the case was hopeless, and had therefore reiterated his original intention.

The vote for General Cass was at first almost exclusively from Western and Southern States, but there was little significance in this fact. All the candidates were against the Wilmot Proviso, — they were all classed as "Northern men with Southern principles," — and the preferences of delegates were personal rather than political. The nomination was made unanimous with enthusiasm. In the evening the convention proceeded to vote for a candidate for Vice-President. On the first trial, General William O. Butler of Kentucky had 114; General John A. Quitman of Mississippi had 74; John Y. Mason of Virginia, 24; William R. King of Alabama, 25; James J. McKay of North Carolina, 13; Jefferson Davis of Mississippi, 1. As 169 were necessary for a choice, the convention proceeded to vote a second time. General William O. Butler was nominated, receiving 169 votes to 62 for Quitman and 22 for all others. This nomination was also made unanimous.

On the fifth and last day of the convention, the platform was reported. The resolutions were, for the most part, a repetition of those of 1844. The first was modified to read as follows : —

Resolved, That the American Democracy place their trust in the intelligence, the patriotism, and the discriminating justice of the American people.

Then followed the resolutions adopted in 1840 and 1844, as arranged in the platform of 1844, except that to the fifth resolution (see p. 200) are appended the words: "And for the gradual but certain extinction of the debt created by the prosecution of a just and necessary war, after peaceful relations shall have been restored." The convention added to an already ample platform the following new resolutions : —

Resolved, That the war with Mexico, provoked on her part by years of insult and injury, was commenced by her army crossing the Rio Grande, attacking the American troops, and invading our sister State of Texas ; and that, upon all the principles of patriotism and the laws of nations, it is a just and necessary war upon our part, in which every American citizen should have shown himself on the side of his country, and neither morally nor physically, by word or deed, have given aid and comfort to the enemy.

Resolved, That we should be rejoiced at the assurance of a peace with Mexico founded on the just principles of indemnity for the past and security for the future ; but that, while the ratification of the liberal treaty offered to Mexico remains in doubt, it is the duty of the country to sustain the administration in every measure necessary to provide for the vigorous prosecution of the war should that treaty be rejected.

Resolved, That the officers and soldiers who have carried the arms of their country into Mexico have crowned it with imperishable glory. Their unconquerable courage, their daring enterprise, their unfaltering perseverance and fortitude when assailed on all sides by innumerable foes, — and that more formidable enemy, the diseases of the climate, — exalt their devoted patriotism into the highest heroism, and give them a right to the profound gratitude of their country and the admiration of the world.

Resolved, That the Democratic National Convention of thirty States, composing the American Republic, tender their fraternal congratulations to the National Convention of the Republic of France, now assembled as the free suffrage representatives of the sovereignty of thirty-five millions of republicans, to establish governments on those eternal principles of equal rights for which their Lafayette and our Washington fought side by side in their struggle for our national independence ; and we would especially convey to them and to the whole people of France our earnest wishes for the consolidation of their liberties, through the wisdom that shall guide their counsels, on the basis of a democratic constitution, not derived from the grants or concessions of kings or dynasties, but originating from the only true source of political power recognized in the States of this Union, — the inherent and inalienable rights of the people, in their sovereign capacity, to make and to amend their forms of government in such a manner as the welfare of the community may require.

Resolved, That with the recent development of this grand political truth, — of the sovereignty of the people and their capacity and power for self-government, which is prostrating thrones and erecting republics on the ruins of despotism in the Old World, — we feel that a high and sacred duty is devolved, with increased responsibility, upon the Democratic party of this country, as the party of the people, to sustain and advance among us constitutional liberty, equality, and fraternity, by continuing to resist all monopolies and exclusive legislation for the benefit of the few at the expense of the many, and by a vigilant and constant adherence to those principles and compromises of the Constitution which are broad enough and strong enough to embrace and uphold the Union as it was, the Union as it is, and the Union as it shall be, in the full expansion of the energies and capacity of this great and progressive people.

Resolved, That a copy of these resolutions be forwarded, through the American minister at Paris, to the National Convention of the Republic of France.

Resolved, That the fruits of the great political triumph of 1844, which elected James K. Polk and George M. Dallas President and Vice-President of the United States, have fulfilled the hopes of the Democracy of the Union in defeating the declared purposes of their opponents to create a national bank; in preventing the corrupt and unconstitutional distribution of the land proceeds, from the common treasury of the Union, for local purposes; in protecting the currency and labor of the country from ruinous fluctuations, and guarding the money of the people for the use of the people; by the establishment of the constitutional treasury; in the noble impulse given to the cause of free trade by the repeal of the tariff of 1842, and the creation of the more equal, honest, and productive tariff of 1846; and that, in our opinion, it would be a fatal error to weaken the hands of a political organization by which these great reforms have been achieved, and risk them in the hands of their known adversaries, with whatever delusive appeals they may solicit our surrender of that vigilance which is the only safeguard of liberty.

Resolved, That the confidence of the Democracy of the Union in the principles, capacity, firmness, and integrity of James K. Polk, manifested by his nomination and election in 1844, has been signally justified by the strictness of his adherence to sound Democratic doctrines, by the purity of purpose, the energy and ability, which have characterized his administration in all our affairs at home and abroad; that we tender to him our cordial congratulations upon the brilliant success which has hitherto crowned his patriotic efforts, and assure him in advance that, at the expiration of his presidential term, he will carry with him to his retirement the esteem, respect, and admiration of a grateful country.

Resolved, That this convention hereby present to the people of the United States Lewis Cass, of Michigan, as the candidate of the Democratic party for the office of President, and William O. Butler, of Kentucky, as the candidate of the Democratic party for Vice-President of the United States.

Mr. Yancey, of Alabama, offered the following resolution as an addition to the platform: —

Resolved, That the doctrine of non-interference with the rights of property of any portion of the people of this confederacy, be it in the States or Territories thereof, by any other than the parties interested in them, is the true republican doctrine recognized by this body.

The resolution was rejected by a vote of yeas, 36; nays,

216.   All the affirmative votes were given by delegates from the slave States.   It is an illustration of the temporizing character of the politics of the time that some of the Southern Democrats explained their vote against the resolution by saying that they deemed it unnecessary, because the same doctrine was otherwise expressed in the platform.   This explanation would do for Southern consumption; meanwhile it was hoped that the Northern members of the party could be held to their allegiance by having it pointed out to them that the extremists were defeated in their purpose to commit the party to the Southern view of "the rights of property."

The Whig national convention met at Philadelphia on the 7th of June.   John A. Collier, of New York, was the temporary chairman, and ex-Governor John M. Morehead, of North Carolina, was the permanent president.   All the States were represented fully, save two.   South Carolina had a partial delegation; Texas sent no delegates, but its state convention authorized the delegates from Louisiana to cast the vote of Texas.   Inasmuch as the Louisiana delegation was strongly in favor of Taylor, the question whether the proxy-voting should be permitted was made a test of the strength of the general; but when it came to the vote, the request of Texas was granted without a division.   The convention reached the point of voting for candidates on the evening of the second day.   Four ballots were taken on that and the following day, when General Taylor was nominated.   Before the voting began, a letter was read from Taylor, in which he said that his friends would withdraw his name if the choice of the convention should fall upon some one else.   The result of the four votes was as follows: —

	1st.	2d.	3d.	4th.
Whole number of votes . . .	279	278	279	280
Necessary for a choice . . .	140	140	140	141
Zachary Taylor, Louisiana . . .	111	118	133	171
Henry Clay, Kentucky	97	85	74	32
Winfield Scott, New Jersey . .	43	49	54	63
Daniel Webster, Massachusetts .	22	22	17	14
John McLean, Ohio	2	–	–	–
John M. Clayton, Delaware . .	4	4	1	–

The vote for General Taylor on the first ballot came from all parts of the country.   There were only eight of the thirty

States then in the Union from which he received no votes. The New England States, except Maine, supported either Mr. Webster or Mr. Clay, and gave Taylor but six votes. Maine had a grievance against Mr. Webster in that he had negotiated the Ashburton Treaty, by which the northeastern boundary question was settled, involving the loss of a large slice of territory to which Maine had asserted a claim, and had defended it in what is still known as the "Aroostook War." The speech nominating General Taylor was made by ex-Governor Edward Kent, of Maine. On the final vote Taylor had at least one vote from every State. The convention, after giving itself up for a time to enthusiasm, proceeded to vote for a candidate for Vice-President. A large number of nominations was made. On the first ballot, Millard Fillmore, of New York, had 115; Abbott Lawrence, of Massachusetts, 109; and 51 votes were divided among ten other candidates. On the second vote Fillmore had 173; Lawrence, 87; and all others, 6. Mr. Fillmore's nomination was then declared, and, after a season of speech-making, the convention adjourned. No committee on resolutions was appointed, and the convention made no declaration of principles whatever. Its attitude of non-committalism was by no means approved by a large section of the party; and it was late in the canvass, when some additional letters from General Taylor had been published, giving assurance that he really sympathized — mildly, at least — with the purposes of the party, before some of the prominent Whig leaders came cordially to his support. Daniel Webster, indeed, had promptly pronounced the nomination one "not fit to be made."

The "Barnburners," who had withdrawn from the Baltimore convention with a frank avowal of their purpose not to accept the nomination of General Cass, took active measures to oppose his candidacy. They held a state convention at Utica on June 22 and 23, in which delegates from Massachusetts, Connecticut, Ohio, and Wisconsin participated, and nominated Martin Van Buren for President, and Henry Dodge, of Wisconsin, for Vice-President. Mr. Van Buren accepted the nomination, although with evident reluctance. Senator Dodge declined, and supported General Cass. Also on June 22 an Ohio state convention of persons dissatisfied with both the nominations recommended and called a national convention, which was held at Buffalo, August 9. Charles Francis Adams, of Massachusetts, was made permanent president of the convention, which contained representatives of seventeen States, and seems to have had a membership of about 300. On a ballot for a candidate for President, Martin Van Buren had 159 votes, and John P. Hale, of New Hampshire, 129. Charles Francis Adams, of Massachusetts, was nominated by acclamation for Vice-President. The convention adopted the following resolutions : —

Whereas, We have assembled in convention, as a union of free-men for the sake of freedom, forgetting all past political differences, in common resolve to maintain the rights of free labor against the aggressions of the slave power, and to secure free soil for a free people; and

Whereas, The political conventions recently assembled at Baltimore and Philadelphia, the one stifling the voice of a great constituency entitled to be heard in its deliberations, and the other abandoning its distinctive principles for mere availability, have dissolved the national party organizations heretofore existing, by nominating for the chief magistracy of the United States, under the slaveholding dictation, candidates neither of whom can be supported by the opponents of slavery extension, without a sacrifice of consistency, duty, and self-respect; and

Whereas, These nominations so made furnish the occasion and demonstrate the necessity of the union of the people under the banner of free democracy, in a solemn and formal declaration of their independence of the slave power, and of their fixed determination to rescue the federal government from its control, —

Resolved, therefore, that we, the people here assembled, remembering the example of our fathers in the days of the first Declaration of Independence, putting our trust in God for the triumph of our cause, and invoking his guidance in our endeavors to advance it, do now plant ourselves upon the national platform of freedom, in opposition to the sectional platform of slavery.

Resolved, That slavery in the several States of this Union which recognize its existence depends upon state laws alone, which cannot be repealed or modified by the federal government, and for which laws that government is not responsible. We therefore propose no interference by Congress with slavery within the limits of any State.

Resolved, That the proviso of Jefferson, to prohibit the existence of slavery after 1800 in all the Territories of the United States, southern and northern; the votes of six States and sixteen delegates, in the Congress of 1784 for the proviso, to three States and seven delegates against it; the actual exclusion of slavery from the

Northwestern Territory by the Ordinance of 1787, unanimously adopted by the States in Congress; and the entire history of that period, — clearly show that it was the settled policy of the nation not to extend, nationalize, or encourage, but to limit, localize, and discourage slavery; and to this policy, which should never have been departed from, the government ought to return.

Resolved, That our fathers ordained the Constitution of the United States in order, among other great national objects, to establish justice, promote the general welfare, and secure the blessings of liberty, but expressly denied to the federal government, which they created, all constitutional power to deprive any person of life, liberty, or property without due legal process.

Resolved, That, in the judgment of this convention, Congress has no more power to make a slave than to make a king; no more power to institute or establish slavery than to institute or establish a monarchy. No such power can be found among those specifically conferred by the Constitution, or derived by any just implication from them.

Resolved, That it is the duty of the federal government to relieve itself from all responsibility for the existence or continuance of slavery wherever the government possesses constitutional authority to legislate on that subject, and is thus responsible for its existence.

Resolved, That the true and in the judgment of this convention the only safe means of preventing the extension of slavery into territory now free is to prohibit its existence in all such territory by an act of Congress.

Resolved, That we accept the issue which the slave power has forced upon us; and to their demand for more slave States and more slave territory our calm but final answer is, no more slave States and no more slave territory. Let the soil of our extensive domains be ever kept free for the hardy pioneers of our own land, and the oppressed and banished of other lands seeking homes of comfort and fields of enterprise in the New World.

Resolved, That the bill lately reported by the committee of eight in the Senate of the United States was no compromise, but an absolute surrender of the rights of the non-slaveholders of all the States; and while we rejoice to know that a measure which, while opening the door for the introduction of slavery into territories now free, would also have opened the door to litigation and strife among the future inhabitants thereof, to the ruin of their peace and prosperity, was defeated in the House of Representatives, its passage in hot haste, by a majority embracing several senators who voted in open violation of the known will of their constituents, should warn the people to see to it that their representatives be not suffered to betray them.   There must be no more compromises with slavery; if made, they must be repealed.

Resolved, That we demand freedom and established institutions for our brethren in Oregon, now exposed to hardships, peril, and massacre by the reckless hostility of the slave power to the establishment of free government for free territory, and not only for them, but for our new brethren in New Mexico and California.

And whereas, It is due not only to this occasion, but to the whole people of the United States, that we should declare ourselves on certain other questions of national policy; therefore

Resolved, That we demand cheap postage for the people; a retrenchment of the expenses and patronage of the federal government; the abolition of all unnecessary offices and salaries; and the election by the people of all civil officers in the service of the government, so far as the same may be practicable.

Resolved, That river and harbor improvements, whenever demanded by the safety and convenience of commerce with foreign nations or among the several States, are objects of national concern; and that it is the duty of Congress, in the exercise of its constitutional powers, to provide therefor.

Resolved, That the free grant to actual settlers, in consideration of the expenses they incur in making settlements in the wilderness, which are usually fully equal to their actual cost, and of the public benefits resulting therefrom, of reasonable portions of the public lands, under suitable limitations, is a wise and just measure of public policy which will promote, in various ways, the interests of all the States of this Union; and we therefore recommend it to the favorable consideration of the American people.

Resolved, That the obligations of honor and patriotism require the earliest practicable payment of the national debt; and we are, therefore, in favor of such a tariff of duties as will raise revenue adequate to defray the necessary expenses of the federal government, and to pay annual instalments of our debt, and the interest thereon.

Resolved, That we inscribe on our banner, " Free Soil, Free Speech, Free Labor, and Free Men," and under it will fight on, and fight ever, until a triumphant victory shall reward our exertions.

There was much in this platform which must have made Martin Van Buren wince when he read it.   No doubt his candidacy of a party professing such principles was grotesque. Speaking of the Free Soil campaign of 1848, William Allen Butler says : " Mr. Van Buren's name was in it, but not his head nor his heart.   Great words were inscribed on its banners :

' Free Soil, Free Speech, Free Labor, and Free Men.' But they were words of advance and not of strategy, and Mr. Van Buren was too deeply intrenched in his old political notions to utter them in earnest."

Nevertheless his vote in New York exceeded that for Cass, and the division which his candidacy caused defeated the Democratic candidate, as it was intended to do. The canvass was short. On the part of the Whigs it was spirited and confident, while on the Democratic side it was conducted with little hope of success. The early elections showed that the Whigs must carry the country. The number of States which took part in this election was thirty. Florida had been admitted as a State on March 3, 1845; Texas on December 29, 1845; Iowa on December 28, 1846; and Wisconsin on May 29, 1848. For the first time all the electors, except those from Massachusetts, were appointed on one day. This was in accordance with an act passed in 1845, which, by the way, was a party measure, and debated in Congress in an intensely partisan spirit. The act was as follows : —

Be it enacted, etc., That the electors of President and Vice-President shall be appointed in each State on the Tuesday next after the first Monday in the month of November of the year in which they are to be appointed :

Provided, That each State may by law provide for the filling of any vacancy or vacancies which may occur in its college of electors when such college meets to give its electoral vote :

And provided also, When any State shall have held an election for the purpose of choosing electors, and shall fail to make a choice on the day aforesaid, then the electors may be appointed on a subsequent day in such manner as the State may by law provide.

In all the States except New Hampshire and Massachusetts, a plurality was sufficient to effect a choice. New Hampshire gave a majority to Cass over both the others. In Massachusetts there was no choice, and the legislature met and chose the Taylor electors. The aggregate vote at this election was 2,871,906 against 2,698,605, — an increase of 173,301 over that of 1844. But of these additional votes 83,609 were cast in the four new States, so that the increase in the old States was but 89,692, or barely three per cent. in four years. This fact proves, not that slight interest was taken in the election, but that the result was foreseen, and that in many States less effort than usual to poll a full vote was put forth. The count of electoral votes proceeded in the usual manner, and was devoid of incident.

The popular and electoral votes in 1848 were as follows: —

STATES.	POPULAR VOTE.			ELECTORAL VOTE.	
	Zachary Taylor, Louisiana.	Lewis Cass, Michigan.	Martin Van Buren, New York.	Taylor and Fillmore.	Cass and Butler.
Alabama	30,482	31,363	–	–	9
Arkansas	7,588	9,300	–	–	3
Connecticut	30,314	27,046	5,005	6	–
Delaware	6,421	5,898	80	3	–
Florida	3,116	1,847	–	3	–
Georgia	47,544	44,802	-	10	–
Illinois	53,047	56,300	15,774	–	9
Indiana	69,907	74,745	8,100	–	12
Iowa	11,084	12,093	1,126	–	4
Kentucky	67,141	49,720	–	12	–
Louisiana	18,217	15,370	–	6	–
Maine	35,125	39,880	12,096	–	9
Maryland	37,702	34,528	125	8	–
Massachusetts . . .	61,070	35,281	38,058	12	–
Michigan	23,940	30,687	10,389	–	5
Mississippi	25,922	26,537	–	–	6
Missouri	32,671	40,077	–	–	7
New Hampshire . .	14,781	27,763	7,560	–	6
New Jersey	40,015	36,901	829	7	–
New York	218,603	114,318	120,510	36	–
North Carolina . . .	43,550	34,869	–	11	–
Ohio	138,360	154,775	35,354	–	23
Pennsylvania . . .	185,513	171,176	11,263	26	–
Rhode Island . . .	6,779	3,646	730	4	–
South Carolina * . .	–	–	–	–	9
Tennessee	64,705	58,419	–	13	–
Texas	4,509	10,668	–	–	4
Vermont	23,122	10,948	13,837	6	–
Virginia	45,124	46,586	9	–	17
Wisconsin	13,747	15,001	10,418	–	4
Total	1,360,099	1,220,544	291,263	163	127

* Electors appointed by the legislature.

XIX

THE DEMOCRATS REUNITED

To a large number of Whigs, the result of their second victory was almost as disappointing as was the administration of Mr. Tyler. Throughout the North the Whig party was anti-slavery, — not abolitionist, not even unanimously against slavery extension, but almost everywhere controlled by the anti-slavery sentiment. General Taylor was a Virginian by birth, and a slaveholder. The Southern Whigs supported him willingly ; the Northern contingent of the party gave him its vote with misgivings, and with the expectation that he would do nothing to resist "the aggressions of slavery." Fillmore, on the other hand, had a consistent record as an Anti-Slavery man, and was expected to be firm and unyielding, should the circumstances which did occur place him in the position of responsibility. Taylor lived long enough to make it evident that slavery as a political force could not rely upon him to assist it in its struggle with Northern sentiment ; Fillmore, on his accession, became an active agent in promoting the "compromise" measures which the Anti-Slavery men abhorred.

To say that the slavery question dominated the politics of the country, from the inauguration of Taylor until the outbreak of the Civil War, is to put the case mildly. It substantially excluded all other topics from consideration. The sketch of the leading events of the time which can be given in this place is necessarily of the most meagre and barren character. Much that excited a powerful influence upon the general history of the country must be omitted altogether, and those events only can be selected which had a certain direct bearing upon our main topic, the presidency. By far the best account hitherto written of the political events from the election of Harrison until secession is to be found in Rhodes's History.

The first session of the Thirty-first Congress was a memorable one. It witnessed the last appearance in the senatorial arena of the three intellectual giants, — Clay, Calhoun, and Webster. They had entered Congress almost together, two in 1811, and the other in 1813 ; each had been Secretary of State, one had been Vice-President ; all had had most promising aspirations to the presidency ; none had reached the goal. Clay introduced the compromise resolutions ; Webster supported them ; Calhoun opposed them. Calhoun died before the session closed, and Clay and Webster retired from the Senate forever, the one to engage in a combat which admitted of no compromise, — with incurable disease, — the other to take the chief place in Mr. Fillmore's cabinet. It was not their disappearance from the great stage of national public life that gave the signal for the stern and strenuous contest which compromise had long postponed; but it was well for Clay and Webster that they did not see the failure of the plans which their love for the Union persuaded them would restore peace to the country.

At the beginning of the administration, a problem confronted Congress and the President which compelled a consideration of the slavery question. A vast territory had been acquired from Mexico, and it was necessary to organize a government over it. Mexican law excluded slavery, but the territory had been obtained for the express purpose of extending the area of slavery. Mr. Clay, in January, 1850, introduced in the Senate a series of eight resolutions, embracing the following propositions : the admission of California as a free State ; the new Territories to be organized without restriction as to slavery ; the boundary to be established between Texas and New Mexico ; the United States to pay the public debt of Texas ; slavery not to be abolished in the District of Columbia ; the slave trade to be abolished in the District; a fugitive slave law to be passed ; Congress to declare that it had no power to interfere with the slave trade between the States. All the great senators debated these resolutions. Webster supported them in his famous Seventh of March speech, which cost him the favor of the anti-slavery Whigs of the North, and gave him no perceptible additional strength in the South. No act of any American public man is worthy of more careful historical study than the stand Webster took on this occasion. That it destroyed the last chance for the nomination and election of the great man is all that can be said of it here.

The resolutions were discussed until the 18th of April, when they were referred to a committee of thirteen senators, of which Mr. Clay was chairman. The committee reported bills covering all the points mentioned in the resolution. Three of the recommendations were combined in a single measure, which the President called an " omnibus bill." By successive amendments it was pared down to a measure for organizing the Territory of Utah; its opponents, in derision, declared that the omnibus was upset. Nevertheless, the Senate eventually passed all the measures in separate bills. A most interesting analysis of the votes in the Senate is given by Rhodes.[1] Some of the bills had the support of the slave States with a sprinkling of Northern senators; others were supported chiefly by Northern men. Four senators only voted for all the bills; yet the closest division was a vote of two to one on the admission of California. During the debate, which dragged on for nearly four months, President Taylor died and Mr. Fillmore succeeded him. The policy of the administration was reversed. General Taylor had been opposed to the compromise; the new President favored it strongly. The House of Representatives devoted little time to discussion. In less than a month the whole series of bills had been passed; and they were signed promptly by President Fillmore.

Those who are curious in searching for the small and seemingly insignificant causes of great events, ascribe Mr. Fillmore's attitude on this important series of measures to the personal relations between him and Governor Seward. Offices have always played a great part in New York politics, whatever party was in power. Seward became a senator when Fillmore became Vice-President. Who was to have the distribution of the patronage in New York? A division seemed the natural solution of the problem. But Seward early obtained a great hold upon President Taylor, and was regarded as the most influential of his advisers. He suggested the position which the President should take upon public questions, and, incidentally, he took all the New York offices. Mr. Fillmore was driven into an attitude of almost open hostility to the administration, and, when he became President, took the course, both on the great public questions and incidentally with reference to the offices, most distasteful to Mr. Seward.

The compromise measures became law. Those who carried

[1] History, vol. i. p. 181.

them through Congress, and those who supported them on the stump and in the press, deluded themselves with the idea that they were a finality ; that they took away all matters of difference, or at least established the principles upon which all future questions arising out of them were to be decided; and that the people would regard a reopening of the agitation as meddlesome and unpatriotic.

Acquiescence in the settlement was really quite general in the Democratic party. The two wings of the party reunited, and carried most of the elections, as against the Whigs, who lost the unswerving Abolition and Anti-Slavery vote. It was evident that the Democrats would go into the election of 1852 a united party, provided a candidate unobjectionable to both wings could be found. It was equally evident that anything like a hearty union of Whigs was out of the question.

There was much preparation, and there was a great deal of discussion and intrigue, in each party, months before the time of nomination. The leading candidate on the Democratic side was General Cass, who had been defeated four years before. Mr. James Buchanan also was strongly supported ; and Stephen A. Douglas and William L. Marcy each had many friends. But it does not seem to have been confidently anticipated that either of these gentlemen would succeed in securing the necessary two thirds, and the experience of 1844 was frequently in men's minds.

The Whigs were in a worse case. Mr. Webster was the greatest of their statesmen, but after his Seventh of March speech he was impossible as a candidate to that wing of the party which regarded the compromise measures of 1850 with abhorrence. On the other hand, the Southern members of the party were firmly resolved not to accept any candidate who was not in favor of those measures. Mr. Fillmore, although an accidental President, had stood by them, and they were in favor of nominating him for reëlection. But as General Taylor had loomed up four years before as a colorless and non-committal candidate, so now there was a strong movement in favor of General Winfield Scott. No one knew what was his position on the subject of the " compromises," and there was a careful and successful effort to keep the Whig public in the dark. But, as has happened before and since that time, the most energetic movements in favor of the candidate who was eventually to be nominated came from States which could not be expected to give him an electoral vote.

Yet it is not easy to see what course could have been taken to avert the fate which awaited the Whigs in 1852. Had a candidate been chosen who was identified with the compromise of 1850, like Mr. Webster or Mr. Fillmore, he would have been slaughtered remorselessly in the North; had an opponent of these measures been selected, he would have failed to secure an electoral vote in the South; and no other non-committal candidate would have succeeded better than General Scott did.

The Democratic national convention, the first to be held, met at Baltimore on June 1, 1852. Although its session was protracted until the 6th, it was not an interesting convention. John W. Davis, of Indiana, was the permanent president. Two days were occupied in organizing, and in adopting the two-thirds rule, which was agreed to by an overwhelming majority, after a short debate. Inasmuch as there was no contest over principles, it was agreed to make the nominations before considering the platform; and on the third day voting for candidates began. On the first ballot General Cass had 116; James Buchanan, 93; William L. Marcy, 27; Stephen A. Douglas, 20; Joseph Lane, 13; Samuel Houston, 8; and there were 4 scattering. The number necessary for a choice was 188. In the succeeding ballots the vote for Mr. Cass fell off, while the number of delegates who voted for Mr. Douglas steadily increased, until, on the twenty-ninth trial, the votes were: for Cass, 27; for Buchanan, 93; for Douglas, 91; and no other candidate had more than 26. At this point Cass began to recover his strength, and reached his largest number on the thirty-fifth trial, namely, 131. On that same ballot, Virginia gave 15 votes to Franklin Pierce. Mr. Pierce gained 15 more votes on the thirty-sixth trial; but at that point his increase ceased, and was then slowly resumed, as the weary repetition of balloting without effect went on. The forty-eighth trial resulted as follows: for Cass, 73; for Buchanan, 28; for Douglas, 33; for Marcy, 90; for Pierce, 55; for all others, 8. The forty-ninth trial was the last. There was a "stampede" for Pierce, and he received 282 votes to 6 for all others. There is no doubt that the nomination of General Pierce was carefully planned before the convention met. The originator of the scheme was James W. Bradbury, then a senator from Maine,[1] a college mate and lifelong friend of Pierce.

[1] In 1898 he still survives, the only senatorial contemporary of Clay and Webster.

Ten persons received votes in the nomination of a candidate for Vice-President, — William R. King of Alabama had 126; S. U. Downs of Louisiana, 30; John B. Weller of California, 28; William O. Butler of Kentucky, 27; Gideon J. Pillow of Tennessee, 25; David R. Atchison of Missouri, 25; Robert Strange of North Carolina, 23; T. J. Rusk of Texas, 12; Jefferson Davis of Mississippi, 2; Howell Cobb of Georgia, 2. On the second ballot, William R. King of Alabama was unanimously nominated.

The platform adopted was made up of the previous platforms of the party, with some additions. It was identical with that of 1848, up to and including the resolution respecting slavery, numbered seven in the platform of 1840 (p. 200), following which are these two resolutions: —

Resolved, That the foregoing proposition covers, and is intended to embrace, the whole subject of slavery agitated in Congress; and therefore the Democratic party of the Union, standing on this national platform, will abide by, and adhere to, a faithful execution of the acts known as the "compromise" measures settled by the last Congress, — the act for reclaiming fugitives from service or labor included; which act, being designed to carry out an express provision of the Constitution, cannot with fidelity thereto be repealed, nor so changed as to destroy or impair its efficiency.

Resolved, That the Democratic party will resist all attempts at renewing, in Congress or out of it, the agitation of the slavery question, under whatever shape or color the attempt may be made.

Then follow the resolutions in former platforms respecting the distribution of the proceeds of land sales, that respecting the veto power, and these additions: —

Resolved, That the Democratic party will faithfully abide by and uphold the principles laid down in the Kentucky and Virginia resolutions of 1798, and in the report of Mr. Madison to the Virginia legislature in 1799; that it adopts those principles as constituting one of the main foundations of its political creed, and is resolved to carry them out in their obvious meaning and import.

Resolved, That the war with Mexico, upon all the principles of patriotism and the law of nations, was a just and necessary war on our part, in which no American citizen should have shown himself opposed to his country, and neither morally nor physically, by word or deed, given aid and comfort to the enemy.

Resolved, That we rejoice at the restoration of friendly relations with our sister republic of Mexico, and earnestly desire for her all the blessings and prosperity which we enjoy under republican

institutions; and we congratulate the American people on the results of that war, which have so manifestly justified the policy and
conduct of the Democratic party, and insured to the United States
indemnity for the past and security for the future.

Resolved, That, in view of the condition of popular institutions
in the Old World, a high and sacred duty is devolved, with increased responsibility, upon the Democracy of this country, as the
party of the people, to uphold and maintain the rights of every
State, and thereby the union of States, and to sustain and advance
among them constitutional liberty, by continuing to resist all monopolies and exclusive legislation for the benefit of the few at the
expense of the many, and by a vigilant and constant adherence to
those principles and compromises of the Constitution which are
broad enough and strong enough to embrace and uphold the Union
as it is, and the Union as it should be, in the full expansion of the
energies and capacity of this great and progressive people.

The platform was adopted with but a few dissenting voices.
The resolution relating to the compromise measures set the convention wild with delight.   A re-reading of it was demanded,
and the applause with which it was received was vociferous
and prolonged.

The Whig convention met at Baltimore on the 16th of June.
All the States were represented.   John G. Chapman, of Maryland, was the permanent president.   The convention was, from
the beginning, a theatre of intrigue.   On the first day of the
session the Southern delegates held a caucus and adopted a
platform, thus forestalling the action of the convention.   It
is said that the platform was subsequently submitted to the
friends of Mr. Webster, and accepted by them.   Mr. Fillmore
was the candidate preferred by the Southerners; General Scott
was the favorite in the North; Mr. Webster had the greater
part of New England, but no votes from Maine, where his
negotiation of the Ashburton Treaty was still treasured up
against him.   There is said to have been a secret understanding that, if the platform drawn up by the Southern caucus
should be accepted by the convention, a sufficient number of
Southern delegates would go over to Scott and nominate him.
But there was still another scheme.   A careful canvass was
made by the Southern friends of Mr. Webster, and it was believed that when Fillmore — for whom many of the Southerners were instructed — should be abandoned, twenty-two of
them would probably go for Scott, but that one hundred and
six could be counted for Webster.   If then the Northern men

could secure forty-one delegates, there would be enough to nominate him. The necessary number could not be found. Two Massachusetts men held out against Webster: not one vote would Maine give him.[1]

To return to the record of the convention. On the first ballot for a candidate for President, Mr. Fillmore had 133; General Scott, 131; and Mr. Webster, 29. The convention voted fifty times before any material change took place. At no time, in the first forty-nine votes, did General Scott fall below his original 131, or receive more than 139. Mr. Fillmore did not once receive more than 133 or fewer than 122. Mr. Webster's highest vote was 32, his lowest 28. But from the fiftieth vote on to the fifty-third, General Scott drew ahead with 142, 142, 146, and 159, which last number was 12 more than was necessary to a choice. William A. Graham of North Carolina was nominated for Vice-President on the second ballot.

The platform, although reported by the committee on resolutions almost unanimously, was not adopted without a struggle. It was as follows: —

The Whigs of the United States, in convention assembled, adhering to the great conservative principles by which they are controlled and governed, and now, as ever, relying upon the intelligence of the American people, with an abiding confidence in their capacity for self-government, and their devotion to the Constitution and the Union, do proclaim the following as the political sentiments and determination for the establishment and maintenance of which their national organization as a party was effected: —

First. The government of the United States is of a limited character, and it is confined to the exercise of powers expressly granted by the Constitution, and such as may be necessary and proper for carrying the granted powers into full execution, and that powers not granted or necessarily implied are reserved to the States respectively and to the people.

Second. The state governments should be held secure to their reserved rights, and the general government sustained on its constitutional powers, and that the Union should be revered and watched over as the palladium of our liberties.

Third. That while struggling freedom everywhere enlists the warmest sympathy of the Whig party, we still adhere to the doctrines of the Father of his Country, as announced in his Farewell Address, of keeping ourselves free from all entangling alliances

[1] See Rhodes's History, vol. i. p. 259

with foreign countries, and of never quitting our own to stand upon foreign ground; that our mission as a republic is not to propagate our opinions, or impose on other countries our forms of government by artifice or force; but to teach by example, and show by our success, moderation and justice, the blessings of self-government, and the advantage of free institutions.

Fourth. That, as the people make and control the government, they should obey its Constitution, laws, and treaties, as they would retain their self-respect and the respect which they claim and will enforce from foreign powers.

Fifth. That the government should be conducted on principles of the strictest economy; and revenue sufficient for the expenses thereof, in time of peace, ought to be mainly derived from a duty on imports, and not from direct taxes; and in laying such duties sound policy requires a just discrimination, and protection from fraud by specific duties, when practicable, whereby suitable encouragement may be afforded to American industry, equally to all classes and to all portions of the country.

Sixth. The Constitution vests in Congress the power to open and repair harbors, and remove obstructions from navigable rivers, whenever such improvements are necessary for the common defence and for the protection and facility of commerce with foreign nations or among the States, — said improvements being in every instance national and general in their character.

Seventh. The federal and state governments are parts of one system, alike necessary for the common prosperity, peace, and security, and ought to be regarded alike with a cordial, habitual, and immovable attachment. Respect for the authority of each, and acquiescence in the just constitutional measures of each, are duties required by the plainest considerations of national, state, and individual welfare.

Eighth. That the series of acts of the Thirty-second Congress, the act known as the Fugitive Slave Law included, are received and acquiesced in by the Whig party of the United States as a settlement in principle and substance of the dangerous and exciting questions which they embrace; and, so far as they are concerned, we will maintain them, and insist upon their strict enforcement, until time and experience shall demonstrate the necessity of further legislation to guard against the evasion of the laws on the one hand and the abuse of their powers on the other, not impairing their present efficiency; and we deprecate all further agitation of the question thus settled, as dangerous to our peace, and will discountenance all efforts to continue or renew such agitation, whenever, wherever, or however the attempt may be made; and we will maintain this system as essential to the nationality of the Whig party and the integrity of the Union.

The objection was, of course, to the last resolution of the series. It was strongly opposed, but was adopted by a vote of 212 to 70. The negative vote was given exclusively by Northern delegates, and by supporters of Scott as against Fillmore and Webster.

The nomination of Pierce was well received by the Democrats; that of Scott had a cold reception in many parts of the North, and was nowhere welcomed in a spirit which gave promise of victory. The action of the Whig convention was criticised by many of the party papers. The platform was distasteful to the Northern wing of the party, and the candidate excited no enthusiasm anywhere. He was esteemed as a gallant soldier, but he was not recognized as a statesman, and his views were too little known to inspire either section with confidence. On the other hand, Mr. Pierce, if not a very prominent man, was known to have opinions in accordance with the Democratic platform, upon which the party was substantially united.

The Anti-Slavery organization, the Free Soil Democrats, though a much less important political factor than they had been four years earlier, held their convention in Pittsburg on August 11. Henry Wilson of Massachusetts presided. John P. Hale of New Hampshire was nominated for President, and George W. Julian of Indiana for Vice-President, and the following platform was adopted : —

Having assembled in national convention as the Democracy of the United States; united by a common resolve to maintain right against wrong and freedom against slavery; confiding in the intelligence, patriotism, and discriminating justice of the American people; putting our trust in God for the triumph of our cause, and invoking his guidance in our endeavors to advance it, — we now submit to the candid judgment of all men the following declaration of principles and measures : —

1. That governments deriving their just powers from the consent of the governed are instituted among men to secure to all those unalienable rights of life, liberty, and the pursuit of happiness with which they are endowed by their Creator, and of which none can be deprived by valid legislation, except for crime.

2. That the true mission of American Democracy is to maintain the liberties of the people, the sovereignty of the States, and the perpetuity of the Union, by the impartial application to public affairs, without sectional discriminations, of the fundamental principles of human rights, strict justice, and an economical administration.

3. That the federal government is one of limited powers, derived solely from the Constitution, and the grants of power therein ought to be strictly construed by all the departments and agents of the government, and it is inexpedient and dangerous to exercise doubtful constitutional powers.

4. That the Constitution of the United States, ordained to form a more perfect Union, to establish justice, and secure the blessings of liberty, expressly denies to the general government all power to deprive any person of life, liberty, or property without due process of law; and, therefore, the government, having no more power to make a slave than to make a king, and no more power to establish slavery than to establish a monarchy, should at once proceed to relieve itself from all responsibility for the existence of slavery wherever it possesses constitutional power to legislate for its extinction.

5. That, to the persevering and importunate demand of the slave power for more slave States, new slave Territories, and the nationalization of slavery, our distinct and final answer is: No more slave States, no slave Territory, no nationalized slavery, and no national legislation for the extradition of slaves.

6. That slavery is a sin against God, and a crime against man, which no human enactment or usage can make right; and that Christianity, humanity, and patriotism alike demand its abolition.

7. That the fugitive slave act of 1850 is repugnant to the Constitution, to the principles of the common law, to the spirit of Christianity, and to the sentiments of the civilized world. We therefore deny its binding force upon the American people, and demand its immediate and total repeal.

8. That the doctrine that any human law is a finality, and not subject to modification or repeal, is not in accordance with the creed of the founders of our government, and is dangerous to the liberties of the people.

9. That the acts of Congress known as the "compromise" measures of 1850, — by making the admission of a sovereign State contingent upon the adoption of other measures demanded by the special interest of slavery; by their omission to guarantee freedom in the free Territories; by their attempt to impose unconstitutional limitations on the power of Congress and the people to admit new States; by their provisions for the assumption of five millions of the state debt of Texas, and for the payment of five millions more, and the cession of a large territory to the same State under menace, as an inducement to the relinquishment of a groundless claim; and by their invasion of the sovereignty of the States and the liberties of the people, through the enactment of an unjust oppressive, and unconstitutional fugitive slave law, — are proved

to be inconsistent with all the principles and maxims of Democracy, and wholly inadequate to the settlement of the questions of which they are claimed to be an adjustment.

10. That no permanent settlement of the slavery question can be looked for except in the practical recognition of the truth that slavery is sectional and freedom national; by the total separation of the general government from slavery, and the exercise of its legitimate and constitutional influence on the side of freedom; and by leaving to the States the whole subject of slavery and the extradition of fugitives from service.

11. That all men have a natural right to a portion of the soil; and that, as the use of the soil is indispensable to life, the right of all men to the soil is as sacred as their right to life itself.

12. That the public lands of the United States belong to the people, and should not be sold to individuals nor granted to corporations, but should be held as a sacred trust for the benefit of the people, and should be granted in limited quantities, free of cost, to landless settlers.

13. That a due regard for the federal Constitution and a sound administrative policy demands that the funds of the general government be kept separate from banking institutions; that inland and ocean postage should be reduced to the lowest possible point; that no more revenue should be raised than is required to defray the strictly necessary expenses of the public service, and to pay off the public debt; and that the power and patronage of the government should be diminished, by the abolition of all unnecessary offices, salaries, and privileges, and by the election, by the people, of all civil officers in the service of the United States, so far as may be consistent with the prompt and efficient transaction of the public business.

14. That river and harbor improvements, when necessary to the safety and convenience of commerce with foreign nations or among the several States, are objects of national concern; and it is the duty of Congress, in the exercise of its constitutional powers, to provide for the same.

15. That emigrants and exiles from the Old World should find a cordial welcome to homes of comfort and fields of enterprise in the New; and every attempt to abridge their privilege of becoming citizens and owners of soil among us ought to be resisted with inflexible determination.

16. That every nation has a clear right to alter or change its own government, and to administer its own concerns, in such a manner as may best secure the rights and promote the happiness of the people; and foreign interference with that right is a dangerous violation of the laws of nations, against which all independent

governments should protest, and endeavor by all proper means to prevent; and especially is it the duty of the American government, representing the chief republic of the world, to protest against, and by all proper means to prevent, the intervention of kings and emperors against nations seeking to establish for themselves republican or constitutional governments.

17. That the independence of Hayti ought to be recognized by our government, and our commercial relations with it placed on a footing of the most favored nation.

18. That as, by the Constitution, the "citizens of each State shall be entitled to all the privileges and immunities of citizens in the several States," the practice of imprisoning colored seamen of other States, while the vessels to which they belong lie in port, and refusing the exercise of the right to bring such cases before the Supreme Court of the United States, to test the legality of such proceedings, is a flagrant violation of the Constitution, and an invasion of the rights of the citizens of other States, utterly inconsistent with the professions made by the slaveholders, that they wish the provisions of the Constitution faithfully observed by every State in the Union.

19. That we recommend the introduction into all treaties hereafter to be negotiated between the United States and foreign nations, of some provision for the amicable settlement of difficulties by a resort to decisive arbitration.

20. That the Free Democratic party is not organized to aid either the Whig or the Democratic wing of the great slave-compromise party of the nation, but to defeat them both; and that, repudiating and renouncing both as hopelessly corrupt and utterly unworthy of confidence, the purpose of the Free Democracy is to take possession of the federal government, and administer it for the better protection of the rights and interests of the whole people.

21. That we inscribe on our banner, "Free soil, free speech, free labor, and free men!" and under it will fight on and fight ever until a triumphant victory shall reward our exertions.

22. That upon this platform the convention presents to the American people as a candidate for the office of President of the United States, John P. Hale of New Hampshire, and as a candidate for the office of Vice-President of the United States, George W. Julian of Indiana, and earnestly commends them to the support of all free men and all parties.

The canvass was not a spirited one. All the early autumn elections were favorable to the Democrats, and the result in November was a crushing defeat of the Whigs in the popular vote and one still more decisive in the electoral vote. Thirty-

one States took part in the election, California having been
admitted to the Union September 9, 1850. A new apportionment, based on the census of 1850, changed the number of
electoral votes of many of the States. The popular and elec
toral votes were as follows: —

| STATES. | POPULAR VOTE. | | | ELECTORAL VOTE. | |
	Franklin Pierce, New Hampshire.	Winfield Scott, New Jersey.	John P. Hale, New Hampshire.	Pierce and King.	Scott and Graham.
Alabama	26,881	15,038	–	9	–
Arkansas	12,173	7,404	–	4	–
California	40,626	35,407	100	4	–
Connecticut	33,249	30,359	3,160	6	–
Delaware	6,318	6,293	62	3	–
Florida	4,318	2,875	–	3	–
Georgia *	34,705	16,660	–	10	–
Illinois	80,597	64,934	9,966	11	–
Indiana	95,340	80,901	6,929	13	–
Iowa	17,763	15,856	1,604	4	–
Kentucky	53,806	57,068	265	–	12
Louisiana	18,647	17,255	–	6	–
Maine	41,609	32,543	8,030	8	–
Maryland	40,020	35,066	281	8	–
Massachusetts † . .	44,569	52,683	28,023	–	13
Michigan	41,842	33,859	7,237	6	–
Mississippi	26,876	17,548	–	7	–
Missouri	38,353	29,984	–	9	–
New Hampshire . .	29,997	16,147	6,695	5	–
New Jersey . . .	44,305	38,556	350	7	–
New York . . .	262,083	234,882	25,329	35	–
North Carolina . .	39,744	39,058	59	10	–
Ohio	169,220	152,526	31,682	23	–
Pennsylvania . . .	198,568	179,174	8,525	27	–
Rhode Island . .	8,735	7,626	644	4	–
South Carolina ‡ . .	–	–	–	8	–
Tennessee	57,018	58,898	–	–	12
Texas	13,552	4,995	–	4	–
Vermont	13,044	22,173	8,621	–	5
Virginia	73,858	58,572	291	15	–
Wisconsin	33,658	22,240	8,814	5	–
Total	1,601,474	1,386,580	156,667	254	42

* A Webster ticket received 5324 votes in Georgia; an independent Pierce ticket, 5811
† Massachusetts gave Webster 1670 votes. ‡ Electors appointed by the legislature.

XX

THE NEW REPUBLICAN PARTY

The election of 1852 gave a death-blow to the Whig party. That organization had outlived its usefulness. It was unable to cope with the one vital issue of the day, that of slavery in the Territories. The Democratic party was controlled by its Southern contingent; the Whig by its Northern members. Both parties declared that the question was decided by the compromises of 1850, and was eliminated from politics. Although the extremists of the South had opposed the measures, they speedily began to assume that the settlement was a concession of their own contention, and to bring forward propositions which would make the introduction of slavery into the Territories easy and its exclusion therefrom impossible. In this view of the matter they were, in a certain sense, sustained by the anti-slavery men of the North, who, while they resisted the new measures and declared them to be a violation of the agreement, continued to denounce the acts of 1850 as a surrender to the slaveholders. The Southern leaders put forth the proposition that the natural right of every American citizen permitted him to settle in any Territory, with his property of every kind, including slaves, and entitled him to protection of that property; that no power was or could be given to a territorial government to exclude slavery; and that only when the people came together to form a state constitution could the power originate to decide whether slavery should or should not be allowed to exist. Events in Kansas and elsewhere led ultimately to a division of the Democratic party. Senator Douglas held that the people of a Territory had the power to exclude slavery. This was his doctrine of "popular sovereignty," or "squatter sovereignty," as its opponents called it. In one or the other form the principle was adopted by the Democratic party, although it was rejected in both forms by a great body of its Northern members. The Northern Whig party was overwhelmingly against the extension of slavery, but it could not so declare itself without self-destruction. To do so would at once drive out of the party almost all its Southern supporters; it would alienate a great many Northern men whom an apprehension of the terrible consequences of a sectional issue rendered timid; and at the same time it would draw into the party neither the anti-slavery Democrats, who differed from the Whigs on every question save this, nor the Abolitionists, who went much further in opposition to slavery than either Whigs or Democrats could go.

The only course left open for the Whig party was to delude itself and to attempt to delude the country by asserting that the slavery issue was decided. This was merely to live in the past, to abandon the true function of an opposition. The government was controlled by a party which, in spite of its protestations to the contrary, supported the aggression of the slave interest. The Whig party failed in the South because it made the contest on an issue in which the people were not interested; in the North because it had not the courage to avow opinions which a large majority of the party held. But the Whig pretence, that the slavery question was settled by the compromise measures of 1850, was kept up for some years longer, until it became no longer possible to practise self-deception.

The delusion soon after the election of 1852 took a new phase. Native Americanism had been a favorite doctrine in certain parts of the North for many years, and of late it had been a growing sentiment. It was confined to no party; and the political method of those who believed in the principle that "Americans must rule America," and who were animated by hostility to the Roman Catholic Church, was to choose between candidates already nominated. Occasionally, in the cities of New York and Philadelphia, they nominated candidates of their own, and succeeded in electing them to local offices. The membership was carefully guarded; for the societies were secret, and the initiated were bound by oaths. The order which existed before 1850 was superseded, early in Pierce's administration, by a new one, the Order of United Americans, which became popularly known as the Know-Nothing Order, from the ignorance, even of the existence of such an association, which was professed by all its members. A large number of the Whigs, hoping to transfer the political issue from slavery to Native Americanism, joined the order, which for some years had extraordinary success in state elections; but, as Horace Greeley predicted at the time when it was at the height of its power, it was destined " to run its career rapidly, and vanish as suddenly as it appeared. It *may* last through the next presidential canvass; but hardly longer than that. . . . It would seem as devoid of the elements of persistence as an anti-cholera or an anti-potato-rot party would be." It was chiefly confined to the East at first; later it extended to the South, even as far as Texas, where it became strong enough to carry one election; but it never had much success, nor an organization, in the Northwest.

It was impossible to keep the slavery question out of sight. Mr. Pierce congratulated the country, at the beginning of his administration, that the agitation had ceased, and both parties were pledged to treat a revival of the controversy as an unpatriotic act; but it was revived at once by the proposition to organize the Territories of Kansas and Nebraska, in which was a declaration that the compromises of 1850 superseded the Missouri Compromise, which was accordingly no longer operative. The bill was referred to by anti-slavery orators and journals as a "repeal" of the Missouri Compromise, and it stirred popular sentiment at the North most profoundly. It virtually created three factions in the Democratic party; for beside the Southern extremists there was now a new element, the members of which became known as " Anti-Nebraska Democrats," and another which tried to stand between the two, headed by Senator Stephen A. Douglas. Mr. Douglas was chairman of the Senate committee on Territories, and assumed a position of extraordinary prominence in the politics of the country. The struggle between the pro-slavery and the anti-slavery factions over Kansas, both within and without the Territory, was one of unexampled bitterness and violence; but during the early part of Mr. Pierce's term the opponents of the administration were without effective organization.

The Republican party originated in the West. A mass meeting at Ripon, Wisconsin, early in 1854, followed soon afterward by a mass state convention at Jackson, Michigan; and state conventions in July in Vermont, Wisconsin, Ohio and Indiana, brought the new party into being, with its present name, and with opposition to the extension of slavery as the one issue that united its members. Past differences were forgotten; the jealousies that might be expected to arise in the selection of candidates on account of those differences, were strikingly absent. A Republican organization was not effected in many States of the North in 1854, but the Anti-Nebraska party, if we may so term it, under many names and with various forms of fusion, had many successes at the polls.[1]

A fresh example of the determination of the Southern leaders to force the fighting and to obtain additional territory for the extension of slavery was given in the "Ostend Manifesto." At the instance of the Secretary of State, Mr. Marcy, of New York, a meeting of the United States ministers to Great Britain, France, and Spain, Mr. James Buchanan, Mr. John Y. Mason, and Mr. Pierre Soulé, was held to consider the relation of the island of Cuba to the United States. They came together at Ostend, Belgium, and drew up a report to the effect that Cuba was territorially a part of the United States, that its possession by a foreign power was detrimental to our interest, that an offer should be made to Spain to purchase it, and that in case Spain were to refuse to sell, "by every law, human and divine, we shall be justified in wresting it from Spain, if we possess the power." The "Ostend Manifesto" is referred to repeatedly in the state and national platforms of the Republican party.

At the close of 1855 the situation was extremely complicated. In the Eastern States there were four parties, — the Democrats, the Whigs, the Know-Nothings, and the Republicans. The Democrats and Whigs were inclined to coalesce in order to withstand the common enemy, the Republicans, whose party was acquiring gigantic strength. The days of the Know-Nothing, or American, party were numbered, and most of the members had fallen away to the Republican party. In the West, — except in Ohio, where a remnant of the Whig party survived, — the parties were two only, the Democratic and the Republican. In the South the American party was at the time of its greatest success, having absorbed most of the Whig strength. Although the Whig party had not formally acknowledged that it had ceased to exist, it was really only a memory, and the members merely accepted and voted for the candidates of the Know-Nothings.

The first convention preliminary to the election of 1856 was that of the Americans. It was held at Philadelphia, on

---

[1] For a full and admirable analysis of the elections of 1854, see *Rhodes's History*, vol. ii. pp. 58 *et seq.*

Washington's birthday, February 22, 1856. But already the "National Council" of the order had been in session three days, beginning on the 19th of the month, and had adopted the platform of the party. This platform was as follows: —

1. An humble acknowledgment of the Supreme Being, for His protecting care vouchsafed to our fathers in their successful revolutionary struggle, and hitherto manifested to us, their descendants, in the preservation of their liberties, the independence and the union of these States.

2. The perpetuation of the Federal Union and Constitution, as the palladium of our civil and religious liberties and the only sure bulwark of American independence.

3. Americans must rule America; and to this end native-born citizens should be selected for all state, federal, and municipal offices of government employment, in preference to all others. Nevertheless,

4. Persons born of American parents residing temporarily abroad should be entitled to all the rights of native-born citizens.

5. No person should be selected for political station (whether of native or foreign birth) who recognizes any allegiance or obligation of any description to any foreign prince, potentate, or power, or who refuses to recognize the federal and state Constitutions (each within its sphere) as paramount to all other laws as rules of political action.

6. The unqualified recognition and maintenance of the reserved rights of the several States, and the cultivation of harmony and fraternal good will between the citizens of the several States, and, to this end, non-interference by Congress with questions appertaining solely to the individual States, and non-intervention by each State with the affairs of any other State.

7. The recognition of the right of native-born and naturalized citizens of the United States, permanently residing in any Territory thereof, to frame their constitution and laws, and to regulate their domestic and social affairs in their own mode, subject only to the provisions of the Federal Constitution, with the privilege of admission into the Union whenever they have the requisite population for one representative in Congress; *provided, always*, that none but those who are citizens of the United States, under the Constitution and laws thereof, and who have a fixed residence in any such Territory, ought to participate in the formation of a constitution or in the enactment of laws for said Territory or State.

8. An enforcement of the principle that no State or Territory ought to admit others than citizens to the right of suffrage, or of holding political offices of the United States.

9. A change in the laws of naturalization, making a continued residence of twenty-one years, of all not heretofore provided for, an indispensable requisite for citizenship hereafter, and excluding all paupers and persons convicted of crime from landing upon our shores ; but no interference with the vested rights of foreigners.

10. Opposition to any union between Church and State; no interference with religious faith or worship, and no test oaths for office.

11. Free and thorough investigation into any and all alleged abuses of public functionaries, and a strict economy in public expenditures.

12. The maintenance and enforcement of all laws constitutionally enacted, until said laws shall be repealed or shall be declared null and void by competent judicial authority.

13. Opposition to the reckless and unwise policy of the present Administration in the general management of our national affairs, and more especially as shown in removing " Americans " (by designation) and conservatives in principle from office, and placing foreigners and ultraists in their places ; as shown in a truckling subserviency to the stronger, and an insolent and cowardly bravado toward the weaker powers; as shown in reopening sectional agitation, by the repeal of the Missouri Compromise; as shown in granting to unnaturalized foreigners the right of suffrage in Kansas and Nebraska; as shown in its vacillating course on the Kansas and Nebraska question ; as shown in the corruptions which pervade some of the departments of the government ; as shown in disgracing meritorious naval officers through prejudice or caprice ; and as shown in the blundering mismanagement of our foreign relations.

14. Therefore, to remedy existing evils, and to prevent the disastrous consequences otherwise resulting therefrom, we would build up the " American Party " upon the principles hereinbefore stated.

15. That each State Council shall have authority to amend their several constitutions, so as to abolish the several degrees, and substitute a pledge of honor, instead of other obligations, for fellowship and admission into the party.

16. A free and open discussion of all political principles embraced in our platform.

The convention, which met on the 22d, consisted of 227 delegates from 27 States of the Union, — all except Maine, Vermont, South Carolina, and Georgia. Having organized by the choice of Ephraim Marsh, of New Jersey, as President, and having decided cases of contested seats, the convention became involved in a long and angry discussion of the right of the

National Council to make the platform of the party. A resolution was presented : —

That the National Council has no authority to prescribe a platform of principles for this nominating convention, and that no
candidates for President and Vice-President who are not in favor
of interdicting slavery in territory north of 36° 30′, by congressional action, shall be nominated by this Convention.

A motion to lay this resolution on the table was accepted
as a test of the strength of the two wings of the party. The
motion was carried by a vote of 141 to 59. A motion to proceed to nominate a candidate for President was successful, 151
to 51. Thereupon nearly all the delegates from New England
and Ohio, and a part of those from Pennsylvania, Illinois, and
Iowa, withdrew from the convention. An informal ballot
gave Millard Fillmore 71 votes; George Law, of New York, 27;
Garrett Davis, of Kentucky, 13; and 32 votes were given to
seven other candidates, from one to eight each. On the formal
vote Mr. Fillmore had 179; Mr. Law 24; Kenneth Raynor, of
North Carolina, 14; Judge John McLean, of Ohio, 13; Garrett
Davis 10; and Samuel Houston, of Texas, 3. Mr. Fillmore
had a majority and was nominated. On the first ballot for a
candidate for Vice-President, Andrew J. Donelson, of Tennessee, had 181; Henry J. Gardner, of Massachusetts, 12; Kenneth
Raynor 8; and Percey Walker, of Alabama, 8. Mr. Donelson
was declared nominated ; and the convention adjourned. Soon
after this the seceding delegates met and nominated for President Colonel John C. Frémont, of California, and for Vice-
President ex-Governor William F. Johnston, of Pennsylvania.

The meeting of the Democratic national convention was
looked forward to with much interest. A great many members still adhered to the party, who were not disposed to yield
to what the general drift of sentiment in the Northern States
regarded as the arrogant and unreasonable demands of the slave
interest. The division of the party was most serious in New
York, where the two factions were now known as the "hards"
and the "softs." Mr. Pierce was in high favor with the Southern delegates and with the Southern people ; the Northern and
more moderate wing of the party preferred Mr. Buchanan;
while Mr. Douglas had a strong hold upon the popular heart,
and was regarded as the most natural successor to Mr. Pierce's
strength, should that gentleman's nomination become impossible. The excitement at Cincinnati, where the convention was

to meet, ran high on the days before the session began, and it was freely said that the Northern delegates would bolt if Mr. Buchanan should be defeated. The preliminary intriguing has probably never been greater in any national nominating convention than it was at that time.

The convention met on the 2d of June. All the States were fully represented, and two sets of delegates appeared from each of the States of New York and Missouri. The opponents of Senator Benton were the " regulars " from Missouri. The contestants signalized their advent by knocking down the door-keeper, who endeavored to prevent them from entering the hall. The scene was an incipient riot. When order had been restored, the presiding officer administered to the intruders such a stinging rebuke for their lawless conduct that they retired, and, as the committee on credentials reported against their claim, they were seen no more. The " hards " and " softs " of New York were quite as bitter in their quarrel as the more turbulent Missourians; but they waited peaceably, and finally both delegations were admitted, each delegate to have half a vote. The permanent chairman was John E. Ward, of Georgia. There was no opposition to the two-thirds rule. On the first vote for a candidate for President, James Buchanan had 135; Franklin Pierce 122; Stephen A. Douglas 33; and Lewis Cass 5. The Southern States gave on this vote 72 to Mr. Pierce; 29 to Mr. Buchanan; and 14 to Mr. Douglas. The North gave 106 to Buchanan; 50 to Pierce; 19 to Douglas; and 5 to Cass. On the second and succeeding votes Mr. Buchanan's strength increased very slowly but steadily; Mr. Pierce's fell off rapidly, and the most of his loss was Mr. Douglas's gain; on the sixteenth trial the result was, for Mr. Buchanan 168; for Mr. Pierce none; for Mr. Douglas 121; and for General Cass 6. Mr. Buchanan had had a majority on the tenth vote, and he now lacked but eighteen of two thirds. On the seventeenth vote the delegations began changing in his favor, he received all the votes, 296, and was declared nominated. Ten candidates were voted for as candidates for Vice-President on the first trial. The leader was John A. Quitman, of Mississippi, with 59 votes, closely followed by John C. Breckinridge, of Kentucky, with 55. Linn Boyd, of Kentucky, had 33; Herschel V. Johnson, of Georgia, 31; James A. Bayard, of Delaware, 31; Aaron V. Brown, of Tennessee, 29; James C. Dobbin, of North Carolina, 13;

Benjamin Fitzpatrick, of Alabama, 11; Trusten Polk, of Missouri, 5; and Thomas J. Rusk, of Texas, 2. On the second vote the names of General Quitman and of most of the other leading candidates were withdrawn, and Mr. Breckinridge was unanimously nominated.

The platform, which was adopted without opposition, begins with the preamble first adopted in 1844, and repeated in subsequent platforms. Then follow ten of the resolutions which form a part of previous platforms, namely, the first five of 1840, in order, and those relating to the proceeds of the public lands; against a national bank; in favor of a separate treasury; regarding the veto power; and against abridgment of the privileges of aliens to become citizens. To these the following were added: —

And whereas, Since the foregoing declaration was uniformly adopted by our predecessors in national convention, an adverse political and religious test has been secretly organized by a party claiming to be exclusively American, and it is proper that the American Democracy should clearly define its relations thereto, and declare its determined opposition to all secret political societies, by whatever name they may be called,

Resolved, That the foundation of this Union of States having been laid in, and its prosperity, expansion, and preëminent example of free government built upon, entire freedom in matters of religious concernment, and no respect of persons in regard to rank or place, or birth, no party can be justly deemed national, constitutional, or in accordance with American principles which bases its exclusive organization upon religious opinions and accidental birthplace. And hence a political crusade in the nineteenth century, and in the United States of America, against Catholics and foreign-born, is neither justified by the past history or future prospects of the country, nor in unison with the spirit of toleration and enlightened freedom which peculiarly distinguishes the American system of popular government.

Resolved, That we reiterate with renewed energy of purpose the well-considered declarations of former conventions upon the sectional issue of domestic slavery and concerning the reserved rights of the States, —

1. That Congress has no power under the Constitution to interfere with or control the domestic institutions of the several States, and that all such States are the sole and proper judges of everything appertaining to their own affairs not prohibited by the Constitution; that all efforts of the Abolitionists or others made to induce Congress to interfere with questions of slavery, or to take

incipient steps in relation thereto, are calculated to lead to the most alarming and dangerous consequences, and that all such efforts have an inevitable tendency to diminish the happiness of the people and endanger the stability and permanency of the Union, and ought not to be countenanced by any friend of our political institutions.

2. That the foregoing covers, and was intended to embrace, the whole subject of slavery agitation in Congress; and therefore the Democratic party of the Union, standing on this national platform, will abide by and adhere to a faithful execution of the acts known as the "compromise" measures, settled by the Congress of 1850, the act for reclaiming fugitives from service or labor included; which act, being designed to carry out an express provision of the Constitution, cannot, with fidelity thereto, be repealed, or so changed as to destroy or impair its efficiency.

3. That the Democratic party will resist all attempts at renewing, in Congress or out of it, the agitation of the slavery question, under whatever shape or color the attempt may be made.

4. The Democratic party will faithfully abide by and uphold the principles laid down in the Kentucky and Virginia resolutions of 1798, and in the report of Mr. Madison to the Virginia legislature in 1799; that it adopts these principles as constituting one of the main foundations of its political creed, and is resolved to carry them out in their obvious meaning and import.

And that we may more distinctly meet the issue on which a sectional party, subsisting exclusively on slavery agitation, now relies to test the fidelity of the people, North and South, to the Constitution and the Union, —

1. *Resolved*, That, claiming fellowship with and desiring the cooperation of all who regard the preservation of the Union under the Constitution as the paramount issue, and repudiating all sectional issues and platforms concerning domestic slavery which seek to embroil the States and incite to treason and armed resistance to law in the Territories, and whose avowed purpose, if consummated, must end in civil war and disunion, the American Democracy recognize and adopt the principles contained in the organic laws establishing the Territories of Nebraska and Kansas as embodying the only sound and safe solution of the slavery question, upon which the great national idea of the people of this whole country can repose in its determined conservation of the Union, and non-interference of Congress with slavery in the Territories or in the District of Columbia.

2. That this was the basis of the compromise of 1850, confirmed by both the Democratic and Whig parties in national conventions, ratified by the people in the election of 1852, and rightly applied to the organization of the Territories in 1854.

3. That by the uniform application of the Democratic principle to the organization of Territories, and the admission of new States with or without domestic slavery, as they may elect, the equal rights of all the States will be preserved intact, the original compacts of the Constitution maintained inviolate, and the perpetuity and expansion of the Union insured to its utmost capacity of embracing, in peace and harmony, every future American State that may be constituted or annexed with a republican form of government.

Resolved, That we recognize the right of the people of all the Territories, including Kansas and Nebraska, acting through the legally and fairly expressed will of the majority of the actual residents, and whenever the number of their inhabitants justifies it, to form a constitution, with or without domestic slavery, and be admitted into the Union upon terms of perfect equality with the other States.

Resolved, Finally, that in view of the condition of popular institutions in the Old World (and the dangerous tendencies of sectional agitation, combined with the attempt to enforce civil and religious disabilities against the rights of acquiring and enjoying citizenship in our own land), a high and sacred duty is devolved, with increased responsibility, upon the Democratic party of this country, as the party of the Union, to uphold and maintain the rights of every State, and thereby the Union of the States; and to sustain and advance among us constitutional liberty, by continuing to resist all monopolies and exclusive legislation for the benefit of the few at the expense of the many ; and by a vigilant and constant adherence to those principles and compromises of the Constitution which are broad enough and strong enough to embrace and uphold the Union as it was, the Union as it is, and the Union as it shall be, in the full expansion of the energies and capacity of this great and progressive people.

1. *Resolved*, That there are questions connected with the foreign policy of this country which are inferior to no domestic question whatever. The time has come for the people of the United States to declare themselves in favor of free seas, and progressive free trade throughout the world, and by solemn manifestations to place their moral influence at the side of their successful example.

2. *Resolved*, That our geographical and political position with reference to the other states of this continent, no less than the interest of our commerce and the development of our growing power, requires that we should hold sacred the principles involved in the Monroe doctrine. Their bearing and import admit of no misconstruction, and should be applied with unbending rigidity.

3. *Resolved*, That the great highway, which nature as well as the assent of states most immediately interested in its maintenance

has marked out for free communication between the Atlantic and the Pacific oceans, constitutes one of the most important achievements realized by the spirit of modern times, in the unconquerable energy of our people; and that result would be secured by a timely and efficient exertion of the control which we have the right to claim over it ; and no power on earth should be suffered to impede or clog its progress by any interference with relations that it may suit our policy to establish between our government and the governments of the states within whose dominions it lies. We can, under no circumstances, surrender our preponderance in the adjustment of all questions arising out of it.

4. *Resolved*, That, in view of so commanding an interest, the people of the United States cannot but sympathize with the efforts which are being made by the people of Central America to regenerate that portion of the continent which covers the passage across the inter-oceanic isthmus.

5. *Resolved*, That the Democratic party will expect of the next administration that every proper effort be made to insure our ascendency in the Gulf of Mexico, and to maintain permanent protection to the great outlets through which are emptied into its waters the products raised out of the soil and the commodities created by the industry of the people of our Western valleys and of the Union at large.

Resolved, That the administration of Franklin Pierce has been true to Democratic principles, and therefore true to the great interests of the country. In the face of violent opposition he has maintained the laws at home, and vindicated the rights of American citizens abroad; and therefore we proclaim our unqualified admiration of his measures and policy.

The first Republican national convention was the outcome of a preliminary convention held at Pittsburg on Washington's Birthday, February 22, 1856. The Pittsburg meeting was called by the chairmen of the Republican state committees of Maine, Vermont, Massachusetts, New York, Pennsylvania, Ohio, Indiana, Michigan, and Wisconsin. There were representatives of twenty-three States in attendance. A long address " to the people of the United States " was adopted ; and it was voted to call a convention for the nomination of candidates for President and Vice-President, to meet at Philadelphia on the 17th of June, the anniversary of Bunker Hill.

The convention met on the day named. The delegates were too enthusiastic and united in their purpose to be careful about the proportionate representation of the States, or to scrutinize closely the credentials of their fellow-members. All the Northern States were represented, as were also Delaware, Maryland, Virginia, and Kentucky, the Territories of Minnesota, Nebraska, and Kansas, and the District of Columbia. It was reported that more than one thousand delegates were in attendance, but the vote for candidates disclosed less than six hundred. New York cast 96 votes, Pennsylvania 81, and Ohio 69; but many of the more remote States were underrepresented. Robert Emmet, of New York, formerly a Democrat, was the temporary chairman, and Colonel Henry S. Lane, of Indiana, the permanent president. The enthusiasm and the hopefulness of the delegates were unbounded. For the first time they found themselves in a party united by what they deemed a great moral purpose, and not by considerations of temporary expediency. The convention gave itself up to a season of speech-making of the most earnest and enthusiastic character. The extraordinary success of the new party, barely two years old, seemed to justify them in their expectation of an immediate national victory.

Much depended, for such a party even more than for an old and established party, upon the quality of the candidate. William H. Seward, of New York, no doubt represented the attitude of the Republican party on public questions better and more prominently than any other public man; but he had seen the formation of the party with reluctance, and, not being so optimistic as to expect an election, declined to be a candidate. The next choice might have been Senator Salmon P. Chase, of Ohio; but he had been so fully identified with the Democratic party that his ability to carry Ohio was doubtful, and he withdrew. John McLean, also of Ohio, Postmaster-General under Monroe and Adams, and a Justice of the Supreme Court since 1829, was regarded as a strong candidate, but his name was also withdrawn. The only remaining candidate who had been prominently mentioned was Colonel John C. Frémont, whose political experience was limited to a brief service as senator from California, and whose political opinions were almost unknown. Upon an urgent representation that Frémont would be unable to carry Pennsylvania, Judge McLean was again brought forward as a candidate. On an informal ballot Frémont received 359 votes, Judge McLean 196, Charles Sumner, of Massachusetts, 2, and William H. Seward, of New York, 1. Colonel Frémont was thereupon unanimously nominated. An informal ballot was likewise taken for a candidate for Vice-President. William L. Dayton, of New Jersey, had 259; Abraham Lincoln, of Illinois, 110; Nathaniel P. Banks, of Massachusetts, 46; and twelve other candidates received some votes each. Mr. Dayton was then unanimously nominated. The selection of Frémont was due in no small degree to the fact that he had already been nominated by the seceding Know-Nothings, and a communication from the officers of the convention which placed him in nomination was frequently referred to, but was not read. Governor Johnston, who was nominated by the seceding Americans for Vice-President, received two votes only in the Republican convention.

The following platform was adopted : —

This convention of delegates, assembled in pursuance of a call addressed to the people of the United States, without regard to past political differences or divisions, who are opposed to the repeal of the Missouri Compromise, to the policy of the present administration, to the extension of slavery into free territory ; in favor of admitting Kansas as a free State, of restoring the action of the federal government to the principles of Washington and Jefferson ; and who purpose to unite in presenting candidates for the offices of President and Vice-President, do resolve as follows : —

Resolved, That the maintenance of the principles promulgated in the Declaration of Independence and embodied in the federal Constitution is essential to the preservation of our Republican institutions, and that the federal Constitution, the rights of the States, and the union of the States, shall be preserved.

Resolved, That with our republican fathers we hold it to be a self-evident truth, that all men are endowed with the unalienable rights to life, liberty, and the pursuit of happiness, and that the primary object and ulterior designs of our federal government were to secure these rights to all persons within its exclusive jurisdiction ; that, as our republican fathers, when they had abolished slavery in all our national territory, ordained that no person should be deprived of life, liberty, or property without due process of law, it becomes our duty to maintain this provision of the Constitution against all attempts to violate it for the purpose of establishing slavery in any Territory of the United States, by positive legislation prohibiting its existence or extension therein ; that we deny the authority of Congress, of a territorial legislature, of any individual or association of individuals, to give legal existence to slavery in any Territory of the United States, while the present Constitution shall be maintained.

Resolved, That the Constitution confers upon Congress sovereign power over the Territories of the United States, for their government, and that in the exercise of this power it is both the right and the duty of Congress to prohibit in the Territories those twin relics of barbarism, polygamy and slavery.

Resolved, That while the Constitution of the United States was ordained and established by the people in order to form a more perfect Union, establish justice, ensure domestic tranquillity, provide for the common defence, and secure the blessings of liberty, and contains ample provision for the protection of the life, liberty, and property of every citizen, the dearest constitutional rights of the people of Kansas have been fraudulently and violently taken from them; their territory has been invaded by an armed force; spurious and pretended legislative, judicial, and executive officers have been set over them, by whose usurped authority, sustained by the military power of the government, tyrannical and unconstitutional laws have been enacted and enforced; the rights of the people to keep and bear arms have been infringed; test oaths of an extraordinary and entangling nature have been imposed as a condition of exercising the right of suffrage and holding office; the right of an accused person to a speedy and public trial by an impartial jury has been denied; the right of the people to be secure in their persons, houses, papers, and effects against unreasonable searches and seizures has been violated; they have been deprived of life, liberty, and property without due process of law; the freedom of speech and of the press has been abridged; the right to choose their representatives has been made of no effect; murders, robberies, and arsons have been instigated and encouraged, and the offenders have been allowed to go unpunished; — that all these things have been done with the knowledge, sanction, and procurement of the present administration; and that for this high crime against the Constitution, the Union, and humanity, we arraign the administration, the President, his advisers, agents, supporters, apologists, and accessories, either before or after the fact, before the country and before the world, and that it is our fixed purpose to bring the actual perpetrators of these atrocious outrages, and their accomplices, to a sure and condign punishment hereafter.

Resolved, That Kansas should be immediately admitted as a State of the Union, with her present free Constitution, as at once the most effectual way of securing to her citizens the enjoyment of the rights and privileges to which they are entitled, and of ending the civil strife now raging in her territory.

Resolved, That the highwayman's plea, that "might makes right," embodied in the Ostend circular, was in every respect unworthy of American diplomacy, and would bring shame and dishonor upon any government or people that gave it their sanction.

Resolved, That a railroad to the Pacific Ocean, by the most central and practicable route, is imperatively demanded by the interests of the whole country, and that the Federal government ought to render immediate and efficient aid in its construction; and, as an auxiliary thereto, the immediate construction of an emigrant route on the line of the railroad.

Resolved, That appropriations by Congress for the improvement of rivers and harbors, of a national character, required for the accommodation and security of our existing commerce, are authorized by the Constitution, and justified by the obligation of government to protect the lives and property of its citizens.

Resolved, That we invite the affiliation and coöperation of the men of all parties, however differing from us in other respects, in support of the principles herein declared; and believing that the spirit of our institutions as well as the Constitution of our country guarantees liberty of conscience and equality of rights among citizens, we oppose all legislation impairing their security.

One other convention was held, that of the Whigs, at Baltimore, on the 17th of September, in which there was a more or less full representation of twenty-six States. No delegates were present from Michigan, Iowa, Wisconsin, Texas, or California. Edward Bates, of Missouri, was the president. The proceedings were brief and uninteresting. The nominations of Fillmore and Donelson were accepted by resolution, and the following platform was adopted: —

Resolved, That the Whigs of the United States, now here assembled, hereby declare their reverence for the Constitution of the United States, their unalterable attachment to the national Union, and a fixed determination to do all in their power to preserve them for themselves and their posterity. They have no new principles to announce, no new platform to establish, but are content to broadly rest — where their fathers rested — upon the Constitution of the United States, wishing no safer guide, no higher law.

Resolved, That we regard with the deepest interest and anxiety the present disordered condition of our national affairs, — a portion of the country ravaged by civil war, large sections of our population embittered by mutual recriminations; and we distinctly trace these calamities to the culpable neglect of duty by the present national administration.

Resolved, That the government of the United States was formed by the conjunction in political unity of widespread geographical sections, materially differing not only in climate and products, but in social and domestic institutions; and that any cause that shall permanently array the different sections of the Union in political hostility and organized parties, founded only on geographical distinctions, must inevitably prove fatal to a continuance of the national Union.

Resolved, That the Whigs of the United States declare, as a fundamental rule of political faith, an absolute necessity for avoiding geographical parties. The danger so clearly discerned by the Father of his Country has now become fearfully apparent in the agitation now convulsing the nation, and must be arrested at once if we would preserve our Constitution and our Union from dismemberment, and the name of America from being blotted out from the family of civilized nations.

Resolved, That all who revere the Constitution and the Union must look with alarm at the parties in the field in the present presidential campaign, — one claiming only to represent sixteen Northern States, and the other appealing mainly to the passions and prejudices of the Southern States; that the success of either faction must add fuel to the flame which now threatens to wrap our dearest interests in a common ruin.

Resolved, That the only remedy for an evil so appalling is to support a candidate pledged to neither of the geographical sections now arrayed in political antagonism, but holding both in a just and equal regard. We congratulate the friends of the Union that such a candidate exists in Millard Fillmore.

Resolved, That, without adopting or referring to the peculiar doctrines of the party which has already selected Mr. Fillmore as a candidate, we look to him as a well-tried and faithful friend of the Constitution and the Union, eminent alike for his wisdom and firmness; for his justice and moderation in our foreign relations; for his calm and pacific temperament, so well becoming the head of a great nation; for his devotion to the Constitution in its true spirit; his inflexibility in executing the laws; but, beyond all these attributes, in possessing the one transcendent merit of being a representative of neither of the two sectional parties now struggling for political supremacy.

Resolved, That, in the present exigency of political affairs, we are not called upon to discuss the subordinate questions of administration in the exercising of the constitutional powers of the government. It is enough to know that civil war is raging, and that the Union is imperilled; and we proclaim the conviction that the restoration of Mr. Fillmore to the presidency will furnish the best if not the only means of restoring peace.

The canvass which followed was an extraordinary one. It was sluggish enough in the South, where the only candidates were Mr. Buchanan and Mr. Fillmore; for Mr. Buchanan had the support of the entire slaveholding interest, and of all who were concerned for the maintenance of the political power of the slavery system. But in the North the Republicans conducted a canvass rivalling that of 1840 in enthusiasm, and having behind it what the "hard cider" campaign lacked, — a definite moral purpose and a clearly understood policy. Great political clubs were organized, which marched from place to place visiting each other, uniformed and bearing torches. Immense public meetings were held, and the Northern heart was fired as it had never been before. Nevertheless the Republican canvass was destined to end in defeat, although the earlier elections of the autumn indicated a Republican victory. In Vermont more than three fourths of the votes were Republican; and Maine, which had been carried in 1855 by a fusion party of Democrats and "straight" Whigs, was now carried by the Republicans by almost 18,000 majority. But the October elections were unfavorable; for, while Ohio gave a Republican majority, Indiana was lost, and Pennsylvania gave the Democratic candidates on the state ticket a majority over the Republican and Whig vote combined. "The Quakers did not come out," it was said; but all who could read the signs of the time knew that the election was lost for the Republicans.

Thirty-one States participated in the election. The popular and electoral votes are given on the next page.

The count of the electoral vote was enlivened by a scene unlike any which had ever occurred. The usual resolution for counting the votes was adopted. If it was known in advance that there was anything unusual in the certificate of any State, it does not so appear from the record; but, in point of fact, the electors for Wisconsin had not met on the day fixed by law, which day, says the Constitution itself, "shall be the same throughout the United States," but on the next day after. A severe snowstorm had prevented the electors from reaching the capital of the State in season to give their votes on the 3d of December, and they had met and voted on the 4th.

When the votes of Wisconsin were presented at the joint meeting of the two Houses, an objection was made to counting them. The president *pro tempore* of the Senate, the Hon. James M. Mason, of Virginia, ruled that debate was not in order while the tellers were counting the votes. The

STATES.	POPULAR VOTE.			ELECTORAL VOTE.		
	James Buchanan, Pennsylvania.	John C. Frémont, California.	Millard Fillmore, New York.	Buchanan and Breckinridge.	Frémont and Dayton.	Fillmore and Donelson.
Alabama	46,739	–	28,552	9	–	–
Arkansas	21,910	–	10,787	4	–	–
California . . .	53,365	20,691	36,165	4	–	–
Connecticut . . .	34,995	42,715	2,615	–	6	–
Delaware	8,004	308	6,175	3	–	–
Florida	6,358	–	4,833	3	–	–
Georgia	56,578	–	42,228	10	–	–
Illinois	105,348	96,189	37,444	11	–	–
Indiana	118,670	94,375	22,386	13	–	–
Iowa	36,170	43,954	9,180	–	4	–
Kentucky	74,642	314	67,416	12	–	–
Louisiana	22,164	–	20,709	6	–	–
Maine	39,080	67,379	3,325	–	8	–
Maryland . . .	39,115	281	47,460	–	–	8
Massachusetts . .	39,240	108,190	19,626	–	13	–
Michigan	52,136	71,762	1,660	–	6	–
Mississippi . . .	35,446	–	24,195	7	–	–
Missouri	58,164	–	48,524	9	–	–
New Hampshire .	32,789	38,345	422	–	5	–
New Jersey . . .	46,943	28,338	24,115	7	–	–
New York . . .	195,878	276,007	124,604	–	35	–
North Carolina . .	48,246	–	36,886	10	–	–
Ohio	170,874	187,497	28,126	–	23	–
Pennsylvania . .	230,710	147,510	82,175	27	–	–
Rhode Island . .	6,680	11,467	1,675	–	4	–
South Carolina * .	–	–	–	8	–	–
Tennessee . . .	73,638	–	66,178	12	–	–
Texas	31,169	–	15,639	4	–	–
Vermont	10,569	39,561	545	–	5	–
Virginia	89,706	291	60,310	15	–	–
Wisconsin	52,843	66,090	579	–	5	–
Total	1,838,169	1,341,264	874,534	174	114	8

* Electors appointed by the legislature.

count having been concluded, Mr. Letcher, of Virginia, of the House of Representatives, inquired if it would then be in order to move that the votes of Wisconsin be excluded. The president ruled that it was not in order. Senator Crittenden, of Kentucky, asked if the chair decided " that Congress, in no form, has power to decide upon the validity or invalidity of a vote." The president, having disclaimed the intention to make any such decision, proceeded to recapitulate the votes, giving Buchanan and Breckinridge 174 each, and Frémont and Dayton 114 each (which included the votes of Wisconsin), and to declare the election of the Democratic candidates. Protests were raised on all sides, from both parties and by members of both Houses. In spite of the declaration of the presiding officer that no debate was in order, a long and rambling debate ensued, in which the most diverse views were advanced. The discussion was at last cut short by the withdrawal of the Senate. The matter was immediately resumed in each House, and discussion was continued for two days. The debates on that occasion are the most valuable for the student of political history, as to this *casus omissus* of the Constitution, that have ever taken place, because the question was considered without a spirit of partisanship. The vote of Wisconsin would not affect the result, whether counted or rejected. There was much ignorance of the Constitution displayed by many of the speakers; but, on the other hand, some of them discussed the question with profound learning and with great ability.

It is impossible here to give a sketch of this most interesting debate. Nothing more can be done than to summarize some of the views advanced. On the main question, Republicans generally thought the votes of Wisconsin ought to be counted; Democrats, for the most part, took the contrary view. Upon the question who, under the Constitution, should count, that is, who decide what were votes, the divergence of opinion was amazing. Some contented themselves with asserting that the power was in Congress to decide upon the validity of votes, leaving the method of exercising the power to be determined by law. But it was maintained in the Senate, by Mr. Thompson, of Kentucky, that the "votes are to be returned to *us*, and counted by *us*, and the House of Representatives are admitted to be present at the count to prevent a combination, a clandestine operation, a secret session, a *coup d'état*. . . . The votes are to be returned to the Senate, and counted by the Senate." On the other hand, Mr. Humphrey Marshall, of Kentucky, maintained in the House that that body was the sole judge, and Mr. Henry Winter Davis, of Maryland, took the same view. The ground of this opinion was, that it was for the House to decide whether or not to go into an election of President.

There was still another point on which the difference of opinion was decided. The president of the Senate stoutly affirmed that he had neither counted nor rejected the votes, although he had said: "The state of the votes as delivered by the tellers is . . . for John C. Frémont, of California, 114 votes." Many senators sustained the assertion of Mr. Mason that he had not counted the votes, while others declared that he had counted them. Numerous resolutions were offered in each branch, but the debate produced nothing more than a resolution of formal notification to Messrs. Buchanan and Breckinridge that they had been elected. The opinion that the whole subject ought to be taken up and considered, and the doubtful points determined by law, was generally expressed; but, as soon as the matter in hand was disposed of, the subject was dropped. The Congress was then in the last month of its term, and it was too busy to take further notice of a danger past which might never return. Consequently the disputed point was left for a Republican Congress to decide, according to the political exigency of the hour, in the midst of a civil war.

XXI

THE LAST STRUGGLE OF SLAVERY

DURING the whole of Mr. Buchanan's administration the country was drifting steadily toward civil war. The issue between slavery and anti-slavery was joined at all points. The Dred Scott decision, promulgated by the Supreme Court soon after the new President was inaugurated, sustained the Southerners' contention as to their rights of property so fully as to justify the bitter comment upon it that it made "Slavery national, Freedom sectional." The Republicans would not accept the *dictum* as final. If the Constitution must be taken to support the view taken by the court, they would refuse to obey the Constitution and follow the "higher law" proclaimed by Seward.

The struggle over Kansas, which had begun in the first year of Pierce's administration, continued under his successor until early in 1861, after secession had begun, when the State was admitted without slavery. The story of the contest fills one of the darkest pages of American political history. It is a record of perfidy and violence. The attempt to force the Lecompton constitution upon the people, under the patronage of the executive department of the government, was matched in baseness by the offer by Congress of a bribe to the people if they would accept it. The South, struggling as it was to maintain the political power of the section and of its social system, and backed by the highest judicial authority in the land, had a technical justification for every claim which it put forth to the possession of Kansas as a field for the extension of slavery. But, on the other hand, the moral sense of the Northern people was outraged by the effort to force slavery upon an unwilling people, and by the repeated violations of good faith which were resorted to in order to make the attempt successful. Kansas had seven governors in five years. One of them was removed because he would not be made the tool of the pro-slavery party. Another, a

Mississippian, an ex-senator, and Secretary of the Treasury during the whole of Polk's administration, resigned because the President would not keep officially the pledge which he had made verbally to the governor, that the people of Kansas should be allowed to vote on the whole Lecompton constitution.

The line which separated the Republican and the Democratic parties was broad; but there was a great variety of opinion within the ranks of each party.   Even the Abolitionists were beginning to think that an organization had been formed which they could join with consistency, one from which they might hope great things.   There was a wide difference, nevertheless, between them and the most conservative Republicans, who would not go beyond a firm and decided conviction that slavery could not exist in any Territory in opposition either to the will of Congress or to that of the people of the Territory.   But while the Republicans, being a party in opposition, could and did act together, the Democrats were split into two factions.   Senator Douglas, who had been a leader for the South in the repeal of the Missouri Compromise, revolted against the attempt to force the Lecompton constitution upon the people of Kansas.   Public opinion in the North was so strong as to carry almost the whole of the Democratic party of that section with him.   In the South he had some followers, and in the North many Democrats opposed his "popular sovereignty" doctrine and accepted the Southern view.   The office-holders stood by the administration, which opposed Douglas, with a reasonable apprehension of the consequences of taking another course.   No doubt there were many men at the North who were intellectually convinced that the constitutional position assumed in defence of slavery extension was correct; while others were with the administration because it was the administration, and favored the Southern view because the ascendency of slavery as a political power, if secured by their assistance, would give them office and standing in the party.

Since the time of Andrew Jackson the personal qualities of the President had had little influence upon the course of public events.   But now the weakness of Mr. Buchanan encouraged the Southern extremists to press their advantage; it made possible the formation of a strong Northern faction in open revolt against administration measures, and it rendered the

Republicans more resolute in their opposition to all the aggressions of slavery. Before the President was inaugurated, many of his moderate Northern supporters had hoped that he would incline toward a conservative policy, and resist the extremists of both sections. They saw him resign himself into the hands of the slavery propagandists and work their will. It is easy to see, after the event, that the conflict, which assumed the form of open war soon after his term closed, was really irrepressible, and that sooner or later it would have come to that, no matter who had been President. Yet there can be no doubt that Buchanan's lack of force hastened the war by sustaining one party in its greatest pretensions, and by goading the other party to more desperate resistance.

Douglas won the applause of the Republicans by his opposition to the administration's programme in Kansas, but he soon showed that his course was not prompted by hostility to slavery. He adhered to his " popular sovereignty " theories, and admitted that he did not care whether slavery "was voted up or voted down." The great series of debates between him and Abraham Lincoln, in the canvass of 1858, each of the disputants being the candidate of his party for the Illinois senatorship, brought out in the clearest possible light the wide difference between even Douglas's Democracy and the conservative Republicanism of Lincoln. Incidentally, while it strengthened Douglas as the favorite of the Northern Democrats for the presidency, it disclosed to the astonished eyes of the Republicans a leader worthy to take rank with the foremost.

The four years' term of Mr. Buchanan was filled with most important events, which tended to embitter politics and to prepare men for the great civil conflict that was impending. Beside those already mentioned, the John Brown raid at Harper's Ferry was the most startling. The tragic death of Senator Broderick, of California, a supporter of Douglas, in a duel with an adherent of the administration, stirred the people of the North profoundly. These occurrences and many others which cannot even be mentioned kept the popular pulse beating fast, and indicated to those who could read the signs of the times the profound crisis in the health of the body politic which was soon to come. There were large numbers of men, North and South, who observed the growing strife between the two sections of the country with almost agonized sorrow. Beside the old Whigs, whom time in its rapid flight had left behind the age, and the Native Americans of the South, who hated the Democrats, and yet could not join the Republican party, there were hosts of well-meaning men, all over the country, who feared that the bitter conflict would end in war. They deemed it a duty to the Union to endeavor to restore harmony. In the North they feared disunion more than they feared slavery; in the South they hated disunion almost as much as they hated abolition. The several elements mentioned above became temporarily united in the Constitutional Union party, as patriotic a party as was ever organized, but one which could not succeed in its mission because the time had come when the self-preservation of the South, as a political power, and the moral sense of the North, demanded that the pending question be settled finally and forever.

A series of momentous conventions began when the delegates of the Democratic party assembled at Charleston, South Carolina, on the 23d of April, 1860. There was a full delegation from every State of the Union, and contesting delegations appeared from New York and Illinois. In New York the "hards," led by Fernando Wood, had been elected by districts; while the "softs," who were favorable to Senator Douglas, were chosen by a state convention, which met at Syracuse in the autumn of 1859. The two Illinois delegations were respectively for and against Mr. Douglas. As soon as Mr. Francis B. Flournoy, of Arkansas, had taken the chair as temporary presiding officer of the convention, an angry debate began upon the contested seats, for the national committee had given tickets of admission, in each case, to the Douglas delegates, and had shut out their opponents.

On the first day of the convention nothing was done except to appoint committees. On the second day Mr. Caleb Cushing, of Massachusetts, was made the permanent presiding officer; a committee on resolutions was appointed; and it was voted not to vote for candidates of the party until a platform had been adopted. The third day was occupied in deciding the contests for seats, — in favor of the New York "softs," and the Douglas men from Illinois. It was only on the 27th of April, the fifth day of the convention, that the committee on resolutions reported to the assembly a majority and two or three minority sets of resolutions. Two days of fierce debate, and of numerous propositions to amend, followed; and, on the 28th, a motion was carried to recommit the whole subject to the committee.

Later on the same day the committee reported back a series of resolutions, asserting, as the previous majority report had done, the extreme Southern view of the question of slavery in the Territories. These resolutions were subsequently adopted by the convention of seceders some months later, and will be found on page 287. A minority report was presented, which, although signed by less than one half of the members of the platform committee, represented more than one half the electoral votes of the whole country. Gen. Benjamin F. Butler, of Massachusetts, who throughout the convention occupied an attitude peculiar to himself, presented a second minority report, which consisted of the Cincinnati platform of 1856, without any change whatever. Much debate, and a determined effort to postpone the vote on the substitution of the minority reports, followed; but on Monday, the 30th, a vote was reached. General Butler's platform was rejected, by yeas 105, nays 198. The minority resolutions presented by Mr. Samuels, of Iowa, were then substituted for those of the majority, by 165 to 138. These resolutions were in the following terms: —

1. *Resolved*, That we, the Democracy of the Union, in convention assembled, hereby declare our affirmance of the resolutions unanimously adopted and declared as a platform of principles by the Democratic convention at Cincinnati in the year 1856, believing that Democratic principles are unchangeable in their nature when applied to the same subject-matters; and we recommend as the only further resolutions the following: —

Inasmuch as differences of opinion exist in the Democratic party as to the nature and extent of the powers of a territorial legislature, and as to the powers and duties of Congress, under the Constitution of the United States, over the institution of slavery within the Territories, —

2. *Resolved*, That the Democratic party will abide by the decisions of the Supreme Court of the United States on the questions of constitutional law.

3. *Resolved*, That it is the duty of the United States to afford ample and complete protection to all its citizens, whether at home or abroad, and whether native or foreign.

4. *Resolved*, That one of the necessities of the age, in a military, commercial, and postal point of view, is speedy communication between the Atlantic and Pacific States; and the Democratic party pledge such constitutional government aid as will insure the construction of a railroad to the Pacific coast at the earliest practicable period.

5. *Resolved*, That the Democratic party are in favor of the acquisition of the island of Cuba, on such terms as shall be honorable to ourselves and just to Spain.

6. *Resolved*, That the enactments of state legislatures to defeat the faithful execution of the fugitive slave law are hostile in character, subversive of the Constitution, and revolutionary in their effects.

This series having been substituted for the majority set, the several resolutions were then considered singly, and, with the exception of that numbered two, which was rejected, they were adopted by an almost unanimous vote. This action was the signal for the withdrawal of a large number of the Southern delegates. Alabama led off with a formal protest. The delegation had been instructed not to waive the issue, and, as the convention had decided against the Southern view, they had no alternative but to withdraw. Mississippi, Florida, and Texas followed, with their entire delegations; and all but two of those from Louisiana, all but three from South Carolina, three from Arkansas, and two from Delaware joined the seceders. On the next day, May 1st, 28 of the 36 delegates who cast the 10 votes of Georgia also withdrew. This made a loss of about 45 votes out of 303.

The convention, after listening to some remarkable speeches by Southern men who did not secede, voted that two thirds of a full convention, that is, 202 votes, should be necessary to effect a nomination. The first vote for President resulted : —

Stephen A. Douglas, of Illinois 145½
R. M. T. Hunter, of Virginia 42
James Guthrie, of Kentucky 35
Andrew Johnson, of Tennessee 12
Daniel S. Dickinson, of New York 7
Joseph Lane, of Oregon 6
Isaac Toucey, of Connecticut 2½
Jefferson Davis, of Mississippi. 1½
James A. Pearce, of Maryland. 1

The convention took, on that and the following day, 57 votes. Mr. Douglas's strength rose slowly to 152½ on the 32d trial, then dropped to 151½, and remained at the same point from the 36th to the 57th vote. Mr. Hunter dropped slowly to 16 votes, which was his almost uniform number during the last twenty trials. Mr. Guthrie, who gained most of the votes lost by Mr. Hunter, reached 66½ on the 39th trial, and had 65½ on the 57th. The strength of no other candidate reached 21 votes on any one of the 57 contests. The last vote of this series was : for Douglas, 151½ ; Guthrie, 65½ ; Hunter, 16 ; Lane, 14 ; Dickinson, 4 ; Davis, 1.

On the 3d of May, the tenth day of the convention, a resolution was adopted to adjourn to meet in Baltimore on the 18th of June, and that it be recommended to Democrats to fill the vacancies made by the withdrawal of delegates. This resolution was carried by 195 votes to 55. The only Southern votes given, on both sides of this question, were : Maryland, 8 ; Virginia, 15 ; North Carolina, 14 ; Kentucky, 2 ; Tennessee, 12 ; Missouri, 9 ; Arkansas, 1 ; total 61, of the 120 to which the South was entitled.

Meantime the seceders from the regular convention had met in another hall in Charleston, organized by the choice of Senator James A. Bayard, of Delaware, as president, and adopted as a platform the resolutions reported by the majority of the committee on resolutions of the national convention (see page 287). After a session of four days they adjourned to meet in Richmond, Va., on the 11th of June. On reassembling at that time and place, Mr. John Erwin, of Alabama, was made president, and a resolution was adopted to adjourn again until the 21st of the month. At the adjourned session nothing was done until the 23d, when what was left of the body adopted the nominations of Breckinridge and Lane, made by the seceders at Baltimore, and adjourned without day.

The regular convention reassembled at Baltimore on the 18th of June. The president, Caleb Cushing, on taking the chair, made a long address, in which he stated the condition of business, the significant part of which was an intimation that the adoption of the platform was subject to reconsideration. The first business in order was the admission of delegates from those States whose representatives had withdrawn at Charleston. Three whole days were occupied in the settlement of these questions ; for in some cases the original delegates had presented themselves for readmission, and in other cases there were contesting delegations. The action of the convention was in most instances in favor of the delegates pledged to Mr. Douglas, and accordingly, as soon as the membership of the convention was fully decided, a portion of the Virginia delegation set the example of a second secession. They were followed by most of the remaining members from the Southern States, and by a few from the North ; and Mr. Cushing, the president, also withdrew and resigned the chair, which was taken by Governor Tod, of Ohio. The convention then proceeded to vote again for a candidate for President. On the first vote Douglas received $173\frac{1}{2}$ votes; Guthrie 10; and John C. Breckinridge 5, and three votes were divided among four other candidates. All the Southern States combined cast but 35 votes, and 15 of these were given by the contesting delegates just admitted to the convention. On the announcement of the result, Mr. Sanford E. Church, of New York, moved a resolution that, as Mr. Douglas had received two thirds of the vote given in this convention, he be declared the regular nominee of the party. The objection was raised that the resolution indirectly rescinded the rule requiring two thirds of a full convention to effect a nomination ; but the resolution was declared in order, and a long debate took place upon it. Finally it was withdrawn to allow another vote to be taken, which resulted in Mr. Douglas receiving $181\frac{1}{2}$; Mr. Breckinridge $7\frac{1}{2}$; and Mr. Guthrie $5\frac{1}{2}$ votes. The resolution of Mr. Church was then taken up and passed. Benjamin Fitzpatrick, of Alabama, was nominated for Vice-President on the first vote, with almost complete unanimity. The following resolution, proposed from the floor, was adopted with only two dissenting votes, as an addition to the platform : —

Resolved, That it is in accordance with the interpretation of the Cincinnati platform, that, during the existence of the Territorial governments, the measure of restriction, whatever it may be, imposed by the Federal Constitution on the power of the Territorial legislature over the subject of the domestic relations, as the same has been, or shall hereafter be, finally determined by the Supreme Court of the United States, should be respected by all good citizens, and enforced with promptness and fidelity by every branch of the general government.

This finished the proceedings of the convention. Mr. Fitzpatrick declined the nomination for Vice-President, and Herschel V. Johnson, of Georgia, was nominated by the National Committee.

Upon leaving the convention hall the seceders proceeded to organize a rival convention. They were joined by some delegates who had withdrawn from the convention at Charleston, and by the excluded contesting delegates. Mr. Cushing presided over the convention. Twenty-one States were wholly or partially represented, but no delegates were present from the States of Maine, New Hampshire, Rhode Island, Connecticut, New Jersey, South Carolina, Ohio, Michigan, Indiana, Illinois, Iowa, and Wisconsin. The convention made short work. It adopted the platform reported by the majority of the committee on resolutions of the Charleston convention, nominated John C. Breckinridge, of Kentucky, for President, and Joseph Lane, of Oregon, for Vice-President, both by a unanimous vote, and adjourned. The platform adopted was as follows : —

Resolved, That the platform adopted by the Democratic party at Cincinnati be affirmed, with the following explanatory resolutions : —

1. That the government of a Territory organized by an act of Congress is provisional and temporary; and, during its existence, all citizens of the United States have an equal right to settle with their property in the Territory, without their rights, either of person or of property, being destroyed or impaired by congressional legislation.

2. That it is the duty of the federal government, in all its departments, to protect, when necessary, the rights of persons and property in the Territories, and wherever else its constitutional authority extends.

3. That when the settlers in a Territory, having an adequate population, form a state constitution, the right of sovereignty commences, and, being consummated by admission into the Union, they stand on an equal footing with the people of other States; and the State thus organized ought to be admitted into the federal Union, whether its Constitution prohibits or recognizes the institution of slavery.

4. That the Democratic party are in favor of the acquisition of the island of Cuba, on such terms as shall be honorable to ourselves and just to Spain, at the earliest practicable moment.

5. That the enactments of state legislatures to defeat the faithful execution of the fugitive slave law are hostile in character, subversive of the Constitution, and revolutionary in their effect.

6. That the Democracy of the United States recognize it as the imperative duty of this government to protect the naturalized citizen in all his rights, whether at home or in foreign lands, to the same extent as its native-born citizens.

Whereas, One of the greatest necessities of the age, in a political, commercial, postal, and military point of view, is a speedy communication between the Pacific and Atlantic coasts, —

Therefore be it resolved, That the Democratic party do hereby pledge themselves to use every means in their power to secure the passage of some bill, to the extent of the constitutional authority of Congress, for the construction of a Pacific railroad from the Mississippi River to the Pacific Ocean, at the earliest practicable moment.

This brief and meagre summary of the proceedings of the Democrats gives no idea of the intense excitement that attended the sessions of the convention, nor of the breathless interest with which the country watched its proceedings. The " irrepressible conflict " existed even in the party which had upheld the Southern cause, although that party had been already more than decimated in the North by secession to the Republican ranks. The two-thirds rule had wrecked the convention. The party had two sets of candidates, neither of which could claim regularity of nomination according to ordinary Democratic usage ; and two platforms, the one supported by a majority as represented in the original convention, the other expressing the views of a great majority of those who could give electoral votes to Democratic candidates. It was evident to every one that, unless the two factions could get together on election day, probably even if they were able to patch up their differences, the cause was lost and a Republican triumph was assured. The Republicans themselves were delighted at a situation which gave them such an opportunity. The southern Democrats sent forth emphatic warning of the course they would pursue should a Republican President be chosen, and began to prepare for the grim struggle. Douglas's followers maintained their ground. They had gone as far as they would go in concession to the South.

Soon after the Charleston convention adjourned, to reassemble in Baltimore, the Constitutional Union party held its first and only general convention, at Baltimore, on the 9th of May. Most of the States were represented, though not in all cases by delegates duly elected in primary meetings and conventions. Young as it was, the party was divided into two wings. The Southerners, mostly representatives of the still surviving Native American sentiment, desired to nominate General Sam Houston, of Texas. The old Whigs of the North did not relish such a candidacy. They were adjured not to pay too much attention to gentility, but to take a candidate who, rough as he might be, would carry many of the southern States. Although the party was, by its very name, one of union, it had no sooner organized, by the choice of Washington

Hunt, of New York, as president, than it fell into a bitter debate as to the manner of voting, and as to the number of votes which delegations might cast. The Houston party was present in great force, and it was feared that, unless a strict rule were adopted, that candidate might be thrust upon the convention. When this difficulty had been surmounted, the committee on resolutions made a report, which was unanimously adopted, and the following platform was accepted : —

Whereas, Experience has demonstrated that platforms adopted by the partisan conventions of the country have had the effect to mislead and deceive the people, and at the same time to widen the political divisions of the country by the creation and encouragement of geographical and sectional parties, therefore, —

Resolved, That it is both the part of patriotism and of duty to recognize no political principle other than the Constitution of the country, the union of the States, and the enforcement of the laws, and that, as representatives of the Constitutional Union men of the country in national convention assembled, we hereby pledge ourselves to maintain, protect, and defend, separately and unitedly, these great principles of public liberty and national safety, against all enemies at home and abroad, believing that thereby peace may once more be restored to the country, the rights of the people and of the States reëstablished, and the government again placed in that condition of justice, fraternity, and equality which, under the example and Constitution of our fathers, has solemnly bound every citizen of the United States to maintain a more perfect union, establish justice, insure domestic tranquillity, provide for the common defence, promote the general welfare, and secure the blessings of liberty to ourselves and our posterity.

Two votes only were necessary to effect a nomination of a candidate for President. They resulted as follows : —

	First.	Second.
John Bell, of Tennessee	68½	138½
Samuel Houston, of Texas	57	68
John J. Crittenden, of Kentucky	28	8⅓
Edward Everett, of Massachusetts	25	9⅓
John McLean, of Ohio	22	—
William A. Graham, of North Carolina	22	18½
William C. Rives, of Virginia	13	—
John M. Botts, of Virginia	9½	5½
William L. Sharkey, of Mississippi	6	5
William L. Goggin, of Virginia	3	—

The number necessary for a choice on the second vote was 127, and Mr. Bell was accordingly nominated. Edward Everett, of Massachusetts, was the only person proposed as a candidate for Vice-President, and he was unanimously nominated. Not a little enthusiasm was manifested over the two nominations, which, if they did not insure a vigorous treatment of the questions of the day, did certainly represent the desire of the convention that the country should have union and peace.

All the political interest of the country was now concentrated upon the Republican convention called to meet at Chicago on the 16th of May. While the Democrats were divided and discordant, and were evidently unable to unite upon a platform or a candidate, the Republicans were confident. They had been successful in every Northern State in which an election was held, in 1859, save four: California; Oregon, where the adverse majority was only 59; New York, where the combined vote of the Democrats and third party men was less than 2000 more than that of the Republicans; and Rhode Island, where they were defeated by a fusion of all the opposition. Mr. Seward was the leading candidate. A large, influential, and well-organized body of delegates went to Chicago with a determination to effect his nomination. But the party was far from being united in his support. He had the bitter hostility of Horace Greeley, whose "Tribune" was the most powerful newspaper organ of Republican opinion; but that opposition did not count for so much as did the calmer and less virulent objection of a large section of the party which, though not unfriendly to Mr. Seward, and though grateful for his services, questioned the wisdom of putting in the field a candidate whose views were so pronounced, and whose attitude might alienate some elements which needed to be conciliated.

The political conditions were so favorable that the list of willing candidates was a long one. Senator Chase was hardly less prominent in politics than Mr. Seward, although his support was neither so large nor so general as that of the New York candidate. Mr. Greeley supported Edward Bates, of Missouri. Pennsylvania presented the name of Simon Cameron, for trading purposes. But it was seen early in the preliminary canvass that the only man who could be pitted against Seward with hope of success was the rugged "rail-splitter" of Illinois the champion who had not hesitated to match himself against the foremost debater of the Democratic party, and had emerged from the logical conflict with a reputation not inferior to that of his antagonist, — Abraham Lincoln.

When the convention assembled there were delegates present from all the free States, also from Delaware, Maryland, Virginia, Kentucky, Missouri, and Texas, and from the Territories of Kansas, Nebraska, and the District of Columbia. David Wilmot, of Pennsylvania, was the temporary chairman, and George Ashmun, of Massachusetts, the permanent president. There was a contest over the standing of the delegates from some of the Southern States, owing to a strong suspicion that they represented nobody but themselves, and were Republicans of the States which they claimed as their own, for convention purposes only. The convention took a liberal view, and allowed the delegates to retain their seats with a somewhat diminished voting strength in some cases.

On the second day there was a debate over the question whether a majority of the whole number of delegates, were all the States of the Union fully represented, or only a majority of the delegates voting, should be necessary to nominate. The first proposition, which would have been almost equivalent to the two-thirds rule of the Democrats, was rejected by 331 votes to 130.

The platform was reported, amended, and adopted as follows : —

Resolved, That we, the delegated representatives of the Republican electors of the United States, in convention assembled, in discharge of the duty we owe to our constituents and our country, unite in the following declarations : —

1. That the history of the nation, during the last four years, has fully established the propriety and necessity of the organization and perpetuation of the Republican party, and that the causes which called it into existence are permanent in their nature, and now, more than ever before, demand its peaceful and constitutional triumph.

2. That the maintenance of the principles promulgated in the Declaration of Independence and embodied in the Federal Constitution, — " that all men are created equal ; that they are endowed by their Creator with certain unalienable rights ; that among these are life, liberty, and the pursuit of happiness ; that, to secure these rights, governments are instituted among men, deriving their just

powers from the consent of the governed " — is essential to the preservation of our republican institutions; and that the federal Constitution, the rights of the States, and the union of the States must and shall be preserved.

3. That to the union of the States this nation owes its unprecedented increase in population, its surprising development of material resources, its rapid augmentation of wealth, its happiness at home, and its honor abroad; and we hold in abhorrence all schemes for disunion, come from whatever source they may; and we congratulate the country that no Republican member of Congress has uttered or countenanced the threats of disunion so often made by Democratic members, without rebuke and with applause from their political associates; and we denounce those threats of disunion, in case of a popular overthrow of their ascendency, as denying the vital principles of a free government, and as an avowal of contemplated treason, which it is the imperative duty of an indignant people sternly to rebuke and forever silence.

4. That the maintenance inviolate of the rights of the States, and especially the right of each State to order and control its own domestic institutions according to its own judgment exclusively, is essential to that balance of power on which the perfection and endurance of our political fabric depends; and we denounce the lawless invasion by armed force of the soil of any State or Territory, no matter under what pretext, as among the gravest of crimes.

5. That the present Democratic administration has far exceeded our worst apprehensions, in its measureless subserviency to the exactions of a sectional interest, as especially evinced in its desperate exertions to force the infamous Lecompton constitution upon the protesting people of Kansas; in construing the personal relation between master and servant to involve an unqualified property in person; in its attempted enforcement, everywhere, on land and sea, through the intervention of Congress and of the Federal courts, of the extreme pretensions of a purely local interest; and in its general and unvarying abuse of the power intrusted to it by a confiding people.

6. That the people justly view with alarm the reckless extravagance which pervades every department of the federal government; that a return to rigid economy and accountability is indispensable to arrest the systematic plunder of the public treasury by favored partisans; while the recent startling developments of frauds and corruptions at the Federal metropolis show that an entire change of administration is imperatively demanded.

7. That the new dogma that the Constitution, of its own force, carries slavery into any or all of the Territories of the United States,

is a dangerous political heresy, at variance with the explicit provisions of that instrument itself, with contemporaneous exposition, and with legislative and judicial precedent; is revolutionary in its tendency, and subversive of the peace and harmony of the country.

8. That the normal condition of all the territory of the United States is that of freedom; that as our republican fathers, when they had abolished slavery in all our national territory, ordained that no person should be deprived of life, liberty, or property without due process of law, it becomes our duty, by legislation, whenever such legislation is necessary, to maintain this provision of the Constitution against all attempts to violate it; and we deny the authority of Congress, of a territorial legislature, or of any individual, to give legal existence to slavery in any Territory of the United States.

9. That we brand the recent reopening of the African slave-trade, under the cover of our national flag, aided by perversions of judicial power, as a crime against humanity, and a burning shame to our country and age; and we call upon Congress to take prompt and efficient measures for the total and final suppression of that execrable traffic.

10. That in the recent vetoes, by their federal governors, of the acts of the legislatures of Kansas and Nebraska, prohibiting slavery in those Territories, we find a practical illustration of the boasted Democratic principle of non-intervention and popular sovereignty, embodied in the Kansas-Nebraska Bill, and a demonstration of the deception and fraud involved therein.

11. That Kansas should of right be immediately admitted as a State under the Constitution recently formed and adopted by her people and accepted by the House of Representatives.

12. That, while providing revenue for the support of the general government by duties upon imports, sound policy requires such an adjustment of these imposts as to encourage the development of the industrial interests of the whole country; and we commend that policy of national exchanges which secures to the workingmen liberal wages, to agriculture remunerating prices, to mechanics and manufacturers an adequate reward for their skill, labor, and enterprise, and to the nation commercial prosperity and independence.

13. That we protest against any sale or alienation to others of the public lands held by actual settlers, and against any view of the free-homestead policy which regards the settlers as paupers or suppliants for public bounty; and we demand the passage by Congress of the complete and satisfactory homestead measure which has already passed the House.

14. That the Republican party is opposed to any change in our naturalization laws, or any state legislation by which the rights of

citizenship hitherto accorded to immigrants from foreign lands shall be abridged or impaired; and in favor of giving a full and efficient protection to the rights of all classes of citizens, whether native or naturalized, both at home and abroad.

15. That appropriations by Congress for river and harbor improvements of a national character, required for the accommodation and security of our existing commerce, are authorized by the Constitution, and justified by the obligations of government to protect the lives and property of its citizens.

16. That a railroad to the Pacific Ocean is imperatively demanded by the interests of the whole country; that the federal government ought to render immediate and efficient aid in its construction; and that, as preliminary thereto, a daily overland mail should be promptly established.

17. Finally, having thus set forth our distinctive principles and views, we invite the coöperation of all citizens, however differing on other questions, who substantially agree with us in their affirmance and support.

The second resolution as originally reported did not contain the passage from the Declaration of Independence therein quoted. It was proposed by Mr. Joshua R. Giddings, of Ohio, to insert it in the form of a separate resolution, "that we solemnly reassert the self-evident truth that all men," etc.; but the motion was defeated. Mr. George William Curtis, of New York, afterward moved to insert the passage in its present place, and the motion prevailed. On the third day of the convention the names of candidates for President were formally presented, but no speeches were allowed to be made by those who nominated the candidates. Three votes were taken amid increasing excitement, with the following result: —

	1st.	2d.	3d.
Whole number of votes	465	465	465
Necessary for a choice	233	233	233
William H. Seward, of New York . . .	173½	184½	180
Abraham Lincoln, of Illinois	102	181	231½
Simon Cameron, of Pennsylvania	50½	2	–
Salmon P. Chase, of Ohio	49	42½	24½
Edward Bates, of Missouri	48	35	22
William L. Dayton, of New Jersey . . .	14	10	1
John McLean, of Ohio	12	8	5
Jacob Collamer, of Vermont	10	–	–
Scattering	6	2	1

Mr. Lincoln was within one and a half votes of a nomination when the roll-call was completed. Ohio quickly transferred four votes to him, and then delegation after delegation changed in his favor until he had 354 in all. On motion of Mr. W. M. Evarts, of New York, seconded by Mr. John A. Andrew, of Massachusetts, the nomination was made unanimous with the greatest enthusiasm.

At a later session on the same day the convention voted twice for a candidate for Vice-President, with this result: —

	First.	Second.
Hannibal Hamlin, of Maine	194	367
Cassius M. Clay, of Kentucky	101½	86
John Hickman, of Pennsylvania	58	13
Andrew H. Reeder, of Pennsylvania	51	–
Nathaniel P. Banks, of Massachusetts	38½	–
Scattering	15	–

The nomination of Mr. Hamlin having been made unanimous, the convention closed its proceedings by the adoption of the following resolution, offered by Mr. Giddings, of Ohio: —

Resolved, That we deeply sympathize with those men who have been driven, some from their native States and others from the States of their adoption, and are now exiled from their homes on account of their opinions; and we hold the Democratic party responsible for the gross violation of that clause of the Constitution which declares that citizens of each State shall be entitled to all the privileges and immunities of citizens of the several States.

The canvass which ensued after these several nominations had been made was fierce and exciting. On the part of the Republicans there was a well-grounded confidence that they were to be victorious. The nomination of Mr. Lincoln, like that of General Harrison twenty years before, was exceedingly popular with young men; although, of course, the remark is true in the later case of the young men in the Northern half of the country only. The tactics which had been so efficacious in the successful Whig campaigns were again resorted to, and the Northern States were alive with processions, torch-light parades, and mass-meetings. In the South there was a grim determination to win the victory if possible, but in no event to submit to defeat. The mutterings of secession and war, should Mr. Lincoln be elected, were frequently heard; the supporters of the Republican party refused to believe that the South would be guilty of such madness. In the Northern section of the Democratic party there was an earnest effort to fuse all the elements in support of a union ticket of electors, with the implied, and in some cases the expressed, agreement that in case the ticket should command a majority the electoral votes should be given to that candidate who should come the nearest to an election. This course was pursued in the close States only. Where there was no hope that fusion would give the Democrats a majority, the two wings of the party had each its own electoral ticket. All the planning was without avail. Had there been complete fusion in every State, the Republicans would have lost no electoral votes save those of California and Oregon. The early elections in Maine, Ohio, Indiana, and Pennsylvania, to say nothing of other States where the contest was not so close, foreshadowed the certain election of Mr. Lincoln, and the result in November more than justified the deductions from the September and October elections. Every Northern State except New Jersey was carried by the Republicans, and even that State gave a divided electoral vote. The decision was hardly made by the people of the country before the South began to carry out the threats which had been only muttered before the election; and the new President succeeded to the administration of a government which was to fight for its very existence.

Thirty-three States took part in this election. Minnesota had been admitted to the Union on the 11th of May, 1858, and Oregon on the 12th of February, 1859. The popular and electoral vote, together with the details of fusion, are given on the next page.

The official record of the electoral count contains nothing of interest. The proceedings were in strict accordance with precedent. Nevertheless a single remark made by a member of the House of Representatives after the count was over indicates the condition of affairs at the time. Some trouble had been feared on the occasion of the count of votes, and no doubt precautions were taken against violence at any time, and particularly at that time. At all events, the Southerners scented hostile preparations; and Mr. Hindman, of Arkansas, suggested that the committee to wait on the President-elect " be directed to inform General Scott that there is no further need for his janizaries about the Capitol, the votes being counted and the result proclaimed." The only attention paid to the sneer was in a retort from Mr. Grow, of Pennsylvania, that " gentlemen seem to trouble themselves a good deal about General Scott on all occasions." The proceedings then terminated.

STATES.	POPULAR VOTE.				ELECTORAL VOTE.			
	Abraham Lincoln, Illinois.	Stephen A. Douglas, Illinois.	John C. Breckinridge, Kentucky.	John Bell, Tennessee.	Lincoln and Hamlin.	Douglas and Johnson.	Breckinridge and Lane.	Bell and Everett.
Alabama	–	13,651	48,831	27,875	–	–	9	–
Arkansas	–	5,227	28,732	20,094	–	–	4	–
California	39,173	38,516	34,334	6,817	4	–	–	–
Connecticut . . .	43,792	15,522	14,641	3,291	6	–	–	–
Delaware	3,815	1,023	7,337	3,864	–	–	3	–
Florida	–	367	8,543	5,437	–	–	3	–
Georgia	–	11,590	51,889	42,886	–	–	10	–
Illinois	172,161	160,215	2,404	4,913	11	–	–	–
Indiana	139,033	115,509	12,295	5,306	13	–	–	–
Iowa	70,409	55,111	1,048	1,763	4	–	–	–
Kentucky	1,364	25,651	53,143	66,058	–	–	–	12
Louisiana	–	7,625	22,861	20,204	–	–	6	–
Maine	62,811	26,693	6,368	2,046	8	–	–	–
Maryland	2,294	5,966	42,482	41,760	–	–	8	–
Massachusetts . .	106,533	34,372	5,939	22,331	13	–	–	–
Michigan	88,480	65,057	805	405	6	–	–	–
Minnesota . . .	22,069	11,920	748	62	4	–	–	–
Mississippi . . .	–	3,283	40,797	25,040	–	–	7	–
Missouri	17,028	58,801	31,317	58,372	–	9	–	–
New Hampshire .	37,519	25,881	2,112	441	5	–	–	–
New Jersey . . .	58,324	62,801*	–	–	4†	3†	–	–
New York	362,646	312,510*	–	–	35	–	–	–
North Carolina . .	–	2,701	48,539	44,990	–	–	10	–
Ohio	231,610	187,232	11,405	12,194	23	–	–	–
Oregon	5,270	3,951	5,006	183	3	–	–	–
Pennsylvania . .	268,030	16,765	178,871*	12,776	27	–	–	–
Rhode Island . .	12,244	7,707*	–	–	4	–	–	–
South Carolina‡ .	–	–	–	–	–	–	8	–
Tennessee	–	11,350	64,709	69,274	–	–	–	12
Texas	–	–	47,548	15,438	–	–	4	–
Vermont	33,808	8,649	1,866	217	5	–	–	–
Virginia	1,929	16,290	74,323	74,681	–	–	–	15
Wisconsin . . .	86,110	65,021	888	161	5	–	–	–
Total	1,866,452	1,376,957	849,781	588,879	180	12	72	39

* Vote for fusion tickets. † Although the Fusion ticket in New Jersey received a
popular majority, four of the candidates were defeated by "scratching," and four
Lincoln electors had a plurality. ‡ Electors appointed by the legislature.

XXII

LINCOLN RE-ELECTED

SEVEN of the Southern States had taken the step of secession before the inauguration of President Lincoln. A futile attempt to save the Union was made by the Peace Convention which met in Washington on February 4, 1861, at the call of Virginia. Within six weeks after the attack upon Fort Sumter, Virginia and three other "Border" States had joined their more Southern sisters. The outbreak of the war almost obliterated parties. The South was eliminated from the politics of the country. Hundreds of thousands of Democrats eagerly adopted the view expressed by Douglas, " There can be no neutrals in this war, — only patriots and traitors." Many of the War Democrats became merged in the Republican party; others retained their political independence, but cordially supported all the war measures of the administration, and furnished to the army their due share of officers and men. There were, it is true, many Democrats who offered a persistent and unrelenting opposition to the war, and were querulous critics of the method of its prosecution. Not all who were denounced as " Southern sympathizers " were really desirous of the success of disunion; but the Northern temper was naturally intolerant, and, exaggerating the offence of those who opposed the administration, classed them all as " traitors." The favorite term of opprobrium was " Copperhead," the name of a venomous reptile. As the war proceeded, the spirit of acquiescence in the conduct of affairs diminished greatly, and a strong political opposition developed. The effective prosecution of a civil war necessarily involved the use of harsh and summary measures against men who were suspected of giving aid to the enemy. Nevertheless the suspension of the writ of *habeas corpus*, and the arbitrary arrests of citizens, drove into opposition many men whose loyalty could not be suspected. It was their misfortune that they were forced to make a political alliance with the more virulent enemies of the administration, not a few of whom rendered themselves obnoxious to the patriotic by rejoicing openly over defeats of the Union armies. The opposition was also ever ready to espouse the cause of generals who for any cause fell into disfavor at Washington. This was especially the case with respect to General McClellan, who became more and more a favorite with Democrats as the real or fancied wrongs which he suffered at the hands of the President increased. In 1862 the Republican party met with many reverses, the most important of which gave the great State of New York to the Democrats.

The President's trials did not come from those alone who regarded his acts, and those of his officers and agents, as arbitrary and tyrannical. He was beset also by an active minority of his own party, who chafed at his conservatism and his unwillingness to adopt the radical measures which they were persuaded would hasten the success of the Union arms. They urged the enrollment of colored troops and the complete emancipation of the slaves. Mr. Lincoln moved slowly, because public sentiment was slower still. The people at large learned to trust his calmness and good sense. If they did not approve all his acts, they were sure of his high purpose, and they pardoned much to the terrible exigency that forced him to sanction doubtful or objectionable measures. The firmness with which he withstood the demand for emancipation, when it was clamorously urged upon him, made them all the more ready to accept his judgment as to the wisdom of the step when at last and with deliberation he proclaimed that all the slaves within the territory held by the Confederacy were thenceforth free. His wisdom and strength commended him to thoughtful men, and his quaint shrewdness in word and act brought him near to the common people.

Mr. Lincoln neither obtrusively urged himself as a candidate for reëlection nor made any coy professions of unwillingness to be chosen again. He was simply and frankly a candidate. He believed that it was best for the country, in the circumstances, that he should be continued in office. It was not good policy, he said, — and the phrase made the one argument which in any case would have turned the scale in his favor, — " to swap horses while crossing a stream."

The certainty that the Republican convention — which was called on February 22, 1864, to meet in Baltimore on the 7th of June — would nominate Mr. Lincoln led certain radical opponents of his administration in various parts of the country to attempt to forestall its action by calling a convention to meet on an earlier day at Cleveland. Several calls were published, all of them inviting the people to meet in mass convention in that city on the 31st of May. Among the signers of these calls were the Rev. Dr. George B. Cheever, of New York, B. Gratz Brown, of Missouri, Lucius Robinson, of New York, and other gentlemen then or since prominent in public affairs. Wendell Phillips, Frederick Douglass, and others sent letters approving the objects of the convention.

In answer to these calls, about three hundred and fifty persons met in Cleveland on the appointed day. General John Cochrane, of New York, was made president. A platform was adopted as follows : —

First. That the Federal Union shall be preserved.

Second. That the Constitution and laws of the United States must be observed and obeyed.

Third. That the rebellion must be suppressed by force of arms, and without compromise.

Fourth. That the rights of free speech, free press, and the *habeas corpus* be held inviolate, save in districts where martial law has been proclaimed.

Fifth. That the rebellion has destroyed slavery, and the Federal Constitution should be amended to prohibit its reëstablishment, and to secure to all men absolute equality before the law.

Sixth. That integrity and economy are demanded at all times in the administration of the government, and that in time of war the want of them is criminal.

Seventh. That the right of asylum, except for crime and subject to law, is a recognized principle of American liberty; that any violation of it cannot be overlooked, and must not go unrebuked.

Eighth. That the national policy known as the " Monroe Doctrine " has become a recognized principle, and that the establishment of an anti-republican government on this continent by any foreign power cannot be tolerated.

Ninth. That the gratitude and support of the nation are due to the faithful soldiers and the earnest leaders of the Union army and navy for their heroic achievements of deathless valor in defence of our imperilled country and civil liberty.

Tenth. That the one-term policy for the presidency adopted by the people is strengthened by the force of the existing crisis, and should be maintained by constitutional amendments.

Eleventh. That the Constitution should be so amended that the President and Vice-President shall be elected by a direct vote of the people.

Twelfth. That the question of the reconstruction of the rebellious States belongs to the people, through their representatives in Congress, and not to the executive.

Thirteenth. That the confiscation of the lands of the rebels, and their distribution among the soldiers and actual settlers, is a measure of justice.

General John C. Frémont was nominated by acclamation for President, and General John Cochrane, a few dissenting, for Vice-President. In letters dated at New York, June 4, both gentlemen accepted these nominations. As a manifestation of one phase of the opposition to Mr. Lincoln, these proceedings and those which followed are interesting; but the candidacy of General Frémont came to nothing. On August 20 a letter was addressed to him by citizens of Boston, asking him if, " in case Mr. Lincoln will withdraw, you will do so," and "unite the thorough and earnest friends of a vigorous prosecution of the war in a new convention." The ultimate result of this movement, although Mr. Lincoln did nothing to promote it, was the withdrawal of both General Frémont and General Cochrane on the 21st of September, and the union of the Republican party in support of its regular candidates.

The call for the Republican national convention was worded, as the calls for many of the state conventions had been, so as to include in the invitation to participate in it all, of whatever former party relations, who would stand by the administration and its measures. It was addressed to those " who desire the unconditional maintenance of the Union, the supremacy of the Constitution, and the complete suppression of the existing rebellion, with the cause thereof, by vigorous war, and all apt and efficient means." The convention met at Baltimore, June 7, 1864, and was presided over temporarily by the Rev. Dr. Robert J. Breckinridge, of Kentucky, and, as permanent president, by ex-Governor William Dennison, of Ohio. The platform was reported by Mr. Henry J. Raymond, of New York, and was adopted unanimously, as follows : —

1. *Resolved,* That it is the highest duty of every American citizen to maintain against all their enemies the integrity of the Union, and the permanent authority of the Constitution and laws of the United States ; and that, laying aside all differences of political opinion, we pledge ourselves as Union men, animated by a common sentiment and aiming at a common object, to do everything in our power to aid the government in quelling by force of arms

the rebellion now raging against its authority, and in bringing to the punishment due to their crimes the rebels and traitors arrayed against it.

2. *Resolved*, That we approve the determination of the government of the United States not to compromise with rebels, or to offer them any terms of peace except such as may be based upon an unconditional surrender of their hostility and a return to their just allegiance to the Constitution and laws of the United States; and that we call upon the government to maintain this position, and to prosecute the war with the utmost possible vigor to the complete suppression of the rebellion, in full reliance upon the self-sacrificing patriotism, the heroic valor, and the undying devotion of the American people to their country and its free institutions.

3. *Resolved*, That, as slavery was the cause and now constitutes the strength of this rebellion, and as it must be, always and everywhere, hostile to the principles of republican government, justice and the national safety demand its utter and complete extirpation from the soil of the republic; and that, while we uphold and maintain the acts and proclamations by which the government, in its own defence, has aimed a death-blow at this gigantic evil, we are in favor, furthermore, of such amendment to the Constitution, to be made by the people in conformity with its provisions, as shall terminate and forever prohibit the existence of slavery within the limits or the jurisdiction of the United States.

4. *Resolved*, That the thanks of the American people are due to the soldiers and sailors of the army and navy who have perilled their lives in defence of their country and in vindication of the honor of its flag; that the nation owes to them some permanent recognition of their patriotism and their valor, and ample and permanent provision for those of their survivors who have received disabling and honorable wounds in the service of the country; and that the memories of those who have fallen in its defence shall be held in grateful and everlasting remembrance.

5. *Resolved*, That we approve and applaud the practical wisdom, the unselfish patriotism, and the unswerving fidelity with which Abraham Lincoln has discharged, under circumstances of unparalleled difficulty, the great duties and responsibilities of the presidential office; that we approve and indorse, as demanded by the emergency and essential to the preservation of the nation and as within the provisions of the Constitution, the measures and acts which he has adopted to defend the nation against its open and secret foes; that we approve, especially, the proclamation of emancipation and the employment as Union soldiers of men heretofore held in slavery; and that we have full confidence in his determination to

carry these and all other constitutional measures essential to the salvation of the country into full and complete effect.

6. *Resolved*, That we deem it essential to the general welfare that harmony should prevail in the national councils, and we regard as worthy of public confidence and official trust those only who cordially indorse the principles proclaimed in these resolutions, and which should characterize the administration of the government.

7. *Resolved*, That the government owes to all men employed in its armies, without regard to distinction of color, the full protection of the laws of war; and that any violation of these laws, or of the usages of civilized nations in time of war, by the rebels now in arms, should be made the subject of prompt and full redress.

8. *Resolved*, That foreign immigration, which in the past has added so much to the wealth, development of resources, and increase of power to this nation, — the asylum of the oppressed of all nations, — should be fostered and encouraged by a liberal and just policy.

9. *Resolved*, That we are in favor of a speedy construction of the railroad to the Pacific coast.

10. *Resolved*, That the national faith, pledged for the redemption of the public debt, must be kept inviolate, and that for this purpose we recommend economy and rigid responsibility in the public expenditures, and a vigorous and just system of taxation; and that it is the duty of every loyal State to sustain the credit and promote the use of the national currency.

11. *Resolved*, That we approve the position taken by the government, that the people of the United States can never regard with indifference the attempt of any European power to overthrow by force, or to supplant by fraud, the institutions of any republican government on the Western Continent; and that they will view with extreme jealousy, as menacing to the peace and independence of their own country, the efforts of any such power to obtain new footholds for monarchical governments, sustained by foreign military force, in near proximity to the United States.

On a formal vote for a candidate for President, Mr. Lincoln received all the votes of every State, except those of Missouri, which were cast, in accordance with instructions, for General U. S. Grant. The nomination was then made unanimous. On the first ballot for a candidate for Vice-President, Andrew Johnson, of Tennessee, received 200; Hannibal Hamlin, of Maine, 150; Daniel S. Dickinson, of New York, 108; and seven other candidates an aggregate of 61. Before the vote was declared, a great many changes took place, and the final result was: for Johnson, 494 votes; for Dickinson, 17; for Hamlin, 9. Mr. Johnson was declared the candidate.

The Democratic convention met on August 29, at Chicago. Ex-Governor William Bigler, of Pennsylvania, was the temporary president, and Governor Horatio Seymour, of New York, the permanent president. The platform was reported by Mr. James Guthrie, of Kentucky, as follows: —

Resolved, That in the future, as in the past, we will adhere with unswerving fidelity to the Union under the Constitution as the only solid foundation of our strength, security, and happiness as a people, and as a framework of government equally conducive to the welfare and prosperity of all the States, both Northern and Southern.

Resolved, That this convention does explicitly declare, as the sense of the American people, that after four years of failure to restore the Union by the experiment of war, during which, under the pretence of a military necessity, or war power higher than the Constitution, the Constitution itself has been disregarded in every part, and public liberty and private right alike trodden down, and the material prosperity of the country essentially impaired, — justice, humanity, liberty, and the public welfare demand that immediate efforts be made for a cessation of hostilities, with a view to an ultimate convention of the States, or other peaceable means, to the end that, at the earliest practicable moment, peace may be restored on the basis of the federal Union of the States.

Resolved, That the direct interference of the military authorities of the United States in the recent elections held in Kentucky, Maryland, Missouri, and Delaware was a shameful violation of the Constitution; and a repetition of such acts in the approaching election will be held as revolutionary, and resisted with all the means and power under our control.

Resolved, That the aim and object of the Democratic party is to preserve the federal Union and the rights of the States unimpaired; and they hereby declare that they consider that the administrative usurpation of extraordinary and dangerous powers not granted by the Constitution; the subversion of the civil by military law in States not in insurrection; the arbitrary military arrest, imprisonment, trial, and sentence of American citizens in States where civil law exists in full force; the suppression of freedom of speech and of the press; the denial of the right of asylum; the open and avowed disregard of state rights; the employment of unusual test oaths; and the interference with and denial of the right of the people to bear arms in their defence, — are calculated to prevent a restoration of the Union and the perpetuation of a government deriving its just powers from the consent of the governed.

Resolved, That the shameful disregard of the administration of
its duty in respect to our fellow-citizens who are now, and long have
been, prisoners of war and in a suffering condition, deserves the
severest reprobation, on the score alike of public policy and common humanity.

Resolved, That the sympathy of the Democratic party is heartily and earnestly extended to the soldiery of our army and the sailors of our navy, who are and have been, in the field and on the sea,
under the flag of our country ; and, in the event of its attaining
power, they will receive all the care, protection, and regard that
the brave soldiers and sailors of the republic have so nobly
earned.

On the first ballot* for a candidate for President, General
George B. McClellan was nominated.   He had been repeatedly
mentioned in connection with the nomination for many months,
and the sentiments of the Democratic party were concentrated in his favor long before the convention met.   The vote
as first taken resulted in 174 votes for McClellan ; 38 for
Thomas H. Seymour, of Connecticut ; 12 for Horatio Seymour,
of New York ; $\frac{1}{2}$ vote for Charles O'Conor, of New York ; and
$1\frac{1}{2}$ votes blank.   But before the result was announced several
changes were made, and the announcement was : for McClel-
lan, $202\frac{1}{2}$ votes; for Thomas H. Seymour, $28\frac{1}{2}$.   All the votes
for Mr. Seymour were given by delegates from Ohio, Indiana,
and the " border States."   The nomination of General Mc-
Clellan was made unanimous, on motion of Mr. Vallandigham
of Ohio.

The first vote for a candidate for Vice-President resulted
as follows : James Guthrie, of Kentucky, $65\frac{1}{2}$; George H.
Pendleton, of Ohio, $55\frac{1}{2}$; Lazarus W. Powell, of Kentucky,
$32\frac{1}{2}$; George W. Cass, of Pennsylvania, 26 ; Daniel W.
Voorhees, of Indiana, 13 ; John D. Caton, of Illinois, 16 ;
Augustus C. Dodge, of Iowa, 9 ; John S. Phelps, of Missouri,
8 ; blank, $\frac{1}{2}$ vote.   On the second trial, Mr. Guthrie's name
having been withdrawn, the friends of all the other candidates,
except those of Mr. Pendleton, withdrew their names also, and
Mr. Pendleton was unanimously nominated.

The canvass that followed was one of great spirit.   The
attention of the country was, it is true, earnestly fixed upon
the progress of the war, and it could not be greatly or for a
long time diverted to a political contest ; but the reëlection of
Mr. Lincoln was regarded and treated by the Republicans as

one of the important campaigns of the war ; and they held that those who were not with them in-the accomplishment of that object were against the Union. They denounced the Democratic platform as a base and cowardly surrender to the enemy, and as an encouragement to those in arms against the old flag to persevere in their hostilities until the peace party should be in a position to make terms with them on the basis of a peaceable secession. The Republicans had called their convention as one of Union men. War Democrats took a prominent part in the proceedings of that assembly, and one of them was the candidate for the Vice-Presidency on the ticket with Mr. Lincoln. They called upon all Union men to support the armies in the field by voting down the party which would make a disgraceful peace.

The Democratic platform, unpopular from its first promulgation, became more so as the canvass proceeded. General McClellan repudiated its obvious meaning in his letter of acceptance. Where the convention had demanded "a cessation of hostilities with a view to an ultimate convention of the States," the candidate expressed the belief that so " soon as it is clear, or even probable, that our present adversaries are ready for peace on the basis of the Union, we should exhaust all the resources of statesmanship . . . to secure such peace." The convention had proclaimed "four years of failure to restore the Union by the experiment of war ; " General McClellan wrote : " I could not look in the face of my gallant comrades of the army and navy, who have survived so many bloody battles, and tell them that their labors and the sacrifice of so many of our slain and wounded brethren had been in vain ; that we had abandoned that Union for which we have so often perilled our lives." The convention said : Peace first, and Union afterward, if it can be had. General McClellan said : The Union first, and then peace ; " no peace can be permanent without union." The convention said that the war had been a failure ; General McClellan could not look his old comrades in the face and say that.

His open repudiation of the expressed sentiments of the party saved to General McClellan many of the votes which would otherwise have been given to Mr. Lincoln. But although the party held its forces together much more generally than might have been expected, the plain common sense of the people taught them that Mr. Lincoln was the candidate whose election meant earnest and uncompromising war until the power of the rebellion was destroyed and the Union was restored, and they supported him. The general result was at no time in doubt.

In some of the States, provision had been made, before the war broke out, for taking the votes of soldiers absent from their respective States with the army. Other States adopted

STATES.	POPULAR VOTE.		SOLDIERS' VOTE.		ELECTORAL VOTE.	
	Abraham Lincoln, Illinois.	George B. McClellan, New Jersey.	Lincoln.	McClellan.	Lincoln and Johnson.	McClellan and Pendleton.
California . .	62,134	43,841	2,600	237	5	–
Connecticut . .	44,693	42,288	–	–	6	
Delaware . .	8,155	8,767	–	–	–	3
Illinois . . .	189,487	158,349	–	–	16	–
Indiana . . .	150,422	130,233	–	–	13	–
Iowa	87,331	49,260	15,178	1,364	8	–
Kansas . .	14,228	3,871	–	–	3	–
Kentucky . .	27,786	64,301	1,194	2,823	–	11
Maine	72,278	47,736	4,174	741	7	–
Maryland . .	40,153	32,739	2,800	321	7	–
Massachusetts	126,742	48,745	–	–	12	–
Michigan . .	85,352	67,370	9,402	2,959	8	–
Minnesota . .	25,060	17,375	–	–	4	–
Missouri . . .	72,991	31,026	–	–	11	–
Nevada . . .	9,826	6,594	–	–	2*	–
New Hampshire	36,595	33,034	2,066	690	5	–
New Jersey . .	60,723	68,014	–	–	–	7
New York . .	368,726	361,986	–	–	33	–
Ohio	265,154	205,568	41,146	9,757	21	–
Oregon . . .	9,888	8,457	–	–	3	–
Pennsylvania .	296,389	276,308	26,712	12,349	26	–
Rhode Island .	14,343	8,718	–	–	4	–
Vermont . .	42,422	13,325	243	49	5	–
West Virginia .	23,223	10,457	–	–	5	–
Wisconsin . .	79,564	63,875	11,372	2,458	8	–
Totals . . .	2,213,665	1,802,237	116,887	33,748	212	21

* Nevada chose three electors, one of whom died before the election.

similar provisions before the election took place. The army votes for President in 1864, which were counted in canvassing the returns for electors, are, in the table on the preceding page, separated from the home vote. It will be seen that in no case does the addition of the two change the result.

The total vote *counted*, including both the home and the army votes, was 4,166,537, and Mr. Lincoln's plurality was 494,567. The army votes of Kansas and Minnesota, which arrived too late to be counted, and certain votes rejected for informality in Wisconsin, would have brought up the total to about 4,175,000, and Mr. Lincoln's majority to a number in excess of half a million.

This was the first election since the adoption of the Constitution at which any State had deliberately neglected to appoint electors. In 1864 the authority of the United States was denied in, and complete sovereignty was claimed by the regular governments of, eleven States. But in some of them there had been set up rival governments, asserting their own loyalty to the Union, and claiming the recognition of Congress as the true government of those States. In one case, at least, the question presented was a puzzling one. The consent of the State of Virginia to the erection of the State of West Virginia within its territory — consent which was required by the terms of the Constitution — was given by one of these mushroom governments. After the creation of that new State, however, the territory and the population which admitted the authority of this government of Virginia were so small that Congress refused to recognize the claims of those who presented themselves as senators and representatives.

Nevertheless, pretended elections had been held in Louisiana and Tennessee, and the question was evidently to be pressed upon Congress whether or not the electoral votes cast in those States by a handful of men, many of them mere adventurers, were to be received. No such question had ever arisen before. Never had there been offered, at the joint meeting of the two Houses of Congress, a certificate of electoral votes which it was clearly the duty of Congress to reject, if Congress had any power to reject. In most such cases a decision of the question whether or not the disputed votes should be counted had been evaded; but in all these instances a determination either way could not affect the result. Nor would the admission or the rejection of the Southern votes in

1864 change the result. But if the votes were allowed, the act would be equivalent to a declaration that the governments by whose authority they were given were valid and regular, and such a declaration might make trouble when the time for reconstruction should come.

In these circumstances, and in order to fix the status of the seceded States until their governments had been duly reconstructed by Congress, a joint resolution was passed by both Houses a week before the count was to take place, as follows:—

Whereas, The inhabitants and local authorities of the States of Virginia, North Carolina, South Carolina, Georgia, Florida, Alabama, Mississippi, Louisiana, Texas, Arkansas, and Tennessee rebelled against the government of the United States, and were in such condition on the 8th day of November, 1864, that no valid election of electors for President and Vice-President of the United States, according to the Constitution and laws thereof, was held therein on said day; therefore —

Be it resolved, By the Senate and House of Representatives of the United States of America in Congress assembled, that the States mentioned in the preamble to this joint resolution are not entitled to representation in the Electoral College for the choice of President and Vice-President of the United States for the term commencing on the 4th day of March, 1865, and no electoral votes shall be received or counted from said States concerning the choice of President and Vice-President for said term of office.

The President was committed to the validity and regularity of the governments of Louisiana and Tennessee. A state government was in full operation in Louisiana, with Governor Hahn at its head, and the election in Tennessee had been ordered by Governor Andrew Johnson, Mr. Lincoln's associate on the ticket. Accordingly, the President was earnestly opposed to the resolution just recited, which virtually declared the invalidity of governments which he recognized, although Congress did not. But the Republicans in Congress were resolved that the votes should not be counted, and they determined that if they could not exclude Louisiana and Tennessee by law, they would do so by joint action of the two Houses in counting the vote. Owing to a fear that the President would not sign the joint resolution, the "twenty-second joint rule," which governed the count of electoral votes until it threatened anarchy in 1877, was hastily drawn and hastily adopted by both branches. At the same time great pressure was brought to bear upon the President to approve the joint resolution. He finally yielded on the day the count was to take place, February 8, but not in time formally to notify Congress that he had done so. The joint rule, which would have been unnecessary if he had signed the resolution promptly, and which was to make much mischief in after years, served the same purpose. It was as follows: —

The two Houses shall assemble in the hall of the House of Representatives at the hour of one o'clock P. M., on the second Wednesday in February next succeeding the meeting of the electors of President and Vice-President of the United States, and the President of the Senate shall be their presiding officer. One teller shall be appointed on the part of the Senate, and two on the part of the House of Representatives, to whom shall be handed, as they are opened by the President of the Senate, the certificates of the electoral votes; and said tellers, having read the same in the presence and hearing of the two Houses then assembled, shall make a list of the votes as they shall appear from the said certificates; and the votes having been counted, the result of the same shall be delivered to the President of the Senate, who shall thereupon announce the state of the vote and the names of the persons, if any, elected; which announcement shall be deemed a sufficient declaration of the persons elected President and Vice-President of the United States, and, together with a list of the votes, be entered on the journals of the two Houses.

If, upon the reading of any such certificate by the tellers, any question shall arise in regard to counting the votes therein certified, the same having been stated by the presiding officer, the Senate shall thereupon withdraw, and said question shall be submitted to that body for its decision; and the Speaker of the House of Representatives shall, in like manner, submit said question to the House of Representatives for its decision; and no question shall be decided affirmatively, and no vote objected to shall be counted, except by the concurrent votes of the two Houses, which being obtained, the two Houses shall immediately reassemble, and the presiding officer shall then announce the decision of the question submitted, and upon any such question there shall be no debate in either House; and any other question pertinent to the object for which the two houses are assembled may be submitted and determined in like manner.

At such joint meeting of the two Houses, seats shall be provided as follows: for the President of the Senate, the Speaker's chair; for the Speaker, a chair immediately upon his left; for the senators, in the body of the hall, upon the right of the presiding officer; for the

representatives, in the body of the hall not occupied by the senators; for the tellers, Secretary of the Senate, and Clerk of the House
i Representatives, at the Clerk's desk; for the other officers of the two Houses, in front of the Clerk's desk, and upon either side of the Speaker's platform.

Such joint meeting shall not be dissolved until the electoral votes are all counted and the result declared; and no recess shall be taken unless a question shall have arisen in regard to counting any of such votes, in which case it shall be competent for either House, acting separately, in the manner hereinbefore provided, to direct a recess, not beyond the next day at the hour of one o'clock P. M.

The power assumed by Congress in the adoption of this joint resolution has frequently been assailed as an invention of the Republican party, and as a power never before asserted. But by reference to the proceedings in Congress in the year 1800 (p. 64 *et seq.*), it will be seen that a bill making permanent provision for counting the electoral vote failed only because the Senate then insisted that either branch of Congress might reject a vote, while the House of Representatives maintained that it should be rejected only by a concurrent vote. The act of 1887, which is now in force, permits the rejection of the vote of a State by concurrent action of both branches.

On the 8th of February the joint meeting was held. The Vice-President, Mr. Hamlin, presided. The votes were opened by him and read by the tellers. When all the returns had been read, and the result was about to be declared, Senator Cowan of Pennsylvania inquired if there were any more returns to be counted, and if so, " why they are not submitted to this body in joint convention, which alone is capable of determining whether they should be counted or not." The Vice-President replied : —

The chair has in his possession returns from the States of Louisiana and Tennessee, but, in obedience to the law of the land, the chair holds it to be his duty not to present them to the convention.

Senator Cowan thereupon asked if the joint resolution had become a law by the signature of the President, to which the Vice-President responded that it had been signed, but there had been no official notification of the act. A debate ensued upon the question whether the proceedings should have been had under the joint resolution or under the joint rule. The

Vice-President ultimately acted under the resolution, and did not present the doubtful votes. The election of Abraham Lincoln, of Illinois, as President, and of Andrew Johnson, of Tennessee, as Vice-President, for the term commencing March 4, 1865, was then proclaimed, and the joint convention was dissolved.

XXIII

GENERAL GRANT

EVENTS moved rapidly between the time of Mr. Lincoln's
election and that of his entering upon his second term.   The
South was exhausted by the struggle, and its army was hemmed
in on all sides.   Although, in his second inaugural address, " no
prediction is ventured " as to the issue of the war, it was believed that the civil war was virtually at an end, and already
plans of " reconstruction " were much discussed.   No one was
in favor of restoring to power, or of leaving in power, those
who had governed the States while they were in insurrection.
Nevertheless there was room for a wide diversity of opinion
as to the extent to which the disfranchisement of the former
voters in those States should be carried.   Mr. Lincoln's own
views were much more liberal than those of most of the
Northern statesmen.   There was even some apprehension of
a political conflict between him and Congress.   Six weeks
after the inauguration the President was assassinated, and
Andrew Johnson became President.   A man could not have
been found less fitted than he to enter into the plans of those
who, having determined the policy of the country during the
war, were resolved that the fruits of the war should be secured.   Compliance was not in his nature.   He lacked that
characteristic of greatness which enables strong popular leaders
to persuade their followers to support measures which their
judgment does not approve.   Jackson dragged his party after
him in his attack on the Bank, and ultimately inspired them
with such zeal for the war that his conduct in that affair has
been held up for popular applause for more than half a century after the conflict ended.   Yet it was not praiseworthy
in its motive, in its conduct, or in its results.   Lincoln would
probably have carried his liberal policy, in spite of Thaddeus
Stevens, Senator Ben Wade, and all the radicals, because the
people believed in Lincoln, in his motives, and in his wisdom.   They saw, and history sees, in President Johnson much

obstinacy, little wisdom, and no tact. But a combination of circumstances alienated him, almost at the beginning of his administration, from those to whom he owed his election, and made him a more strenuous opponent of the conditions devised by their leaders for the readmission of the southern States than Mr. Lincoln could ever have been.

The four years of Mr. Johnson's administration were a period scarcely less agitated than the four years which preceded secession. Civil war between the two sections, North and South, was succeeded by war, bloodless but severe, between the executive and legislative departments of the government. Mr. Johnson's training had been that of a southern state-rights Democrat; and although his patriotism was strong enough to keep him loyal when Tennessee voted herself out of the Union, no sooner was the military conquest of the Southern Confederacy accomplished than his former principles reasserted themselves. The more radical Republicans of the North, remembering the experience of the Whigs with Mr. Tyler, were only too ready to see evidence that he was to betray the party in all that Mr. Johnson did. They began to suspect him and to criticise him unpleasantly upon the appearance of his first proclamations. They feared the worst when he made known his selection of provisional governors of the seceded States. Little by little his adherence to his lifelong political principles, and the unnecessarily persistent and violent opposition of the radical Republicans, widened the breach; and at last he found himself in full sympathy with the Democratic party.

The chief cause of the difference between President and Congress was the extra-constitutional position in which the seceded States were left when armed hostility to the Union was extinguished. War had been waged against them, or rather against their inhabitants, upon the theory that a State had no right to secede. The logical sequence of this proposition was that, since no State had seceded, the "States lately in rebellion," as the phrase ran, were still members of the Union; and that their laws and acts, so far as they were not contrary to the Constitution of the United States, were in full force. Under this view of the case the white men of the South, and they alone, would be entitled to reëstablish relations with the other States, to send senators and members to Congress, and, in short, to resume the position which they had abandoned in 1861, suffering no political penalty whatever for their attempt to dissolve the Union.

It need not be said that not even the most moderate Republicans allowed the theory of the indissoluble nature of the Union to overcome the practical necessity of imposing conditions to the reinstatement of the South in that Union. The President's views, to which he referred as "my policy," were that the States were already restored to their old position when they chose to exercise their right by the election of senators and members. Congress rejected this policy absolutely, and, by a series of measures known as the reconstruction acts, required the southern States to abjure all the principles for which they had contended on the field of battle. The States were placed under military governors until they should have complied with the conditions of readmission. Thorough revision of the state constitutions was required ; the assent of the States to the amendments to the Constitution of the United States was also a necessary preliminary to restoration. The enfranchisement of the negroes, and the disfranchisement of those who had been in arms against the Union, deprived the former ruling class of its privileges. These measures and others, some of which were subsequently declared unconstitutional by the Supreme Court, made almost every southern State Republican by the simple expedient of excluding the Democrats who had participated in the war against the Union from the exercise of the elective franchise.

Congress carried through its measures of reconstruction only by overcoming a succession of vetoes. The President expressed his constitutional views, which were shared by no Republicans, in returning the bills : " to provide for the more efficient government of the rebel States," to establish the Freedmen's Bureau, to secure civil rights, to admit Colorado and Nebraska to the Union, and many others. He tried to remove Republicans from office, and to fill their places with Democrats ; and Congress retorted upon him with the tenure-of-office bill, which Mr. Johnson returned without his signature, and which Congress promptly passed over the veto. By this act the power of removal, always previously conceded to the President, was denied, and the consent of the Senate to the removal was required. The savage contest with Secretary Stanton, whom the President was resolved to remove from the war office and from the cabinet, his correspondence with General Grant, the

disrespectful manner in which he spoke of Congress in
" swinging round the circle," — all these events aggravated a
contest which culminated in the impeachment of the President
by the House of Representatives and his trial by the Senate.
During all this time the Republicans in Congress were strongly
supported in the North, which then, constitutionally or not,
governed the country without assistance from the South. The
resolution that the long struggle against rebellion should not be
fruitless was firm and unchangeable, and the Republicans had
the satisfaction of seeing all their measures adopted, ineffectual
as some of them have since proved to be.

During this period another set of questions began to be discussed, and some of them were to be the basis of a new party
and of a new school of politicians, and to form the issue on
which future elections were to be decided. In the prosecution
of the war a great debt had been created, and a part of this
debt consisted of treasury notes, made a legal tender for all
public and private debts, except duties on imports and the
interest of the public debt. An attempt in the early part of
Mr. Johnson's term to reduce the amount of legal-tender notes,
or greenbacks, outstanding, had resulted in a temporary strin-
gency in the money market, and had led to action by Congress
which forbade a further reduction of the volume of the currency. The heavy taxation caused by the war, the high premium on gold, and the rapidly increasing value of government
bonds which were drawing gold interest, induced some politicians
to propose a variety of schemes which would lighten the burden
of the taxpayer at the cost of a virtual breach of faith on the
part of the government. One of the propositions was the taxation of bonds, which were by their terms expressly exempted
from state and municipal taxation. Taxation of them by
national authority would have been the same thing as reducing
the rate of interest which had been promised upon them. The
most popular form of attack upon the bondholders was a
proposition to pay the principal of the bonds in greenbacks.
The letter of the law did not forbid this, but the Republicans
maintained that the spirit of the law was against it, and that
it would be virtual repudiation. A large number of Democrats, particularly in the West, took up this proposition with
great enthusiasm. One of the most prominent among them
was Mr. Pendleton, of Ohio, who had been General McClellan's associate on the national ticket in 1864, and was now

regarded as the leading candidate for the first place in 1868. While this view of public policy was most prevalent among Democrats, there were many Republicans also who shared it. Thaddeus Stevens was the most conspicuous example of dissent from the general opinion of the party, yet even he finally voted in favor of a bill to strengthen the public credit, which President Johnson defeated by a " pocket veto." It was in the canvass preliminary to the election of 1868 that the Democrats first manifested that preference for the greenback currency which continued to be a principle of the controlling wing of the party until it transferred its affections to silver.

A great many circumstances united to make General Ulysses S. Grant the natural and inevitable choice of the Republicans for a candidate for President. The chief of these reasons were his military success, and the conspicuous position into which he was thrust by the controversy with Mr. Johnson. But added to these recommendations was the confidence reposed in his judgment in the choice of men; and the fact that he was no politician increased not a little his popularity with the people, who were tired of the wrangles of the past few years. General Grant, it was well known, had never voted for Republican candidates in his life. There were many persons who feared that the risk was too great in taking for the leader of the party, at such a time, a man whose political principles were thought not to be well defined, and that the Republicans might be about to repeat their own mistake of 1864. But nothing could stay the tide of public sentiment in General Grant's favor, and the warnings of the dissentients were drowned in the nearly universal demand that he should be selected. The wisest and most cautious men of the party convinced themselves by General Grant's letters and private conversation that he was fully to be trusted, and their confidence was not misplaced.

The question of the candidacy for the first place being fully decided by the action of the state and district conventions, as well as by popular sentiment, all the interest in the Republican convention was concentrated upon the vice-presidency and the platform. The vote of the Senate upon the impeachment of the President had been taken the week before the convention met. Inasmuch as several Republican senators had voted for acquittal on the eleventh article, which had been taken for a test, some of the more radical and impulsive delegates were in favor of expressing decided condemnation of the act which had rendered the removal of the President impossible. In spite of the vehemence of the more hot-headed members of the party, the proposed action was defeated, and the convention contented itself with expressing the opinion that those who voted for conviction were in the right.

There was a long list of candidates for the nomination for Vice-President, including Mr. Hamlin, who had been left off the ticket four years before in order to give a representation to the loyalty of the South; Mr. Benjamin F. Wade, senator from Ohio, who was President of the Senate during a part of the time that the war between the President and Congress was waging; Mr. Colfax, the Speaker of the House of Representatives; Senators Fenton, of New York, and Wilson, of Massachusetts, Governor Curtin, of Pennsylvania, and other candidates of less prominence.

Prior to the meeting of the national convention of the Republicans, a convention of soldiers and sailors was held at Chicago. It was presided over by General John A. Logan, and was full of enthusiasm for General Grant. The Republican convention met on May 20 at Chicago, and completed its work in two days. General Carl Schurz was the temporary presiding officer, and General Joseph R. Hawley, of Connecticut, was made permanent president. The first day was occupied with preliminaries. On the morning of the second day the committee on resolutions reported a platform, which was adopted. Two additional resolutions were afterwards appended to the platform, having been moved from the floor by Mr. Schurz, and unanimously approved. The platform in full was as follows: —

The National Republican party of the United States, assembled in national convention in the city of Chicago, on the twenty-first day of May, 1868, make the following declaration of principles: —

1. We congratulate the country on the assured success of the reconstruction policy of Congress, as evinced by the adoption, in the majority of the States lately in rebellion, of constitutions securing equal civil and political rights to all; and it is the duty of the government to sustain those institutions, and to prevent the people of such States from being remitted to a state of anarchy.

2. The guarantee by Congress of equal suffrage to all loyal men at the South was demanded by every consideration of public safety,

of gratitude, and of justice, and must be maintainêd; while the question of suffrage in all the loyal States properly belongs to the people of those States.

3. We denounce all forms of repudiation as a national crime; and the national honor requires the payment of the public indebtedness in the uttermost good faith to all creditors at home and abroad, not only according to the letter, but the spirit of the laws under which it was contracted.

4. It is due to the labor of the nation that taxation should be equalized, and reduced as rapidly as the national faith will permit.

5. The national debt, contracted as it has been for the preservation of the Union for all time to come, should be extended over a fair period for redemption; and it is the duty of Congress to reduce the rate of interest thereon whenever it can be honestly done.

6. That the best policy to diminish our burden of debt is so to improve our credit that capitalists will seek to loan us money at lower rates of interest than we now pay, and must continue to pay, so long as repudiation, partial or total, open or covert, is threatened or suspected.

7. The government of the United States should be administered with the strictest economy; and the corruptions which have been so shamefully nursed and fostered by Andrew Johnson call loudly for radical reform.

8. We profoundly deplore the untimely and tragic death of Abraham Lincoln, and regret the accession to the presidency of Andrew Johnson, who has acted treacherously to the people who elected him and the cause he was pledged to support; who has usurped high legislative and judicial functions; who has refused to execute the laws; who has used his high office to induce other officers to ignore and violate the laws; who has employed his executive powers to render insecure the property, the peace, the liberty and life of the citizen; who has abused the pardoning power; who has denounced the national legislature as unconstitutional; who has persistently and corruptly resisted, by every means in his power, every proper attempt at the reconstruction of the States lately in rebellion; who has perverted the public patronage into an engine of wholesale corruption; and who has been justly impeached for high crimes and misdemeanors, and properly pronounced guilty thereof by the vote of thirty-five senators.

9. The doctrine of Great Britain and other European powers, that because a man is once a subject he is always so, must be resisted at every hazard by the United States as a relic of feudal times, not authorized by the laws of nations, and at war with our national honor and independence. Naturalized citizens are entitled

to protection in all their rights of citizenship, as though they were native born; and no citizen of the United States, native or naturalized, must be liable to arrest and imprisonment by any foreign power for acts done or words spoken in this country; and, if so arrested and imprisoned, it is the duty of the government to interfere in his behalf.

10. Of all who were faithful in the trials of the late war, there were none entitled to more special honor than the brave soldiers and seamen who endured the hardships of campaign and cruise, and imperilled their lives in the service of the country; the bounties and pensions provided by the laws for these brave defenders of the nation are obligations never to be forgotten; the widows and orphans of the gallant dead are the wards of the people, — a sacred legacy bequeathed to the nation's protecting care.

11. Foreign immigration, which in the past has added so much to the wealth, development, and resources, and increase of power to this republic, — the asylum of the oppressed of all nations, — should be fostered and encouraged by a liberal and just policy.

12. This convention declares itself in sympathy with all oppressed peoples struggling for their rights.

13. We highly commend the spirit of magnanimity and forbearance with which men who have served in the rebellion, but who now frankly and honestly coöperate with us in restoring the peace of the country and reconstructing the southern state governments upon the basis of impartial justice and equal rights, are received back into the communion of the loyal people; and we favor the removal of the disqualifications and restrictions imposed upon the late rebels in the same measure as the spirit of disloyalty will die out, and as may be consistent with the safety of the loyal people.

14. We recognize the great principles laid down in the immortal Declaration of Independence as the true foundation of democratic government; and we hail with gladness every effort toward making these principles a living reality on every inch of American soil.

When the convention was ready to proceed with its nominations, General Logan presented the name of General Grant in a brief but stirring speech, and, the roll of the States being called, every vote — 650 in all — was given to him. While the enthusiasm of the convention was at its height, a large portrait of General Grant was uncovered behind the president's chair, and the delegates again went wild with cheering. Five votes were necessary to effect a nomination for the second place on the ticket. The result of the several votes is shown in the following table : —

	1st.	2d.	3d.	4th.	5th.
Benjamin F. Wade, Ohio	147	170	178	206	38
Reuben E. Fenton, New York	126	144	139	144	69
Henry Wilson, Massachusetts	119	114	101	87	–
Schuyler Colfax, Indiana	115	145	165	186	541
Andrew G. Curtin, Pennsylvania	51	45	40	–	–
Hannibal Hamlin, Maine	28	30	25	25	–
James Speed, Kentucky	22	–	–	–	–
James Harlan, Iowa	16	–	–	–	–
John A. J. Creswell, Maryland	14	–	–	–	–
Samuel C. Pomeroy, Kansas	6	–	–	–	–
William D. Kelley, Pennsylvania	4	–	–	–	–

The nomination of Mr. Colfax, the youngest candidate of all, was made unanimous, and the convention adjourned.

The Democratic convention was called to meet at Tammany Hall, New York, on the fourth of July. Democratic soldiers and sailors were invited to meet on the same day, also in New York. The interest centred wholly in the nomination of a candidate for the presidency, and it was from the first a contest of "the field" against Mr. Pendleton. Other candidates had strong supporters. The sentiment in the soldiers' convention was all in favor of General Winfield S. Hancock, who commended himself to those who had favored the war by his own gallant services, and to Democrats by his action as military commander at New Orleans during Mr. Johnson's administration. The Southern delegations were at least outwardly for Mr. Johnson himself. There was an undercurrent in favor of Chief Justice Chase. Most of the delegates from the Eastern States were not bound by instructions, and were prepared to support any candidate — except perhaps Mr. Pendleton — who seemed to have a chance of success.

Meantime, the Northwest was strong for Mr. Pendleton, though, as the event proved, the feeling was not deep. A day or two before the convention a body of three hundred men — the "Pendleton Escort" — arrived from Ohio, and marched through New York, each man wearing, pinned to his breast, a flag on which was a representation of a five-dollar greenback, and an inscription demanding the payment of the five-twenty bonds in that currency.

The fourth of July fell on Saturday. The convention organized by the choice of Henry S. Palmer, of Wisconsin, as temporary chairman. Governor Horatio Seymour, of New York, was permanent president. The convention was from the first extremely, suspicious of the Pendleton men. A motion that the rules of the national House of Representatives be the rules of the convention was offered, and voted down because it was proposed by an Ohio man, and because of a fear that it might mean an abrogation of the two-thirds rule. The two-thirds rule was adopted without opposition. On the first day the supporters of Mr. Pendleton were in favor of prompt work, that a ballot might be taken before their opponents could have an opportunity to concentrate; but they were defeated, and the convention adjourned until Monday. Afterward the Pendleton men were in favor of all possible delay, and on Monday they " filibustered " to retard the progress of business. It was not until Tuesday that the committee on resolutions was ready to report. The platform was unanimously reported and unanimously adopted, as follows : —

The Democratic party, in national convention assembled, reposing its trust in the intelligence, patriotism, and discriminating justice of the people, standing upon the Constitution as the foundation and limitation of the powers of the government, and the guarantee of the liberties of the citizen, and recognizing the questions of slavery and secession as having been settled, for all time to come, by the war, or the voluntary action of the Southern States in constitutional conventions assembled, and never to be renewed or reagitated, do, with the return of peace, demand, —

1. Immediate restoration of all the States to their rights in the Union under the Constitution, and of civil government to the American people.

2. Amnesty for all past political offences, and the regulation of the elective franchise in the States by their citizens.

3. Payment of the public debt of the United States as rapidly as practicable ; all moneys drawn from the people by taxation, except so much as is requisite for the necessities of the government, economically administered, being honestly applied to such payment, and where the obligations of the government do not expressly state upon their face, or the law under which they were issued does not provide, that they shall be paid in coin, they ought, in right and in justice, to be paid in the lawful money of the United States.

4. Equal taxation of every species of property according to its real value, including government bonds and other public securities.

5. One currency for the government and the people, the laborer and the office-holder, the pensioner and the soldier, the producer and the bondholder.

6. Economy in the administration of the government; the re

duction of the standing army and navy; the abolition of the freed-men's bureau, and all political instrumentalities designed to secure negro supremacy; simplification of the system, and discontinuance of inquisitorial modes of assessing and collecting internal revenue, so that the burden of taxation may be equalized and lessened; the credit of the government and the currency made good; the repeal of all enactments for enrolling the state militia into national forces in time of peace; and a tariff for revenue upon foreign imports, and such equal taxation under the internal revenue laws as will afford incidental protection to domestic manufacturers, and as will, without impairing the revenue, impose the least burden upon, and best promote and encourage, the great industrial interests of the country.

7. Reform of abuses in the administration, the expulsion of corrupt men from office, the abrogation of useless offices, the restoration of rightful authority to, and the independence of, the executive and judicial departments of the government, the subordination of the military to the civil power, to the end that the usurpations of Congress and the despotism of the sword may cease.

8. Equal rights and protection for naturalized and native-born citizens, at home and abroad; the assertion of American nationality which shall command the respect of foreign powers, and furnish an example and encouragement to peoples struggling for national integrity, constitutional liberty, and individual rights, and the maintenance of the rights of naturalized citizens against the absolute doctrine of immutable allegiance, and the claims of foreign powers to punish them for alleged crime committed beyond their jurisdiction.

In demanding these measures and reforms, we arraign the Radical party for its disregard of right, and the unparalleled oppression and tyranny which have marked its career.

After the most solemn and unanimous pledge of both Houses of Congress to prosecute the war exclusively for the maintenance of the government and the preservation of the Union under the Constitution, it has repeatedly violated that most sacred pledge under which alone was rallied that noble volunteer army which carried our flag to victory. Instead of restoring the Union it has, so far as in its power, dissolved it, and subjected ten States, in the time of profound peace, to military despotism and negro supremacy. It has nullified there the right of trial by jury; it has abolished the *habeas corpus,* that most sacred writ of liberty; it has overthrown the freedom of speech and the press; it has substituted arbitrary seizures and arrests, and military trials and secret star-chamber inquisitions, for the constitutional tribunals; it has disregarded, in time of peace, the right of the people to be free from searches and seizures; it has entered the post and telegraph offices, and even the private rooms of individuals, and seized their private papers and letters without any specific charge or notice or affidavit, as required by the organic law; it has converted the American Capitol into a bastille; it has established a system of spies and official espionage to which no constitutional monarchy of Europe would now dare to resort; it has abolished the right of appeal, on important constitutional questions, to the supreme judicial tribunals, and threatened to curtail or destroy its original jurisdiction, which is irrevocably vested by the Constitution; while the learned chief justice has been subjected to the most atrocious calumnies, merely because he would not prostitute his high office to the support of the false and partisan charges preferred against the President. Its corruption and extravagance have exceeded anything known in history, and, by its frauds and monopolies, it has nearly doubled the burden of the debt created by the war. It has stripped the President of his constitutional power of appointment, even of his own cabinet. Under its repeated assaults the pillars of the government are rocking on their base, and should it succeed in November next, and inaugurate its President, we will meet, as a subjected and conquered people, amid the ruins of liberty and the scattered fragments of the Constitution.

And we do declare and resolve that, ever since the people of the United States threw off all subjection to the British crown, the privilege and trust of suffrage have belonged to the several States, and have been granted, regulated, and controlled exclusively by the political power of each State respectively, and that any attempt by Congress, on any pretext whatever, to deprive any State of this right, or interfere with its exercise, is a flagrant usurpation of power, which can find no warrant in the Constitution, and, if sanctioned by the people, will subvert our form of government, and can only end in a single centralized and consolidated government, in which the separate existence of the States will be entirely absorbed, and unqualified despotism be established in place of a federal Union of coequal States. And that we regard the reconstruction acts (so called) of Congress, as such, as usurpations, and unconstitutional, revolutionary, and void.

That our soldiers and sailors, who carried the flag of our country to victory against a most gallant and determined foe, must ever be gratefully remembered, and all the guarantees given in their favor must be faithfully carried into execution.

That the public lands should be distributed as widely as possible among the people, and should be disposed of either under the preemption or homestead laws, or sold in reasonable quantities, and to none but actual occupants, at the minimum price established by the government. When grants of the public lands may be allowed, necessary for the encouragement of important public improvements, the proceeds of the sale of such lands, and not the lands themselves, should be so applied.

That the President of the United States, Andrew Johnson, in exercising the powers of his high office in resisting the aggressions of Congress upon the constitutional rights of the States and the people, is entitled to the gratitude of the whole American people, and in behalf of the Democratic party we tender him our thanks for his patriotic efforts in that regard.

Upon this platform the Democratic party appeal to every patriot, including all the conservative element and all who desire to support the Constitution and restore the Union, forgetting all past differences of opinion, to unite with us in the present great struggle for the liberties of the people; and that to all such, to whatever party they may have heretofore belonged, we extend the right hand of fellowship, and hail all such coöperating with us as friends and brethren.

To this platform two additional resolutions were subsequently appended, on motion, as follows: —

Resolved, That this convention sympathize cordially with the workingmen of the United States in their efforts to protect the rights and interests of the laboring classes of the country.

Resolved, That the thanks of the convention are tendered to Chief Justice Salmon P. Chase for the justice, dignity, and impartiality with which he presided over the court of impeachment on the trial of President Andrew Johnson.

Voting for a candidate then began, and continued until Thursday. The whole number of votes — each delegate having one half a vote — was 317; and 212, two thirds of the whole, were necessary for a choice. A few only of the twenty-two separate trials are necessary to show the increase and decrease of strength of the respective candidates: —

	1st.	8th.	16th.	18th.	19th.	21st.
George H. Pendleton, Ohio	105	156½	107½	56½	–	–
Andrew Johnson, Tennessee	65	6	5½	10	–	5
Winfield S. Hancock, Pennsylvania	33½	28	113½	144½	135½	135½
Sanford E. Church, New York	33	–	–	–	–	–
Asa Packer, Pennsylvania	26	26	–	–	22	–
Joel Parker, New Jersey	13	7	7	3½	–	–
James E. English, Connecticut	16	6	–	–	6	19
James R. Doolittle, Wisconsin	13	12	12	12	12	12
Thomas A. Hendricks, Indiana	2½	75	70½	87	107½	132
Salmon P. Chase, Ohio	–	–	–	½	½	½
All others	9	½	–	3½	33	12½

Great excitement had prevailed during the voting. On several occasions, delegates from States which had instructed their members to vote " as a unit," insisted upon their right to a record of their individual votes, but it was uniformly decided that the delegations as a whole were empowered to decide how the votes should be cast, and that only one spokesman from a State could be heard. There was much intriguing during the three days of voting. The New York and Pennsylvania delegations, with a combined vote of 59, assisted by the delegations from other Eastern States, prevented a nomination more than once by abandoning candidates, whose strength was increasing, when they were becoming too dangerous. On the twenty-first vote the contest was apparently narrowed down to Hancock and Hendricks, neither of whom was acceptable to New York. At this point a sensation was created. When the votes of a few States had been recorded at the twenty-second trial, some votes were given to Horatio Seymour, the president of the convention. Mr. Seymour promptly refused to be a candidate, but there was a hurried consultation, and the vote was persisted in. More votes were given to Seymour, and a " stampede" began. Mr. Seymour withdrew from the chair, and the changes of votes went on, amid the greatest excitement and enthusiasm, until he was made the nominee of the convention by 317 votes, — a full convention. It was asserted then, as it has been on every other occasion of a nomination suddenly made after a long contest, from that of Mr. Polk in 1844 to that of General Garfield in 1880, that the whole affair was carefully planned and rehearsed beforehand. In some cases the assertion was true. But if it was so in 1868, and not a line of evidence was ever adduced to prove it, a few persons only could have been in the secret, and the enthusiasm of the delegates was genuine and sincere. Indeed, the convention had selected one of the strongest men in the party.

General Francis P. Blair, Jr., of Missouri, was nominated unanimously for Vice-President at the first trial. Mr. Blair had just brought himself into prominence by a violent, not to say a revolutionary letter, addressed to Colonel J. O. Brodhead, dated a few days before the convention met. The nomination seemed to be, and probably was, a result of that letter.

The canvass was shorter than usual, and, although one-sided, was decidedly interesting. The fame of General Grant, and the high regard in which he was held, did not allow the result to be doubtful; but there were already some noteworthy defections from the Republican party at the North on account of the radical character of its Southern legislation; and a new element of discord in politics appeared in the shape of the movement, already mentioned, to pay the five-twenty bonds in greenbacks. It was never seriously believed that Governor Seymour was in favor of that measure, yet he "stood upon the platform," and declared, in accepting the nomination, that the resolutions "are in accord with my views." The Republicans made much of the virtual repudiation which such a financial policy as the resolutions demanded would effect, and, while they lost some votes of a certain class, they gained many others which were better worth having, even if they did not count any more. Toward the end of the canvass there was a strong movement by business men to defeat the Democrats, which contributed not a little to the overwhelming success of General Grant.

The South was secure for the Republicans. Reconstruction with negro suffrage, protected by the general government, and with extensive disfranchisement of those who had joined in the rebellion, made the triumph of the Republican electoral ticket a certainty. Delaware, Maryland, Kentucky, and Louisiana only, of all the Southern States, gave Governor Seymour a majority; but some of the States were not, under the act of Congress, entitled to representation in Congress, and consequently not to electoral votes. The votes of thirty-three States were counted; that of Georgia was treated as the vote of Missouri had been in 1820. Nebraska having been admitted to the Union, — the proclamation declaring its admission was dated March 1, 1867, — the number of States became thirty-seven. All the Southern States, except Virginia, Mississippi, and Texas, had been readmitted to representation in Congress, and to the right to choose electors. The position of Georgia was in doubt. In the reorganization of South Carolina the practice of a choice of electors by the legislature was abandoned; but Florida adopted the discarded system, and accordingly there was not as yet complete uniformity. The electoral and popular votes of the States, including Georgia, were as follows : —

STATES.	Ulysses S. Grant, Illinois.	Horatio Seymour, New York.	Grant and Colfax.	Seymour and Blair.
	POPULAR VOTE.		ELECTORAL VOTE.	
Alabama	76,366	72,086	8	–
Arkansas	22,152	19,078	5	–
California	54,592	54,078	5	–
Connecticut	50,641	47,600	6	–
Delaware	7,623	10,980	–	3
Florida *	–	–	3	–
Georgia	57,134	102,822	–	9
Illinois	250,293	199,143	16	–
Indiana	176,552	166,980	13	–
Iowa	120,399	74,040	8	–
Kansas	31,049	14,019	3	–
Kentucky	39,566	115,889	–	11
Louisiana	33,263	80,225	–	7
Maine	70,426	42,396	7	–
Maryland	30,438	62,357	–	7
Massachusetts	136,477	59,408	12	–
Michigan	128,550	97,069	8	–
Minnesota	43,542	28,072	4	–
Mississippi †	–	–	–	–
Missouri	85,671	59,788	11	–
Nebraska	9,729	5,439	3	–
Nevada	6,480	5,218	3	–
New Hampshire	38,191	31,224	5	–
New Jersey	80,121	83,001	–	7
New York	419,883	429,883	–	33
North Carolina	96,226	84,090	9	–
Ohio	280,128	238,700	21	–
Oregon	10,961	11,125	–	3
Pennsylvania	342,280	313,382	26	–
Rhode Island	12,993	6,548	4	–
South Carolina	62,301	45,237	6	–
Tennessee	56,757	26,311	10	–
Texas †	–	–	–	–
Vermont	44,167	12,045	5	–
Virginia †	–	–	–	–
West Virginia	29,025	20,306	5	–
Wisconsin	108,857	84,710	8	–
Total	3,012,833	2,703,249	214	80

* Electors appointed by the legislature.　　　　† No vote in the State.

There were many charges of gross fraud in the election. Aside from the irregularities alleged in the Southern States, the most famous case was that of New York. At the time the election took place, the " Tweed Ring " was in full power; and some telegrams which the Republicans regarded as highly suspicious passed between members of the Democratic State Central Committee and certain prominent politicians. It will be observed that the vote as canvassed gave a majority of exactly ten thousand to Mr. Seymour. This result, it was believed by many persons, was brought about intentionally, with a view to saving certain large wagers upon the Democratic majority in New York.

Reference has already been made to the fact that some of the southern States were, while others according to the legislation of Congress were not, entitled to vote for electors of President and Vice-President. Congress had passed a joint resolution declaring that no State of those lately in rebellion should be entitled to electoral votes unless, at the time prescribed for the election, such State had adopted a constitution since the 4th of March, 1867, under which a state government had been organized; unless the election was held under the authority of that government; and unless the State had become entitled to representation in Congress under the reconstruction laws. President Johnson vetoed the resolution on July 20, 1868. Both Houses of Congress passed it over his veto, the Senate by 45 to 8, and the House of Representatives by 134 to 36, and it was proclaimed a law. Under the resolution, Virginia, Mississippi, and Texas were excluded absolutely from the election. All the other seceded States, except Georgia, had been admitted to representation in Congress and were entitled to vote for President. The question whether or not Georgia had complied with the terms of the act authorizing a representation of that State in Congress was in dispute. Accordingly, on the 6th of February, 1869, two days before the count of electoral votes was to take place, Mr. Edmunds, of Vermont, introduced in the Senate a concurrent resolution, which does not require the approval of the President, in the following terms : —

Whereas, The question whether the State of Georgia has become and is entitled to representation in the two Houses of Congress is now pending and undetermined; and whereas by the joint resolution of Congress, passed July 20, 1868, entitled " resolution excluding from the electoral college votes of States lately in rebellion which shall not have been reorganized," it was provided that no electoral votes from any of the States lately in rebellion should be received or counted for President or Vice-President of the United States until, among other things, such State should have become entitled to representation in Congress pursuant to acts of Congress in that behalf; therefore

Resolved, That, on the assembling of the two Houses on the second Wednesday of February, 1869, for the counting of the electoral votes for President and Vice-President, as provided by law and the joint rules, if the counting or omitting to count the electoral votes, if any, which may be presented as of the State of Georgia, shall not essentially change the result, in that case they shall be reported by the President of the Senate in the following manner : Were the votes presented as of the State of Georgia to be counted, the result would be, for —— for President of the United States —— votes ; if not counted, for —— for President of the United States —— votes ; but, in either case, —— is elected President of the United States ; and in the same manner for Vice-President.

Mr. Hendricks, of Indiana, was the only senator who took an active part in the debate against this resolution ; although Mr. Trumbull, of Illinois, expressed the opinion that it would be best to count the vote of Georgia and say nothing about it, and finally voted — alone among the Republicans — against the resolution. It was passed by the House of Representatives on the same day under a suspension of the rules. It is worth noting that three of the candidates on presidential tickets in 1884 — Messrs. Blaine, Logan, and Butler — voted in the affirmative in the House on the passage of this resolution, while a fourth — Mr. Hendricks — voted against it in the Senate.

The count of the electoral votes took place on the 10th of February. It proceeded regularly until the votes of Louisiana were presented, when a member from Tennessee objected to them, under the twenty-second joint rule (see page 310), and the two Houses separated to consider the matter. Although no debate was in order, much time was consumed by the Senate in agreeing upon a form in which the decision of the question should be put. In the end the Senate voted to admit the votes by 51 to 7. The House promptly decided the question the same way by 137 to 63. The count was then resumed, and all the votes were opened and recorded, except

those of Georgia. On the presentation of the votes of that
State, General Butler, of Massachusetts, arose and objected
in writing to them on four distinct grounds : first, that the
votes were not given on the day fixed by law, — the electoral
college of Georgia had met on the 9th instead of the 2d of
December, 1868 ; secondly, because at the date of the election
Georgia had not been admitted to representation in Congress ;
thirdly, because Georgia had not complied with the reconstruction acts ; and, fourthly, because the election had not been
fair and free. The question arose at once whether the concurrent resolution of the Senate and House, directing how the
vote of Georgia should be treated, or the joint rule, was to
govern. The presiding officer, Senator Wade, of Ohio, was at
first inclined to hold the two Houses to the concurrent resolution ; but, as the situation became complicated, he led the
Senate back to its chamber.

The House of Representatives quickly decided, without
debate, — 150 to 41, — that the vote of Georgia should not
be counted. In the Senate there was a long and somewhat
ungoverned discussion. Mr. Wade explained that the reason
why he had yielded his first position in the joint meeting was
that two of Mr. Butler's objections were not of the kind contemplated by the concurrent resolution directing how the votes
of Georgia should be declared. Many propositions were made ;
and at last the Senate voted, by 28 votes against 25, " that,
under the special order of the two Houses respecting the electoral vote from the State of Georgia, the objections made to
the counting of the vote of the electors for the State of Georgia
are not in order." The action of each House having been
communicated to the other, the Senate returned to the Representatives' Hall. Then ensued one of the most remarkable
and disgraceful scenes ever enacted in Congress. Mr. Wade,
on taking the chair, remarked that the objections of the gentleman from Massachusetts had been overruled by the Senate,
and that the vote would be announced according to the terms
of the concurrent resolution. General Butler said that the
House had sustained the objections, and proposed to offer a
resolution, remarking, " I do not understand that we are to be
overruled by the Senate in that way." The President of the
Senate refused to entertain the resolution, and General Butler
appealed from the decision of the chair. The President
declined to entertain the appeal. A scene of indescribable
disorder and confusion followed, several members speaking at

once, Mr. Butler distinguishing himself by the violence of his language, and, as General Garfield said in the debate which followed the joint meeting, by "a manner and bearing of unparalleled insolence." Some of his remarks were omitted in the revised version, which appears in the "Congressional Globe;" but they were referred to in the debate just mentioned. His last remark, as revised, is thus reported : —

Mr. BUTLER, of Massachusetts : I move that this convention now be dissolved, and that the Senate have leave to retire. [Continued cries of "Order !" "Order !"] And on that motion I demand a vote. [Cries of "Order !" "Order !" from various parts of the hall.] We certainly have the right to clear the hall of interlopers.

The presiding officer, not noticing these interruptions, proceeded to sum up the result, as directed by the concurrent resolution, and declared Grant and Colfax elected. The Senate then retired.

As soon as the House was by itself, Mr. Butler rose to a question of privilege, and offered a resolution that "the House protest that the counting of the vote of Georgia by the order of the Vice-President *pro tempore* was a gross act of oppression and an invasion of the rights and privileges of the House." Upon this resolution a long and most acrimonious debate took place, which lasted three days. It contributed little or nothing to the settlement of the constitutional questions that have arisen in regard to the count of votes. The position of affairs was quite novel, and the gentlemen who took part in the debate seemed, without exception, to give hasty impressions rather than the result of careful study. The only point which was made clear was that the Constitution and the action of Congress left room for a variety of views, and that no member need be at a loss for precedents to sustain his own opinion. General Butler changed his resolution several times before a vote was taken. In one of its forms it proposed to abrogate the twenty-second joint rule, — a proposition which was received with derision by many Republican members, who declared that it was not possible for one House to rescind a joint rule. Nevertheless, eight years later the Senate rescinded the same rule, and refused to be bound by it, although the House was then in favor of acting under it. General Butler's resolution, greatly toned down, and providing for the reference of the subject to a select committee, was at last brought to a vote, on a motion to lay it on the table, which was carried by 130 to 55, and the matter was dropped.

XXIV

THE GREELEY CAMPAIGN

THE reconstruction of the southern States had been substantially completed before the term of General Grant as President began. It remained for three States only to comply with the conditions already established. This they did soon afterward, and before the third session of the Forty-first Congress began, every State in the Union was fully represented. But the Southern question was not yet settled. The constitutions of the re-admitted States contained guaranties of the right of the people to vote without distinction on account of race, color, or previous condition of servitude; but, in effect, both the political and social rights of the colored people were much restricted. A state of terrorism existed in some parts of the South, where a secret organization known as the Ku-Klux-Klan committed outrages upon the colored people, intended to intimidate them and to prevent them from voting. To defeat the schemes of those who endeavored by lawless acts to render the legislation of Congress nugatory, the act for the enforcement of the Fourteenth Amendment to the Constitution, commonly known as the Ku-Klux Act, was passed. This measure, although it seemed necessary at the time, gave the Democrats an opportunity, which they were not slow to improve, to sneer at the inefficiency of a party which, with unlimited power, had not been able in five years since the war closed to finish its work with the South. Military force was constantly necessary to uphold the southern state governments, and the internal condition of some districts was sadly disturbed.

Beside the Southern question, there were others which now began to assume political importance. The first act signed by President Grant pledged the faith of the government to the payment of the interest-bearing bonds of the United States in coin, and to an early resumption of specie payments. For the time being, the opposition confined their attacks upon the financial system to the national banks. The annexation of Santo

Domingo to the United States was a favorite scheme with the President, and he did all that was in his power, both publicly and privately, to accomplish it. In the course of his negotiations to that end, and by other measures, he alienated the support of Mr. Sumner and of Horace Greeley, whose standing as Republicans and as public men was almost unique, and whose adhesion to the opposition in the ensuing canvass was deemed at the time to be most disastrous to the Republicans.

There was another issue, which had its origin at this time, which has since played an important part in congressional and presidential elections. The principle tersely expressed by Mr. Marcy to justify the wholesale removals from office practised by General Jackson, that "to the victors belong the spoils of the enemy," had been adopted by every Democratic and opposition administration which followed that of Jackson. On the accession of Mr. Lincoln, the Democratic officers were driven out and Republicans took their places, in every department of the government, from the foreign minister to the country postmaster. Mr. Johnson had been restrained from substituting Democrats for them all by the tenure-of-office act. General Grant found few Democrats to expel from public positions; but an evil which had grown up with that of a partisan civil service now took on alarming proportions. Certain gentlemen, usually one for each State, became practically recognized as dispensers of patronage within those States, and, by the exercise of the power which the virtual right to dismiss and appoint to office gave them, made themselves "bosses" and dictators of Republican politics in their respective States. The heads of the custom-houses, the post-offices, and other government offices were in many cases the servants of these bosses, and were forced to work in the interest of the personal fortunes of their protectors, and to employ the subordinates under them to promote the same object, — all under the penalty of removal. Manipulation of the offices for private purposes developed a demand for a reform of the civil service, and emphasized the objections of many who had been sturdy Republicans to the administration of General Grant.

The supporters of the administration were, however, neither few nor inactive. In addition to those who cordially approved the public acts of Grant, there were many others who were not prepared to abandon it on account of its mistakes. They set down some of the President's errors to his inexperience in civil life; and while other errors could not be so explained, the Republicans generally held that for certain tasks which they thought remained to be done before the South could be safely left to itself General Grant was the best executive the country could have. While, therefore, the elements existed for an unusually powerful opposition to the Republican party, the leaders of that party had no doubt of their ability to carry the election of 1872.

The beginning of a united opposition was made in Missouri in 1870, when a part of the Republicans united with the Democrats in a "liberal" movement, and carried the state election. It was further developed the next year. Meetings were held in St. Louis and Cincinnati in the spring, in which opposition to the reëlection of General Grant was freely expressed; for even then it was assumed that he would expect to be nominated for reëlection. About the same time Mr. Vallandigham, of Ohio, who had been identified with the most extreme form of Democratic opposition to the war for the Union, and had been equally radical in his condemnation of Republican reconstruction and treatment of the South, presented and supported in a local caucus in Ohio a series of resolutions looking to a union of all elements of opposition on the basis of a full acceptance of the results of the war, the legislation already enacted, and the three amendments made to the Constitution. Finally, at a mass meeting of Liberal Republicans of Missouri, held at Jefferson City in January, 1872, in which nearly all the counties of the State were represented, it was voted to call a national convention of Liberal Republicans, to be held at Cincinnati on the 1st of May.

The first conventions for making nominations for the presidency were held at Columbus, Ohio, in February. The Labor Reformers met on the 21st of that month, with representatives present from seventeen States. The party had its origin in Massachusetts, where a trade union of shoemakers, who took the name of Knights of St. Crispin, formed the nucleus of a Labor Reform party. The reference in the sixth resolution of the platform which follows, indicates this origin. A Massachusetts manufacturer who had trouble with his "Crispin" hands brought a car-load of Chinese from California to operate his machinery. Mr. E. M. Chamberlin, of Massachusetts, who was the permanent president of the convention, had been the candidate of the party for governor.

The convention was in session two days, and adopted the following platform: —

We hold that all political power is inherent in the people, and free government is founded on their authority and established for their benefit; that all citizens are equal in political rights, entitled to the largest religious and political liberty compatible with the good order of society, as also to the use and enjoyment of the fruits of their labor and talents; and no man or set of men is entitled to exclusive separable endowments and privileges, or immunities from the government, but in consideration of public services; and any laws destructive of these fundamental principles are without moral binding force, and should be repealed. And believing that all the evils resulting from unjust legislation now affecting the industrial classes can be removed by the adoption of the principles contained in the following declaration, therefore,

Resolved, That it is the duty of the government to establish a just standard of distribution of capital and labor by providing a purely national circulating medium, based on the faith and resources of the nation, issued directly to the people without the intervention of any system of banking corporations; which money shall be legal tender in the payment of all debts, public and private, and interchangeable at the option of the holder for government bonds bearing a rate of interest not to exceed 3.65 per cent., subject to future legislation by Congress.

2. That the national debt should be paid in good faith, according to the original contract, at the earliest option of the government, without mortgaging the property of the people or the future earnings of labor, to enrich a few capitalists at home and abroad.

3. That justice demands that the burdens of government should be so adjusted as to bear equally on all classes, and that the exemption from taxation of government bonds bearing extortionate rates of interest is a violation of all just principles of revenue laws.

4. That the public lands of the United States belong to the people, and should not be sold to individuals nor granted to corporations, but should be held as a sacred trust for the benefit of the people, and should be granted to landless settlers only, in amounts not exceeding one hundred and sixty acres of land.

5. That Congress should modify the tariff so as to admit free such articles of common use as we can neither produce nor grow, and lay duties for revenue mainly upon articles of luxury and upon such articles of manufacture as will, we having the raw materials in abundance, assist in further developing the resources of the country.

6. That the presence in our country of Chinese laborers, imported by capitalists in large numbers for servile use, is an evil,

entailing want and its attendant train of misery and crime on all classes of the American people, and should be prohibited by legislation.

7. That we ask for the enactment of a law by which all mechanics and day-laborers employed by or on behalf of the government, whether directly or indirectly, through persons, firms, or corporations, contracting with the State, shall conform to the reduced standard of eight hours a day, recently adopted by Congress for national employees, and also for an amendment to the acts of incorporation for cities and towns, by which all laborers and mechanics employed at their expense shall conform to the same number of hours.

8. That the enlightened spirit of the age demands the abolition of the system of contract labor in our prisons and other reformatory institutions.

9. That the protection of life, liberty, and property are the three cardinal principles of government, and the first two are more sacred than the latter; therefore money needed for prosecuting wars should, as it is required, be assessed and collected from the wealth of the country, and not entailed as a burden upon posterity.

10. That it is the duty of the government to exercise its power over railroads and telegraph corporations, that they shall not in any case be privileged to exact such rates of freight, transportation, or charges, by whatever name, as may bear unduly or unequally upon the producer or consumer.

11. That there should be such a reform in the civil service of the national government as will remove it beyond all partisan influence, and place it in the charge and under the direction of intelligent and competent business men.

12. That as both history and experience teach us that power ever seeks to perpetuate itself by every and all means, and that its prolonged possession in the hands of one person is always dangerous to the interests of a free people, and believing that the spirit of our organic laws and the stability and safety of our free institutions are best obeyed on the one hand, and secured on the other, by a regular constitutional change in the chief of the country at each election; therefore, we are in favor of limiting the occupancy of the presidential chair to one term.

13. That we are in favor of granting general amnesty and restoring the Union at once on the basis of equality of rights and privileges to all, the impartial administration of justice being the only true bond of union to bind the States together and restore the government of the people.

14. That we demand the subjection of the military to the civil

authorities, and the confinement of its operations to national purposes alone.

15. That we deem it expedient for Congress to supervise the
patent laws, so as to give labor more fully the benefit of its own
ideas and inventions.

16. That fitness, and not political or personal considerations,
should be the only recommendation to public office, either appointive or elective, and any and all laws looking to the establishment
of this principle are heartily approved.

One informal and three formal ballots were required to effect
the nomination of a candidate for President.   These several
votes were as follows : —

	Informal.	1st.	2d.	3d.
John W. Geary, Pennsylvania . .	60	–	–	–
Horace H. Day, New York . .	59	21	59	3
David Davis, Illinois	47	88	93	201
Wendell Phillips, Massachusetts .	13	76	12	–
J. M. Palmer, Illinois	8	–	–	–
Joel Parker, New Jersey . . .	7	7	7	7
George W. Julian, Indiana . . .	6	1	5	–
B. Gratz Brown, Missouri . .	–	–	14	–
Horace Greeley, New York . .	–	–	11	–

On the first vote for a candidate for Vice-President, E. M.
Chamberlin, of Massachusetts, had 72 ; Joel Parker, of New
Jersey, 70 ; Alanson M. West, of Mississippi, 18 ; Thomas
Ewing, of Ohio, 31 ; and W. G. Bryan, of Tennessee, 10.   On
the second trial, Parker had 112, Chamberlin 57, and Ewing
22.

The candidates were men of eminent ability and of high
standing, and would have dignified almost any convention
that might put them in nomination.   But the Labor Reform
convention, although some of its members were able men,
was for the most part made up of trade union bosses and
political adventurers.   Its platform seemed at the time the
utterance of madmen ; yet it is far less radical than other
platforms since adopted by much more important political
bodies.   But no other convention would have failed to per-
ceive that when it resolved that the money needed for war
purposes should not be " entailed as a burden upon posterity," posterity might be more than willing to bear the burden ;

or would have spoken of a "bond of union to bind the States together;" or would have asked Congress to "supervise" the patent laws, instead of asking it to revise them. But if the convention went mad in its platform, it was evidently directed by skilful tacticians in making its nominations. Judge Davis was popularly credited with having political aspirations, and was known to be no longer in full sympathy with the Republican party. It seems to have been hoped that the united opposition would adopt this ticket. Judge Davis sent a non-committal dispatch to the convention, thanking it for the honor without accepting the nomination. In June both he and Judge Parker formally declined. The convention was called together again, but only a small number of delegates attended. Charles O'Conor, of New York, was nominated for President, and no nomination was made for the second place on the ticket.

Another party, destined to have a long life, although the part it has played in national politics has not been an important one, made its first appearance in this canvass. The advocates of the prohibition of the sale of intoxicating liquor had formed a more or less distinct group in the politics of many States since the "Maine law" agitation in the early fifties. During the civil war, all other issues save that of the Union were thrust aside. But now the agitation was renewed, and the Prohibition party met in national convention at Columbus, Ohio, on February 22. One hundred and ninety-four delegates were present, from nine States. Samuel Chase, of Ohio, was the president. A very long platform was reported and adopted by the convention, of which the newspapers of the day give but a brief abstract. In addition to a declaration in favor of the main principle of the party, — the legislative prohibition of the sale of intoxicating liquor, — the resolutions declare that sobriety is one of the main qualifications for a public officer; that officers should not be removed for political reasons; that public servants should be paid fixed salaries, and not by fees; that all possible measures should be adopted to prevent corruption in the government; that Congress should pass laws which will secure a sound national currency convertible at the will of the holder into gold and silver coin; that the rates of inland and ocean postage, and the charges for transportation by railway and water conveyances, and for communication by telegraph, should be as low as possible; that there should be no discrimination in favor of capital against labor; that monopoly and class legislation are evils; that the right of suffrage should be conferred without regard to sex; that the common-school system should be fostered; and that all judicious means should be employed to promote immigration.

The names of James Black, of Pennsylvania, as a candidate for President, and of John Russell, of Michigan, for Vice-President, were presented by a committee on nominations, and accepted by acclamation by the convention.

The Liberal Republican convention attracted much attention, and caused not a little uneasiness in advance among the friends of the administration. It was evident that the Democrats were ready to take up with any good candidates whom the dissatisfied Republicans might nominate. Suggestions were numerous, but unity of purpose there was not. Some of the most influential politicians and newspapers which supported the movement were strongly in favor of a free-trade policy; Mr. Greeley and his "Tribune" being almost the only conspicuous exceptions. Of candidates there was a full supply. Illinois furnished no less than three, — Judge David Davis, Governor John M. Palmer, and Senator Lyman Trumbull. Missouri brought forward her favorite son, B. Gratz Brown. Ohio suggested ex-Secretary Jacob D. Cox, and Chief Justice Chase was not forgotten. The candidate most spoken of at the East was Mr. Charles Francis Adams, of Massachusetts. The aspirations of Mr. Greeley were well known, but, even when the convention met, the idea of nominating him was treated almost as a joke.

Just before sailing for Europe, as arbitrator at Geneva on the Alabama Claims, Mr. Adams addressed a letter to Mr. David A. Wells, which was made public a day or two before the convention. The writer expressed his indifference in regard to the nomination, and declared his unwillingness to authorize any one to speak for him, except that, if he was expected to give any pledges or assurances of his own honesty, "you will please to draw me out of that crowd." In spite of the cautious way in which Mr. Adams refused to commit himself to the movement, which alienated many who might have supported him, his nomination was urgently pressed by his friends upon the members of the convention as they arrived. On the other hand some of the most influential Democrats in Congress and elsewhere sent word that, should Mr. Adams be nominated, they would oppose the acceptance of the Cincinnati ticket by the Democratic convention. As the Liberal Republicans felt confident that, with the assistance of the Democrats, victory was assured, the several cliques made great exertions to secure the nominations for their respective favorites.

The convention was a mass meeting. Except in a few places the Liberal Republicans had no organization, and the members were all volunteers. Mr. Stanley Matthews, of Ohio, was made temporary chairman. The question of membership was a puzzling one, certain States having but a small, and others a large, number of representatives, while in the case of New York there were two distinct and opposing factions. It was finally determined that the membership should be on the basis of two delegates for each senator and representative to which a State was entitled; that if a smaller number of members were present from any State, they should be allowed to cast the full vote of the State; and that delegations too numerous should meet and designate the delegates. The New York quarrel was composed. The organization was completed by the choice of Gen. Carl Schurz, of Missouri, as permanent president. Although the free-traders were a majority of the convention, the importance of uniting all who were opposed to General Grant was recognized, and, greatly to the chagrin of the most earnest advocates of free trade, a resolution on the subject of the tariff, which had been prepared by Mr. Greeley, was adopted. The convention issued an address to the people of the country and a platform of principles, which are given in full: —

The administration now in power has rendered itself guilty of wanton disregard of the laws of the land, and of usurping powers not granted by the Constitution; it has acted as if the laws had binding force only for those who were governed, and not for those who govern. It has thus struck a blow at the fundamental principles of constitutional government and the liberties of the citizen.

The President of the United States has openly used the powers and opportunities of his high office for the promotion of personal ends.

He has kept notoriously corrupt and unworthy men in places of power and responsibility, to the detriment of the public interest.

He has used the public service of the government as a machinery of corruption and personal influence, and has interfered with tyrannical arrogance in the political affairs of States and municipalities.

He has rewarded with influential and lucrative offices men who had acquired his favor by valuable presents, thus stimulating the demoralization of our political life by his conspicuous example.

He has shown himself deplorably unequal to the task imposed upon him by the necessities of the country, and culpably careless of the responsibilities of his high office.

The partisans of the administration, assuming to be the Republican party and controlling its organization, have attempted to justify such wrongs and palliate such abuses to the end of maintaining partisan ascendency.

They have stood in the way of necessary investigations and indispensable reforms, pretending that no serious fault could be found with the present administration of public affairs, thus seeking to blind the eyes of the people.

They have kept alive the passions and resentments of the late civil war, to use them for their own advantage; they have resorted to arbitrary measures in direct conflict with the organic law, instead of appealing to the better instincts and latent patriotism of the Southern people by restoring to them those rights the enjoyment of which is indispensable to a successful administration of their local affairs, and would tend to revive a patriotic and hopeful national feeling.

They have degraded themselves and the name of their party, once justly entitled to the confidence of the nation, by a base sycophancy to the dispenser of executive power and patronage, unworthy of republican freemen; they have sought to silence the voice of just criticism, and stifle the moral sense of the people, and to subjugate public opinion by tyrannical party discipline.

They are striving to maintain themselves in authority for selfish ends by an unscrupulous use of the power which rightfully belongs to the people, and should be employed only in the service of the country.

Believing that an organization thus led and controlled can no longer be of service to the best interests of the republic, we have resolved to make an independent appeal to the sober judgment, conscience, and patriotism of the American people.

We, the Liberal Republicans of the United States, in national convention assembled at Cincinnati, proclaim the following principles as essential to just government:—

1. We recognize the equality of all men before the law, and hold that it is the duty of government, in its dealings with the people, to mete out equal and exact justice to all, of whatever nativity, race, color, or persuasion, religious or political.

2. We pledge ourselves to maintain the union of these States, emancipation, and enfranchisement, and to oppose any reopening of the questions settled by the Thirteenth, Fourteenth, and Fifteenth Amendments of the Constitution.

3. We demand the immediate and absolute removal of all disabilities imposed on account of the rebellion, which was finally subdued seven years ago, believing that universal amnesty will result in complete pacification in all sections of the country.

4. Local self-government, with impartial suffrage, will guard the rights of all citizens more securely than any centralized power. The public welfare requires the supremacy of the civil over the military authority, and the freedom of the person under the protection of the *habeas corpus*. We demand for the individual the largest liberty consistent with public order, for the State self-government, and for the nation a return to the methods of peace and the constitutional limitations of power.

5. The civil service of the government has become a mere instrument of partisan tyranny and personal ambition, and an object of selfish greed. It is a scandal and reproach upon free institutions, and breeds a demoralization dangerous to the perpetuity of republican government. We therefore regard a thorough reform of the civil service as one of the most pressing necessities of the hour; that honesty, capacity, and fidelity constitute the only valid claims to public employment; that the offices of the government cease to be a matter of arbitrary favoritism and patronage and that public station shall become again a post of honor. To this end it is imperatively required that no President shall be a candidate for reëlection.

6. We demand a system of federal taxation which shall not unnecessarily interfere with the industry of the people, and which shall provide the means necessary to pay the expenses of the government, economically administered, the pensions, the interest on the public debt, and a moderate reduction annually of the principal thereof; and, recognizing that there are in our midst honest but irreconcilable differences of opinion with regard to the respective systems of protection and free trade, we remit the discussion of the subject to the people in their congressional districts and the decision of Congress thereon, wholly free from executive interference or dictation.

7. The public credit must be sacredly maintained, and we denounce repudiation in every form and guise.

8. A speedy return to specie payments is demanded alike by the highest considerations of commercial morality and honest government.

9. We remember with gratitude the heroism and sacrifices of the

soldiers and sailors of the republic, and no act of ours shall ever detract from their justly earned fame or the full rewards of their patriotism.

10. We are opposed to all further grants of lands to railroads or other corporations. The public domain should be held sacred to actual settlers.

11. We hold that it is the duty of the government in its intercourse with foreign nations to cultivate the friendships of peace by treating with all on fair and equal terms, regarding it alike dishonorable to demand what is not right or submit to what is wrong.

12. For the promotion and success of these vital principles, and the support of the candidates nominated by this convention, we invite and cordially welcome the coöperation of all patriotic citizens, without regard to previous political affiliations.

Mr. Greeley was nominated for President on the sixth vote. The several votes were as follows : —

	1st.	2d.	3d.	4th.	5th.	6th.
Charles Francis Adams, Massachusetts . . .	203	243	264	279	258	324
Horace Greeley, New York	147	245	258	251	309	332
Lyman Trumbull, Illinois	110	148	156	141	81	19
B. Gratz Brown, Missouri	95	2	2	2	2	–
David Davis, Illinois	92½	75	41	51	30	6
Andrew G. Curtin, Pennsylvania	62	–	–	–	–	–
Salmon P. Chase, Ohio	2½	1	–	–	24	32

Before the result of the sixth trial was announced, members began to change their votes. When the changes had been made the result stood, for Greeley 482, for Adams 187. On a motion that the nomination of Mr. Greeley be made unanimous, the negative votes were numerous. Two votes only were required to effect a nomination of a candidate for Vice-President. They were as follows : —

	1st.	2d.
B. Gratz Brown, Missouri	237	435
Lyman Trumbull, Illinois	158	175
George W. Julian, Indiana	134½	–
Gilbert C. Walker, Virginia	84½	75
Cassius M. Clay, Kentucky	34	–
Jacob D. Cox, Ohio	25	–
John M. Scoville, New Jersey	12	–
Thomas W. Tipton, Nebraska	8	3
John M. Palmer, Illinois	–	8

The nomination of Mr. Brown was then made unanimous, and the convention adjourned. Its work was received by Republicans throughout the country with a shout of derision. Greatly as Mr. Greeley was esteemed for his sincerity and respected for his ability, he had always been regarded as an erratic man, and there were few persons who credited him with the cool judgment and tact needed in a President. But the cry of "anybody to beat Grant" had been raised; and although many members of the Cincinnati convention were chagrined at the failure to present acceptable candidates, and although many Democrats did not conceal their disappointment, it soon became evident that the Democratic convention would adopt both the platform and the candidates of that convention. The Tennessee Democratic convention, held the week after Greeley and Brown had been nominated, instructed its delegates to the Baltimore convention to support that ticket. The New York Democrats did the same thing a week or two later, and sixteen other Democratic state conventions held in June followed the example. Accordingly it was not doubtful, when the Democratic convention met, what its action would be.

The interest in the Republican convention was confined to the question of the vice-presidency. The renomination of General Grant by a unanimous vote was a foregone conclusion. There was no dissatisfaction with Mr. Colfax as Vice-President. He had been most assiduous in his attention to the few duties of his office, and had given general satisfaction as presiding officer of the Senate. The scandal which involved him and others at a later date had not then been whispered. But Mr. Colfax had given offence to certain of the fraternity of Washington correspondents, and they determined to use all their power to prevent his nomination. They were assisted in their work by the presentation of the name of Mr. Henry Wilson as a candidate by the Republicans of Massachusetts. Considering the closeness of the vote in the convention, it is not too much to say that Mr. Wilson owed his nomination to these correspondents.

The convention met at Philadelphia on June 5, and did its work with promptness and harmony. Mr. Morton McMichael, of Pennsylvania, was the temporary chairman, and Judge Thomas Settle, of North Carolina, the permanent president of the convention. The committee on resolutions reported the following platform, which was unanimously adopted : —

The Republican party of the United States, assembled in national convention in the city of Philadelphia on the fifth and sixth days of June, 1872, again declares its faith, appeals to its history, and announces its position upon the questions before the country.

1. During eleven years of supremacy it has accepted with grand courage the solemn duties of the time. It suppressed a gigantic rebellion, emancipated four millions of slaves, decreed the equal citizenship of all, and established universal suffrage. Exhibiting unparalleled magnanimity, it criminally punished no man for political offences, and warmly welcomed all who proved loyalty by obeying the laws and dealing justly with their neighbors. It has steadily decreased with firm hand the resultant disorders of a great war, and initiated a wise and humane policy toward the Indians. The Pacific Railroad and similar vast enterprises have been generously aided and successfully conducted, the public lands freely given to actual settlers, immigration protected and encouraged, and a full acknowledgment of the naturalized citizens' rights secured from European powers. A uniform national currency has been provided, repudiation frowned down, the national credit sustained under the most extraordinary burdens, and new bonds negotiated at lower rates. The revenues have been carefully collected and honestly applied. Despite annual large reductions of the rates of taxation, the public debt has been reduced during General Grant's presidency at the rate of a hundred millions a year. Great financial crises have been avoided, and peace and plenty prevail throughout the land. Menacing foreign difficulties have been peacefully and honorably composed, and the honor and power of the nation kept in high respect throughout the world. This glorious record of the past is the party's best pledge for the future. We believe the people will not entrust the government to any party or combination of men composed chiefly of those who have resisted every step of this beneficent progress.

2. The recent amendments to the national Constitution should be cordially sustained because they are right, not merely tolerated because they are law, and should be carried out according to their spirit by appropriate legislation, the enforcement of which can safely be entrusted only to the party that secured these amendments.

3. Complete liberty and exact equality in the enjoyment of all civil, political, and public rights should be established and effectually maintained throughout the Union by efficient and appropriate state and federal legislation. Neither the law nor its administration should admit any discrimination in respect of citizens by reason of race, creed, color, or previous condition of servitude.

4. The national government should seek to maintain honorable

peace with all nations, protecting its citizens everywhere, and sympathizing with all peoples who strive for greater liberty.

5. Any system of the civil service under which the subordinate positions of the government are considered rewards for mere party zeal is fatally demoralizing, and we therefore favor a reform of the system by laws which shall abolish the evils of patronage and make honesty, efficiency, and fidelity the essential qualifications for public positions, without practically creating a life-tenure of office.

6. We are opposed to further grants of the public lands to corporations and monopolies, and demand that the national domain be set apart for free homes for the people.

7. The annual revenue, after paying current expenditures, pensions, and the interest on the public debt, should furnish a moderate balance for the reduction of the principal, and that revenue, except so much as may be derived from a tax upon tobacco and liquors, should be raised by duties upon importations, the details of which should be so adjusted as to aid in securing remunerative wages to labor, and promote the industries, prosperity, and growth of the whole country.

8. We hold in undying honor the soldiers and sailors whose valor saved the Union. Their pensions are a sacred debt of the nation, and the widows and orphans of those who died for their country are entitled to the care of a generous and grateful people. We favor such additional legislation as will extend the bounty of the government to all soldiers and sailors who were honorably discharged, and who, in the line of duty, became disabled, without regard to the length of service or cause of such discharge.

9. The doctrine of Great Britain and other European powers concerning allegiance — "Once a subject always a subject" — having at last, through the efforts of the Republican party, been abandoned, and the American idea of the individual right to transfer allegiance having been accepted by European nations, it is the duty of our government to guard with jealous care the rights of adopted citizens against the assumption of unauthorized claims by their former governments, and we urge continued careful encouragement and protection of voluntary immigration.

10. The franking privilege ought to be abolished, and the way prepared for a speedy reduction in the rates of postage.

11. Among the questions which press for attention is that which concerns the relations of capital and labor, and the Republican party recognizes the duty of so shaping legislation as to secure full protection and the amplest field for capital, and for labor, the creator of capital, the largest opportunities and a just share of the mutual profits of these two great servants of civilization.

12. We hold that Congress and the President have only fulfilled an imperative duty in their measures for the suppression of violent and treasonable organizations in certain lately rebellious regions, and for the protection of the ballot-box; and therefore they are entitled to the thanks of the nation.

13. We denounce repudiation of the public debt, in any form or disguise, as a national crime. We witness with pride the reduction of the principal of the debt, and of the rates of interest upon the balance, and confidently expect that our excellent national currency will be perfected by a speedy resumption of specie payment.

14. The Republican party is mindful of its obligations to the loyal women of America for their noble devotion to the cause of freedom. Their admission to wider spheres of usefulness is viewed with satisfaction; and the honest demand of any class of citizens for additional rights should be treated with respectful consideration.

15. We heartily approve the action of Congress in extending amnesty to those lately in rebellion, and rejoice in the growth of peace and fraternal feeling throughout the land.

16. The Republican party proposes to respect the rights reserved by the people to themselves as carefully as the powers delegated by them to the States and to the federal government. It disapproves of the resort to unconstitutional laws for the purpose of removing evils by interference with the rights not surrendered by the people to either the state or the national government.

17. It is the duty of the general government to adopt such measures as may tend to encourage and restore American commerce and ship-building.

18. We believe that the modest patriotism, the earnest purpose, the sound judgment, the practical wisdom, the incorruptible integrity, and the illustrious services of Ulysses S. Grant have commended him to the heart of the American people, and with him at our head we start to-day upon a new march to victory.

19. Henry Wilson, nominated for the vice-presidency, known to the whole land from the early days of the great struggle for liberty as an indefatigable laborer in all campaigns, an incorruptible legislator, and representative man of American institutions, is worthy to associate with our great leader and share the honors which we pledge our best efforts to bestow upon them.

General Grant was nominated by the unanimous vote of all the delegates, amid great enthusiasm. A single trial was sufficient to give the nomination as Vice-President to Mr. Wilson, who received $364\frac{1}{2}$ votes, to $321\frac{1}{2}$ for Mr. Colfax.

In spite of their apparent unanimity, the Democrats were

not really united in the movement for Greeley and Brown. Nevertheless most of the leaders believed that nothing better remained to be done than to adopt the principles and the candidates of the Liberal Republicans, and they had gone too far to recede. The convention met at Baltimore on July 9. Mr. Thomas Jefferson Randolph, of Virginia, was the temporary chairman, and ex-Senator James R. Doolittle, of Wisconsin, the permanent president. The committee on resolutions reported the Cincinnati platform without change. Its acceptance was strongly opposed by Senator Thomas F. Bayard, of Delaware, but the platform was adopted by a vote of 670 to 62. It was decided not to nominate candidates by acclamation, but to take the vote as usual. Mr. Greeley received 686 votes; Jeremiah S. Black, of Pennsylvania, 21; Thomas F. Bayard, of Delaware, 16; William S. Groesbeck, of Ohio, 2; and 7 votes were cast blank. Mr. Greeley was thus nominated by much more than the necessary two thirds. On a vote for a candidate for Vice-President, Mr. Brown received 713; John W. Stephenson, of Kentucky, 6; and 13 votes were blank.

Although this result of the convention had been universally expected, there was great dissatisfaction with it in many Democratic circles. Some members of the party were outspoken in their objection to what they regarded as a cowardly surrender of principle for the sake of a possible victory. Others said little, but it was easy to see that they had not much heart in the " new departure," and would not cordially support Mr. Greeley, even if they should so far overcome their repugnance as to vote the ticket. The open opposition to the Greeley movement found expression in a call for a straight Democratic convention, which was held at Louisville, Kentucky, on September 3, and was well attended. Mr. James Lyon, of Virginia, was the president. The following resolutions were adopted : —

Whereas, A frequent recurrence to first principles, and eternal vigilance against abuses, are the wisest provisions for liberty, which is the source of progress, and fidelity to our constitutional system is the only protection for either; therefore,

Resolved, That the original basis of our whole political structure is a consent in every part thereof. The people of each State voluntarily created their State, and the States voluntarily formed the Union; and each State has provided, by its written Constitution, for everything a State should do for the protection of life, liberty, and property within it; and each State, jointly with the others, provided a Federal Union for foreign and inter-state relations.

Resolved, That all government powers, whether state or federal, are trust powers coming from the people of each State; and that they are limited to the written letter of the Constitution and the laws passed in pursuance of it, which powers must be exercised in the utmost good faith, the Constitution itself providing in what manner they may be altered and amended.

Resolved, That the interests of labor and capital should not be permitted to conflict, but should be harmonized by judicious legislation. While such a conflict continues, labor, which is the parent of wealth, is entitled to paramount consideration.

Resolved, That we proclaim to the world that principle is to be preferred to power; that the Democratic party is held together by the cohesion of time-honored principles which they will never surrender in exchange for all the offices which presidents can confer. The pangs of the minorities are doubtless excruciating; but we welcome an eternal minority under the banner inscribed with our principles, rather than an almighty and everlasting majority purchased by their abandonment.

Resolved, That, having been betrayed at Baltimore into a false creed and a false leadership by the convention, we repudiate both, and appeal to the people to approve our platform and to rally to the polls and support the true platform, and the candidates who embody it.

Resolved, That we are opposed to giving public lands to corporations, and favor their disposal to actual settlers only.

Resolved, That we favor a judicious tariff for revenue purposes only, and that we are unalterably opposed to class legislation which enriches a few at the expense of the many under the plea of protection.

The convention nominated Mr. Charles O'Conor for President, and John Quincy Adams, of Massachusetts, for Vice-President. Mr. Adams had written a letter, in which he said that, while he did not wish for the nomination, he would not refuse it if Mr. O'Conor should head the ticket. Mr. O'Conor, on being notified by telegraph of his nomination, declined peremptorily. The convention then hastily passed a vote nominating Mr. Lyon, the president of the convention, in his place; but Mr. Lyon wisely declined. Mr. Adams also refused to take any but the second place, and not even that, unless Mr. O'Conor were to stand at the head of the ticket. Under these circumstances, the convention returned to Mr.

O'Conor, and left the ticket as it had been originally arranged, whether its candidates would accept or decline.

The result of the canvass was at no time in doubt. Some of the Democrats deluded themselves with the idea that there was a chance for Mr. Greeley, and that gentleman departed from the usual custom of candidates by going "on the stump." The early elections showed clearly the drift of public opinion ; and General Grant was elected by a larger majority than he had received at his first election. As in 1868, thirty-seven States formed the Union ; and on this occasion, for the first time in the history of the government, all the States chose electors by a popular vote. The apportionment which followed the census of 1870 enlarged the number of electors. Mr. Greeley died a few days after the choice of electors had been made, and the Democratic electors cast their votes without serious attempt at concentration. The popular vote is given on the next page.

It will be observed that the popular vote of Louisiana is given in two forms. Political affairs in the State were in a chaotic condition, both then and subsequently. The governor, Henry C. Warmoth, had been elected as a Republican, but had joined the Greeley movement, and was disposed to do all that lay in his power to give the vote of the State to the Democratic candidates. The votes of the State were at that time canvassed by a " returning board," consisting of the governor, lieutenant-governor, secretary of state, and two others. The lieutenant-governor and one of the unofficial members became disqualified by being candidates for office. The governor then removed the secretary of state and appointed another man in his place ; and he, with this new secretary, proceeded to fill up the vacancies in the returning board. But the old secretary of state, before his removal, and the remaining unofficial member of the board, had previously filled the vacancies. Accordingly there were two returning boards. The official returns were canvassed by that board only of which the governor was the head ; the other board made up returns from the best sources of information it could command. Each board seems to have manipulated the figures so as to bring about a desired result. This is a very brief account of a long and complicated controversy, full particulars of which may be found in the newspapers and in official documents of the time. Two sets of electors met, voted, and forwarded their

STATES.	Ulysses S. Grant, Illinois.	Horace Greeley, New York.	Charles O'Conor, New York.	James Black, Pennsylvania.
Alabama	90,272	79,444	–	–
Arkansas	41,373	37,927	–	–
California	54,020	40,718	1,068	–
Connecticut	50,638	45,880	204	206
Delaware	11,115	10,206	487	–
Florida	17,763	15,427	–	–
Georgia	62,550	76,356	4,000	–
Illinois	241,944	184,938	3,058	–
Indiana	186,147	163,632	1,417	–
Iowa	131,566	71,196	2,221	–
Kansas	67,048	32,970	596	–
Kentucky	88,766	99,995	2,374	–
Louisiana *	71,663	57,029	–	–
Louisiana †	59,975	66,467	–	–
Maine	61,422	29,087	–	–
Maryland	66,760	67,687	19	–
Massachusetts	133,472	59,260	–	–
Michigan	138,455	78,355	2,861	1,271
Minnesota	55,117	34,423	–	–
Mississippi	82,175	47,288	–	–
Missouri	119,196	151,434	2,439	–
Nebraska	18,329	7,812	–	–
Nevada	8,413	6,236	–	–
New Hampshire	37,168	31,424	100	200
New Jersey	91,656	76,456	630	–
New York	440,736	387,281	1,454	201
North Carolina	94,769	70,094	–	–
Ohio	281,852	244,321	1,163	2,100
Oregon	11,819	7,730	572	–
Pennsylvania	349,589	212,041	–	1,630
Rhode Island	13,665	5,329	–	–
South Carolina	72,290	22,703	187	–
Tennessee	85,655	94,391	–	–
Texas	47,468	66,546	2,580	–
Vermont	41,481	10,927	593	–
Virginia	93,468	91,654	42	–
West Virginia	32,315	29,451	600	–
Wisconsin	104,997	86,477	834	–
Total	3,597,132	2,834,125	29,489	5,608

* "Custom-house" count.   The total vote of the country, as given above, includes these returns.

† Count by the Warmoth returning board.   If these returns should be substituted for the others, the total vote of the country would be: for Grant, 3,585,444 ; Greeley, 2,843,563.

returns to Washington ; but the vote of the State was excluded, as will be noticed in the report of the electoral count. The votes of the electoral colleges as actually cast, including both the votes of Louisiana, are given below. These and all others which were rejected by Congress are marked with an asterisk : —

STATES.	PRESIDENT.						VICE-PRESIDENT.								
	Ulysses S. Grant, Ill.	Thomas A. Hendricks, Ind.	B. Gratz Brown, Mo.	Horace Greeley, N. Y.	Charles J. Jenkins, Ga.	David Davis, Ill.	Henry Wilson, Mass.	B. Gratz Brown, Mo.	George W. Julian, Ind.	Alfred H. Colquitt, Ga.	John M. Palmer, Ill.	Thomas E. Bramlette, Ky.	Nathaniel P. Banks, Mass.	William S. Groesbeck, O.	Willis B. Machen, Ky.
Alabama . . .	10	–	–	–	–	–	10	–	–	–	–	–	–	–	–
Arkansas . .	6*	–	–	–	–	–	6*	–	–	–	–	–	–	–	–
California . .	6	–	–	–	–	–	6	–	–	–	–	–	–	–	–
Connecticut . .	6	–	–	–	–	–	6	–	–	–	–	–	–	–	–
Delaware . . .	3	–	–	–	–	.	3	–	–	–	–	–	–	–	–
Florida . . .	4	–	–	–	–	–	4	–	–	–	–	–	–	–	–
Georgia . . .	–	–	6	3*	2	–	–	5	–	5	–	–	1	–	–
Illinois . . .	21	–	–	–	–	–	21	–	–	–	–	–	–	–	–
Indiana . . .	15	–	–	–	–	–	15	–	–	–	–	–	–	–	–
Iowa	11	–	–	–	–	–	11	–	–	–	–	–	–	–	–
Kansas . . .	5	–	–	–	–	–	5	–	–	–	–	–	–	–	–
Kentucky . .	–	8	4	–	–	–	–	8	–	–	–	3	–	–	1
Louisiana † . .	8*	–	–	–	–	–	8*	–	–	–	–	–	–	–	–
Louisiana ‡ . .	–	–	–	–	–	–	–	8*	–	–	–	–	–	–	–
Maine . . .	7	–	–	–	–	–	7	–	–	–	–	–	–	–	–
Maryland . .	–	8	–	–	–	–	–	8	–	–	–	–	–	–	–
Massachusetts .	13	–	–	–	–	–	13	–	–	–	–	–	–	–	–
Michigan . .	11	–	–	–	–	–	11	–	–	–	–	–	–	–	–
Minnesota . .	5	–	–	–	–	–	5	–	–	–	–	–	–	–	–
Mississippi . .	8	–	–	–	–	–	8	–	–	–	–	–	–	–	–
Missouri . . .	–	6	8	–	–	1	–	6	5	–	3	–	–	1	–
Nebraska . . .	3	–	–	–	–	–	3	–	–	–	–	–	–	–	–
Nevada . . .	3	–	–	–	–	–	3	–	–	–	–	–	–	–	–
New Hampshire	5	–	–	–	–	–	5	–	–	–	–	–	–	–	–
New Jersey . .	9	–	–	–	–	–	9	–	–	–	–	–	–	–	–
New York . .	35	–	–	–	–	–	35	–	–	–	–	–	–	–	–
North Carolina	10	–	–	–	–	–	10	–	–	–	–	–	–	–	–
Ohio	22	–	–	–	–	–	22	–	–	–	–	–	–	–	–
Oregon . . .	3	–	–	–	–	–	3	–	–	–	–	–	–	–	–
Pennsylvania .	29	–	–	–	–	–	29	–	–	–	–	–	–	–	–
Rhode Island .	4	–	–	–	–	–	4	–	–	–	–	–	–	–	–
South Carolina .	7	–	–	–	–	–	7	–	–	–	–	–	–	–	–
Tennessee . .	–	12	–	–	–	–	–	12	–	–	–	–	–	–	–
Texas	–	8	–	–	–	–	–	8	–	–	–	–	–	–	–
Vermont . . .	5	–	–	–	–	–	5	–	–	–	–	–	–	–	–
Virginia . . .	11	–	–	–	–	–	11	–	–	–	–	–	–	–	–
West Virginia .	5	–	–	–	–	–	5	–	–	–	–	–	–	–	–
Wisconsin . .	10	–	–	–	–	–	10	–	–	–	–	–	–	–	–
Total as declared	286	42	18	–	2	1	286	47	5	5	3	3	1	1	1

* Rejected by Congress. † " Custom-house " electors. ‡ Warmoth electors.

Many questions arose during the count of electoral votes, which took place on February 12, 1873, was conducted in accordance with the twenty-second joint rule, and occupied seven hours. The first objection was made by Mr. Hoar, of Massachusetts, to counting the three votes cast in Georgia for Horace Greeley, on the ground that Mr. Greeley was dead at the time the votes were given. This raised the question whether Congress might take cognizance of the ineligibility of a candidate for the presidential office. The next objection was raised by Senator Trumbull, of Illinois, to the vote of Mississippi, on the ground that the certificates did not state that the electors voted by ballot. Mr. Potter, of New York, also objected especially to one vote of Mississippi, cast by an elector chosen to fill a vacancy, the choice of whom was certified only by the secretary of state of Mississippi, and by him only upon information and not of his own knowledge. Upon these three objections the two Houses separated. The House of Representatives voted to reject the Greeley votes in Georgia; the Senate voted to accept them; under the joint rule they were cast out and not counted. Each House overruled both objections to the vote of Mississippi, and it was counted. Upon the resumption of the count, when the State of Missouri was reached, attention was called to the fact that votes were cast for Mr. Brown both as President and as Vice-President, but the objection that this was contrary to the provision of the Constitution that electors shall vote for two persons, " one of whom, at least, shall not be an inhabitant of the same State with themselves," was obviated by reading the concluding part of the certificate, that no person who voted for Mr. Brown as President also voted for him as Vice-President. The vote of Texas was next objected to, on the ground that the choice of the electors was certified to only by the acting secretary of state, and not, as the law required, by the governor. A second objection was made on the ground that four of the eight electors (not a majority) had met and filled vacancies. Both objections were overruled by each House, and the vote of Texas was counted.

The count then proceeded until the only votes remaining to be counted were those of Arkansas and Louisiana. The votes of both States were objected to. The returns for Arkansas were certified to by the secretary of state only, and his office seal was the only one which the papers bore. Both sets of electors for Louisiana were objected to. The two Houses having separated, the Senate passed a resolution that the votes of Arkansas should not be counted; the House of Representatives agreed to admit them. The vote in the Senate was a consequence of the bad rule that no debate should be allowed. In fact the only seal in use in the State was that of the secretary of state; and the rejection of the vote was a hasty act upon the most frivolous of pretexts. Both Houses voted not to count any votes from Louisiana. The result of this action, under the twenty-second joint rule, was that the votes of Arkansas and Louisiana were excluded. The joint session of Congress was then resumed, and the result of the election was declared.

XXV

THE DISPUTED ELECTION

WHEN slavery had been overthrown by the convulsion of war, and when the fruits of victory had been secured, so far as legislation could secure them, the original mission of the Republican party was accomplished. The more or less successful solution of the great moral and political problems which caused the party to come into being was followed by several changes that must be noticed briefly, since they explain the political reverses that began during General Grant's second term.

It was not yet time for the revival of old issues, the tariff, for example, to send back into the Democratic party men who had seceded from it when slavery became the predominant question before the people. That change was to come later. Many "war Democrats" who had acted with the Republicans now felt that the reconstruction measures were too radical, and many of them returned to their old party allegiance. But in the main the *personnel* of the Republican party remained unchanged. There was, nevertheless, an internal modification that was to work mischief in the future. The long possession of power increased the appetite for power, and led some of the politicians to employ objectionable means for retaining it, — means that were possibly justified when the life of the nation and its future well-being seemed to depend upon the continuance of the Republican policy, but which were reprehensible when no such necessity existed. All this implied an alteration which is perhaps too harshly described as moral degeneration. The demoralization did not affect the body of the party, save that the change was regarded with too much toleration ; but the leaders became overbearing and reckless. The party suffered greatly, also, by reason of the character of its membership in the South. The great body of the party in that section consisted of the newly enfranchised blacks, — not too well qualified to exercise the right of suffrage, — who were permitted by the white men to vote when and where only their votes would not change the result of an election. The white contingent of the party, a handful only, was made up of "carpet-baggers" and "scallawags." Carpet-baggers were Northern men who had removed — with hand-luggage only, it was sarcastically asserted by the Democrats — to the South in order to get elected to office by negro votes. Scallawags were Southern-born men who had braved the social ostracism that followed their non-conformity to the formula that "this is a white man's government," for the same purpose of obtaining office.

The overturn which resulted in the election of a Democratic House of Representatives in 1874 was by no means caused wholly by the changes just noted. A much more direct cause was the great financial panic of 1873. There had been no serious effort to reform the disordered currency, the excessive volume of which produced an era of speculation and extension of credit. When the crash came, there was widespread disaster and insolvency. A season of hard times set in; and, as is usually the case, the party in power was held responsible for the evil. It was then that a party sprang up in many parts of the country, particularly in the West, which held that the cause of the disaster was not too much but too little paper money; and it urged not merely the retention of the greenbacks as the permanent money of the country, but a large — even an unlimited — increase of the amount.

As if the Republican party had even then not enough to bear, the startling revelation of the condition of the public service which was popularly supposed to be given by the discovery of the complicity of high officers in the "whiskey ring" frauds upon the revenue, and the acts of General Belknap, the Secretary of War, — more sinned against than sinning, as the true history of the affair shows, — were scandals of a most serious character. The people began, too, to be somewhat weary of the Southern question, — of "waving the bloody shirt," as it was called, — and no longer responded eagerly to demands upon their loyalty to support further legislation, in order that the blood spilled in the war might not be wasted. Inasmuch as the Southern States themselves had become almost "solid" already in the support of the Democratic party, it required but a slight change in the North to give a majority to the opposition.

Before entering upon a chronicle of the events of 1876, it is advisable to record the efforts made in Congress to modify the electoral system and to regulate the count of votes.

At the beginning of the session of 1874–5, Senator Oliver P. Morton called up, and endeavored to secure action upon, several propositions which had for their object to remedy the constitutional defects which ninety years of experience had developed. The first of these was a proposition to amend the Constitution, the origin of which was this: Under a resolution offered by Mr. Morton in March, 1873, the committee on privileges and elections, of which he was chairman, was directed to examine and report at the next session upon the best and most practicable mode of electing the President and Vice-President, and providing a tribunal to adjust and decide all contested questions connected therewith. The committee reported, May 28, 1874, a proposition to amend the Constitution by the adoption of the following new article: —

1. The President and Vice-President shall be elected by the direct vote of the people in the manner following: Each State shall be divided into districts, equal in number to the number of Representatives to which the State may be entitled in the Congress, to be composed of contiguous territory, and to be as nearly equal in population as may be; and the person having the highest number of votes in each district for President shall receive the vote of that district, which shall count one presidential vote.

2. The person having the highest number of votes for President in a State shall receive two presidential votes from the State at large.

3. The person having the highest number of presidential votes in the United States shall be President.

4. If two persons have the same number of votes in any State, it being the highest number, they shall receive each one presidential vote from the State at large; and if more than two persons shall have each the same number of votes in any State, it being the highest number, no presidential vote shall be counted from the State at large. If more persons than one shall have the same number of votes, it being the highest number in any district, no presidential vote shall be counted from that district.

5. The foregoing provisions shall apply to the election of Vice-President.

6. The Congress shall have the power to provide for holding and conducting the elections of President and Vice-President, and to establish tribunals for the decision of such elections as may be contested.

7. The State shall be divided into districts by the legislatures thereof, but the Congress may at any time by law make or alter the same.

The report which accompanied this proposition was one of great ability and thoroughness. It was the work of Senator Morton himself, who probably devoted more time and though to this part of the Constitution than have been given to it by any other statesman of any period in our history. The resolution of amendment was called up in the Senate on the 20th of January, 1875, and Mr. Morton made a long speech in favor of it, pointing out once more in forcible language what he regarded as the evils and dangers of the existing system. He maintained that the twenty-second joint rule was grossly unconstitutional. Senators Thurman, Conkling, and Anthony followed. They all agreed that some change was absolutely necessary, but the general judgment was that the greatest danger lay in the matter of the electoral count. Mr. Anthony went so far as to say that " all the machinery of the existing system is absurd." But notwithstanding the concurrence of the leaders of the Senate in the opinion that some measure should be passed, the resolution was laid aside and debate upon it was never resumed.

A few days later, however, the Senate began a discussion of a resolution, also submitted by Mr. Morton, that the twenty-second joint rule be repealed. Subsequently he modified this resolution. He proposed to amend, not to repeal the rule, and to make an affirmative vote of both Houses necessary for the rejection of an electoral vote. A long debate took place upon this proposition; and the resolution was finally referred to the committee on privileges and elections. The committee reported speedily a bill, which, if enacted, would take the place of the joint rule. For the most part it followed the language of that rule, but with these exceptions : no vote could be rejected except by the concurrent vote of the two Houses ; if more than one return should be presented from a State, that one was to be accepted which the two Houses acting separately should determine to be the true return ; and when the Houses separated to decide upon any objection, debate was to be allowed, each member being permitted to speak for ten minutes, once only. When the debate had lasted two hours the House was to have the right, by a majority vote, to order the main question to be put. This bill was fully debated. Numerous amendments were offered, but none were adopted, except for the purpose of perfecting the language. The only important suggestion of amendment was made by Mr. Edmunds, of Vermont, who proposed to substitute for the whole bill a plan for a joint committee, resembling the grand committee provided for in the bill of the year 1800 (see p. 64 *et seq.*). The bill was passed by a vote of 28 to 20. All the affirmative votes were given by Republicans, but six members of that party, including Senators Carpenter, Conkling, Edmunds, and Windom, voted against the bill. It was never taken up in the House of Representatives.

Mr. Morton was greatly in earnest in regard to this matter. Immediately on the reassembling of Congress — it was a new Congress, and the House of Representatives was Democratic — he again introduced the bill. It was referred and reported back, and on the 13th of March, 1876, a debate began which occupied a large part of nearly every daily session until the 24th of the month, when it was passed, 32 to 26. Although this was nearly a party vote, Mr. Thurman supported the bill. But he had an objection to one feature of it, and therefore moved that the vote passing it be reconsidered for the purpose of amendment. The motion was agreed to late in April, and the bill was then laid aside. It was again taken up, just at the close of the session, in August, but no action was had upon the bill, and of course it failed.

It began to be rumored in 1875 that General Grant would be a candidate for a third term. Since the time of Washington it had been an unwritten law that eight years should be the limit of any man's service at the head of the government. The idea that the rule established by the Father of his Country was to be broken was highly displeasing to a large body of Republicans, and still more so to all Democrats. There was much public and private discussion on the subject. The President himself allowed it to be understood that he was not disposed to refuse a third term if it should be offered him. In a letter addressed to General Harry White, of Pennsylvania, he expressed himself in terms that could not be misunderstood. The Republican state convention, over which General White presided, had passed a resolution of unalterable " opposition to the election to the presidency of any person for a third term." This drew from General Grant the letter referred to, in which he said : " Now for the third term. I do not want it any more than I did the first;" but he also remarked that the people were not restricted to two terms by the Constitution; that the time might come when it would be unfortunate to make a change at the end of eight years; and that he "would not accept a nomination if it were tendered, unless it should come under such circumstances as to make it an imperative duty, — circumstances not likely to arise." The universal interpretation of these phrases was that General Grant's friends were at liberty to make it appear the imperative duty of the Republicans to nominate him again, and of the President to accept the nomination. But the idea made little headway except among the officials of the government and the most devoted adherents of the President. There was, nevertheless, much apprehension that the close organization of the official class would make it possible to manipulate the primary meetings and secure his nomination. A death-blow to the movement was dealt soon after the opening of Congress, in December, 1875. A Democratic member from Illinois offered a resolution, "that, in the opinion of this House, the precedent established by Washington and other Presidents of the United States, in retiring from the presidential office after their second term, has become, by universal concurrence, a part of our republican system of government, and that any departure from this time-honored custom would be unwise, unpatriotic, and fraught with peril to our free institutions." This resolution was passed by the immense majority of 234 to 18. Not only did all the Democrats present support it, but 70 out of the 88 Republicans voting were also found in the affirmative.

Nothing more was heard that year of the third term, and the Republicans who had been willing to entertain the idea turned their attention to other candidates, while the Republican leaders who had been special friends of the administration felt themselves at liberty to become candidates for the Republican nomination. There were many candidates. The favor of the administration was believed to have gone chiefly to Senator Conkling, of New York, when General Grant himself was put out of the running; but there was no hostility to Senator Morton, of Indiana, who ultimately secured most of the southern delegations. Both of these gentlemen had been ardent defenders of the President whenever he had been attacked, and trustworthy supporters of all administration measures.

The strongest movement, outside of the official circles, was in favor of Mr. James G. Blaine, of Maine. Mr. Blaine had been six years Speaker of the House of Representatives, and had gained extraordinary popularity among members of Congress. At the beginning of the Forty-fourth Congress, in 1875, the control of the House having passed into the hands of the Democrats, he had become the natural leader of the minority on the floor, and had drawn the attention of the country by some brilliant parliamentary victories. Many Republicans, however, regretted that in so doing he had revived memories of the war which they were entirely willing should be forgotten. When the movement to make him the Republican candidate became formidable some of them felt constrained to oppose him. Soon afterward whispers were heard that his public career was not free from acts which, if not corrupt, involved corrupt motives and desires; and these insinuations took a form which led to an investigation into Mr. Blaine's connection with the Little Rock and Fort Smith Railroad Company and the Union Pacific Railroad Company. In brief, Mr. Blaine had, as Speaker, given a decision which facilitated the passage of a bill authorizing the State of Arkansas to aid in the construction of the Fort Smith road. Afterward he had become interested in the securities of the company; and it was asserted that he had traded upon the service he had rendered to the company to obtain specially favorable terms from those who had the disposal of the securities. Mr. Blaine's prominence in public affairs, and the strong position he occupied as a candidate for the Republican nomination, caused the scandal to attract general attention. The letters he had written upon the subject were in hostile hands. Mr. Blaine obtained possession of them, and in a memorably dramatic scene read them, with his own explanation, to the House of Representatives. The effect was precisely what might have been expected : those who were previously convinced of his guilt saw in them proof of the charges against him; his ardent admirers, of whom there was a host in all parts of the country, accepted them as a complete exoneration. The present writer, who enjoyed a lifelong personal friendship, and for many years was on terms of intimacy, with Mr. Blaine, always believed in his innocence not only of the charges here referred to, but of others which his political opponents made against him. The unpleasant chapter in his history is recorded here because it had an important bearing upon his aspirations to the presidency, but with keen regret that a perpetuation of it is necessary.

A strong movement was organized in the party in favor of Mr. Benjamin H. Bristow, the Secretary of the Treasury. Mr. Bristow had won the high opinion of the country by his vigorous proceedings against the western "whiskey rings." The heavy tax upon distilled spirit was a great temptation to fraud in its manufacture. Evidence was obtained that many western distilleries were enabled by collusion with government officers to manufacture vast amounts of whiskey upon which no tax was paid. They secured a great profit, which profit was divided between those who committed the frauds and those who permitted them. Certain persons near the administration were implicated, or at least open to serious suspicion. The President directed that the prosecutions should be pressed with all vigor; but Mr. Bristow received most of the credit for the unrelenting vigor with which the prosecutions were carried to a successful issue. Accordingly he became the favorite candidate of those who were most opposed to what it was the fashion to call "Cæsarism" and "Grantism."

Ohio presented her governor, Rutherford B. Hayes, a general in the Union army during the war, formerly a member of Congress, and in 1876, for the third time, governor of Ohio. Governor John F. Hartranft, of Pennsylvania, and Mr. Marshall Jewell, who had been governor of Connecticut, minister to Russia, and Postmaster-general, were also candidates.

The leading candidate on the Democratic side was Governor Samuel J. Tilden, of New York, but his supremacy was not undisputed. Mr. Hendricks, of Indiana, who had received most of the votes of Democratic electors in 1872, after the death of Mr. Greeley, had strong western support. General Hancock was a favorite of the soldiers, as he had been in 1868. Ohio was in the field with ex-Governor William Allen, who had carried the State in 1873. But as the state and district conventions made Mr. Blaine the leading candidate on the Republican side, so those of the Democrats placed Mr. Tilden far in advance of all competitors. Mr. Tilden had gained a high reputation by his warfare against the "Tweed ring" in New York city some years before, and had added to it by his career as governor of the State of New York. But he was opposed most warmly by the Tammany organization in his own city, and this was deemed by many a sufficient reason why he should not be nominated. Such was the situation when the season of national conventions began, in May, 1876.

The first convention of the series was that of the Prohibitionists, which was held in Cleveland, Ohio, on the 17th of May. This convention nominated, for President, Green Clay Smith, of Kentucky, and, for Vice-President, G. T. Stewart, of Ohio ; and adopted the following platform : —

The Prohibition Reform party of the United States, organized in the name of the people to revive, enforce, and perpetuate in the government the doctrines of the Declaration of Independence, submit in this centennial year of the republic, for the suffrages of all good citizens, the following platform of national reforms and measures : —

1. The legal prohibition in the District of Columbia, the Territories, and in every other place subject to the laws of Congress, of the importation, exportation, manufacture, and traffic of all alcoholic beverages as high crimes against society ; an amendment of the national Constitution to render these prohibitory measures universal and permanent ; and the adoption of treaty stipulations with foreign powers to prevent the importation and exportation of all alcoholic beverages.

2. The abolition of class legislation and of special privileges in the government, and of the adoption of equal suffrage and eligibility to office without distinction of race, religious creed, property, or sex.

3. The appropriation of the public lands in limited quantities to actual settlers only ; the reduction of the rates of inland and ocean postage ; of telegraphic communication ; of railroad and water transportation and travel to the lowest practicable point by force of law, wisely and justly framed, with reference not only to the interests of capital employed, but to the higher claims of the general good.

4. The suppression by law of lottery and gambling in gold, stocks, produce, and every form of money and property, and the penal inhibition of the use of the public mails for advertising schemes of gambling and lotteries.

5. The abolition of those foul enormities, polygamy and the social evil, and the protection of purity, peace, and happiness of homes by ample and efficient legislation.

6. The national observance of the Christian Sabbath, established by laws prohibiting ordinary labor and business in all departments of public service and private employment (works of necessity, charity, and religion excepted) on that day.

7. The establishment by mandatory provisions in national and state constitutions, and by all necessary legislation, of a system of free public schools for the universal and forced education of all the youth of the land.

8. The free use of the Bible, not as a ground of religious creeds, but as a text-book of the purest morality, the best liberty, and the noblest literature, in our public schools, that our children may grow up in its light, and that its spirit and principles may pervade the nation.

9. The separation of the government in all departments and institutions, including the public schools and all funds for their maintenance, from the control of every religious sect or other association, and the protection alike of all sects by equal laws, with entire freedom of religious faith and worship.

10. The introduction into all treaties hereafter negotiated with foreign governments of a provision for the amicable settlement of international difficulties by arbitration.

11. The abolition of all barbarous modes and instruments of punishment; the recognition of the laws of God and the claims of humanity in the discipline of jails and prisons, and of that higher and wiser civilization worthy of our age and nation, which regards the reform of criminals as a means for the prevention of crime.

12. The abolition of executive and legislative patronage, and the election of President, Vice-President, United States senators, and of all civil officers, so far as practicable, by the direct vote of the people.

13. The practice of a friendly and liberal policy to immigrants from all nations, the guarantee to them of ample protection, and of equal rights and privileges.

14. The separation of the money of government from all banking institutions. The national government only should exercise the high prerogative of issuing paper money, and that should be subject to prompt redemption on demand in gold and silver, the only equal standards of value recognized by the civilized world.

15. The reduction of the salaries of public officers in a just ratio with the decline of wages and market prices, the abolition of sine-cures, unnecessary offices, and official fees and perquisites; the practice of strict economy in government expenses, and a free and thorough investigation into any and all alleged abuses of public trusts.

Reference has been made already, in this chapter, to the rise and growth of a party favorable to a paper money régime. It had its origin as early as 1868, when the retirement of greenbacks was prohibited by Congress on the ground that a contraction of the currency was injurious to business. It found expression in the canvass of that year, in the demand that the bonds of the United States should be made payable in greenbacks. After the panic of 1873 the secretary of the treasury issued a part of the notes retired six years before, taking the position that the forty-four million dollars so retired were a "reserve." It was urged on the one hand that the volume of the currency ought to be still further, and largely, increased; and on the other that "inflation" was but feeding the financial disease, and that steps should be taken to resume specie payments, suspended since 1862. The controversy was severe. The sharp commercial and industrial distress disposed Congress to accede to the call for more paper money, and in 1874 a bill was passed by both branches which authorized an increase. The bill was vetoed by the President, and failed. The advocates of resumption of specie payments took courage from the veto, and an act was passed, as a Republican measure, in 1875, which not only fixed January 1, 1879, as the date on which the government would redeem in coin all its notes on demand, but clothed the secretary of the treasury with practically unlimited authority to borrow money in preparation for redemption, and to maintain specie payments afterward. The resumption act was most vigorously opposed; but it was passed, approved by the President, and ultimately carried into effect. During the period of the agitation over the question a "greenback" convention was held in Indianapolis, which adopted what was then known as "the Ohio idea," — in brief that paper money was less fluctuating in value than coin, and that the volume of the currency should be "equal to the demands of business." Many of the "greenbackers," as they were called, favored "fiat" money, that is, "coined paper," — which was not to be redeemed in coin, but was to be stamped as full legal tender and kept in circulation by the fiat of the government. It may be remarked here that the party which was organized to oppose resumption and to perpetuate the paper money régime is the Populist party of later times, under a new name, with kindred purposes, although it now espouses the cause of silver instead of greenbacks. It will be noticed that in the first platform adopted by the party, three years after "the crime of 1873," — as the act discontinuing the coinage of the silver dollar has been called, — but before the "crime" had aroused the indignation of the members of the party, the bonds then being issued for resumption purposes were spoken of as "gold bonds." Indeed, this platform is worthy of notice in many points, by those who would study the silver question historically.

The first national convention of the Independent National, or Greenback, party, was held at Indianapolis, on May 18, 1876. Ignatius Donnelly, of Minnesota, was the temporary chairman, and Thomas J. Durant, of Washington, D. C., the permanent president. Peter Cooper, of New York, was nominated on the first ballot for President, and Senator Newton Booth, of California, for Vice-President. Mr. Booth declined the nomination, and General Samuel F. Cary, of Ohio, was substituted. This convention, in which nineteen States were represented by 239 delegates, adopted the following platform : —

The Independent party is called into existence by the necessities of the people, whose industries are prostrated, whose labor is deprived of its just reward, by a ruinous policy which the Republican and Democratic parties refuse to change, and in view of the failure of these parties to furnish relief to the depressed industries of the country, thereby disappointing the just hopes and expectations of the suffering people, we declare our principles, and invite all independent and patriotic men to join our ranks in this movement for financial reform and industrial emancipation.

1. We demand the immediate and unconditional repeal of the specie-resumption act of January 14, 1875, and the rescue of our industries from ruin and disaster resulting from its enforcement; and we call upon all patriotic men to organize, in every congressional district of the country, with a view of electing representatives to Congress who will carry out the wishes of the people in this regard, and stop the present suicidal and destructive policy of contraction.

2. We believe that a United States note, issued directly by the government, and convertible on demand into United States obligations, bearing a rate of interest not exceeding one cent a day on each one hundred dollars, and exchangeable for United States notes at par, will afford the best circulating medium ever devised. Such United States notes should be full legal tender for all purposes except for the payment of such obligations as are, by existing contracts, especially made payable in coin, and we hold that it is the duty of the government to provide such circulating medium, and insist, in the language of Thomas Jefferson, that bank paper must be suppressed, and the circulation restored to the nation, to whom it belongs.

3. It is the paramount duty of the government, in all its legislation, to keep in view the full development of all legitimate business, agricultural, mining, manufacturing, and commercial.

4. We most earnestly protest against any further issue of gold

bonds, for sale in foreign markets, by which we would be made, for a long period, hewers of wood and drawers of water for foreigners, especially as the American people would gladly and promptly take, at par, all bonds the government may need to sell, provided they are made payable at the option of the holder, and bearing interest at 3.65 per cent. per annum, or even a lower rate.

5. We further protest against the sale of government bonds for the purpose of purchasing silver, to be used as a substitute for our more convenient and less fluctuating fractional currency, which, although well calculated to enrich owners of silver mines, yet in operation it will still further oppress, in taxation, an already overburdened people.

The Republican convention met at Cincinnati on June 14. As the day approached, the public interest in the meeting became very great. The delegates elected in most of the States were pledged to one or another of the candidates. Each of the three largest States had a candidate of its own. New York, with 70 delegates, was substantially unanimous for Mr. Conkling; Pennsylvania, with 58 delegates, was instructed to vote for General Hartranft; Ohio, whose delegates numbered 44, was united in support of Governor Hayes. These three candidates thus held 172 votes out of the 756 to which all the States and Territories were entitled. Mr. Morton had, in addition to the 30 votes of his own Indiana delegation, nearly 100 more pledged to him, every one of which was from the Southern States. The Bristow strength was unknown, but was believed to be about 100 votes. It was evident from the beginning that, if the forces of these five candidates could be united, the defeat of Mr. Blaine, whose delegates were more than twice as numerous as those of any other candidate, was assured. The party was roughly divided into two wings, one of which was warmly in favor of the Grant administration, while the other desired "reform within the party." The prevailing sentiment was decidedly hostile to a perpetuation of the Grant administration under a new head. The administration strength was represented, accurately enough, by the Conkling and Morton contingents. The rest of the delegates were, for the most part, opposed to any one who might seem to be the political heir of the President. Many of the adherents of Mr. Bristow were as strongly opposed to Mr. Blaine as they were to what they called "the Grant dynasty." The charges brought against Mr. Blaine were in process of investigation almost up to the very day that the convention met. Many delegates believed the charges to be true; and although a large majority of the delegates probably disbelieved them, some of them deemed it bad policy to nominate a man who was so seriously assailed. On the Sunday morning before the convention, Mr. Blaine suffered a sunstroke, and was, for a day or two, believed to be dangerously ill. This also was unfortunate for him, and probably cost him some votes.

Theodore M. Pomeroy, of New York, was temporary chairman of the convention, and Edward McPherson, of Pennsylvania, was the permanent president. On the second day the adoption of the rules drafted by the committee on rules introduced some important reforms in national convention work. It was decided that the report of the committee on credentials should be disposed of first, the platform next, and only then should the nomination of candidates be in order. Another rule put an end to the practice of "stampeding," by providing that the roll-call should in no case be dispensed with; and that after the vote of a State for candidates was announced it should not be changed on that ballot.

There were several contested elections, but the only important case was that of Alabama, where one delegation, headed by Senator Spencer, was in favor of Mr. Morton, the other, headed by Mr. Haralson, a colored member of Congress, was divided between Mr. Blaine and Mr. Bristow. The Spencer delegation was refused admittance by a vote of 375 to 354, and the Haralson delegation was admitted. The following platform was then reported by Gen. Joseph R. Hawley, of Connecticut: —

When, in the economy of Providence, this land was to be purged of human slavery, and when the strength of government of the people, by the people, and for the people, was to be demonstrated, the Republican party came into power. Its deeds have passed into history, and we look back to them with pride. Incited by their memories to high aims for the good of our country and mankind, and looking to the future with unfaltering courage, hope, and purpose, we, the representatives of the party in national convention assembled, make the following declaration of principles: —

1. The United States of America is a nation, not a league. By the combined workings of the national and state governments, under their respective constitutions, the rights of every citizen are secured, at home and abroad, and the common welfare promoted.

2. The Republican party has preserved these governments to the

hundredth anniversary of the nation's birth, and they are now embodiments of the great truths spoken at its cradle, "That all men are created equal; that they are endowed by their Creator with certain unalienable rights, among which are life, liberty, and the pursuit of happiness; that for the attainment of these ends governments have been instituted among men, deriving their just powers from the consent of the governed." Until these truths are cheerfully obeyed, or, if need be, vigorously enforced, the work of the Republican party is unfinished.

3. The permanent pacification of the Southern section of the Union, and the complete protection of all its citizens in the free enjoyment of all their rights, is a duty to which the Republican party stands sacredly pledged. The power to provide for the enforcement of the principles embodied by the recent constitutional amendments is vested by those amendments in the Congress of the United States, and we declare it to be the solemn obligation of the legislative and executive departments of the government to put into immediate and vigorous exercise all their constitutional powers for removing any just causes of discontent on the part of any class, and for securing to every American citizen complete liberty and exact equality in the exercise of all civil, political, and public rights. To this end we imperatively demand a Congress and a Chief Executive whose courage and fidelity to these duties shall not falter until these results are placed beyond dispute or recall.

4. In the first act of Congress signed by President Grant, the national government assumed to remove any doubts of its purpose to discharge all just obligations to the public creditors, and "solemnly pledged its faith to make provision, at the earliest practicable period, for the redemption of the United States notes in coin." Commercial prosperity, public morals, and national credit demand that this promise be fulfilled by a continuous and steady progress to specie payment.

5. Under the Constitution the President and heads of departments are to make nominations for office; the Senate is to advise and consent to appointments, and the House of Representatives is to accuse and prosecute faithless officers. The best interest of the public service demands that these distinctions be respected; that senators and representatives, who may be judges and accusers, should not dictate appointments to office. The invariable rule in appointments should have reference to the honesty, fidelity, and capacity of the appointees, giving to the party in power those places where harmony and vigor of administration require its policy to be represented, but permitting all others to be filled by persons selected with sole reference to the efficiency of the public service, and the right of all citizens to share in the honor of rendering faithful service to the country.

6. We rejoice in the quickened conscience of the people concerning political affairs, and will hold all public officers to a rigid responsibility, and engage that the prosecution and punishment of all who betray official trusts shall be swift, thorough, and unsparing.

7. The public-school system of the several States is a bulwark of the American Republic, and, with a view to its security and permanence, we recommend an amendment to the Constitution of the United States forbidding the application of any public funds or property for the benefit of any schools or institutions under sectarian control.

8. The revenue necessary for current expenditures and the obligations of the public debt must be largely derived from duties upon importations, which, so far as possible, should be adjusted to promote the interests of American labor and advance the prosperity of the whole country.

9. We reaffirm our opposition to further grants of the public land to corporations and monopolies, and demand that the national domain be devoted to free homes for the people.

10. It is the imperative duty of the government so to modify existing treaties with European governments that the same protection shall be afforded to the adopted American citizen that is given to the native-born; and that all necessary laws should be passed to protect emigrants, in the absence of power in the States for that purpose.

11. It is the immediate duty of Congress fully to investigate the effect of immigration and importation of Mongolians upon the moral and material interests of the country.

12. The Republican party recognizes with its approval the substantial advances recently made toward the establishment of equal rights for women by the many important amendments effected by Republican legislatures in the laws which concern the personal and property relations of wives, mothers, and widows, and by the appointment and election of women to the superintendence of education, charities, and other public trusts. The honest demands of this class of citizens for additional rights, privileges, and immunities should be treated with respectful consideration.

13. The Constitution confers upon Congress sovereign power over the Territories of the United States for their government, and in the exercise of this power it is the right and duty of Congress to prohibit and extirpate, in the Territories, that relic of barbarism, polygamy; and we demand such legislation as shall secure this end and the supremacy of American institutions in all the Territories.

14. The pledges which the nation has given to her soldiers and sailors must be fulfilled, and a grateful people will always hold

those who imperilled their lives for the country's preservation in the kindest remembrance.

15. We sincerely deprecate all sectional feeling and tendencies. We therefore note with deep solicitude that the Democratic party counts, as its chief hope of success, upon the electoral vote of a united South, secured through the efforts of those who were recently arrayed against the nation; and we invoke the earnest attention of the country to the grave truth that a success thus achieved would reopen sectional strife and imperil national honor and human rights.

16. We charge the Democratic party with being the same in character and spirit as when it sympathized with treason; with making its control of the House of Representatives the triumph and opportunity of the nation's recent foes; with reasserting and applauding in the national Capitol the sentiments of unrepentant rebellion; with sending Union soldiers to the rear, and promoting Confederate soldiers to the front; with deliberately proposing to repudiate the plighted faith of the government; with being equally false and imbecile upon the overshadowing financial questions; with thwarting the ends of justice by its partisan mismanagement and obstruction of investigation; with proving itself, through the period of its ascendency in the lower House of Congress, utterly incompetent to administer the government; and we warn the country against trusting a party thus alike unworthy, recreant, and incapable.

17. The national administration merits commendation for its honorable work in the management of domestic and foreign affairs, and President Grant deserves the continued hearty gratitude of the American people for his patriotism and his eminent services, in war and in peace.

18. We present as our candidates for President and Vice-President of the United States two distinguished statesmen, of eminent ability and character, and conspicuously fitted for those high offices, and we confidently appeal to the American people to entrust the administration of their public affairs to Rutherford B. Hayes and William A. Wheeler.

The last resolution, of course, was added to the series after the nominations had been made. When the resolutions had been read, Mr. Edward L. Pierce, of Massachusetts, moved to strike out the eleventh resolution, relating to the Chinese. After a brief debate the motion was rejected, yeas 215, nays 532. Mr. E. J. Davis, of Texas, moved to strike out the fourth resolution, and to substitute the following: —

That it is the duty of Congress to provide for carrying out the act known as the Resumption Act of Congress, to the end that the resumption of specie payments may not be longer delayed.

A debate took place upon this proposition also, but the motion was rejected without a count, and the platform was then adopted. The proceedings of the second day closed with the formal nomination of candidates. Some of the speeches were remarkable efforts, and excited the partisans of the several candidates to the highest pitch of enthusiasm.

On the third day the nominations were made. On the first vote Mr. Blaine received 285; Mr. Morton 125; Mr. Bristow 113; Mr. Conkling 99; Mr. Hayes 61; Mr. Hartranft 58; Mr. Jewell 11; and Mr. William A. Wheeler, of New York, 3. Mr. Blaine's strength was made up of 77 votes from the South, and of 208 from Northern States, including some votes from almost every State except those which presented candidates of their own. Mr. Morton had 30 votes from Indiana, and 95 from Southern States. Mr. Bristow's votes were given by seventeen States and one Territory, and were strictly scattering, except the votes of Kentucky, his own State, 17 from Massachusetts, and 10 from Tennessee. Mr. Conkling's 99 were made up of 69 from New York and a few scattering votes from nine other States; the South contributing 25 of the 30. Mr. Hayes had 17 votes from other States than Ohio. The other candidates received no votes except from their respective States. Seven trials were necessary to effect a choice. They resulted as follows: —

	1st.	2d.	3d.	4th.	5th.	6th.	7th.
Blaine	285	296	293	292	286	308	351
Morton	125	120	113	108	95	85	–
Bristow	113	114	121	126	114	111	21
Conkling	99	93	90	84	82	81	–
Hayes	61	64	67	68	104	113	384
Hartranft	58	63	68	71	69	50	–
Jewell	11	–	–	–	–	–	–
Scattering	3	4	3	5	5	5	–
Whole number	754	754	755	754	755	755	756
Necessary	378	378	378	378	378	378	379

The nomination of Mr. Hayes was made unanimous. It seemed to be inevitable when the fifth ballot was announced.

Mr. Hayes was the only candidate who had made a gain on every vote; and as he was entirely unobjectionable to the friends of all other candidates, it was less difficult to concentrate votes upon him than upon any other person in the list.   Mr. Blaine, who was informed by telegraph at his house in Washington of the progress of the voting, wrote a dispatch congratulating Mr. Hayes immediately on receiving the result of the fifth vote.

During the progress of the voting a stormy scene took place upon the demand of four Pennsylvania delegates to have their votes separately recorded.   The delegation had been instructed to vote " as a unit," and these delegates claimed the right to vote for themselves.   Mr. McPherson, the president of the convention, sustained their demand, and, on an appeal, his decision was affirmed, 395 to 354.   Thus was broken the famous " unit rule," which, after one more contest at Chicago, four years later, was abandoned by the Republicans, no doubt forever.

Several candidates were presented for the nomination for Vice-President, but, as the voting proceeded, nearly all the votes were for William A. Wheeler, of New York.   The other candidates were thereupon withdrawn, and Mr. Wheeler was unanimously nominated.   The convention soon afterward adjourned, with cheers for the ticket.

The Democrats met at St. Louis two weeks later.   The convention was deprived of much of its interest by the fact that Mr. Tilden's lead for the nomination was so great.   He was known to have more than four hundred delegates out of the whole convention of 744, and, while his candidacy was opposed, the opposition came from States which nevertheless sent delegations unanimously in his favor.   The delegates who were not for him were not against him.   His nomination was therefore universally expected, except by the more sanguine friends of other candidates.

Mr. Henry Watterson, of Kentucky, was the temporary chairman, and General John A. McClernand, of Illinois, the permanent president.   On the second day the platform was reported by Mr. Dorsheimer, of New York, as follows: —

We, the delegates of the Democratic party of the United States, in national convention assembled, do hereby declare the administration of the federal government to be in urgent need of immediate reform; do hereby enjoin upon the nominees of this convention, and of the Democratic party in each State, a zealous effort and coöperation to this end; and do hereby appeal to our fellow-citizens of every former political connection to undertake with us this first and most pressing patriotic duty.

For the Democracy of the whole country, we do here reaffirm our faith in the permanence of the federal Union, our devotion to the Constitution of the United States, with its amendments universally accepted as a final settlement of the controversies that engendered civil war, and do here record our steadfast confidence in the perpetuity of republican self-government.

In absolute acquiescence in the will of the majority, — the vital principle of republics; in the supremacy of the civil over the military authority; in the total separation of Church and State, for the sake alike of civil and religious freedom; in the equality of all citizens before just laws of their own enactment; in the liberty of individual conduct, unvexed by sumptuary laws; in the faithful education of the rising generation, that they may preserve, enjoy, and transmit these best conditions of human happiness and hope, — we behold the noblest products of a hundred years of changeful history; but, while upholding the bond of our Union and great charter of these our rights, it behooves a free people to practice also that eternal vigilance which is the price of liberty.

Reform is necessary to rebuild and establish in the hearts of the whole people the Union, eleven years ago happily rescued from the danger of a secession of States, but now to be saved from a corrupt centralism which, after inflicting upon ten States the rapacity of carpet-bag tyrannies, has honeycombed the offices of the federal government itself with incapacity, waste, and fraud; infected States and municipalities with the contagion of misrule, and locked fast the prosperity of an industrious people in the paralysis of hard times.

Reform is necessary to establish a sound currency, restore the public credit, and maintain the national honor.

We denounce the failure, for all these eleven years of peace, to make good the promise of the legal tender notes, which are a changing standard of value in the hands of the people, and the non-payment of which is a disregard of the plighted faith of the nation.

We denounce the improvidence which, in eleven years of peace, has taken from the people in federal taxes thirteen times the whole amount of the legal tender notes, and squandered four times their sum in useless expense without accumulating any reserve for their redemption.

We denounce the financial imbecility and immorality of that party which, during eleven years of peace, has made no advance toward resumption, no preparation for resumption, but instead has obstructed resumption, by wasting our resources and exhausting all our surplus income ; and, while annually professing to intend a speedy return to specie payments, has annually enacted fresh hindrances thereto. As such hindrance, we denounce the resumption clause of the act of 1875, and we here demand its repeal.

We demand a judicious system of preparation by public economy, by official retrenchment, and by wise finance, which shall enable the nation soon to assure the whole world of its perfect ability and its perfect readiness to meet any of its promises at the call of the creditor entitled to payment.

We believe such a system, well devised, and, above all, entrusted to competent hands for its execution, creating at no time an artificial scarcity of currency, and at no time alarming the public mind into a withdrawal of that vaster machinery of credit by which ninety-five per cent. of all business transactions are performed, — a system open, public, and inspiring general confidence, — would, from the day of its adoption, bring healing on its wings to all our harassed industries, set in motion the wheels of commerce, manufactures, and the mechanic arts, restore employment to labor, and renew in all its natural resources the prosperity of the people.

Reform is necessary in the sum and modes of federal taxation, to the end that capital may be set free from distrust, and labor lightly burdened.

We denounce the present tariff, levied upon nearly four thousand articles, as a masterpiece of injustice, inequality, and false pretence. It yields a dwindling, not a yearly rising revenue. It has impoverished many industries to subsidize a few. It prohibits imports that might purchase the products of American labor. It has degraded American commerce from the first to an inferior rank on the high seas. It has cut down the sales of American manufactures at home and abroad and depleted the returns of American agriculture, — an industry followed by half our people. It costs the people five times more than it produces to the treasury, obstructs the processes of production, and wastes the fruits of labor. It promotes fraud, fosters smuggling, enriches dishonest officials, and bankrupts honest merchants. We demand that all custom-house taxation shall be only for revenue.

Reform is necessary in the scale of public expense, — federal, state, and municipal. Our federal taxation has swollen from sixty millions gold, in 1860, to four hundred and fifty millions currency, in 1870; our aggregate taxation from one hundred and fifty-four millions gold, in 1860, to seven hundred and thirty millions currency, in 1870; or in one decade from less than five dollars per head to more than eighteen dollars per head. Since the peace, the people have paid to their tax-gatherers more than thrice the sum of the national debt, and more than twice that sum for the federal government alone. We demand a rigorous frugality in every department, and from every officer of the government.

Reform is necessary to put a stop to the profligate waste of the public lands, and their diversion from actual settlers by the party in power, which has squandered two hundred million acres upon railroads alone, and out of more than thrice that aggregate has disposed of less than a sixth directly to tillers of the soil.

Reform is necessary to correct the omissions of a Republican Congress, and the errors of our treaties and diplomacy, which have stripped our fellow-citizens of foreign birth and kindred race, re-crossing the Atlantic, of the shield of American citizenship, and have exposed our brethren of the Pacific Coast to the incursions of a race not sprung from the same great parent stock, and, in fact, now by law denied citizenship through naturalization as being neither accustomed to the traditions of a progressive civilization nor exercised in liberty under equal laws. We denounce the policy which thus discards the liberty-loving German and tolerates a revival of the cooly trade in Mongolian women imported for immoral purposes, and Mongolian men held to perform servile labor-contracts, and demand such modification of the treaty with the Chinese empire or such legislation within constitutional limitations as shall prevent further importation or immigration of the Mongolian race.

Reform is necessary, and can never be effected but by making it the controlling issue of the elections, and lifting it above the two false issues with which the office-holding class and the party in power seek to smother it: —

1. The false issue with which they would enkindle sectarian strife in respect to the public schools, of which the establishment and support belong exclusively to the several States, and which the Democratic party has cherished from their foundation, and is resolved to maintain without prejudice or preference for any class, sect, or creed, and without largesses from the treasury to any.

2. The false issue by which they seek to light anew the dying embers of sectional hate between kindred peoples once estranged, but now reunited in one indivisible republic and a common destiny.

Reform is necessary in the civil service. Experience proves that efficient, economical conduct of the governmental business is not possible if its civil service be subject to change at every election; be a prize fought for at the ballot-box; be a brief reward of party zeal, instead of posts of honor assigned for proved competency, and held for fidelity in the public employ; that the dispensing of patronage should neither be a tax upon the time of all our public men, nor the instrument of their ambition. Here, again, promises falsified in the performance attest that the party in power can work out no practical or salutary reform.

Reform is necessary even more in the higher grades of the public service. President, Vice-President, judges, senators, representatives, cabinet officers, — these and all others in authority are the people's servants. Their offices are not a private perquisite; they are a public trust.

When the annals of this republic show the disgrace and censure of a Vice-President; a late Speaker of the House of Representatives marketing his rulings as a presiding officer; three senators profiting secretly by their votes as law-makers; five chairmen of the leading committees of the House of Representatives exposed in jobbery; a late secretary of the treasury forcing balances in the public accounts; a late attorney-general misappropriating public funds; a secretary of the navy enriched or enriching friends by percentages levied off the profits of contractors with his department; an ambassador to England censured in a dishonorable speculation; the President's private secretary barely escaping conviction upon trial for guilty complicity in frauds upon the revenue; a secretary of war impeached for high crimes and misdemeanors, — the demonstration is complete that the first step in reform must be the people's choice of honest men from another party, lest the disease of one political organization infect the body politic, and lest, by making no change of men or parties, we get no change of measures and no real reform.

All these abuses, wrongs, and crimes, the product of sixteen years' ascendency of the Republican party, create a necessity for reform confessed by Republicans themselves; but their reformers are voted down in convention and displaced from the cabinet. The party's mass of honest voters is powerless to resist the eighty thousand office-holders, its leaders and guides.

Reform can only be had by a peaceful civic revolution. We demand a change of system, a change of administration, a change of parties, that we may have change of measures and of men.

Resolved, That this convention, representing the Democratic party of the United States, do cordially indorse the action of the present House of Representatives in reducing and curtailing the expenses of the federal government, in cutting down salaries, extravagant appropriations, and in abolishing useless offices and places not required by the public necessities: and we shall trust to the firmness of the Democratic members of the House that no committee of conference, and no misinterpretation of the rules, shall be allowed to defeat these wholesome measures of economy demanded by the country.

Resolved, That the soldiers and sailors of the republic, and the widows and orphans of those who have fallen in battle, have a just claim upon the care, protection, and gratitude of their fellow-citizens.

When the report was read, General Thomas Ewing, of Ohio, moved to strike from the platform, in the eighth paragraph, the words, " As such hindrance, we denounce the resumption clause of the act of 1875, and we here demand its repeal," in order to insert the words : " The law for the resumption of specie payments on the 1st of January, 1879, having been enacted by the Republican party without deliberation in Congress or discussion before the people, and being both ineffective to secure its objects and highly injurious to the business of the country, ought to be forthwith repealed." This was in accordance with a minority report signed by eight members of the committee on resolutions, representing the " Ohio idea." The amendment was rejected, ayes 219, noes 550 ; and the platform as reported was adopted, ayes 651, noes 83.

The convention then proceeded to the work of nominating a candidate for President. After the formal presentation of names, two votes were taken amid great excitement, with the following result : —

	First.	Second.
Samuel J. Tilden, New York	417	535
Thomas A. Hendricks, Indiana	140	60
Winfield S. Hancock, Pennsylvania . . .	75	59
William Allen, Ohio	56	54
Thomas F. Bayard, Delaware	33	11
Joel Parker, New Jersey	18	18
Allen G. Thurman, Ohio	—	7

The whole number of votes on the second ballot being 744, the number necessary to a choice was 496, — the two-thirds rule having been adopted. Mr. Tilden was accordingly nominated, and the choice was enthusiastically made unanimous. On the next day Thomas A. Hendricks was nominated for Vice-President by a unanimous vote, though the Indiana delegation protested that they did not know if he would accept the second place on the ticket, and the convention shortly afterward adjourned.

The canvass which followed was comparatively spiritless. Mr. Hayes was not sufficiently well known to arouse enthusiasm, and Mr. Tilden, though commanding respect for his ability, was not a candidate to draw to himself strong personal supporters. The Republicans were on the defensive; but this fact served to make the political discussion of the time more strictly a debate about measures and policies than it had been for many years. The Democrats denounced the record of the Republicans; the Republicans derided the reform professions of their opponents as insincere. Great efforts were made by the Republicans to cast discredit upon Mr. Tilden for his connection with certain railroad enterprises; and a suit was brought against him for income tax alleged to be due by him to the government. The Democrats sneered at Mr. Hayes as an unknown man, and roundly denounced the political assessments which were levied mercilessly upon the office-holders for funds to carry the elections. The Republicans made much of the opposition of the Democrats to the resumption policy, though it was well known that Mr. Tilden was a " hard-money man." But on the whole there was less than the usual amount of excitement during the canvass, and less of the usual fireworks of presidential campaigns. Not many Republicans were confident of success, and the result of the early elections, particularly that of Indiana in October, indicated that the Democrats would have enough Northern votes, together with the " solid South," to give them a victory.

Thirty-eight States participated in the election. Colorado had been admitted to the Union in August, 1876, and, in order to save an additional election, the choice of electors for that occasion was conferred upon the legislature. All the other States appointed them by popular vote. The polls had hardly closed on the day of election, the 7th of November, when the Democrats began to claim the presidency. The returns came in so unfavorably for the Republicans that there was hardly a newspaper organ of the party which did not, on the following morning, concede the election of Mr. Tilden. He was believed to have carried every Southern State, as well as New York, Indiana, New Jersey, and Connecticut. The whole number of electoral votes was 369. If the above estimate were correct, the Democratic candidates would have 203 votes, and the Republican candidates 166 votes. But word was sent out on the same day from Republican headquarters at Washington that Hayes and Wheeler were elected by one majority; that the States of South Carolina, Florida, and Louisiana had chosen Republican electors.

Then began the most extraordinary contest that ever took place in the country. The only hope of the Republicans was in the perfect defence of their position. The loss of a single vote would be fatal. An adequate history of the four months between the popular election and the inauguration of Mr. Hayes would fill volumes. Space can be given here for a bare reference only to some of the most important events. Neither party was over-scrupulous, and no doubt the acts of some members of each party were grossly illegal and corrupt. Attempts were even made to find a Republican elector who would vote for Mr. Tilden in consideration of a large sum of money as a bribe. The funds were provided, and mysterious correspondence by telegraph was held between men who were connected with Democratic political committees and those in the several States who were seeking for a venal elector. The whole scandal came to light afterward when the key to the famous "cipher dispatches" was discovered.

In four States, South Carolina, Florida, Louisiana, and Oregon, there were double returns. In South Carolina there were loud complaints that detachments of the army, stationed near the polls, had prevented a fair and free election. Although the board of state canvassers certified to the choice of the Hayes electors, who were chosen on the face of the returns, the Democratic candidates for electors met on the day fixed for the meeting of electors and cast ballots for Tilden and Hendricks. In Florida there were allegations of fraud on both sides. The canvassing board and the governor certified to the election of the Hayes electors, but, fortified by a court decision in their favor, the Democratic electors also met and voted. In Louisiana there was anarchy. There were two governors, two returning boards, two sets of returns showing different results, and two electoral colleges. In Oregon the Democratic governor adjudged one of the Republican electors ineligible, and gave a certificate to the highest candidate on the Democratic list. The Republican electors, having no certificate from the governor, met and voted for Hayes and Wheeler. The Democratic elector, whose appointment was certified to by the governor, appointed two others to fill the vacancies, since the two Republican electors would not meet with him, and the three voted for Tilden and Hendricks. All of these cases were extremely complicated in their incidents, and a brief account which should convey an intelligible idea of what occurred is impossible. For the first and only time in the history of the country, the election ended in such a way as to leave the result in doubt; and in two States the number of legal votes given for the electors was in dispute. In these States the returns were also open to the suspicion of having been manipulated by each party to bring about a desired result. The table of the popular vote on the next page shows both returns in the disputed States.

As soon as the electoral votes had been cast it became a question of the greatest importance how they were to be counted. Congress was divided, politically. The Senate and its President *pro tempore*, Mr. Ferry, of Michigan, were Republican; the House of Representatives was Democratic. It was evident that the Senate would refuse to be governed by the twenty-second joint rule, — in fact the Senate voted to rescind the rule, — and it was further evident that if the count were to take place in accordance with that rule it would result in throwing out electoral votes on both sides on the most frivolous pretexts. It was asserted by the Republicans that, under the Constitution, the President of the Senate alone had the right to count, in spite of the fact that the joint rule, the work of their party, had assumed the power for the two Houses of Congress. On the other hand, the Democrats, who had always denounced that rule as unconstitutional, now maintained that the right to count was conferred upon Congress. A compromise became necessary, and the moderate men on both sides determined to effect the establishment of a tribunal, as evenly divided politically as might be, which should decide all disputed questions so far as the Constitution gave authority to Congress to decide them. The outcome of their efforts was the Electoral Commission law of 1877, which was passed as originally reported, as follows: —

An act to provide for and regulate the counting of votes for President and Vice-President, and the decision of questions arising thereon, for the term commencing March 4, A. D. 1877.

Be it enacted, etc., That the Senate and House of Representatives shall meet in the hall of the House of Representatives at the hour of one o'clock, post meridian, on the first Thursday in February, A. D. 1877, and the President of the Senate shall be their presiding officer. Two tellers shall be previously appointed on the part of the Senate, and two on the part of the House of Representatives, to whom shall be handed, as they are opened by the

STATES.	Samuel J. Tilden, New York.	Rutherford B. Hayes, Ohio.	Peter Cooper, New York.	Green Clay Smith, Kentucky.
Alabama	102,989	68,708	–	–
Arkansas	58,071	38,669	289	–
California	76,468	78,322	44	–
Colorado*	–	–	–	–
Connecticut	61,934	59,034	774	378
Delaware	13,381	10,752	–	–
Florida†	22,927	23,849	–	–
Florida‡	24,434	24,340	–	–
Georgia	130,088	50,446	–	–
Illinois	258,601	278,232	9,533	–
Indiana	213,526	208,011	17,233	141
Iowa	112,121	171,326	9,901	36
Kansas	37,902	78,322	7,776	110
Kentucky	159,696	97,156	1,944	818
Louisiana†	70,508	75,315	–	–
Louisiana‡	83,723	77,174	–	–
Maine	49,917	66,300	663	–
Maryland	91,780	71,981	33	10
Massachusetts . . .	108,777	150,063	779	84
Michigan	141,095	166,534	9,060	766
Minnesota	40,799	72,902	2,311	72
Mississippi	112,173	52,605	–	–
Missouri	203,077	145,029	3,498	64
Nebraska	17,554	31,916	2,320	1,599
Nevada	9,308	10,383	–	–
New Hampshire . . .	38,509	41,539	76	–
New Jersey	115,962	103,517	712	43
New York	521,949	489,207	1,987	2,359
North Carolina . . .	125,427	108,417	–	–
Ohio	323,182	330,698	3,057	1,636
Oregon	14,149	15,206	510	–
Pennsylvania . . .	366,204	384,184	7,187	1,319
Rhode Island . . .	10,712	15,787	68	60
South Carolina . . .	90,896	91,870	–	–
Tennessee	133,166	89,566	–	–
Texas	104,803	44,803	–	–
Vermont	20,350	44,428	–	–
Virginia	139,670	95,558	–	–
West Virginia	56,495	42,046	1,373	–
Wisconsin	123,926	130,070	1,509	27
Total Republican count	4,285,992	4,033,768	81,737	9,522
Total Democratic count	4,300,590	4,036,298	81,737	9,522

* Electors appointed by the legislature. † Republican count. ‡ Democratic count.

President of the Senate, all the certificates and papers purporting to be certificates of electoral votes, which certificates and papers shall be opened, presented, and acted upon in the alphabetical order of the States, beginning with the letter A; and said tellers having then read the same in the presence and hearing of the two Houses, shall make a list of the votes as they shall appear from the said certificates; and the votes having been ascertained and counted as in this act provided, the result of the same shall be delivered to the President of the Senate, who shall thereupon announce the state of the vote and the names of the persons, if any, elected, which announcement shall be deemed a sufficient declaration of the persons elected President and Vice-President of the United States, and, together with a list of the votes, shall be entered upon the journals of the two Houses. Upon such reading of any such certificate or paper, when there shall be only one return from a State, the President of the Senate shall call for objections, if any. Every objection shall be made in writing, and shall state clearly and concisely, and without argument, the ground thereof, and shall be signed by at least one senator and one member of the House of Representatives, before the same shall be received. When all objections so made to any vote or paper from a State shall have been received and read, the Senate shall thereupon withdraw, and such objections shall be submitted to the Senate for its decision, and the speaker of the House of Representatives shall in like manner submit such objections to the House of Representatives for its decision, and no electoral vote or votes from any State from which but one return has been received shall be rejected except by the affirmative vote of the two Houses. When the two Houses have voted they shall immediately again meet, and the presiding officer shall then announce the decision of the question submitted.

Sec. 2. That if more than one return or paper, purporting to be a return from a State, shall have been received by the President of the Senate, purporting to be the certificates of the electoral votes given at the last preceding election for President and Vice-President in such State, unless they shall be duplicates of the same return, all such returns and papers shall be opened by him in the presence of the two Houses, when met as aforesaid, and read by the tellers; and all such returns and papers shall thereupon be submitted to the judgment and decision, as to which is the true and lawful electoral vote of such State, of a commission constituted as follows, namely: —

During the session of each House on the Tuesday next preceding the first Thursday in February, A. D. 1877, each House shall by *viva voce* vote appoint five of its members, who, with the five associate justices of the Supreme Court of the United States, to be ascertained as hereinafter provided, shall constitute a commission for the decision of all questions upon or in respect of such double returns named in this section. On the Tuesday next preceding the first Thursday in February, A. D. 1877, or as soon thereafter as may be, the associate justices of the Supreme Court of the United States, now assigned to the first, third, eighth, and ninth circuits, shall select, in such manner as a majority of them shall deem fit, another of the associate justices of said court, which five persons shall be members of the said commission; and the person longest in commission of said five justices shall be the president of said commission. Members of said commission shall respectively take and subscribe the following oath: —

"I, ——, do solemnly swear (or affirm, as the case may be) that I will impartially examine and consider all questions submitted to the commission of which I am a member, and a true judgment give thereon, agreeably to the Constitution and the laws, so help me God."

Which oath shall be filed with the secretary of the Senate. When the commission shall have been thus organized it shall not be in the power of either House to dissolve the same, or to withdraw any of its members; but if any such senator or member shall die, or become physically unable to perform the duties required by this act, the fact of such death or physical inability shall be by said commission, before it shall proceed further, communicated to the Senate or House of Representatives, as the case may be, which body shall immediately and without debate proceed by *viva voce* vote to fill the place so vacated, and the person so appointed shall take and subscribe the oath hereinbefore prescribed, and become a member of said commission; and, in like manner, if any of said justices of the Supreme Court shall die or become physically incapable of performing the duties required by this act, the other of said justices, members of the said commission, shall immediately appoint another justice of said court a member of said commission (and in such appointments regard shall be had to the impartiality and freedom from bias sought by the original appointments to said commission), who shall thereupon immediately take and subscribe to the oath hereinbefore prescribed, and become a member of said commission to fill the vacancy so occasioned.

All the certificates and papers purporting to be certificates of the electoral votes of each State shall be opened in the alphabetical order of the States as provided in section 1 of this act; and when there shall be more than one such certificate or paper, as the certificates or papers from such State shall so be opened (excepting duplicates of the same return), they shall be read by the tellers, and thereupon the president of the Senate shall call for objections if any. Every objection shall be made in writing, and shall state clearly and concisely, and without argument, the ground thereof, and shall be signed by at least one senator and one member of the House of Representatives before the same shall be received. When all such objections so made to any certificates, vote, or paper from a State shall have been received and read, all such certificates, votes, and papers so objected to, and all papers accompanying the same, together with such objections, shall be forthwith submitted to said commission, which shall proceed to consider the same, with the same powers, if any, now possessed for that purpose by the two Houses, acting separately or together, and, by a majority of votes, decide whether any and what votes from such State are the votes provided for by the Constitution of the United States, and how many and what persons were duly appointed electors in such State; and may therein take into view such petitions, depositions, and other papers, if any, as shall, by the Constitution and now existing law, be competent and pertinent in such consideration, which decision shall be made in writing, stating briefly the ground thereof, and signed by the members of said commission agreeing therein; whereupon the two Houses shall again meet, and such decision shall be read and entered in the journal of each House, and the counting of the votes shall proceed in conformity therewith, unless, upon objection made thereto in writing by at least five senators and five members of the House of Representatives, the two Houses shall separately concur in ordering otherwise, in which case such concurrent order shall govern. No votes or papers from any other State shall be acted upon until the objections previously made to the votes or papers from any State shall have been finally disposed of.

Sec. 3. That while the two Houses shall be in meeting, as provided in this act, no debate shall be allowed, and no question shall be put by the presiding officer, except to either House on a motion to withdraw, and he shall have power to preserve order.

Sec. 4. That when the two Houses separate to decide upon an objection that may have been made to the counting of any electoral vote or votes from any State, or upon objection to a report of said commission, or other question arising under this act, each senator or representative may speak to such objection or question ten minutes, and not oftener than once; but, after such debate shall have lasted two hours, it shall be the duty of each House to put the main question without further debate.

Sec. 5. That at such joint meeting of the two Houses, seats shall be provided as follows: for the President of the Senate, the Speaker's chair; for the Speaker, immediately upon his left; for the senators in the body of the hall, upon the right of the presiding officer; for the representatives, in the body of the hall not provided for the senators; for the tellers, secretary of the Senate, and clerk of the House of Representatives, at the clerk's desk; for the other officers of the two Houses, in front of the clerk's desk, and upon each side of the speaker's platform. Such joint meeting shall not be dissolved until the count of the electoral votes shall be completed and the result declared; and no recess shall be taken unless a question shall have arisen in regard to counting any such votes or otherwise under this act, in which case it shall be competent for either House, acting separately in the manner hereinbefore provided, to direct a recess of such House, not beyond the next day, Sunday excepted, at the hour of ten o'clock in the forenoon; and while any question is being considered by said commission, either House may proceed with its legislative or other business.

Sec. 6. That nothing in this act shall be held to impair or affect any right now existing under the Constitution and laws to question by proceeding in the judicial courts of the United States the right or title of the person who shall be declared elected, or who shall claim to be President or Vice-President of the United States, if any such right exists.

Sec. 7. That said commission shall make its own rules, keep a record of its proceedings, and shall have power to employ such persons as may be necessary for the transaction of its business and the execution of its powers.

In neither House was the bill treated as a partisan measure. In the House of Representatives 191 members voted in favor of it, of whom there were 158 Democrats and 33 Republicans; 86 members — 68 Republicans and 18 Democrats — voted in the negative. In the Senate an attempt was made to forbid the commission to " go behind the returns," but the amendment was rejected, yeas 18, all Republicans; nays 47, of whom 27 were Democrats and 20 Republicans. The bill was passed by the Senate, yeas 47, — 26 Democrats and 21 Republicans; nays 17, — 16 Republicans and 1 Democrat. The bill became a law, by the approval of the President, on the 29th of January. On the next day each House proceeded to choose five members of the commission. The Senate made choice of Senators George F. Edmunds, Oliver P. Morton, and Frederick T. Frelinghuysen, Republicans, and Allen G. Thurman and Thomas F. Bayard, Democrats. The House of Representatives chose Messrs. Henry B. Payne, Eppa Hunton, and Josiah G. Abbott, Democrats, and James A. Garfield and George F.

Hoar, Republicans.   The four justices of the Supreme Court designated by the act were Justices Nathan Clifford, William Strong, Samuel F. Miller, and Stephen J. Field, of whom Messrs. Clifford and Field were Democrats in national politics; and they selected Justice Joseph P. Bradley as the fifth member of the commission on the part of the Supreme Court.   Mr. Bradley was a Republican.   The natural choice of the justices would have been their associate, David Davis; but he had been elected five days before as a senator from Illinois, and it was regarded by him and by others as improper that he should serve.   Thus the commission consisted of eight Republicans and seven Democrats.   If Judge Davis had been selected, the majority would have been reversed, and the ultimate result might have been different.

When the count began, on the 1st of February, 1877, each party was confident of victory.   The Democrats relied upon a great variety of objections which had been prepared, the sustaining of any one of which would be sufficient to give the election to Mr. Tilden.   The Republican hope was in a refusal of the commission to "go behind the returns."   Senator Thomas W. Ferry, of Michigan, President *pro tempore* of the Senate, was the presiding officer, Vice-President Wilson having died in 1875.   The count proceeded, under the law, in the alphabetical order of the States.   When the vote of Florida was reached, the certificates of the Hayes and also those of the Tilden electors were read.   Objections were made to each.   The Democrats asserted that the Hayes electors were not duly chosen; that the certificate of the governor to their election was the result of a conspiracy; that its validity, if any, had been annulled by a subsequent certificate by the governor, to the effect that the Tilden electors were chosen; that a court decision made certain the election of the Democratic electors; and that one of the Republican electors was a shipping commissioner under appointment from the government of the United States at the time of his election, and was therefore disqualified.   The Republican objection to the Tilden votes was that the returns were not duly authenticated by any person holding at the time an office under the State of Florida. It was only on the 7th of February that the commission, after long arguments by eminent counsel selected to appear for the two parties, decided the case of Florida.   The decision was that it was not competent for the commission " to go into evidence *aliunde* the papers opened by the President of the Senate, to prove that other persons than those regularly certified to by the governor " were appointed. With reference to the case of the elector alleged to have been disqualified, it was decided that the evidence did not show that he held an office on the day of his appointment. The several votes were passed by eight to seven, — all the Republicans being on one side, and all the Democrats on the other. The formal decision, which was submitted to the two Houses, was that the four Hayes electors, naming them, were duly appointed electors, and that their votes were the constitutional votes. The Houses met on February 10, and received this decision. Formal objection was then made to the decision of the Electoral Commission, and the Houses separated to consider it. The Senate, by a strict party vote, decided that the votes should be counted. The House of Representatives, by a vote which was on party lines, except that one Democrat voted with the Republicans, voted that the electoral votes given by the Tilden electors should be counted. The two Houses not having agreed in rejecting the decision of the commission, it stood, and the joint session was resumed.

The votes of Florida having been recorded, the count proceeded until Louisiana was reached. The Republican objections to the Tilden votes from Louisiana were, like those to the votes of Florida, brief and formal. The government, of which W. P. Kellogg was the head, had been recognized by every department of the government of the United States as the true government of Louisiana, and the certificates of the Hayes electors certified by him were in due form. The Democrats made a great variety of objections to the Hayes votes. They asserted that John McEnery was the lawful governor of the State; that the certificates asserting the appointment of the Hayes electors were false; and that the canvass of votes by the returning board was without jurisdiction and void. Special objection was made to three of the electors : to two of them as being disqualified, under the Constitution ; and to the third, Governor Kellogg, because he certified to his own election. Several days were consumed in argument before the commission. On the 16th of February the commission voted, once more by eight to seven, that the evidence offered to prove that the Tilden electors were chosen be not received, and that the certificates of the Hayes electors were the true votes of

Louisiana. The decision having been communicated to the two Houses, the count was resumed on the 19th. Objection was made to the decision of the commission, and the two Houses separated again to act upon them. The Senate voted, by 41 to 28, that the decision of the commission should stand. The House voted that the electoral votes cast by the Hayes electors for Louisiana ought not to be counted, — 173 to 99. In each case this was a party vote except that two Republicans in the House voted with the Democrats.

The Houses then met again on the 20th, and resumed the count, which proceeded without dispute as far as the State of Michigan, when objection was made from the Democratic side to one vote from that State, on the ground that one of the persons chosen by the people held a Federal office at the time of his appointment, and that the act of the other electors in filling the alleged vacancy caused by his failure to act was not justified. This not being a case of double returns, the two Houses separated to decide it for themselves. The objection was overruled by each House. A somewhat similar case of an elector for Nevada was the next stumbling-block in the count, and it too was decided in favor of the elector objected to. Oregon was reached in the count on the 21st. An outline sketch of the extremely complicated situation of affairs in Oregon has been given already. There were objections from both sides to the votes, and the papers were referred to the Electoral Commission, by whom further argument was heard. The commission unanimously rejected the made-up vote of the Tilden board of electors, but decided, eight to seven, that the full board of Hayes electors were the legal electors for the State. The decision was objected to, when communicated to the two Houses. Once more they separated, and each decided, substantially by a party vote, as before, — the Senate for accepting the decision, and the House of Representatives for rejecting it. They then met again, and resumed the count. In the vote of Pennsylvania another case was encountered of an elector alleged to have been ineligible by reason of his having been a centennial commissioner. The other electors treated the place as vacant, and chose another person to act in it. The Senate agreed, without a division, to a resolution that the vote be counted. The House rejected it, 135 to 119, the affirmative consisting entirely of Democrats, and the negative containing only 15 of that party. The full vote of Pennsylvania was accordingly counted under the law, the two Houses not having agreed to reject. Rhode Island furnished a case not very different, but the two Houses this time concurred unanimously in deciding that the disputed vote should be counted.

To the Hayes votes in South Carolina the Democrats next objected that there was no legal election in the State, that there was not, in South Carolina, during the year 1876, a republican form of government, and that the army and the United States deputy marshals stationed at and near the polls prevented the free exercise of the right of suffrage. The Republicans asserted that the Tilden board was not duly appointed, and that the certificates were wholly defective in form and lacking the necessary official certification. The papers having been referred to the Electoral Commission, that body met again on the 26th. Senator Thurman was obliged to retire from service upon the commission, on account of illness, and Senator Francis Kernan took his place. After a day devoted to arguments, the commission voted unanimously that the Tilden electors were not the true electors of South Carolina, and, by the old majority of eight to seven, that the Hayes electors were the constitutional electors duly appointed. The two Houses separated upon renewed objections to the decision of the commission, and as before the Senate sustained the finding; the House voted to reject it.

There were two further objections, the first to a vote cast by an elector for Vermont, substituted for an ineligible person who had been chosen by the people, on which the result was the same as in the other similar cases; the other was a case of the same kind in Wisconsin, which was decided in like manner. The Vermont case was complicated by the presentation, by Mr. Hewitt, of New York, of a packet purporting to contain a return of electoral votes given in Vermont. The President of the Senate having received no such vote, nor any vote different from that of the regularly chosen Hayes electors, refused to receive it.

The count had begun on the first day of February, and the final vote upon Wisconsin was not reached until the early morning of March 2. As question after question was decided uniformly in favor of the Republicans, it became evident to the Democrats that their case was lost. They charged gross partisanship upon the Republican members of the Electoral Commission, in determining every point involved in the dual returns for their own party, though as a matter of fact there does not seem to have been much room for choice between the two parties on the score of partisanship. Each member of the commission favored by his vote that view which would result in adding to the electoral vote of his own party. But as the result of the count became more and more certainly a Republican triumph, the anger of the Democrats rose. Some of them were for discontinuing the count; and the symptoms of a disposition to filibuster so that there should be no declaration of the result gave reason for public disquietude. But the conservative members of the party were too patriotic to allow the failure of a law which they had been instrumental in passing to lead to anarchy or revolution, and they sternly discountenanced all attempts to defeat the conclusion of the count. The summing up of the votes was read by Mr. Allison, of Iowa, one of the tellers on the part of the Senate, at a little after four o'clock, on the morning of the 2d of March, amid great excitement. That result, as declared, was as follows:—

STATES.	Hayes and Wheeler.	Tilden and Hendricks.	STATES.	Hayes and Wheeler.	Tilden and Hendricks.
Alabama	–	10	Missouri	–	15
Arkansas	–	6	Nebraska	3	–
California	6	–	Nevada	3	–
Colorado	3	–	New Hampshire	5	–
Connecticut	–	6	New Jersey	–	9
Delaware	–	3	New York	–	35
Florida	4	–	North Carolina	–	10
Georgia	–	11	Ohio	22	–
Illinois	21	–	Oregon	3	–
Indiana	–	15	Pennsylvania	29	–
Iowa	11	–	Rhode Island	4	–
Kansas	5	–	South Carolina	7	–
Kentucky	–	12	Tennessee	–	12
Louisiana	8	–	Texas	–	8
Maine	7	–	Vermont	5	–
Maryland	–	8	Virginia	–	11
Massachusetts	13	–	West Virginia	–	5
Michigan	11	–	Wisconsin	10	–
Minnesota	5	–			
Mississippi	–	8	Total	185	184

Mr. Ferry thereupon declared Rutherford B. Hayes elected President, and William A. Wheeler Vice-President, of the United States. The decision was acquiesced in peaceably by the whole country, and by men of every party. But the Democrats have never ceased to denounce the whole affair as a fraud, and some newspapers have steadily refused to speak of Mr. Hayes as having ever been rightfully in possession of the presidential office. Their anger at the time was very great, and it was excusable, since they honestly believed that Mr. Tilden was fairly elected. It is to be hoped that the patriotism of the American people and their love of peace may never again be put to so severe a test as was that to which they were subjected in 1876 and 1877.

XXVI

A REPUBLICAN REVIVAL

THE circumstances that attended the election of 1876 led to the introduction in Congress of many propositions intended to render impossible a recurrence of the danger which was then met and overcome, and to forestall other evils which have often been apprehended, but have never happened. Certain difficulties that arose in consequence of the silence of the Constitution might be obviated by law; others must be cured by amendment of the Constitution itself. Although the warning was a serious one, and although many members brought forward measures to meet the case, not one of the bills and resolutions introduced was acted upon finally. Nevertheless, it may be well to notice the suggestions which were made during Mr. Hayes's administration, — during the special session of Congress, October 15, 1877, and the regular session, which followed without an interval.

Mr. Cravens, of Arkansas, offered a resolution of amendment to the Constitution, providing that the people should vote directly for President and Vice-President. Each State was to have a number of presidential votes equal to its electoral votes under the present system, which votes were to be apportioned in each State among the several candidates, in the proportion of the votes given to each; the legislature of each State was to direct the manner in which the presidential vote of that State was to be ascertained; on a day to be fixed by Congress, or, in case of disagreement between the two Houses, on a day to be named by the President, not less than fifteen nor more than thirty days before the 4th of March, a joint meeting of the two Houses was to be held, the President of the Senate was to open the presidential votes certified to by the governor of the State, and one list from each State was then to be counted under the direction of the two Houses; a majority of all the presidential votes was requisite to a choice. In case

no choice had been made by such a majority, then the two
Houses, in joint convention, were to elect a President by *viva
voce* vote, each senator and member having one vote, the
choice being limited to the two highest on the list, unless two
persons should have an equal number of votes next to the
highest ; one senator and a majority of the representatives
from two thirds of the States were to constitute a quorum for
the purposes of this election. In case no person should receive a majority of the Congress so voting, the President in
office was to continue to be President until a choice was
effected. The election of Vice-President. was to be made in
the same manner and at the same time as that of President.
Whenever the office of Vice-President became vacant, there
was to be an election by joint convention of Congress, within
ten days after the next meeting of Congress, or within twenty
days if Congress should be in session at the time the vacancy
occurred.

Mr. Springer, of Illinois, made a proposition, of which the
leading features were : a presidential term of six years, the
President not to be immediately reëligible ; each State to have a
number of presidential votes equal to its electoral votes according to the present system, except that States having but one
representative in Congress were to have but one presidential
vote, and States having but two representatives were to have
but three votes; a direct vote for President and Vice-President; a canvassing board in each State, with ministerial
powers only, — consisting of the governor, secretary of state,
and chief justice of the highest court, — to aggregate the votes,
apportion to each candidate his proportional part of the presidential votes of the State, and to make return thereof to the
president of the Senate ; the two Houses to be in session on
the third Monday in January after a presidential election ; a
joint meeting to be held, to be presided over by the president
of the Senate, unless he should be a candidate for the office
of President, and in that case by the speaker of the House of
Representatives, and, if he were similarly disqualified, then by
a presiding officer chosen by the joint convention ; a plurality
of votes to elect both the President and the Vice-President;
the joint convention to be the judge of the returns and qualifications of the persons who shall be President and Vice-President. If no conclusion upon the returns should be reached
by the second Monday in February, the convention was to

vote *viva voce* upon the question who was constitutionally elected President and who Vice-President, — a majority of those present to determine all questions.

Mr. Maish, of Pennsylvania, proposed a popular election of President, without the intervention of electors. The votes were to be returned to the secretary of state of each State and to be by him opened in the presence of the governor and the chief justice of the highest court, and these three officers were to apportion electoral votes to each candidate in accordance with the returns. The proposition did not deal with the matter of a count of the votes.

Mr. Finley, of Ohio, proposed a direct vote of all the people for President and Vice-President, disregarding state lines altogether; a plurality of votes was to elect in each case; but if two persons had an equal and the highest number of votes, then the House of Representatives was to choose the President from those two; or, if the failure was in relation to the vice-presidency, then the Senate was to make the choice. The voting was to be *viva voce*, and each member was to have one vote; the canvass of returns for President and Vice-President was to be made by Congress in a manner to be determined by joint rules or by law, and, if the two Houses could not agree, the matter in dispute was to be referred to the Supreme Court for final decision.

Mr. Eaton, of Connecticut, proposed in the Senate an amendment constituting a tribunal for the decision of controverted questions arising out of the presidential election. Not less than twelve months before the occurrence of such an election, the governor of each State was to appoint, with the consent of the Senate of the State, five qualified persons, who were to hear and determine all questions of contests in relation to the choice of electors, and to transmit their report, sealed, to the president of the Senate.

A resolution offered by Mr. Riddle, of Tennessee, proposed a direct election by the people, a clear majority being required for a choice. In case such majority should not be obtained, then a second election was to be held within two months of the time of the first vote, when the choice should be limited to the two highest on the list. In case of no choice, by reason of a tie, on the second trial, the two Houses of Congress, in joint convention, each member having one vote, were to elect.

Mr. Sampson, of Iowa, proposed that the relative electoral

power of the States should be as it now is; that the people should vote directly for the executive; that the persons having a plurality for the offices of President and Vice-President in any State should receive the full presidential vote of that State, or, in case of a tie, that the votes should be equally divided among those having the highest number; and if no person received a majority of presidential votes, the choice of either President or Vice-President was to be made in the same manner as the Constitution now provides for cases where the electors have not made a choice.

In May, 1878, Mr. Southard, of Ohio, from a committee of the House of Representatives, appointed for the purpose, reported a plan. It dispensed with secondary electors. Each State was to be entitled to as many presidential votes as it would have electors under the present system. The people having voted directly for President and Vice-President, the vote for each candidate in any State was to be ascertained by multiplying the number of votes given for any person by the number of presidential votes assigned to the State, and dividing the product by the whole number of votes cast; and the fractions were to be ascertained to the third place of decimals. The returns were to be made to the secretary of state of each State, who was to open them in the presence of the governor and the state auditor or controller; and the apportionment of presidential votes was to be made by them as a canvassing board. Disputed questions might be passed upon by the highest judicial tribunal in each State, and the decision was to be sent to the president of the Senate at Washington. The votes were to be counted by the two Houses of Congress, assembled under the presidency of the president of the Senate, and all votes were to be counted unless the two Houses concurred in rejecting them; or, if there was a decision by the highest court of the State upon a contest, that decision was to stand unless the two Houses concurred in overruling it. If there were dual returns, or two decisions purporting to be by the highest court, that was to be accepted which the two Houses should decide to be the true return or the true decision. A plurality of votes was to elect the President, and in case of a tie the election was to be made in the manner now provided for the case of a failure to elect by the electors. This proposition was never even debated in the House.

A determined effort was made by the Senate, during the

session of 1878–79, to amend the law relative to the count of votes, by a statute covering the whole subject. The bill was managed by Mr. Edmunds, of Vermont. A brief account of its provisions only can be given. It changed the time for the appointment of electors in the several States to the first Tuesday of October in every fourth year. If a vacancy should occur in both the offices of President and Vice-President more than two months before the first Tuesday of October in any year other than that in which electors would be regularly appointed, a new election was to be held. The time for the meeting and voting of the electors was to be the second Monday in January following their appointment. The fourth section was as follows : —

Each State may provide by law enacted prior to the day in this act named for the appointment of the electors, for the trial and determination of any controversy concerning the appointment of electors, before the time fixed for the meeting of the electors, in any manner it may deem expedient. Every such determination made pursuant to such law so enacted before said day, and made prior to the said time of meeting of the electors, shall be conclusive evidence of the lawful title of the electors who shall have been so determined to have been appointed, and shall govern in the counting of the electoral votes, as provided in the Constitution and as hereinafter regulated.

The provisions of the bill in relation to the count followed in general the custom of Congress under the twenty-second joint rule, with these exceptions : No vote from a State from which there was but one return could be rejected without a concurrent vote of the two Houses. If there were two or more returns, that only should be counted which was decided to be the true return in the manner provided in the section just quoted. If there were no such determination, or if there were two or more decisions purporting to have been made in accordance with a law passed in conformity with that section, that return, or that decision only, could be accepted which the two Houses acting separately should decide by affirmative vote to be in accordance with the Constitution and the laws. When the two Houses separated to consider objections to electoral votes, each member of either House might speak once only, for five minutes, and at the expiration of two hours it would become the duty of the presiding officer to put the main question. After several days of debate this bill was passed by the

Senate, 35 to 26. The negative vote consisted entirely of Democrats; the majority was made up of Republicans, with the exception of Messrs. Bayard, Merrimon, and Morgan, Democrats, and Judge Davis, of Illinois, Independent. It was referred in the House of Representatives to the select committee having the subject in charge, but no report was made upon it. We shall see that the principles of this bill, little changed in detail, were all adopted and enacted in the law of 1887, which is given in a subsequent chapter, and which is now in force.

In May, 1880, the Democrats having a majority in the Senate, Mr. Morgan, of Alabama, reported from a select committee a joint rule for the government of the two Houses in counting the electoral votes. It differed from the rescinded twenty-second rule in several particulars. No vote from a State which sent but one return was to be rejected except by the affirmative action of both branches of Congress. If two or more returns should be offered, neither was to be counted unless the two Houses agreed in deciding that one of them was the true and correct return. Provision was made for one hour's debate in each House upon objections, no member to speak more than once, or longer than ten minutes; and also for debate by unanimous consent in the joint meeting. It was further provided that an appeal might be taken from a decision by the presiding officer, which was to be overruled only by concurrent action of both Houses. This proposed rule was considered at length. Mr. Edmunds moved his bill, already summarized, with some changes, as a substitute for the rule. The motion was defeated, all other amendments were rejected, and the rule was adopted by the Senate, by a vote of 25 to 14, — a party vote, except that Mr. Davis, of Illinois, voted with the Democrats. In the House, the Republicans endeavored to have the rule referred to a committee, but their motions having that object in view were rejected. Finally the matter was postponed until the first Monday in December, 1880. It was under consideration several times during the session, but the Republicans persistently opposed it, and on the last day that it was considered, January 26, 1881, they filibustered successfully against its passage.

Early in February of the same year a resolution was adopted, which carried the conduct of the count back to the method so long in use before the twenty-second joint rule was adopted.

It provided, however, for two tellers on the part of the Senate, which was an innovation introduced by the Electoral Commission Law of 1877. The second resolution directed that in case it should appear that the electoral vote of any State had been given on any other day than that fixed by law, the declaration of the result should be in the alternative form first introduced in 1821, with respect to the vote of Missouri. This rule was adopted by both Houses. In the Senate there was no division. In the House the second resolution was opposed by 77 members, of whom six were Democrats and three Greenbackers. The count of 1881 took place under that rule.

Mr. Hayes, upon taking office, at once reversed the policy of his predecessor in respect of the Republican governments of South Carolina and Louisiana. He withdrew the military assistance which had protected them from overthrow by the white minority. The Democratic governments took instant advantage of the opportunity; and the last state governments representative of negro and "carpet-bag" control were driven from the capitals. The President's act practically eliminated the Southern question from politics by the simple expedient of non-resistance to the demands of those who proclaimed their determination to restore white men's government at all hazards, and by violence if necessary. It was not at all to the liking of many Republican statesmen who, however disposed they might be to concede the failure of the negro rule introduced by universal suffrage, believed that the faith of their party was pledged to the maintenance of the rights of the colored people. Mr. Hayes did not strengthen his own political position by the move. The Democrats were willing to profit by it; but they had as yet hardly become willing to acknowledge Mr. Hayes as a legal President. A large faction of the Republican party became estranged from him. The South was made "solid" for the Democrats. In the Forty-sixth Congress, elected in 1878, four Republicans only were elected to the House of Representatives in all the South; there were 102 Democrats.

No other President — save Mr. Johnson, who was not elected to the position, but succeeded to it on the death of Mr. Lincoln — has been so unfortunate as was Mr. Hayes in the political complexion of Congress during his term. The House of Representatives was against him the first two years, and both branches were Democratic during the last two years. Although he was not possessed of great tact and exhibited little skill in his management of men, yet his intentions were so honorable and his standards so high that his administration bears well a comparison with that of some men much more able than he was. His cabinet was a strong one. There were no scandals. Mr. Hayes was the first President to discourage and to forbid the political activity of the civil servants of the government. If he did not win applause for himself by his administration, he did raise the tone of his party. He introduced, without fuss, the reforms for which the Democrats clamored obstreperously in their platform. And when the time came for him to retire from office the people had recovered the confidence in the Republican party which they had well-nigh lost when he was elected.

Nevertheless the administration was not a quiet but a turbulent one. There was a struggle during his whole term over the question of attaching political legislation to appropriation bills. The Democrats in Congress were determined to root out the last remnants of Republican law which gave the general government any supervision of elections in the South. In the Forty-fifth Congress the contest was between the Senate and the House. The Democrats endeavored to withhold the necessary funds for the purposes of government unless the Republicans would consent to the " riders " upon appropriation bills, to prohibit the presence of United States troops near the polls, to regulate the impaneling of juries, and to prevent the appointment of deputy marshals for elections at which representatives were to be chosen. In the Forty-sixth Congress the bills went to the President with the riders attached, and the veto power was necessary to prevent their enactment. The laws which it was then sought in vain to repeal afterward fell into disuse, and the last vestige of them was removed from the statute book under President Cleveland.

Financial questions were much discussed during this administration. A great effort was made to repeal the act for the resumption of specie payments. The House of Representatives passed a repealing bill, but the Senate rejected it; and resumption took place successfully, and with great advantage to business, on January 1, 1879. The silver question was first agitated at the beginning of Mr. Hayes's term ; and on February 28, 1878, the act for the coinage of silver dollars was passed over the President's veto. Another question which became prominent in politics at this time was that of

Chinese immigration. A bill forbidding such immigration was passed, but was vetoed, and failed to obtain the necessary two-thirds majority.

Mr. Hayes was not a candidate for reëlection. But there was no lack of candidates on the Republican side. Two of them were extremely strong. Many persons who had been strongly opposed to a third consecutive term for General Grant saw no objection to electing him after an interval of four years, and a numerous body of his adherents in all parts of the country brought him forward with great enthusiasm. Mr. Blaine was again prominent as a candidate in the West, and indeed throughout the land. Those who were opposed to both Grant and Blaine favored, some Mr. John Sherman, Secretary of the Treasury, and others Senator George F. Edmunds. On the Democratic side there was no concentration of opinion. In the early stages of the preliminary canvass it was universally conceded that Mr. Tilden would be nominated if he would accept the candidacy; but his health was known to be infirm, and, as he gave no indication of his intentions, his opponents worked secretly and successfully to secure delegates who were opposed to him.

The Republican convention met at Chicago on the 2d of June. Senator George F. Hoar, of Massachusetts, was the temporary and also the permanent president. Three days were occupied in preliminaries and in deciding cases of contesting delegates, of whom there were many. The opposition which the candidacy of General Grant encountered was significantly indicated by the following resolution introduced by Senator Conkling, who managed the Grant canvass : —

Resolved, As the sense of this convention, that every member of it is bound in honor to support its nominee, whoever that nominee may be, and that no man should hold his seat here who is not ready so to agree.

After a brief debate, this resolution was passed by a vote of 716 to 3; the negative votes were given by delegates from West Virginia. Mr. Conkling offered a resolution that those who had voted in the negative " do not deserve and have forfeited their votes in this convention." To this summary way of disfranchising delegates there were numerous objections, and, in view of the possible rejection of the resolution, Mr. Conkling withdrew it.

On the fourth day General James A. Garfield reported from

the committee on rules a code consisting for the most part of the rules of the convention of 1876. One important amendment was made, to the effect that when the vote of any State should be announced by the chairman, if any exception should be taken to the announcement, "the president of the convention shall direct the roll of members of such delegation to be called, and the result recorded in accordance with the votes individually given." This was a direct and fatal blow at the "unit rule." A minority report was presented by General George H. Sharpe, of New York, on behalf of himself and eight other members of the committee, recommending the retention of the rule as it had been adopted by the convention of 1876. The delegation from New York had been instructed to vote as a unit for General Grant, and the adoption of the new rule would allow several members of that delegation, who were not in favor of the ex-President, to vote individually for the person whom they might prefer. The minority report was rejected without a division. An amendment having been adopted directing the national committee to prescribe a method for the election of delegates to the convention of 1884, the rules were adopted. The platform was then reported, as follows, by Mr. Edwards Pierrepont, of New York : —

The Republican party in national convention assembled, at the end of twenty years since the federal government was first committed to its charge, submits to the people of the United States this brief report of its administration. It suppressed the rebellion which had armed nearly a million of men to subvert the national authority. It reconstructed the Union of the States with freedom instead of slavery as its corner-stone. It transformed four millions of human beings from the likeness of things to the rank of citizens. It relieved Congress from the infamous work of hunting fugitive slaves, and charged it to see that slavery does not exist. It has raised the value of our paper currency from thirty-eight per cent. to the par of gold. It has restored upon a solid basis payment in coin for all the national obligations, and has given us a currency absolutely good and equal in every part of our extended country. It has lifted the credit of the nation from the point where six per cent. bonds sold at eighty-six per cent. to that where four per cent. bonds are eagerly sought at a premium. Under its administration railways have increased from thirty-one thousand miles in 1860 to more than eighty-two thousand miles in 1879. Our foreign trade has increased from seven hundred million dollars to one billion one hundred and fifty million dollars in the same time, and our exports, which were twenty million dollars less than our imports in 1860, were two hundred and sixty-four million more than our imports in 1879. Without resorting to loans, it has, since the war closed, defrayed the ordinary expenses of government beside the accruing interest on the public debt, and has annually disbursed more than thirty million dollars for soldiers' pensions. It has paid eight hundred and eighty-eight million dollars of the public debt, and, by refunding the balance at lower rates, has reduced the annual interest charged from nearly one hundred and fifty-one million dollars to less than eighty-nine million dollars. All the industries of the country have revived, labor is in demand, wages have increased, and throughout the entire country there is evidence of a coming prosperity greater than we have ever enjoyed.

Upon this record the Republican party asks for the continued confidence and support of the people, and this convention submits for their approval the following statement of the principles and purposes which will continue to guide and inspire its efforts : —

1. We affirm that the work of the last twenty-one years has been such as to commend itself to the favor of the nation, and that the fruits of the costly victories which we have achieved through immense difficulties should be preserved; that the peace regained should be cherished ; that the dissevered Union, now happily restored, should be perpetuated, and that the liberties secured to this generation should be transmitted undiminished to future generations; that the order established and the credit acquired should never be impaired; that the pensions promised should be extinguished by the full payment of every dollar thereof ; that the reviving industries should be further promoted, and that the commerce, already so great, should be steadily encouraged.

2. The Constitution of the United States is a supreme law, and not a mere contract : out of confederated States it made a sovereign nation. Some powers are denied to the nation, while others are denied to the States ; but the boundary between the powers delegated and those reserved is to be determined by the national, and not by the State tribunals.

3. The work of popular education is one left to the care of the several States, but it is the duty of the national government to aid that work to the extent of its constitutional duty. The intelligence of the nation is but the aggregate of the intelligence in the several States, and the destiny of the nation must be guided, not by the genius of any one State, but by the average genius of all.

4. The Constitution wisely forbids Congress to make any law respecting an establishment of religion, but it is idle to hope that the nation can be protected against the influences of sectarianism

while each State is exposed to its domination. We therefore recommend that the Constitution be so amended as to lay the same prohibition upon the legislature of each State, and to forbid the appropriation of public funds to the support of sectarian schools.

5. We affirm the belief avowed in 1876, that the duties levied for the purpose of revenue should so discriminate as to favor American labor; that no further grant of the public domain should be made to any railway or other corporation; that, slavery having perished in the States, its twin barbarity, polygamy, must die in the Territories; that everywhere the protection accorded to citizens of American birth must be secured to citizens by American adoption; and that we esteem it the duty of Congress to develop and improve our watercourses and harbors, but insist that further subsidies to private persons or corporations must cease; that the obligations of the Republic to the men who preserved its integrity in the hour of battle are undiminished by the lapse of the fifteen years since their final victory, — to do them perpetual honor is, and shall forever be, the grateful privilege and sacred duty of the American people.

6. Since the authority to regulate immigration and intercourse between the United States and foreign nations rests with Congress, or with the United States and its treaty-making powers, the Republican party, regarding the unrestricted immigration of the Chinese as an evil of great magnitude, invoke the exercise of those powers to restrain and limit that immigration by the enactment of such just, humane, and reasonable provisions as will produce that result.

7. That the purity and patriotism which characterized the earlier career of Rutherford B. Hayes in peace and war, and which guided the thoughts of our immediate predecessors to him for a presidential candidate, have continued to inspire him in his career as Chief Executive, and that history will accord to his administration the honors which are due to an efficient, just, and courteous discharge of the public business, and will honor his interposition between the people and proposed partisan laws.

We charge upon the Democratic party the habitual sacrifice of patriotism and justice to a supreme and insatiable lust of office and patronage; that to obtain possession of the national and State governments and the control of place and position they have obstructed all efforts to promote the purity and to conserve the freedom of suffrage, and have devised fraudulent certifications and returns; have labored to unseat lawfully elected members of Congress, to secure at all hazards the vote of a majority of the States in the House of Representatives; have endeavored to occupy by force and fraud the places of trust given to others by the people of

Maine, and rescued by the courageous action of Maine's patriotic sons; have, by methods vicious in principle and tyrannical in practice, attached partisan legislation to appropriation bills, upon whose passage the very movements of the government depend, and have crushed the rights of individuals; have advocated the principles and sought the favor of rebellion against the nation, and have endeavored to obliterate the sacred memories of the war, and to overcome its inestimably valuable results of nationality, personal freedom, and individual equality.

The equal, steady, and complete enforcement of laws, and the protection of all our citizens in the enjoyment of all privileges and immunities guaranteed by the Constitution, are the first duties of the nation. The dangers of a solid South can only be averted by a faithful performance of every promise which the nation has made to the citizen. The execution of the laws and the punishment of all those who violate them are the only safe methods by which an enduring peace can be secured and genuine prosperity established throughout the South. Whatever promises the nation makes, the nation must perform, and the nation cannot with safety delegate this duty to the States. The solid South must be divided by the peaceful agencies of the ballot, and all opinions must there find free expression, and to this end the honest voter must be protected against terrorism, violence, or fraud.

And we affirm it to be the duty and the purpose of the Republican party to use every legitimate means to restore all the States of this Union to the most perfect harmony that may be practicable; and we submit it to the practical, sensible people of the United States to say whether it would not be dangerous to the dearest interests of our country at this time to surrender the administration of the national government to the party which seeks to overthrow the existing policy under which we are so prosperous, and thus bring distrust and confusion where there are now order, confidence, and hope.

The platform was adopted unanimously, as was also the following resolution offered by Mr. J. M. Barker, of Massachusetts : —

The Republican party, adhering to principles affirmed by its last national convention of respect for the constitutional rule covering appointments to office, adopts the declaration of President Hayes, that the reform of the civil service should be thorough, radical, and complete. To this end it demands the coöperation of the legislative with the executive department of the government, and that Congress shall so legislate that fitness, ascertained by proper practical tests, shall admit to the public service.

The day's and the week's session was concluded with the formal presentation of the names of candidates. On Monday the voting began, and twenty-eight trials to nominate a candidate were made on that day. General Grant was the leading candidate, with 304 votes, and during that day his number fluctuated only between 302 and 309. Mr. Blaine came next, with 284 votes on the first ballot; his number varied on the first day from 285, the highest, to 275, the lowest. Mr. Sherman began with 93 and ended with 91, having meanwhile dropped to 88 and risen to 97. Mr. Elihu B. Washburne, of Illinois, had 31 votes at the beginning, rose to 36, and had 35 on the twenty-eighth ballot. Senator Edmunds had 33 votes at the start, dropped to 32 on the second ballot, to 31 on the eighth, and held that number unchanged through twenty more ballots. Senator William Windom, of Minnesota, had ten votes, those of his own State, on every ballot. The number of votes necessary to a choice was in every case 378. The convention ended the day's voting without having made any progress toward a nomination.

On the morning of Tuesday there was a slight change. About twenty of the supporters of Mr. Edmunds, joined by a few others, transferred their votes to Mr. Sherman, giving him 116. His number rose to 120 on the thirtieth ballot; but, inasmuch as not the slightest impression was made upon the Grant and Blaine forces, the movement came to nothing, and on the next trial his strength began to decline again. On the thirty-fourth ballot 17 votes were given to James A. Garfield. General Garfield had received one vote on the second ballot, the day before, and thereafter had received sometimes one vote, sometimes two votes, and sometimes none. He was present in the convention as a delegate and as the manager of Mr. Sherman's canvass, and had been a conspicuous figure in the proceedings of the convention. When he suddenly sprang into prominence on the thirty-fourth ballot, the idea of making him the candidate met with great favor. On the thirty-fifth ballot a number of Mr. Blaine's delegates transferred their votes to him, and gave him 50 votes. On the next trial, — the thirty-sixth, — he received 399, and was nominated. The history of the voting will be sufficiently exhibited by showing in a table the result of the 1st, the 28th, the 30th, the 34th, the 35th, and the 36th trials: —

	1st.	28th.	30th.	34th.	35th.	36th.
Ulysses S. Grant, Illinois . . .	304	307	306	312	313	306
James G. Blaine, Maine	284	279	279	275	257	42
John Sherman, Ohio	93	91	120	107	99	3
George F. Edmunds, Vermont . .	33	31	11	11	11	–
Elihu B. Washburne, Illinois . .	31	35	33	30	23	5
William Windom, Minnesota . .	10	10	4	4	3	–
James A. Garfield, Ohio	–	2	2	17	50	399

The nomination was received with great enthusiasm by the most of the members of the convention, and with general satisfaction throughout the country. Garfield had been a gallant general during the civil war, and after the close of that conflict he had served continuously as a member of Congress, where he had risen to a position of honorable leadership. More than once he had exhibited, in addition to talents of a high order, great political courage. When the greenback movement made such inroads into the Republican party of Ohio that he was threatened with defeat unless he yielded to it, he openly declared that he would suffer defeat rather than give up his convictions. At the time of his nomination he had been elected a senator from Ohio for the term beginning in 1881. It was thought by many persons at the time that he was in honor bound not to allow himself to be nominated, since he was the accredited and recognized champion of Mr. Sherman. It is true he protested against being made the candidate, but he did not hesitate to accept the nomination when it was tendered. One must nevertheless not forget that Mr. Sherman's candidacy was hopeless; and the prize was a great one.

While the Republicans everywhere hailed the nomination as a good and strong one, some of the prominent leaders of the Grant movement were sullen and discontented. A consultation took place between politicians of the two wings, and the nomination of a candidate for the vice-presidency was conceded to those who had been upholding the cause of General Grant. Senator Conkling, who was recognized as the chief spokesman for the ex-President, named Mr. Chester A. Arthur, of New York. Mr. Arthur's only service in the national government had been rendered as collector of the port of New York, from which position he had been removed by Mr. Hayes.

The first ballot for a candidate resulted as follows: For Chester A. Arthur, 468; Elihu B. Washburne, of Illinois, 199; Marshall Jewell, of Connecticut, 43; Horace Maynard, of Tennessee, 30; Edmund J. Davis, of Texas, 20; Blanche K. Bruce, of Mississippi, 8; James L. Alcorn, of Mississippi, 4; Thomas Settle, of Florida, 2; Stewart L. Woodford, of New York, 1. The nomination of Mr. Arthur was made unanimous, and the convention adjourned.

The nomination of Mr. Arthur was most coldly received. Indeed it was regarded in some quarters with dismay. The events of the succeeding four years greatly modified public opinion, and enabled Mr. Arthur to deserve and to win universal respect. Nevertheless at that time he was deemed by a large section of the party unfitted, by his political instincts and training, for the office of Vice-President. But those who were dissatisfied with that part of the ticket were so well pleased with General Garfield that, after once giving vent to their feelings, they prepared to support both Garfield and Arthur with zeal. Some of those who had set their hearts upon the nomination of General Grant were not so easily reconciled to the situation.

The next convention in the order of time was that of the Greenbackers. It met at Chicago on the 9th of June. The Rev. Gilbert De La Matyr, of Indiana, was the temporary chairman, and Richard Trevellick, of Michigan, was the permanent president. On the second day the following platform was reported and adopted: —

1. That the right to make and issue money is a sovereign power to be maintained by the people for the common benefit. The delegation of this right to corporations is a surrender of the central attribute of sovereignty, void of constitutional sanction, conferring upon a subordinate irresponsible power absolute dominion over industry and commerce. All money, whether metallic or paper, should be issued and its volume controlled by the government, and not by or through banking corporations, and, when so issued, should be a full legal tender for all debts, public and private.

2. That the bonds of the United States should not be refunded, but paid as rapidly as practicable, according to contract. To enable the government to meet these obligations, legal tender currency should be substituted for the notes of the national banks, the national banking system abolished, and the unlimited coinage of silver, as well as gold, established by law.

3. That labor should be so protected by national and State

authority as to equalize its burdens and insure a just distribution of its results; the eight-hour law of Congress should be enforced; the sanitary condition of industrial establishments placed under rigid control; the competition of contract labor abolished; a bureau of labor statistics established; factories, mines, and workshops inspected; the employment of children under fourteen years of age forbidden; and wages paid in cash.

4. Slavery being simply cheap labor, and cheap labor being simply slavery, the importation and presence of Chinese serfs necessarily tends to brutalize and degrade American labor; therefore immediate steps should be taken to abrogate the Burlingame treaty.

5. Railroad land grants forfeited by reason of non-fulfilment of contract should be immediately reclaimed by government; and henceforth the public domain reserved exclusively as homes for actual settlers.

6. It is the duty of Congress to regulate interstate commerce. All lines of communication and transportation should be brought under such legislative control as shall secure moderate, fair, and uniform rates for passenger and freight traffic.

7. We denounce, as destructive to prosperity and dangerous to liberty, the action of the old parties in fostering and sustaining gigantic land, railroad, and money corporations, invested with, and exercising, powers belonging to the government, and yet not responsible to it for the manner of their exercise.

8. That the Constitution, in giving Congress the power to borrow money, to declare war, to raise and support armies, to provide and maintain a navy, never intended that the men who loaned their money for an interest consideration should be preferred to the soldier and sailor who perilled their lives and shed their blood on land and sea in defence of their country; and we condemn the cruel class legislation of the Republican party, which, while professing great gratitude to the soldier, has most unjustly discriminated against him and in favor of the bondholder.

9. All property should bear its just proportion of taxation; and we demand a graduated income tax.

10. We denounce as most dangerous the efforts everywhere manifest to restrict the right of suffrage.

11. We are opposed to an increase of the standing army in time of peace, and the insidious scheme to establish an enormous military power under the guise of militia laws.

12. We demand absolute democratic rules for the government of Congress, placing all representatives of the people upon an equal footing, and taking away from committees a veto power greater than that of the President.

Read

13. We demand a government of the people, by the people, and for the people, instead of a government of the bondholders, by the bondholders, and for the bondholders; and we denounce every attempt to stir up sectional strife as an effort to conceal monstrous crimes against the people.

14. In the furtherance of these ends we ask the coöperation of all fair-minded people. We have no quarrel with individuals, wage no war upon classes, but only against vicious institutions. We are not content to endure further discipline from our present actual rulers, who, having dominion over money, over transportation, over land and labor, and largely over the press and the machinery of government, wield unwarrantable power over our institutions, and over our life and property.

15. That every citizen of due age, sound mind, and not a felon be fully enfranchised, and that this resolution be referred to the States, with recommendation for their favorable consideration.

An informal vote was taken for a candidate for President, with the following result: James B. Weaver, of Iowa, had 224½; Hendrick B. Wright, of Pennsylvania, 126½; Stephen D. Dillaye, of New York, 119; Benjamin F. Butler, of Massachusetts, 95; Solon Chase, of Maine, 89; Edward P. Allis, of Wisconsin, 41; Alexander Campbell, of Illinois, 21. The delegations began changing as soon as the strong lead of Mr. Weaver was known, and that gentleman was unanimously nominated. On a vote for a candidate for Vice-President, B. J. Chambers, of Texas, had 403, and Alanson M. West, of Mississippi, had 311. Mr. Chambers was thereupon unanimously nominated.

The Prohibitionists held a convention at Cleveland, Ohio, on the 17th of June. It attracted so little attention that no report of its proceedings was published in the leading newspapers of the country. Twelve States were represented by 142 delegates. A platform presenting the principles of the party, in much the same form as they were announced in 1876, was adopted. General Neal Dow, of Maine, was nominated for President, and A. M. Thompson, of Ohio, for Vice-President.

The series of national conventions was closed by that of the Democrats at Cincinnati on the 22d of June. What that convention would do was a matter of great uncertainty. Mr. Tilden had still not indicated what was his wish in respect of the nomination. It is probable that, if he had frankly allowed it to be understood that he would be a candidate, he could have secured enough delegates to make him the nominee on the first ballot. Since he neither encouraged nor discouraged his friends, and left them in the dark as to his purposes, hardly a third of the delegates went to Cincinnati for Tilden as their first choice. A great many Southern members of the convention were in favor of Senator Thomas F. Bayard, of Delaware. General Hancock was brought forward by Pennsylvania, and had strong support in other States. Ohio presented Senator Thurman; and Mr. Hendricks, as well as other leaders of the party, Mr. Henry B. Payne, of Ohio, Speaker Samuel J. Randall, and Judge Stephen J. Field, had their friends. A movement was begun in favor of Mr. Horatio Seymour, and it made not a little progress in a quiet way. Mr. Seymour was captured by an "interviewer," and expressed himself in such terms that it was believed that he really would not accept the nomination if it should be tendered; and although he received a few votes there was no opportunity to test his actual strength in the convention.

Simultaneously with the assembling of the convention came a letter from Mr. Tilden, in which he "renounced" the nomination. The phraseology of the letter was such that it left room for both the friends and the opponents of Mr. Tilden to say that he would not refuse the nomination if it should be tendered to him; but the prevailing tendency of opinion was to take him at his word.

Mr. George Hoadly, of Ohio, was the temporary chairman of the convention, which did not effect its permanent organization until the second day, after the contested seats had been passed upon. There were several cases of contest. Two sets of delegates made their appearance from Massachusetts, and the case was decided by admitting both sets, with a half vote for each delegate. A more difficult case was that of New York. Here, too, there were two full delegations, one chosen by the "regular" Democrats; the other, the "Tammany" delegation. The attitude of the Tammany organization towards Mr. Tilden in 1876, and the open declaration of Mr. John Kelly and other members of the contesting delegation, that if that candidate should be nominated again they would not support him, did not give the delegation favor in the eyes of the convention; and the committee on credentials reported against giving them any recognition whatever. A minority of the committee reported in favor of granting their request to be allowed twenty of the seventy votes of New York. After a debate the minority report was rejected by a vote of yeas 205½, nays 457. The New York delegation was excused from voting at its own request. Thus Tammany was excluded from the convention altogether.

Ex-Governor John W. Stevenson, of Kentucky, having been chosen permanent president of the convention, the platform was reported by Mr. Henry Watterson, of Kentucky, and unanimously adopted. It was as follows : —

The Democrats of the United States, in convention assembled, declare —

1. We pledge ourselves anew to the constitutional doctrines and traditions of the Democratic party, as illustrated by the teachings and example of a long line of Democratic statesmen and patriots, and embodied in the platform of the last national convention of the party.

2. Opposition to centralizationism and to that dangerous spirit of encroachment which tends to consolidate the powers of all the departments in one, and thus to create, whatever be the form of government, a real despotism. No sumptuary laws ; separation of church and state for the good of each; common schools fostered and protected.

3. Home rule ; honest money, consisting of gold and silver, and paper convertible into coin on demand; the strict maintenance of the public faith, state and national; and a tariff for revenue only.

4. The subordination of the military to the civil power, and a general and thorough reform of the civil service.

5. The right to a free ballot is the right preservative of all rights, and must and shall be maintained in every part of the United States.

6. The existing administration is the representative of conspiracy only, and its claim of right to surround the ballot-boxes with troops and deputy marshals, to intimidate and obstruct the electors, and the unprecedented use of the veto to maintain its corrupt and despotic power, insult the people and imperil their institutions.

7. The great fraud of 1876–77, by which, upon a false count of the electoral votes of two States, the candidate defeated at the polls was declared to be President, and, for the first time in American history, the will of the people was set aside under a threat of military violence, struck a deadly blow at our system of representative government; the Democratic party, to preserve the country from a civil war, submitted for a time in firm and patriotic faith that the people would punish this crime in 1880 ; this issue precedes and dwarfs every other ; it imposes a more sacred duty upon the people of the Union than ever addressed the conscience of a nation of freemen.

8. We execrate the course of this administration in making places in the civil service a reward for political crime, and demand a reform by statute which shall make it forever impossible for the defeated candidate to bribe his way to the seat of a usurper by billeting villains upon the people.

9. The resolution of Samuel J. Tilden not again to be a candidate for the exalted place to which he was elected by a majority of his countrymen, and from which he was excluded by the leaders of the Republican party, is received by the Democrats of the United States with sensibility, and they declare their confidence in his wisdom, patriotism, and integrity, unshaken by the assaults of a common enemy, and they further assure him that he is followed into the retirement he has chosen for himself by the sympathy and respect of his fellow-citizens, who regard him as one who, by elevating the standards of public morality, merits the lasting gratitude of his country and his party.

10. Free ships and a living chance for American commerce on the seas and on the land. No discrimination in favor of transportation lines, corporations, or monopolies.

11. Amendment of the Burlingame treaty. No more Chinese immigration, except for travel, education, and foreign commerce, and therein carefully guarded.

12. Public money and public credit for public purposes solely, and public land for actual settlers.

13. The Democratic party is the friend of labor and the laboring man, and pledges itself to protect him alike against the cormorant and the commune.

14. We congratulate the country upon the honesty and thrift of a Democratic Congress, which has reduced the public expenditure forty million dollars a year; upon the continuation of prosperity at home and the national honor abroad; and, above all, upon the promise of such a change in the administration of the government as shall insure us genuine and lasting reform in every department of the public service.

The business of the convention was transacted so expeditiously that the formal presentation of the candidates took place on the second day, and one ballot for a candidate for President was taken. It showed a slight lead for General Hancock over Mr. Bayard; yet the combined vote for both these candidates did not constitute a majority of the convention. A second ballot was taken the next morning, when General Hancock gained nearly one hundred and fifty votes, and the delegations then began changing in his favor, and he was nominated. The hand of Mr. Tilden was detected, or rather suspected, in the voting, but if he had any part in the affair he suffered a defeat. The vote of New York was at first cast for Mr. Payne, of Ohio, who was believed to be Mr. Tilden's heir ; but, on the second ballot, New York and nearly all the recognized friends of Tilden voted for Mr. Randall, who was also supposed to be a favorite of Mr. Tilden. It was mentioned as a queer feature of the convention that none of the delegates seemed to be enthusiastically in favor of their respective candidates, and it was said that those who voted at the beginning for General Hancock were ready to abandon him if any other person should have a lead over him. Accordingly, although he had been presented as a candidate and had received votes in the conventions of 1868 and 1876, and although he was so prominent prior to the convention of 1880, his nomination had all the effect of a surprise. The two ballots, the second as it stood originally and also as it was when the changes had been made, were as follows : —

CANDIDATES.	1st.	2d.	After changes.
Winfield S. Hancock, Pennsylvania . . .	171	320	705
Thomas F. Bayard, Delaware	153½	113	2
Henry B. Payne, Ohio	81	–	–
Allen G. Thurman, Ohio	68½	50	–
Stephen J. Field, California	65	65½	
William R. Morrison, Illinois	62	–	–
Thomas A. Hendricks, Indiana	50¼	31	30
Samuel J. Tilden, New York	38	6	1
Horatio Seymour, New York	8	–	–
Samuel J. Randall, Pennsylvania	–	128½	–
Scattering	31	22	–

The names of two gentlemen as candidates for the vice-presidency were presented : that of William H. English, of Indiana, and that of Richard M. Bishop, of Ohio, " your uncle Dick," as he was termed by the delegate who nominated him, in an unsuccessful attempt to arouse enthusiasm. The preference for Mr. English was so strongly expressed as the voting proceeded, that Mr. Bishop's name was withdrawn, and Mr. English was nominated by acclamation.

The canvass of 1880 was a remarkable one in several ways. First, for the savage assaults that were made upon General Garfield by the opposition. He was accused of numerous improprieties in his conduct as a member of the House of

Representatives, of complicity in corrupt contracts, and of having been concerned in the Credit Mobilier, which had made a great sensation in Congress in the years 1872 and 1873. At one time the number " 329 " was painted, chalked, and printed everywhere, on sidewalks, doors and dead-walls, and in the opposition newspapers ; that being the number of dollars he was alleged to have received as a Credit Mobilier dividend. It probably had little effect. Neither Democrats nor Republicans believed that General Garfield was corrupt. In the last days of the canvass the famous " Morey Letter " was forged and scattered broadcast, particularly in the Pacific States. That letter, in which General Garfield's handwriting was counterfeited with some success, addressed to a mythical person named Morey, asserted principles on the Chinese question which, if they had been held by General Garfield, would have made him unpopular in California and the other States where " Chinese cheap labor " was regarded as a crying evil. It was lithographed and printed in vast numbers, and scattered among the voters in the Pacific States at a time when an effective denial of its authenticity was impossible; and it had a great effect.

Another feature of the canvass was the sudden importation of the tariff question into the political discussion a few weeks before the election. The Democratic platform had declared in favor of " a tariff for revenue only." Republican speakers seized upon this as an assertion of the baldest free-trade doctrine, and they denounced it with surprising vigor as assailing the interests of American industry. The Democrats could not make an effective reply, at least they did not; and they would not defend the phrase in its obvious meaning. No one really supposed that General Hancock was a free-trader, but some unfortunate sentences which were written and spoken by him gave an opportunity to the Republicans to jeer at his supposed ignorance upon all tariff questions.

The canvass was remarkable also for the conspicuous absence of agitation upon Southern questions ; and indeed those questions had less influence upon the result than upon that of any other election since the Abolitionists defeated Henry Clay in 1844. Another fact was the failure of the Democrats to excite the interest of the people in the " fraud issue," meaning the result of the Electoral Commission law of 1877, which issue, the Democratic platform had said, " precedes and dwarfs

STATES.	POPULAR VOTE.				ELECTORAL VOTE.	
	James A. Garfield, Ohio.	Winfield S. Hancock, Pennsylvania.	James B. Weaver, Iowa.	Neal Dow, Maine.	Garfield and Arthur.	Hancock and English.
Alabama	56,221	91,185	4,642	–	–	10
Arkansas	42,436	60,775	4,079	–	–	6
California . . .	80,348	80,426	3,392	–	1	5
Colorado	27,450	24,647	1,435	–	3	–
Connecticut . . .	67,071	64,415	868	409	6	–
Delaware	14,133	15,275	120	–	–	3
Florida	23,654	27,964	–	–	–	4
Georgia	54,086	102,470	969	–	–	11
Illinois	318,037	277,321	26,358	443	21	–
Indiana	232,164	225,522	12,986	–	15	–
Iowa	183,927	105,845	32,701	592	11	–
Kansas	121,549	59,801	19,851	25	5	–
Kentucky	106,306	149,008	11,499	258	–	12
Louisiana	*38,637	65,067	439	–	–	8
Maine	74,039	† 65,171	4,408	93	7	–
Maryland	78,515	93,706	818	–	–	8
Massachusetts . .	165,205	111,960	4,548	682	13	–
Michigan	185,341	131,597	34,895	942	11	–
Minnesota	93,903	53,315	3,267	286	5	–
Mississippi . . .	34,854	75,750	5,797	–	–	8
Missouri	153,567	208,600	35,135	–	–	15
Nebraska	54,979	28,523	3,950	–	3	–
Nevada	8,732	9,613	–	–	–	3
New Hampshire . .	44,852	40,794	528	180	5	–
New Jersey . . .	120,555	122,565	2,617	191	–	9
New York	555,544	534,511	12,373	1,517	35	–
North Carolina . .	115,874	124,208	1,126	–	–	10
Ohio	375,048	340,821	6,456	2,616	22	–
Oregon	20,619	19,948	249	–	3	–
Pennsylvania . . .	444,704	407,428	20,668	1,939	29	–
Rhode Island . . .	18,195	10,779	236	20	4	–
South Carolina . .	58,071	112,312	566	–	–	7
Tennessee	107,677	128,191	5,917	43	–	12
Texas	57,893	156,428	27,405	–	–	8
Vermont	45,567	18,316	1,215	–	5	–
Virginia	84,020	‡128,586	–	–	–	11
West Virginia . .	46,243	57,391	9,079	–	–	5
Wisconsin	144,400	114,649	7,986	69	10	–
Total	4,454,416	4,444,952	308,578	10,305	214	155

* Two Republican tickets were voted for.

† Votes for a fusion electoral ticket, made up of three Democrats and four Greenbackers. A "straight" Greenback ticket was also voted for.

‡ Two Democratic tickets were voted for in Virginia. The regular ticket received 96,912, and was successful; the "Readjusters" polled 31,674 votes.

every other." The canvass was, finally, singular for the discord and sullenness among the Grant men in the Republican party at the outset, followed, after a reverse in Maine in September, by a restoration of harmony and an increase of vigor which immediately thereafter gave energy to the canvass, carried Ohio and Indiana in October, and made General Garfield President. Reference must also be made to the scandals connected with the contributions of funds to the Republican treasury, which brought into unpleasant prominence the contributions of certain officials who were afterwards shown to have obtained their money by corrupt or otherwise improper acts.

General Garfield had but an insignificant plurality of the popular vote over Hancock, and much less than a majority of all; but this was largely the result of abstention, voluntary or enforced, on the part of Republican voters in the South. Thirty-eight States took part in the election; in each the appointment of electors was by popular vote. The popular and electoral votes are given on the preceding page.

The count of votes took place under the resolution already cited. The electoral votes of Georgia were counted in the alternative manner first devised in 1821, as they had been cast on the second Wednesday of December. The vote was so close in California that one of the Republican electors was chosen by "split tickets." The electoral count was entirely devoid of incident, and General Garfield was duly proclaimed elected.

XXVII

THE MUGWUMP CAMPAIGN

THERE has never been a time in the history of the country when party lines were so indistinct, and so easily and frequently crossed, as during the four years that preceded the election of 1884. During all that time there was hardly a vote passed by either House of Congress in which the division was strictly on party lines. There were no sharply defined party issues; and political matters were in such a condition that if any fresh question of absorbing interest had arisen, there must have been extensive changes of party association, if not a complete reconstruction of both the great historical organizations. In the absence of such questions, men continued to act, each with his own party, merely as a matter of habit, and, up to the spring of 1884, there was nothing to portend the violence and fury with which the canvass of that year was to be conducted.

A brief survey of the leading events of the years from 1881 to 1884 will indicate how little occurred that had an influence upon the result in the presidential year. There was, first of all, the dissension in the Republican party caused by some of Mr. Garfield's appointments, chiefly in New York, which deeply offended Mr. Conkling, and led to the formation of two factions, one of which called itself "Stalwart" and stigmatized the other as "Half-breed." The assassination, the lingering sickness, and the death of President Garfield; the accession of Mr. Arthur, the scandal of the "Star route" mail contracts, and the offensive incidents of the trial of the assassin of the President, — these are chapters in our history which every patriotic student would gladly forget.

The only important legislation during Mr. Arthur's administration consisted of laws aimed at polygamy in Utah, and at Chinese immigration; the creation of the Tariff Commission in 1882, and the passage of a new tariff law in 1883; and the Civil Service Reform Act. While this was all, in one sense, political legislation, it was not, in the strict sense, party legislation. The Tariff Act was an exception, for it divided Congress nearly on party lines. In the Senate, one Democrat only voted for the bill, and two Republicans against it; while, in the House of Representatives, fifteen Democrats and nine Republicans separated themselves from their respective parties. The Civil Service Reform Act was passed in each branch by large majorities; but in the Senate all the five negative votes were given by Democrats, and in the House of Representatives seven only of the forty-seven negative votes were given by Republicans. Neither of these important acts was regarded as a party measure to such an extent that any member lost political standing by placing himself in opposition to the general opinion of his associates; and neither had a perceptible effect upon the election of 1884.

Events, nevertheless, were occurring which weakened the Republicans and prepared the way for the impending defeat of the party. There was a feeling which found expression in various ways that " the machine " was becoming too prominent in the management of affairs, and that the " bosses " were defiant of the better sentiment of the party in the selection of candidates. In many States, the election of 1882 resulted in Democratic victories which were largely due to a revolt against what was, rightly or wrongly, deemed the arrogant dictation of self-constituted leaders. Pennsylvania defeated the Republican candidate for governor, to whom no one objected on personal grounds; and New York gave to Grover Cleveland, the Democratic candidate for governor, the unprecedented majority of one hundred and ninety thousand. Yet the opposing candidate was Mr. Folger, the Secretary of the Treasury, formerly the chief judge of the New York Court of Appeals, and a gentleman of the highest character, against whom nothing could be said, except that he was a candidate chosen for the Republicans, and not by them. These defeats were regarded as warnings to the Republicans that they could win the coming contest only by nominating good candidates, without the intervention of the " machine " and the " bosses."

A step in the direction of greater freedom within the party, and in curtailment of the powers sometimes exercised by leaders in disregard of the popular will, was taken at a meeting of the Republican national committee held in 1883. An attempt was made so to change the basis of the national convention as to enlarge the influence of the States and communities giving Republican majorities, and to diminish correspondingly the relative strength of those parts of the country where the party was in a hopeless minority. Two propositions were submitted. According to the first, the national convention would consist of delegates from each State as follows: (1) Four delegates at large; (2) One delegate for each Congress-district; (3) One delegate for each twelve thousand votes given in the State in 1880 for the Republican electoral ticket. The other plan proposed for each State: (1) Four delegates at large; (2) One delegate at large for each Republican senator representing the State; (3) One delegate for each Congress-district; (4) One additional delegate for each district represented in Congress by a Republican. Each of these propositions was rejected, and the old basis of a national convention was readopted.

But a radical change was made in the method of choosing delegates. A time was prescribed for electing them, and the right of districts to choose their own delegates was recognized and secured. It was voted that the state conventions should be held not less than thirty nor more than sixty days before the time of meeting of the national convention, and after not less than twenty days' public, advertised notice. District delegates were to be elected either by separate district conventions or by subdivision of the state convention. If separate conventions were to be held, they were to meet within fifteen days prior to the state convention; and in any case their credentials were to be given and certified by district officers. By the first of these provisions, security was given against forestalling the action of the national convention by early conventions in some of the States; by the other, an opportunity was given to minorities to make their influence felt, and power was taken from a majority in the State to stifle opposition.

The first national convention held in 1884 was that of the Anti-Monopoly party, which met in Chicago, May 14. The party had no prior nor subsequent history. The attendance was not large. Only seventeen States and the District of Columbia were represented on the Committee on Resolutions. Mr. Alson J. Streeter was the temporary chairman, and John F. Henry the permanent president of the convention. The following platform was reported, and adopted by a vote of eighty-five to twenty-nine: —

The Anti-Monopoly organization of the United States, in convention assembled, declares : —

1. That labor and capital should be allies; and we demand justice for both, by protecting the rights of all against privileges for the few.

2. That corporations, the creatures of law, should be controlled by law.

3. That we propose the greatest reduction practicable in public expenses.

4. That in the enactment and vigorous execution of just laws, equality of rights, equality of burdens, equality of privileges, and equality of powers in all citizens will be secured. To this end, we declare : —

5. That it is the duty of the government to immediately exercise its constitutional prerogative to regulate commerce among the States. The great instruments by which this commerce is carried on are transportation, money, and the transmission of intelligence. They are now mercilessly controlled by giant monopolies, to the impoverishment of labor, the crushing out of healthful competition, and the destruction of business security. We hold it, therefore, to be the imperative and immediate duty of Congress to pass all needful laws for the control and regulation of those great agents of commerce, in accordance with the oft-repeated decisions of the Supreme Court of the United States.

6. That these monopolies, which have exacted from enterprise such heavy tribute, have also inflicted countless wrongs upon the toiling millions of the United States; and no system of reform should commend itself to the support of the people which does not protect the man who earns his bread by the sweat of his face. Bureaus of labor-statistics must be established, both state and national; arbitration take the place of brute force in the settlement of disputes between employer and employed; the national eight-hour law be honestly enforced; the importation of foreign labor under contract be made illegal; and whatever practical reforms may be necessary for the protection of united labor must be granted, to the end that unto the toiler shall be given that proportion of the profits of the thing or value created which his labor bears to the cost of production.

7. That we approve and favor the passage of an Interstate Commerce bill. Navigable waters should be improved by the government, and be free.

8. We demand the payment of the bonded debt as it falls due; the election of United States senators by the direct vote of the people of their respective States; a graduated income tax; and a tariff, which is a tax upon the people, that shall be so levied as to

bear as lightly as possible upon necessaries. We denounce the present tariff as being largely in the interest of monopoly, and demand that it be speedily and radically reformed in the interest of labor, instead of capital.

9. That no further grants of public lands shall be made to corporations. All enactments granting lands to corporations should be strictly construed, and all land grants should be forfeited where the terms upon which the grants were made have not been strictly complied with. The lands must be held for homes for actual settlers, and must not be subject to purchase or control by non-resident foreigners or other speculators.

10. That we deprecate the discrimination of American legislation against the greatest of American industries, — agriculture, — by which it has been deprived of nearly all beneficial legislation, while forced to bear the brunt of taxation ; and we demand for it the fostering care of government, and the just recognition of its importance in the development and advancement of our land ; and we appeal to the American farmer to coöperate with us in our endeavors to advance the national interests of the country and the overthrow of monopoly in every shape, whenever and wherever found.

General Benjamin F. Butler, of Massachusetts, was nominated as candidate for President on the first vote. He received 122 votes, to 7 for Allen G. Thurman, of Ohio, and 1 for Solon Chase, of Maine. The nomination of a candidate for Vice-President was left with the national committee, who adopted the candidate of the National or Greenback party, General Alanson M. West, of Mississippi.

The National party — Greenbackers — held its convention in Indianapolis, on the 28th of May. John Tyler, of Florida, was the temporary chairman, and General James B. Weaver, of Iowa, permanent president. The following platform was adopted : —

Eight years ago, our young party met in this city for the first time, and proclaimed to the world its immortal principles, and placed before the American people as a presidential candidate that great philanthropist and spotless statesman, Peter Cooper. Since that convention, our party has organized all over the Union, and through discussion and agitation has been educating the people to a sense of their rights and duties to themselves and their country. These labors have accomplished wonders. We now have a great, harmonious party, and thousands who believe in our principles in the ranks of other parties.

" We point with pride to our history." We forced the remonetization of the silver dollar; prevented the refunding of the public debt into long-time bonds; secured the payment of the bonds, until "the best banking system the world ever saw," for robbing the producer, now totters because of its contracting foundation; we have stopped the wholesale destruction of the greenback currency, and secured a decision of the Supreme Court of the United States establishing forever the right of the people to issue their own money.

Notwithstanding all this, never in our history have the banks, land-grant railroads, and other monopolies been more insolent in their demands for further privileges — still more class legislation. In this emergency, the dominant parties are arrayed against the people, and are the abject tools of the corporate monopolies.

In the last Congress, they repealed over twelve million dollars of annual taxes for the banks, throwing the burden upon the people to pay, or pay interest thereon.

Both old parties in the present Congress vie with each other in their efforts to further repeal taxes in order to stop the payment of the public debt and save the banks whose charters they have renewed for twenty years. Notwithstanding the distress of business, the shrinkage of wages, and panic, they persist in locking up, on various pretexts, four hundred million dollars of money, every dollar of which the people pay interest upon, and need, and most of which should be promptly applied to pay bonds now payable.

The old parties are united — as they cannot agree what taxes to repeal — in efforts to squander the income of the government upon every pretext rather than pay the debt.

A bill has already passed the United States Senate making the banks a present of over fifty million dollars more of the people's money, in order to enable them to levy a still greater burden of interest taxes.

A joint effort is being made by the old party leaders to overthrow the sovereign constitutional power of the people to control their own financial affairs and issue their own money, in order to forever enslave the masses to bankers and other business. The House of Representatives has passed bills reclaiming nearly one hundred million acres of lands granted to and forfeited by railroad companies. These bills have gone to the Senate, a body composed largely of aristocratic millionaires, who, according to their own party papers, generally purchased their elections in order to protect great monopolies which they represent. This body has thus far defied the people and the House, and refused to act upon these bills in the interest of the people.

Therefore we, the National party of the United States, in national convention assembled, this twenty-ninth day of May, A. D. 1884, declare : —

1. That we hold the late decision of the Supreme Court on the legal tender question to be a full vindication of the theory which our party has always advocated on the right and authority of Congress over the issue of legal tender notes, and we hereby pledge ourselves to uphold said decision, and to defend the Constitution against alterations or amendments intended to deprive the people of any rights or privileges conferred by that instrument. We demand the issue of such money in sufficient quantities to supply the actual demand of trade and commerce, in accordance with the increase of population and the development of our industries. We demand the substitution of greenbacks for national bank notes, and the prompt payment of the public debt. We want that money which saved our country in time of war, and which has given it prosperity and happiness in peace. We condemn the retirement of the fractional currency and the small denomination of greenbacks, and demand their restoration. We demand the issue of the hoards of money now locked up in the United States treasury, by applying them to the payment of the public debt now due.

2. We denounce, as dangerous to our republican institutions, those methods and policies of the Democratic and Republican parties which have sanctioned or permitted the establishment of land, railroad, money, and other gigantic corporate monopolies; and we demand such governmental action as may be necessary to take from such monopolies the powers they have so corruptly and unjustly usurped, and restore them to the people, to whom they belong.

3. The public lands being the natural inheritance of the people, we denounce that policy which has granted to corporations vast tracts of land, and we demand that immediate and vigorous measures be taken to reclaim from such corporations, for the people's use and benefit, all such land grants as have been forfeited by reason of non-fulfilment of contract, or that may have been wrongfully acquired by corrupt legislation, and that such reclaimed lands and other public domain be henceforth held as a sacred trust, to be granted only to actual settlers in limited quantities; and we also demand that the alien ownership of land, individual or corporate, be prohibited.

4. We demand congressional regulation of interstate commerce. We denounce " pooling," stock watering, and discrimination in rates and charges, and demand that Congress shall correct these abuses, even, if necessary, by the construction of national railroads. We also demand the establishment of a government postal telegraph system.

5. All private property, all forms of money and obligations to pay money, should bear their just proportion of the public taxes. We demand a graduated income tax.

6. We demand the amelioration of the condition of labor, by enforcing the sanitary laws in industrial establishments, by the abolition of the convict labor system, by a rigid inspection of mines and factories, by a reduction of the hours of labor in industrial establishments, by fostering educational institutions, and by abolishing child labor.

7. We condemn all importations of contracted labor, made with a view of reducing to starvation wages the workingmen of this country, and demand laws for its prevention.

8. We insist upon a constitutional amendment reducing the terms of United States senators.

9. We demand such rules for the government of Congress as shall place all representatives of the people upon an equal footing, and take away from committees a veto power greater than that of the President.

10. The question as to the amount of duties to be levied upon various articles of import has been agitated and quarrelled over, and has divided communities, for nearly a hundred years. It is not now, and never will be, settled, unless by the abolition of indirect taxation. It is a convenient issue, always raised when the people are excited over abuses in their midst. While we favor a wise revision of the tariff laws, with a view to raising a revenue from luxuries rather than necessities, we insist that, as an economic question, its importance is insignificant as compared with financial issues; for whereas we have suffered our worst panics under low and also under high tariffs, we have never suffered from a panic, nor seen our factories and workshops closed, while the volume of money in circulation was adequate to the needs of commerce. Give our farmers and manufacturers money as cheap as you now give it to our bankers, and they can pay high wages to labor, and compete with all the world.

11. For the purpose of testing the sense of the people upon the subject, we are in favor of submitting to a vote of the people an amendment to the Constitution in favor of suffrage regardless of sex, and also on the subject of the liquor traffic.

12. All disabled soldiers of the late war should be equitably pensioned, and we denounce the policy of keeping a small army of office-holders, whose only business is to prevent, on technical grounds, deserving soldiers from obtaining justice from the government they helped to save.

13. As our name indicates, we are a national party, knowing no East, no West, no North, no South. Having no sectional prejudices, we can properly place in nomination for the high offices of state, as candidates, men from any section of the Union.

14. We appeal to all people who believe in our principles, to aid us by voice, pen, and votes.

The first vote for a candidate for President resulted as follows: — General Benjamin F. Butler, of Massachusetts, 322; Jesse Harper, of Illinois, 99; Solon Chase, of Maine, 2; Edward P. Allis, of Wisconsin, 1; David Davis, of Illinois, 1. General Butler was declared nominated. A motion to make the nomination unanimous was declared adopted, though it was received with hisses and shouts of " no." General Alanson M. West, of Mississippi, was nominated for Vice-President by acclamation.

As the time set for the meeting of the Republican convention approached, there was the usual activity among the partisans of the several candidates. General Arthur had succeeded to the presidency in trying circumstances, and had acquitted himself in his high office with great credit. His moderation had won for him the praise of many men who had heard of his nomination for the vice-presidency, in 1880, with dismay. The President was frankly a candidate for reëlection. He had hosts of friends and few enemies in the party. General John A. Logan had not only the support of the Republicans of his own State of Illinois, but many strong partisans among the volunteer soldiers of the civil war. Senator John Sherman was supported by a compact body of Ohio Republicans. Senator George F. Edmunds, of Vermont, was a favorite candidate with many of those members of the party who regarded civil service reform as the great issue. But the candidate who had the strongest, the most enthusiastic, and, as the event proved, the prevailing body of followers, was Mr. James G. Blaine, of Maine. This gentleman had been secretary of state under General Garfield, the President's most intimate friend, and his chief political adviser. He had narrowly missed the nomination in 1876 and again in 1880, on his own merits; and he was now regarded as the natural heir of the assassinated President. His own State supported him, but he had no great strength in the other New England States. But elsewhere, — everywhere else, — his partisans were numerous, enthusiastic, and devoted. From the northwest, the southwest, the Pacific coast States, from New York and Pennsylvania, they gathered, and they had even successfully disputed the claim of Ohio's and Illinois's " favorite sons " to united delegations. It was evident, before the convention met, that the supporters of Mr. Blaine and of General Arthur constituted a large majority of the delegates. It was also evident that Mr.

Blaine was the leading candidate. His success was sure, unless all the opposing elements, those which were simply more friendly to other candidates, as well as that element which was unalterably opposed to his candidacy, could be held together and concentrated upon one man.

The convention met at Chicago on June 3. The national committee had named ex-Senator Powell Clayton, of Arkansas, as the temporary chairman of the convention. This selection was supposed to be in the interest of Mr. Blaine. A nomination of the Hon. John R. Lynch, of Mississippi, a distinguished colored man, was made from the floor, and the convention, on a vote by delegates, elected him to the position, by 431 votes to 387 given for Mr. Clayton. On the next day, no other business was transacted beyond the choice of the Hon. John B. Henderson, of Missouri, as permanent president.

On the third day, the rules of the convention were reported and adopted. One important rule was adopted, concerning the constitution of the national committee, and the election of future conventions. It provided that " no person shall be a member of the committee who is not eligible as a member of the electoral college." This provision excludes from the committee all persons who hold offices of trust or profit under the United States, as well as all senators and representatives, and removes every opportunity to influence the action of the party directly through the elected or appointed official class. The same rule provides that all delegates at large shall be chosen by state conventions, and that in each Congress-district the delegates shall be elected " in the same way as the nomination of a member of Congress is made in said district." This provision abolishes altogether the practice of subdividing a state convention to choose district delegates, and makes each district absolutely free. An attempt was made to change the basis of representation in the convention, but it met with small encouragement, and the matter was not brought to a vote.

The following platform was reported and adopted : —

1. The Republicans of the United States, in national convention assembled, renew their allegiance to the principles upon which they have triumphed in six successive presidential elections, and congratulate the American people on the attainment of so many results in legislation and administration by which the Republican party has, after saving the Union, done so much to render its institutions just, equal, and beneficent; the safeguard of liberty, and

the embodiment of the best thought and highest purposes of our citizens. The Republican party has gained its strength by quick and faithful response to the demands of the people for the freedom and equality of all men; for a united nation, assuring the rights of all citizens; for the elevation of labor; for an honest currency; for purity in legislation; and for integrity and accountability in all departments of the government. And it accepts anew the duty of leading in the work of progress and reform.

2. We lament the death of President Garfield, whose sound statesmanship, long conspicuous in Congress, gave promise of a strong and successful administration, a promise fully realized during the short period of his office as President of the United States. His distinguished services in war and in peace have endeared him to the hearts of the American people.

3. In the administration of President Arthur we recognize a wise, conservative, and patriotic policy, under which the country has been blessed with remarkable prosperity; and we believe his eminent services are entitled to, and will receive, the hearty approval of every good citizen.

4. It is the first duty of a good government to protect the rights and promote the interests of its own people. The largest diversity of industry is most productive of general prosperity and of the comfort and independence of the people. We therefore demand that the imposition of duties on foreign imports shall be made, not for revenue only, but that, in raising the requisite revenues for the government, such duties shall be so levied as to afford security to our diversified industries, and protection to the rights and wages of the laborers, to the end that active and intelligent labor, as well as capital, may have its just reward, and the laboring man his full share in the national prosperity.

5. Against the so-called economical system of the Democratic party, which would degrade our labor to the foreign standard, we enter our most earnest protest. The Democratic party has failed completely to relieve the people of the burden of unnecessary taxation by a wise reduction of the surplus.

6. The Republican party pledges itself to correct the irregularities of the tariff and to reduce the surplus, not by the vicious and indiscriminate process of horizontal reduction, but by such methods as will relieve the taxpayer without injuring the laborer or the great productive interests of the country.

7. We recognize the importance of sheep husbandry in the United States, the serious depression which it is now experiencing, and the danger threatening its future prosperity; and we therefore respect the demands of the representatives of this important agricultural interest for a readjustment of duties upon

foreign wool, in order that such industry shall have full and adequate protection.

8. We have always recommended the best money known to the civilized world, and we urge that an effort be made to unite all commercial nations in the establishment of an international standard which shall fix for all the relative value of gold and silver coinage.

9. The regulation of commerce with foreign nations and between the States is one of the most important prerogatives of the general government, and the Republican party distinctly announces its purpose to support such legislation as will fully and efficiently carry out the constitutional power of Congress over interstate commerce.

10. The principle of the public regulation of railway corporations is a wise and salutary one for the protection of all classes of the people, and we favor legislation that shall prevent unjust discrimination and excessive charges for transportation, and that shall secure to the people and to the railways alike the fair and equal protection of the laws.

11. We favor the establishment of a national bureau of labor; the enforcement of the eight-hour law; a wise and judicious system of general education, by adequate appropriation from the national revenues wherever the same is needed. We believe that everywhere the protection of a citizen of American birth must be secured to citizens by American adoption, and we favor the settlement of national differences by international arbitration.

12. The Republican party, having its birth in a hatred of slave labor, and in a desire that all men may be truly free and equal, is unalterably opposed to placing our workingmen in competition with any form of servile labor, whether at home or abroad. In this spirit we denounce the importation of contract labor, whether from Europe or Asia, as an offence against the spirit of American institutions, and we pledge ourselves to sustain the present law restricting Chinese immigration, and to provide such further legislation as is necessary to carry out its purposes.

13. Reform of the civil service, auspiciously begun under Republican administration, should be completed by the further extension of the reformed system already established by law to all the grades of the service to which it is applicable. The spirit and purpose of the reform should be observed in all executive appointments, and all laws at variance with the objects of existing reformed legislation should be repealed, to the end that the dangers to free institutions which lurk in the power of official patronage may be wisely and effectively avoided.

14. The public lands are a heritage of the people of the United

States, and should be reserved, as far as possible, for small holdings by actual settlers. We are opposed to the acquisition of large tracts of these lands by corporations or individuals, especially where such holdings are in the hands of non-resident aliens, and we will endeavor to obtain such legislation as will tend to correct this evil. We demand of Congress the speedy forfeiture of all land-grants which have lapsed by reason of non-compliance with acts of incorporation, in all cases where there has been no attempt in good faith to perform the conditions of such grants.

15. The grateful thanks of the American people are due to the Union soldiers and sailors of the late war ; and the Republican party stands pledged to suitable pensions for all who were disabled, and for the widows and orphans of those who died in the war. The Republican party also pledges itself to the repeal of the limitation contained in the arrears act of 1879, so that all invalid soldiers shall share alike, and their pensions begin with the date of disability, and not with the date of the application.

16. The Republican party favors a policy which shall keep us from entangling alliances with foreign nations, and which gives us the right to expect that foreign nations shall refrain from meddling in American affairs, — the policy which seeks peace and trade with all powers, but especially with those of the western hemisphere.

17. We demand the restoration of our navy to its old-time strength and efficiency, that it may in any sea protect the rights of American citizens and the interests of American commerce. We call upon Congress to remove the burdens under which American shipping has been depressed, so that it may again be true that we have a commerce which leaves no sea unexplored, and a navy which takes no law from superior force.

18. That appointments by the President to offices in the Territories should be made from the *bona-fide* citizens and residents of the Territories wherein they are to serve.

19. That it is the duty of Congress to enact such laws as shall promptly and effectually suppress the system of polygamy within our Territories, and divorce the political from the ecclesiastical power of the so-called Mormon Church, and that the law so enacted should be rigidly enforced by the civil authorities, if possible, and by the military, if need be.

20. The people of the United States, in their organized capacity, constitute a nation, and not a mere confederacy of States. The national government is supreme within the sphere of its national duties, but the States have reserved rights which should be faithfully maintained, and which should be guarded with jealous care, so that the harmony of our system of government may be preserved and the Union kept inviolate.

21. The perpetuity of our institutions rests upon the mainte-nance of a free ballot, an honest count, and correct return. We denounce the fraud and violence practised by the Democracy in southern States, by which the will of the voter. is defeated, as dangerous to the preservation of free institutions; and we solemnly arraign the Democratic party as being the guilty recipient of the fruits of such fraud and violence.

22. We extend to the Republicans of the South, regardless of their former party affiliations, our cordial sympathy, and pledge to them our most earnest efforts to promote the passage of such legislation as will secure to every citizen, of whatever race and color, the full and complete recognition, possession, and exercise of all civil and political rights.

An evening session was held, at which the speeches were made, putting the several candidates in nomination, but no vote was taken until the next morning, Friday, June 6. Four votes only were required to effect the nomination of Mr. Blaine, which was then made unanimous. The votes were as follows : —

	1st.	2d.	3d.	4th.
James G. Blaine, Maine	334½	349	375	541
Chester A. Arthur, New York	278	276	274	207
George F. Edmunds, Vermont.	93	85	69	41
John A. Logan, Illinois	63½	61	53	7
John Sherman, Ohio	30	28	25	–
Joseph R. Hawley, Connecticut	13	13	13	15
Robert T. Lincoln, Illinois	4	4	8	2
William T. Sherman, Missouri	2	2	2	–

At an evening session, John A. Logan, of Illinois, was nominated for Vice-President by 779 votes to 7 for Lucius Fairchild, of Wisconsin, and 6 for Walter Q. Gresham, of Indiana, and the convention adjourned.

Although there had been certain vague warnings in a part of the Republican press that the party might forfeit the support of many of its members in case the convention should adopt a course contrary to that which the "reform element" of the party desired, yet no one seems to have been prepared for the extensive bolt which followed immediately upon the adjournment of the convention. Several important party organs, and a large number of prominent Republicans, chiefly in the

Eastern States, announced, formally, that they would not support the candidates nominated.   Independent committees were at once organized in New York and Boston, for the purpose of concentrating the Republican opposition to Mr. Blaine; and these committees, which had the coöperation of committees and of independent voters in other cities, turned to the Democrats with assurances that if they would make nominations acceptable to the reformers, they could have the support of those who were opposed to Mr. Blaine, and to what they deemed the reckless disregard of good political morals by the Republican convention.

The Republican revolt had a strong effect upon the action of the Democrats.   While most of the candidates who had received votes for the nomination in 1880 were again in the field with supporters in considerable numbers, — Bayard, Thurman, Randall, and others, — Democratic public opinion had already fixed upon Grover Cleveland, governor of New York, as the strongest candidate.   He was the candidate who had obtained the enormous majority of 190,000 in 1882, and he had a large majority of the New York delegation, which was instructed by the state convention to act as a unit on all questions.   He was, moreover, the favorite candidate of the Republican dissidents, who looked upon him as a sincere reformer, who would carry into practice the principles which he and they professed.   There was, in New York, nevertheless, not a little opposition, chiefly of a personal nature, to Governor Cleveland, for the powerful organization of Tammany Hall was against him.

The convention met at Chicago, on July 8, and effected a temporary organization, with Richard D. Hubbard, of Texas, as chairman.   The rules of the last Democratic convention were adopted with one modification, namely, a provision that after a State had given its vote for a candidate for President or Vice-President, it should not change its vote until the roll-call should be completed.   The "two-thirds rule" was, of course, adopted with the rest.   The leader of the Tammany opposition to Grover Cleveland endeavored to secure the adoption of a rule that when any member of a state delegation disputed the correctness of the vote of that State, as announced by the chairman, the secretary should call the roll, and that "their individual preferences as expressed shall be recorded as the vote of the State."   The object, of course, was to break down the unit rule, and particularly to allow the minority of the New York delegation to be heard. The proposition was defeated by about one hundred majority, and, although attempts were afterward made to cause the actual vote of the New York delegates to be recorded, the presiding officer declared himself bound to accept the vote of that delegation as a unit, in accordance with the instructions of the state convention.

On the second day of the convention, William F. Vilas, of Wisconsin, was elected permanent president; and the several candidates were presented to the convention, in nominating speeches. An evening session was held, and the following platform was reported and adopted : —

The Democratic party of the Union, through its representatives in national convention assembled, recognizes that, as the nation grows older, new issues are born of time and progress, and old issues perish; but the fundamental principles of the Democracy, approved by the united voice of the people, remain, and will ever remain, as the best and only security for the continuance of free government. The preservation of personal rights; the equality of all citizens before the law; the reserved rights of the States; and the supremacy of the federal government within the limits of the Constitution, will ever form the true basis of our liberties, and can never be surrendered without destroying that balance of rights and powers which enables a continent to be developed in peace, and social order to be maintained by means of local self-government. But it is indispensable for the practical application and enforcement of these fundamental principles that the government should not always be controlled by one political party. Frequent change of administration is as necessary as constant recurrence to the popular will. Otherwise, abuses grow, and the government, instead of being carried on for the general welfare, becomes an instrumentality for imposing heavy burdens on the many who are governed, for the benefit of the few who govern. Public servants thus become arbitrary rulers. This is now the condition of the country; hence, a change is demanded.

The Republican party, so far as principle is concerned, is a reminiscence. In practice it is an organization for enriching those who control its machinery. The frauds and jobbery which have been brought to light in every department of the government are sufficient to have called for reform within the Republican party; yet those in authority, made reckless by the long possession of power, have succumbed to its corrupting influence, and have placed in nomination a ticket against which the independent portion of the party are in open revolt. Therefore a change is demanded. Such a change was alike necessary in 1876, but the will of the people was then defeated by a fraud which can never be forgotten nor condoned. Again, in 1880, the change demanded by the people was defeated by the lavish use of money contributed by unscrupulous contractors and shameless jobbers, who had bargained for unlawful profits or high office. The Republican party, during its legal, its stolen, and its bought tenures of power, has steadily decayed in moral character and political capacity. Its platform promises are now a list of its past failures. It demands the restoration of our navy; it has squandered hundreds of millions to create a navy that does not exist. It calls upon Congress to remove the burdens under which American shipping has been depressed; it imposed and has continued these burdens. It professes the policy of reserving the public lands for small holdings by actual settlers; it has given away the people's heritage, till now a few railroads and non-resident aliens, individual and corporate, possess a larger area than that of all our farms between the two seas. It professes a preference for free institutions; it organized and tried to legalize a control of state elections by federal troops. It professes a desire to elevate labor; it subjected American workingmen to the competition of convict and imported contract labor. It professes gratitude to all who were disabled or died in the war, leaving widows and orphans; it left to a Democratic House of Representatives the first effort to equalize both bounties and pensions. It professes a pledge to correct the irregularities of our tariff; it created and has continued them. Its own tariff commission confessed the need of more than twenty per cent. reduction; its Congress gave a reduction of less than four per cent. It professes the protection of American manufactures; it has subjected them to an increasing flood of manufactured goods and a hopeless competition with manufacturing nations, not one of which taxes raw materials. It professes to protect all American industries; it has impoverished many, to subsidize a few. It professes the protection of American labor; it has depleted the returns of American agriculture, an industry followed by half our people. It professes the equality of all men before the law, attempting to fix the status of colored citizens; the acts of its Congress were overset by the decisions of its courts. It "accepts anew the duty of leading in the work of progress and reform;" its caught criminals are permitted to escape through contrived delays or actual connivance in the prosecution. Honeycombed with corruption, out-breaking exposures no longer shock its moral sense. Its honest members, its independent journals, no longer maintain a successful contest for authority in its canvasses or a veto upon bad nominations. That change is necessary is proved by an existing surplus of more than $100,000,000, which has yearly been collected from a suffering people. Unnecessary taxation is unjust taxation. We denounce the Republican party for having failed to relieve the people from crushing war taxes, which have paralyzed business, crippled industry, and deprived labor of employment and of just reward.

The Democracy pledges itself to purify the administration from corruption, to restore economy, to revive respect for law, and to reduce taxation to the lowest limit consistent with due regard to the preservation of the faith of the nation to its creditors and pensioners. Knowing full well, however, that legislation affecting the occupations of the people should be cautious and conservative in method, not in advance of public opinion, but responsive to its demands, the Democratic party is pledged to revise the tariff in a spirit of fairness to all interests. But, in making reduction in taxes, it is not proposed to injure any domestic industries, but rather to promote their healthy growth. From the foundation of this government, taxes collected at the custom-house have been the chief source of federal revenue. Such they must continue to be. Moreover, many industries have come to rely upon legislation for successful continuance, so that any change of law must be at every step regardful of the labor and capital thus involved. The process of reform must be subject in the execution to this plain dictate of justice: all taxation shall be limited to the requirements of economical government. The necessary reduction in taxation can and must be effected without depriving American labor of the ability to compete successfully with foreign labor, and without imposing lower rates of duty than will be ample to cover any increased cost of production which may exist in consequence of the higher rate of wages prevailing in this country. Sufficient revenue to pay all the expenses of the federal government, economically administered, including pensions, interest and principal of the public debt, can be got under our present system of taxation from custom-house taxes on fewer imported articles, bearing heaviest on articles of luxury, and bearing lightest on articles of necessity. We therefore denounce the abuses of the existing tariff; and, subject to the preceding limitations, we demand that federal taxation shall be exclusively for public purposes, and shall not exceed the needs of the government economically administered.

The system of direct taxation, known as the "internal revenue," is a war tax, and, so long as the law continues, the money derived therefrom should be sacredly devoted to the relief of the people from the remaining burdens of the war, and be made a fund to defray the expenses of the care and comfort of worthy soldiers disabled in the line of duty in the wars of the Republic, and for the payment of such pensions as Congress may from time to time grant to such soldiers, a like fund for the sailors having been already provided; and any surplus should be paid into the Treasury.

We favor an American continental policy, based upon more intimate commercial and political relations with the fifteen sister republics of North, Central, and South America, but entangling alliances with none.

We believe in honest money, the gold and silver coinage of the Constitution, and a circulating medium convertible into such money without loss.

Asserting the equality of all men before the law, we hold that it is the duty of the government, in its dealings with the people, to mete out equal and exact justice to all citizens, of whatever nativity, race, color, or persuasion, religious or political.

We believe in a free ballot and a fair count; and we recall to the memory of our people the noble struggle of the Democrats in the Forty-fifth and Forty-sixth Congresses, by which a reluctant Republican opposition was compelled to assent to legislation making everywhere illegal the presence of troops at the polls, as the conclusive proof that a Democratic administration will preserve liberty with order.

The selection of federal officers for the Territories should be restricted to citizens previously resident therein.

We oppose sumptuary laws, which vex the citizens and interfere with individual liberty.

We favor honest civil service reform and the compensation of all United States officers by fixed salaries, the separation of Church and State, and the diffusion of free education by common schools, so that every child in the land may be taught the rights and duties of citizenship.

While we favor all legislation which will tend to the equitable distribution of property, to the prevention of monopoly, and to the strict enforcement of individual rights against corporate abuses, we hold that the welfare of society depends upon a scrupulous regard for the rights of property as defined by law.

We believe that labor is best rewarded where it is freest and most enlightened. It should, therefore, be fostered and cherished. We favor the repeal of all laws restricting the free action of labor, and the enactment of laws by which labor organizations may be incorporated, and of such legislation as will tend to enlighten the people as to the true relation of capital and labor.

We believe that the public land ought, as far as possible, to be kept as homesteads for actual settlers; that all unearned lands heretofore improvidently granted to railroad corporations by the action of the Republican party should be restored to the public domain, and that no more grants of land shall be made to corporations or be allowed to fall into the ownership of alien absentees.

We are opposed to all propositions which, upon any pretext, would convert the general government into a machine for collecting taxes to be distributed among the States or the citizens thereof.

In reaffirming the declaration of the Democratic platform of 1856, that "the liberal principles embodied by Jefferson in the Declaration of Independence, and sanctioned in the Constitution, which makes ours the land of liberty and the asylum of the oppressed of every nation, have ever been cardinal principles in the Democratic faith," we nevertheless do not sanction the importation of foreign labor or the admission of servile races, unfitted by habits, training, religion, or kindred, for absorption into the great body of our people, or for the citizenship which our laws confer. American civilization demands that against the immigration or importation of Mongolians to these shores our gates be closed.

The Democratic party insists that it is the duty of this government to protect with equal fidelity and vigilance the rights of its citizens, native and naturalized, at home and abroad; and, to the end that this protection may be assured, United States papers of naturalization, issued by courts of competent jurisdiction, must be respected by the executive and legislative departments of our own government and by all foreign powers. It is an imperative duty of this government to efficiently protect all the rights of persons and property of every American citizen in foreign lands, and demand and enforce full reparation for any invasion thereof. An American citizen is only responsible to his own government for any act done in his own country or under her flag, and can only be tried therefor on her own soil and according to her laws; and no power exists in this government to expatriate an American citizen to be tried in any foreign land for any such act.

This country has never had a well-defined and executed foreign policy, save under Democratic administration. That policy has ever been in regard to foreign nations, so long as they do no act detrimental to the interests of the country or hurtful to our citizens, to let them alone. As the result of this policy, we recall the acquisition of Louisiana, Florida, California, and the adjacent Mexican territory by purchase alone, and contrast these grand acquisitions of Democratic statesmanship with the purchase of Alaska, the sole fruit of a Republican administration of nearly a quarter of a century.

The federal government should care for and improve the Mississippi River and other great waterways of the republic, so as to secure for the interior States easy and cheap transportation to tide-water.

Under a long period of Democratic rule and policy, our merchant marine was fast overtaking and on the point of outstripping that of Great Britain. Under twenty years of Republican rule and policy, our commerce has been left to British bottoms, and the American flag has almost been swept off the high seas. Instead of the Republican party's British policy, we demand for the people of the United States an American policy. Under Democratic rule and policy, our merchants and sailors, flying the Stars and Stripes in every port, successfully searched out a market for the various products of American industry; under a quarter of a century of Republican rule and policy, despite our manifest advantages over all other nations, in high-paid labor, favorable climates, and teeming soils; despite freedom of trade among all these United States; despite their population by the foremost races of men, and an annual immigration of the young, thrifty, and adventurous of all nations; despite our freedom here from the inherited burdens of life and industry in Old World monarchies, their costly war navies, their vast tax-consuming, non-producing standing armies; despite twenty years of peace — that Republican rule and policy have managed to surrender to Great Britain, along with our commerce, the control of the markets of the world. Instead of the Republican party's British policy, we demand, in behalf of the American Democracy, an American policy. Instead of the Republican party's discredited scheme and false pretence of friendship for American labor, expressed by imposing taxes, we demand, in behalf of the Democracy, freedom for American labor by reducing taxes, to the end that these United States may compete with unhindered powers for the primacy among nations in all the arts of peace and fruits of liberty.

With profound regret we have been apprised by the venerable statesman, through whose person was struck that blow at the vital principle of republics, acquiescence in the will of the majority, that he cannot permit us again to place in his hands the leadership of the Democratic hosts, for the reason that the achievement of reform in the administration of the Federal government is an undertaking now too heavy for his age and failing strength. Rejoicing that his life has been prolonged until the general judgment of our fellow-countrymen is united in the wish that that wrong were righted in his person, for the Democracy of the United States we offer to him, in his withdrawal from public cares, not only our respectful sympathy and esteem, but also that best of homage of freemen, — the pledge of our devotion to the principles and the cause now inseparable in the history of this Republic from the labors and the name of Samuel J. Tilden.

With this statement of the hopes, principles, and purposes of the Democratic party, the great issue of reform and change in administration is submitted to the people in calm confidence that the popular voice will announce in favor of new men, and new and more favorable conditions for the growth of industry, the extension of trade, the employment and due reward of labor and of capital, and the general welfare of the whole country.

When the foregoing platform was reported, General Benjamin F. Butler, of Massachusetts, proposed to substitute a series of resolutions embodying certain ideas of his own, which he had previously offered to the committee on resolutions. The position which General Butler occupied was peculiar. He had, a few years before, abandoned the Republican party, with which he had acted since the civil war, and, after several failures, had been elected governor of Massachusetts, in 1882, as a Democrat. He now appeared as a delegate to the Democratic national convention, supported by a majority of his fellow-delegates from Massachusetts, urging his own nomination as a candidate for the presidency, to which position he had already received two nominations, as has been recorded in this chapter. To a notification of one of the nominations, he had written a reply, in which he had adroitly omitted to say whether or not he accepted the candidacy. His resolutions were rejected, — yeas, $97\frac{1}{2}$, nays, $714\frac{1}{2}$, — and the platform as reported was adopted without a division. General Butler's name was not presented to the convention as a candidate, and he received no votes.

Two ballots only were necessary to effect the nomination of a candidate for President. They resulted as follows: —

	1st.	2d.
Grover Cleveland, New York	392	683
Thomas F. Bayard, Delaware	170	$81\frac{1}{2}$
Thomas A. Hendricks, Indiana	–	$145\frac{1}{2}$
Allen G. Thurman, Ohio	88	4
Samuel J. Randall, Pennsylvania	78	4
Joseph E. McDonald, Indiana	56	2
John G. Carlisle, Kentucky	27	–
Roswell P. Flower, New York	4	–
George Hoadly, Ohio	3	–
Samuel J. Tilden, New York	1	–

Governor Cleveland, it will be seen, had less than a majority on the first vote, although he led all the other candidates. When the second roll-call was completed he still lacked 72 votes of the necessary two thirds, but numerous changes were made, and his nomination was effected.

Several persons were named to the convention as candidates for the nomination for Vice-President, — John C. Black, of Illinois, William S. Rosecrans, of California, and George W. Glick, of Kansas. The names were all withdrawn, and Thomas A. Hendricks, of Indiana, was nominated by a unanimous vote. This completed the work of the convention.

Two conventions were held by Prohibitionists. The first, which seems to have been, not a representative body, but rather a mass convention of the whole party, was held at Chicago, June 19, under the name of the American Prohibition National Convention. It was presided over by J. L. Barlow, of Connecticut, and adopted the following platform : —

We hold: 1. That ours is a Christian and not a heathen nation, and that the God of the Christian Scriptures is the author of civil government.

2. That the Bible should be associated with books of science and literature in all our educational institutions.

3. That God requires and man needs a Sabbath.

4. That we demand the prohibition of the importation, manufacture, and sale of intoxicating drinks.

5. That the charters of all secret lodges granted by our federal and state legislatures should be withdrawn and their oaths prohibited by law.

6. We are opposed to putting prison labor or depreciated contract labor from foreign countries in competition with free labor to benefit manufacturers, corporations, and speculators.

7. We are in favor of a thorough revision and enforcement of the law concerning patents and inventions, for the prevention and punishment of frauds either upon inventors or the general public.

8. We hold to and will vote for woman suffrage.

9. We hold that civil equality secured to all American citizens by articles thirteen, fourteen, and fifteen of our amended national Constitution should be preserved inviolate, and the same equality should be extended to Indians and Chinamen.

10. That international differences should be settled by arbitration.

11. That land and other monopolies should be discouraged.

12. That the general government should furnish the people with an ample and sound currency.

13. That it should be the settled policy of the government to reduce the tariffs and taxes as rapidly as the necessities of revenue and vested business interests will allow.

14. That polygamy should be immediately suppressed by law, and that the Republican party is censurable for its long neglect of its duty in respect to this evil.

15. And, finally, we demand for the American people the abolition of electoral colleges, and a direct vote for President and Vice-President of the United States.

The convention nominated Samuel C. Pomeroy, of Kansas, for President, by 72 votes, to 12 for all others, and nominated John A. Conant, of Connecticut, for Vice-President. It does not appear that an electoral ticket was presented at the polls in any State in support of the nominees of this convention.

The convention of the regular National Prohibition party was held at Pittsburg, July 23. William Daniel, of Maryland, was the temporary chairman, and Samuel Dickie, of Michigan, the permanent president of the convention, which adopted the following platform : —

The Prohibition-Home-Protection party, in national convention assembled, acknowledge Almighty God as the rightful sovereign of all men, from whom the just powers of government are derived, and to whose laws human enactments should conform. Peace, prosperity, and happiness only can come to the people when the laws of their national and state governments are in accord with the divine will.

That the importation, manufacture, supply, and sale of alcoholic beverages, created and maintained by the laws of the national and state governments, during the entire history of such laws, is everywhere shown to be the promoting cause of intemperance, with resulting crime and pauperism ; making large demands upon public and private charity ; imposing large and unjust taxation and public burdens for penal and sheltering institutions upon thrift, industry, manufactures, and commerce ; endangering the public peace ; causing desecration of the sabbath ; corrupting our politics, legislation, and administration of the laws ; shortening lives ; impairing health ; and diminishing productive industry ; causing education to be neglected and despised ; nullifying the teachings of the Bible, the church, and the school, the standards and guides of our fathers and their children in the founding and growth under God of our widely extended country ; and, while imperilling the perpetuity of our civil and religious liberties, are baleful fruits by which we know that these laws are alike contrary to God's laws, and contravene our happiness ; and we call upon our fellow-citizens to aid in the repeal of these laws and in the legal suppression of this baneful liquor traffic.

The fact that, during the twenty-four years in which the Republican party has controlled the general government and that of many of the States, no effort has been made to change this policy; that Territories have been created from the national domain, and governments from them established, and States admitted into the Union, in no instance in either of which has this traffic been forbidden, or the people of these Territories or States been permitted to prohibit it; that there are now over two hundred thousand distilleries, breweries, wholesale and retail dealers in these drinks, holding certificates and claiming the authority of government for the continuation of a business which is so destructive to the moral and material welfare of the people, together with the fact that they have turned a deaf ear to remonstrance and petition for the correction of this abuse of civil government, is conclusive that the Republican party is insensible to or impotent for the redress of those wrongs, and should no longer be intrusted with the powers and responsibilities of government; that although this party, in its late national convention, was silent on the liquor question, not so were its candidates, Messrs. Blaine and Logan. Within the year past, Mr. Blaine has publicly recommended that the revenues derived from the liquor traffic shall be distributed among the States, and Senator Logan has by bill proposed to devote these revenues to the support of schools. Thus, both virtually recommend the perpetuation of the traffic, and that the State and its citizens shall become partners in the liquor crime.

The fact that the Democratic party has, in its national deliverances of party policy, arrayed itself on the side of the drink makers and sellers, by declaring against the policy of prohibition of such traffic under the false name of "sumptuary laws," and, when in power in some of the States, in refusing remedial legislation, and, in Congress, of refusing to permit the creation of a board of inquiry to investigate and report upon the effects of this traffic, proves that the Democratic party should not be intrusted with power or place.

There can be no greater peril to the nation than the existing competition of the Republican and Democratic parties for the liquor vote. Experience shows that any party not firmly opposed to the traffic will engage in this competition, will court the favor of the criminal classes, will barter away the public morals, purity of the ballot, and every trust and object of good government, for party success; and patriots and good citizens should find in this practice sufficient cause for immediate withdrawal from all connection with their party.

That we favor reforms in the administration of the government, in the abolition of all sinecures, useless offices and officers, in the election by the people of officers of the government instead of appointment by the President. That competency, honesty, and sobriety are essential qualifications for holding civil office, and we oppose the removal of such persons from mere administrative offices, except so far as it may be absolutely necessary to secure effectiveness to the vital issues on which the general administration of the government has been intrusted to a party.

That the collection of revenue from alcohol, liquors, and tobacco should be abolished, as the vices of men are not a proper subject for taxation; that revenues for custom duties should be levied for the support of the government, economically administered; and when so levied, the fostering of American labor, manufactures, and industries should constantly be held in view.

That the public lands should be held for homes for the people and not for gifts to corporations, or to be held in large bodies for speculators upon the needs of actual settlers.

That all money, coin and paper, should be made, issued, and regulated by the general government, and should be a legal tender for all debts, public and private.

That grateful care and support should be given to our soldiers and sailors, their dependent widows and orphans, disabled in the service of the country.

That we repudiate as un-American, contrary to and subversive of the principle of the Declaration of Independence, from which our government has grown to be the government of fifty-five millions of people, and a recognized power among nations, that any person or people shall or may be excluded from residence or citizenship with all others who may desire the benefits which our institutions confer upon the oppressed of all nations.

That while there are important reforms that are demanded for purity of administration and the welfare of the people, their importance sinks into insignificance when compared with the reform of the drink traffic, which annually wastes eight hundred million dollars of the wealth created by toil and thrift, and drags down thousands of families from comfort to poverty; which fills jails, penitentiaries, insane asylums, hospitals, and institutions for dependency; which destroys the health, saps industry, and causes loss of life and property to thousands in the land, lowers intellectual and physical vigor, dulls the cunning hand of the artisan, is the chief cause of bankruptcy, insolvency, and loss in trade, and, by its corrupting power, endangers the perpetuity of free institutions.

That Congress should exercise its undoubted power, and prohibit the manufacture and sale of intoxicating beverages in the District of Columbia, in the Territories of the United States, and in all places over which the government has exclusive jurisdiction; that hereafter no State shall be admitted into the Union until its constitution shall expressly prohibit polygamy and the manufacture and sale of intoxicating beverages.

We earnestly call the attention of the laborer and mechanic, the miner and manufacturer, and ask investigation of the baneful effects upon labor and industry caused by the needless liquor business, which will be found the robber who lessens wages and profits, the destroyer of happiness and the family welfare of the laboring man, and that labor and all legitimate industry demand deliverance from the taxation and loss which this traffic imposes, and that no tariff or other legislation can so healthily stimulate production or increase a demand for capital and labor, or produce so much of comfort and content, as the suppressing of this traffic would bring to the laboring man, mechanic, or employer of labor throughout the land.

That the activity and coöperation of the women of America for the promotion of temperance has, in all the history of the past, been a strength and encouragement which we gratefully acknowledge and record. In the later and present phase of the movement for the prohibition of the licensed traffic by the abolition of the drinking-saloon, the purity of purpose and method, the earnestness, zeal, intelligence, and devotion of the mothers and daughters of the Women's Christian Temperance Union has been eminently blessed by God. Kansas and Iowa have been given her as "sheaves of rejoicing;" and the education and arousing of the public mind, and the demand for constitutional amendment now prevailing, are largely the fruit of her prayers and labors, and we rejoice to have our Christian women unite with us in sharing the labor that shall bring the abolition of this traffic to the polls; she shall join in the grand " Praise God, from whom all blessings flow," when by law our boys and friends shall be free from legal drink temptation.

That we believe in the civil and political equality of the sexes, and that the ballot in the hand of woman is a right for her protection, and would prove a powerful ally for the abolition of the drinking-saloon, the execution of law, the promotion of reform in civil affairs, and the removal of corruption in public life; and thus believing, we relegate the practical outworking of this reform to the discretion of the Prohibition party in the several States, according to the condition of public sentiment in those States; that gratefully we acknowledge and praise God for the presence of his Spirit, guiding our counsels and granting the success which has been vouchsafed in the progress of temperance reform, and, looking to Him from whom all wisdom and help come, we ask the voters of the United States to make the principles of the above declaration a ruling principle in the government of the nation and of the States.

Resolved, That henceforth the Prohibition-Home-Protection party shall be called by the name of the Prohibition party.

John P. St. John, of Kansas, was unanimously nominated as the candidate of the party for President, and William Daniel, of Maryland, was chosen with like unanimity for Vice-President.

It became evident, as soon as all the nominations had been made, that the canvass was to differ in important respects from all that had preceded it. The defection of the independent Republicans, who soon became known as "Mugwumps," took much of the spirit out of the party in the early days of the contest. These men would not be wooed back into the ranks of their former associates. They repeated the old charges against Mr. Blaine, and added to them objections based upon his course as secretary of state, which, they insisted, had a tendency to involve the country in war. On the other hand, serious personal accusations were brought against Mr. Cleveland. The Mugwumps openly supported Mr. Cleveland, but for the most part asserted that they were still Republicans, that they opposed Mr. Blaine only, and that Mr. Cleveland was "better than his party." As a matter of history it may be mentioned here that large numbers of them followed Mr. Cleveland to the end, and became members of the Democratic party. The canvass was, from first to last, conducted on personal grounds. The candidates were mercilessly lampooned, and false accusations of the most preposterous character were made against them. The earnest efforts of many Republicans to introduce questions of principle, to direct the attention of the people to the records and the tendencies of the two parties, and thus to change the character of the canvass, were unavailing.

This was not the only peculiarity of the election contest. The candidacy of General Butler was at times a source of uneasiness to the Democrats, who feared that the support of him by Tammany leaders and other malcontents in New York might result in the loss of that State. But before the day of election, Tammany yielded, and gave its support to Mr. Cleveland. On the other hand, the Republicans were greatly weakened by the Prohibition party; for that organization successfully invited many Republicans who would not support Mr. Blaine, and who could not bring themselves to the point of voting for a Democrat, to give their votes to Mr. St. John.

It would not be true, despite all these disturbing conditions, to say that the canvass was not an enthusiastic one on both sides. The Republican defection certainly chilled and well-nigh paralyzed the party in Massachusetts, and caused a serious loss in other New England States and in New York. But in the rest of the country the defection was not great. In the West, the enthusiasm for Mr. Blaine was almost unprecedented. During the canvass he made a tour from his home in Maine through many of the States of the West, and was met and cheered everywhere by enormous crowds of people. The Democrats, jubilant over the accession of a fresh contingent of voters, and hopeful of returning to power after many years of exclusion therefrom, made a bold and confident fight.

Yet all observers could see that the result of the contest was to be extremely close. The whole number of electoral votes was 401. The Democrats, as usual, were sure of the "solid South" with 153 votes, and they accordingly needed to gain only 48 votes in the North. The October election i Ohio showed that in the States usually Republican there wa likely to be no change; in short, the Republicans could d pend upon all the Northern States except Connecticut, Ne York, New Jersey, and Indiana, — that is, upon 182 vote The 66 votes of four States would decide the result. No o could tell how these States would go. Each party hoped ar feared. For although in three of them the Republicans had lost many strong supporters, Mr. Blaine was popular among the Irish voters, and no one could guess whether from that quarter enough recruits might not be found to offset the Mugwump defection.

Just on the eve of the election, an incident occurred which dashed this hope of the Republicans. A delegation of clergymen met Mr. Blaine in New York, as he was returning from the tour already mentioned, and one of their number made an address to the candidate, in the course of which he said in effect that the Republican canvass was directed against "Rum, Romanism, and Rebellion." The phrase was immediately used with great effect to drive back the Irish supporters of Mr. Blaine into the Democratic ranks. He had not used the

STATES.	POPULAR VOTE.				ELECTORAL VOTE.	
	Grover Cleveland, New York.	James G. Blaine, Maine.	Benjamin F. Butler, Massachusetts.	John P. St. John, Kansas.	Cleveland and Hendricks.	Blaine and Logan.
Alabama	93,951	59,591	873	612	10	–
Arkansas	72,927	50,895	1,847	–	7	–
California	89,288	102,416	2,017	2,920	–	8
Colorado . . .	27,723	36,290	1,953	761	–	3
Connecticut . . .	67,199	65,923	1,688	2,305	6	–
Delaware	16,964	12,951	6	55	3	–
Florida	31,766	28,031	–	72	4	–
Georgia	94,667	48,603	145	195	12	–
Illinois	312,355	337,474	10,910	12,074	–	22
Indiana	244,990	238,463	8,293	3,028	15	–
Iowa	177,316	197,089	–	1,472	–	13
Kansas	90,132	154,406	16,341	4,495	–	9
Kentucky	152,961	118,122	1,691	3,139	13	–
Louisiana	62,540	46,347	–	–	8	–
Maine	52,140	72,209	3,953	2,160	–	6
Maryland	96,932	85,699	531	2,794	8	–
Massachusetts . .	122,481	146,724	24,433	10,026	–	14
Michigan	149,835	192,669	42,243	18,403	–	13
Minnesota . . .	70,144	111,923	3,583	4,684	–	7
Mississippi . . .	76,510	43,509	–	–	9	–
Missouri	235,988	202,929	–	2,153	16	–
Nebraska	54,391	79,912	–	2,899	–	5
Nevada	5,578	7,193	26	–	–	3
New Hampshire .	39,183	43,249	552	1,571	–	4
New Jersey . . .	127,798	123,440	3,496	6,159	9	–
New York . . .	563,154	562,005	16,994	25,016	36	–
North Carolina . .	142,952	125,068	–	454	11	–
Ohio	368,280	400,082	5,179	11,069	–	23
Oregon	24,604	26,860	726	492	–	3
Pennsylvania . .	392,785	473,804	16,992	15,283	–	30
Rhode Island . .	12,391	19,030	422	928	–	4
South Carolina . .	69,890	21,733	–	–	9	–
Tennessee . . .	133,258	124,078	957	1,131	12	–
Texas	225,309	93,141	3,321	3,534	13	–
Vermont	17,331	39,514	785	1,752	–	4
Virginia	185,497	139,356	–	138	12	–
West Virginia . .	67,317	63,096	810	939	6	–
Wisconsin	146,459	161,157	4,598	7,656	–	11
Total	4,874,986	4,851,981	175,370	150,369	219	182

phrase, — indeed, it is doubtful if, in the confusion, he even heard it as it was uttered; but it was employed as though it had been an expression of his own, and there is scarcely a doubt that it affected enough votes in New York, which was most closely divided, to change the whole result, and to elect Mr. Cleveland instead of Mr. Blaine, — for the vote of New York was decisive.

The excitement of the canvass did not die out with the election, for the result was in great doubt. The early returns showed that Mr. Cleveland had carried all the Southern States, together with Connecticut, New Jersey, and Indiana. In all the other Northern States, except New York, the Republicans had been successful. The vote in New York was so close that both parties claimed its electoral vote for several days, and the corrected returns as they came in, showing differences from the first hasty returns of a score or two, first in favor of one party, then in favor of the other, were studied with intense anxiety. But the final result, a plurality of 1149 in a total vote of nearly 1,200,000, ended all doubt, and gave a President to the Democratic party for the first time since the close of Mr. Buchanan's administration.

No State had been admitted since 1876, but a new apportionment on the basis of the census of 1880 had increased the number of electors. The result of the popular vote, and of the vote by electors, has been given.

The count of electoral votes took place on February 11, 1885, in accordance with a joint resolution adopted by both Houses of Congress without opposition. The resolution was in the identical words of the first part of the resolution of 1881, and simply provided for the opening of the certificates by two tellers on the part of each House, and a declaration of the result by the president of the Senate. The count was undisturbed by any event calling for notice.

XXVIII

TWO IMPORTANT QUESTIONS DECIDED

THE quadrennial period which completed the first century of government under the Constitution was distinguished by the passage of two acts of constitutional importance. By one of them, the method of counting the electoral votes was settled on principles so reasonable and equitable that there seems no reason to apprehend that it will ever be changed, so long as the system of electing the President indirectly is pursued. Thus the famous *casus omissus* of the Constitution has been supplied so far as that can be done without a formal amendment. The amendment is unnecessary so long as parties are willing to abide by a fair settlement of a much disputed point, and it could not be adopted were either party opposed to it. By the other act, the presidential succession has been completely changed.

The history of the adoption of these measures contains little that is interesting. Neither was carried as a party measure, and when brought to a vote the opposition to either was little more than a symptom of that conservatism which usually resists all change.

The Presidential Succession Act was the first in order of time. The law of 1792 made the President *pro tempore* of the Senate the successor to the office of President in the event of the removal, death, resignation, or disability of both the President and the Vice-President; [1] and, after the President of the Senate, the Speaker of the House of Representatives. The Constitution conferred upon Congress the duty of designating what officer shall act as President in such cases. There was, from the beginning, a doubt if the President *pro tempore* of the Senate, or the Speaker, was an " officer," within the meaning of the Constitution. But certain considerations of personal politics at the time the act was passed caused Con-

[1] See page 36.

gress not to take the members of the Cabinet, the natural successors of the President and Vice-President in case of vacancy, but to vest the succession in the President *pro tempore* of the Senate and the Speaker of the House of Representatives. Fortunately, the case has never occurred which called for an application of the law of 1792. Nevertheless, on more than one occasion the country was perilously near a crisis, owing to the fact that the death of one person would cause the presidency to lapse, since no one then held the position either of President *pro tempore* or of Speaker.

It was this consideration, rather than the doubt if the law of 1792 was in conformity with the Constitution, that led to the enactment of the law of 1886. Another reason was that neither of the presiding officers of Congress designated for the succession is necessarily or invariably a member of the party which has been successful in electing the President; and it is universally admitted that political fair dealing demands that the party which has carried the election shall not be deprived of its victory by the death of the President and Vice-President.

The Presidential Succession bill was reported from the Committee on the Judiciary, of the Senate, as early as June 19, 1882. It was considered and passed January 19, 1883; but was not taken up for consideration in the House of Representatives before the expiration of the Forty-seventh Congress, March 4, 1883. A bill with identical provisions was passed by the Senate on December 17, 1885, without a division. It was taken up January 12, 1886, by the House of Representatives, and, after several proposed amendments had been rejected, the bill was passed as it came from the Senate by a vote of 185 to 77. The affirmative vote was given by 146 Democrats and 39 Republicans; the negative, by 75 Republicans and 2 Democrats. The act was approved January 19, 1886, and is in the following words: —

Be it enacted, etc., that in case of the removal, death, resignation, or inability of both the President and Vice-President of the United States, the Secretary of State, or if there be none, or in case of his removal, death, resignation, or inability, then the Secretary of the Treasury, or if there be none, or in case of his removal, death, resignation, or inability, then the Secretary of War, or if there be none, or in case of his removal, death, resignation, or inability, then the Attorney-General, or if there be none, or in case of his removal, death, resignation, or inability, then the Postmaster-General, or if there be none, or in case of his removal, death, resignation, or inability, then the Secretary of the Navy, or if there be none, or in case of his removal, death, resignation, or inability, then the Secretary of the Interior shall act as President until the disability of the President or Vice-President is removed, or a President shall be elected: *provided*, that whenever the powers and duties of the office of President of the United States shall devolve upon any of the persons named herein, if Congress be not then in session, or if it would not meet in accordance with law within twenty days thereafter, it shall be the duty of the person upon whom said powers and duties shall devolve to issue a proclamation convening Congress in extraordinary session, giving twenty days' notice of the time of meeting.

SECTION 2. That the preceding section shall only be held to describe and apply to such officers as shall have been appointed by the advice and consent of the Senate to the offices therein named, and such as are eligible to the office of President under the Constitution, and not under impeachment by the House of Representatives of the United States at the time the powers and duties of the office shall devolve upon them respectively.

SECTION 3. That sections 146, 147, 148, 149, and 150 of the Revised Statutes are hereby repealed.

The final settlement of the mode of counting the electoral votes stands as Chapter 9 of the Acts of the Forty-ninth Congress, approved February 3, 1887. Its history is even less eventful than that of the Presidential Succession Act, though agreement upon the terms of the bill was only reached after much consideration, many amendments, and the work of a conference committee. Into this act, as will be seen from an examination of its provisions, has been introduced the principle that a State may finally determine every contest arising out of a presidential election. Such determination must be made in accordance with a law passed before the electors are chosen, and the decision must have been made at least six days before the meeting of the electors; but under these conditions the two Houses of Congress cannot reverse the decision so reached. The only case in which such a determination can be subverted is when there is a conflict of tribunals, and the two Houses cannot agree in deciding which of them is the lawful tribunal. As to votes not made secure by a judicial determination, the general principle is that none can be rejected except by concurrent vote of the two Houses. This is different from the principle of the old " twenty-second joint rule," which allowed either House to reject votes.   The act in full is as follows : —

Be it enacted, etc., that the electors of each State shall meet and give their votes on the second Monday in January next following their appointment, at such place in each State as the Legislature of such State shall direct.

SECTION 2. That if any State shall have provided, by laws enacted prior to the day fixed for the appointment of the electors, for its final determination of any controversy or contest concerning the appointment of all or any of the electors of such State, by judicial or other methods of procedure, and such determination shall have been made at least six days before the time fixed for the meeting of the electors, such determination made pursuant to such law so existing on said day, and made at least six days prior to the said time of meeting of the electors, shall be conclusive, and shall govern in the counting of the electoral votes as provided in the Constitution, as hereinafter regulated, so far as the ascertainment of the electors appointed by such State is concerned.

SECTION 3. That it shall be the duty of the executive of each State, as soon as practicable after the conclusion of the appointment of electors in such State, by the final ascertainment under and in pursuance of the laws of such State providing for such ascertainment, to communicate under the seal of the State, to the secretary of state of the United States, a certificate of such ascertainment of the electors appointed, setting forth the names of such electors and the canvass or other ascertainment, under the laws of such State, of the number of votes given or cast for each person for whose appointment any and all votes have been given or cast; and it shall also thereupon be the duty of the executive of each State to deliver to the electors of such State, on or before the day on which they are required, by the preceding section, to meet, the same certificate, in triplicate, under the seal of the State; and such certificate shall be inclosed and transmitted by the electors at the same time and in the same manner as is provided by law for transmitting by such electors to the seat of government the lists of all persons voted for as President, and of all persons voted for as Vice-President: and Section 136 of the Revised Statutes is hereby repealed; and if there shall have been any final determination in the State of a controversy or contest, as provided for in Section 2 of this act, it shall be the duty of the executive of such State, as soon as practicable after such determination, to communicate, under the seal of the State, to the secretary of state of the United States, a certificate of such determination, in form and manner as the same shall have been made; and the secretary of state of the United States, as soon as practicable after the receipt at the State Department of each of the certificates hereinbefore directed to be transmitted to the secretary of state, shall publish, in such public newspaper as he shall designate, such certificates in full; and at the first meeting of Congress, thereafter, he shall transmit to the two Houses of Congress copies in full of each and every such certificate so received theretofore at the State Department.

SECTION 4. That Congress shall be in session on the second Wednesday in February succeeding every meeting of the electors. The Senate and House of Representatives shall meet in the hall of the House of Representatives at the hour of one o'clock in the afternoon, on that day, and the President of the Senate shall be their presiding officer. Two tellers shall be previously appointed on the part of the Senate, and two on the part of the House of Representatives, to whom shall be handed, as they are opened by the President of the Senate, all the certificates and papers purporting to be the certificates of the electoral vote, which certificates and papers shall be opened, presented, and acted upon in the alphabetical order of the States, beginning with the letter A; and said tellers, having then read the same in the presence and hearing of the two Houses, shall make a list of the votes as they shall appear from the said certificates, and, the votes having been ascertained and counted in the manner and according to the rules in this act provided, the result of the same shall be delivered to the President of the Senate, who shall thereupon announce the state of the vote, which announcement shall be deemed a sufficient declaration of the persons, if any, elected President and Vice-President of the United States, and, together with a list of the votes, be entered on the journals of the two Houses. Upon such reading of any such certificate or paper, the President of the Senate shall call for objections, if any. Every objection shall be made in writing, and shall state clearly and concisely, and without argument, the ground thereof, and shall be signed by at least one senator and one member of the House of Represenatives before the same shall be received. When all objections so made to any vote or paper from a State shall have been received and read, the Senate shall thereupon withdraw, and such objections shall be submitted to the Senate for its decision; and the Speaker of the House of Representatives shall, in like manner, submit such objections to the House of Representatives for its decision; and no electoral vote or votes from any State which shall have been regularly given by electors, whose appointment has been lawfully certified to according to Section 3 of this act, from which but one return has been received, shall be rejected; but the two Houses concurrently may reject the vote or votes when they agree that such vote or votes have not been so regularly given by electors whose appointment has been so certified. If more than one return or paper purporting to be a return from a State shall have been received by the President of the Senate, those votes, and those only, shall be counted which shall have been regularly given by the electors who are shown by the determination mentioned in Section 2 of this act to have been appointed, if the determination in said section provided for shall have been made, or by such successors, or substitutes, in case of a vacancy in the board of electors so ascertained, as have been appointed to fill such vacancy in the mode provided by the laws of the State; but in case there shall arise a question which of two or more of such State authorities determining what electors have been appointed, as mentioned in Section 2 of this act, is the lawful tribunal of such State, the votes regularly given of those electors, and those only, of such State shall be counted whose title as electors the two Houses, acting separately, shall concurrently decide is supported by the decision of such State so authorized by its laws; and in such case of more than one return or paper purporting to be a return from a State, if there shall have been no such determination of the question in the State aforesaid, then those votes, and those only, shall be counted which the two Houses shall concurrently decide were cast by lawful electors appointed in accordance with the laws of the State, unless the two Houses, acting separately, shall concurrently decide such votes not to be the lawful votes of the legally appointed electors of such State. But if the two Houses shall disagree in respect of the counting of such votes, then and in that case the votes of the electors whose appointment shall have been certified by the Executive of the State, under the seal thereof, shall be counted. When the two Houses have voted, they shall immediately again meet, and the presiding officer shall then announce the decision of the questions submitted. No votes or papers from any other State shall be acted upon until the objections previously made to the votes or papers from any State shall have been finally disposed of.

Section 5. That while the two Houses shall be in meeting as provided in this act, the President of the Senate shall have power to preserve order : and no debate shall be allowed and no question shall be put by the presiding officer, except to either House on a motion to withdraw.

Section 6. That when the two Houses separate to decide upon an objection that may have been made to the counting of any electoral vote or votes from any State, or other question arising in the matter, each Senator and Representative may speak to such objection or question five minutes, and not more than once; but after such debate shall have lasted two hours, it shall be the duty of the presiding officer of each House to put the main question without further debate.

SECTION 7. Such joint meeting shall not be dissolved until the count of electoral votes shall be completed and the result declared; and no recess shall be taken unless a question shall have arisen in regard to counting any such votes, or otherwise under this act, in which case it shall be competent for either House, acting separately, in the manner hereinbefore provided, to direct a recess of such House not beyond the next calendar day, Sunday excepted, at the hour of ten o'clock in the forenoon. But if the counting of the electoral votes and the declaration of the result shall not have been completed before the fifth calendar day next after such first meeting of the two Houses, no further or other recess shall be taken by either House.

During the same period of four years which witnessed the passage of these two important acts, propositions to amend the Constitution relative to the office of President were introduced in unusual number and variety. Some of the old suggestions were received, such as the lengthening of the term, forbidding reëlection, and changing the mode of election so that voters should cast their votes directly and without the intervention of electors. Other schemes, some of them highly fanciful, were added to the list. But not one of them all, old or new, had even the success implied in a favorable report by a committee; and no proposition of amendment excited the smallest interest on the part of the general public.

XXIX

THE SECOND HARRISON

WHEN a political party acquires control of the executive department of the government after passing twenty-four years in the cold shade of the opposition, a redistribution of offices is naturally the matter that first engages its attention. Mr. Cleveland, entering upon the duties of President, found himself in a peculiar position. He owed his election as much to a body of dissident Republicans as to the Democratic party. His "Mugwump" supporters were for the most part thorough believers in the principles of civil service reform, and had supported him in the belief that he agreed with them on that issue. They were totally opposed to a "clean sweep" of the appointive officers of the government. On the other hand, the main body of his adherents regarded the offices as the fruits of victory, and would not be satisfied so long as Republicans were drawing salaries from the Treasury. Mr. Cleveland so shaped his course as not wholly to disappoint either wing of his supporters. That he did not wholly satisfy either wing is involved in this statement. Removals from office for political reasons were numerous; and at the end of the four years' term a large proportion of the incumbents were Democrats. But in one case Mr. Cleveland reappointed a Republican to an important office; the removals were not made with too unseemly haste; and in many instances Republicans were suffered to serve out the full term of four years for which they had been appointed. There was not much friction between the President and the Senate, although the Republicans controlled that branch of Congress during Mr. Cleveland's term of office. The Senate usually acquiesced in the removals, and confirmed the President's appointments; and before his term had half expired, it concurred with the Democratic House of Representatives in repealing the Tenure of Office Act, which had been devised to limit President Johnson's power of removal from office, and which, in a modified form, had been retained on the statute book ever since.

Although the Senate interposed no great obstacles to the President's distribution of the offices according to his pleasure, it set up an effectual barrier to the enactment of legislation of a political character. There was no serious attempt to draw up the two great parties in line of battle during the continuance of the Forty-ninth Congress. The party wrangling took place for the most part over the executive acts of the President, the Democrats upholding and the Republicans denouncing the disposition he made of the offices, and his use of the veto power, which he exercised with unexampled freedom. Inasmuch as a large number of the bills returned to Congress without the approval of the President were private pension bills, the effort was made, not without a measure of success, to represent Mr. Cleveland as but a half-hearted sympathizer with the soldiers ; and the accusation that the interests of the former defenders of the flag were regarded by him in a too calculating spirit was used against him in the ensuing canvass.

But all other political questions were thrust completely out of sight by the unusual and startling act of the President at the beginning of the Fiftieth Congress. The question of the tariff had been brought forward during the Forty-ninth Congress in the so-called " Morrison bill," — Mr. Morrison, of Illinois, was the chairman of the Committee on Ways and Means, — but the division in the ranks of the Democratic party on this issue had been deep enough to prevent the passage of the bill even by the House of Representatives, in which the Democrats had a clear majority of forty members. At the beginning of the first session of the Fiftieth Congress, in December, 1887, the President, in disregard of unbroken precedent, omitted altogether from his annual message a review of government operations and a statement of international relations during the year past, and devoted the whole document to a plea for a revision of the tariff. The party lines were formed at once. The Republicans detected in Mr. Cleveland's message an attack upon the principle of a protective tariff, and closed up their ranks to defend the system of which they had been the champions for a quarter of a century. Mr. Blaine, who was making a long sojourn in Europe, in an " interview " with an American newspaper correspondent examined Mr.

Cleveland's argument in detail, and set forth the Republican side of the discussion in a way which made his "Paris message," as it was called, the "keynote" of the Republican defence of the protective tariff. The Democrats recognized in the President's message a summons to move forward to the attack. They responded to the call. The leaders resolved to be no longer tolerant of differences. Those who would not fight the battle of the Democracy must be coerced, or treated as enemies and driven out of the camp. The measure which the Democratic members of the Ways and Means Committee prepared under the leadership of Mr. Mills, the chairman, after long deliberation and consultation, was made a *quasi* test of party loyalty. Support of its main features, and support of the bill itself after the work of amendment was completed, was required of all Democrats in the House of Representatives. Those who refused to give it their votes forfeited the favors which it was in the power of the administration and the party to bestow. The party became so well united in the support of the Mills bill that when that measure came up on its passage in the House of Representatives, four Democrats only voted against it. When that vote was given, on July 21, 1888, the great conventions had already been held, and the candidates were before the people.

Six months before the meeting of the nominating conventions it seemed to be certain that the presidential contest of 1888 would be between the same candidates who had been pitted against each other in 1884, — Cleveland and Blaine. The President made no public manifestation of his wish to be nominated for reëlection, but it was not necessary that he should do so. It appeared to be the well-nigh universal wish of his party that he should be again the leader of their forces, and he was understood to be entirely willing to accept the position.

On the other hand, the desire of the Republicans that Mr. Blaine should head the ticket once more found overwhelming expression among them. The unanimity of sentiment was surprising. It is probably safe to say that had the delegates to the convention been elected in December, 1887, there would not have been chosen a dozen in all the country who would have preferred any other candidate to Mr. Blaine. Great, therefore, was the confusion into which the party was thrown by the withdrawal of Mr. Blaine from the contest. On January 25, 1888, he addressed, from Florence, Italy, a letter to the chairman of the Republican national committee, in which, on account of "considerations entirely personal to myself," he announced that his name would not be presented to the national convention. At the same time he congratulated the party upon its cheering prospects, foretold that the tariff was to be the great issue of the canvass, and expressed confidence that the result could not be in doubt. Republicans were surprised and disappointed by this letter. They saw that it was a genuine and sincere refusal to accept the nomination, yet many of his friends, in the earnestness of their wish that he should be again the candidate, persuaded themselves that he would accept the mandate of the party if it were expressed with great unanimity. But while these excessively zealous champions persisted in their purpose to choose and send to the convention delegates who were for Mr. Blaine, "first, last, and all the time," the acceptance of his withdrawal as a finality by the party at large resulted in the coming forward of many candidates. The unwillingness of Mr. Blaine's most ardent friends to give up the hope of nominating him placed that gentleman in a position of embarrassment from which he extricated himself by a second letter, dated at Paris, May 17. He had learned that some of his former supporters had not taken his Florence letter as "absolutely conclusive in ultimate and possible contingencies," as he had intended it to be; and on the strength of it canvasses had been begun for other candidates. Therefore, if the nomination could by any chance be offered to him, "I could not accept it without leaving in the minds of thousands of these men [friends of other candidates] the impression that I had not been free from indirection; and therefore I could not accept it at all." Even after this there were some men who did not abandon hope that Mr. Blaine might be nominated; but the canvass within the Republican party proceeded on the theory that the leading favorite was entirely out of the contest.

Two conventions were held simultaneously in Cincinnati, beginning on the 15th of May. These conventions were held by two factions of the Labor party, known respectively as the "Union Labor" and the "United Labor" party.

The Union Labor convention was made up of about two hundred and twenty delegates, representing twenty States. S. F. Norton was the temporary chairman, and John Seitz the permanent president. The following platform was reported by the committee on resolutions, and adopted after a long discussion : —

General discontent prevails on the part of the wealth-producer. Farmers are suffering from a poverty which has forced most of them to mortgage their estates, and the prices of products are so low as to offer no relief, except through bankruptcy, and laborers are sinking into greater dependence. Strikes are resorted to without bringing relief, because of the inability of employers in many cases to pay living wages, while more and more are driven into the street. Business men find collections almost impossible, and, meantime, hundreds of millions of idle public money, which is needed for relief, is locked up in the United States Treasury, or placed without interest in favored banks in grim mockery of distress. Land monopoly flourishes as never before, and more owners of the soil are daily becoming tenants. Great transportation corporations still succeed in extorting their profits on watered stock through unjust charges. The United States Senate has become an open scandal, its membership being purchased by the rich in open defiance of the popular will. Various efforts are made to squander the public money, which are designed to empty the Treasury without paying the public debt. Under these and other alarming conditions we appeal to the people of our country to come out of old party organizations, whose indifference to the public welfare is responsible for this distress, and aid the Union Labor party to repeal existing class legislation, and relieve the distress of our industries by establishing the following principles : —

Land. — While we believe that the proper solution of the financial question will greatly relieve those now in danger of losing their homes by mortgages and foreclosures, and enable all industrious persons to secure a home as the highest result of civilization, we oppose land monopoly in every form, demand the forfeiture of unearned grants, the limitation of land ownership, and such other legislation as will stop speculations in land, and holding it unused from those whose necessities require it.

We believe the earth was made for the people, and not to enable an idle aristocracy to subsist, through rents, upon the toil of the industrious, and that corners in land are as bad as corners in food, and that those who are not residents or citizens should not be allowed to own lands in the United States. A homestead should be exempt, to a limited extent, from execution or taxation.

Transportation. — The means of communication and transportation should be owned by the people, as is the United States postal service.

Money. — The establishment of a national monetary system in the interest of the producer, instead of the speculator and usurer, by which the circulating medium, in necessary quantity and full legal tender, shall be issued directly to the people, without the intervention of banks, or loaned to citizens upon land security at a low rate of interest, to relieve them from extortions of usury, and enable them to control the money supply. Postal savings banks should be established. While we have free coinage of gold, we should have free coinage of silver. We demand the immediate application of all the money in the United States Treasury to the payment of the bonded debt, and condemn the further issue of interest-bearing bonds, either by the national government or by States, Territories, or municipalities.

Labor. — Arbitration should take the place of strikes and other injurious methods of settling labor disputes. The letting of convict labor to contractors should be prohibited, the contract system be abolished in public works, the hours of labor in industrial establishments be reduced commensurate with the increased production by labor-saving machinery, employees protected from bodily injury, equal pay for equal work for both sexes, and labor, agricultural, and coöperative associations be fostered and encouraged by law. The foundation of a republic is in the intelligence of its citizens, and children who are driven into workshops, mines, and factories are deprived of the education which should be secured to all by proper legislation.

Pensions. — We demand the passage of a service pension bill to every honorably discharged soldier and sailor of the United States.

Income Tax. — A graduated income tax is the most equitable system of taxation, placing the burden of government on those who can best afford to pay, instead of laying it on the farmers and producers, and exempting millionaire bondholders and corporations.

United States Senate. — We demand a constitutional amendment making United States senators elective by a direct vote of the people.

Contract Labor. — We demand the strict enforcement of laws prohibiting the importation of subjects of foreign countries under contract.

Chinese. — We demand the passage and enforcement of such legislation as will absolutely exclude the Chinese from the United States.

Woman Suffrage. — The right to vote is inherent in citizenship, irrespective of sex, and is properly within the province of state legislation.

Paramount Issues. — The paramount issues to be solved in the interests of humanity are the abolition of usury, monopoly, and trusts, and we denounce the Democratic and Republican parties for creating and perpetuating these monstrous evils.

Alson J. Streeter, of Illinois, was nominated for President. by acclamation. Samuel Evans, of Texas, was nominated for Vice-President on the first trial. He received 124 votes to 44 for T. P. Rynders, of Pennsylvania, and 32 for Charles R. Cunningham, of Arkansas.

The United Labor party held what the chairman of the national committee said was rather a conference than a convention. The number in attendance was small. The chairman, both temporary and permanent, was William B. Ogden, of Kentucky, and the Rev. Edward McGlynn, of New York, was the chairman of the committee on resolutions.

The following platform was reported and adopted : —

We, the delegates of the United Labor party of the United States, in national convention assembled, hold that the corruptions of government and the impoverishment of the masses result from neglect of the self-evident truths proclaimed by the founders of this Republic, that all men are created equal, and are endowed with inalienable rights. We aim at the abolition of the system which compels men to pay their fellow-creatures for the use of the common bounties of nature, and permits monopolizers to deprive labor of natural opportunities for employment.

We see access to farming land denied to labor, except on payment of exorbitant rent or the acceptance of mortgage burdens, and labor, thus forbidden to employ itself, driven into the cities. We see the wage-workers of the cities subjected to this unnatural competition, and forced to pay an exorbitant share of their scanty earnings for cramped and unhealthful lodgings. We see the same intense competition condemning the great majority of business and professional men to a bitter and often unavailing struggle to avoid bankruptcy; and that, while the price of all that labor produces ever falls, the price of land ever rises.

We trace these evils to a fundamental wrong, — the making of the land on which all must live the exclusive property of but a portion of the community. To this denial of natural rights are due want of employment, low wages, business depressions, that intense competition which makes it so difficult for the majority of men to get a comfortable living, and that wrongful distribution of wealth which is producing the millionaire on one side and the tramp on the other.

To give all men an interest in the land of their country; to enable all to share in the benefits of social growth and improvement;

to prevent the shutting out of labor from employment by the monopolization of natural opportunities ; to do away with the one-sided competition which cuts down wages to starvation rates ; to restore life to business, and prevent periodical depressions ; to do away with that monstrous injustice which deprives producers of the fruits of their toil while idlers grow rich ; to prevent the conflicts which are arraying class against class, and which are fraught with menacing dangers to society, — we propose so to change the existing system of taxation that no one shall be taxed on the wealth he produces, nor any one suffered to appropriate wealth he does not produce by taking to himself the increasing values which the growth of society adds to land.

What we propose is not the disturbing of any man in his holding or title ; but, by taxation of land according to its value and not according to its area, to devote to common use and benefit those values which arise, not from the exertion of the individual, but from the growth of society, and to abolish all taxes on industry and its products. This increased taxation of land values must, while relieving the working farmer and small homestead owner of the undue burdens now imposed upon them, make it unprofitable to hold land for speculation, and thus throw open abundant opportunities for the employment of labor and the building up of homes. We would do away with the present unjust and wasteful system of finance which piles up hundreds of millions of dollars in treasury vaults while we are paying interest on an enormous debt; and we would establish in its stead a monetary system in which a legal tender circulating medium should be issued by the government, without the intervention of banks.

We wish to abolish the present unjust and wasteful system of ownership of railroads and telegraphs by private corporations, — a system which, while failing to supply adequately public needs, impoverishes the farmer, oppresses the manufacturer, hampers the merchant, impedes travel and communication, and builds up enormous fortunes and corrupting monopolies that are becoming more powerful than the government itself. For this system we would substitute government ownership and control for the benefit of the whole people instead of private profit.

While declaring the foregoing to be the fundamental principles and aims of the United Labor party, and while conscious that no reform can give effectual and permanent relief to labor that does not involve the legal recognition of equal rights to natural opportunities, we, nevertheless, as measures of relief from some of the evil effects of ignoring those rights, favor such legislation as may tend to reduce the hours of labor, to prevent the employment of children of tender years, to avoid the competition of convict labor with honest industry, to secure the sanitary inspection of tenements, factories, and mines, and to put an end to the abuse of conspiracy laws.

We desire also to simplify the procedure of our courts and diminish the expense of legal proceedings, that the poor may therein be placed on an equality with the rich, and the long delays which now result in scandalous miscarriages of justice may be prevented. Since the ballot is the only means by which, in our Republic, the redress of political and social grievances is to be sought, we especially and emphatically declare for the adoption of what is known as the Australian system of voting, in order that the effectual secrecy of the ballot, and the relief of candidates for public office from the heavy expenses now imposed upon them, may prevent bribery and intimidation, do away with practical discriminations in favor of the rich and unscrupulous, and lessen the pernicious influence of money in politics.

We denounce the Democratic and Republican parties as hopelessly and shamelessly corrupt, and, by reason of their affiliation with monopolies, equally unworthy of the suffrages of those who do not live upon public plunder; we therefore require of those who would act with us that they sever all connection with both.

In support of these aims, we solicit the coöperation of all patriotic citizens, who, sick of the degradation of politics, desire by constitutional methods to establish justice, to preserve liberty, to extend the spirit of fraternity, and to elevate humanity.

Robert H. Cowdrey, of Illinois, was nominated for President, and W. H. T. Wakefield, of Kansas, for Vice-President.

The National Prohibition party began its convention at Indianapolis on May 20. The gathering was a large one. It was estimated that there were at least four thousand members of the party in attendance on the convention, beside the delegates. Nearly all the States were represented, and the committee on credentials reported that there were one thousand and twenty-nine delegates present. A feature of the meeting was the presence of James Black, candidate of the party for President in 1872; Neal Dow, the candidate in 1880; and John P. St. John, the candidate in 1884; as well as two of the party's former candidates for Vice-President. The Rev. H. A. Delano, of Connecticut, was the temporary chairman, and John P. St. John, of Kansas, was the permanent president, of the convention. The following platform was adopted. As at first reported, the tariff plank did not contain the implied declaration in favor of protection; but it was amended on motion from the floor, as noted hereafter : —

The Prohibition party, in national convention assembled, acknowledging Almighty God as the source of all power in government, do hereby declare: —

1. That the manufacture, importation, exportation, transportation, and sale of alcoholic beverages should be made public crimes, and punished as such.

2. That such prohibition must be secured through amendments of our national and state constitutions, enforced by adequate laws adequately supported by administrative authority; and to this end the organization of the Prohibition party is imperatively demanded in State and Nation.

3. That any form of license, taxation, or regulation of the liquor traffic is contrary to good government; that any party which supports regulation, license, or tax enters into alliance with such traffic, and becomes the actual foe of the state's welfare; and that we arraign the Republican and Democratic parties for their persistent attitude in favor of the licensed iniquity, whereby they oppose the demand of the people for prohibition, and, through open complicity with the liquor cause, defeat the enforcement of law.

4. For the immediate abolition of the internal revenue system, whereby our national government is deriving support from ·our greatest national vice.

5. That, an adequate public revenue being necessary, it may properly be raised by impost duties and by an equitable assessment upon the property and the legitimate business of the country, but import duties should be so reduced that no surplus shall be accumulated in the treasury; and that the burdens of taxation shall be removed from foods, clothing, and other comforts and necessaries of life, and imposed on such other articles of import as will give protection both to the manufacturing employee and the producing laborer against the competition of the world.

6. That civil service appointments for all civil offices, chiefly clerical in their duties, should be based upon moral, intellectual, and physical qualifications, and not upon party service or party necessity.

7. That the right of suffrage rests on no mere circumstance of race. color, sex, or nationality, and that where, from any cause, it has been held from citizens who are of suitable age and mentally and morally qualified for the exercise of an intelligent ballot, it should be restored by the people through the legislatures of the several States on such educational basis as they may deem wise.

8. For the abolition of polygamy and the establishment of uniform laws governing marriage and divorce.

9. For prohibiting all combinations of capital to control and to increase the cost of products for popular consumption.

10. For the preservation and defence of the Sabbath as a civil institution without oppressing any who religiously observe the same on any other day than the first day of the week.

11. That arbitration is the Christian, wise, and economic method of settling national differences, and the same method should, by judicious legislation, be applied to the settlement of disputes between large bodies of employees and employers; that the abolition of the saloons would remove the burdens, moral, physical, pecuniary, and social, which now oppress labor and rob it of its earnings, and would prove to be the wise and successful way of promoting labor reform; and we invite labor and capital to unite with us for the accomplishment thereof; that monopoly in land is a wrong to the people, and the public land should be reserved to actual settlers, and that men and women should receive equal wages for equal work.

12. That our immigration laws should be so enforced as to prevent the introduction into our country of all convicts, inmates of other dependent institutions, and of others physically incapacitated for self-support, and that no person should have the ballot in any State who is not a citizen of the United States.

Recognizing and declaring that prohibition of the liquor traffic has become the dominant issue in national politics, we invite to full party fellowship all those who, on this one dominant issue, are with us agreed, in the full belief that this party can and will remove sectional differences, promote national unity, and insure the best welfare of our entire land.

The only contest in the convention took place upon the woman suffrage plank of the platform, — the paragraph numbered seven. There was a long debate upon the subject in the session of the committee on resolutions, and the matter was brought before the full convention by a minority report, in which was recommended the substitution of a declaration in favor of leaving the question to the action of States, promising that "as rapidly as we come into power we will submit this question to a vote of the people in the several States, to be settled by them at the ballot-box." This resolution was defeated by an overwhelming vote.

An addition was made to the platform on a motion from the floor, which was not opposed. To the tariff plank, the paragraph numbered five, these words were appended : —

. . . "and imposed on such other articles of import as will give protection both to the manufacturing employee and the producing laborer against the competition of the world."

The platform, with this amendment, was adopted without a division.

Clinton B. Fisk, of New Jersey, was made the candidate for President, and John A. Brooks, of Missouri, for Vice-President. Both nominations were made unanimously and by acclamation.

The Democrats assembled in national convention at St. Louis on the 5th of June. Notwithstanding the certainty of Mr. Cleveland's nomination, there was an enormous gathering of prominent members of the party from North and South. S. M. White, of California, acted as temporary chairman, and Patrick A. Collins, of Massachusetts, was made permanent president. The rules of the convention of 1884 were adopted, with a slight change in the phraseology of the rule intended to discourage a stampede. In its new form the rule provided "that, in voting for candidates for President and Vice-President, no State shall be allowed to change its vote until the roll of the States has been called, and every State has cast its vote."

There was a contest within the committee on resolutions as to the extent to which the convention should "indorse" the Mills bill. While not only all the members of the committee, but all the delegates who composed the convention, were in favor of a strong declaration for " tariff reform," there were some who deemed it inexpedient in explicit terms to express approval of the bill at that moment pending before the House of Representatives. But the general sentiment of the committee was that the Mills bill, as it stood, should be made a party question. The minority yielded, and the committee made a unanimous report. Nevertheless there was a half compromise; for the indorsement of the Mills bill was not made a part of the platform proper. The committee on resolutions expressed its approval of three resolutions to be offered from the floor, and one of the three was an unqualified expression in favor of the Mills bill. The platform, as reported and adopted, is as follows : —

The Democratic party of the United States, in national convention assembled, renews the pledge of its fidelity to Democratic faith, and reaffirms the platform adopted by its representatives in the convention of 1884, and indorses the views expressed by President Cleveland in his last earnest message to Congress as the correct interpretation of that platform upon the question of tariff reduction ; and also indorses the efforts of our Democratic representatives in Congress to secure a reduction of excessive taxation. Chief among its principles of party faith are the maintenance of an indissoluble union of free and indestructible States, now about to enter upon its second century of unexampled progress and renown ; devotion to a plan of government regulated by a written constitution strictly specifying every granted power, and expressly reserving to the States or people the entire ungranted residue of power; the encouragement of a jealous popular vigilance, directed to all who have been chosen for brief terms to enact and execute the laws, and are charged with the duty of preserving peace, insuring equality, and establishing justice.

The Democratic party welcomes an exacting scrutiny of the administration of the executive power which, four years ago, was committed to its trust in the election of Grover Cleveland as President of the United States; but it challenges the most searching inquiry concerning its fidelity and devotion to the pledges which then invited the suffrages of the people. During a most critical period of our financial affairs, resulting from over-taxation, the anomalous condition of our currency, and a public debt unmatured, it has, by the adoption of a wise and conservative policy, not only averted a disaster, but greatly promoted the prosperity of the people. It has reversed the improvident and unwise policy of the Republican party touching the public domain, and has reclaimed from corporations and syndicates, alien and domestic, and restored to the people, nearly one hundred millions of acres of valuable land to be sacredly held as homesteads for our citizens.

While carefully guarding the interests of the taxpayers and conforming strictly to the principles of justice and equity, it has paid out more for pensions and bounties to the soldiers and sailors of the Republic than was ever paid before during an equal period.

It has adopted and consistently pursued a firm and prudent foreign policy, preserving peace with all nations, while scrupulously maintaining all the rights and interests of our own government and people at home and abroad. The exclusion from our shores of Chinese laborers has been effectually secured under the provisions of a treaty the operation of which has been postponed by the action of a Republican majority in the Senate.

Honest reform in the civil service has been inaugurated and maintained by President Cleveland, and he has brought the public service to the highest standard of efficiency, not only by rule and precept, but by the example of his own untiring and unselfish administration of public affairs.

In every branch and department of the government under Democratic control the rights and welfare of all the people have been guarded and defended; every public interest has been protected, and the equality of all our citizens before the law, without regard to race or color, has been steadfastly maintained.

Upon its record thus exhibited,· and upon a pledge of a continuance to the people of these benefits, the Democracy invokes a renewal of popular trust by the reëlection of a Chief Magistrate who has been faithful, able, and prudent. We invoke, in addition to that trust, the transfer also to the Democracy of the entire legislative power.

The Republican party, controlling the Senate and resisting in both Houses of Congress a reformation of unjust and unequal tax laws which have outlasted the necessities of war, and are now undermining the abundance of a long peace, denies to the people equality before the law, and the fairness and the justice which are their right. Thus the cry of American labor for a better share in the rewards of industry is stifled with false pretences, enterprise is fettered and bound down to home markets, capital is discouraged with doubt, and unequal, unjust laws can neither be properly amended nor repealed. The Democratic party will continue with all the power confided to it the struggle to reform these laws, in accordance with the pledges of its last platform, indorsed at the ballot-box by the suffrages of the people.

Of all the industrious freemen of our land, the immense majority, including every tiller of the soil, gain no advantage from excessive tax laws, but the price of nearly everything they buy is increased by the favoritism of an unequal system of tax legislation. All unnecessary taxation is unjust taxation. It is repugnant to the creed of Democracy that by such taxation the cost of the necessaries of life should be unjustifiably increased to all our people. Judged by Democratic principles, the interests of the people are betrayed when, by unnecessary taxation, trusts and combinations are permitted to exist which, while unduly enriching the few that combine, rob the body of our citizens by depriving them of the benefits of natural competition. Every Democratic rule of governmental action is violated when, through unnecessary taxation, a vast sum of money, far beyond the needs of an economical administration, is drawn from the people and the channels of trade, and accumulated as a demoralizing surplus in the national treasury. The money now lying idle in the federal treasury, resulting from superfluous taxation, amounts to more than one hundred and twenty-five million dollars, and the surplus collected is reaching the sum of more than sixty millions annually. Debauched by this immense temptation, the remedy of the Republican party is to meet and exhaust by extravagant appropriations and expenses, whether constitutional or not, the accumulation of extravagant taxation. The Democratic policy is to enforce frugality in public expense, and to abolish unnecessary taxation. Our established domestic industries and enterprises should not, and need not, be endangered by the reduction and correction of the burdens of taxation. On the contrary, a fair and careful revision of our tax laws, with due allowance for the difference between the wages of American and foreign labor, must promote and encourage every branch of such industries and enterprises, by giving them assurance of extended markets and steady and continuous operations in the interests of American labor, which should in no event be neglected. The revision of our tax laws contemplated by the Democratic party should promote the advantage of such labor, by cheapening the cost of the necessaries of life in the home of every workman, and at the same time securing to him steady and remunerative employment. Upon this question of tariff reform, so closely concerning every phase of our national life, and upon every question involved in the problem of good government, the Democratic party submits its principles and professions to the intelligent suffrages of the American people.

The following are the three resolutions mentioned above, offered with the sanction of the committee on resolutions, and adopted unanimously by the convention : —

Resolved, That this convention hereby indorses and recommends the early passage of the bill for the reduction of the revenue now pending in the House of Representatives.

Resolved, That a just and liberal policy should be pursued in reference to the Territories; that right of self-government is inherent in the people, and guaranteed under the Constitution; that the Territories of Washington, Dakota, Montana, and New Mexico are, by virtue of population and development, entitled to admission into the Union as States, and we unqualifiedly condemn the course of the Republican party in refusing statehood and self-government to their people.

Resolved, That we express our cordial sympathy with the struggling people of all nations in their efforts to secure for themselves the inestimable blessings of self-government, and civil and religious liberty, and we especially declare our sympathy with the efforts of those noble patriots, who, led by Gladstone and Parnell, have conducted their grand and peaceful contest for home rule in Ireland.

For the first time since 1840, when Martin Van Buren was nominated for reëlection by resolution, and not by the individual votes of delegates, there was no formal vote for a candidate for President. A motion was made and carried with great enthusiasm to place Grover Cleveland in nomination for a second term. The death of Vice-President Hendricks in the first year of his term had left the second place on the ticket open to a contest. Several candidates had appeared, but, before the convention met, the sentiment of the delegates was setting strongly in favor of Allen G. Thurman, of Ohio. The brief contest over the nomination of a candidate for Vice-President gave rise to the most picturesque incidents that characterized the St. Louis convention. During Judge Thurman's long service in the Senate the country had become accustomed to hear much about the "red bandanna" of which he was in the habit of making use after indulging in a pinch of snuff. The friends of Governor Gray, of Indiana, were present in strong force, all wearing high white hats as badges. But the advocates of Judge Thurman had provided themselves with a great quantity of red pocket-handkerchiefs, and these articles proved to be far more popular badges than the white hats. When the voting for a candidate was about to begin, the California delegation displayed the bandanna at the top of a long pole, and the appearance of the emblem was received with the wildest cheering. The Indiana delegation strove in vain to offset the demonstration by elevating a white hat on another pole. The red bandannas fluttered in all parts of the immense hall, and delegates and spectators cheered until they were hoarse for the flag of the "noble old Roman," as the Democrats affectionately designated Mr. Thurman. The victory had, in reality, been won by Judge Thurman already. The vote for a candidate showed an immense majority in his favor. It resulted: for Allen G. Thurman, of Ohio, 690; for Isaac P. Gray, of Indiana, 105; for John C. Black, of Illinois, 25.

The Republican convention was held at Chicago, June 19. John M. Thurston, of Nebraska, was the temporary chairman, and M. M. Estee, of California, was the permanent president. The following platform was reported and adopted : —

The Republicans of the United States, assembled by their delegates in national convention, pause on the threshold of their proceedings to honor the memory of their first great leader, the immortal champion of liberty and the rights of the people, Abraham Lincoln, and to cover also with wreaths of imperishable remembrance and gratitude the heroic names of our later leaders, who have more recently been called away from our councils, —

Grant, Garfield, Arthur, Logan, Conkling. May their memories be faithfully cherished ! We also recall, with our greetings and with prayer for his recovery, the name of one of our living heroes, whose memory will be treasured in the history both of Republicans and of the Republic, the name of that noble soldier and favorite child of victory, Philip H. Sheridan.

In the spirit of these great leaders, and of our own devotion to human liberty, and with that hostility to all forms of despotism and oppression which is the fundamental idea of the Republican party, we send fraternal congratulations to our fellow-Americans of Brazil upon their great act of emancipation, which completed the abolition of slavery throughout the two American continents. We earnestly hope that we may soon congratulate our fellow-citizens of Irish birth upon the peaceful recovery of home rule for Ireland.

We reaffirm our unswerving devotion to the national Constitution, and to the indissoluble union of the States ; to the autonomy reserved to the States under the Constitution ; to the personal rights and liberties of citizens in all the States and Territories in the Union, and especially to the supreme and sovereign right of every lawful citizen, rich or poor, native or foreign born, white or black, to cast one free ballot in public elections, and to have that ballot duly counted. We hold the free and honest popular ballot, and the just and equal representation of all the people, to be the foundation of our republican government, and demand effective legislation to secure the integrity and purity of elections, which are the fountains of public authority. We charge that the present administration and the Democratic majority in Congress owe their existence to the suppression of the ballot by a criminal nullification of the Constitution and laws of the United States.

We are uncompromisingly in favor of the American system of protection. We protest against its destruction, as proposed by the President and his party. They serve the interests of Europe ; we will support the interests of America. We accept the issue, and confidently appeal to the people for their judgment. The protective system must be maintained. Its abandonment has always been followed by disaster to all interests, except those of the usurer and the sheriff. We denounce the Mills bill as destructive to the general business, the labor, and the farming interests of the country, and we heartily indorse the consistent and patriotic action of the Republican representatives in Congress opposing its passage. We condemn the proposition of the Democratic party to place wool on the free list, and we insist that the duties thereon shall be adjusted and maintained so as to furnish full and adequate protection to that industry. The Republican party would effect all needed reduction of the national revenue by repealing the taxes upon tobacco, which are an annoyance and burden to agriculture, and the tax upon spirits used in the arts and for mechanical purposes, and by such revision of the tariff laws as will tend to check imports of such articles as are produced by our people, the production of which gives employment to our labor, and release from import duties those articles of foreign production, except luxuries, the like of which cannot be produced at home. If there shall still remain a larger revenue than is requisite for the wants of the government, we favor the entire repeal of internal taxes, rather than the surrender of any part of our protective system, at the joint behest of the whiskey trusts and the agents of foreign manufacturers.

We declare our hostility to the introduction into this country of foreign contract labor, and of Chinese labor, alien to our civilization and our Constitution, and we demand the rigid enforcement of the existing laws against it, and favor such immediate legislation as will exclude such labor from our shores.

We declare our opposition to all combinations of capital, organized in trusts or otherwise, to control arbitrarily the condition of trade among our citizens, and we recommend to Congress and the state legislatures, in their respective jurisdictions, such legislation as will prevent the execution of all schemes to oppress the people by undue charges on their supplies, or by unjust rates for the transportation of their products to market. We approve the legislation by Congress to prevent alike unjust burdens and unfair discriminations between the States.

We reaffirm the policy of appropriating the public lands of the United States to be homesteads for American citizens and settlers, not aliens, which the Republican party established in 1862, against the persistent opposition of the Democrats in Congress, and which has brought our great Western domain into such magnificent development. The restoration of unearned railroad land grants to the public domain for the use of actual settlers, which was begun under the administration of President Arthur, should be continued. We deny that the Democratic party has ever restored one acre to the people, but declare that by the joint action of the Republicans and Democrats about fifty millions of acres of unearned lands, originally granted for the construction of railroads, have been restored to the public domain, in pursuance of the conditions inserted by the Republican party in the original grants. We charge the Democratic administration with failure to execute the laws securing to settlers title to their homesteads, and with using appropriations made for that purpose to harass innocent settlers with spies and prosecutions under the false pretence of exposing frauds and vindicating the law.

The government by Congress of the Territories is based upon necessity only, to the end that they may become States in the Union; therefore, whenever the conditions of population, material resources, public intelligence, and morality are such as to insure a stable local government therein, the people of such Territories should be permitted, as a right inherent in them, the right to form for themselves constitutions and state governments, and be admitted into the Union. Pending the preparation for statehood, all officers thereof should be selected from the *bona fide* residents and citizens of the Territory wherein they are to serve. South Dakota should, of right, be immediately admitted as a State under the constitution framed and adopted by her people, and we heartily indorse the action of the Republican Senate in twice passing bills for her admission. The refusal of the Democratic House of Representatives, for partisan purposes, favorably to consider these bills is a wilful violation of the sacred American principle of local self-government, and merits the condemnation of all just men. The pending bills in the Senate for acts to enable the people of Washington, North Dakota, and Montana Territories to form Constitutions and establish state governments should be passed without unnecessary delay. The Republican party pledges itself to do all in its power to facilitate the admission of the Territories of New Mexico, Wyoming, Idaho, and Arizona to the enjoyment of self-government as States, such of them as are now qualified as soon as possible, and the others as soon as they become so.

The political power of the Mormon Church in the Territories as exercised in the past is a menace to free institutions, a danger no longer to be suffered; therefore we pledge the Republican party to appropriate legislation asserting the sovereignty of the nation in all Territories where the same is questioned, and in furtherance of that end to place upon the statute books legislation stringent enough to divorce the political from the ecclesiastical power, and thus stamp out the attendant wickedness of polygamy.

The Republican party is in favor of the use of both gold and silver as money, and condemns the policy of the Democratic administration in its efforts to demonetize silver.

We demand the reduction of letter postage to one cent per ounce.

In a republic like ours, where the citizen is the sovereign and the official the servant, where no power is exercised except by the will of the people, it is important that the sovereign and the people should possess intelligence. The free school is the promoter of that intelligence which is to preserve us a free nation: therefore the State or nation, or both combined, should support free institutions of learning, sufficient to afford to every child growing up in the land the opportunity of a good common-school education.

We earnestly recommend that prompt action be taken by Congress in the enactment of such legislation as will best secure the rehabilitation of our American merchant marine; and we protest against the passage by Congress of a free-ship bill, as calculated to work injustice to labor by lessening the wages of those engaged in preparing materials as well as those directly employed in our shipyards.

We demand appropriations for the early rebuilding of our navy; for the construction of coast fortifications and modern ordnance, and other approved modern means of defence for the protection of our defenceless harbors and cities; for the payment of just pensions to our soldiers; for necessary works of national importance in the improvement of harbors and the channels of internal, coastwise, and foreign commerce; for the encouragement of the shipping interests of the Atlantic, Gulf, and Pacific States, as well as for the payment of the maturing public debt. This policy will give employment to our labor; activity to our various industries; increase the security of our country; promote trade; open new and direct markets for our produce, and cheapen the cost of transportation. We affirm this to be far better for our country than the Democratic policy of loaning the government's money, without interest, to "pet banks."

The conduct of foreign affairs by the present administration has been distinguished by its inefficiency and its cowardice. Having withdrawn from the Senate all pending treaties effected by Republican administration for the removal of foreign burdens and restrictions upon our commerce, and for its extension into better markets, it has neither effected nor proposed any others in their stead. Professing adherence to the Monroe doctrine, it has seen, with idle complacency, the extension of foreign influence in Central America and of foreign trade everywhere among our neighbors. It has refused to charter, sanction, or encourage any American organization for constructing the Nicaragua Canal, — a work of vital importance to the maintenance of the Monroe doctrine, and of our national influence in Central and South America, and necessary for the development of trade with our Pacific territory, with South America, and with the islands and farther coasts of the Pacific Ocean.

We arraign the present Democratic administration for its weak and unpatriotic treatment of the fisheries question, and its pusillanimous surrender of the essential privileges to which our fishing vessels are entitled in Canadian ports under the treaty of 1818, the reciprocal maritime legislation of 1830, and the comity of nations, and which Canadian fishing vessels receive in the ports of the United States. We condemn the policy of the present administration and the Democratic majority in Congress towards our fisheries as unfriendly and conspicuously unpatriotic, and as tending to destroy a valuable national industry and an indispensable resource of defence against a foreign enemy.

The name of American applies alike to all citizens of the republic, and imposes upon all alike the same obligation of obedience to the laws. At the same time that citizenship is and must be the panoply and safeguard of him who wears it, and protects him, whether high or low, rich or poor, in all his civil rights, it should and must afford him protection at home, and follow and protect him abroad, in whatever land he may be, on a lawful errand.

The men who abandoned the Republican party in 1884, and continue to adhere to the Democratic party, have deserted not only the cause of honest government, of sound finance, of freedom, of purity of the ballot, but especially have deserted the cause of reform in the civil service. We will not fail to keep our pledges because they have broken theirs, nor because their candidate has broken his. We therefore repeat our declaration of 1884, to wit : " The reform of the civil service auspiciously begun under the Republican administration should be completed by the further extension of the reform system, already established by law, to all the grades of the service to which it is applicable. The spirit and purpose of the reform should be observed in all executive appointments, and all laws at variance with the object of existing reform legislation should be repealed, to the end that the dangers to free institutions, which lurk in the power of official patronage, may be wisely and effectively avoided."

The gratitude of the nation to the defenders of the Union cannot be measured by laws. The legislation of Congress should conform to the pledge made by a loyal people, and be so enlarged and extended as to provide against the possibility that any man who honorably wore the Federal uniform shall become an inmate of an almshouse or dependent upon private charity. In the presence of an overflowing treasury, it would be a public scandal to do less for those whose valorous services preserved the government. We denounce the hostile spirit shown by President Cleveland, in his numerous vetoes of measures for pension relief, and the action of the Democratic House of Representatives in refusing even a consideration of general pension legislation.

In support of the principles herewith enunciated, we invite the coöperation of patriotic men of all parties, and especially of all workingmen, whose prosperity is seriously threatened by the free-trade policy of the present administration.

The withdrawal of Mr. Blaine, as has been explained, had left the field open for all contestants. Not only was there an unusually large number of "favorite sons," but several prominent public men, who were not brought forward as candidates by the delegates representing the respective States of their residence, were mentioned as possible candidates in case the contest should be long and the difficulty of agreeing upon a nominee great. Pervading the convention at all times, up to the moment that a nomination was effected, was a feeling that the name of Mr. Blaine might be presented in such a way, at a critical period, that the convention would be carried away by an outburst of irrepressible enthusiasm, and that he would be summoned to lead the party again by a call so vociferous that he could not decline. Mr. Blaine gave no countenance nor help to this movement. At the opening of the convention, having learned that some of his indiscreet friends were making unauthorized use of his name, and were assuming to declare what he would do in certain contingencies, Mr. Blaine requested the London correspondent of the "New York Tribune" to say that all rumors "pretending to give letters or dispatches from him or any of his party touching political topics of any kind may be promptly discredited unless signed by Mr. Blaine himself;" and, further, that he had written nothing concerning the presidential nominations except the two published letters from Florence and Paris, and that he had held no correspondence of any kind with any one on political subjects. Even this did not prevent many men from thinking that the nomination of Mr. Blaine was the most probable outcome of the contest. Some of the delegates persisted in voting for him from first to last; and a Blaine stampede was the event which the whole country expected. But the fitting moment for it never came, and the judgment of the cooler members of the convention was against it at all times, chiefly because they saw what Mr. Blaine had said so clearly, that he could not honorably accept the nomination, even if it were thrust upon him.

The first vote for a candidate showed an extraordinary lack of concentration. Senator John Sherman, who led all other candidates, had but little more than one half of the number necessary to nominate. Judge Gresham, the next on the list, had less than half as many as Mr. Sherman, and not one of the delegates from his own State of Indiana was among his supporters. The votes were divided among thirteen candidates, and even on the fourth trial the number had been reduced only to ten. How greatly the votes were scattered may be seen from the statement that, on the first vote for a candidate, Senator Sherman received more or less support from twenty-three States and Territories, Judge Gresham from twenty-three, Mr. Harrison from twenty-three, Mr. Alger from twenty, Mr. Allison from nineteen, Mr. Depew from sixteen, and Mr. Blaine from thirteen. Only nine States of the Union gave a solid vote to any candidate, and five of the nine presented "favorite sons" as candidates.

The session of the convention was one of the longest in the history of the country. It began on June 19. The platform was adopted on the 21st. Two votes for a presidential candidate were taken on the 22d, three on the 23d, and three on the 25th (the 24th was Sunday). The history of former conventions was repeated; the leading candidate did not greatly increase his vote, and a concentration took place gradually upon one who had at the beginning a small but a compact and aggressive body of followers. General Benjamin Harrison, of Indiana, was nominated upon the eighth vote. The result on each of the votes is shown in the following table: —

	1st.	2d.	3d.	4th.	5th.	6th.	7th.	8th.
John Sherman, Ohio	229	249	244	235	224	244	231	118
Walter Q. Gresham, Indiana	111	108	123	98	87	91	91	59
Chauncey M. Depew, New York	99	99	91	–	–	–	–	–
Russel A. Alger, Michigan	84	116	122	135	142	137	120	100
Benjamin Harrison, Indiana	80	91	94	217	213	231	278	544
William B. Allison, Iowa	72	75	88	88	99	73	76	–
James G. Blaine, Maine	35	33	35	42	48	40	15	5
John J. Ingalls, Kansas	28	16	–	–	–	–	–	–
Jeremiah M. Rusk, Wisconsin	25	20	16	–	–	–	–	–
William W. Phelps, New Jersey	25	18	5	–	–	–	–	–
E. H. Fitler, Pennsylvania	24	–	–	–	–	–	–	–
Joseph R. Hawley, Connecticut	13	–	–	–	–	–	–	–
Robert T. Lincoln, Illinois	3	2	2	1	–	–	2	–
William McKinley, Jr., Ohio	2	3	8	11	14	12	16	4
Samuel F. Miller, Iowa	–	–	2	–	–	–	–	–
Frederick Douglass	–	–	–	1	–	–	–	–
Joseph B. Foraker, Ohio	–	–	–	1	–	1	1	–
Frederick D. Grant, New York	–	–	–	–	–	1	–	–
Creed Haymond, California	–	–	–	–	–	–	1	–
Whole number of votes	830	830	830	829	827	830	831	830
Necessary for a choice	416	416	416	415	414	416	416	416

Levi P. Morton, of New York, was nominated for Vice-President on the first vote. He received 591 votes to 119 for William Walter Phelps, of New Jersey; 103 for William O.

Bradley, of Kentucky ; 11 for Blanche K. Bruce, of Mississippi; and 1 for Walter F. Thomas, of Texas.

The following resolution, which was offered from the floor,
at the close of the proceedings of the convention, was adopted
with but one dissenting vote : —

The first concern of all good government is the virtue and
sobriety of the people, and the purity of their homes. The Republican party cordially sympathizes with all wise and well-directed
efforts for the promotion of temperance and morality.

A convention of a party which adopted the name of American was held at Washington on the 14th of August. It was
attended by 126 delegates, of whom 65 represented New York,
and 15 were from California. On the second day of the convention a contest which had divided the meeting from the first
led to a split, and all the members except those from New
York and California seceded and held a convention of their
own. The issue which broke up the convention was the apportionment of votes. The two States most strongly represented
desired that each delegate should have one vote, while the
minority insisted upon the usual rule of other conventions,
that the State or the Congressional district should be the unit
for voting power, rather than the individual delegate. The
seceders from the convention made no nominations. The New
York and California members who were left completed their
work, not without some friction. They nominated for President
James Langdon Curtis, of New York, and for Vice-President
James R. Greer, of Tennessee. Mr. Greer subsequently declined
the nomination.

The following platform was adopted : —

Resolved, That all law-abiding citizens of the United States of
America, whether native or foreign born, are politically equals
(except as provided by the Constitution), and all are entitled to,
and should receive, the full protection of the laws.

Resolved, That the Constitution of the United States should be
so amended as to prohibit the federal and state governments from
conferring upon any person the right to vote unless such person be
a citizen of the United States.

Resolved, That we are in favor of fostering and encouraging
American industries of every class and kind, and declare that the
assumed issue " Protection " *vs.* " Free Trade " is a fraud and a
snare. The best " protection " is that which protects the labor
and life blood of the republic from the degrading competition with

and contamination by imported foreigners ; and the most dangerous "free trade" is that in paupers, criminals, communists, and an-
archists, in which the balance has always been against the United
States.

Whereas, One of the greatest evils of unrestricted foreign immigration is the reduction of the wages of the American workingman and working-woman to the level of the underfed and under-
paid labor of foreign countries ; therefore

Resolved, That we demand that no immigrant shall be admitted
into the United States without a passport obtained from the American consul at the port from which he sails ; that no passport
shall be issued to any pauper, criminal, or insane person, or to any
person who, in the judgment of the consul, is not likely to become
a desirable citizen of the United States ; and that for each immigrant passport there shall be collected by the consul issuing the
same the sum of one hundred dollars to be by him paid into the
Treasury of the United States.

Resolved, That the present naturalization laws of the United
States should be unconditionally repealed.

Resolved, That the soil of America should belong to Americans;
that no alien non-resident should be permitted to own real estate
in the United States; and that the realty possessions of the resident alien should be limited in value and area.

Resolved, That no flag shall float on any public buildings, municipal, state, or national, in the United States, except the municipal, state, or national flag of the United States, — the flag of the
stars and stripes.

Resolved, That we reassert the American principles of absolute freedom of religious worship and belief, the permanent separation of church and state ; and we oppose the appropriation of
public money or property to any church, or institution administered by a church. We maintain that all church property should
be subject to taxation.

The canvass which followed the nomination of candidates
presented no remarkable features until a short time before the
election. Political clubs took somewhat unusual prominence
in the contest. They were enabled to make their work more
effective by forming state and national leagues, and thus gaining the advantage which is derived from organized and con-
certed effort.

The tariff was the great issue. It was the chief topic upon
which the Republican and Democratic candidates dwelt in their
respective letters of acceptance. It was the subject discussed
from the stump and in the party journals. The Democrats

distinctly pledged themselves that, if they should gain full control of the government, they would reduce the tariff, taking for general principles in the method of reduction the system sketched by the " Mills bill." The Republicans, on the other hand, committed themselves unreservedly by a declaration that they would sweep away the whole internal revenue system before they would abandon any part of the protective duties on imports. The public discussion was earnest. There were, however, prior to the election itself, no decided indications how the battle was going to result. Although each side professed confidence that it would win from the enemy electoral votes of States not counted as doubtful, there was little real expectation on either side of such a result. The Democrats were evidently sure of the entire Southern vote ; and the Republicans had no fear of losing any Northern State, except Connecticut, New York, New Jersey, and Indiana. Upon these States, therefore, most of the energy of both parties was concentrated.

Two weeks before the election a strange incident occurred, and the importance attached to it — for no doubt it had a certain influence in the election — shows how highly wrought was political feeling at that time. A correspondence was published between a person, who adopted the fictitious name of Charles F. Murchison, and Lord Sackville, the British Minister at Washington. The false Murchison represented himself to be a former British subject, now naturalized as an American, but cherishing a love for the mother country, and asking Lord Sackville's advice as to how he should vote at the coming election. The incautious reply of Lord Sackville, who fell into a trap set for him, implied, though it gave no direct advice, that a vote for the Democratic candidate would be rather more friendly to England than one for Mr. Harrison. The correspondence was published on October 24. The Republicans seized upon it as confirming what they had insisted upon, when discussing the Mills bill, that the Democratic tariff policy was good for England's interest, but bad for America. The President quickly perceived the use that was to be made of the incident, and took his measures accordingly. The view was taken that the advice given by Lord Sackville was an interference by a foreign minister with the internal politics of this country, — a repetition on a small scale of the impertinence of Citizen Genet during the administration of Washington. The attention of Lord

STATES.	POPULAR VOTE.				ELECTORAL VOTE.	
	Benjamin Harrison, Indiana.	Grover Cleveland, New York.	Clinton B. Fisk, New Jersey.	Alson J. Streeter, Illinois.	Harrison and Morton.	Cleveland and Thurman.
Alabama . . .	56,197	117,320	583	–	–	10
Arkansas . . .	58,752	85,962	641	10,613	–	7
California* . .	124,816	117,729	5,761	–	8	–
Colorado . . .	50,774	37,567	2,191	1,266	3	–
Connecticut . .	74,584	71,920	4,234	240	–	6
Delaware . .	12,973	16,414	400	–	–	3
Florida . . .	26,657	39,561	423	–	–	4
Georgia . . .	40,496	100,499	1,808	133	–	12
Illinois† . . .	370,473	348,278	21,695	7,090	22	–
Indiana . . .	263,361	261,013	9,881	2,694	15	–
Iowa . . .	211,598	179,887	3,550	9,105	13	–
Kansas . . .	182,934	103,744	6,768	37,726	9	–
Kentucky . .	155,134	183,800	5,225	622	–	13
Louisiana . .	30,484	85,032	160	39	–	8
Maine . . .	73,734	50,481	2,691	1,344	6	–
Maryland . .	99,986	106,168	4,767	–	–	8
Massachusetts .	183,892	151,856	8,701	–	14	–
Michigan . . .	236,370	213,459	20,942	4,541	13	–
Minnesota . .	142,492	104,385	15,311	1,094	7	–
Mississippi . .	30,096	85,471	218	22	–	9
Missouri . . .	236,257	261,974	4,539	18,632	–	16
Nebraska . . .	108,425	80,552	9,429	4,226	5	–
Nevada . . .	7,229	5,362	41	–	3	–
New Hampshire	45,728	43,458	1,593	13	4	–
New Jersey . .	144,344	151,493	7,904	–	–	9
New York‡ . .	648,759	635,757	30,231	626	36	–
North Carolina .	134,784	147,902	2,787	32	–	11
Ohio	416,054	396,455	24,356	3,496	23	–
Oregon . . .	33,291	26,522	1,677	363	3	–
Pennsylvania .	526,091	446,633	20,947	3,873	30	–
Rhode Island .	21,968	17,530	1,250	18	4	–
South Carolina .	13,736	65,825	–	–	–	9
Tennessee . .	138,988	158,779	5,969	48	–	12
Texas	88,422	234,883	4,749	29,459	–	13
Vermont . . .	45,192	16,785	1,460	–	4	–
Virginia . . .	150,438	151,977	1,678	–	–	12
West Virginia .	77,791	79,664	669	1,064	–	6
Wisconsin . .	176,553	155,232	14,277	8,552	11	–
Total	5,439,853	5,540,329	249,506	146,935	233	168

* 1591 for Curtis, American.   † 150 for Cowdrey, United Labor.   ‡ 2668 for Cowdrey

Salisbury was called to the matter; and when the British premier failed to regard Lord Sackville's indiscretion as a serious offence, if indeed he regarded it as an offence at all, the President directed that the British minister be informed that he was no longer *persona grata*, and that his passports should be given to him.   The incident was variously regarded at the time. Some deemed the whole affair an amusing illustration of the tendency to magnify what is really insignificant when an election is pending.   Those who took, or affected to take, a serious view of the matter, vented their indignation, according to the party to which they respectively belonged, upon the sharp politician who prepared a pitfall for the diplomatist, or upon the minister, who, they said, had revealed the partiality of the government he represented for one of the two parties.   Great Britain took the expulsion of Lord Sackville so seriously that it refused to appoint another minister until after the close of Mr. Cleveland's administration.

The number of States participating in the election was, as in 1884, thirty-eight.   The Democrats carried the entire South, together with the States of Connecticut and New Jersey.   The other States of the North, including the doubtful States of New York and Indiana, chose Republican electors.   The popular and electoral votes are given on the preceding page.

The statement of the popular vote is that printed in Appletons' "Annual Cyclopædia" for 1888.   It differs slightly in the vote of several States from that given in McPherson's "Handbook of Politics," and in the New York "Tribune Almanac," edited by Mr. McPherson.   A comparison of the totals is printed on the next page.   The returns were "official" in each case; the reason why they do not agree does not appear.   It may be suggested that the return in the one case is that of the vote for the leading elector on each ticket, and in the other case the average vote for all the electors on each ticket respectively.   This is apparently not the true explanation.   The aggregate difference between the two statements is not large.

There are other returns which differ from both of those given.   Possibly they also may have been obtained from "official" sources.   The discrepancies are not important, but they illustrate the difficulty of obtaining exact statistics when the ultimate authority varies its reply to the same question.

The count of electoral votes following this election was the

	Appletons: Cyclopædia.	McPherson: Handbook and Almanac.
Cleveland	5,540,329	5,536,242
Harrison	5,439,853	5,440,708
Fisk	249,506	246,876
Streator	146,935	146,836
Curtis	1,591	1,591
Cowdrey	2,818	3,073
Socialist and scattering	7,006	9,845
Total vote	11,388,038	11,385,171

first to take place under the act of February 3, 1887, and the first in the history of the government under the Constitution which was regulated by a general law, and did not require previous concurrent action by the two Houses of Congress for the time being. The joint convention for counting the votes was held in the hall of the House of Representatives on February 13, 1889. The proceedings were devoid of striking incident. Mr. Cox, of New York, called attention to a slight deviation from the precise requirements of the law. It appears that Mr. Ingalls, the President *pro tempore* of the Senate, who presided, did not " call for objections, if any," after the reading of each certificate, as directed by section four of the law (see p. 454). The official report of the proceedings does not state whether or not the presiding officer changed his method after attention was called to the matter. When the vote of Indiana was reported, the vote of the President-elect's own State, there was applause, which was quickly suppressed. Mr. Manderson, the first of the Senate tellers, reported the state of the vote in detail, and in a summary; the presiding officer repeated the summary, and added a formula, drawn from the law, that this announcement of the state of the vote " is, by law, a sufficient declaration " that Benjamin Harrison, of the State of Indiana, had been elected President, and Levi P. Morton, of the State of New York, Vice-President, for the ensuing term.

XXX

CLEVELAND'S SECOND ELECTION

THE victory of the Republicans, although narrow, was complete. A safe majority of the electoral vote was supplemented by a meagre majority in both Houses of Congress. A factional quarrel among the Democrats of Delaware threw the legislature of that State into the hands of the Republicans, who thus regained the one Senator, lost in Virginia, needed to give them ascendency in the upper house. The House of Representatives was so closely divided between the two parties as to give some ground for the apprehension that certain Democratic governors in southern States would revise and amend the returns for Congressmen, and withhold certificates from candidates who apparently had received a plurality of votes. In one case only did a governor assume authority to pass judicially upon the county returns, and his act was not sufficient to overcome the Republican majority. The victorious party felt itself returned permanently to power in the country; and the exultant remark was commonly made that, " if we behave ourselves well," the Republicans could not be shaken from their hold upon the government for twenty years to come.

The four years' term of Benjamin Harrison which followed was a period of as bitter party strife as the country has ever seen. It was crowded with events that had a direct bearing upon the ensuing election. The Republicans proceeded to carry through their measures with perfect confidence that they had the people behind them; the Democrats waged an aggressive and unrelenting war upon them. In the end it was evident that the dominant party had exposed itself to attack at too many points. The favor of the people was withdrawn when the administration was at its mid-point, and given to the opposition by an overwhelming majority. At the close of the four years the control of every department of the government, except the judicial, passed into the hands of the Democrats, where it had not been placed since the election of James Buchanan in 1856.

When the Fifty-first Congress met, in December, 1889, the extremely small Republican majority in the House of Representatives, as elected in 1888, was reinforced by the addition of five members from newly admitted States. The two parties had been engaged in a competition for the favor of the people of the Territories clamoring for admission to the Union. For several years Republicans had urged the passage of an enabling act for Dakota. The Democrats, knowing that the proposed new State would be against them, had prevented its admission until the Territory became populous enough, as it was territorially large enough, to claim division, and admission as two States. Then the Democrats proposed to offset the two Dakotas by admitting at the same time Washington and Montana, both of which they expected to control. The Republicans feared that opposition to the admission of Washington and Montana — which they knew would be futile in any event — would insure their becoming Democratic States. Accordingly they gave their support to the " omnibus " bill, which became a law in February, 1889. All four of the States were carried by the Republicans at the first election, and added eight votes to the strength of the party in the Senate, and five — South Dakota elected two members — to the Republican majority in the House of Representatives. But after these five votes were added, the majority in the House was still too small to be effective. The chance absence of a few members might easily convert it into a minority. Moreover, the rules of the House and the — to that time — uniform interpretation of the quorum clause of the Constitution rendered a narrow majority powerless for affirmative action in the face of determined " filibustering."

Mr. Thomas B. Reed, of Maine, who was chosen Speaker, had long held two views directly opposed to accepted parliamentary law. He maintained that the vote of a member was not the only method of revealing his presence in the House as a part of a constitutional quorum; that the House itself, or the Speaker as the organ of the House, might take cognizance of his physical presence and count him as a present member. Under the previously accepted theory, the ruling party could pass no motion if, not mustering a full quorum of its own members, the opposition unanimously refused to vote. Mr.

Speaker Reed acted upon his own theory, prior to the adoption of any rules, by counting as present non-voting members
who were otherwise taking part in the proceedings. The other
point whereon he differed from earlier parliamentary authorities was that of dilatory motions. Congress had long before
limited the " freedom of debate " by a rule which restricted a
member's right to occupy the floor on any motion to the space
of one hour. It had limited his right to make motions by the
"previous question." But it had left open for his use certain
privileged motions which, made alternately and decided in
each case by a roll-call, would put a complete and indefinite
stop to public business. The Speaker proposed a new code of
rules of parliamentary procedure, which included a recognition
of the right to " count a quorum," an absolute prohibition of
dilatory motions, and some minor amendments of the current
parliamentary law. The code was debated with great asperity,
but was finally adopted by a party vote. It made the majority
masters of the House, and enabled them to pass measures which
never would have been brought to a vote under the old system. It added greatly to the power of the Speaker in the
conduct of business, and to his control over legislation. Mr.
Speaker Reed's strong will and undaunted courage, in enforcing his new rules against violent opposition, earned for him
with the Democratic members the title of " Czar." Not a few
of them admitted that his position was sound and logical,
while they condemned his forceful maintenance of it. The
Republicans applauded ; and the whole country saw afterward
that it was upon him, far more than upon any other person,
that the responsibility rested for things done and left undone
by the Fifty-first Congress.

The Republicans proceeded, promptly and mercilessly, to
decide contested elections by ejecting Democrats and giving
the places to members of their own party, thus increasing their
effective majority. The fact that the number, both of contested seats and of members displaced, was unusually large
they explained by asserting that fraud had been unusually rife
in the elections and returns. The opposition accused the majority of using its power to override and reverse the will of
the people expressed at the polls. In many cases the Democrats refused to answer to their names when the resolutions
unseating their members were put to vote ; some of them were
counted, though not voting, to make up the quorum.

Both parties were committed, by platform and by the promises of their candidates and leaders, to a revision of customs duties. A large part of the session was occupied in the elaboration of a tariff bill. It was reported by Mr. McKinley, of Ohio, chairman of the Committee on Ways and Means, in April; was passed by the House of Representatives in May; was passed by the Senate in September; and, after an adjustment of the differences between the two Houses by a conference committee, was sent to the President, by whom it was signed on the 1st of October. The act was popularly styled the "McKinley Bill," and as such played a great part in the political events of the next three years. The principle of the bill was to lighten the burden borne by the people by removing altogether the duty on sugar, the article most productive of revenue of all commodities entered at the custom-houses, and at the same time to make the system of "protection" more thorough by raising the rates of duty on all foreign articles which, under the previous tariff, could compete successfully with similar articles of domestic production. The American sugar-planters were compensated for the withdrawal of tariff protection by means of a bounty on their production. The Tariff Act of 1890 went beyond any previous measure of the kind in its levy of duty on agricultural productions imported from abroad. The avowed intention of its partisans was to give the farmer protection equal to that enjoyed by the manufacturer. The McKinley Act aroused the unmeasured opposition of the Democrats, who could find no words adequate to express their detestation of it, and of what they denounced as the bad faith of the Republicans. In their view the people had demanded a substantial reduction of the tariff, and had given the Republican party a commission to carry out their will. That party had solicited and obtained the privilege of making the reduction in a spirit friendly to the protective system and to the manufacturers. Now, so the Democrats declared, the party in power had violated its pledge by bringing forward a proposition in which increases of the rates of duty were far more numerous than reductions. But the Republicans were unmoved by the criticism, and persisted in their course. Some of their leaders made no secret of an opinion that the measure was too radical. In particular, Mr. Blaine, the Secretary of State, expressed the opinion openly, and directed attention to the fact that while the bill was professedly drawn in the interest of agriculture, it would not open any foreign market to American flour and pork. His influence was sufficient to secure the adoption by the Senate of an amendment, afterward concurred in by the House, authorizing the negotiation of reciprocity treaties providing for the admission of American products, at favorable rates of duty, into the countries with which the treaties might be concluded. It may be remarked here that many such treaties were negotiated under the terms of the McKinley Act, but, as will be seen presently, they were denounced by the Democrats in their national platform; and during the ensuing administration the authorization of such treaties was withdrawn, and the treaties themselves were abrogated.

Another most important measure of this session was the act which subsequently became known as the Sherman Silver Purchase Act. The history of this legislation, and indeed of the whole agitation for the free coinage of silver during the administration of President Harrison, is most interesting. But, save that the act above mentioned served for the time being to keep the Republican party together, it had no distinct bearing upon the election of the next President, and therefore the record of what was done, and prevented, in reference to silver, is reserved for the next chapter.

A third measure, which never became a law, did play a certain part in the election, namely, the bill to regulate national elections, styled by the Democrats the "Force Bill." The bill was passed by the House of Representatives at the first session of the Fifty-first Congress; it failed in the Senate at the second session through the defection of a certain number of Republican senators who favored the free coinage of silver. It was well understood, and indeed not concealed, that there was a temporary alliance between these senators and the Democrats. Some of the Democratic senators showed at the time a toleration toward the silver movement which they did not manifest before nor afterward.

The McKinley tariff act went into effect just before the general congressional elections of November, 1890. The Democrats had succeeded in making it exceedingly unpopular even before it was finally passed; and they followed up its enactment with vigorous assaults upon its promoters, and energetic efforts to convince the people that it was detrimental to their interests. Success was comparatively easy, for the increase of duty on certain articles of common consumption was distinctly perceptible in the retail price. While it is impossible to estimate the exact influence of this event and that in bringing about a political revulsion, and while there can be no doubt that other acts of the Republican party contributed their share toward its overthrow, certainly the quick popular condemnation of the tariff act was the most potent agent in determining the result of the congressional election in 1890. The Republicans were overwhelmed at the polls. They lost more than one half of their strength in the House of Representatives; and the Democrats lacked but a few votes of a three-fourths majority. The sixteen Southern States, returning 121 members, elected but three Republicans. Even New England returned a majority of Democratic members. A highly significant feature of this election was the great stride made by the party which had begun its existence as the "Farmers' Alliance," but which now became known as the "People's Party," or "Populists." In several of the Western States this party made a brave showing as an independent organization, maintaining a separate existence and voting for its own candidates. In others it allied itself with the Democrats. It succeeded in electing nine members of the House of Representatives, and held such a strong position in the legislatures of Kansas and South Dakota as to be able to send two members to the Senate of the United States.

The political situation established by the elections of 1890 changed but slightly during the ensuing two years. The conditions were of course not favorable to legislation, and the Democrats wisely attempted nothing beyond proposing amendments of the tariff. The few elections which took place in 1891 did not indicate that the Republicans had regained the ground lost the year before; but they did show some recovery, and gave the party reason to hope that it might succeed in the coming contest. Ohio and Pennsylvania, in particular, gave evidence of a reaction in favor of the Republican party. The local elections in New York State, and the annual election in Rhode Island, in the spring of 1892, were still more encouraging to them. Indeed, a peculiar situation developed itself about a year before the presidential election. The active politicians of both the great parties were opposed to the leading candidates. On the Democratic side they attributed the loss of the election in 1888 to Mr. Cleveland's forcing the tariff issue; and, although the popular judgment had seemed to be reversed in 1890, they were still afraid to appeal to the people for a fresh verdict on the question of protection or free trade. Moreover, Mr. Cleveland himself was not and had never been personally popular with the men who managed caucuses and conventions. Most important of all, as it then seemed, there was a factional division of the party in New York. Governor David B. Hill was in control of the party machinery. He was himself an avowed candidate for the presidency. Rightly or wrongly, he was accused of having defeated the Democratic electors in New York in 1888, while securing his own election as governor. The electoral vote of New York was deemed absolutely essential to success, and great stress was laid upon the inexpediency of nominating for President a man who was represented to be foredoomed to defeat in that State.

Mr. Harrison, on the other hand, had not gained popularity in his own party, either with the politicians or with the common people. It was understood that there was friction between him and Mr. Blaine, his Secretary of State; and Mr. Blaine's devoted partisans were, for that reason, against the nomination of the President for a second term, without knowing the cause of unpleasantness nor the merits of the case. The President had won the esteem of his party by his administration, but to himself he had attached no large body of personal admirers and adherents. Nevertheless there was a general expectation that he would be again a candidate. The general sentiment of the party may be best described as one of indifference. The rank and file of the party were not opposed to Mr. Harrison, as were many of the leaders, nor were they eager for his nomination for a second term. The opponents of the President endeavored to take advantage of this condition of the public mind, and organized to defeat him. They turned, of course, to Mr. Blaine as the natural candidate in such circumstances. But that gentleman disconcerted them by writing a letter in February, 1892, announcing that he was not a candidate. Had there been no other reason for the decision, Mr. Blaine's health was seriously and permanently impaired. His withdrawal from the field left the opponents of Mr. Harrison no man of sufficient strength and prominence to make headway against him, and, although they continued to protest against his nomination to the last, their defeat was inevitable.

The campaign opened with a startling event. On January 25, almost as soon as the call for the Democratic national convention had been issued, the New York Democratic state committee called the state convention to choose the delegates, to meet on the 22d of February, — four full months before the national convention. The hand of Governor Hill was seen clearly in this action. The plan was, and it was subsequently carried out, to choose a full delegation to Chicago pledged to vote for Mr. Hill and to oppose Mr. Cleveland. A chorus of indignant protest against the " snap convention " was raised at once by Mr. Cleveland's friends, who organized, not to control that convention, which would be hopeless while all the party machinery was in the hands of the enemy, but to send another delegation to Chicago representing, as they asserted, a majority of the Democratic voters of the State. Those who joined in this anti-Hill movement were known popularly as " anti-snappers."

During the spring months the delegates to the several conventions were chosen. On the Republican side the party elections were largely in favor of General Harrison. Nevertheless, the number of uninstructed delegates was so large that his success was by no means assured. The Democratic state and district conventions were overwhelmingly in favor of Mr. Cleveland. It was evident that, unless the Hill delegation from New York could rule the national convention by fear, Mr. Cleveland would receive far more than the necessary two thirds on the first vote.

The convention period was a time of great excitement, despite the fact which all could see, save those who would not see, that the nominations were predetermined. In the case of General Harrison, and equally so in the case of Mr. Cleveland, determined and bitter antagonism was manifested to the evident choice of a majority of delegates until the very end. The opponents of the President endeavored to rally around Mr. Blaine, but his letter declining to be a candidate stood in the way of their success. Although he added nothing to that letter and took nothing away from it, yet some of his adherents declared that he would not refuse a nomination if tendered to him. But others of his oldest and stanchest friends, who had become partisans of Mr. Harrison, after Mr. Blaine's withdrawal, insisted that the Secretary of State would not and could not be a candidate. Three days before the meeting of the Republican convention Mr. Blaine suddenly resigned from the Cabinet. His act threw the whole country into a condition of amazed and wondering bewilderment. What did it mean? Had the relations between the President and the Secretary become intolerable? Had the Secretary changed his intention not to be a candidate? Had his health at last broken down? An authoritative answer to the series of questions has never been given. Every one who discussed it believed that the act of resignation and the time chosen for it had a direct connection with the approach of the time for the meeting of the national convention. But since it was as easy to give the interpretation that Mr. Blaine purposed retiring from public life, as to deem his purposed resignation a mark of willingness again to enter the field, the startling change in the situation gave no help to the opponents of Mr. Harrison, nor did it concentrate their efforts upon an attempt to nominate Mr. Blaine. It simply added to the prevailing confusion.

The Republican convention met at Minneapolis, June 7, 1892. Mr. J. Sloat Fassett, of New York, was the temporary chairman, and Governor William McKinley, Jr., of Ohio, the permanent president. The drafting of the platform was a difficult task, owing to the demands of the partisans of silver money that the party should make a declaration in favor of free coinage. This demand was resisted, and the " plank " relating to the money question was a compromise. The platform, reported and adopted on June 9, was as follows : —

The representatives of the Republicans of the United States, assembled in general convention on the shores of the Mississippi River, the everlasting bond of an indestructible republic, whose most glorious chapter of history is the record of the Republican party, congratulate their countrymen on the majestic march of the nation under the banners inscribed with the principles of our platform of 1888, vindicated by victory at the polls and prosperity in our fields, workshops, and mines, and make the following declaration of principles : —

We reaffirm the American doctrine of protection. We call attention to its growth abroad. We maintain that the prosperous condition of our country is largely due to the wise revenue legislation of the Republican Congress.

We believe that all articles which cannot be produced in the United States, except luxuries, should be admitted free of duty, and that on all imports coming into competition with the products of American labor there should be levied duties equal to the difference between wages abroad and at home.

We assert that the prices of manufactured articles of general consumption have been reduced under the operations of the Tariff Act of 1890.

We denounce the efforts of the Democratic majority of the House of Representatives to destroy our tariff laws piecemeal, as is manifested by their attacks upon wool, lead and lead ores, the chief products of a number of States, and we ask the people for their judgment thereon.

We point to the success of the Republican policy of reciprocity, under which our export trade has vastly increased, and new and enlarged markets have been opened for the products of our farms and workshops.

We remind the people of the bitter opposition of the Democratic party to this practical business measure, and claim that, executed by a Republican administration, our present laws will eventually give us control of the trade of the world.

The American people, from tradition and interest, favor bimetallism, and the Republican party demands the use of both gold and silver as standard money, with such restrictions and under such provisions, to be determined by legislation, as will secure the maintenance of the parity of values of the two metals, so that the purchasing and debt-paying power of the dollar, whether of silver, gold, or paper, shall be at all times equal. The interests of the producers of the country, its farmers and its workingmen, demand that every dollar, paper or coin, issued by the government, shall be as good as any other.

We commend the wise and patriotic steps already taken by our government to secure an international conference to adopt such measures as will insure a parity of value between gold and silver for use as money throughout the world.

We demand that every citizen of the United States shall be allowed to cast one free and unrestricted ballot in all public elections, and that such ballot shall be counted and returned as cast; that such laws shall be enacted and enforced as will secure to every citizen, be he rich or poor, native or foreign born, white or black, this sovereign right guaranteed by the Constitution. The free and honest popular ballot, the just and equal representation of all the people, as well as their just and equal protection under the laws, are the foundation of our republican institutions, and the party will never relax its efforts until the integrity of the ballot and the purity of elections shall be fully guaranteed and protected in every State.

We denounce the continued inhuman outrages perpetrated upon

American citizens for political reasons in certain Southern States of the Union.

We favor the extension of our foreign commerce, the restoration of our mercantile marine by home-built ships, and the creation of a navy for the protection of our national interests and the honor of our flag; the maintenance of the most friendly relations with all foreign powers, entangling alliances with none, and the protection of the rights of our fishermen.

We reaffirm our approval of the Monroe doctrine, and believe in the achievement of the manifest destiny of the republic in its broadest sense.

We favor the enactment of more stringent laws and regulations for the restriction of criminal, pauper, and contract immigration.

We favor efficient legislation by Congress to protect the life and limbs of employees of transportation companies engaged in carrying on interstate commerce, and recommend legislation by the respective States that will protect employees engaged in state commerce, in mining and manufacturing.

The Republican party has always been the champion of the oppressed, and recognizes the dignity of manhood, irrespective of faith, color, or nationality; it sympathizes with the cause of home rule in Ireland, and protests against the persecution of the Jews in Russia.

The ultimate reliance of free popular government is the intelligence of the people and the maintenance of freedom among men. We therefore declare anew our devotion to liberty of thought and conscience, of speech and press, and approve all agencies and instrumentalities which contribute to the education of the children of the land; but, while insisting upon the fullest measure of religious liberty, we are opposed to any union of church and state.

We reaffirm our opposition, declared in the Republican platform of 1888, to all combinations of capital, organized in trusts or otherwise, to control arbitrarily the condition of trade among our citizens. We heartily indorse the action already taken upon this subject, and ask for such further legislation as may be required to remedy any defects in existing laws, and to render their enforcement more complete and effective.

We approve the policy of extending to towns, villages, and rural communities the advantages of the free delivery service, now enjoyed by the larger cities of the country, and reaffirm the declaration contained in the Republican platform of 1888, pledging the reduction of letter postage to one cent, at the earliest possible moment consistent with the maintenance of the Post-office Department, and the highest class of postal service.

We commend the spirit and evidence of reform in the civil service, and the wise and consistent enforcement by the Republican party of the laws regulating the same.

The construction of the Nicaragua Canal is of the highest importance to the American people, both as a measure of national defence and to build up and maintain American commerce, and it should be controlled by the United States government.

We favor the admission of the remaining Territories at the earliest practical date, having due regard to the interests of the people of the Territories and of the United States. All the federal officers appointed for the Territories should be selected from *bona fide* residents thereof, and the right of self-government should be accorded as far as practicable.

We favor cession, subject to the homestead laws, of the arid public lands to the States and Territories in which they lie, under such congressional restrictions as to disposition, reclamation, and occupancy by settlers as will secure the maximum benefits to the people.

The World's Columbian Exposition is a great national undertaking, and Congress should promptly enact such reasonable legislation in aid thereof as will ensure a discharge of the expenses and obligations incident thereto, and the attainment of results commensurate with the dignity and progress of the nation.

In temperance we sympathize with all wise and legitimate efforts to lessen and prevent the evils of intemperance and promote morality.

Ever mindful of the services and sacrifices of the men who saved the life of the nation, we pledge anew to the veteran soldiers of the republic a watchful care and recognition of their just claims upon a grateful people.

We commend the able, patriotic, and thoroughly American administration of President Harrison. Under it the country has enjoyed remarkable prosperity, and the dignity and honor of the nation, at home and abroad, have been faithfully maintained, and we offer the record of pledges kept as a guarantee of faithful performance in the future.

President Harrison was nominated for reëlection on the first vote, June 10. The result of the polling was as follows : —

Whole number of votes	905
Necessary for a choice	453
Benjamin Harrison, Indiana	535$\frac{1}{6}$
James G. Blaine, Maine	182$\frac{5}{6}$
William McKinley, Jr., Ohio	182
Thomas B. Reed, Maine	4
Robert T. Lincoln, Illinois	1

The fractional votes here reported resulted from the division of the voting power between contesting delegates in North Carolina and Mississippi. In the one case the division was into thirds, and in the other into halves of votes. The combination of fractions caused an erroneous appearance of a more minute division than really existed.

Whitelaw Reid, of New York, was nominated for Vice-President by acclamation.

The Democratic convention met at Chicago on June 21. William C. Owens, of Kentucky, was the temporary chairman, and William L. Wilson, of West Virginia, the permanent president. The platform was reported on the evening of June 22. As adopted it was as follows : —

SECTION 1. The representatives of the Democratic party of the United States, in national convention assembled, do reaffirm their allegiance to the principles of the party as formulated by Jefferson, and exemplified by the long and illustrious line of his successors in Democratic leadership, from Madison to Cleveland; we believe the public welfare demands that these principles be applied to the conduct of the federal government through the accession to power of the party that advocates them ; and we solemnly declare that the need of a return to these fundamental principles of a free popular government, based on home rule and individual liberty, was never more urgent than now, when the tendency to centralize all power at the federal capital has become a menace to the reserved rights of the States that strikes at the very roots of our government under the Constitution as framed by the fathers of the republic.

SEC. 2. We warn the people of our common country, jealous for the preservation of their free institutions, that the policy of federal control of elections to which the Republican party has committed itself is fraught with the greatest dangers, scarcely less momentous than would result from a revolution practically establishing monarchy on the ruins of the republic. It strikes at the North as well as the South, and injures the colored citizen even more than the white. It means a horde of deputy marshals at every polling-place armed with federal power, returning boards appointed and controlled by federal authority, the outrage of the electoral rights of the people in the several States, the subjugation of the colored people to the control of the party in power, and the reviving of race antagonisms now happily abated, of the utmost peril to the safety and happiness of all ; a measure deliberately and justly described by a leading Republican senator as "the most infamous bill that ever crossed the threshold of the

Senate." Such a policy, if sanctioned by law, would mean the dominance of a self-perpetuating oligarchy of office-holders, and the party first intrusted with its machinery could be dislodged from power only by an appeal to the reserved right of the people to resist oppression, which is inherent in all self-governing communities. Two years ago, this revolutionary policy was emphatically condemned by the people at the polls; but in contempt of that verdict, the Republican party has defiantly declared in its latest authoritative utterance that its success in the coming elections will mean the enactment of the Force bill, and the usurpation of despotic control over elections in all the States. Believing that the preservation of republican government in the United States is dependent upon the defeat of this policy of legalized force and fraud, we invite the support of all citizens who desire to see the Constitution maintained in its integrity, with the laws pursuant thereto, which have given our country a hundred years of unexampled prosperity ; and we pledge the Democratic party, if it be intrusted with power, not only to the defeat of the Force bill, but also to relentless opposition to the Republican policy of profligate expenditure, which in the short space of two years has squandered an enormous surplus, and emptied an overflowing treasury, after piling new burdens of taxation upon the already overtaxed labor of the country.

SEC. 3. We denounce the Republican protection as a fraud, a robbery of the great majority of the American people for the benefit of the few. We declare it to be a fundamental principle of the Democratic party that the federal government has no constitutional power to impose and collect tariff duties, except for the purposes of revenue only, and we demand that the collection of such taxes shall be limited to the necessities of the government when honestly and economically administered.

We denounce the McKinley tariff law enacted by the Fifty-first Congress as the culminating atrocity of class legislation; we indorse the efforts made by the Democrats of the present Congress to modify its most oppressive features in the direction of free raw materials and cheaper manufactured goods that enter into general consumption, and we promise its repeal as one of the beneficent results that will follow the action of the people in intrusting power to the Democratic party. Since the McKinley tariff went into operation, there have been ten reductions of the wages of laboring men to one increase. We deny that there has been any increase of prosperity to the country since that tariff went into operation, and we point to the dullness and distress, the wage reductions and strikes in the iron trade, as the best possible evidence that no such prosperity has resulted from the McKinley Act.

We call the attention of thoughtful Americans to the fact that, after thirty years of restrictive taxes against the importation of foreign wealth in exchange for our agricultural surplus, the homes and farms of the country have become burdened with a real estate mortgage debt of over $2,500,000,000, exclusive of all other forms of indebtedness; that in one of the chief agricultural States of the West, there appears a real estate mortgage debt averaging $165 per capita of the total population, and that similar conditions and tendencies are shown to exist in the other agricultural exporting States. We denounce a policy which fosters no industry so much as it does that of the sheriff.

SEC. 4. Trade interchange on the basis of reciprocal advantage to the countries participating is a time-honored doctrine of the Democratic faith; but we denounce the sham reciprocity which juggles with the people's desire for enlarged foreign markets and freer exchanges by pretending to establish closer trade relations for a country whose articles of export are almost exclusively agricultural products with other countries that are also agricultural, while erecting a custom-house barrier of prohibitive tariff taxes against the richest countries of the world, that stand ready to take our entire surplus of products, and to exchange therefor commodities which are necessaries and comforts of life among our own people.

SEC. 5. We recognize, in the trusts and combinations which are designed to enable capital to secure more than its just share of the joint product of capital and labor, a natural consequence of the prohibitive taxes which prevent the free competition which is the life of honest trade, but we believe their worst evils can be abated by law; and we demand the rigid enforcement of the laws made to prevent and control them, together with such further legislation in restraint of their abuses as experience may show to be necessary.

SEC. 6. The Republican party, while professing a policy of reserving the public land for small holdings by actual settlers, has given away the people's heritage, till now a few railroad and nonresident aliens, individual and corporate, possess a larger area than that of all our farms between the two seas. The last Democratic administration reversed the improvident and unwise policy of the Republican party touching the public domain, and reclaimed from corporations and syndicates, alien and domestic, and restored to the people, nearly 100,000,000 acres of valuable land, to be sacredly held as homesteads for our citizens, and we pledge ourselves to continue this policy until every acre of land so unlawfully held shall be reclaimed and restored to the people.

SEC. 7. We denounce the Republican legislation known as the

Sherman Act of 1890 as a cowardly makeshift, fraught with possibilities of danger in the future which should make all of its supporters, as well as its author, anxious for its speedy repeal. We hold to the use of both gold and silver as the standard money of the country, and to the coinage of both gold and silver without discrimination against either metal or charge for mintage; but the dollar unit of coinage of both metals must be of equal intrinsic and exchangeable value, or be adjusted through international agreement, or by such safeguards of legislation as shall insure the maintenance of the parity of the two metals, and the equal power of every dollar at all times in the markets and in the payment of debts; and we demand that all paper currency shall be kept at par with and redeemable in such coin. We insist upon this policy as especially necessary for the protection of the farmers and laboring classes, the first and most defenceless victims of unstable money and a fluctuating currency.

SEC. 8. We recommend that the prohibitory ten per cent. tax on state bank issues be repealed.

SEC. 9. Public office is a public trust. We reaffirm the declaration of the Democratic national convention of 1876 for the reform of the civil service, and we call for the honest enforcement of all laws regulating the same. The nomination of a President, as in the recent Republican convention, by delegations composed largely of his appointees, holding office at his pleasure, is a scandalous satire upon free popular institutions, and a startling illustration of the methods by which a President may gratify his ambition. We denounce a policy under which federal office-holders usurp control of party conventions in the States, and we pledge the Democratic party to the reform of these and all other abuses which threaten individual liberty and local self-government.

SEC. 10. The Democratic party is the only party that has ever given the country a foreign policy consistent and vigorous, compelling respect abroad and inspiring confidence at home. While avoiding entangling alliances, it has aimed to cultivate friendly relations with other nations, and especially with our American neighbors on the American continent whose destiny is closely linked with our own, and we view with alarm the tendency to a policy of irritation and bluster which is liable at any time to confront us with the alternative of humiliation or war. We favor the maintenance of a navy strong enough for all purposes of national defence, and to properly maintain the honor and dignity of the country abroad.

SEC. 11. This country has always been the refuge of the oppressed from every land, — exiles for conscience' sake; and in the spirit of the founders of our government, we condemn the oppression practised by the Russian government upon its Lutheran and Jewish subjects, and we call upon our national government, in the interest of justice and humanity, by all just and proper means, to use its prompt and best efforts to bring about a cessation of these cruel persecutions in the dominions of the Czar, and to secure to the oppressed equal rights. We tender our profound and earnest sympathy to those lovers of freedom who are struggling for home rule and the great cause of local self-government in Ireland.

SEC. 12. We heartily approve all legitimate efforts to prevent the United States from being used as the dumping-ground for the known criminals and professional paupers of Europe; and we demand the rigid enforcement of the laws against Chinese immigration, or the importation of foreign workmen under contract, to degrade American labor and lessen its wages; but we condemn and denounce any and all attempts to restrict the immigration of the industrious and worthy of foreign lands.

SEC. 13. This convention hereby renews the expression of appreciation of the patriotism of the soldiers and sailors of the Union in the war for its preservation, and we favor just and liberal pensions for all disabled Union soldiers, their widows and dependents; but we demand that the work of the Pension office shall be done industriously, impartially, and honestly. We denounce the present administration of that office as incompetent, corrupt, disgraceful, and dishonest.

SEC. 14. The federal government should care for and improve the Mississippi River and other great waterways of the republic, so as to secure for the interior States easy and cheap transportation to the tidewater. When any waterway of the republic is of sufficient importance to demand the aid of the government, such aid should be extended for a definite plan of continuous work until permanent improvement is secured.

SEC. 15. For purposes of national defence and the promotion of commerce between the States, we recognize the early construction of the Nicaragua Canal, and its protection against foreign control, as of great importance to the United States.

SEC. 16. Recognizing the World's Columbian Exposition as a national undertaking of vast importance, in which the general government has invited the coöperation of all the powers of the world, and appreciating the acceptance by many of such powers of the invitation extended, and the broadest liberal efforts being made by them to contribute to the grandeur of the undertaking, we are of the opinion that Congress should make such necessary financial provision as shall be requisite to the maintenance of the national honor and public faith.

SEC. 17. Popular education being the only safe basis of popular suffrage, we recommend to the several States most liberal appropriations for the public schools. Free common schools are the nursery of good government, and they have always received the fostering care of the Democratic party, which favors every means of increasing intelligence. Freedom of education, being an essential of civil and religious liberty as well as a necessity for the development of intelligence, must not be interfered with under any pretext whatever. We are opposed to state interference with parental rights and rights of conscience in the education of children, as an infringement of the fundamental Democratic doctrine that the largest individual liberty consistent with the rights of others insures the highest type of American citizenship and the best government.

SEC. 18. We approve the action of the present House of Representatives in passing bills for the admission into the Union as States of the Territories of New Mexico and Arizona, and we favor the early admission of all the Territories having necessary population and resources to admit them to Statehood; and, while they remain Territories, we hold that the officials appointed to administer the government of any Territory, together with the Districts of Columbia and Alaska, should be *bonâ fide* residents of the Territory or District in which their duties are to be performed. The Democratic party believes in home rule, and the control of their own affairs by the people of the vicinage.

SEC. 19. We favor legislation by Congress and state legislatures to protect the lives and limbs of railway employees, and those of other hazardous transportation companies, and denounce the inactivity of the Republican party, and particularly the Republican Senate, for causing the defeat of measures beneficial and protective to this class of wage-workers.

SEC. 20. We are in favor of the enactment by the States of laws for abolishing the notorious sweating system, for abolishing contract convict labor, and for prohibiting the employment in factories of children under fifteen years of age.

SEC. 21. We are opposed to all sumptuary laws as an interference with the individual rights of the citizen.

SEC. 22. Upon this statement of principles and policies, the Democratic party asks the intelligent judgment of the American people. It asks a change of administration and a change of party in order that there may be a change of system and a change of methods, thus assuring the maintenance unimpaired of institutions under which the republic has grown great and powerful.

The platform as originally reported contained, instead **of** the first paragraph of Section 3 above, the following : —

We reiterate the oft-repeated doctrines of the Democratic party that the necessity of the government is the only justification for taxation, and whenever a tax is unnecessary it is unjustifiable; that when custom-house taxation is levied upon articles of any kind produced in this country, the difference between the cost of labor here and labor abroad, when such a difference exists, fully measures any possible benefits to labor; and the enormous additionkl impositions of the existing tariff fall with crushing force upon our farmers and workingmen, and, for the mere advantage of the few whom it enriches, exact from labor a grossly unjust share of the expenses of the government; and we demand such a revision of the tariff laws as will remove their iniquitous inequalities, lighten their oppressions, and put them on a constitutional and equitable basis. But in making reduction in taxes, it is not proposed to injure any domestic industries, but rather to promote their healthy growth. From the foundation of this government, taxes collected at the custom-house have been the chief source of federal revenue. Such they must continue to be. Moreover, many industries have come to rely upon legislation for successful continuance, so that any change of law must be at every step regardful of the labor and capital thus involved. The process of reform must be subject in the execution to this plain dictate of justice.

There had been a prolonged struggle, at a meeting of the committee on resolutions, over the tariff " plank." The paragraph just recited was, it will be perceived, an echo of the tariff plank of 1884, with an implied promise to the " protected industries " that there should be no sweeping reduction of duties to destroy their business. It was so far less aggressive than the attitude of the party during the preceding six years warranted as to seem like a complete change of front on the tariff question. The radical tariff reformers, defeated in committee, carried the contest into the convention, and on a motion from the floor the paragraph was struck out, and the paragraph printed in the platform was substituted, by a vote of yeas 564, nays 342. An excited debate preceded the vote. An impassioned appeal to the members to avow openly their real opinions was received with applause, and carried the day.

After the adoption of the platform, at a late hour in the evening, the convention proceeded at once to the work of nominating a candidate for President. Grover Cleveland was nominated on the first vote. The result of the polling was as follows : —

Whole number of votes 909½
Necessary for a choice (two thirds) 607
Grover Cleveland, New York 617⅓
David B. Hill, New York 114
Horace Boies, Iowa 103
Arthur P. Gorman, Maryland 36½
Adlai E. Stevenson, Illinois 16⅔
John G. Carlisle, Kentucky 14
William R. Morrison, Illinois 3
James E. Campbell, Ohio 2
William C. Whitney, New York 1
William E. Russell, Massachusetts 1
Robert E. Pattison, Pennsylvania 1

The nomination of a candidate for Vice-President was post-poned until the following day, when the polling resulted as follows : —

Whole number of votes 909
Necessary for a choice (two thirds) 606
Adlai E. Stevenson, Illinois 402
Isaac P. Gray, Indiana 343
Allen B. Morse, Michigan 86
John L. Mitchell, Wisconsin 45
Henry Watterson, Kentucky 26
Bourke Cockran, New York 5
Lambert Tree, Illinois 1
Horace Boies, Iowa 1

A motion was then made and adopted that Adlai E. Stevenson, of Illinois, be the candidate for Vice-President.

The National Prohibition party held its convention at Cincinnati, beginning on June 29. John P. St. John, of Kansas, was the temporary chairman, and Eli Ritter, of Indiana, the permanent president. The convention was in session only two days. The platform as originally reported by the committee on resolutions was as follows : —

The Prohibition party, in National Convention assembled, acknowledging Almighty God as the source of all true government, and his law as the standard to which all human enactments must conform to secure the blessings of peace and prosperity, presents the following declaration of principles : —

1. The liquor traffic is a foe to civilization, the arch enemy of popular government, and a public nuisance. It is the citadel of the forces that corrupt politics, promote poverty and crime, degrade the nation's home life, thwart the will of the people, and

deliver our country into the hands of rapacious class interests. All laws that, under the guise of regulation, legalize and protect this traffic, or make the government share in its ill-gotten gains, are "vicious in principle and powerless as a remedy."

We declare anew for the entire suppression of the manufacture, sale, importation, exportation, and transportation of alcoholic liquors as a beverage, by federal and state legislation; and the full powers of the government should be exerted to secure this result. Any party that fails to recognize the dominant nature of this issue in American politics is undeserving of the support of the people.

2. No citizen should be denied the right to vote on account of sex, and equal labor should receive equal wages, without regard to sex.

3. The money of the country should be gold, silver, and paper, and be issued by the general government only, and in sufficient quantities to meet the demands of business and give full opportunity for the employment of labor. To this end an increase in the volume of money is demanded, and no individual or corporation should be allowed to make any profit through its issue. It should be made a legal tender for the payment of all debts, public and private. Its volume should be fixed at a definite sum per capita, and made to increase with our increase in population.

4. We favor the free and unlimited coinage of silver and gold.

5. Tariffs should be levied only as a defence against foreign governments which put tariffs upon or bar our products from their markets, revenue being incidental. The residue of means necessary to an economical administration of the government should be raised by levying a burden on what the people possess instead of upon what we consume.

6. Railroad, telegraph, and other public corporations should be controlled by the government in the interest of the people, and no higher charges allowed than necessary to give fair interest on the capital actually invested.

7. Foreign immigration has become a burden upon industry, one of the factors in depressing wages and causing discontent; therefore our immigration laws should be revised and strictly enforced. The time of residence for naturalization should be extended, and no naturalized person should be allowed to vote until one year after he becomes a citizen.

8. Non-resident aliens should not be allowed to acquire land in this country, and we favor the limitation of individual and corporate ownership of land. All unearned grants of lands to railroad companies or other corporations should be reclaimed.

9. Years of inaction and treachery on the part of the Republican

and Democratic parties have resulted in the present reign of mob law, and we demand that every citizen be protected in the right of trial by constitutional tribunals.

10. All men should be protected by law in their right to one day's rest in seven.

11. Arbitration is the wisest and most economical and humane method of settling national differences.

12. Speculations in margins, the cornering of grain, money, and products, and the formation of pools, trusts, and combinations for the arbitrary advancement of prices, should be suppressed.

13. We pledge that the Prohibition party if elected to power will ever grant just pensions to disabled veterans of the Union army and navy, their widows and orphans.

14. We stand unequivocally for the American public school, and opposed to any appropriation of public moneys for sectarian schools. We declare that only by united support of such common schools, taught in the English language, can we hope to become and remain an homogeneous and harmonious people.

15. We arraign the Republican and Democratic parties as false to the standards reared by their founders; as faithless to the principles of the illustrious leaders of the past to whom they do homage with the lips; as recreant to the "higher law," which is as inflexible in political affairs as in personal life; and as no longer embodying the aspirations of the American people, or inviting the confidence of enlightened, progressive patriotism. Their protests against the admission of "moral issues" into politics is a confession of their own moral degeneracy. The declaration of an eminent authority, that municipal misrule is "the one conspicuous failure of American politics," follows as a natural consequence of such degeneracy, and is true alike of cities under Republican and Democratic control. Each accuses the other of extravagance in Congressional appropriations, and both are alike guilty; each protests when out of power against the infraction of the civil service laws, and each when in power violates those laws in letter and spirit; each professes fealty to the interests of the toiling masses, but both covertly truckle to the money power in their administration of public affairs. Even the tariff issue, as represented in the Democratic Mills bill and the Republican McKinley bill, is no longer treated by them as an issue upon great and divergent principles of government, but is a mere catering to different sectional and class interests. The attempt in many States to wrest the Australian ballot system from its true purpose, and to so deform it as to render it extremely difficult for new parties to exercise the rights of suffrage, is an outrage upon popular government. The competition of both the parties for the vote of the slums, and

their assiduous courting of the liquor power and subserviency to the money power, have resulted in placing those powers in the position of practical arbiters of the destinies of the nation. We renew our protest against these perilous tendencies, and invite all citizens to join us in the upbuilding of a party that, as shown in five national campaigns, prefers temporary defeat to an abandonment of the claims of justice, sobriety, personal rights, and the protection of American homes.

A minority of the committee presented substitutes for the financial and the tariff planks of the platform, and also offered an additional resolution, which was ultimately adopted. The platform as printed above was adopted, except the fourth resolution, relating to the free coinage of silver, which was defeated by a vote of 596 to 335. The additional resolution referred to was as follows : —

Recognizing and declaring that prohibition of the liquor traffic has become the dominant issue in national politics, we invite to full party fellowship all those who on this one dominant issue are with us agreed, in the full belief that this party can and will remove sectional differences, promote nationality, and insure the best welfare of our entire land.

John Bidwell, of California, was nominated for President. The first and only vote was as follows : —

Whole number of votes	911
Necessary for a choice	456
John Bidwell, California	590
Gideon T. Stewart, Ohio	179
W. Jennings Demorest, New York	139
H. Clay Bascom	3

J. B. Cranfill, of Texas, was nominated for Vice-President by the following vote : —

Whole number of votes	811
Necessary for a choice	406
J. B. Cranfill, Texas	417
Joshua Levering, Maryland	351
W. W. Satterly, Minnesota	26
Thomas R. Carskodon, West Virginia	19

The first national convention of the " People's party " was held at Omaha, on July 2. C. H. Ellington, of Georgia, was the temporary chairman, and H. L. Loucks, of South Dakota, the permanent president. The platform, reported and adopted on July 4, was as follows : —

Assembled upon the 116th anniversary of the Declaration of Independence, the People's party of America, in their first national convention, invoking upon their action the blessing of Almighty God, puts forth, in the name and on behalf of the people of this country, the following preamble and declaration of principles : —

The conditions which surround us best justify our coöperation : we meet in the midst of a nation brought to the verge of moral, political, and material ruin. Corruption dominates the ballot-box, the legislature, the Congress, and touches even the ermine of the bench. The people are demoralized; most of the States have been compelled to isolate the voters at the polling-places to prevent universal intimidation or bribery. The newspapers are largely subsidized or muzzled; public opinion silenced; business prostrated; our homes covered with mortgages; labor impoverished; and the land concentrating in the hands of the capitalists. The urban workmen are denied the right of organization for self-protection ; imported pauperized labor beats down their wages; a hireling standing army, unrecognized by our laws, is established to shoot them down, and they are rapidly degenerating into European conditions. The fruits of the toil of millions are boldly stolen to build up colossal fortunes for a few, unprecedented in the history of mankind; and the possessors of these, in turn, despise the republic and endanger liberty. From the same prolific womb of governmental injustice we breed the two great classes of tramps and millionaires.

The national power to create money is appropriated to enrich bondholders ; a vast public debt, payable in legal tender currency, has been funded into gold-bearing bonds, thereby adding millions to the burdens of the people. Silver, which has been accepted as coin since the dawn of history, has been demonetized to add to the purchasing power of gold by decreasing the value of all forms of property as well as human labor ; and the supply of currency is purposely abridged to fatten usurers, bankrupt enterprise, and enslave industry. A vast conspiracy against mankind has been organized on two continents, and it is rapidly taking possession of the world. If not met and overthrown at once, it forebodes terrible social convulsions, the destruction of civilization, or the establishment of an absolute despotism.

We have witnessed for more than a quarter of a century the struggles of the two great political parties for power and plunder, while grievous wrongs have been inflicted upon the suffering people. We charge that the controlling influences dominating both these parties have permitted the existing dreadful condition to develop without serious effort to prevent or restrain them.

Neither do they now promise us any substantial reform. They have agreed together to ignore in the campaign every issue but one. They propose to drown the outcries of a plundered people with the uproar of a sham battle over the tariff, so that capitalists, corporations, national banks, rings, trusts, watered stock, the demonetization of silver, and the oppressions of the usurers may all be lost sight of. They propose to sacrifice our homes, lives, and children on the altar of mammon; to destroy the multitude in order to secure corruption funds from the millionaires.

Assembled on the anniversary of the birthday of the nation, and filled with the spirit of the grand general chief who established our independence, we seek to restore the government of the Republic to the hands of "the plain people," with whose class it originated. We assert our purposes to be identical with the purposes of the National Constitution, "to form a more perfect union and establish justice, insure domestic tranquillity, provide for the common defence, promote the general welfare, and secure the blessings of liberty for ourselves and our posterity." We declare that this republic can only endure as a free government while built upon the love of the whole people for each other and for the nation; that it cannot be pinned together by bayonets; that the civil war is over, and that every passion and resentment which grew out of it must die with it; and that we must be in fact, as we are in name, one united brotherhood of freemen.

Our country finds itself confronted by conditions for which there is no precedent in the history of the world: our annual agricultural productions amount to billions of dollars in value, which must, within a few weeks or months, be exchanged for billions of dollars of commodities consumed in their production; the existing currency supply is wholly inadequate to make this exchange; the results are falling prices, the formation of combines and rings, the impoverishment of the producing class. We pledge ourselves, if given power, we will labor to correct these evils by wise and reasonable legislation, in accordance with the terms of our platform. We believe that the powers of government — in other words, of the people — should be expanded (as in the case of the postal service) as rapidly and as far as the good sense of an intelligent people and the teachings of experience shall justify, to the end that oppression, injustice, and poverty shall eventually cease in the land.

While our sympathies as a party of reform are naturally upon the side of every proposition which will tend to make men intelligent, virtuous, and temperate, we nevertheless regard these questions — important as they are — as secondary to the great issues now pressing for solution, and upon which not only our individual prosperity but the very existence of free institutions depends; and we ask all men to first help us to determine whether we are to have a republic to administer before we differ as to the conditions upon which it is to be administered; believing that the forces of reform this day organized will never cease to move forward until every wrong is remedied, and equal rights and equal privileges securely established for all the men and women of this country.

We declare, therefore, —

First. That the union of the labor forces of the United States this day consummated shall be permanent and perpetual; may its spirit enter all hearts for the salvation of the republic and the uplifting of mankind!

Second. Wealth belongs to him who creates it, and every dollar taken from industry without an equivalent is robbery. "If any will not work, neither shall he eat." The interests of rural and civic labor are the same; their enemies are identical.

Third. We believe that the time has come when the railroad corporations will either own the people or the people must own the railroads; and, should the government enter upon the work of owning and managing all railroads, we should favor an amendment to the Constitution by which all persons engaged in the government service shall be placed under a civil service regulation of the most rigid character, so as to prevent the increase of the power of the national administration by the use of such additional government employees.

We demand, —

First, A national currency, safe, sound, and flexible, issued by the general government only, a full legal tender for all debts, public and private, and that, without the use of banking corporations, a just, equitable, and efficient means of distribution direct to the people, at a tax not to exceed two per cent. per annum, to be provided as set forth in the sub-treasury plan of the Farmers' Alliance, or a better system; also, by payments in discharge of its obligations for public improvements.

(*a*) We demand free and unlimited coinage of silver and gold at the present legal ratio of sixteen to one.

(*b*) We demand that the amount of circulating medium be speedily increased to not less than fifty dollars per capita.

(*c*) We demand a graduated income tax.

(*d*) We believe that the money of the country should be kept as much as possible in the hands of the people, and hence we demand that all state and national revenues shall be limited to the necessary expenses of the government economically and honestly administered.

(*e*) We demand that postal savings banks be established by the government for the safe deposit of the earnings of the people and to facilitate exchange.

Second, Transportation. Transportation being a means of exchange and a public necessity, the government should own and operate the railroads in the interest of the people.

(a) The telegraph and telephone, like the post-office system, being a necessity for the transmission of news, should be owned and operated by the government in the interest of the people.

Third, Land. The land, including all the natural sources of wealth, is the heritage of the people, and should not be monopolized for speculative purposes, and alien ownership of land should be prohibited. All land now held by railroads and other corporations in excess of their actual needs, and all lands now owned by aliens, should be reclaimed by the government and held for actual settlers only.

Subsequently the committee on resolutions made a supplementary report, submitting a series of resolutions which it was explained are not to be regarded as a part of the party platform, but as expressive of the opinion of the party, as follows : —

Whereas, Other questions have been presented for our consideration, we hereby submit the following, not as a part of the platform of the People's party, but as resolutions expressive of the sentiment of this convention.

1. *Resolved*, That we demand a free ballot and a fair count in all elections, and pledge ourselves to secure it to every legal voter without federal intervention, through the adoption by the States of the unperverted Australian or secret ballot system.

2. *Resolved*, That the revenue derived from a graduated income tax should be applied to the reduction of the burden of taxation now resting upon the domestic industries of this country.

3. *Resolved*, That we pledge our support to fair and liberal pensions to ex-Union soldiers and sailors.

4. *Resolved*, That we condemn the fallacy of protecting American labor under the present system, which opens our ports to the pauper and criminal classes of the world, and crowds out our wage-earners; and we denounce the present ineffective laws against contract labor, and demand the further restriction of undesirable immigration.

5. *Resolved*, That we cordially sympathize with the efforts of organized workingmen to shorten the hours of labor, and demand a rigid enforcement of the existing eight-hour law on government work, and ask that a penalty clause be added to the said law.

6. *Resolved*, That we regard the maintenance of a large standing army of mercenaries, known as the Pinkerton system, as a

.menace to our liberties, and we demand its abolition; and we condemn the recent invasion of the Territory of Wyoming by the hired assassins of plutocracy, assisted by federal officials.

7. *Resolved*, That we commend to the favorable consideration of the people and the reform press the legislative system known as the initiative and referendum.

8. *Resolved*, That we favor a constitutional provision limiting the office of President and Vice-President to one term, and providing for the election of senators of the United States by a direct vote of the people.

9. *Resolved*, That we oppose any subsidy or national aid to any private corporation for any purpose.

General James B. Weaver, of Iowa, was nominated for President. The vote stood: —

Whole number of votes	1263
Necessary for a choice	632
James B. Weaver, Iowa	995
James H. Kyle, South Dakota	265
Mann Page, Virginia	1
Leland Stanford, California	1
—— Norton	1

For Vice-President, James G. Field, of Virginia, was nominated. The vote was as follows: —

Whole number of votes	1287
Necessary for a choice	644
James G. Field, Virginia	733
Ben. S. Terrell, Texas	554

The representation in this convention was irregular, as may be seen from the fact that Texas cast 60 votes, New York 59, Pennsylvania 21, Massachusetts 28, Illinois 83, and North Dakota 25.

A Socialist Labor convention was held at New York on August 28, by which Simon Wing, of Massachusetts, was nominated for President, and Charles H. Matchett, of New York, for Vice-President. The following platform was adopted: —

Social Demands: 1. Reduction of the hours of labor in proportion to the progress of production.

2. The United States shall obtain possession of the railroads, canals, telegraphs, telephones, and all other means of public transportation and communication.

3. The municipalities to obtain possession of the local railroads,

ferries, water-works, gas-works, electric plants, and all industries requiring municipal franchises.

4. The public lands to be declared inalienable. Revocation of all land grants to corporations or individuals, the conditions of which have not been complied with.

5. Legal incorporation by the States of local trade unions which have no national organization.

6. The United States to have the exclusive right to issue money.

7. Congressional legislation providing for the scientific management of forests and waterways, and prohibiting the waste of the natural resources of the country.

8. Inventions to be free to all; the inventors to be remunerated by the nation.

9. Progressive income tax and tax on inheritances; the smaller incomes to be exempt.

10. School education of all children under fourteen years of age to be compulsory, gratuitous, and accessible to all by public assistance in meals, clothing, books, etc., where necessary.

11. Repeal of all pauper, tramp, conspiracy, and sumptuary laws. Unabridged right of combination.

12. Official statistics concerning the condition of labor. Prohibition of the employment of children of school age, and of the employment of female labor in occupations detrimental to health or morality. Abolition of the convict labor contract system.

13. All wages to be paid in lawful money of the United States. Equalization of women's wages with those of men where equal service is performed.

14. Laws for the protection of life and limb in all occupations, and an efficient employers' liability law.

Political Demands: 1. The people to have the right to propose laws and to vote upon all measures of importance, according to the referendum principle.

2. Abolition of the Presidency, Vice-Presidency, and Senate of the United States. An Executive Board to be established, whose members are to be elected, and may at any time be recalled, by the House of Representatives, as the only legislative body. The States and municipalities to adopt corresponding amendments to their constitutions and statutes.

3. Municipal self-government.

4. Direct vote and secret ballots in all elections. Universal and equal right of suffrage, without regard to color, creed, or sex. Election days to be legal holidays. The principle of minority representation to be introduced.

5. All public officers to be subject to recall by their respective constituencies.

6. Uniform civil and criminal law throughout the United States. Administration of justice to be free of charge. Abolition of capital punishment.

The canvass developed few features of special interest. The result seemed to be in doubt, and both parties were hopeful. The opposition which had existed, prior to the conventions, to the President and the ex-President, the candidates of their respective parties, disappeared for the most part. The Republicans had been placed in a minority by the disaster of 1890; but their leaders, their orators, their journalists, and the rank and file of the party made no doubt that the defection was temporary. The ticket did not arouse great enthusiasm; but the Republicans built great hopes upon the situation of the Democrats in New York. There seemed to be an irreparable breach in that State. An eloquent advocate of the nomination of Governor Hill had said, in a speech before the Democratic convention at Chicago, that Mr. Cleveland could not carry New York. Tammany Hall protested its loyalty to the ticket; but the "anti-snapper" wing of the party feared, and the Republicans hoped, that the protestations were insincere. An element of humor was imparted to the canvass in New York by an ostentatiously disingenuous attempt on the part of those Democrats who did not subscribe to the free-trade-plank in the platform to make it appear that "negro domination" would ensue upon the success of the Republicans. The New York "Sun," which disliked Mr. Cleveland almost beyond its by no means deficient power of expression, made "No Force Bill!" its campaign cry, to excuse its support of the Democratic candidate.

The growth of the Populist party in the West and in some parts of the South led to coalitions which render an exact division of the votes among the several parties quite impossible. In five States — Colorado, Idaho, Kansas, North Dakota, and Wyoming — the Democrats nominated no electors, but voted for the Populist candidates. It was deemed possible that neither party might secure a majority of electors. In that case the election of President would devolve upon the House of Representatives already chosen, in which the Democrats controlled a large majority of the state delegations. Consequently, for their purposes, a defeat of the Republicans, by the success of the Populists in a few of the States, was as serviceable as the election of a full majority of Democratic electors. In

Nevada the Democrats nominated an electoral ticket, but almost the whole voting strength of the party was given to the Populists. In Oregon one of the four Populist electors was placed on the Democratic ticket. In Minnesota there was a fusion of Democrats and Populists on four candidates for electors. The members of each party voted for their own candidates for the other five electors. In the South the alliances of the Populists were with Republicans. The fusion in Alabama was incomplete, but in Louisiana the electoral ticket was divided between the two parties, — four electors for each party. This fusion explains why the popular vote in Louisiana for Harrison and for Weaver, in the following table, is substantially the same. The vote for the fusion electors was 26,563. An independent electoral ticket, by the so-called "Lily White" faction of the Republican party of Texas, received 3,969 votes.

Still another complication was introduced at this election by the action of the Democratic legislature of Michigan chosen in the "landslide" year, 1890. An act was passed by that legislature reëstablishing the system of choosing electors by districts. Maryland, the last State to cling to this method, had abandoned it in 1836. It was a device, in the case of Michigan, to enable a party which was conscious of being in a minority to secure a few electors. The constitutionality of the measure was attacked; but it was clearly within the power of the legislature to pass the act, and the Supreme Court of Michigan so decided.

The result of the election was a great surprise to men of all parties. Not only was the South "solid" once more for the Democratic candidates, not only did all the usually doubtful States support Mr. Cleveland by large majorities, but Illinois, Wisconsin, and California were drawn into the Democratic ranks. Even Ohio, which had not given an electoral vote to a Democrat since there had been a Republican party, was so closely divided that one Cleveland elector slipped in. The fusion against the Republicans was successful in Colorado, Idaho, Kansas, and Nevada. It was partially successful in North Dakota and Oregon. The popular vote for the several candidates is given in the following table, as nearly as it can be stated, but the "official returns" vary so greatly as to render absolute accuracy impossible. The appended figures are made up by a careful comparison of several sets of "official" returns, and a choice of those that seem most trustworthy. It should

STATES.	Grover Cleveland, New York.	Benjamin Harrison, Indiana.	James B. Weaver, Iowa.	John Bidwell, California.	Simon Wing, Massachusetts.	Cleveland and Stevenson.	Harrison and Reid.	Weaver and Field.
	POPULAR VOTE.					ELECTORAL VOTE.		
Alabama	138,138	9,197	85,181	239	–	11	–	–
Arkansas	87,834	46,884	11,831	113	–	8	–	–
California . . .	117,908	117,618	25,226	8,056	–	8	1	–
Colorado	–	38,620	53,584	1,638	–	–	–	4
Connecticut . . .	82,395	77,025	806	4,025	329	6	–	–
Delaware . . .	18,581	18,083	13	565	–	3	–	–
Florida	30,143	–	4,843	475	–	4	–	–
Georgia	129,361	48,305	42,937	988	–	13	–	–
Idaho	–	8,599	10,520	288	–	–	–	3
Illinois	426,281	399,288	22,207	25,870	–	24	–	–
Indiana	262,740	255,615	22,208	13,050	–	15	–	–
Iowa	196,367	219,795	20,595	6,402	–	–	13	–
Kansas	–	157,237	163,111	4,539	–	–	–	10
Kentucky . . .	175,461	135,441	23,500	6,442	–	13	–	–
Louisiana . . .	87,922	13,281	13,282	–	–	8	–	–
Maine	48,044	62,931	2,381	3,062	336	–	6	–
Maryland . . .	113,866	92,736	796	5,877	27	8	–	–
Massachusetts . .	176,813	202,814	3,210	1,539	649	–	15	–
Michigan	202,296	222,708	19,892	14,069	–	5	9	–
Minnesota . . .	100,920	122,823	29,313	12,182	–	–	9	–
Mississippi . . .	40,237	1,406	10,256	910	–	9	–	–
Missouri	268,398	226,918	41,213	4,331	–	17	–	–
Montana	17,581	18,851	7,334	549	–	–	3	–
Nebraska . . .	24,943	87,227	83,134	4,902	–	–	8	–
Nevada	714	2,811	7,264	89	–	–	–	3
New Hampshire .	42,081	45,658	292	1,297	–	–	4	–
New Jersey . . .	171,042	156,068	969	8,131	1,337	10	–	–
New York . . .	654,868	609,350	16,429	38,190	17,956	36	–	–
North Carolina . .	132,951	100,342	44,736	2,636	–	11	–	–
North Dakota . .	–	17,519	17,700	899	–	1	1	1
Ohio	404,115	405,187	14,850	26,012	–	1	22	–
Oregon	14,243	35,002	26,965	2,281	–	–	0	1
Pennsylvania . .	452,264	516,011	8,714	25,123	898	–	32	–
Rhode Island .	24,335	26,972	228	1,654	–	–	4	–
South Carolina . .	54,692	13,345	2,407	–	–	9	–	–
South Dakota . .	9,081	34,888	26,544	–	–	–	4	–
Tennessee . . .	138,874	100,331	23,447	4,851	–	12	–	–
Texas	239,148	81,444	99,688	2,165	–	15	–	–
Vermont	16,325	37,992	43	1,415	–	–	4	–
Virginia	163,977	113,202	12,275	2,738	–	12	–	–
Washington . . .	29,802	36,460	19,165	2,542	–	–	4	–
West Virginia . .	84,467	80,293	4,166	2,145	–	6	–	–
Wisconsin . . .	177,335	170,791	9,909	13,132	–	12	–	–
Wyoming . . .	–	8,454	7,722	530	–	–	3	–
Total	5,556,543	5,175,582	1,040,886	255,841	21,532	277	145	22

be borne in mind that the Populist vote is overstated, and the Democratic vote understated, by reason of the alliances just mentioned.

Forty-four States participated in the election, six new States having been admitted since the previous election, — North and South Dakota, Montana, Idaho, Washington, and Wyoming. In all the States, electors were chosen by popular vote ; in all, save Michigan, on a general ticket.   The popular and electoral votes are included in the same table.

The count of the electoral vote took place on February 8, 1893.   The proceedings of 1889 were followed exactly.   No incident occurred to enliven the occasion more important than a round of Democratic applause when the vote of Illinois was announced.

XXXI

THE FREE SILVER CAMPAIGN

THE four years which cover the second term of Grover Cleveland may be characterized as the most momentous period, in a time of peace, in the history of the country, and as the most interesting, from a political point of view, in either war or peace. The prominence assumed by our foreign relations would alone have distinguished it from preceding administrations; and yet the diplomatic questions that confronted us, although important, far-reaching, and exciting, became almost insignificant in comparison with the domestic problems and conditions with which public men had to deal. An attempt which, since it was but partially successful, was not successful at all, to introduce a new principle in the levy of import duties; a steady and large deficit in the revenue, not corrected by additional taxation; a currency hopelessly disordered, while no party was strong enough either to restore it to soundness or to introduce a new element of confusion; commercial disaster and private distress, manifesting itself in demonstrations that always excited apprehension, and in some cases lapsed into lawlessness which the local authorities could not or would not suppress, — such, in brief, were the evil conditions that prevailed during that eventful period. It was a time full of surprises, the last and greatest of which was the sudden rise, to an issue of overwhelming importance and interest, of a question that had troubled the peace of American politicians for twenty years, but had previously been dallied with and avoided, never met squarely and with courage.

At the very beginning of the administration the President signified his disagreement with his predecessor on a question of foreign policy by withdrawing from consideration by the Senate the treaty for the annexation of Hawaii. The position ultimately taken by the new administration was that the revolution in the island kingdom had been accomplished by an improper use of the armed forces of the United States, and that the wrong should be righted by a restoration of the queen to her throne.   Upon the question of fact on which the policy was based there was an exceedingly warm controversy; yet there can be little doubt that, whatever opinion men held as to the conduct of our minister at Honolulu, the restoration of a monarchy by the armed intervention, or under the protecting authority, of the United States was repugnant to the general sentiment of the people.

The vigorous interference of the government in the difficulty between Great Britain and Venezula was the most dramatic passage in our recent diplomatic history.   When it seemed certain that England would put an end to the dispute, that had been running more than half a century, as to the true boundary between Venezuela and her possession of British Guiana, by seizing the territory in question, the President brought the subject to the attention of Congress in a message that contained the broadest assertion of the Monroe doctrine ever made in a state paper.   The United States had been endeavoring for years to bring about a settlement of the quarrel by arbitration. The suggestion of the President was, in effect, that if the contending parties could not come to terms, this government should undertake a judicial investigation of the matter, and sustain whatever rights it might find Venezuela to possess.   The message was received in some quarters as presaging war with Great Britain ; and its first effect was to inflict almost absolute paralysis upon business.   In the end, after much negotiation, just before the close of Mr. Cleveland's administration, Great Britain and the United States agreed upon an arbitration of the boundary question on nearly the terms originally proposed by this country, — the most signal victory of American diplomacy in modern times.   Had not domestic questions quite overshadowed all matters of foreign policy, and left the administration without a party to support it, this grand success, giving the Monroe doctrine both a wider scope and a stronger legal standing than ever before, must have played a great part in the election of 1896.

On the other hand, the outbreak of a fresh insurrection in Cuba increased greatly the perplexities of the administration. The outspoken sympathy with the insurgents, more or less sincere, of journals and politicians, expressed itself, among other ways, in heated denunciation of the President for his strict observance of a friendly attitude toward Spain, and for the

steps which he took to prevent filibustering and other violations of the neutrality laws. In a position of extreme difficulty
he succeeded in avoiding complications that might lead to war,
but he did not and could not succeed in pleasing Spain, or the
Cubans, or their sympathizers in this country.

Another incident of the diplomatic history of this administration must be alluded to, although it ultimately came to nothing, and had no marked bearing upon party politics or upon
the presidential election. Mr. Olney, the Secretary of State,
negotiated a treaty of general arbitration with Sir Julian
Pauncefote, the British minister at Washington, under which
all questions arising between the two governments were to be
submitted to international tribunals. The treaty was most
warmly attacked by many persons as placing the interests of
the country in jeopardy; and on the other hand it was urged,
both wisely and unwisely, by men who thought they saw in it
the germ of a principle that was to put an end to war. The
treaty was not acted upon by the Senate before the close of
Mr. Cleveland's administration; and, although his successor in
office recommended it most earnestly, it was rejected.

The most cursory review of this remarkable administration
would be incomplete without a reference to these stirring
events in our foreign relations. Nevertheless not one of them
had the least influence in shaping the canvass of 1896, or in
determining its result. Two acts of Congress, passed in the
year 1890, were the special object of attack by the Democratic
party in the election of 1892. The result of that election was
to give full power to the Democrats in the legislative as well
as the executive department of the government, and the President soon began the promised campaign for the repeal of those
obnoxious acts. The so-called "Sherman Silver-Purchase
Act" was a measure of concession by Republicans to the sentiment that "something ought to be done for silver." Both
parties, Republican and Democratic alike, were paralyzed by
the advocates of silver free-coinage. A majority of Democrats
favored, and a majority of Republicans opposed, the policy.
But it was difficult, and, as the event proved, impossible, to
persuade the opponents of the measure to act in harmony.
Some of them were even alarmed lest, should they agree upon
nothing to increase the use of silver money, the advocates of
free coinage would carry their point. Out of this situation
arose the compromise contained in the act of 1890. The

Silver Republicans accepted it as the least that would satisfy them ; the anti-Silver members persuaded themselves that it was safe ; and it was carried through as a party measure.   As for the Democrats, not one of them supported it, — the Free Silver wing treating it with scorn, as a delusion ; the " Sound Money " wing, as it came afterward to be known, regarding it as a long step toward free coinage, if not a surrender to the Silver Republicans.

The working of the act satisfied neither the Silver party nor their opponents.   The Democrats denounced it in terms, in their national platform, as a " cowardly makeshift," and were pledged to its repeal.   When, however, in the spring and early summer of 1893, the consequences of the execution of the act began to make themselves felt, a line of division different from the party line was established.   All those who were opposed to free coinage, Republicans as well as Democrats, were anxiously and earnestly in favor of repeal.   The advocates of free coinage, on the other hand, while maintaining consistently that it was far short of the measure which they desired, protested against repeal unless something quite as favorable to silver were simultaneously enacted in its stead.   Something like a panic seized the banking and mercantile communities of the money centres, and the alarm lest the country should fall to a silver standard was widespread.   In these circumstances the President, who was well known to be opposed to further legislation in favor of silver, and strongly against free coinage, called Congress together in extraordinary session for the purpose of repealing the silver-purchase clauses of the act of 1890.   The situation was a peculiar one.   It may perhaps be most briefly explained by a statement of what occurred.   The act of repeal was passed by the House of Representatives on August 28, 1893, three weeks after the session began.   It did not pass the Senate until October 30.   It was successful in the lower House because the Speaker, Mr. Crisp, a silver advocate both before and afterward, gave it his support and the weight of all the influence a Speaker could exert.   In the Senate the bill was managed by Mr. Voorhees, also a free-coinage man.

The fact that, in spite of the passage of this bill, there was a majority in each House of Congress in favor of free coinage, was proved abundantly at the subsequent regular sessions ; but owing to the difficulty of carrying any measure through both Houses in the face of a determined minority, nothing was accomplished.   A bill was, nevertheless, passed to " coin the seigniorage." This act encountered a veto by the President, May 27, 1894, and the two-thirds majority, necessary to pass the bill notwithstanding his objections, could not be obtained. The bill proposed to coin so much of the silver purchased under the act of 1890 as represented the difference between the price paid for the silver and its coining value, and to use the coin for the current expenses of the government; and afterward to coin the rest of the silver owned by the Treasury for the purpose of redeeming the treasury notes issued against the silver purchased.   This measure, to which Mr. Abram S. Hewitt applied the catching phrase " coining a vacuum," was the only one touching the silver question which reached the President after the repealing act already mentioned.   But the temper of Congress was well shown by its absolute refusal to sanction an issue of bonds payable, principal and interest, in gold.   The matter was brought to the attention of Congress by the President at a time when a large issue of bonds was pending ; and a proposition by a bankers' syndicate to take the bonds on much more favorable terms, provided the promise were made to pay in gold what was to be lent in gold, was submitted at the same time ; but Congress refused to allow the promise to be made. A resolution authorizing an issue of gold bonds was rejected by a large majority.

The significance of all these events, in their bearing upon the election of a President in 1896, lies in the fact of a constantly increasing difference between Mr. Cleveland and the majority of his party as represented in Congress.   At the beginning of the administration, there were enough Silver Democrats, who joined with the Gold Democrats, to give a majority of the party in the House of Representatives in favor of the repeal act of 1893.   In the Senate the Democrats who opposed the President were exactly as many as those who supported him.   Included among his supporters were seven senators who were far more disposed to vote for free coinage than for the repealing act.   The President's influence was sufficient to secure their vote for the bill.   But this was the last occasion on which they conceded anything to him or yielded their opinion in the slightest degree.

As soon as the Silver-Purchase Repeal Act had been passed, the President bent all his energies to the fulfilment of the second pledge of his party, — the repeal of the McKinley Tariff

Act, and the passage of a customs revenue law " to reduce taxation." The protective system had been denounced in 1892 from every Democratic stump, and Mr. Cleveland had been elected with a distinct understanding that his victory would signify a purpose to go as far as prudence would warrant in the direction of free trade, or a " tariff for revenue only." Accordingly, at the beginning of the regular session of Congress in December, 1893, the President summoned his party to the performance of this duty. The apparent unanimity of the Democrats on this question, moreover, seemed to promise an opportunity to heal the breach caused by the contest over silver. The result made manifest a party division no less deplorable from a political point of view than that which had been revealed at the extraordinary session, and one which filled with humiliation those who wished honestly and faithfully to redeem the party pledge. A tariff bill framed as nearly in conformity to the principle which the voters of the country were supposed to have approved, as could be expected of any party, was brought into the House by Mr. Wilson, Chairman of the Committee on Ways and Means, and was promptly passed by that branch of Congress. When it reached the Senate a singular state of affairs appeared. A coterie of Democratic senators made an informal alliance with the Republicans for the purpose of saving the protective duties upon certain classes of goods in which the people of their respective States were interested. Neither threats nor persuasion, and no consideration of party loyalty, availed to break this alliance. The Democratic leaders were forced to accept the amendments dictated by the wayward members of their own party, including some that were insisted upon by the Republicans as the price of their assistance. In these circumstances, the bill as it was passed by the Senate was one which consistent upholders of the Democratic principle declared they could never accept. Nevertheless, it was soon made evident to them that no changes would be permitted, — that the choice lay between taking the bill as the Senate had passed it, or taking nothing, and thus leaving the McKinley act in force. With unconcealed reluctance they took the Senate bill. The only consolation they permitted themselves was the fact that the bill made wool free of duty; and the wool duty was regarded as the keystone of the protection arch. The President would neither approve the bill nor become responsible for the failure of tariff legislation by vetoing it. He allowed the bill to become law by lapse of time, without his signature.

During the ensuing two years the financial and business situation became steadily worse. Each reacted upon the other. The lower duties imposed by the new tariff act were not followed by such an increase of importations as to make good the loss of revenue. Foreign distrust in the stability of our affairs led to a withdrawal of foreign investments, and this caused a heavy exportation of gold, which was drawn from the Treasury. The gold borrowed on government loans to make good the reserve maintained to insure the redeemability of the paper money was quickly lost; for the greenbacks paid out in excess of revenue were again presented for redemption, to procure more gold for export. The President, in calling the attention of Congress to the subject, likened the process to the operation of an " endless chain." The constant imperilling of the gold reserve caused frequent panics and a paralysis of business. The labor situation became serious. Great strikes took place, attended with extreme violence. One in particular on certain great lines of railway centring in Chicago led to a direct intervention of the national authority and the employment of the army to protect the running of trains, on the theory that it was necessary to continue the operation of the postal service. The use of the government troops was not solicited by the governor of Illinois, who publicly protested that the intervention of the national authority, by command of the President, prior to a request therefor by the governor, was an unconstitutional invasion of State rights.

The generally deplorable condition of affairs, which, as is usually the case, was popularly attributed to the inefficiency and failure of the party in power, caused a violent reaction from the great Democratic victory of 1892. The Congress elections of 1894 gave the Republicans a majority of more than two to one in the House. Hardly a dozen Democratic members were returned from all the Northern States. The situation of the Democratic party did not improve, and at the beginning of 1896 was as hopeless as it had been at any time during the second administration of Mr. Cleveland. It was at this time a common remark by Republicans, which their opponents ventured only mildly to contradict, that they " could nominate a rag baby and elect it President " that year.

Yet events so shaped themselves as to render the contest one of the sharpest, most memorable, and for a brief season the most doubtful, of all that have taken place since the election of Mr. Lincoln in 1860. That which brought about the change was the intrusion of the silver question into the canvass as the dominant issue, in opposition to the wishes and efforts of those who, in each of the old historic parties, had previously exercised a controlling influence in its councils. It is easy to understand why they took this attitude of opposition. As apostles of the gospel of success, they dreaded the division which a plain and unmistakable pronouncement on the subject of silver would cause. The Populist party alone was united on that issue. The growing strength of that organization had filled all the old politicians with alarm. In some of the Western States it had even become formidable to the extent of outnumbering both the old parties combined. It was evident that, if the silver question were to become the foremost issue in the canvass, the old policy of a " straddling " platform would not do ; since in that case all those who were resolved to have free coinage at all hazards would flock to the Populist standard. Out of this situation developed a sensational contest for the control of the Democratic organization. The Eastern section of the party was dominated by the advocates of the gold standard ; the Free Coinage wing was overwhelmingly strong in the West and South ; and the great battle-ground was the central Western States. The national administration employed all its influence to secure the election to the national convention of delegates who would oppose the demands of the Silver men. Kentucky was the scene of the fiercest conflict ; and when the primary elections resulted in a brilliant victory for free silver, it was evident that the contest was ended, and that the only hope of the opponents of free coinage was that the victors might be persuaded not to carry their advantage to extremes, — a hope which was destined to be disappointed. The earnestness with which the struggle was carried on may be judged from the fact that the Democratic conventions of no less than thirty States resolved in distinct and emphatic language in favor of the free coinage of silver at the ratio of sixteen to one. Fourteen state conventions opposed free coinage, and ten of them declared in set terms for the gold standard. One convention only, that of Florida, expressed no opinion on the silver question. The sectional division on this issue is indicated by the fact that the fourteen anti-Silver States were the New England States, New York, New Jersey, Pennsylvania, Delaware, and Maryland, with Michigan, Wisconsin, and Minnesota.

Meantime another contest had been attracting deep interest throughout the country, — a contest, not of principle, but between rival candidates for the Republican nomination. Major William McKinley, of Ohio, and the Speaker of the House of Representatives, Thomas B. Reed, of Maine, had long been avowed candidates for the nomination. Months before the convention was to be held, the agents and partisans of each were at work laying plans, conducting correspondence, and dispatching emissaries to all parts of the country — particularly into the Southern States — in order to secure the election of delegates. By far the better organized, more aggressive and systematic campaign was carried on in behalf of Major McKinley, under the direction of his friend Marcus A. Hanna, whose name became familiar as household words in the mouths of all the stump speakers before the presidential canvass ended. Mr. McKinley was proclaimed "the advance agent of prosperity;" and, in the renewed popularity of the protective system, no cry was more effective than the demand for "Bill McKinley and the McKinley Bill." Mr. Reed's immense and universally admitted services to his party, his talents, his iron will, and his almost undisputed leadership, gave him a host of supporters. New York brought forward her governor, the former Vice-President, Levi P. Morton. Iowa presented as a worthy candidate her senator, William B. Allison; and Pennsylvania named Senator Matthew S. Quay. The efforts in behalf of the minor candidates availed little save in their respective States; the hopes of their supporters hardly went further than this: that they might make such a display of strength as to suggest that, if neither Mr. McKinley nor Mr. Reed could carry the convention, one of them would be available as a "dark horse." But it became evident long before the convention, although the partisans of the other candidates would not admit it, that a strong majority of the delegates favored the nomination of Mr. McKinley. During the whole of this preliminary skirmishing in the Republican party, the silver question was thrust into the background as much as possible. Twenty-two state conventions, it is true, declared against free coinage; but many even of these gave greater prominence and vigor to their expressions on the tariff than to their views on the money standard. Here also the gospel of success prevailed. The States of the extreme West, the "mining States," were practically unanimous in favor of silver. If the Democrats could count as usual on a " solid South," if they could hold the doubtful States of the Northwest, and if they could win over the new States of the far Northwest by taking ground in favor of free coinage while the Republicans opposed it, the canvass was already decided against the Republicans. It was announced by the Republican leaders in Colorado, Idaho, and other States that their electoral votes were irretrievably lost to the party if the national convention did not show itself more "friendly to silver" than the Minneapolis convention of 1892. This consideration caused many of the managers to do their utmost to retain the tariff as the leading issue, and to contemplate a "straddle" on the silver question. Their plans and purposes were overturned by influences too strong for them to resist.

Affairs were in this interesting situation when the time arrived for holding the national conventions. The results of these great assemblies were surprising to those even who had gauged accurately the intensity of the public feeling on the silver question. Never before were conventions so inharmonious, and never were there so many "splits" and "bolts" in parties. The first convention to be held was that of the Prohibition party, which met at Pittsburg on May 27, 1896. Mr. A. A. Stevens, of Pennsylvania, was the temporary chairman, and Mr. Oliver W. Stewart, of Illinois, the permanent president of the convention.

The assembly was divided from the first into two factions, — the "narrow gaugers" and the "broad gaugers." The real contest was over the silver question. The "broad gaugers" favored a platform made up of resolutions on many topics, upon which they held views closely approaching those of the Populists. The "narrow gaugers," opposing particularly the adoption of a free coinage "plank," contended for a platform which should make the prohibition of the manufacture and sale of intoxicating liquors the only issue upon which the party should appeal to the people. So sharp was the contest between the two factions that a disruption was foreseen before the convention was called to order. Leading men on each side had announced that if their faction were defeated, they would not support either platform or candidates. There was war between them in the choice of presiding officers ; and the two presidential candidates ultimately named had been agreed upon in rival caucuses before the first session of the convention.

The platform was reported on the second day of the session. A majority of the committee consisted of " narrow gaugers," and all the resolutions, six in number, were aimed at the liquor traffic. A minority of the committee presented fifteen additional resolutions, the first of which demanded the free and unlimited coinage of silver at the ratio of sixteen to one. The convention, in order that it might consider the question as a whole, first voted, yeas 492, nays 310, to append the minority resolutions to those reported by the majority, and then proceeded to consider the resolutions *seriatim*. The first six were adopted with unanimity. The next,[1] opposing all bank currency, and advocating the free coinage of silver, was warmly debated, and was rejected by a vote of yeas 387, nays 427. A motion was then made, and carried almost unanimously, to substitute for the resolutions already adopted the following, which became the platform of the convention : —

We, the members of the Prohibition party, in National Convention assembled, renewing our declaration of allegiance to Almighty God as the rightful Ruler of the universe, lay down the following as our declaration of political purpose : —

The Prohibition party, in National Convention assembled, declares its firm conviction that the manufacture, exportation, importation, and sale of alcoholic beverages has produced such social, commercial, industrial, and political wrongs, and is now so threatening the perpetuity of all our social and political institutions, that the suppression of the same, by a national party organized therefor, is the greatest object to be accomplished by the voters of our country, and is of such importance that it of right ought to control the political actions of all our patriotic citizens until such suppression is accomplished.

The urgency of this course demands the union, without further delay, of all citizens who desire the prohibition of the liquor traffic, therefore be it

Resolved, That we favor the legal prohibition by state and national legislation of the manufacture, importation, and sale of alcoholic beverages. That we declare our purpose to organize and unite all the friends of prohibition into one party, and in order to accomplish this end we deem it of right to leave every Prohibitionist the freedom of his own convictions upon all other political

[1] See the third resolution of the National party, p. 531.

questions, and trust our representatives to take such action upon other political questions as the changes occasioned by prohibition and the welfare of the whole people shall demand.

The following additional resolution was moved from the floor and unanimously adopted; but in order to save the consistency of the " narrow gaugers," it was voted that the resolution should not be a part of the platform : —

Resolved, That the right of suffrage ought not to be abridged on account of sex.

Immediately after the adoption of the substitute platform and the defeat of the " broad gaugers," a delegate requested all members of the convention who " wanted to work for humanity " to withdraw. Thereupon the " broad gaugers " retired from the hall. Those who remained proceeded to make nominations. Joshua Levering, of Maryland, was chosen as the candidate for President of the United States by acclamation. A vote was taken for a candidate for Vice-President, and Hale Johnson, of Illinois, was chosen. He received 309 votes, to 132 for T. C. Hughes, of Arizona.

The seceders from the Prohibition convention met in Pittsburg on the evening of May 28, chose Mr. A. L. Moore, of Michigan, chairman, and proceeded to organize the " National " party. The following platform was adopted. The six resolu· tions of the Prohibition platform were condensed into one ; the declaration in favor of woman suffrage was appended ; and the other eleven " planks " were taken from the report of the minority of the platform committee of the Prohibition convention : —

The National party, recognizing God as the author of all just power in government, presents the following declaration of principles, which it pledges itself to enact into effective legislation when given the power to do so : —

1. The suppression of the manufacture and sale, importation, exportation, and transportation of intoxicating liquors for beverage purposes. We utterly reject all plans for regulating or compromising with this traffic, whether such plans be called local option, taxation, license, or public control. The sale of liquors for medicinal and other legitimate uses should be conducted by the State, without profit, and with such regulations as will prevent fraud or evasion.

2. No citizen should be denied the right to vote on account of sex.

3. All money should be issued by the general government only, and without the intervention of any private citizen, corporation, or banking institution. It should be based upon the wealth, stability, and integrity of the nation. It should be a full legal tender for all debts, public and private, and should be of sufficient volume to meet the demands of the legitimate business interests of the country. For the purpose of honestly liquidating our outstanding coin obligations, we favor the free and unlimited coinage of both silver and gold, at the ratio of 16 to 1, without consulting any other nation.

4. Land is the common heritage of the people and should be preserved from monopoly and speculation. All unearned grants of land subject to forfeiture should be reclaimed by the government, and no portion of the public domain should hereafter be granted except to actual settlers, continuous use being essential to tenure.

5. Railroads, telegraphs, and other natural monopolies should be owned and operated by the government, giving to the people the benefit of service at actual cost.

6. The national Constitution should be so amended as to allow the national revenues to be raised by equitable adjustment of taxation on the properties and incomes of the people, and import duties should be levied as a means of securing equitable commercial relations with other nations.

7. The contract convict labor system, through which speculators are enriched at the expense of the State, should be abolished.

8. All citizens should be protected by law in their right to one day of rest in seven, without oppressing any who conscientiously observe any other than the first day of the week.

9. The American public schools, taught in the English language, should be maintained, and no public funds should be appropriated for sectarian institutions.

10. The President, Vice-President, and United States senators should be elected by direct vote of the people.

11. Ex-soldiers and sailors of the United States army and navy, their widows and minor children, should receive liberal pensions, graded on disability and term of service, not merely as a debt of gratitude, but for service rendered in the preservation of the Union.

12. Our immigration laws should be so revised as to exclude paupers and criminals. None but citizens of the United States should be allowed to vote in any State, and naturalized citizens should not vote until one year after naturalization papers have been issued.

13. The initiative and referendum, and proportional representation, should be adopted.

The Rev. Charles E. Bentley, of Nebraska, was nominated by acclamation for President of the United States; and James H. Southgate, of North Carolina, for Vice-President. Representatives of twenty-seven States took part in the convention. A roll-call showed the presence of 299 seceding delegates accredited to the Prohibition convention. All the proceedings of this assembly were completed at a single sitting, which lasted until the dawn of May 29.

The Republican convention met at St. Louis on June 16. The nomination of Major McKinley was a foregone conclusion; but the formation of the platform excited the most intense interest among the delegates and throughout the country. The complete victory of the Free Silver wing of the Democratic party in the choice of delegates to the convention soon to assemble, and the determination expressed by its leaders to declare for free coinage in the most radical terms, placed before the Republican politicians for solution a puzzling problem. Should they try to evade the issue about to be set forth by their enemies, and endeavor to make the canvass on the tariff issue? Or should they boldly anticipate the new issue and declare against free coinage and in favor of the gold standard? A small but compact and persistent group of delegates from the extreme West urged a third course, namely, a declaration in favor of free coinage; but that was manifestly out of the question, since a vast majority of the leaders and of those whom they represented was unalterably opposed to that policy.

The advocates of a timorous policy were defeated in the first preliminary skirmish. Two facts which were set forth most clearly convinced a great majority of the convention that there was nothing to be gained and much to be lost by a "straddle," — the first, that such a course would not pacify the Free Silver delegates or keep them in the convention; and the second, that the advocates of the policy of saying plainly what almost all the delegates except those from the "Silver States" thought, would carry the contest into the convention if they were defeated in the committee. In these circumstances most of the opposition to the insertion of the word "gold" in the platform ceased. Even the phraseology of the resolution, which was afterward changed but slightly, was agreed upon and published.

Nevertheless, after the convention met and organized, by the choice of Mr. Charles W. Fairbanks, of Indiana, as temporary chairman, and Mr. John M. Thurston, of Nebraska, as permanent president, the contest was renewed in the committee on resolutions. It was not until the third day of the session, June 18, that the platform was reported, as follows : —

The Republicans of the United States, assembled by their representatives in national convention, appealing for the popular and historical justification of their claims to the matchless achievements of the thirty years of Republican rule, earnestly and confidently address themselves to the awakened intelligence, experience, and conscience of their countrymen in the following declaration of facts and principles : —

For the first time since the Civil War the American people have witnessed the calamitous consequences of full and unrestricted Democratic control of the government. It has been a record of unparalleled incapacity, dishonor, and disaster. In administrative management it has ruthlessly sacrificed indispensable revenue, entailed an unceasing deficit, eked out ordinary current expenses with borrowed money, piled up the public debt by $262,000,000 in time of peace, forced an adverse balance of trade, kept a perpetual menace hanging over the redemption fund, pawned American credit to alien syndicates, and reversed all the measures and results of successful Republican rule.

In the broad effect of its policy it has precipitated panic, blighted industry and trade with prolonged depression, closed factories, reduced work and wages, halted enterprise, and crippled American production while stimulating foreign production for the American market. Every consideration of public safety and individual interest demands that the government shall be rescued from the hands of those who have shown themselves incapable of conducting it without disaster at home and dishonor abroad, and shall be restored to the party which for thirty years administered it with unequalled success and prosperity, and in this connection we heartily indorse the wisdom, the patriotism, and the success of the administration of President Harrison.

We renew and emphasize our allegiance to the policy of protection as the bulwark of American industrial independence and the foundation of American development and prosperity. This true American policy taxes foreign products and encourages home industry; it puts the burden of revenue on foreign goods; it secures the American market for the American producer ; it upholds the American standard of wages for the American workingman ; it puts the factory by the side of the farm, and makes the American farmer less dependent on foreign demand and price ; it diffuses general thrift, and founds the strength of all on the strength of each. In its reasonable application it is just, fair, and impartial, equally opposed to foreign control and domestic monopoly, to sec-tional discrimination and individual favoritism.

We denounce the present Democratic tariff as sectional, injurious to the public credit, and destructive to business enterprise. We demand such an equitable tariff on foreign imports which come into competition with American products as will not only furnish adequate revenue for the necessary expenses of the government, but will protect American labor from degradation to the wage level of other lands. We are not pledged to any particular schedules. The question of rates is a practical question, to be governed by the conditions of the time and of production; the ruling and uncompromising principle is the protection and development of American labor and industry. The country demands a right settlement, and then it wants rest.

We believe the repeal of the reciprocity arrangements negotiated by the last Republican administration was a national calamity, and we demand their renewal and extension on such terms as will equalize our trade with other nations, remove the restrictions which now obstruct the sale of American products in the ports of other countries, and secure enlarged markets for the products of our farms, forests, and factories.

Protection and reciprocity are twin measures of Republican policy and go hand in hand. Democratic rule has recklessly struck down both, and both must be reëstablished. Protection for what we produce; free admission for the necessaries of life which we do not produce; reciprocity agreements of mutual interests which gain open markets for us in return for our open market to others. Protection builds up domestic industry and trade, and secures our own market for ourselves; reciprocity builds up foreign trade and finds an outlet for our surplus.

We condemn the present administration for not keeping faith with the sugar-producers of this country. The Republican party favors such protection as will lead to the production on American soil of all the sugar which the American people use, and for which they pay other countries more than $100,000,000 annually.

To all our products — to those of the mine and the fields, as well as those of the shop and factory; to hemp, to wool, the product of the great industry of sheep husbandry, as well as to the finished woollens of the mills — we promise the most ample protection.

We favor restoring the early American policy of discriminating duties for the upbuilding of our merchant marine and the protection of our shipping in the foreign carrying trade, so that American ships — the product of American labor, employed in American shipyards, sailing under the stars and stripes, and manned, officered, and owned by Americans — may regain the carrying of our foreign commerce.

The Republican party is unreservedly for sound money. It caused the enactment of the law providing for the resumption of specie payments in 1879 ; since then every dollar has been as good as gold.

We are unalterably opposed to every measure calculated to debase our currency or impair the credit of our country. We are, therefore, opposed to the free coinage of silver, except by international agreement with the leading commercial nations of the world, which we pledge ourselves to promote, and until such agreement can be obtained the existing gold standard must be preserved. All our silver and paper currency must be maintained at parity with gold, and we favor all measures designed to maintain inviolably the obligations of the United States and all our money, whether coin or paper, at the present standard, the standard of the most enlightened nations of the earth.

The veterans of the Union armies deserve and should receive fair treatment and generous recognition. Whenever practicable they should be given the preference in the matter of employment, and they are entitled to the enactment of such laws as are best calculated to secure the fulfilment of the pledges made to them in the dark days of the country's peril. We denounce the practice in the Pension Bureau, so recklessly and unjustly carried on by the present administration, of reducing pensions and arbitrarily dropping names from the rolls, as deserving the severest condemnation of the American people.

Our foreign policy should be at all times firm, vigorous, and dignified, and all our interests in the Western hemisphere carefully watched and guarded. The Hawaiian islands should be controlled by the United States, and no foreign power should be permitted to interfere with them ; the Nicaragua Canal should be built, owned and operated by the United States ; and by the purchase of the Danish islands we should secure a proper and much-needed naval station in the West Indies.

The massacres in Armenia have aroused the deep sympathy and just indignation of the American people, and we believe that the United States should exercise all the influence it can properly exert to bring these atrocities to an end. In Turkey, American residents have been exposed to the gravest dangers and American property destroyed. There and everywhere American citizens and American property must be absolutely protected at all hazards and at any cost.

We reassert the Monroe doctrine in its full extent, and we reaffirm the right of the United States to give the doctrine effect by responding to the appeal of any American State for friendly intervention in case of European encroachment. We have not interfered and shall not interefere with the existing possessions of any European power in this hemisphere, but those possessions must not on any pretext be extended. We hopefully look forward to the eventual withdrawal of the European powers from this hemisphere, and to the ultimate union of all English-speaking parts of the continent by the free consent of its inhabitants.

From the hour of achieving their own independence, the people of the United States have regarded with sympathy the struggles of other American people to free themselves from European domination. We watch with deep and abiding interest the heroic battle of the Cuban patriots against cruelty and oppression, and our best hopes go out for the full success of their determined contest for liberty.

The government of Spain, having lost control of Cuba, and being unable to protect the property or lives of resident American citizens, or to comply with its treaty obligations, we believe that the government of the United States should actively use its influence and good offices to restore peace and give independence to the island.

The peace and security of the republic and the maintenance of its rightful influence among the nations of the earth demand a naval power commensurate with its position and responsibility. We therefore favor the continued enlargement of the navy and a complete system of harbor and seacoast defences.

For the protection of the quality of our American citizenship and of the wages of our workingmen against the fatal competition of low-priced labor, we demand that the immigration laws be thoroughly enforced, and so extended as to exclude from entrance to the United States those who can neither read nor write.

The civil-service law was placed on the statute book by the Republican party, which has always sustained it, and we renew our repeated declarations that it shall be thoroughly and honestly enforced and extended wherever practicable.

We demand that every citizen of the United States shall be allowed to cast one free and unrestricted ballot, and that such ballot shall be counted and returned as cast.

We proclaim our unqualified condemnation of the uncivilized and barbarous practice, well known as lynching, or killing of human beings suspected or charged with crime, without process of law.

We favor the creation of a national Board of Arbitration to settle and adjust differences which may arise between employers and employees engaged in interstate commerce.

We believe in an immediate return to the free-homestead policy of the Republican party, and urge the passage by Congress of a satisfactory free-homestead measure such as has already passed the House, and is now pending in the Senate.

We favor the admission of the remaining Territories at the earliest practicable date, having due regard to the interests of the people of the Territories and of the United States. All the Federal officers appointed for the Territories should be selected from *bonâ fide* residents thereof, and the right of self-government should be accorded as far as practicable.

We believe the citizens of Alaska should have representation in the Congress of the United States, to the end that needful legislation may be intelligently enacted.

We sympathize with all wise and legitimate efforts to lessen and prevent the evils of intemperance and promote morality.

The Republican party is mindful of the rights and interests of women. Protection of American industries includes equal opportunities, equal pay for equal work, and protection to the home. We favor the admission of women to wider spheres of usefulness, and welcome their coöperation in rescuing the country from Democratic and Populist mismanagement and misrule.

Such are the principles and policies of the Republican party. By these principles we will abide and these policies we will put into execution. We ask for them the considerate judgment of the American people. Confident alike in the history of our great party and in the justice of our cause, we present our platform and our candidates in the full assurance that the election will bring victory to the Republican party and prosperity to the people of the United States.

Immediately after the reading of the platform Senator Henry M. Teller, of Colorado, the leader of the Silver forces, took the floor, and in behalf of a minority of the Committee on Resolutions offered the following as a substitute for the declaration in the platform on the subject of currency and coinage : —

The Republican party favors the use of both gold and silver as equal standard money, and pledges its power to secure the free, unrestricted, and independent coinage of gold and silver at our mints at the ratio of sixteen parts of silver to one of gold.

Mr. Teller pleaded for his substitute in an earnest speech, which virtually recognized the impending defeat of the motion, and left no doubt that an adverse vote would be followed by the withdrawal of himself and his associates from the convention.

At the close of his speech a motion to lay the substitute on the table, which was equivalent to rejecting it, was carried by 818½ ayes to 105½ noes. Sixty-seven of the negative votes were given by delegates from States west of the Missouri River; 33½ by delegates from Southern States; and five by delegates from the Middle West. A separate vote was then taken on the adoption of the financial plank reported by the majority. The result was: ayes 812½, noes 110½. The rest of the platform was adopted by acclamation and with unanimity. Mr. Frank Cannon, United States Senator from Utah, then read a carefully prepared protest signed by many members of the Silver wing of the party, after which thirty-four members of the convention, including four United States senators and two representatives in Congress, with Mr. Teller at their head, solemnly withdrew from the convention.

William McKinley, of Ohio, was nominated as the candidate for President on the first vote, which resulted as follows: —

Whole number of votes	906
Necessary for a choice	453½
William McKinley, Ohio	661½
Thomas B. Reed, Maine	84½
Matthew S. Quay, Pennsylvania	61½
Levi P. Morton, New York	58
William B. Allison, Iowa	35½
J. Donald Cameron, Pennsylvania	1
Blank	4

Garret A. Hobart, of New Jersey, was nominated as the candidate for Vice-President by the following vote: —

Whole number of votes	895
Necessary for a choice	448
Garret A. Hobart, New Jersey	535½
Henry Clay Evans, Tennessee	277½
Morgan G. Bulkeley, Connecticut	39
James A. Walker, Virginia	24
Charles W. Lippitt, Rhode Island	8
Thomas B. Reed, Maine	3
Chauncey M. Depew, New York	3
John M. Thurston, Nebraska	2
Frederick D. Grant, New York	2
Levi P. Morton, New York	1

The Socialist Labor party held a convention in New York city, beginning on the 4th of July and continuing for six days.

Inasmuch as the Democratic convention was close at hand, the newspapers paid but slight attention to its proceedings. No exact statement can be made as to the number of members, or the States from which they came. The following platform was adopted : —

The Socialist Labor party of the United States, in convention assembled, reasserts the inalienable right of all men to life, liberty, and the pursuit of happiness.

With the founders of the American republic, we hold that the purpose of government is to secure every citizen in the enjoyment of this right; but in the light of our social conditions, we hold, furthermore, that no such right can be exercised under a system of economic inequality, essentially destructive of life, of liberty, and of happiness.

With the founders of this republic, we hold that the true theory of politics is that the machinery of government must be owned and controlled by the whole people; but in the light of our industrial development we hold, furthermore, that the true theory of economics is that the machinery of production must likewise belong to the people in common.

To the obvious fact, that our despotic system of economics is the direct opposite of our democratic system of politics, can plainly be traced the existence of a privileged class, the corruption of government by that class, the alienation of public property, public franchises, and public functions to that class, and the abject dependence of the mightiest nations upon that class.

Again, through the perversion of democracy to the ends of plutocracy, labor is robbed of the wealth which it alone produces, is denied the means of self-employment, and, by compulsory idleness in wage slavery, is even deprived of the necessaries of life. Human power and natural forces are thus wasted that the plutocracy may rule. Ignorance and misery, with all their concomitant evils, are perpetuated, that the people may be kept in bondage. Science and invention are diverted from their humane purpose to the enslavement of women and children.

Against such a system the Socialist Labor party once more enters its protest. Once more it reiterates its fundamental declaration, that private property in the natural sources of production and in the instruments of labor is the obvious cause of all economic servitude and political dependence.

The time is fast coming when, in the natural course of social evolution, this system, through the destructive action of its failures and crises on the one hand, and the constructive tendencies of its trusts and other capitalistic combinations on the other hand, shall have worked out its own downfall.

We therefore call upon the wage-workers of the United States, and upon all other honest citizens, to organize under the banner of the Socialist Labor party into a class-conscious body, aware of its rights and determined to conquer them by taking possession of the public powers; so that, held together by an indomitable spirit of solidarity under the most trying conditions of the present class struggle, we may put a summary end to that barbarous struggle by the abolition of classes, the restoration of the land, and of all the means of production, transportation, and distribution to the people as a collective body, and the substitution of the coöperative commonwealth for the present state of planless production, industrial war, and social disorder; a commonwealth in which every worker shall have the free exercise and full benefit of his faculties, multiplied by all the modern factors of civilization.

With a view to immediate improvement in the condition of labor we present the following demands: —

1. Reduction of the hours of labor in proportion to the progress of production.

2. The United States to obtain possession of the mines, railroads, canals, telegraphs, telephones, and all other means of public transportation and communication; the employees to operate the same coöperatively under control of the federal government and to elect their own superior officers, but no employee shall be discharged for political reasons.

3. The municipalities to obtain possession of the local railroads, ferries, water-works, gas-works, electric plants, and all industries requiring municipal franchises; the employees to operate the same coöperatively under control of the municipal administration and to elect their own superior officers, but no employee shall be discharged for political reasons.

4. The public lands to be declared inalienable. Revocation of all land grants to corporations or individuals, the conditions of which have not been complied with.

5. The United States to have the exclusive right to issue money.

6. Congressional legislation providing for the scientific management of forests and waterways, and prohibiting the waste of the natural resources of the country.

7. Inventions to be free to all; the inventors to be remunerated by the nation.

8. Progressive income tax and tax on inheritances; the smaller incomes to be exempt.

9. School education of all children under fourteen years of age to be compulsory, gratuitous, and accessible to all by public assistance in meals, clothing, books, etc., where necessary.

10. Repeal of all pauper, tramp, conspiracy, and sumptuary laws. Unabridged right of combination.

11. Prohibition of the employment of children of school age, and the employment of female labor in occupations detrimental to health or morality. Abolition of the convict labor contract system.

12. Employment of the unemployed by the public authorities (county, city, state, and nation).

13. All wages to be paid in lawful money of the United States. Equalization of women's wages with those of men where equal service is performed.

14. Laws for the protection of life and limb in all occupations, and an efficient employers' liability law.

15. The people to have the right to propose laws and to vote upon all measures of importance, according to the *referendum* principle.

16. Abolition of the veto power of the executive (national, state, and municipal) wherever it exists.

17. Abolition of the United States Senate and all upper legislative chambers.

18. Municipal self-government.

19. Direct vote and secret ballots in all elections. Universal and equal right of suffrage without regard to color, creed, or sex. Election days to be legal holidays. The principle of proportional representation to be introduced.

20. All public officers to be subject to recall by their respective constituencies.

21. Uniform civil and criminal law throughout the United States. Administration of justice to be free of charge. Abolition of capital punishment.

On the sixth day of the session, July 9, the convention made its nominations. It is reported that there was a serious — in the sense of sober, it is to be presumed, as well as in the sense of active — contest for the nomination for President; not that either of the candidates expected to be elected, but because the victory of the party not later than the year 1925 was confidently expected, and it was to be an honor to be the standard-bearer of the party in 1896. Mr. Charles H. Matchett, of New York, was nominated, receiving 43 votes to 23 for Matthew Maguire, of New Jersey, and 4 for William Watkins, of Ohio. Matthew Maguire, of New Jersey, was nominated by acclamation for Vice-President.

The result of the Republican convention intensified public interest in the Democratic national convention, which met at Chicago on July 7. The explicit declaration at St. Louis in favor of the gold standard strengthened the position of the

Silver wing of the Democratic party, which, having a sufficient majority of the delegates, intended in any event to use its power to the utmost.   Meanwhile the control of the national committee was in the hands of the anti-Silver wing, and most of the " old-liners " of the North and West were on the same side.   A strenuous effort was determined on to prevent, if possible, the adoption of a free-coinage resolution.   All the arts known to politicians were resorted to; as the event proved, without avail.   The national committee proposed as temporary chairman Senator David B. Hill, of New York.   His election was challenged on the floor of the convention, and after a heated debate Senator John W. Daniel, of Virginia, the candidate of the Free Silver men, was chosen in his stead by a vote of 556 to 349.   On this, as on most other votes in the convention, the unit rule was observed; that is, the majority of a state delegation cast the whole vote of the State for or against a motion, or for a particular candidate.   On the second day of the session the Silver forces were augmented by three changes in the membership proposed in the report of the Committee on Credentials :   (1) the representation of each Territory was increased from two members to six ;   (2) the Gold Standard delegation from Nebraska was unseated and a delegation favorable to Silver, headed by Mr. William J. Bryan, was admitted ; and (3) four Silver delegates were substituted for four Gold delegates from Michigan, which gave the Silver party the control of the twenty-eight votes of that State. After these changes had been made, Senator Stephen M. White, of California, was made permanent president of the convention.

On the third day of the session the platform was reported as follows : —

We, the Democrats of the United States in national convention assembled, do reaffirm our allegiance to those great essential principles of justice and liberty, upon which our institutions are founded, and which the Democratic party has advocated from Jefferson's time to our own, — freedom of speech, freedom of the press, freedom of conscience, the preservation of personal rights, the equality of all citizens before the law, and the faithful observance of constitutional limitations.

During all these years the Democratic party has resisted the tendency of selfish interests to the centralization of governmental power, and steadfastly maintained the integrity of the dual scheme of government established by the founders of this republic of republics. Under its guidance and teachings, the great principle of local self-government has found its best expression in the maintenance of the rights of the States, and in its assertion of the necessity of confining the general government to the exercise of the powers granted by the Constitution of the United States.

The Constitution of the United States guarantees to every citizen the rights of civil and religious liberty. The Democratic party has always been the exponent of political liberty and religious freedom, and it renews its obligations and reaffirms its devotion to these fundamental principles of the Constitution.

Recognizing that the money question is paramount to all others at this time, we invite attention to the fact that the federal Constitution names silver and gold together as the money metals of the United States, and that the first coinage law passed by Congress under the Constitution made the silver dollar the money unit, and admitted gold to free coinage at a ratio based upon the silver dollar unit.

We declare that the act of 1873 demonetizing silver without the knowledge or approval of the American people has resulted in the appreciation of gold and a corresponding fall in the prices of commodities produced by the people; a heavy increase in the burden of taxation and of all debts, public and private; the enrichment of the money-lending class at home and abroad; the prostration of industry and impoverishment of the people.

We are unalterably opposed to monometallism, which has locked fast the prosperity of an industrial people in the paralysis of hard times. Gold monometallism is a British policy, and its adoption has brought other nations into financial servitude to London. It is not only un-American, but anti-American, and it can be fastened on the United States only by the stifling of that spirit and love of liberty which proclaimed our political independence in 1776 and won it in the war of the Revolution.

We demand the free and unlimited coinage of both silver and gold at the present legal ratio of sixteen to one without waiting for the aid or consent of any other nation. We demand that the standard silver dollar shall be a full legal tender, equally with gold, for all debts, public and private, and we favor such legislation as will prevent for the future the demonetization of any kind of legal tender money by private contract.

We are opposed to the policy and practice of surrendering to the holders of the obligations of the United States the option reserved by law to the government of redeeming such obligations in either silver coin or gold coin.

We are opposed to the issuing of interest-bearing bonds of the United States in time of peace, and condemn the trafficking with banking syndicates, which, in exchange for bonds and at enormous profit to themselves, supply the federal treasury with gold to maintain the policy of gold monometallism.

Congress alone has the power to coin and issue money, and President Jackson declared that this power could not be delegated to corporations or individuals. We therefore denounce the issuance of notes intended to circulate as money by national banks as in derogation of the Constitution, and we demand that all paper which is made a legal tender for public and private debts, or which is receivable for duties to the United States, shall be issued by the government of the United States and shall be redeemable in coin.

We hold that tariff duties should be levied for purposes of revenue, such duties to be so adjusted as to operate equally throughout the country, and not discriminate between class or section, and that taxation should be limited by the needs of the government honestly and economically administered.

We denounce as disturbing to business the Republican threat to restore the McKinley law, which has twice been condemned by the people in national elections, and which, enacted under the false plea of protection to home industry, proved a prolific breeder of trusts and monopolies, enriched the few at the expense of the many, restricted trade, and deprived the producers of the great American staples of access to their natural markets.

Until the money question is settled we are opposed to any agitation for further changes in our tariff laws, except such as are necessary to meet the deficit in revenue caused by the adverse decision of the Supreme Court on the income tax. But for this decision by the Supreme Court, there would be no deficit in the revenue under the law passed by a Democratic Congress in strict pursuance of the uniform decisions of that court for nearly one hundred years, that court having in that decision sustained constitutional objections to its enactment which had previously been overruled by the ablest judges who have ever sat on that bench. We declare that it is the duty of Congress to use all the constitutional power which remains after that decision, or which may come from its reversal by the court as it may hereafter be constituted, so that the burdens of taxation may be equally and impartially laid, to the end that wealth may bear its due proportion of the expenses of the government.

We hold that the most efficient way of protecting American labor is to prevent the importation of foreign pauper labor to compete with it in the home market, and that the value of the home market to our American farmers and artisans is greatly reduced by a vicious monetary system which depresses the prices of their products below the cost of production, and thus deprives them of the means of purchasing the products of our home manufactories; and, as labor creates the wealth of the country, we demand the passage of such laws as may be necessary to protect it in all its rights.

We are in favor of the arbitration of differences between employers engaged in interstate commerce and their employees, and recommend such legislation as is necessary to carry out this principle.

The absorption of wealth by the few, the consolidation of our leading railroad systems, and the formation of trusts and pools require a stricter control by the federal government of those arteries of commerce. We demand the enlargement of the powers of the interstate commerce commission, and such restrictions and guarantees in the control of railroads as will protect the people from robbery and oppression.

We denounce the profligate waste of the money wrung from the people by oppressive taxation and the lavish appropriations of recent Republican Congresses, which have kept taxes high, while the labor that pays them is unemployed and the products of the people's toil are depressed in price till they no longer repay the cost of production. We demand a return to that simplicity and economy which befits a democratic government and a reduction in the number of useless offices, the salaries of which drain the substance of the people.

We denounce arbitrary interference by federal authorities in local affairs as a violation of the Constitution of the United States and a crime against free institutions, and we especially object to government by injunction as a new and highly dangerous form of oppression by which federal judges, in contempt of the laws of the States and rights of citizens, become at once legislators, judges, and executioners; and we approve the bill passed at the last session of the United States Senate, and now pending in the House of Representatives, relative to contempts in federal courts and providing for trials by jury in certain cases of contempt.

No discrimination should be indulged in by the government of the United States in favor of any of its debtors. We approve of the refusal of the Fifty-third Congress to pass the Pacific Railroad funding bill, and denounce the effort of the present Republican Congress to enact a similar measure.

Recognizing the just claims of deserving Union soldiers, we heartily indorse the rule of the present Commissioner of Pensions, that no name shall be arbitrarily dropped from the pension roll; and the fact of enlistment and service should be deemed conclusive evidence against disease and disability before enlistment.

We favor the admission of the Territories of New Mexico, Arizona, and Oklahoma into the Union as States, and we favor the early admission of all the Territories having the necessary population and resources to entitle them to statehood, and, while they remain Territories, we hold that the officials appointed to administer the government of any Territory, together with the District of Columbia and Alaska, should be *bonâ fide* residents of the Territory or District in which the duties are to be performed. The Democratic party believes in home rule, and that all public lands of the United States should be appropriated to the establishment of free homes for American citizens.

We recommend that the Territory of Alaska be granted a delegate in Congress, and that the general land and timber laws of the United States be extended to said Territory.

The Monroe doctrine, as originally declared and as interpreted by succeeding Presidents, is a permanent part of the foreign policy of the United States, and must at all times be maintained.

We extend our sympathy to the people of Cuba in their heroic struggle for liberty and independence.

We are opposed to life tenure in the public service, except as provided in the Constitution. We favor appointments based upon merit, fixed terms of office, and such an administration of the civil service laws as will afford equal opportunities to all citizens of ascertained fitness.

We declare it to be the unwritten law of this republic, established by custom and usage of a hundred years, and sanctioned by the examples of the greatest and wisest of those who founded and have maintained our government, that no man should be eligible for a third term of the presidential office.

The federal government should care for and improve the Mississippi River and other great waterways of the republic, so as to secure for the interior States easy and cheap transportation to tidewater. When any waterway of the republic is of sufficient importance to demand aid of the government, such aid should be extended upon a definite plan of continuous work until permanent improvement is secured.

Confiding in the justice of our cause and the necessity of its success at the polls, we submit the foregoing declaration of principles and purposes to the considerate judgment of the American people. We invite the support of all citizens who approve them, and who desire to have them made effective, through legislation, for the relief of the people and the restoration of the country's prosperity.

A minority of the Committee on Resolutions, consisting of the members from sixteen States, submitted a dissenting report, expressing their inability to give their assent to " many declarations " of the platform. " Some are ill-considered and ambiguously phrased, while others are extreme and revolutionary of the well-recognized principles of the party." They offered two amendments, the first a substitute for the financial plank, as follows : —

We declare our belief that the experiment on the part of the United States alone of free silver coinage and a change in the existing standard of value, independently of the action of other great nations, would not only imperil our finances, but would retard, or entirely prevent, the establishment of international bimetallism, to which the efforts of the government should be steadily directed.

It would place this country at once upon a silver basis, impair contracts, disturb business, diminish the purchasing power of the wages of labor, and inflict irreparable evils upon our nation's commerce and industry.

Until international coöperation among leading nations for the coinage of silver can be secured, we favor the rigid maintenance of the existing gold standard as essential to the preservation of our national credit, the redemption of our public pledges, and the keeping inviolate of our country's honor.

We insist that all our paper currency shall be kept at a parity with gold. The Democratic party is the party of hard money, and is opposed to legal tender paper money as a part of our permanent financial system, and we therefore favor the gradual retirement and cancellation of all United States notes and treasury notes, under such legislative provisions as will prevent undue contraction.

We demand that the national credit shall be resolutely maintained at all times and under all circumstances.

The other resolution was offered as an addition to the platform : —

We commend the honesty, economy, courage, and fidelity of the present Democratic administration.

A most earnest debate ensued upon the Free Silver policy, the most dramatic and interesting event of which was an impassioned speech by Mr. William J. Bryan, of Nebraska. This gentleman excited the Silver men to the highest pitch of enthusiasm by his oratory, and at once leaped into prominence as a presidential candidate. Indeed, it was believed that, if a vote had been taken on that day, he would have been nominated almost by acclamation. The financial plank offered by the minority was rejected by ayes 303, noes 626; and the resolution commendatory of President Cleveland's administration was defeated by ayes 357, noes 564. In all the votes thus far reported, the minority consisted of the members from New England, — except a few from Maine and Massachusetts, — the coast States as far south as Maryland, and the delegates from Wisconsin, Minnesota, and South Dakota. Senator Hill had offered, in addition to the amendments proposed by the minority of the committee, two other amendments. The first proposed to insert at the end of the clause opposing "the demonetization of any kind of legal tender money by private contract" the following proviso: —

But it should be carefully provided by law at the same time that any change in the monetary standard should not apply to existing contracts.

The other amendment was to add at the end of the financial plank the following pledge: —

Our advocacy of the independent free coinage of silver being based on the belief that such coinage will effect and maintain a parity between gold and silver at the ratio of sixteen to one, we declare as a pledge of our sincerity that, if such free coinage shall fail to effect such parity within one year from its enactment by law, such coinage shall thereupon be suspended.

Both of these amendments were rejected without a division, and the platform as a whole, unamended, was then adopted by yeas 628, nays 301.

The overwhelming victory of the Silver wing of the party made it certain that the defeated minority would be unable to prevent a nomination under the two-thirds rule always governing Democratic conventions. The delegates who had contended so earnestly against the adoption of the free coinage plank were for the most part not men to yield their convictions because they had been outvoted. They did not withdraw from the convention, but on every convenient occasion they reiterated their determination not to accept the platform adopted, and not to take part in the nomination of candidates. On the first vote for a candidate for President, 178 delegates refused to be recorded, including the entire delegations of three States. William J. Bryan, of Nebraska, was nominated for President on the fifth vote. The successive trials resulted as follows: —

	1st.	2d.	3d.	4th.	5th.
Whole number of votes	752	768	768	769	768
Necessary for a choice (two thirds) . .	502	512	512	513	512
William J. Bryan, Nebraska	119	190	219	280	500
Richard P. Bland, Missouri.	235	283	291	241	106
Robert E. Pattison, Pennsylvania . .	95	100	97	97	95
Horace Boies, Iowa	85	41	36	33	26
Joseph S. C. Blackburn, Kentucky . .	83	41	27	27	–
John R. McLean, Ohio	54	53	54	46	–
Claude Matthews, Indiana	37	33	34	36	31
Benjamin R. Tillman, South Carolina .	17	–	–	–	–
Sylvester Pennoyer, Oregon	8	8	–	–	–
Henry M. Teller, Colorado	8	8	–	–	–
Adlai E. Stevenson, Illinois	7	10	9	8	8
William E. Russell, Massachusetts . .	2	–	–	–	–
James E. Campbell, Ohio	1	–	–	–	–
David B. Hill, New York	1	1	1	1	1
David Turpie, Indiana	–	–	–	–	1
Not voting	178	162	162	162	162

The fifth vote, it will be seen, left Mr. Bryan twelve votes short of a nomination. After the roll-call was completed and before the result was announced, 78 delegates who had supported other candidates transferred their votes to Mr. Bryan and gave him the nomination. Arthur Sewall, of Maine, was nominated for Vice-President. Five trials were necessary to effect this nomination. They resulted as follows : —

	1st.	2d.	3d.	4th.	5th.
Whole number of votes	670	675	675	677	679
Necessary for a choice (two thirds) . .	447	450	450	452	453
Arthur Sewall, Maine	100	37	97	261	568
Joseph C. Sibley, Pennsylvania . . .	163	113	50	–	–
John R. McLean, Ohio	111	158	210	296	32
George F. Williams, Massachusetts . .	76	16	15	9	9
Richard P. Bland, Missouri.	62	294	255	–	–
Walter A. Clark, North Carolina . .	50	22	22	46	22
John R. Williams, Illinois	22	13	–	–	–
William F. Harrity, Pennsylvania . .	21	21	19	11	11
Horace Boies, Iowa	20	–	–	–	–
Joseph S. C. Blackburn, Kentucky . .	20	–	–	–	–
John W. Daniel, Virginia	11	1	6	54	36
James H. Lewis, Washington	11	–	–	–	–
Robert E. Pattison, Pennsylvania . .	–	1	1	1	1
Henry M. Teller, Colorado	1	–	–	–	–
Stephen M. White, California	1	–	–	–	–
George W. Fithian, Illinois	1	–	–	–	–
Not voting.	260	255	255	253	251

It long had been evident that this canvass was to witness an unexampled shifting of the line between parties. In those parts of the country where the silver idea was almost universally dominant, there had been an instant bolt of Republicans from the platform of the St. Louis convention. And now a revolt of Democrats set in, not only greater in extent than any other in the history of American politics, but distinctly unlike all others. Many of the oldest and most consistent Democratic journals proclaimed in emphatic terms their determination not to continue their support of the party, and not a few of them boldly advocated the election of Mr. McKinley. The dissension extended to all parts of the country; and, although it was most pronounced in the Eastern section, it was so widespread that even in Kentucky, where the victory of the Silver wing had virtually enabled that faction to carry its point in the national convention, there was at the beginning of the canvass not one daily newspaper that advocated the election of Mr. Bryan. At first, — so strong and aggressive were the opponents of platform and candidates within the party, — it was said openly by the leaders that in certain of the Eastern States no electors would even be nominated by the Democrats. The modification of this situation belongs to a later stage of the canvass.

The next conventions in point of time were those of the People's party, commonly called the Populists, and of the Silver party, both of which met at St. Louis on July 22. If the Chicago convention had driven out of the Democratic party thousands of its oldest members and leaders, it had made easy the coöperation of other thousands of Populists; indeed, in the view of many of the leaders of the party, the principles of the Populists were most effectively to be promoted by accepting the candidates nominated at Chicago. Yet there was an earnest faction of the party which deprecated alliance or association with any other organization. The picturesque term " Middle-of-the-road men " was applied to and adopted by them, as indicating the independent course between the two old historic parties which they thought it judicious to take. The acceptance of the Democratic ticket involved the support of Mr. Sewall as the candidate for Vice-President, — a nomination which was especially obnoxious to them. The convention organized by the choice of Senator Marion C. Butler, of North Carolina, as temporary chairman. Senator William V. Allen, of Nebraska, was the permanent president. A test of strength between the " Middle-of-the-road " Populists and those who were favorable to an alliance with the Democrats was made upon an amendment offered to the report of the

Committee on Rules. The Middle-of-the-road wing proposed that the usual order of proceeding should be reversed, and that a candidate for Vice-President be nominated before the candidate for President. The motion was carried by ayes 785, noes 615. The platform was reported on July 24, as follows : —

The People's party, assembled in national convention, reaffirms its allegiance to the principles declared by the founders of the republic, and also to the fundamental principles of just government as enunciated in the platform of the party in 1892.

We recognize that through the connivance of the present and preceding administrations the country has reached a crisis in its national life as predicted in our declaration four years ago, and that prompt and patriotic action is the supreme duty of the hour. We realize that while we have political independence our financial and industrial independence is yet to be attained by restoring to our country the constitutional control and exercise of the functions necessary to a people's government, which functions have been basely surrendered by our public servants to corporate monopolies. The influence of European money-changers has been more potent in shaping legislation than the voice of the American people. Executive power and patronage have been used to corrupt our legislatures and defeat the will of the people, and plutocracy has been enthroned upon the ruins of democracy. To restore the government intended by the fathers and for the welfare and prosperity of this and future generations, we demand the establishment of an economic and financial system which shall make us masters of our own affairs, and independent of European control, by the adoption of the following declaration of principles : —

FINANCE.

1. We demand a national money, safe and sound, issued by the general government only, without the intervention of banks of issue, to be a full legal tender for all debts, public and private ; a just, equitable, and efficient means of distribution direct to the people and through the lawful disbursements of the government.

2. We demand the free and unrestricted coinage of silver and gold at the present legal ratio of sixteen to one, without waiting for the consent of foreign nations.

3. We demand that the volume of circulating medium be speedily increased to an amount sufficient to meet the demands of business and population and to restore the just level of prices of labor and production.

4. We denounce the sale of bonds and the increase of the interest-bearing debt made by the present administration as unnecessary and without authority of law, and demand that no more bonds be issued except by specific act of Congress.

5. We demand such legislation as will prevent the demonetization of the lawful money of the United States by private contract.

6. We demand that the government, in payment of its obligations, shall use its option as to the kind of lawful money in which they are to be paid, and we denounce the present and preceding administrations for surrendering this option to the holders of government obligations.

7. We demand a graduated income tax, to the end that aggregated wealth shall bear its just proportion of taxation; and we regard the recent decision of the Supreme Court relative to the income tax law as a misinterpretation of the Constitution, and an invasion of the rightful powers of Congress over the subject of taxation.

8. We demand that postal savings banks be established by the government for the safe deposit of the savings of the people and to facilitate exchange.

TRANSPORTATION.

1. Transportation being a means of exchange and a public necessity, government should own and operate the railroads in the interests of the people and on a non-partisan basis, to the end that all may be accorded the same treatment in transportation, and that the tyranny and political power now exercised by the great railroad corporations, which result in the impairment, if not the destruction, of the political rights and personal liberties of the citizen, may be destroyed. Such ownership is to be accomplished gradually, in a manner consistent with sound public policy.

2. The interest of the United States in the public highways, built with public moneys, and the proceeds of extensive grants of land to the Pacific railroads should never be alienated, mortgaged, or sold, but guarded and protected for the general welfare as provided by the laws organizing such railroads. The foreclosure of existing liens of the United States on these roads should at once follow default in the payment thereof by the debtor-companies; and at the foreclosure sales of said roads the government shall purchase the same if it become necessary to protect its interests therein, or if they can be purchased at a reasonable price; and the government shall operate said railroads as public highways for the benefit of the whole people, and not in the interest of the few, under suitable provisions for protection of life and property, giving to all transportation interests equal privileges and equal rates for fares and freight.

3. We denounce the present infamous schemes for refunding these debts, and demand that the laws now applicable thereto be executed and administered according to their true intent and spirit.

4. The telegraph, like the post-office system, being a necessity for the transmission of news, should be owned and operated by the government in the interest of the people.

LAND.

1. The true policy demands that national and state legislation shall be such as will ultimately enable every prudent and industrious citizen to secure a home, and therefore the lands should not be monopolized for speculative purposes. All lands now held by railroads and other corporations in excess of their actual needs should by lawful means be reclaimed by the government and held for actual settlers only, and subject to the right of every human being to acquire a home upon the soil, and private land monopoly, as well as alien ownership, should be prohibited.

2. We condemn the frauds by which the land grants to the Pacific railroad companies have, through the connivance of the interior department, robbed multitudes of actual *bonâ fide* settlers of their homes and miners of their claims, and we demand legislation by Congress which will enforce the exemption of mineral land from such grants after as well as before the patent.

3. We demand that *bonâ fide* settlers on all public lands be granted free homes as provided in the national homestead law, and that no exception be made in the case of Indian reservations when opened for settlement, and that all lands not now patented come under this demand.

DIRECT LEGISLATION.

We favor a system of direct legislation through the initiative and *referendum* under proper constitutional safeguards.

GENERAL PROPOSITIONS.

1. We demand the election of President, Vice-President, and United States senators by a direct vote of the people.

2. We tender to the patriotic people of Cuba our deepest sympathy in their heroic struggle for political freedom and independence, and we believe the time has come when the United States, the great republic of the world, should recognize that Cuba is and of right ought to be, a free and independent state.

3. We favor home rule in the Territories and the District of Columbia, and the early admission of Territories as States.

4. All public salaries should be made to correspond to the price of labor and its products.

5. In times of great industrial depression, idle labor should be employed on public works as far as practicable.

6. The arbitrary course of the courts in assuming to imprison citizens for indirect contempt, and ruling by injunction, should be prevented by proper legislation.

7. We favor just pensions for our disabled Union soldiers.

8. Believing that the elective franchise and an untrammeled ballot are essential to a government of, for, and by the people, the People's party condemn the wholesale system of disfranchisement adopted in some of the States, as unrepublican and undemocratic, and we declare it to be the duty of the several state legislatures to take such action as will secure a full, free, and fair ballot and an honest count.

9. While the foregoing propositions constitute the platform upon which our party stands, and for the vindication of which its organization will be maintained, we recognize that the great and pressing issue of the present campaign upon which the present presidential election will turn is the financial question, and upon this great and specific issue between the parties we cordially invite the aid and coöperation of all organizations and citizens agreeing with us upon this vital question.

There were three distinct minority reports from the Committee on Resolutions, each proposing amendments to the platform. All of them, together with several independent motions to amend, were rejected, and the platform as printed above was adopted.

Thomas E. Watson, of Georgia, was nominated for Vice-President on the first vote, which resulted, on the roll-call, as follows : —

Whole number of votes	1337
Necessary for a choice	669
Thomas E. Watson, Georgia	$539\frac{3}{4}$
Arthur Sewall, Maine	$257\frac{1}{8}$
Frank Burkett, Mississippi	$190\frac{3}{4}$
Harry Skinner, North Carolina	$142\frac{1}{4}$
A. L. Mimms, Tennessee	$118\frac{5}{16}$
Mann Page, Virginia	$89\frac{5}{16}$

After the votes of all the States were announced, numerous changes took place, and Mr. Watson was declared nominated. No final declaration of the actual numbers seems to have been made.

William J. Bryan, of Nebraska, was nominated for President. The first vote resulted as follows : —

```
Whole number of votes . . . . . . . . . . 1375
Necessary for a choice . . . . . . . . . . .  698
William J. Bryan, Nebraska  . . . . . . . . 1042
S. F. Norton, Illinois . . . . . . . . . . .  321
Eugene V. Debs, Indiana . . . . . . . . . .    8
Ignatius Donnelly, Minnesota . . . . . . . .    3
J. S. Coxey, Ohio  . . . . . . . . . . . . .    1
```

It should be said with reference to the membership of this convention that the representation was on a different basis from that of the conventions of the older parties.   Texas, entitled in those conventions to 30 votes, had 103 votes in the Populist assembly, while New York had but 36.   Kansas had 92 votes, Connecticut but 6.   The number of delegates was determined by the strength of the party in state elections.

The convention of the National Silver party was held at St. Louis on July 22, simultaneously with that of the Populists. Frank G. Newlands, of Nevada, was the temporary chairman, and William P. St. John, of New York, the permanent president.   No vote was taken during the session of the convention which disclosed the number of persons taking part in it, or the States of which they were citizens.   The members, indeed, did not appear as duly accredited delegates, but rather as individual members of the party.   The platform, which was reported on July 23, was as follows : —

The National Silver party of America, in convention assembled, hereby adopts the following declaration of principles : —

First, the paramount issue at this time in the United States is indisputably the money question.   It is between the British gold standard, gold bonds, and bank currency on the one side, and the bimetallic standard, no bonds, government currency, and an American policy on the other.

On this issue we declare ourselves to be in favor of a distinctive American financial system.   We are unalterably opposed to the single gold standard, and demand the immediate return to the constitutional standard of gold and silver, by the restoration by this government, independently of any foreign power, of the unrestricted coinage of both gold and silver into standard money, at the ratio of sixteen to one, and upon terms of exact equality, as they existed prior to 1873; the silver coin to be of full legal tender, equally with gold, for all debts and dues, public and private ; and we demand such legislation as will prevent for the future the destruction of the legal tender quality of any kind of money by private contract.

We hold that the power to control and regulate a paper currency is inseparable from the power to coin money, and hence that all currency intended to circulate as money should be issued, and its volume controlled, by the general government only, and should be a legal tender.

We are unalterably opposed to the issue by the United States of interest-bearing bonds in time of peace, and we denounce as a blunder worse than a crime the present treasury policy, concurred in by a Republican House of Representatives, of plunging the country into debt by hundreds of millions in the vain attempt to maintain the gold standard by borrowing gold; and we demand the payment of all coin obligations of the United States as provided by existing laws, in either gold or silver coin, at the option of the government, and not at the option of the creditor.

The demonetization of silver in 1873 enormously increased the demand for gold, enhancing its purchasing power and lowering all prices measured by that standard; and, since that unjust and indefensible act, the prices of American products have fallen, upon an average, nearly fifty per cent., carrying down with them proportionately the money value of all other forms of property.

Such fall of prices has destroyed the profits of legitimate industry, injuring the producer for the benefit of the non-producer; increasing the burden of the debtor, swelling the gains of the creditor, paralyzing the productive energies of the American people, relegating to idleness vast numbers of willing workers, sending the shadows of despair into the home of the honest toiler, filling the land with tramps and paupers, and building up colossal fortunes at the money centres.

In the effort to maintain the gold standard the country has, within the last two years, in a time of profound peace and plenty, been loaded down with $262,000,000 of additional interest-bearing debt under such circumstances as to allow a syndicate of native and foreign bankers to realize a net profit of millions on a single deal.

It stands confessed that the gold standard can be only upheld by so depleting our paper currency as to force the prices of our products below the European, and even below the Asiatic, level to enable us to sell in foreign markets, thus aggravating the very evils of which our people so bitterly complain, degrading American labor and striking at the foundations of our civilization itself.

The advocates of the gold standard persistently claim that the real cause of our distress is overproduction, — that we have produced so much that it made us poor, — which implies that the true remedy is to close the factory, abandon the farm, and throw a multitude of people out of employment, — a doctrine that leaves us unnerved and disheartened, and absolutely without hope for the future.

We affirm it to be unquestioned that there can be no such economic paradox as overproduction, and at the same time tens of thousands of our fellow-citizens remaining half-clothed and half-fed, and piteously clamoring for the common necessities of life.

Over and above all other questions of policy, we are in favor of restoring to the people of the United States the time-honored money of the Constitution, — gold and silver, not one but both, — the money of Washington, and Hamilton, and Jefferson, and Monroe, and Jackson, and Lincoln, to the end that the American people may receive honest pay for an honest product; that the American debtor may pay his just obligations in an honest standard, and not in a dishonest and unsound standard, appreciated one hundred per cent. in purchasing power, and no appreciation in debt-paying power; and to the end, further, that silver standard countries may be deprived of the unjust advantage they now enjoy, in the difference in exchange between gold and silver, an advantage which tariff legislation cannot overcome.

We therefore confidently appeal to the people of the United States to hold in abeyance all other questions, however important and even momentous they may appear, to sunder, if need be, all former party ties and affiliations, and unite in one supreme effort to free themselves and their children from the domination of the money power, — a power more destructive than any which has ever been fastened upon the civilized men of any race or in any age. And upon the consummation of our desires and efforts we invoke the aid of all patriotic American citizens, and the gracious favor of Divine Providence.

William J. Bryan, of Nebraska, was nominated for President, and Arthur Sewall, of Maine, for Vice-President. Both nominations were made by acclamation.

Immediately after the adjournment of the Democratic convention a movement was set on foot to organize into a party those whom that convention had turned, politically, out of doors. There were thousands of such men, who would not accept a platform which their spokesmen at Chicago had pronounced "extreme" and "revolutionary," and who nevertheless felt that it would be impossible to vote for the Republican candidates. The result of repeated conferences among the leaders of this group was a delegate convention which was held at Indianapolis on September 2. Forty-one States and three Territories were represented. There were no delegates pre-

sent from Idaho, Nevada, Utah and Wyoming. The name
of National Democratic party was adopted as a designation.
Governor Roswell P. Flower, of New York, was the temporary chairman, and Senator Donelson Caffery, of Louisiana,
the permanent president, of the convention. The platform,
reported September 3 and unanimously adopted, was as follows : —

This convention has assembled to uphold the principles on
which depend the honor and welfare of the American people, in
order that Democrats throughout the Union may unite their patriotic efforts to avert disaster from their country and ruin from
their party.

The Democratic party is pledged to equal and exact justice to
all men, of every creed and condition; to the largest freedom of
the individual consistent with good government; to the preservation of the federal government in its constitutional vigor, and
to the support of the States in all their just rights ; to economy in
the public expenditures; to the maintenance of the public faith
and sound money; and it is opposed to paternalism and all class
legislation.

The declarations of the Chicago convention attack individual
freedom, the right of private contract, the independence of the
judiciary, and the authority of the President to enforce Federal
laws. They advocate a reckless attempt to increase the price of
silver by legislation, to the debasement of our monetary standard,
and threaten unlimited issues of paper money by the government.
They abandon for Republican allies the Democratic cause of tariff
reform, to court the favor of protectionists to their fiscal heresy.

In view of these and other grave departures from Democratic
principles, we cannot support the candidates of that convention
nor be bound by its acts.

The Democratic party has survived defeats, but could not sur-
vive a victory won in behalf of the doctrine and policy proclaimed
in its name at Chicago.

The conditions, however, which make possible such utterances
from a national convention are the direct result of class legislation by the Republican party. It still proclaims, as it has for
years, the power and duty of government to raise and maintain
prices by law, and it proposes no remedy for existing evils, except
oppressive and unjust taxation.

The national Democracy here convened therefore renews its
declaration of faith in Democratic principles, especially as applicable to the conditions of the times. Taxation — tariff, excise, or
direct — is rightfully imposed only for public purposes, and not

for private gain. Its amount is justly measured by public expenditures, which should be limited by scrupulous economy. The sum derived by the Treasury from tariff and excise levies is affected by the state of trade and volume of consumption. The amount required by the Treasury is determined by the appropriations made by Congress. The demand of the Republican party for an increase in tariff taxation has its pretext in the deficiency of revenue, which has its causes in the stagnation of trade and reduced consumption, due entirely to the loss of confidence that has followed the Populist threat of free coinage and depreciation of our money, and the Republican practice of extravagant appropriations beyond the needs of good government.

We arraign and condemn the Populist conventions of Chicago and St. Louis for their coöperation with the Republican party in creating these conditions, which are pleaded in justification of a heavy increase of the burdens of the people by a further resort to protection. We therefore denounce protection and its ally, free coinage of silver, as schemes for the personal profit of a few at the expense of the masses, and oppose the two parties which stand for these schemes as hostile to the people of the republic, whose food and shelter, comfort and prosperity, are attacked by higher taxes and depreciated money. In fine, we reaffirm the historic Democratic doctrine of tariff for revenue only.

We demand that henceforth modern and liberal policies toward American shipping shall take the place of our imitation of the restricted statutes of the eighteenth century, which were long ago abandoned by every maritime power but the United States, and which, to the nation's humiliation, have driven American capital and enterprise to the use of alien flags and alien crews, have made the Stars and Stripes almost an unknown emblem in foreign ports, and have virtually extinguished the race of American seamen. We oppose the pretence that discriminating duties will promote shipping; that scheme is an invitation to commercial warfare upon the United States, un-American in the light of our great commercial treaties, offering no gain whatever to American shipping, while greatly increasing ocean freights on our agricultural and manufactured products.

The experience of mankind has shown that, by reason of their natural qualities, gold is the necessary money of the large affairs of commerce and business, while silver is conveniently adapted to minor transactions, and the most beneficial use of both together can be insured only by the adoption of the former as a standard of monetary measure, and the maintenance of silver at a parity with gold by its limited coinage under suitable safeguards of law. Thus the largest possible enjoyment of both metals is gained with a value universally accepted throughout the world, which constitutes the only practical bimetallic currency, assuring the most stable standard, and especially the best and safest money for all who earn their livelihood by labor or the produce of husbandry. They cannot suffer when paid in the best money known to man, but are the peculiar and most defenceless victims of a debased and fluctuating currency, which offers continual profits to the money changer at their cost.

Realizing these truths, demonstrated by long and public inconvenience and loss, the Democratic party, in the interests of the masses and of equal justice to all, practically established by the legislation of 1834 and 1853 the gold standard of monetary measurement, and likewise entirely divorced the government from banking and currency issues. To this long-established Democratic policy we adhere, and insist upon the maintenance of the gold standard, and of the parity therewith of every dollar issued by the government, and are firmly opposed to the free and unlimited coinage of silver and to the compulsory purchase of silver bullion. But we denounce also the further maintenance of the present costly patchwork system of national paper currency as a constant source of injury and peril. We assert the necessity of such intelligent currency reform as will confine the government to its legitimate functions, completely separated from the banking business, and afford to all sections of our country uniform, safe, and elastic bank currency under governmental supervision, measured in volume by the needs of business.

The fidelity, patriotism, and courage with which President Cleveland has fulfilled his great public trust, the high character of his administration, its wisdom and energy in the maintenance of civil order and the enforcement of the laws, its equal regard for the rights of every class and every section, its firm and dignified conduct of foreign affairs, and its sturdy persistence in upholding the credit and honor of the nation, are fully recognized by the Democratic party, and will secure to him a place in history beside the fathers of the republic.

We also commend the administration for the great progress made in the reform of the public service, and we indorse its effort to extend the merit system still further. We demand that no backward step be taken, but that the reform be supported and advanced until the un-Democratic spoils system of appointments shall be eradicated.

We demand strict economy in the appropriations and in the administration of the government.

We favor arbitration for the settlement of international disputes.

We favor a liberal policy of pensions to deserving soldiers and sailors of the United States.

The Supreme Court of the United States was wisely established by the framers of our Constitution as one of the three coördinate branches of the government. Its independence and authority to interpret the law of the land without fear or favor must be maintained. We condemn all efforts to degrade that tribunal or impair the confidence and respect which it has deservedly held.

The Democratic party ever has maintained, and ever will maintain, the supremacy of law, the independence of its judicial administration, the inviolability of contracts, and the obligations of all good citizens to resist every illegal trust, combination, or attempt against the just rights of property and the good order of society, in which are bound up the peace and happiness of our people.

Believing these principles to be essential to the well-being of the republic, we submit them to the consideration of the American people.

John M. Palmer, of Illinois, was nominated for President on the first vote. He received $769\frac{1}{2}$ votes; General Edward S. Bragg, of Wisconsin, $118\frac{1}{2}$ votes. General Simon B. Buckner, of Kentucky, was nominated by acclamation for Vice-President.

The canvass so remarkably begun continued to be unique and sensational to the end. The Republicans who seceded from the convention at St. Louis, and most of those who agreed with them on the silver question, made common cause with the Democrats. The dissident Democrats were divided in their course of action, but were animated by one and the same purpose, namely, to defeat the regular candidates of their own party in the only possible way, by helping the election of Mr. McKinley. Where a separate organization seemed to promise to draw away more votes from Mr. Bryan, they rallied around the "National Democratic" standard. Where direct support of the Republican candidates seemed necessary, they were ready to give that support. Many of them participated in the nomination of National Democratic candidates for office, and even addressed audiences on the stump in favor of them, in order to draw away votes from Mr. Bryan; but they themselves voted for McKinley. The Prohibition party, never large, was divided; the faction which had insisted at the national convention, that the question of the sale of intoxicating liquor was the great issue before the people, could not hold its own members to that position; the other faction was strongly attracted, in a body, toward the coalesced forces of Free Silver. Even the Populists were in a state of hopeless dissension. It was apparent to the merest tyro in politics that a separate electoral ticket in any State for Bryan and Watson was as little in favor of Bryan as the ticket for Palmer and Buckner. In short, the " Middle-of-the-road " programme was one of practical though undeclared hostility to the head of the ticket it professed to support. This fact was recognized by many of the leaders of the party, especially by those who had been intrusted with authority to speak in the name of the party. Mr. Watson, the candidate for Vice-President, reproached them for taking a course which he regarded as resulting in a sacrifice of himself, of the principles of the Populist party, and of its separate organization. It does not seem unjust to them to surmise that they were, in fact, chiefly desirous of the election of Mr. Bryan, and that at any cost to Mr. Watson they would do that which they thought would contribute most to the success of the head of the ticket.

At first sight the action of the Democratic convention, in taking a position where a great number of the members of the party could not support platform and candidates without a tremendous sacrifice of principle, might seem the height of political folly. Examined more carefully and critically, the reason of their action and the justification of it are obvious. The leaders in the Silver movement had no hope of success in a canvass based on the tariff issue. There was therefore nothing to lose by shifting the field of contest. In taking a firm stand in favor of free coinage, these men doubtless had two things in view, as to both of which the event showed their judgment to have been sound : first, that, whether it were self-consistent or not, the great body of the party would continue to support the ticket; and, secondly, that an addition of the Populist vote to the Democratic vote would in many of the States convert a minority into a majority. They were sure, moreover, that all the so-called " Silver States " would give their electoral votes to the Silver candidate; and were confident that in all the States there were many Silver Republicans who would leave their party rather than vote for the gold standard. In the early days of the canvass these facts impressed themselves so strongly upon the Republicans that many of them believed Mr. Bryan's chances of election to be alarmingly good. The voters had never stood up to be counted on the silver question. Democrats who had declared most solemnly that they could never be drawn into the support of Free Silver went back into the party; some who would not give their assent to the platform nevertheless announced their purpose to vote for the candidates. The whole of the extreme West and the Pacific coast seemed so devoted to the cause of Free Silver that Republicans were inclined to concede all those States to Mr. Bryan.

The first notable event of the canvass was the appearance of Mr. Bryan in New York city, where he made a speech. The time was midsummer, the most unpropitious season that could have been chosen, and the extreme heat that prevailed made against the candidate. Before the speech the Republicans were in a state of alarm as to the result in November; after it they hardly regarded Mr. Bryan as a dangerous antagonist. A week or two later, indications of the impending result began to appear. Alabama and Arkansas elected state officers in August. In each of the States the Democratic majority showed an increase over that of preceding elections; but no special significance was attached to the fact in any quarter, save in so far as it gave reason for thinking that the new departure of the Democratic party would not cause it a loss of electoral votes in the Southern States. In September Vermont gave a Republican majority of more than 29,000 over all other parties combined — by far the largest majority ever given in a Vermont state election. Next came the election in Maine, where the Republican candidate for governor received more than two thirds of the whole vote, and had a majority of 42,000 over the combined opposition. In these States the result alarmed the Democrats as little as the Southern elections had disturbed the Republicans. Nevertheless, after the event we can see that it foreshadowed the election of Mr. McKinley. It indicated the drift of public sentiment throughout the North. The causes which produced the great majorities in the two New England States were operating with equal force in Connecticut, New York, New Jersey, and Indiana, — the four doubtful States of the North in former elections, — as well as in the large States of the central Northwest. Yet the supporters of Mr. Bryan looked forward with confidence to the verdict of the people. They were assured that thousands of the voters in every State were concealing their intentions, and while professing to be in favor of Mr. McKinley, and even wearing his badges, would nevertheless cast a quiet vote for Mr. Bryan on election day. Their confidence was fostered by the extraordinary thronging of the people to hear Mr. Bryan, who was travelling almost incessantly for several months in all parts of the country, and addressing many audiences every day. Mr. Bryan's physical endurance under the tremendous strain of his protracted and busy campaign, and the eager desire of the people to see and hear him, were two of the most remarkable incidents of the canvass.

The days and weeks passed in the most intense popular excitement. Almost nothing was discussed but the silver question ; almost nothing excited interest save the prospects of the two candidates. Mr. McKinley's part in the canvass was as active as Mr. Bryan's, although quite different in method. He remained at his home in Canton, Ohio, where he received and addressed hundreds of visiting parties. Excursions to Canton were organized not only all over Ohio, but in other and in some far-distant States. Parties consisting of a large number of persons went in many cases hundreds of miles to call upon Mr. McKinley, to assure him of their support, and to be addressed by him. The Republican candidate was inclined at first to lay more stress upon the tariff policy of his party than upon the importance of maintaining the gold standard. But the paramount interest in the financial question did not allow him to continue on that line, and when he spoke upon the money issue he spoke boldly and courageously.

The Silver forces effected an almost complete fusion. The Populist managers disregarded to a great extent the policy which their national convention had favored, — the " Middle-of-the-road " policy. They were deaf to the somewhat frantic expostulations of Mr. Watson, and effected a close alliance with the Democrats. In twenty-six of the States they made a division of the electors, but in eighteen of these States they allowed the Democrats to have a majority of the candidates on the ticket; in four there was an equal division, and in the other four the Populists had one majority in each. In all the twenty-six States there were 197 Democratic electors and 79 Populist electors on the fusion tickets. Mr. Watson was not so blind as not to see that, even if Mr. Bryan were elected, there

would be no choice of a Vice-President by the electors; that
Mr. Hobart and Mr. Sewall would be the two candidates eligible, under the Constitution, to be voted for by the Senate;
and that Mr. Sewall would probably be elected.   The Populist managers also were fully aware of this fact, but they did
not intend to imperil any chance Mr. Bryan might have by
presenting separate electoral tickets in order to please Mr.
Watson.   In a few States, nevertheless, the " Middle-of-the-
road " men refused to be " sold out " to the Democrats and set
up independent tickets.   For the most part, however, the two
parties worked in harmony.   Indeed, the word " Popocrat "
was invented to describe the combined forces of the two
parties who, on other issues beside that of silver, — notably
the " government by injunction," and the income tax, — were
in full agreement.   The following table shows how, had the
coalition been successful, the electoral votes for Vice-President
would have been distributed in the twenty-six States where
there was a fusion : —

STATES.	Democratic Electors.	Populist Electors.	STATES.	Democratic Electors.	Populist Electors.
Arkansas	5	3	Montana	1	2
California	5	4	Nebraska	4	4
Colorado *	2	2	New Jersey . . .	9	1
Connecticut . . .	5	1	North Carolina . .	5	6
Idaho *	2	1	Ohio	18	5
Illinois	20	4	Oregon	2	2
Indiana	10	5	Pennsylvania . . .	28	4
Iowa	10	3	Utah	1	2
Kentucky	11	2	Washington . . .	2	2
Louisiana	4	4	West Virginia . .	4	2
Massachusetts . .	13	2	Wisconsin	9	3
Michigan	9	4	Wyoming	2	1
Minnesota	4	5			
Missouri	13	4	Total	198	78

* The Populist electors in Colorado and Idaho, and some others in other States voted
for Mr. Sewall for Vice-President.

At the close of the canvass the people were wrought up to
the highest pitch of excitement.   Never before was the display of political emblems so profuse.   The city streets were
decorated from end to end with huge flags and banners bearing
the names of the candidates.   Lithograph portraits of McKinley

or of Bryan were exhibited in the front windows of dwellings and shops. Buttons showing the familiar features were worn in the lappels of their coats by hundreds of thousands, if not by millions, of men and boys.

Almost fourteen million citizens went to the polls. The number of votes given in the table on the next page is 13,936,957, — by far the largest number ever cast at a popular election in any country. Throughout the country the polling was orderly. Although the indications of a great Republican victory had been apparent for weeks, even months, to the most casual observer, many of the supporters of Mr. Bryan entertained hopes, some of them were even confident, of success to the last. The earliest returns gave assurance of an overwhelming majority for Mr. McKinley, and the prognostication was confirmed as one State after another was heard from. The Eastern, Middle, and Central Northwestern States were carried by the Republicans, without an exception, by unprecedented majorities. The South even was not "solid" for Bryan. Only during the reconstruction period had the Republicans ever obtained any electoral votes in the States from Delaware to Texas. Now Delaware, Maryland, and West Virginia gave McKinley substantial majorities; and even Kentucky, the "dark and bloody ground" of the Democratic conflict between the Gold and the Silver forces, yielded him a narrow margin. No northern State east of the Missouri River gave Bryan a single electoral vote, and even on the Pacific slope the Republicans won California and Oregon.

On the other hand the Democrats wrested from the Republicans Kansas and Nebraska, together with the whole group of mining States, except California; and their majority in such States as Arkansas, Alabama, Missouri, and Texas, was immense.

In presenting the accompanying table of the popular vote, it is proper to say that it differs from any other table published. Errors more or less numerous are discoverable in all the tables published by the political almanacs and by Appleton's Annual Cyclopædia. Where the figures given in these tables differ, an attempt has been made to obtain from state authorities the final official figures. In a few cases no response has been made to requests for the true returns. It cannot be claimed for the returns which follow that they are absolutely correct, but they are believed to be more nearly so

POPULAR VOTE.

STATES.	William McKinley, Ohio.	William J. Bryan, Nebraska.	Bryan and Watson.*	John M. Palmer, Illinois.	Joshua Levering, Maryland.	Charles E. Bentley, Nebraska.	Charles H. Matchett, New York.
Alabama	54,737	131,226	24,089	6,462	2,147	–	–
Arkansas . . .	37,512	110,103	–	839	893	–	
California . . .	146,688	144,766	21,730	2,006	2,573	1,047	1,611
Colorado	26,271	161,269	2,389	1	1,717	386	160
Connecticut . . .	110,285	56,740	–	4,336	1,806	–	1,223
Delaware	20,452	16,615	–	966	602	–	–
Florida	11,257	31,958	1,977	1,772	644	–	–
Georgia	60,091	94,672	440	2,708	5,716	–	–
Idaho	6,324	23,192	–		181	–	–
Illinois	607,130	464,523	1,090	6,390	9,796	793	1,147
Indiana	323,754	305,573	–	2,145	3,056	2,267	324
Iowa	289,293	223,741	–	4,516	3,192	352	453
Kansas	159,541	171,810	46,194	1,209	1,921	630	–
Kentucky . . .	218,171	217,890	–	5,114	4,781	–	–
Louisiana . . .	22,037	77,175	–	1,915	–	–	–
Maine	80,461	34,587	2,387	1,866	1,589	–	–
Maryland . . .	136,978	104,746	–	2,507	5,922	136	588
Massachusetts . .	278,976	105,711	15,181	11,749	2,998	–	2,114
Michigan	293,582	237,268	–	6,968	5,025	1,995	297
Minnesota . . .	193,503	139,735	–	3,222	4,363	–	954
Mississippi . . .	5,123	63,793	7,517	1,071	485	–	–
Missouri	304,940	363,652	–	2,355	2,169	293	599
Montana	10,494	42,537	–	–	186	–	–
Nebraska	103,064	115,999	–	2,797	1,243	797	186
Nevada	1,938	8,377	575	–	–	–	–
New Hampshire .	57,444	21,650	379	3,520	779	49	228
New Jersey . . .	221,367	133,675	–	6,373	5,614	–	3,985
New York . . .	819,838	551,369	–	18,950	16,052	–	17,667
North Carolina .	155,222	174,488	–	578	676	245	–
North Dakota . .	26,335	20,686	–	–	358	–	–
Ohio	525,991	477,497	2,615	1,858	5,068	2,716	1,167
Oregon	48,779	46,662	–	977	919	–	–
Pennsylvania . .	728,300	433,230	11,176	10,921	19,274	870	1,683
Rhode Island . .	37,437	14,459	–	1,166	1,160	5	558
South Carolina . .	9,313	58,801	–	824	–	–	–
South Dakota . .	41,042	41,225	–	–	683	–	–
Tennessee . . .	148,773	166,268	4,525	1,951	3,098	–	–
Texas	167,520	370,434	79,572	5,046	1,786	–	–
Utah	13,491	64,607	–	21	–	–	–
Vermont	50,991	10,607	461	1,329	728	–	–
Virginia	135,388	154,985	–	2,127	2,350	–	115
Washington . . .	39,153	51,646	–	1,668	968	148	–
West Virginia . .	104,414	92,927	–	677	1,203	–	–
Wisconsin . . .	268,135	165,523	286	4,584	7,509	346	1,314
Wyoming . . .	10,072	10,655	286	–	136	–	–
Total . . .	7,111,607	6,509,052	222,583	134,645	131,312	13,968	36,373

* Bryan and Watson's vote is included in the vote for W. J. Bryan.

than any previous table. They are made up upon the principle of giving the highest vote for any name on the electoral

ELECTORAL VOTE.

STATES.	PRESIDENT.		VICE-PRESIDENT.		
	McKinley.	Bryan.	Hobart.	Sewall.	Watson.
Alabama	–	11	–	11	–
Arkansas	–	8	–	5	3
California	8	1	8	1	–
Colorado	–	4	–	4	–
Connecticut	6	–	6	–	–
Delaware	3	–	3	–	–
Florida	–	4	–	4	–
Georgia	–	13	–	13	–
Idaho	–	3	–	3	–
Illinois	24	–	24	–	–
Indiana	15	–	15	–	–
Iowa	13	–	13	–	–
Kansas	–	10	–	10	–
Kentucky	12	1	12	1	–
Louisiana	–	8	–	4	4
Maine	6	–	6	–	–
Maryland	8	–	8	–	–
Massachusetts	15	–	15	–	–
Michigan	14	–	14	–	–
Minnesota	9	–	9	–	–
Mississippi	–	9	–	9	–
Missouri	–	17	–	13	4
Montana	–	3	–	2	1
Nebraska	–	8	–	4	4
Nevada	–	3	–	3	–
New Hampshire	4	–	4	–	–
New Jersey	10	–	10	–	–
New York	36	–	36	–	–
North Carolina	–	11	–	6	5
North Dakota	3	–	3	–	–
Ohio	23	–	23	–	–
Oregon	4	–	4	–	–
Pennsylvania	32	–	32	–	–
Rhode Island	4	–	4	–	–
South Carolina	–	9	–	9	–
South Dakota	–	4	–	2	2
Tennessee	–	12	–	12	–
Texas	–	15	–	15	–
Utah	–	3	–	2	1
Vermont	4	–	4	–	–
Virginia	–	12	–	12	–
Washington	–	4	–	2	2
West Virginia	6	–	6	–	–
Wisconsin	12	–	12	–	–
Wyoming	–	3	–	2	1
Total	271	176	271	149	27

ticket, and not for the first name on the ticket. The vote for Bryan is the combined vote for Bryan and Sewall, and for Bryan and Watson. The Bryan and Watson vote is given separately, but is to be disregarded in making up the total vote.

According to the figures here presented the plurality for Mr. McKinley was 602,555, and his majority over all the candidates combined was 286,257.

The electoral vote, which is given in a separate table, reflects the closeness of the vote in California and Kentucky, in each of which States one elector voted for Bryan and Sewall.

The electoral count took place on the 10th of February, 1897. It was conducted in accordance with the law, and was strictly without incident. The inauguration of Mr. McKinley on the 4th of March was made the occasion of a great popular demonstration by the Republicans, who flocked to Washington in large numbers to witness the ceremony.

The immediate subsidence of excitement after the result of the election was ascertained, and the good-humored acceptance of that result by all save a few grievously disappointed leaders of the defeated party, is not a new experience in American political life. We have seen it after other historic struggles. The Federalists thought that all was lost when Jefferson was elected. Jackson's triumph seemed to his opponents a victory of evil over good. The Democrats lost faith in popular government when Harrison was chosen. To the supporters of Mr. Tilden the declaration that Mr. Hayes was elected was nothing short of a great political crime. Yet after a momentary loss of temper all these good people recovered themselves and devoted their energies to the public service with zeal and with undiminished hope and confidence. So it was in 1896. In some respects the result was the greatest trial of the temper of the defeated party the country has ever known. The aims of the Democratic party were, — not to use the phrase offensively, — in a certain sense revolutionary. They were intended to array the weak, the poor, the debtors, the employed, against the men who were designated as plutocrats. The failure of such an attack is sometimes almost as dangerous to society as its success. The fact that, when the American people had spoken at the polls upon questions that involved the highest interests of society, the decision was quietly accepted as conclusive until a new occasion should arise for passing upon them in the orderly American way, is most creditable to them, and a happy augury for the future.

INDEX